MODERN PHILOSOPHY: *Descartes to Kant*

A HISTORY OF PHILOSOPHY

Etienne Gilson, GENERAL EDITOR

ANCIENT PHILOSOPHY
By Anton Pegis

MEDIEVAL PHILOSOPHY
By Armand A. Maurer, c.s.b.

MODERN PHILOSOPHY: Descartes to Kant
By Etienne Gilson and Thomas Langan

RECENT PHILOSOPHY: Hegel to the Present
By Etienne Gilson, Thomas Langan, and Armand A. Maurer, c.s.b.

MODERN

PHILOSOPHY

Descartes to Kant

❋ ❋ ❋ ❋ ❋ ❋ ❋ ❋

ETIENNE GILSON
Pontifical Institute of Mediaeval Studies, Toronto

THOMAS LANGAN
Indiana University

 RANDOM HOUSE · NEW YORK

FIRST PRINTING

© COPYRIGHT, 1963, BY RANDOM HOUSE, INC.

ALL RIGHTS RESERVED UNDER INTERNATIONAL AND PAN-AMERICAN COPY-
RIGHT CONVENTIONS. PUBLISHED IN NEW YORK BY RANDOM HOUSE, INC.,
AND SIMULTANEOUSLY IN TORONTO, CANADA, BY RANDOM HOUSE OF
CANADA, LIMITED.

LIBRARY OF CONGRESS CATALOG CARD NUMBER: 62-16201

MANUFACTURED IN THE UNITED STATES OF AMERICA
BY THE COLONIAL PRESS INC., CLINTON, MASSACHUSETTS

INTRODUCTION TO
A HISTORY OF PHILOSOPHY

ETIENNE GILSON, GENERAL EDITOR

This *History of Philosophy* is intended as an introduction to philosophy itself. The approaches to philosophy are many, but if one aims to give the reader, beyond mere factual information, a genuine philosophical formation, the historical approach becomes a necessity. Much more important than knowledge about philosophy is a true notion of what it is to philosophize. And what better way is there to learn to philosophize than to observe the great philosophers of the past? If one has the understanding and the patience to follow the discussions of Plato, Aristotle, Thomas Aquinas, or Kant, he cannot fail to appreciate what it means to philosophize. And, equally important, he will have a standard of philosophical excellence that will deter him from confusing a shabby piece of philosophy with one that is first-rate.

Those who take philosophy seriously must have some knowledge of its history, because philosophy is a collective enterprise in which no one can pretend to take part unless he is first properly introduced. Before playing a game, one must learn its rules, must even practice for a long time under the coaching of some expert. The same can be said of the future philosopher, or of any educated man who wishes to share in a philosophical discussion without incurring ridicule. In our own day, philosophy is to be found everywhere; it is hardly an exaggeration to say that it dominates our political life, since Hegel, Marx, and materialistic scientism provide some of our greatest political powers with the ideology they need to justify their actions. At the very least, an equally well thought out ideology is necessary to meet this challenge and, if possible, submit it to a rational critique.

Why is its history a necessary introduction to philosophy? Because philosophy is actually a continuous chain of philosophers who have conducted in the West, for twenty-five centuries, a sort of conversation on the ultimate problems the human mind can ask. What stuff is reality made of? How did it come to be? What is the place of man in the universe? How is knowledge possible? Can we form a sensible opinion concerning our future destiny? Whatever our answer to such questions, it is bound to be a philosophical one. Even to say that they should not be asked and that, anyway, they cannot be answered, is to take a big philosophical chance. These questions, and others like them, have been discussed by countless philosophers, among whom there is at least one point of agreement: that a definite technique be adhered to by all those who want to share in this collective inquiry. First defined by Socrates, followed by Plato and Aristotle, this technique can be found at work in all philosophical doctrines. Two faults will at once disqualify any newcomer to the inquiry: one is not to have learned the technique of philosophical discussion; the other is to want to share in the dialogue without adequate knowledge of the history of philosophy. In the words of the French critic Albert Thibaudet: "Experience shows that during these twenty-five centuries, no self-taught man, no mind uninformed about the work of its predecessors, has been able to make any valuable contribution to philosophy."

A history that aims to make readers feel at home in the great family of philosophers should be neither an accumulation of proper names and dates, which would be better provided by dictionaries and encyclopedias, nor a mere juxtaposition of philosophical doctrines, which would amount to a succession of unrelated monographs. To avoid the first defect, we had to decide which philosophers would be singled out for detailed examination and, within each particular philosophy, what parts of it should be presented. Choice entails arbitrariness; in some cases, other choices could have been made with equal justification. The only rules we have tried to observe were not to omit any really great doctrine and never to mention one of which not enough could be said to relate it to some definite philosophical position. The second defect has been avoided, we hope, by our effort to relate every great doctrine to those with which it was vitally linked. Here, again, enough had to be said to achieve philosophical intelligibility without burdening our history with purely dogmatic considerations.

The last remark leads us to a further question. How should this *History* be used? The answer cannot be the same for all classes of readers. Students will have their teachers to help them make their own selection according to the various kinds of philosophical studies they are engaged in. The only general hypothesis we can visualize is that of the reader who is free to make whatever use of the book he thinks best. To him our advice would be, first, to read the *History* in a rather cursory way so as to gather a general picture of the growth of philosophical doctrines within any one of the four main periods into which it has been divided. A second reading should be both selective and exacting, with the reservation, however, that after making his own choice of the particular philosophy he intends to study more precisely, the reader will not submit it to a hasty criticism. As a rule it takes much more cleverness to understand a philosophy than to refute it. Moreover, no doctrine should be discussed on the basis of its interpretation by any historian, whose role is merely to introduce the reader to the study of the writings of the philosophers themselves. Last, not least, one should always keep in mind that, since philosophy is about ultimate problems, each particular doctrine is determined by its particular way of approaching such problems.

The slightest deviation in the understanding of philosophical principles brings about important differences in the conclusions. In critically assessing a philosophy, therefore, the greatest attention should be paid to its initial data. To discuss a philosopher's conclusion without understanding his principles is a waste of time. However, one will never regret the time and care devoted to a detailed examination of what a philosopher calls philosophy, of the method he advocates and uses in discussing its problems, and, more important still, of his own personal way of understanding these principles. If as much time were spent meditating on our own philosophical ideas as is devoted to refuting those of other philosophers, we would probably realize how much more important it is to set forth truth than to fight error. Hopefully, this *History* will convey to its readers a positive notion of philosophical wisdom, conceived as a never-ceasing effort to deepen the understanding of the first principles of human knowledge. We have planned the *History* as a guide for those who need an introduction to a very wide field of historical information and philosophical speculation. If, as we would like to think, the readers of this *History* want to continue beyond it to some exploring of their own, we trust that they will find themselves at least proceeding in the right direction.

The present general history of philosophical doctrines in the Western world falls naturally into four Parts, and therefore into four volumes: I. *Ancient Philosophy*; II. *Medieval Philosophy*; III. *Modern Philoso-*

phy: Descartes to Kant; IV. *Recent Philosophy: Hegel to the Present.* The distribution of the materials within each Part is dictated by the variations in philosophical thinking itself during the course of centuries, in its way of approaching problems as well as in its mode of expressing them. Even so, the emphasis is always on the doctrinal content of each particular philosophy. Biographical and bibliographical information is limited to what is needed to embark on a personal study of any one of the philosophers, schools, or periods represented. For indeed the very substance of a history of philosophy is philosophy itself. That is why, so far as possible, everything in these four volumes is made to serve this truth.

Etienne Gilson

PREFACE TO *MODERN PHILOSOPHY*

The survival of scholasticism in the fifteenth and sixteenth centuries is a historical fact; yet it cannot be denied that it had been feeding on its own substance for more than two centuries before modern philosophy decisively superseded it. Ever since the death of Ockham, scholasticism had exhausted itself in school controversies, in endless subtleties. Albertists, Thomists, Scotists, Ockhamists, Averroists—all were busy fighting one another, and while each sect was confident of ultimately winning the battle, scholasticism itself was steadily losing it. But it was not killed by modern philosophy. When modern philosophy arose, scholasticism had long been dead, and since the Renaissance philosophers had failed to replace it, its disappearance had created a vacuum which the seventeenth-century philosophers simply filled. Instead of starting from the outdated Aristotelian science in order to form a new philosophical view of the world, they started from what the new astronomy, mathematics, and physics had taught them about the real structure of the universe and the true nature of rational knowledge. The only sense in which modern philosophers can be said to have killed scholasticism is that intimated by the formula of Auguste Comte: the only safe way to destroy something is to replace it.

Modern Philosophy, this third volume of our *History of Philosophy*, tells a twofold story whose moments roughly correspond to the chronological distinction of the seventeenth and of the eighteenth centuries. In reality, however, both its elements were present from the beginning of the seventeenth century. Two names will say it better: Francis Bacon and René Descartes. Bacon was the spokesman for the new ideal of a scientific view of the world based upon observation and experimental reasoning. Descartes was the prophet of modern science to the extent that it has tended to assume the form of mathematical knowledge, not only in physics and biology but in metaphysics. This accounts for the rise of the "Cartesian school," a family of great metaphysicians whose relation to Descartes was less that of disciples to a master than of philosophical geniuses inspired by a common spirit but working independently on the same problems. That common spirit can be defined as their recognition of the primacy of the mathematical method. Descartes, Malebranche, Spinoza, and Leibniz have left us very different systems of philosophy, yet they all agreed that the method of mathematics involved the most perfect exercise of the human mind itself. The *Ethics* of Spinoza even pretended to follow the rules of mathematical demonstration, and when Leibniz decided to substitute a new metaphysics for that of Descartes, he felt justified in his undertaking because, owing to the rise of a new mathematical method still unknown to Descartes, a new philosophy had to be erected on the basis of the infinitesimal calculus. The great "Cartesians" bring to mind the impressive group of great theologians formed earlier by Albert the Great, Thomas Aquinas, Bonaventure, Scotus, and Ockham. Because of the Cartesians, the seventeenth century can be called the golden age of modern metaphysics just as the thirteenth century has been called the golden age of scholasticism.

In both cases, however, a constructive and positively-minded century of speculation was followed by a rather critically-minded one. The eighteenth century devoted itself to destroying the lofty structures of the seventeenth-century metaphysicians. Here again there is similarity in the succession of events. The criticism of Ockham, which spelled the death of scholasticism, had been present in germ as early as the twelfth century, in the form of the Aristotelian nominalism of Roscelin and Abelard; the critical empiricism of the eighteenth century was likewise present before the birth of the Cartesian metaphysics it was later to destroy, in the form of Bacon's own observational ideal of rational knowledge. For, indeed, plain empiricism always spells the death of metaphysics. The two slopes of the road meet in the *New Essays* of Leibniz, where classical metaphysics can be seen fighting a losing battle against the mounting empiricism of Locke. The following period can be called "the age of Locke." It is marked by the complete triumph of empiricism in all domains and by an almost total eclipse of metaphysical speculation. The so-called age of the philosophers, or of the philosophy of Enlightenment, was also the age of a philosophy without metaphysics; deriving its origin from Bacon, it runs through Locke and Condillac, finally losing itself in the poverty-stricken doctrines of the nineteenth-century ideologists.

Metaphysically sterile, the empirical tradition of Bacon and Locke has nevertheless yielded positive results in other fields of philosophical research. In the first place, by making man the proper object of his own philosophical inquiry, Locke initiated the movement that resulted, as early as the eighteenth century, in the creation of what we now call the "human sciences." Descriptive psychology, philosophy of history, the application of the comparative methods of observation in the fields of social and political studies—all these contributions to the creation of new disciplines or to the renovation of ancient ones are typical of an age in which the English poet could state as an immediate evidence that "the proper study of mankind is man." In this respect, "the wise Locke" has left an enduring mark on the history of philosophy, and even as mediocre a philosopher as Voltaire has contributed his share to the progress of sociology by writing his *Essai sur les moeurs*.

But Germany always was the land of "serious" philosophy, and it is there that the philosophy of the Enlightenment was to find its truly philosophical conclusion in the three *Critiques* of Immanuel Kant. Hume had cast doubt on the power of human reason to achieve certitude even in the science of nature; Rousseau had affirmed the primacy of feeling and of moral conscience in the order of morality; Diderot and others had attempted to reduce to some sort of order our conflicting appreciations of beauty; Kant's celebrated *Critiques*, of *Pure Reason*, of *Practical Reason*, and of *Judgment*, were efforts to arbitrate the situation created by the so-called Philosophy of Lights. Kant always wanted to limit (*begrenzen*) in order to found (*begründen*). In the first part of his program, he showed himself the faithful spokesman for the critical spirit of the eighteenth-century philosophers; in fact, he limited speculative philosophy by simply beheading it. Leaving it without the metaphysics that had traditionally been considered its crowning part and had made it a Wisdom, Kant initiated the modern reduction of philosophy to science. By similarly depriving ethics of any objective foundations beyond the mere postulates of moral consciousness, Kant initiated an age of moral faith during which, from Kant to Nietzsche, ethical truth progressively lost its motives of credibility. As for the philosophy of art, which the eighteenth century had attempted to create, this has been confused with aesthetics ever since Kant substituted for objective beauty our own appreciation of it.

Even as a supreme exponent of the critical spirit of his age, Kant has played a positive part in the development of modern philosophy. What had been merely mistrust of metaphysical speculation became in his

work a resolute attempt to make explicit the philosophical grounds
for that mistrust. Instead of simply observing that metaphysics was
dead, Kant undertook to explain and to demonstrate the reasons why,
given the nature of rational knowledge itself, truly metaphysical
knowledge was impossible. The very "spirit of earnestness," that technical thoroughness with which Kant carried out his undertaking, resulted for his successors in a discovery that he himself could not clearly
foresee, although some hints of it could be found in the obscure fragments left uncompleted at the time of his death. Such as it is, Kant's
criticism presupposes, in all orders, arbitrary decisions that can be just
as easily questioned as they were first made—unless one prefers to attempt turning those postulates into rationally justified truths. The second attitude was the only philosophically fruitful one, but could not
be adopted without fully restoring metaphysical speculation. From the
loose skepticism of Voltaire nothing could possibly follow, but we are
indebted to the critical philosophy of Kant for the metaphysical speculation of Fichte, Schelling, Hegel, and Schopenhauer. In this sense,
just as he brought the eighteenth century to its philosophical conclusion,
Kant opened the new age of the German idealism that occupied the
first half of the nineteenth century and is still exercising its influence
on the philosophical and political thought of our own day.

   Recent Philosophy, the fourth part of this *History of Philosophy*, will
deal with the struggle of metaphysics to survive, and with the efforts
of its opponents to transcend it or to replace it by more or less ingen-
iously contrived surrogates. Like a Bergsonian memory, the history of
philosophy gathers within itself its whole past as it proceeds toward
new goals, and nothing in it is ever wholly dead or wholly lost. Descartes and Bacon, Locke and Kant are spiritual forces still active today
even in the minds of men for whom such names are but the symbols of
rather vague notions. To learn better to know what they mean and to
know oneself better, this is for a philosopher one and the same thing.

Contents

xiii

Contents

Part Five

A Golden Age in England

Part Six

The Philosophies of the Human Mind

Part Seven

The Age of the Philosophers

Part Eight

The Philosophies of Society

Contents

Part Nine

Germany, from *Aufklärung* to Criticism

1   THE DAWN OF MODERN TIMES

THE MODERN ERA willed for itself a radical beginning. At the source of the two main parallel traditions running in England and on the Continent through the seventeenth and eighteenth centuries stand two innovators, Francis Bacon and René Descartes, both intent on clearing the ground totally of all the accumulated confusions of past intellectual stumblings to build anew. The structures they wanted erected were as different as the opposition between empiricism and rationalism could make them; but in ambition they were products of the same dream. Each was intended to be the foundation of a new tradition and a new science, each ambitioned to be a structure of truth absolute and unshakable. Each hoped to build, on ground cleared of the ruins of medieval thought, a new palace of scientific philosophy in which man could find lasting shelter from the storms of a half century of religious strife.

I

The Breakdown
of Aristotelianism

ADDED TO THIS "external" reason for a change, there were reasons interior to scholasticism why the association of Aristotle and Christian theology should not last. First, Aristotle himself was a pagan, and the Moslem philosophers, through whom Aristotelian metaphysics had become known to the Western world, had introduced along with it a certain number of doctrines completely unacceptable for Christians. Especially Averroes, who expressly professed to teach philosophy such as he could find it in Aristotle, irrespective of whether what was taught should happen to agree with religion or not. Averroism began with the golden age of scholasticism. In fact, Averroes, as the commentator *par excellence*, was one of the main influences at work in the rise of scholastic theology. What is called "Averroism" is the uninterrupted line of masters in medieval universities who, from the middle of the thirteenth century until the sixteenth century and beyond, insisted that the authentic teaching of Aristotle had been betrayed by the theologians in their effort to adapt it to the needs of Christian apologetics. The main consequence of this was the spreading of the conviction that philosophy is a discipline wholly separate from religion and theology. Many exponents of the Christian tradition allowed themselves to be persuaded of this, with the inevitable result that scholasticism began to break down, disintegrating into its two component elements: a religious faith without philosophy on the one hand and a philosophy without religious faith on the other. In the sixteenth century, scholasticism still survived in European universities, but it was indeed a mere survival.

The breakdown of scholasticism was attended by an important development. Once separated from theology, Aristotelianism found itself on its own. It lost the privilege granted to it by the theologians of being the preferred vehicle of Christian truth. As it became just one philoso-

phy among the others, Aristotelianism was submitted to a stiff competition. The men of the Renaissance created no new philosophy, but
they discovered that antiquity offered them a choice of several other
interesting views of the world besides that of Aristotle. As they became
acquainted with them, they began trying a little of everything.

Platonism had always been familiar to theologians, at least under the
Christianized form it had been given by St. Augustine and by Denys
the Areopagite. In fact, Platonist elements can be detected in all the
great scholastic theologies, with the possible exception of Ockham. At
the end of the Middle Ages, Plato began to be translated into Latin,
read and studied for himself. Marsilio Ficino (1433-1499) had thus
created at Florence a sort of mainly Platonist scholasticism which
heralded a new period in the history of Christian thought.

Plato (and Plotinus) was soon put to a different use, becoming the
starting point, not for a scholasticism, but for personal speculations
largely independent of Christianity and even, on some points, opposed
to it. The reason for this opposition is typical of the times. The men of
the sixteenth century were extremely interested in what we now call
occultism, hermetism, or magic. All that is often considered typically
medieval in the way of sorcery, superstitious practices, and credulity in
magical arts came to the forefront at the time of the Renaissance. Not
that it was not there before, but it had been held in check by the strict
criticism of the theologians; now, however, free to speak up, it became
an open source of philosophical speculation which presently blended
with Platonism, as it had in antiquity, thus adding to it one more source
of impurity. Giordano Bruno (1548-1600) is the best-known exponent
of that syncretism built around a nucleus of Platonism which so well
exemplifies the philosophical disorder of the century. There were
fruitful intuitions lost in that disorder, but they had not reached the
point of precision at which philosophy begins.[1]

Since philosophy had now cut loose from theology, there was no
reason why any and all Greek philosophies should not be tried. Epicureanism had always been at the disposal of the Middle Ages under the
form of Lucretius' poem, "On Nature," but its frank materialism had
kept it from being put to use. The same is true of Stoicism, with this
difference, however, that Seneca had always been read, admired, and
used as a source of moral predication. But not the Stoics' materialistic
view of the world. Yet now in the Renaissance there were philosophers
to profess a combination of Epicurean atomism and elements borrowed

from Stoic physics, capped by a curious brand of universal animism that somehow held great appeal in the sixteenth century. Magic, of course, found there an invitation to enter the system. Two names come to mind in this regard, Telesio (1509-1588)[2] and his admirer and free disciple, Campanella (1568-1639).[3]

In the case of Stoicism as an ethical philosophy, we can almost speak of a Renaissance *school* of philosophy. As we just said, Seneca and moral Stoicism had never been forgotten during the Middle Ages, but now their popularity became widespread. Bruno, Telesio, and Campanella were Italians, and in France the new Christianized Stoicism was soon in much evidence. Moralism has always been popular with French philosophers; but the Stoic Renaissance in the sixteenth century for a while practically became *the* philosophical rage. Guillaume Du Vair (1556-1621),[4] for one, wrote in 1590 a *Traité de la constance et consolation ès calamités publiques* (*On Constancy and Consolation in Public Calamities*), purely Stoic in inspiration and intended as a means of moral education for citizens living in those troubled times. Stoicism then blended with other doctrinal tendencies in the writings of men who, without being exactly Stoics, underwent the influence of Epictetus. Such was the case with Pierre Charron (1541-1603),[5] usually classified as a disciple of Montaigne, which indeed he was, but in whose main work, *Traité de la sagesse* (1601), the Stoic elements already present in Montaigne himself are fully developed. Along with Montaigne, Seneca, Plutarch, and Guillaume Du Vair are among the sources of Charron's moral Stoicism.

The name of Montaigne is a good reminder of the difficulty there is in classifying doctrines in a century when all sorts of influences, representing long-neglected or insufficiently exploited philosophical positions, were at work in every mind. Montaigne's name is usually connected with "skepticism," but it represents many other things and, anyway, skepticism can mean different attitudes.

The Middle Ages had little use for any sort of skepticism; yet there is a kind of religious faith that can put up very easily with philosophical skepticism. The kind is well known: I believe what God says and in very little else. At the end of the Middle Ages, when the schools were divided into philosophical sects endlessly fighting one another, that sort of skepticism was made to order. The *Hypotyposes* of Sextus Empiricus, translated into Latin as early as the thirteenth century, had remained practically unread. In the sixteenth century, the influence of another Greek skeptic, Pyrrho, makes itself strongly felt. The German occultist, Agrippa of Nettesheim,[6] explains that neither philosophy nor sciences are needed, since they are uncertain, especially as compared with religion. The title of his main work is clear enough: *On the uncertainty and vanity of sciences and arts* (1527). Another open-and-shut case of philosophical skepticism following in the wake of religious fideism is that of the Parisian Omer Talon, whose *Academia* (1548) betrays by its very title the predominant influence of Cicero's academicism; that is, a sensible and moderate form of skepticism.[7] In Talon's case, however, skepticism is redeemed by absolute faith in the truth of Christian revelation.

"That nothing is known" is the very title of the treatise published by the physician François Sanchez in 1581: *Quod nil scitur.*[8] The more interesting of his arguments in favor of this conclusion was one already present in the treatise of Nicholas of Cusa on *Learned Ignorance;* to wit, that things are so intimately tied up with one another, as well as with the whole, that the perfect knowledge of one of them would involve the knowledge of all the rest, which cannot be had. It must be noted that, from a certain point of view, the treatise of Sanchez struck a new note. Instead of ending on a purely negative conclusion, this very incomplete skeptic invited his readers to turn from the reading of books to the study of things. Thus to call men to the practice of experience was to enter a way far different from a pure negativism. In fact, this was to take into account the recent discoveries made in the field of natural sciences and to invite philosophers to modify their own methods accordingly.

Le cas Montaigne is the most complicated. Montaigne is not only a perfect example of the effervescent result the unsystematic mating of newly liberated forces could produce, but he himself is such an engaging essayist and altogether unforgettable person that we could not do better in our effort to picture the fertile chaos out of which modern thought was born than to witness these currents meeting in this one figure.

II ❧

Michel Eyquem
de Montaigne

As WE CAN SEE from his name, Michel Eyquem de Montaigne[1] was not a bourgeois. Though no element of the new developments was lost on him, this country aristocrat's instinctive reaction to the Copernican, geographical, social, and religious revolutions was never that of an enthusiast. He was ready to receive their destruction of old dogmatisms, but he was not anxious to replace old faiths with newer and perhaps narrower ones. So posterity has looked on Montaigne as a skeptic, a term that would have not displeased him, although he would have understood the term to mean a doubt aimed ultimately at positive results. Of the Greek skeptic whom, from middle age, he came so much to admire, Montaigne has written: "Pyrrho did not want to make himself into a stone; he wanted to make of himself a living man, discoursing and reasoning, enjoying all pleasures and natural commodities, using all of his corporal and spiritual parts regularly and properly."[2] The Pyrrho envisioned in this quotation is of course the one who retired to the family estate in Périgord at the age of thirty-eight to set about clearing away those dogmatic elements, old and more recent, that still stood in the way of a free spirit's[3] exercise of his corporal and spiritual parts. "There is nothing so beautiful and legitimate," writes this latter-day skeptic in describing the positive goal he was after, "as playing the man well and properly, nor is there science as arduous as knowing how to live this life well and according to nature. The most savage of our illnesses is to despise our being."[4]

The effort of meditation that is to prepare and accompany this endeavor will be no monument of systematic reason. There are too many conflicts in this man to permit that. Conflicts of aristocratic upbringing and bourgeois revelations; of humanist sensibility to the many-faceted spectacle of the human enigma, with the scientist's desire to possess everything absolutely; of the landed man's conviction of the need for roots, with the new class's desire to inquire into all and rebuild everything. This bi-polarity is the result of Montaigne's education, which brought him to drink deeply from every social cup. In infancy his father gave him to peasants to raise "in order to harden me to the lowest and most common manner of life—thinking it better for one to rise from hardships than fall to them." His early education at home was both sweet and fruitful. The whole household actually went to the extent of learning Latin, even the servants addressing Michel in "such Latin words as they scraped together in order to prattle with me." Then, his father giving in to the general opinion that formal schooling was after all necessary, off to the famous Collège de Guyenne, so that from the most enlightened family regime he passed at once to the tyranny of masters "cramming Aristotle down our throats" and raising boys to manhood by brute force. From this time dated Montaigne's craving for the earlier liberty and his disdain for the world's formal learning. Once when asked, "Who was that gentleman I saw you with last night?" he answered, "That was no gentleman, that was a grammarian." His later life, bringing him in touch with Parisian as well as provincial society, at the very epicenter of the violent religious wars, and in the best and the worst of times, permitted him to amass a very rich—almost too rich—quota of experience to assimilate; and incidentally, one of the best private libraries, a balance of modern and classical.

This richness pours into the *Essays*, the abundance of it precluding any pretense at systematization—in fact, Montaigne pokes fun at such organization by attaching pompous titles to sections of this work, announcing subjects that in some instances are not even touched on in the text. What we find there is the whole spectrum of the world without, but especially the incomparable reality of the world within—not the world in the abstract, but Montaigne's world, the microcosm of one rich individual.

It is dogmatism that keeps most people from being able to appreciate this richness. They are afraid of anything that will threaten their narrow systems. They are afraid of diversity—especially the diversity of opinions in the world! Those who persist in the face of this great divergency of opinion do so because they are suffering from the most serious debility of mankind: pride, a base pride with roots in cowardice. Montaigne feels we must be made humble before we can become wise.

How better to humble man than by bringing him to a realization of the limits of the place he occupies in nature. When he realizes that he is one among an infinity of species, and not the semi-divine lord of all he surveys, he might be less inclined to foster St. Bartholomew Day massacres. So Montaigne spends forty pages in *The Apology of Raymond Sebond* [5] vaunting the superiority of the animals—their possession of senses and instincts we do not enjoy; the sureness of their social organization; their exercise of thought processes proud man mistakenly thinks only he possesses, and so on. Then he attacks the feebleness and illusions of our senses, the pretensions and errors of our reason, the narrowness and insufficiency of our opinions. The bookishness of the schoolmen is the result. "There are more books on books than on things. . . . The principal and most famous knowledge of our centuries is to know how to listen to the knowledgeful." [6] Montaigne would change all of this: *Une tête bien faite*, rather than *une tête bien pleine*—a well-made head rather than a well-stuffed one—thus he epitomizes the program he would substitute for a dead scholasticism and a classical humanism gone wild. If people could just be made to *look at themselves* for a change! "I who have no other profession (than knowing myself) find there a profundity and variety so infinite that my learning has no other fruit than to make me feel how much there remains for me to learn." [7] "I study myself more than any other subject; that's my metaphysics; that's my physics." [8] What makes it so hard is that this of all subjects is closest at hand, and, in the words of a contemporary, "What is closest is farthest away." Montaigne puts it this way: "Our condition has it that that which we have in our hands is as far from us, and as much above the clouds, as the stars." [9] A great paradox: To be objective, we must not get too absorbed in the object.

So the spirit needs to learn to proceed with care, to discern the limits of its inquiry, just as it must learn to accept everything, excluding no experience.

It is right to give the human spirit the most constraining barriers possible. In study as in everything else, it must count and regulate its steps, it must carve out artfully the limits of its pursuit. . . . There are certainly few souls so regulated, so strong and so well-born, of whose conduct one can be proud, and which, with moderation and without temerity, can navigate in the liberty of their judgments beyond common opinions. It is more expedient to hand them over to tutelage. [10]

This leads us to the heart of Montaigne's philosophy—his glorification of what he calls "judgment," in contrast with the artificial "reason" the *Apology* was meant to humble—the faculty we must keep royally active in order to live. All this negative preparation—this criticism of common errors made through pride, laziness, stupidity, or voracity—is only intended to lay the ground for one of the first "life" philosophies, here propounded with all the gusto of the Renaissance. The one goal worthy of man's endeavor is *fully conscious* experience, a perfect fusion of consciousness with the world lying about, the most difficult of all goals, demanding complex preparation and perfect discipline, and calling on faculties undervalued by scholastic rationalism.

First of all, it demands submission to the formal organization of the country in which one lives, to the word of God, to the indispensable conditions of society. Legitimate bonds must clearly be distinguished from illegitimate fetters. Montaigne is no social, political, or even religious revolutionary; he is a genuine conservative, both because he knows that external order is necessary for the pursuit of wisdom, and because, believing there are no absolute truths, he thinks feeling our way along practically is the best social as well as intellectual formula. Even his attitude to religion is *stoic;* detesting the confusion unleashed on the world by the Reform,[11] he exhorts his contemporaries to hang on humbly to the revelations of the traditional dispensation while keeping to themselves what Pascal will later call his "idées de derrière la tête." These are voluntary bonds, which paradoxically free the soul for its quest of itself.

That self is *life*—that is why the soul can find itself only by living. Even "truth" itself is witness to this life: the continual change throughout history of the bases for judgment shows that life itself is the very truth of truth. "The laws of consciousness, which we say are born of nature, are born of custom; . . . what is that truth that the course of a river makes into a lie?" The truth is not to be found in any one dogmatic system, but in familiarity with things themselves. "Usage reveals to us the real visage of things." It is this feeling, that life should possess us, rather than that we should attempt to possess life in a closed system of truths, which leads him to underscore the contingency and the unexpectedness in everything, especially in all human creation and noble action ("Nothing noble is ever done without the accidental"), and the element of inspiration in all knowledge, which he urges as more important than any method, as a kind of grace always to be accepted.

"Everyone has felt in himself some image of such agitations (like Socrates' daemon) of a prompt, vehement and fortuitous opinion; I always give them some authority, I, who give so little to our prudence, and who have had such foibles of reason, violent in their persuasiveness, or dissuasiveness, such as those to which Socrates was more accustomed, and which I have let carry me along, so usefully and happily that they could be judged to contain something of divine inspiration." [12]

Montaigne, in other words, is a devotee, in completest contrast to the next generation's Apostles of Method, of what Nietzsche termed "the gay savoir"—the term is almost Montaigne's: "I know by experience that condition of nature which cannot sustain a vehement and laborious premeditation: if it does not proceed gayly and freely, it proceeds to nothing worthwhile. . . . The solicitude to do well, and that condition of a soul too tied up and too tightened to its enterprise, breaks and impedes" [13] the pursuit of the inspiration. Rather the soul needs to be "warned and awakened by occasions foreign, present and fortuitous; if it proceeds all by itself it only drags and languishes; agitation is its life and its grace. I do not hold myself well in my possession and disposition: chance has a greater right over me." [14] Montaigne liked to pretend that he flowed unimpeded into his *Essays,* there to be captured in fresh bloom.

There is but one God, and that is Life—but *poesis* is His prophet! "Did I not see in Plato this divine phrase: 'Nature is nothing but an enigmatic poetry'?" [15] Hence the importance of inspiration, hence the emphasis on style and language, and the very choice of style and language our philosopher has made. "It's the job of words to serve and follow; and if the French can't keep up, let the Gascon come on!" [16] A subversive threat in the sixteenth century! This is not an encouragement for those who would tinker with the language, "searching out affected phrases." Montaigne is quite disgusted with the linguistic fakery of the court and its hired poets. Against the dusty abstractions of scholasticism and the fripperies of courtly gossip Montaigne would unleash the alive language of soldiers and peasants, a language impregnated with the enigmatic poetry of nature that comes from familiarity with "l'usage des choses." "Eloquence does injury to things, turning us away from things and toward itself. . . . The quest for new phrases and words little known derives from a scholastic and puerile ambition. May I only use those which serve *aux Halles de Paris!*" "The speech that I like is a speech simple and naïf, whether on paper or in the mouth, a speech succulent and nervous, curt and tight, not delicate and pained, but vehement and brusque, difficult rather than boring, far from all affectation; unbound and hardy!" [17]

The contrast between the actual language Montaigne employs—earthy, metaphorical, spontaneous, sort of *round*—and that which Descartes will use forty years later—crystalline, careful, clear, and scientific—is startling. What Montaigne would have found to say of Malherbe's disciples' "reform" of the language in the seventeenth century, what he would have said of the *Académie française*! Instead of sorting out differences and arriving at a standardization, Montaigne revels in the varied, the strange, the different, in language, as in nature, or in his friends. The "generous spirit" (the sixteenth and seventeenth centuries' term for the successful man) is full of "admiration, pursuit and ambiguity." [18] He approaches the other person in this spirit. "I free him of the obligation to be according to my conditions and my principles, and consider him simply in himself, comprehending more easily 'the difference than the resemblance in us.'" [19] This man who is made to live must not seek salvation in systems.

> I, who am proud of embracing so curiously and so particularly the commodities of life, find there, when I look carefully, practically nothing but wind. *Mais quoy?* we are everywhere wind! and again the wind, more wisely than us, loves to make noise (*bruyer*) and agitate itself; and is content in its own offices, without desiring stability [or] solidity, qualities which are not his. [20]

This appeal to enjoy the fullness of life, this exhortation to break clear of the false limits of systems, is not, however, an invitation to excess or to the casting off of all reason. Montaigne puts great emphasis on the need for what he terms "judgment" to retain a certain autonomy in our lives.

> The judgment occupies in me a magistral chair, at least it carefully tries to; it lets my appetites go their way, both hate and friendship, even that which I bear toward myself, without altering and corrupting them. If it cannot reform the other parts in keeping with itself, at least it does not let itself be deformed by them; it plays its game apart. [21]

In the *Treatise on the Passions*, Descartes will repeat this Stoic ideal of a judgment that somehow can keep itself clear of the war of passions, like Chimene in *Le Cid*, who is always ready to observe almost scientifically the effects of her passion and therefore to postulate at least the ideal of retaining ultimate control.

This essential quality of soul is not acquired through learning; rather it is the result of a natural quality born into one and developed by one's life experience, which experience depends both on the innate stature necessary to appreciate what we have encountered and on the attentions lavished on us since the cradle.

> My virtue is a virtue, or to put it better, an innocence, accidental and fortuitous. Had I been born of a more disorderly complexion, I am afraid that my case would have been a pitiful one; for I have tried out scarcely any firmness in my soul for resisting passions, whether scarcely or strongly vehement. . . . Therefore I do not have myself to thank for the fact that I find myself without a number of vices.[22]

Of Socrates, he cries, "*Jamais âme si excellente ne se fit elle-mesme—* never did such an excellent soul make itself."[23] Again of the systematizers, of those who think they can arrange all virtues and all truths in neat classifications, he says that such a drive for unity is a function of the arid simplicity of their souls. Only the noble can understand what is noble, and the rest are left to pursuing their poverty-stricken little "wisdom," which Montaigne sarcastically describes as "a structure solid and entire, in which each piece maintains its place and carries its mark: *sola sapientia in se tota conversa est.*"[24] The aristocrat Montaigne never lets us forget: "To judge things grand and lofty, a soul has to be the same; otherwise we attribute to others the vice which is our own."[25] In this regard, Montaigne's view of judgment as a quality of soul, a product of good breeding and good upbringing, of temperament and *moeurs,* over which the formed adult has at that late date little to say and which he cannot then hope to manage through the application of however startling a discovery of "method," is in great contrast with Cartesian reason. Some of his most important "instincts and impressions," declares Montaigne in the chapter from which we have just quoted, he has borne since he was nursed—they are the result, he says, "of little vigor and no art"—and betray a constancy and regularity in *moeurs* scarcely to be found in either his reason or opinion.[26]

Is there, then, nothing to be done about the self we are granted? Are we at the antipodes of Cartesian optimism too? Positively, there is little that can be done. We can try to keep in contact with the greatness of the past and let admiration for the sentiments expressed in the great classics shape our sensibility—but Montaigne is aware of the double problem involved: valid appreciation is impossible to a defective judgment; worse yet, admiration is not a sufficient motive force to change a man's actions; Montaigne himself, for all his love of Cato, still remained at heart what he calls "sluggish and lazy." Negatively, however, there is more room for action. We are not absolutely powerless in the face of those "débordements"—those strong inclinations to this vice or that with which we find ourselves cursed. For one thing, we can keep our judgment free of their influence—we can at least see what is wrong; for another, we can avoid mixing them with other vices toward which we are not so compellingly inclined. Finally, we can seek "to restrict and constrain them to make them as few and as simple as possible." [27]

The art of conducting one's life requires not only deep knowledge of what one, concretely as a person, really is, but also *acceptance* of it. Humble acceptance of the fact of our real limitations and our real abilities is the beginning of all wisdom. If we could just pull ourselves out of the terrible involvements of our daily affairs so that we could see ourselves as we really are! "It's the little souls, enslaved by the weight of affairs, that do not know how to disengage (*desmesler*) themselves, they don't know how to let off for a minute and then start in again." [28] Montaigne's "skepticism" is intended to lead man to care for what really is—the individual's concrete life in all the reality of its givenness—of its "situation." It is better "to love ordinary things more than eminent ones" which we cannot attain. Montaigne's sentiment might have been salutary to Ivan Karamazov: "The most savage sickness is to despise our being." [29] Nothing frightens Montaigne so much, he says, as "the transcendent humours" of those who, wanting to transform themselves into angels, manage to transform themselves into beasts. "Of our sciences," he adds in the same context, "those seem to me the most terrestrial and base which have mounted the highest." The grand climax of the three books of *Essays* is precisely this exhortation to live neither as beast nor angel but as a man. "It is an absolute perfection, and as though divine, to know how to make the most, loyally, of one's being (*de savoir jouir loyalement de son être*)." [30]

Bacon and Descartes both read Montaigne; neither honored his central intentions and intuitions, but they drank deeply of the negative side of his doctrine. Many of Montaigne's criticisms became for the next generations unquestioned givens, so woven were they into the texture of the times—his pushing religion into a corner, his attacks on scholasticism, his doubt that humanist literary culture could provide the answers of life, his emphasis on how hard it is to know anything. This last caused a reaction with which Montaigne would have been totally out of sympathy. Instead of giving up the quest for objective certitude, the next generation was to think it had solved all the problems of Montaigne by finding in science a new way. Thankful to the Sage of Périgord for taking care of the past for them, the moderns will nevertheless refuse to follow him as they turn to the future. Montaigne's root exhortation was largely lost on them: ". . . *méditer et manier vostre vie . . .*"

III

New Ways to Knowledge

Two EVENTS are found at the core of the great change that now took place in the common view of the world; both are events in the history of scientific methods, events distinct, yet interrelated. They are: the development of the methods of observation, especially by means of instruments; the development of the methods of mathematical reasoning.

Observation and Science

THE EARLY seventeenth century witnessed a complete change in the scientific view of the universe. Many influences have been at work to bring about this revolution, but their effects first became visible to all in the life and work of Galileo (1564-1642).[1]

The name of Galileo remains attached to his demonstration of the motion of the earth rotating around the sun, but this discovery, besides having been anticipated many centuries before; did not entail the complete revision of received ideas about the structure of the world which should remain Galileo's main title to fame.

Aristotle had accepted one of the astronomical systems known to his contemporaries, and his own interpretation of it implied a definite notion of the nature of the heavenly bodies as well as of their motion. According to Aristotle, they were made up of matter of a kind entirely different from that of earthly objects and beings. Matter such as we know it is subject to change owing to its continual loss of old and reception of new forms. As the peripatetic put it, matter is in potency with respect to forms, which are its acts. On the contrary, the matter of which the heavenly bodies consist is always perfectly in act, save only with respect to motion. In itself, then, it is immutable and eternal.

Now obviously the same physics could not apply to heavenly bodies
made of one kind of matter and to terrestrial ones made up of another.
But Galileo decided that there was no reason to consider the matter of
heavenly bodies as different from that of the earth, which he decided
is also a heavenly body as much as any. With this, the universe of
Aristotle—and with it, that of all his medieval followers—came to an
end.

According to the system of Eudoxus (*c.* 408-355 B.C.) (as in the
later systems of Hipparchus and Ptolemy), the motion of the planets
and stars had to be as perfect as their matter was supposed to be. Now
circular motion is the most perfect of all, because, its end being in its
beginning, it entails no change of place and is, therefore, the nearest
to immobility. Consequently, it was fitting that an immutable matter
should move in a circular way. It is noteworthy that the basis for such
conclusions was *qualitative*, not quantitative. The matter of heavenly
bodies is immutable, because rest is more *perfect*, or better than change.
The motion of such bodies must needs be circular, because, being self-
sufficient, it is the nearest thing to immobility. It was this kind of argument that seventeenth-century science was beginning to replace by
factual observation and mathematical calculus.

In the old system, all the planets, including the sun and the moon,
were supposed to move according to a circular motion around the
earth, which itself remained immobile at the center of the universe.
However, astronomical observation already in ancient times had soon
shown that their motion could not be perfectly circular. A particularly
disturbing fact was that at certain times the planets seemed to have
moved backward on their orbits. This called for an explanation, and
several clever ones were forthcoming. In the second century after
Christ, Ptolemy imagined a twofold solution to the problem. He decided that the centers of the orbit followed by the planets did not
exactly coincide with the center of the earth; next he imagined that
the motion of each planet was following, not one orbit, but two: the
larger one according to which it revolves around the earth as its approximate center, then a smaller one, whose center is placed on the
larger orbit so that the smaller one moves along with it. Since the
speed of the two revolutions was not the same, the twofold motion of
the planet made it appear to be sometimes fast, sometimes slow with
respect to what should have been its place on the larger orbit. This
kind of added circles (*epicycles*) has become proverbial to signify any

arbitrary hypothesis thought up to maintain an unsatisfactory theory against the testimony of observable facts. When too many "epicycles" are required to uphold it, a theory collapses and worlds change.

This is exactly what happened during the course of the sixteenth century. Modern observation had made it necessary, in order to justify apparent irregularities, to introduce such a large number of epicycles that it became hard to believe in the truth of the Ptolemic system. Important simplification was obtained by the Polish astronomer Copernicus, who substituted the sun for the earth as the approximate center of the world. The result of his observations and calculations was published under the title *De revolutionibus orbium coelestium* in 1543. In 1577, the Danish astronomer Tycho Brahe observed a comet the motion of which was such that, had solid heavenly spheres existed, that heavenly body would have had to go through them in its course. So, he announced, the ancients are wrong again: There were no such solid spheres. So another cog in the traditional machinery was annihilated.

The activities of Galileo began in the last years of the sixteenth century, in 1583, when he observed the uniformity of the oscillations of the pendulum, and continued in the first half of the seventeenth until 1638, when he published his *Mathematical Discourses and Demonstrations Concerning Two New Sciences*. As can be seen from the very title of the latter work, Galileo belongs to the history of sciences as a promoter of the mathematical method as well as of the methods of observation in physics. His activities were indeed many, but three features here deserve particular attention.

First, the name of Galileo remains attached to his invention of an instrument of observation, the telescope (1609). Today such instruments are many; they are being ceaselessly multiplied and brought to a high perfection. In our time a whole family of scientific minds will be tied up with the invention and use of one single instrument of observation. Scientists of this kind need to have good hands as well as good minds. These are not the Einstein type, but they are good at finding facts and, without them, experimental verification would not be possible. Galileo certainly is one of their great ancestors.

Secondly, Galileo has given proof that, by means of careful observation, it is sometimes possible to ascertain correct laws, even if their correct theoretical justification is still lacking. Such was the case when in 1604 he first correctly formulated the law of falling bodies, at a time when its correct interpretation was not yet in sight.

Thirdly, Galileo gave incomparable models of experimental reasoning and, perhaps still more, of the art of intelligently reading facts in interpreting observations. In this regard his *Sidereus nuncius* (The Starry Messenger) remains a model. Published in 1610, the work announces Galileo's first telescopic discoveries and relates, along with his observations, the reasonings he had used in their interpretation. His demonstration of the existence of the satellites of Jupiter can be considered a classic in the history of scientific observation.

The upshot of Galileo's observations and theorizing was to complete the work of the Copernican revolution. Galileo could hardly believe that Copernicus himself had held his position, not as a description of actual reality, but only as a hypothesis accounting for the appearances. The personal outcome of Galileo's efforts have become quite famous. Having mingled biblical arguments, which were not too sound, with his very sound scientific proofs, he managed to get himself condemned. What is of special interest for the history of philosophy is the reason he himself has given for his failure to make his opponents see the truth of his theory. His adversaries were men trained in the philosophy of Aristotle and used to settle all problems by mere dialectical reasonings. Copernicus and Galileo had reached their conclusions after years of observation and calculation; those who were opposing them did not know what scientific observation was and they had not been trained in mathematics. In the Galileo affair the two parties were trying to communicate across the void separating two worlds. "How could I convince those Peripatetics?" Galileo once wrote a friend. "With their minds full of vain propositions, they show themselves unable to follow even the simplest and easiest of demonstrations." The only support he found was among a group of scientifically trained Roman Jesuits; but they were not his judges; so he lost the juridical battle while winning the scientific one.

In 1609, the German astronomer Johann Kepler (1571-1630) had published his monumental *Astronomia nova* in which, starting from the careful observations of Copernicus and by means of circuitous reasonings, he had stumbled upon the key notion that was many years later to open a way out of so many difficulties. The notion was so new that very few contemporaries paid attention to it. According to Kepler, the only way to account for observed facts was to admit that the planetary orbits were not circular but *elliptical;* in short, the earth was not at the center of the world, as Ptolemy still thought it was; but neither was the sun at its center, as Copernicus had suggested; the sun was situated at one focus of its elliptical orbit.

This was decidedly the end of the Greek world. Heavenly bodies were now known to be made up of the same kind of matter as that of the earth; they were moving in the skies by themselves, having lost the support of the solid crystalline spheres by whose circular motion they used to be carried; their orbits had lost their perfection when, owing to Kepler's calculations, they had ceased to be circular; finally, all the eccentric orbits had suddenly disappeared along with their cumbersome epicycles. The heavenly bodies were in new courses; only the Aristotelian professors—and there were still many of them in 1630—could be said to be not yet "in orbit."

The Birth of Modern Mathematics

THE DEVELOPMENT of mathematics that unwound in the sixteenth century and reached its peak in the seventeenth was another decisive cause of the breakdown of Aristotelianism.

Modern mathematics has its source in the writings of Archimedes (*c.* 287-212 B.C.). The old science found in the Renaissance its brand of humanists, too. Here again, however, it must be acknowledged that the waning Middle Ages had already begun to revive old methods, to assimilate the discoveries made by Moslem mathematicians in the field of algebra and, be it ever so shyly, themselves to initiate the application of calculus to problems in physics. In the fourteenth century, Nicole Oresme had shown how the method of longitudes and latitudes, commonly used on geographical spheres, could be used on a plane surface in order to represent the variations of any magnitude whatsoever. The degrees of the variation of the physical phenomenon were what Oresme then called the "latitude of the form" (our modern line of abscissae), while the corresponding times were the "longitude of the form" (our own line of ordinates). The line determined by the points of intersection represents visibly the variations of size and intensity of the magnitude at stake. All this was to prove a fruitful seed indeed, but it remained as yet but a seed.

François Viète (1540-1603) went much further along the same line in the search for ways of representing quantities otherwise than by means of numbers.[2] In his introduction to the art of analysis (*In artem analyticam Isagoge,* 1591) Viète distinguished between arithmetic, conceived as the "logistic of numbers" (*logistica numerosa*), or "numerical logistic," and algebra, which he called a logistic of symbols (*logistica speciosa*). In the latter, letters signify quantities to be combined according to mathematical laws. The analysis of Viète already enabled him systematically to apply algebra to the discussion of geometrical problems. With him, and through his work, the birth of analytical geometry was becoming unavoidable. In fact, the principle of this new mathematical discipline was clearly formulated by the mathematician Pierre Fermat (1601-1665) in his epoch-making *Introduction,* or *Isagoge ad locos planos et solidos.*³ With it, we already find ourselves in an age when all physical magnitudes could be symbolized by signs and calculated by means of algebra. The new era of physico-mathematics was about to begin.

What did this mean for the future of philosophy?

Arithmetic and geometry had never been forgotten during the Middle Ages. Boethius, and after him Thomas Aquinas, had described it as the "discipline" *par excellence.* They had defined it as the science of quantity as such, considered by the mind apart from the material bodies in which it resides. On account of its very abstraction from matter, it was conceived by the scholastics as the most perfectly demonstrable kind of knowledge; in short, as providing the human understanding with a wholly satisfactory set of principles, demonstrations, and conclusions.

It should not be believed that mathematics' essential superiority over other sciences in the certitude of its conclusions had been overlooked by the men of the Middle Ages.⁴ But when the best mathematician of the Society of Jesus, Christopher Clavius,⁵ the "modern Euclid," in the prolegomena to his mathematical works (1611), expressed himself in no uncertain terms on the crushing superiority of mathematical demonstrations over dialectical disputations, this was something altogether different—something definitely bearing the mark of the times. Entrusted by the *Ratio studiorum* of 1586 with the task of organizing the teaching of mathematics in all the colleges of the Society of Jesus, Father Clavius was not only praising mathematics very highly—he was pitting it against scholastic philosophy. Mathematics, Clavius once said,

> . . . truly begets science in the mind of the hearer and completely removes all doubt. This can hardly be said of the other sciences in which, as often as not, the mind remains hesitant and uncertain,

unable to judge of the truth of the conclusions because of the multitude and diversity of the opinions. This is proved by the number of the peripatetic sects (to say now nothing of the other philosophers) that were born of Aristotle, like the limbs of a tree. They disagree between themselves, and even sometimes with Aristotle, who is their source, to such an extent that one feels completely in the dark as to what Aristotle is about. Is it words, or rather perhaps things? Hence it comes about that some of these sects follow the Greek interpreters, others the Latin ones, while still others choose the Arabian ones for their guides; some are nominalists, the rest are those they call realists, and nevertheless, at the same time, they all pride themselves on being peripatetics. How little all this resembles mathematical demonstrations is evident.

Obviously, this is a mathematician speaking. One could not find such an attack against peripateticism in the writings of a thirteenth-century master of arts but, precisely, no algebraist remotely comparable with Clavius could be found among them either. His criticism of the type of philosophy that had led the schoolmen to their endless sterile disputations while startling discoveries in mathematics and science were springing up on all sides could not be ignored by the more intelligent among them. The world of Aristotle was crumbling down; it would have taken a more than human genius to realize that the Christian world of the great scholastics was not affected by the event; they themselves had often mistaken it for the universe whose general notion they had inherited from the Greeks, so the whole fabric went down at once, perennial metaphysics as well as perishable physics. The need was felt for a philosophy fitting the science of the times and not that of a man who had lived four centuries before Christ. Francis Bacon in England and René Descartes in France were to be the spokesmen of their contemporaries and to provide them with the kind of philosophy they were seeking.

2 ❧ THE BEGINNINGS OF MODERN PHILOSOPHY

QUITE GRATEFUL to Montaigne for his attacks on past learning, the new men of the just-beginning seventeenth century refused to go along with his conviction that the systematic quest for certain truth was itself *passé*. Not only is it always hard to dissuade the human mind from seeking after a sure-fire way to capture the truth, but the seventeenth century had just inherited from the sixteenth evidence that *the* way to certain truth had indeed been found. Montaigne's feeling that we must deeply experience in the concrete the infinite richness of reality and that it can consequently never be reduced to any scheme will never disappear entirely from the Western tradition—Pascal is there to inquire beyond Descartes, and Rousseau beyond all rationalists; later, there will be in literature the Romantics, the Goethes, the Barrès; in philosophy the Nietzsches and the Kierkegaards. But for the moment, the quest for a new method, capable of extending the benefits of the new science to the whole of philosophy, will be the great enthusiastic concern.

Two men, as different in personality as Frenchmen can be from Englishmen, initiated this quest. The philosophies of René Descartes and Francis Bacon are quite different, too, except that their aspirations—to discover and put to use a definite method for rightly conducting the reason—were perfectly congenial. A new epistemology, a new view of the world in the light of the scientific results of the new methods, a new and scientific program mapped out for mankind—this is what they wanted. Bacon evolved a method of experimentation as his answer of how to go about it, while Descartes—who actually did himself more experimenting by far than Bacon—sought to find the key in the essence of mathematical reasoning. When Kant will begin a century and a half later his great work of synthesizing the main streams of modern thought, these two giants will still be haunting the tradition waiting to be reconciled with one another.

IV

Francis Bacon

THE FACT THAT Francis Bacon (1561-1626)[1] was neither a
cleric nor even a professional philosophy teacher is in itself
a measure of the change that had overtaken philosophy since the Middle
Ages. Previously, practically all philosophers were both clerics and
professors. Then in the fifteenth and sixteenth centuries lay professors
of philosophy started to appear, especially in Italy (one thinks, for example, of Peter Pomponazzi at Padua and Bologna). In the seventeenth
century, no philosopher of great note, with the exception of Malebranche, will be a priest, and none at all a teacher! As to Bacon—he
was no less than Lord Chancellor of England, and so little the cloistered
type that he managed to get himself fired for accepting bribes.

Like Montaigne, he is a brilliant essayist, a figure with as secure a
place in the history of literature as in the history of philosophy, and
a man of "experience." In other respects, he contrasts markedly with
the sixteenth-century French aristocrat. In Bacon we feel the product
of a slightly less troubled time—there seems more room for confidence.
Nor is the quest for truth held up by him as a monopoly of the noble
soul; it now seems, we might say, something accessible even to the
middle bourgeoisie, provided they can arm themselves with the proper
method. Method is enthroned in the place of authority, genial intuition,
and virtuous exaltation. And method knows no class.

Nature and Division of the Sciences

THE PLANNING to be done in view of assuring the future progress of
the sciences requires a sort of map of the territory already covered in
order to project our course into still uncultivated zones. A good clas-

sification, or division, of the existing sciences is necessary for the advancement of learning. Bacon divides the sciences, or intellectual disciplines, according to a threefold division of the faculties, or powers, of the human soul: memory, imagination, and reason.

Memory gives rise to history, both natural and civil. Natural history includes the observation and recording of all facts and beings, normal or otherwise, to be found in nature. Normal beings express the "liberty" of nature; abnormal beings represent "errors" of nature. What man makes of nature represents still a third order of facts, which are also "natural." Given the importance this third order of facts was to assume in the future, Bacon was not likely to overlook it. He calls it nature in bondage to man, or chained nature: *naturae vincula.*[2] Here as everywhere in his work, the best of Bacon is found in the details of his discussion, so that no conspectus can begin to do it full justice. For instance, in his description of "civil history," he includes, along with two well-recognized types, church and political history, a third one, practically non-existent in his own time, but destined to a brilliant future: literary history. In the nineteenth century, the great French literary critic, Sainte-Beuve, will pay Bacon homage and claim him for one of his predecessors. Except for a few scattered fragments, Bacon considered this *historia literarum* as not yet existent. So far, nobody has attempted to do for "letters"—meaning all the written monuments left behind by the human mind during the course of centuries—what has been often done for the works of nature and for civil and ecclesiastical institutions; yet without it "the history of the world seems to me to be as the statue of Polyphemus with his eye out; that part being wanting which does most show the spirit and life of the person."[3]

Just as history corresponds to the "cell of the mind" called memory, poetry corresponds to imagination. Bacon speaks of poetry as a philosopher. To him it is a "feigned history" which describes things such as we would like them to be or to have been, that they might give us the satisfaction refused us by reality. Poetry is either *narrative, representative,* or *allusive* (i.e., *parabolical*). Narrative poetry is nothing but an imitation of real history, the only difference being that it recounts an imaginary past. Representative poetry "is as a visible history"; it represents actions as if they were happening before us. Allusive or parabolical poetry is destined to express such ideas as deserve or require to be expressed in a refined and subtle way, as well as to be illustrated by fit examples. By and large, this kind of poetry does not mind obscurity; in fact, it uses it to its own end; but there is another kind of parabolical poetry, which, instead of obscuring its object, aims to demonstrate and to clear up the meaning of what it teaches. Such is the case when "the secrets of and mysteries of religion, policy, or philosophy are involved in fables or parables." Bacon is not complaining about the condition of poetry. Like all natural and free-growing products of the soil, it has always been abundant. We actually owe more to it than to philosophy for our knowledge of man, and nearly as much as we owe to orators in the matter of "wit and eloquence." This is in fact so true that we should not tarry in its company! Let us now pass to the third and most important of the three main parts of learning, philosophy, which properly belongs to the faculty of reason.

Philosophy divides into *divine philosophy*, or theology, *natural philosophy*, and *human philosophy*. Bacon observes that there might be still another kind of philosophy; namely, a "prime philosophy," which would be a sort of universal and common science anterior to the point where philosophy begins to divide into the three above-mentioned ways. Bacon is not quite sure whether or not there *really ought* to be such a *philosophia prima*, conceived as the common spring from which all sciences flow. Anyway, it is at best a desideratum, for it certainly does not in fact exist.

Divine philosophy, still called natural theology, is the rudiment of knowledge about God that can be obtained by reason from the consideration of his creatures. Bacon aptly defines its nature and determines its limits: This knowledge "may be truly termed divine in respect of the object, and natural in respect of the light"; as to its bounds, they are "that it suffices to convince atheism, but not to inform religion." [4]

Natural philosophy (or science, or theory) divides into *physics* and *metaphysics*. Obviously, Bacon is careful to retain ancient names while conscious of giving them new, or renovated, meanings.

By "metaphysics" Bacon does not mean to signify that "prime philosophy," the common source of all knowledge, of which we have only rudiments. That *philosophia prima* should deal with the principles and axioms common to all sciences, as well as with the secondary characters of essences (quantity, similitude, diversity, possibility, etc.), conceived not as logical notions but as real properties of things. Nor is metaphysics to be confused with natural theology such as it has just been described. Then what is metaphysics concerned with? This much should be retained of its ancient notion, that "physics should contemplate that which is inherent in matter, and therefore transitory; and metaphysics that which is abstracted and fixed." [5] In more concrete terms, metaphysics handles the formal and final causes; physics handles the material and efficient causes.

The inquiry into formal causes, which belongs to metaphysics, in no way resembles the traditional speculations about the specific forms of beings and things (man, oak, gold, water, air, etc.). What Bacon has in mind seems to be something like the generalities of physics or, in other terms, the knowledge of the properties that enter the common position of the essences of all actually existing things or beings. What are gravity and levity, density and tenuity, heat and cold; in short, all the natures and qualities, limited in number like the letters of the alphabet, that enter the composition of all particular beings as letters enter the composition of innumerable words? [6] We will discover later when we look with some care into Bacon's theory of induction both *that* the notion of form has by then become very obscure and *why*. For the moment, it suffices to realize that what he is thinking of has little to do with traditional metaphysics, and that his notion of "formal cause" would have more affinity with the general laws of physics than with Aristotelian essential "forms."

The consideration of *final* causes is definitely to be excluded from physics, but metaphysics is to continue to interest itself in ends. This kind of inquiry, says Bacon, "I am moved to report not as omitted but as misplaced." The physicists' concern with final causes worked in the past to block the effort required for the investigation of the "real and physical causes." Final causes in physics, he says elsewhere, are like unto virgins consecrated to God. They bear no children. They can serve in making the wisdom of God more admirable, but final causes cannot teach us anything as to the nature of things; so metaphysics is the place for them.[7]

Mathematics also receives a new stature in the Baconian division of sciences. It was traditionally conceived as dealing with "quantity as such." Were it so, its object would be one of those general properties "relative" to essences which Bacon has attributed to that as yet not existent "prime philosophy" we described above. The true object of mathematics is quantity, not undetermined and in a state of complete abstraction, but determined by its proportions. As such, it is found in things, where it causes many effects. Thus understood, quantity "appears to be one of the essential forms of things." Since metaphysics is the science of forms, mathematics should be counted as a distinct part of natural philosophy and as a special branch of metaphysics.[8] Mathematics is either pure, as arithmetic and geometry, or mixed, as when it is used in connection with various orders of physical phenomena, such as light (optics), sound (music), etc. Bacon casually mentions astronomy, cosmography, and engineering without giving any evidence that he suspected the prodigious development of mathematical physics then about to take place. The reason for this blindness we shall see later.

All the above-named sciences are speculative, and each one of them is attended by a corresponding operative science. Speculative sciences are concerned with the investigation of causes; operative sciences are concerned with the production of effects. The operative parts of philosophy, however, are, according to Bacon, still to be invented, as the knowledge of nature they presuppose is still deficient in his time.

After divine philosophy and natural philosophy, the third main part of philosophy is the *human*, which divides into the knowledge (*scientia*) of body and that of mind. The knowledge of body further divides into *medicine*, concerned with health, *athletics* with strength, and *arts voluptuary*. The knowledge of mind, in its turn, divides into two main parts: that of the substance or nature of the soul, which, in the last analysis, loses itself in religion, and the knowledge of the faculties or functions of the soul, which, although it already exists, could be very seriously bettered.

The faculties of man divide into rational and moral. The study of the rational faculties constitutes what is commonly called *logic*. As Bacon conceives it, this science includes the four intellectual arts, distinguished by their diverse ends: the art of *inventing* that which is sought; that of *judging* that which has been invented; that of *retaining* that which has been judged; and that of *delivering* that which has been retained.[9]

The art of invention in the order of arts and sciences was lacking as yet in Bacon's day, which explains why, he says, so few discoveries are made in the sciences, "the art itself of invention and discovery having been passed over." [10] Bacon would certainly be disappointed to learn that in the twentieth century we are still waiting for logic to invent any new science.

The art of examination or judgment will be dealt with in describing scientific method. The arts of custody or memory and that of elocution or tradition provide Bacon with opportunities to display his talents as essayist, which are far from being despicable but which result in developments of unequal interest. At any rate, his treatment of the art of elocution and tradition (transmission) of knowledge is very personal, and debaters could learn something from it.

After the rational faculties of man come his moral faculties; hence, after logic, *moral philosophy*. All the disciplines related to it deal with the human will.[11] Bacon complains that, so far, moralists have rather accumulated examples and models of moral life than taught the way to achieve it. Here again, concrete problems have been neglectd by men eager to jump at conclusions. Yet his own handling of the nature and division of the good is certainly not of a sort to remedy the defect. A more original contribution, however, is Bacon's intention of setting up as a distinct branch of moral philosophy the *cultura animi*, or cultivation of the mind.[12] In attempting to say something about it, he may have realized why that most useful art was still a desideratum and not an accomplished fact. With his remarkable perspicacity in such matters, Bacon observes that here again men want to solve a problem before collecting its data. The starting point is going to have to be "sound and true distributions and descriptions of the characters and tempers of men's natures and dispositions." Once again we know today from the sad state of the much-talked-about science of characterology that Bacon is destined to be disappointed. His remarks on the subject are clever and often of the highest interest, but what he says of others on this occasion also applies to himself: "The distinctions are found (many of them) but we conclude no precepts upon them." In such cases one can always wonder if precepts can possibly be concluded.

In order not to leave any department of learning unclassified, Bacon concludes his division of the sciences with a few remarks concerning the knowledge of man as a social animal, thereby giving what is today called the "social sciences" their due consideration.

This "civil knowledge," as Bacon calls it, has three parts according to the three general activities of social life: *conversation*, or the art of social intercourse, which, perhaps too optimistically for once, he considers competently handled by the moralists; *negotiation*, or the art of conducting business, a most useful art, Bacon says, but which, shamefully enough, remains to be created; thirdly, *government*, of which the Romans were once good professors, although, in that order, nothing compares with the precepts laid down by King Solomon and received among the divinely inspired writings.[13] So, although as a proper science this branch of learning is deficient, the example of Solomon constitutes for it an illustrious precedent. In handling it, one point should be kept uppermost in mind; to wit, "that all those which have written of laws, have written either as philosophers or as lawyers, and none as statesmen." [14]

With this last branch of human philosophy, the description of philosophy has reached its term. By way of conclusion, Bacon comes back to an examination of divinity; that is, of sacred theology. As a rule, he finds no serious lacuna in the way this branch of learning has been handled by theologians, although his personal preferences are in favor of a "positive" theology as free as possible from useless controversies. Sacred theology ultimately rests upon faith in the divine revelation; but there is no harm in letting reason investigate the meaning of revelation, first in order to achieve some understanding of it, next in order to infer from it speculative consequences and practical directions. This is the point where Bacon finds a good project even in that field: an adequate inquiry into, and competent handling of, "the true limits and use of reason in spiritual things, as a kind of divine dialectic." [15] Definitely, Bacon had an unfailing flair for sniffing out difficult problems!

Bacon's free-flowing mode of exposition makes it difficult to do justice to his philosophical positions, but for all that, few doctrines illustrate better the state of mind obtaining at the dawn of modern times. He himself has felicitously described his work when he wrote at the conclusion of his English treatise on the *Advancement of Learning*: "Thus have I made as it were a small globe of the intellectual world, as truly and faithfully as I could discover." In writing his book, Bacon was the spokesman for countless contemporaries who, like himself, could see in front of them a world of knowledge that had been explored only in part and in which marvelous discoveries remained to be made. The case of Bacon is the more remarkable as personally he had very little to contribute to the promotion of scientific learning. He himself was no scientist, but rather contented himself with standing on the sidelines lustily cheering on those who might follow his grand strategy.

Bacon's Clearing Away the Old

THE IDOLS

THE PROPER PRELUDE to the unfolding of his great design is a final attack on the accumulations of the past. This is carried out in three movements: (a) an attack on the debilities and misuse of human reason which have cluttered the path of inquiry with false "idols"; (b) a destruction of extant philosophical systems; (c) a criticism of the traditional logic of demonstration, which Bacon would replace with a new logic, with a *Novum Organum*, no less, methodically correcting all the kinds of errors envisioned in these attacks and leading to "the Great Instauration of Human Control in the Universe."

The most popularly remembered part of all this is probably the theory of the causes of error. Already sketched in the *Advancement of Learning*,[16] it was given full treatment in the *De augmentis*. One of the less worthy reasons it is still remembered is that Bacon gave the four general causes of error rhyming Latin names: *idola tribus, idola specus, idola fori, idola theatri*. He had not forgotten his own remarks on the art of mnemonics! He calls these causes of error *idola* because they are false images which, coming between us and objects, cause in us a distorted view of reality, becoming rooted in the mind until they are to it almost like objects of worship.[17]

Bacon first attacks the idols that result from the inherent weaknesses of human reason. Prominent among these *Idols of the Tribe* is the inclination to conceive the world in a way that would make it handy and cozy for the likes of us.[18] Hence the mind's inclination to "suppose the existence of more order and regularity in the world than it finds"—we think at once of the Aristotelian universe, with man stationed in the ideal center, its perfect spheres and circular motions, turning by means of anthropomorphic attractions and repulsions—a singularly comprehensible and hospitable place for man. The trouble is that science is bogged down by the interference of the will and the affections, which have been allowed too free reign in describing things not the way they are, but as one would have them be.[19] A second disastrous trend of the human intelligence is its readiness at a moment's notice to fly off into the wildest generalization on the flimsiest experiential pretext,[20] which is all the more catastrophic, given the inherent "dullness, incompetency and deceptions of the senses."²¹ These are both reasons for more, not less, careful attention to the data of these senses—for a will to observe, classify, experiment.

Bacon next acknowledges a problem already wonderfully developed by Montaigne—that of idols born of peculiarities of the individual judgment, arising from particularities of background. We are chained in the Cave of our own imaginations, condemned like Plato's spectator to seeing reflections of our own phantasy because we fail to see the need to turn to the things themselves.²² Our worst tyrants are our own creations: a Democritus can see nothing any more but his marvelous atoms. Aristotle must recast everything in the categories of his "Logic." We can also be blinded by our special gifts: those minds that are stronger in distinguishing things never synthesize, and the synthesizers never seem ready to acknowledge real differences; just as those who love what is new refuse honor to what is old, and the reverse. The list, Bacon suggests, could be extended *ad nauseam*.²³

The third class of idols is the most troublesome of all, the *Idols of the Market Place*, the obstacles placed in the path of the understanding by words. "Men believe that their reason governs words; but it is also true that words react on the understanding."²⁴ Philosophers in the modern tradition, from Montaigne, with his sarcastic remark that more books are written on books than on things, all the way to Heidegger, with his insistence that reliance on words worn out by usage in the market place is an essential part of inauthenticity, have pointed to the fact that while in language alone we conceive, reliance on the already-formed language of the past can become a block to our access to things. Bacon's contribution to this tradition is a remarkably precocious one.

The names of things that do not exist (resulting from fantastic suppositions) and the names of things which exist, but which, as the result of faulty and unskillful abstraction, are less helpfully named than misleadingly, constitute, according to Bacon, the two principal categories of Market-Place Idols. "Fortune," "the Prime Mover," "Planetary Orbits," "Elements of Fire" are good examples of the first. As an example of the second, Bacon cites the word *humid*, which actually signifies a whole variety of actions loosely and confusingly lumped together: "It signifies that which easily spreads itself round any body; and that which in itself is indeterminate and cannot solidize; and that which readily yields in any direction; and that which easily divides and scatters itself . . ." Bacon's list goes on and on, showing his reader as concretely as possible how a word can become the lazy substitute for assiduous observation.[25]

The three classes of Idols thus far considered hold influence over all men; and against them the thinking man, the man of science, will have to conduct a by no means hopeless but still never-ending battle. The fourth group, however, those *Idols of the Theater* which are produced by the prancings and pretensions of the philosophers, are not so widespread among humanity and are subject to complete neutralization by a right application of method.[26] These constitute the subject of a new area of attack.

THE DEBILITIES OF TRADITIONAL PHILOSOPHIES

IN CONFRONTING the *Idols of the Theater,* we move to the second aspect of the three-pronged attack on the old cobwebs. Here we can gain precious indications of the kind of general philosophical atmosphere in which Bacon wants the new endeavor to unfold. The first of the three kinds of traditional philosophy to be considered is of course the fashionable butt of all sarcasm, the "sophistical," of which Aristotle's "fashioning the world out of categories" is a good example. The destruction of the other Idols, especially the Idols of the Cave, takes care of this kind, as far as Bacon is concerned, well enough to excuse the need to develop the point any further.

The second sort of philosophy taken to task requires more comment; namely, the *empirical.* At first it might seem strange that the great prophet of close observation of nature should attack "empirical philosophy." The *empiricists,* sneers Bacon, are like ants: They store up observations and then live off them all winter without making anything out of them. That's almost as bad as the *rationalists,* who occupy the other extreme in this regard—they are like spiders, spinning fine systematic webs out of their own substance. What, then, does Bacon propose as an alternative? That the new philosophers gather like bees the nectar from flower and field and, passing it through the organ of the mind, transform it into the most highly usable "honey and wax" of knowledge.

Bacon's position here is complex and extremely interesting because, in an effort to react against a number of extremes in contemporary intellectual trends, he ends up outlining an epistemological position both original and subtle. Looking back on later developments like the actual successes of science, we can now point out both valid and erroneous elements in this epistemology. That he is right in his insistence on the need for a great deal more detailed, accurate observation and in his attack against the overly deductive and verbalistic philosophers of the universities, no one would care to dispute; that he is right, too, in some respects in attacking "empiricism" is also clear: it is true that nature will not yield up its secrets to mere observation. (Bacon goes so far as to suggest that there is no such thing really as sheer observation.) In this regard, Bacon makes a singularly important remark: Nature, he says, yields up her secrets best when "vexed" by experiments, just as a man will show his real mettle best when caught in a difficult situation. He does not elaborate on the remark, but its sense is fairly obvious. To work an experiment, one must have some sort of plan; this directs us deeply into the phenomenon and helps guide our regard. Hobbes will develop the psychology underlying this position, suggesting the guiding role of "desire" in giving a unity to a train of impressions. How true Bacon's idea can be in some cases is illustrated by the example of Bacon's contemporary, William Harvey, who in his anatomical experimenting proceeded almost as though he were using Bacon as a laboratory manual. Not only did he excel in clinical observation and in the invention of ingenious experiments, but he followed another Baconian suggestion for transforming the "nectar" through the mind's intervention: *comparison*. As we shall see in considering the positive program of the "new logic," Bacon attacks the "empiricist" tendency merely to enumerate positive instances; we must, he insists, seek out negative instances, deviations, variations, before we can arrive at a rule of constancy with any hope of exactness and certitude. Harvey was careful to compare his anatomical observations on the human body with results obtained from dissecting apes and other animals. In his work of 1628, *De motu cordis et sanguinis* (Frankfurt, 1628), he is careful to point out that he had been confirming his views "for more than nine years" by "multiple demonstrations."

As an example of the wrong sort of empiricist, the kind who is suffering especially from that "Idol of the Cave" which consists in remaining too tied up with his own little observation, Bacon cites William Gilbert. This worthy had in 1600 published a work, based on his experiments with the magnet, in which he daringly attempted to explain the cohesion of the whole universe in terms of the one phenomenon of magnetism. Such a philosophy has its foundations, declares

Bacon, "in the narrowness and darkness of a few experiments. To those who are daily busied with these experiments, and have infected their imagination with them such a philosophy seems probable and all but certain; to all men else, incredible and vain." [27] The alchemists are cited as nefarious examples in the past, as Gilbert is in the present.

Yet history looks back rather kindly on Gilbert; in fact, to many he now seems a predecessor of Newton in the discovery of universal gravitation. Bacon, as we saw above, was aware of the importance of the challenge of practical imagination—what Hobbes will later term "desire"—in any search for knowledge. But what he failed to see—and this mistake cost him a good chunk of reputation in the history of science—was the extraordinary role the mathematical imagination could and would play in the conquest of nature. Gilbert's invention was in the line of the discoveries to follow; in tending to concentrate on a single, simple force, the scientist's imagination produced a manageable concept, potentially translatable into mathematical terms. Galileo and Kepler were the first actually to make such translations. The mathematically gifted Kepler was able to make order out of the rich harvest of astronomical observations he inherited from Tycho Brahe, because he followed a hunch that order could be achieved through conceiving the planetary orbits as ellipses. Bacon particularly disliked Galileo's method of turning the problem of motion into the problem of geometrical bodies moving in geometrical space. He rebelled against the tendency to leave out complications, like air resistance and the tensions that occur within the moving bodies themselves. He did not sufficiently appreciate the overriding value of mathematical exactness and projection, and failed to realize that, by first leaving out every secondary consideration, the mathematical philosophers would discover simple unifying rules and would then be able to add in later the temporarily set-aside complications. The actual methods followed by the Keplers, Galileos, and Newtons turned out to far outstrip any philosopher's prophetic epistemology; no one really foresaw their actual follow-your-nose development. Bacon does say, "If physics be daily improving, and drawing out new axioms, it will continually be wanting fresh assistance from mathematics," and again, even more strongly, "The investigation of nature is best conducted when mathematics are applied to physics." But the philosophy of nature underlying his detailed program of "new logic" never went more than halfway toward the point where such sentiments could become realities. Mathematics was not Bacon's forte and so remained in his estimation just an instrument.

Before turning to the details of the "new logic" itself, there remains a third sort of traditional philosophizing to be demolished: the "superstitious" or "theological," the kind that freely invents "abstract forms and final causes and first causes, with the omission in most cases of causes intermediate," an "unwholesome mixture of things human and divine." [28] Bacon cites Pythagoras and Plato "and his school" as examples, evidently wishing to make certain that he has fully covered the lot of Christian scholasticisms, whether Platonic or Aristotelian. What is interesting in this regard is Bacon's tremendous narrowing of the field of "philosophy" through the exclusion, not only of mysteries knowable by faith alone, but of all consideration whatever of the nature of God; all finality beyond that necessary for the conduct of human affairs, this finality itself being narrowed to a purely naturalistic and materialistic scope; and all proofs for the existence of a first mover.

Bacon's attitude to religious truth is quite complex. Perhaps we had better say a word more about it before we go on, particularly as his point of view in this regard is often misrepresented. To oppose scholastic philosophy and even scholastic theology, as Bacon very vehemently did, does not, in his view, necessarily entail any opposition to theology as such, much less to religion. Bacon acknowledged that God himself possesses the highest knowledge, knowledge which, since it is not acquired, must not, like ours, be called "learning," but rather wisdom or "sapience." We, however, in our struggle to acquire knowledge, must turn to his works to learn of God. Creation witnesses to the *power* of God, by showing it at work in the creation of matter, and to the *wisdom* of God, by showing it as the cause of the beauty to be observed in the disposition of the form.

Actually the world of creation as Bacon conceived it is not so different from the Middle Ages' notion of a world dependent on God, even to the point of including the "celestial hierarchy" of the pseudo-Dionysius. The patristic tradition has a place in his own notion of learning, and although he thinks the Reformation was willed by God, he does not consider the Church of Rome past mending. On the contrary, Bacon sees the revival of learning and the revival of religion as destined by God to take place together, so that even Roman Catholicism ultimately benefits by it. The eminent part taken by the Society of

Jesus in this revival does not escape his attention: "We see the Jesuits, who partly in themselves and partly by the emulation and provocation of their example, have much quickened and strengthened the state of learning, we see (I say) what notable service and reparation they have done to the Roman see." [29] At any rate, far from finding any opposition between science and Christianity, Bacon thinks that, although a drop of philosophy may invite atheism, a strong dose of it will bring man back to religion.[30] In order not to form a distorted image of Bacon, let us not forget the full title of one of his major works: *Of the Proficience and Advancement of Learning Divine and Human.* The first book is entirely devoted to the consideration of divine learning.

The New Organon

THE METHOD that is to achieve "a true and lawful marriage in perpetuity between the empirical and rational faculty" and thereby become "the mind's machine" for conquering nature must attack first the problem of gathering the nectar from the fields through the weak instruments at our disposal. Heretofore "no search has been made to collect a store of particular observations sufficient either in number, kind, or in certainty to inform the understanding, or in anyway adequate." [31] This is not to say that natural histories have not been gathered—the "great Aristotle," for instance, supported by the wealth of Alexander, composed an "accurate history of animals." But natural histories composed for their own sake are not like those collected with the precise purpose to supply the understanding with information intended to help build up a philosophy. The strength of the new observation, which attempts to achieve this, lies in its alliance with modern mechanical arts. We have seen that just as a man's deep character is best revealed under trying circumstances, "so likewise the secrets of nature reveal themselves more readily under the vexations of art than when they go their own way." [32] If nature has to be tampered with to be made to give up her secrets, why then, we might ask, have not the "mechanics," who have worked practically with her, discovered more material of genuine scientific interest? Because they are just the opposite of those philosophers who take wing on the slightest empirical pretext and fly to the most universal conclusions; "for the mechanic, not troubling himself with the investigation of truth, confines his attention to those things which bear upon his particular work, and will not either raise his mind or stretch out his hand for anything else." [33]

The method usually followed by philosophers should be inverted. Instead of coming down from axioms to particular conclusions, as in syllogistic deduction, the scientist should go instead from particular experiments and observations up to axioms—induction, in other words, should replace deduction.

But scientific induction should be "learned induction," not the hasty inductions of everyday life. Bacon's description of this induction relates it to the logic of the invention of sciences, classified by him among the operations of the rational faculties.[34] Instead of proceeding by simple enumeration of favorable cases, it proceeds by the due rejections and exclusions: *per rejectiones et exclusiones debitas.* The instances to be excluded are often the first ones to catch the eye; they must be rejected if, after careful investigation, they appear as being related to the fact under discussion by a merely accidental tie. The true sign that a supposed cause is the real one is that it alone successfully resists all attempts to eliminate it. Socrates had applied this method of progressive elimination to the determination of ethical notions. This is why Aristotle attributes to him general definition and induction as personal contributions to philosophy; but, concerning nature, Socrates said nothing.[35] Plato applied the same method to the investigation of physical reality, but he did it in a still incomplete way. The method remains to be perfected and generalized.

This result is obtained by subjecting induction to precise rules. Hence the Baconian theory of the *tables of induction.*

In observing facts, the observer should set up three tables. First, a *table of existence,* or *presence.* On it are listed all the instances in which the property under consideration is present; the more varied the circumstances amid which that property is found to be present, the better. The colors of the rainbow, for instance, are found, it should be noted, not only in clouds but also in drops of water or in certain crystals. A second table should list all the observable cases in which facts similar among themselves do not exhibit the property at stake; let us call it the *table of absence.* The third table, or *table of degrees,* should list the variations of the property under discussion; that is to say, all the observable cases in which it can be said to be more intense or less intense.[36] John Stuart Mill will make use of a similar system of tables in his *Logic,* III, viii, but will considerably improve it.

A proper, balanced induction based in rich observation solidly disposed in artful Tables of Discovery, and sufficiently "vexing" to reveal inner secrets: this, then, would be the right kind, the balanced kind of "stretching out the hand." The really central point in Bacon's exposition is that instead of flying from a few particulars to so-called first principles—axioms of the highest generality—and from these deducing the middle axioms, one should proceed "by successive steps, not interrupted or broken," rising from particulars to middle axioms, then from these to wider and wider principles.[37] The lowest axioms are not yet the most fruitful, differing only slightly from bare experience, but they provide a firm base for the middle axioms, which, though not so general as to be "notional and abstract and without solidity," are rather the "living axioms, on which depend the affairs and fortunes of men." [38]

The middle axioms embody the mind's grasp, not of the particulars, but of the universal forms to be found in a real class of particulars. The still more general principles abstract beyond the level of those forms which are real fixed laws of action.

But what exactly does Bacon mean by "form"? Quite obviously final comprehension of the method being offered us depends on a correct answer to this question. Here we touch on a central difficulty in Bacon's positive conception of nature. Central to any scientific philosophy is a sound conception of causality. In routing Aristotelianism, Bacon, as we have already suggested, while retaining the terminology, has really put the four causes in their traditional sense straight to the door. In describing the realm of natural philosophy, we saw that he excludes from its consideration "final" and "efficient" causality, which he would leave, he says, to that "metaphysics" which is concerned with "immutable causes." Bacon conceives of efficiency as a mechanistic shove, and finality—barely mentioned and then explicitly labeled a menace to physics—drops out of sight.

Natural philosophy is concerned only with the material and formal causes. But these fare in Bacon's hands little better than the immutable causes. Bacon seems always to conceive of matter as "some definite kind of stuff," and he has great trouble clarifying his notion of form; this is not too surprising, although, given the centrality of the notion to his whole "logic," it is most unfortunate. The notion of form had been through quite an ordeal during the days of waning scholastic thought. The conception that seems to have impressed itself on Bacon as "the" scholastic conception—and one, therefore, to be avoided at all costs—was that of a formal principle so real in itself that it could exist independently of the realm of concrete things. To distinguish his doctrine from any vestige of tired Renaissance Platonism, Bacon likes to insist that "in nature nothing really exists besides individual bodies," [39] and he suggests that the "form" is somehow a principle of unity—"a fixed law"—accounting for whatever uniformity there is in the operation of a thing and for our ability to induce a primordial unity under the manifold of operations, but without being something that can either be grasped immediately in itself or exist by itself. Bacon is trying to retain the advantages of a scholastic notion of form without being obliged to accept a medieval philosophy of form—an untenable combination of desires that leads to great difficulties in working out a clear and consistent doctrine.

Philosophy for the next one hundred fifty years will continue to be concerned with the problem of reconceiving the relationship of the substance to its qualities and of arriving at a satisfactory description of the "formal" unity underlying consistency in phenomena. The deeper dimensions and the ultimate roots of the problem must be gradually disengaged through the course of our narrative. As a beginning, Bacon's early, rather ambiguous efforts to formulate a modern doctrine of "natures" and forms is quite instructive.

The senses, he declares, are confronted immediately with "natures" through which science is to seek to know the "forms"; that is, the "fixed laws" underlying these natures and responsible for the constancy of their manifestation. There are two types of natures: the simple and the complex; simple natures being qualities like yellowness, transparency, opacity, tenacity, malleability, fixity, etc.;[40] and complex natures constituting substances, like "oak," "gold," "water," "air," etc.[41] To inquire into the form of "complex natures," says Bacon, would be "neither easy nor of any use," for they are infinite in number; besides, they are just complexes of simple natures, and these latter can be studied more easily, as they fortunately "are not many and yet make up and sustain the essences and forms of all the substances." [42] Not only does the reality confronting the scientist thus seem to reduce to a kind of qualitative atomism reminiscent of Anaxagoras and prophetic of Berkeley, but the fact that the number of simple natures is very limited is encouraging; Bacon even contends that among the simple natures some are more primitive than others, and therefore constitute in turn *their* forms, which means that the inductive method has only to happen ultimately upon this small crowd of ultimate notions in order to possess the world!

All of which seems clear enough. But then we encounter a passage like this, in the fifteenth Aphorism of the First Book of the *Novum Organum*:

> There is no soundness in our notions whether logical or physical. Substance, Quality, Action, Passion, Essence itself, are not sound notions: much less are Heavy, Light, Dense, Rare, Moist, Dry, Generation, Corruption, Attraction, Repulsion, Element, Matter, Form and the like; but all are fantastical and ill-defined.

One is forced to admire the range with which this critical mind lashes out; but it must be said, after such an attack, we are not left with much to work with. Where does one turn now? The fourteenth Aphorism would encourage and direct the seeker of truth: Hope lies in obtaining notions that are not "confused and over-hastily abstracted from the facts"—which is to be accomplished by "true induction." But the trouble is that, other than the undeveloped hint about the need to "vex" and "constrain" nature and a few examples of his own efforts at clarification, Bacon has left no systematic program assuring the proper acquisition of sound general notions. The *New Organon's* positive program lays down some basic rules governing the induction of axioms; i.e., of universal principles. But these axioms themselves are composed of terms the soundness of which has to be presupposed before the axioms can be of any value. How are we to come by such notions?

When the Cartesians take up the problem of securing a foundation in certain clear notions, they will proceed by a road altogether different from Bacon's vaguely indicated "induction." The clear and distinct idea analysis will be based, as we shall see, on a conception of "idea" that is far more successful in shaking the dust of peripatetic pathways from its feet than Bacon ever was.

What is perhaps more ironic is the fact that the ultimately most successful scientific tradition, the Galilean-Newtonian, never will share the "father of science's" concern for conceptual and axiomatic induction, nor, as we have already suggested, even his concern for exhaustive observation and enumeration. Instead of securing a base in carefully inducted notions of qualities and states, mathematical physics in the seventeenth and early eighteenth centuries will dispense with them altogether, pinning its well-justified hopes instead on a mathematical system which confines itself to constructions whose clarity and simplicity are assured by its restricted nature.

Where Bacon's remarks will turn out to have the most validity is in the area of the classificatory life sciences. We could suspect that already from the way Bacon understood and appreciated the physician Harvey and completely missed the significance of Gilbert's speculations with magnetism. Be this as it may, men should be appreciated for their positive contributions rather than for their deficiencies. *Non omnia possumus omnes*—we cannot all do everything—and the fact that Bacon himself has often failed to recognize the positive contributions of his predecessors does not justify us for making the same mistake.

He himself was no scientist, so he could speak of scientific research really from hearsay only, yet he correctly weighed the transformation of the philosophical notion of scientific knowledge brought about by the recent development of the methods of observation. Incomplete as it is, his epistemology contains sound elements, particularly concerning the respective merits of deduction and induction as methods of discovery in natural sciences. It has become customary to say that no scientist ever made a single discovery by merely applying the famous three tables of Bacon. This is probably true, but the object of epistemology is not to teach men the art of making discoveries, it is to give a correct description of the way discoveries are made. Bacon has noted this all-important fact, that scientists had begun to make new discoveries at the precise moment they had replaced the *Organon* of Aristotle by a new one. His own task was simply to describe it, and if there is much more in the method of science than the three tables, they certainly are included in it.

Above all, perhaps, Bacon was what Carlyle was to call a "representative man." He epitomizes the boundless ambition to dominate and to exploit the material resources of nature placed by God at the disposal of man. From this very important point of view, it must be observed that the seventeenth century, at the same time as it witnessed the birth of modern science, has seen the beginning of the age of the machines in which we are living still today. Science, mechanics, engineering, and a progressive industrialization of human life were inseparably connected from the very beginning of these events.

In the thirteenth century, the Franciscan Roger Bacon had clearly anticipated the future transformation of human life in consequence of the limitless possibility to invent new machines. In his own utopia, the

New Atlantis, Francis Bacon was in a position to go much farther than his medieval predecessor along this line. For page after page, this unfinished treatise describes life such as it is on the unknown continent of Bensalem and as it will be in the cities of the future when they all possess "engine-houses, where are prepared engines and instruments for all sorts of motions," flying machines, "ships and boats for going under water," and numbers of such marvels. His dream city had "two very long and fair galleries," one sheltering "patterns and samples of all manner of the more rare and excellent inventions," the other containing "the statues of all principal inventors." There now are many such galleries; their existence should help us to understand what was a new and living force in the message of Francis Bacon.

V

Thomas Hobbes

THE SIXTEENTH-CENTURY anti-Aristotelians manifested varying degrees of materialism. Two among the five "innovators"—Telesio, Campanella, Bruno, Gassendi, and Vanni—mentioned by young Descartes in a letter to a friend,[1] namely Vanni[2] and Pierre Gassendi,[3] were pretty thoroughly materialistic. But we have just seen in the example of Bacon that it was possible to be an "innovator," a ferocious anti-Aristotelian, and a man of science, without necessarily espousing the cause of a radical mechanistic explanation of everything.

Still the new conception of the universe as a machine—indeed the discovery that machinery itself held a tremendous potential—provided in the seventeenth century a constant temptation to explain everything as an interplay of "forces." It was Francis Bacon's one-time secretary, Thomas Hobbes,[4] who seems to have most unequivocally yielded to this temptation. He set out to reduce the body to a machine, man to a body, and the state itself to a kind of super-body which itself functioned according to no higher principle. A passage like the following can give an idea of how thoroughly Hobbes is ready to merge the notions of life and machine:

> Nature, the art by which God hath made and governs the world, is by the *art* of man, as in many other things, so in this also imitated, that it can make an artificial animal. For seeing life is but a motion of limbs, the beginning of which is in some principle part within; may we not say, that all *automata* (engines that move themselves by springs and wheels as doth a watch) have an artificial life? For what is the heart, but a spring; and the nerves, but so many strings, and the joints but so many wheels, giving motion to the whole body, such as was intended by the artificer? [5]

Hobbes was in complete agreement with Bacon that "final causes" are "impertinent"—the word is Bacon's—in the quest to understand the material world. Though Bacon had met with numerous difficulties in his effort to substitute some new, more scientific conception of "form" for the Aristotelian formal causes, Hobbes could well feel that he had undercut this whole problem by embracing mechanism, which can explain everything in terms of clearly explicable univocal forces enjoying the inestimable merit of being *measurable*!

The reality of all perceptible objects is made up uniquely of motions of this one sort. The knowable nature of a substance is nothing but an aggregate of "accidents" or appearances, this knowable nature being not the thing in itself, but the bundle of effects the thing has on our senses. In the extramental thing, the accident exists only as motion or rest, figure and extension; but *as known*, the accident is a product of the interaction between the force of the thing and the reacting force of our sensation. Hobbes would find support from both Galileo and Descartes in declaring all secondary qualities subjective, while only the primary qualities of figure and extension, expressing directly the underlying mathematico-mechanical reality of motion, can be considered fundamental. How they escape from being merely subjective—i.e., the result of an interaction between the forces of the thing and the force of sense—is not at all clear.

In keeping with his mechanization of the substance, Hobbes insists that causation be studied "as a whole," rather than classified into kinds of causes. The "entire cause" he then defines as "the sum or aggregate of all such accidents, both in the agents and the patient, as concur to the producing of the effect propounded; all which existing together, it cannot be understood but that the effect exists with them." [6] The aggregate of accidents *moving* is the "efficient" cause; the aggregate *moved*, the "material"; together they can account for the whole movement, or generation—"formal" and "final" causes being nothing but aspects of the efficient causation: *formal* cause designates the production of knowledge in us by the action of the efficient aggregate of the known essence; *final* cause designates the special way sensate beings act as efficient causes. The upshot of this reconstruction is to clear the field of all extraneous, if not to say bogus, considerations, thus leaving philosophy free to pursue a mathematically inspired analysis of mechanical connections between interacting forces.

Hobbes was fifty years old before he launched himself on his philosophical quest, but when he did, it was for a definite reason and with a definite end in mind. Already convinced of the efficacy of the mechanical-mathematical method, with which he had fallen in love in France and the real force of which he had thus only lately discovered, he now suddenly realized that, for all the progress in mechanics terrestrial and celestial, nothing had been done to exploit the possibilities of the method for revealing the *mechanics* of *man*. If only the causes at work in human sensation and reason were to be laid bare, one could then advance from knowledge of the mechanism of the individual to a science of the whole body politic, an enterprise evidently sorely needed, if one were to judge by the contemporary troubles of the Britannic Isles.

In fact, the connection between Hobbes' psychology and political philosophy was designed to be even closer than one between a study first of the unit and then of the whole. Turning Plato's *Republic* around, Hobbes will consider the commonwealth a great artificial "body" designed by men in imitation of their own.[7] Comprehension of the individual human nature, then, is the comprehension of the *model* of the state, prerequisite for understanding the commonwealth itself.

Human Knowledge

HOBBES' MECHANIZATION of man begins with sensation. The cause of sense is the external body, or object, which presses the organ proper to each sense; which motion, by the mediation of the nerves, continues inward to the brain and heart, there causing a resistance, or counter-pressure, or "endeavor of the heart to deliver itself," which endeavor, because outward, appears to us an objective reality (rather than a sub-jective movement). And this "seeming, or fancy," is that which men call sense. Hobbes formally defines sensation: "A phantasm made by the reaction and endeavor outwards in the organ of sense, caused by an endeavor inwards from the object, remaining for some time more or less."[8]

Applying the principle of inertia to these sensible motions, Hobbes concludes that of itself an impression should remain indefinitely, were competing motions not to obscure it.[9] This interference, however, does occur, because the absent object is generally no match for the intensity of the presence of that which is impressing us now. Since new impres-sions are upon us constantly, it follows that the longer the time elapsing since an initial impression, the more it shall have "decayed," or been obscured by subsequent experiences.[10] This decaying sense is the "imagination," and "memory" is just an expression for our recognition, when we attempt to recall something, that it is growing old and dim.

Hobbes' conception of "understanding" is directly based on this conception of sensation. Understanding is nothing more than a special sort of imagination; namely, that which is able to recall past experiences through the aid of words. To understand exactly this function of words, we must realize that our intellection of the world consists not in the sensory formation of single representations, but in the properly intellectual function of *mental discourse*. Our experience is not that of isolated images, but of a continuous, interlocking flow of experience which produces a "train of thought." [11] The residual chain of images produced by the imagination is not a haphazard sequence of fragment after fragment, but a representation of motions "that are relics of those made in the sense; and those motions that immediately succeed one another in the sense, continue also together after the sense."

The train of thoughts, or mental discourse, can be either unguided and without design, as when one's thoughts wander, or *regulated by desire*. By "desire" Hobbes means the strongest originative motion in us, the most constant and the most directing. "From desire ariseth the thought of some means we have seen produce the like of which we aim at," which in turn arouses the thought of a means to that means, and so on "until we come to some beginning within our own power." [12] This is the source of our search for "properties" of things. Desire also works in the other direction, toward discovery of new synthesis. And because desire is so powerful an impetus, one can constantly refer to it, so that the continued presence of the same desire can guide a whole train of thoughts.

Man and the animals share one kind of regulation in common: they can, under appetitive direction, seek out the causes of an imagined effect. Yet man can go a step farther: upon imagining anything whatsoever, he can seek all the possible effects that it might produce. Only man has *foresight*, so only he can be *prudent* and *wise*. Hobbes cautions, however, that in this complex world "such conjecture, through the difficulty of observing all circumstances, [can] be very fallacious."[13] The more experienced individual—i.e., the man who has enjoyed the greatest number of chains of impressions—will be the more "prudent," which means that his conjectures will have a greater chance to turn out, even though the belief that they will is less prudence, really, than presumption, since only God can truly know the future.

Besides sense, decaying sense in imagination, and the train of thoughts in the understanding, there are no other Hobbesian principles of natural cognition. But whence arise the terms used in mathematics and science? How do they fit into the picture? Man, unlike the other animals, can generate in his understanding with the help of speech and method a series of *artificial* motions—which are of special concern to one interested in political society, for without them, and above all without speech, there would be "amongst men, neither commonwealth, nor society, nor contract, nor peace, no more than amongst lions, bears and wolves." [14]

The first use of these artificial motions, or words, is to serve as *notes of remembrance*. The second is to make our thoughts and desires known to others. The truth and the right use of words are inseparable; indeed Hobbes defines "truth" as "the right ordering of names in our affirmations." [15] The effort to be true begins by getting our definitions straight, the way the geometers, practitioners of "the only science that it hath pleased God hitherto to bestow on mankind," [15] are careful to do: we must get it straight what each word stands for, and then see that its usage remains consistent. Then we must be sure that we use them in the right order; that is, that they stand accurately for our real train of thoughts. He deceives who declares "that to be his will which is not." [16]

Because man can "mark" his thoughts with words, he alone enjoys the power of reckoning, or "reason," which is simply the ability to add thoughts to one another or subtract them; i.e., to proceed from many particular thoughts to a general affirmation, and from a generality to descend, or subtract, down to particulars.

> As arithmeticians teach to add and subtract in numbers; so the geometricians teach the same in lines, figures, solid and superficial, angles, proportions, times, degrees of swiftness, force, power, and the like; the logicians teach the same in consequences of words; adding together two names to make an affirmation, and two affirmations to make a syllogism, and many syllogisms to make a demonstration; and from the sum, or conclusion of a syllogism, they subtract one proposition to find the other. Writers of politics add together actions to find men's duties; and lawyers, laws and

facts, to find what is right and wrong in the actions of private men. In sum, in what matter soever there is place for addition and subtraction, there also is place for reason; and where these have no place, there reason has nothing at all to do.[17]

Reckoning is an affair of accumulating forces beginning with the capture of an impression in the movement of a word, and culminating in the drawing of most general conclusions, called *theorems* or *aphorisms*, which capture a great many such movements in a single general statement.

What is Hobbes driving at in this theory of speech and reason? Remember that his great *Leviathan* is really interested in explaining the body politic after the model of the human mechanism. Now by showing that what has traditionally been considered the highest faculty in man can be explained in the same terms as the movements of the body, and that these movements are forces and compounds of forces of greater or lesser degrees of complication, Hobbes has cleared the way for an explanation of the state as just such a mechanism on the grand scale. That this is what he is in fact doing (he explicitly states that it is) becomes, if possible, even more obvious as we approach the center of force in human beings, the passions and the will.

Passion and Voluntary Motion

HOBBES DISTINGUISHES three kinds of motion in man. We have been considering up to now details of the cognitive; as a body moving in the world and moving other bodies, man also possesses the vital motion of a living organism; the third sort of motion possessed by humans is that by which the mind is able to move its own body. This "voluntary motion" has its beginnings in the inward motion of the object impressing itself on the sense and remaining in the imagination. This inward motion or "passion" passes from the brain to the heart, where it either quickens or slows our vital motion, resulting in pleasure or, should it hinder the heart's development of vital motion, pain. These movements generate, respectively, either desire or aversion for the objects originally causing them.

There is of course then no absolute good or evil, any more than there is an absolute truth; all are motions within us, all are relative to the primitive drive of the vital organism, "desire," a *conatus* toward self-preservation. Deliberation works in function of this vital end, seeking to determine what concretely will be to the individual's harm or benefit. The imagination guided by passion is called upon to use its experience through reasoning to foresee the possible good and evil corresponding to our hopes and fears, the deliberation continuing until the action is either done or declared impossible.[18] The last moment in the deliberative series, the one issuing in action or a final denial of it, is termed *will*. Its "freedom" consists only in an absence of physical impediment to the body when it carries out the final result of the deliberation. This conclusion, which is tantamount to denying freedom in any traditional sense, follows perfectly from the mechanistic principles governing Hobbes' whole analysis. The entire psychological process from sensation to voluntary motion has been presented as the development of a univocal kind of movement of the sort outlined in the author's analysis of causes, an interaction of mechanical causes subject to the kind of necessity of which science can conceive. The tendons holding together the great Leviathan—the State—are going to be of no other sort.

The Body Politic

THE MECHANISM of the individual having now been sufficiently analyzed, Hobbes can turn to the study of the composition of those artificial bodies which are human societies. He begins his analysis with a description of the condition of man in the natural state, showing from this the need that gave birth to the ingenious invention which is society and the state.

In their natural condition men are fairly equal in bodily strength, mental powers, and experience; these natural powers are used, by each lone individual, to increase his power and avoid pain—especially the ultimate painful menace, death itself. But though the individual may struggle alone, in fact he is not alone; through no fault of his own, there are others, likewise struggling to make their way, to avoid death, to exercise freely a growing power. Collisions are absolutely unavoidable; in fact, the natural state of these struggling personal *atoms* is a state of war—*bellum omnia contra omnes*. In invoking this primitive state of affairs, Hobbes does not have to consult ancient documents or travelers' accounts of seventeenth-century America. It is enough to see how we lock up our doors at night and sleep tightly under good police protection! And civil war in England—what a fertile source of example!

What keeps this state of affairs from degenerating even further into the domination of the weak by the strongest man is that we are really roughly equal. Hobbes is not thinking of an equality of right, based in a common human nature, but an equality of fact—the crude fact that the weakest man can deal out the *summum malum* to the strongest. Vainglory leads us to overrate our capacities, and under its urging, the passions, though not intrinsically perverse, are soon working havoc with our wills, prompting each man to outdo his brethren, and if he cannot outdo them, to drag them down. The weakest, if driven in this way far enough, can bring down the strongest through an insidious act of homicide.

So the warfare is perpetual; the struggle of several men for one available thing goes on and on, force deciding only temporary superiorities. In this natural state, there is no law; and where there is no law, there are "no arts; no letters; no society; and which is worst of all, continual fear, and danger of violent death; and the life of man, solitary, poor, nasty, brutish and short." [19]

It is above all *fear of death* that drives men to seek a respite from the dog-eat-dog natural situation, but also the desire to make it possible really to enjoy the things necessary for "commodious living." Reason shows us that peace must be obtained and that it can be enjoyed only if the individual is willing to give up some of his "right to all things," thus consenting to a restriction on his liberty.[20] Since this liberty, according to Hobbes, consists in nothing but an unimpeded exercise of the "natural right" to go out in search of what he needs for life, it is obviously a certain amount of precisely this right that he shall have to give up. If he does give up part of his liberty to some person or persons, it is at that moment of transference, *and not before*, that obligation, the "ought," first enters the scene. Justice and injustice begin only when the *contract* involved in the mutual transference of right to a beneficiary is entered into.[21]

This transference does not involve a particular deed by which we give up our right to specific things; it is rather a general determination of the will to transfer liberty perpetually to an authority who will be acknowledged as reigning over one. But what is to guarantee that, once this transfer is made, my bellicose passions will not persuade me to withdraw allegiance? Only a *common power* can achieve this, which it does simply by terrifying men to the point where they will cease to be their own arbitrary judges of when they will or will not obey the common authority.

The commonwealth is that power that comes into existence when enough individuals are ready to give up their previously unrestricted liberty. Hobbes includes this note of "the great multitude" in the formal definition he furnishes for a "commonwealth": ". . . *one person, of whose acts a great multitude, by mutual covenants one with another, have made themselves every one the author, to the end he may use the strength and means of them all, as he shall think expedient, for their peace and common defense.*" [22] Note how Hobbes, in keeping with his notion of the unity that should obtain in causal analysis, has woven all of the causes into this one great unity, the multitude comprising the material cause; their covenant, the efficient; mutual peace and common defense, the final.

One thing in the definition may particularly perplex the democrat— the "one person." Obviously Hobbes holds to no divine-right theory of kings, but is he not nonetheless a bit narrow in his conception of the form a commonwealth is going to have to take? Not at all. In the first place, Hobbes explicitly deplores the idea that we should give up our liberty to another natural person as such, for that would lead straight into slavery. The *sovereign* is to be conceived as an *artificial* person, either one man or an assembly, who functions as authorized representative of the many, within the agreement of the covenant. It should not be concluded from these remarks, however, that Hobbes held to a constitutional conception. The power once turned over to the commonwealth, the state is "that great LEVIATHAN, or rather, to speak more reverently, that *mortal god*, to which we owe under the *immortal God*, our peace and defence." [23] This selection of the sea monster spoken of in the *Book of Job* (chapter 41) will find innumerable echoes in European thought, such as Nietzsche's description of the state as "the coldest of all cold monsters." There is no limitation on the state once established, nor is it even possible to think of a government of checks and balances; the government can be either monarchy, aristocracy, or democracy, depending on whether the "person" to whom power is transferred is one sovereign, a class of men, or a more general assembly. That is almost a detail, a matter to be worked out prudentially in concrete situations; in any event, the power, whatever its form, is absolute, above the law—in fact, source of all law—and however bad the situation that may arise in various governments, it is yet to be preferred to the brutal state of nature without any government at all.

Nevertheless, there is a kind of limit built into the situation of the establishment of the covenant. Since sovereignty is instituted by covenant for the sake of peace and security, there is no obligation to obey governmental commands of a sort that would fundamentally defeat this purpose. A man cannot legitimately be commanded to abstain from self-defense, or to kill or maim himself or his loved ones, or to risk his life in war when he can provide a substitute, or even, adds Hobbes, to testify against himself. (Hobbes would obviously like to find a place for those precious English "civil liberties.") And where the law is silent, we are left at liberty to follow our own decisions.

Moreover, even though the sovereign is under no strict obligations, he (or they) is (or are) a natural person, and as such he does have *duties* to fulfill, duties flowing from his nature: he is bound, in a word, *to follow his reason*. All the detailed duties—the need to keep the state in a condition of preparedness, the need to see to the proper distribution of goods, etc.—are really so many prescriptions of reason in view of the end of a commonwealth. The dictates of reason may seem rather slim protection against the possibility of tyranny, but Hobbes has little else to offer.

The reaction in seventeenth-century England to Hobbes' mechanistic philosophy and to that most impressive of his machines, the Leviathan, was generally one of unmitigated horror. "The Monster of Malmesbury," the ladies in the salons termed the little old man who even in his eighties was still quietly working away—though then on the less dangerous task of translating Homer. But the eighteenth century was to prove the golden age of the machine: the Encyclopedists will lavish seven volumes of the best paper on engravings of every kind of machine in existence; the atmosphere by then will have certainly changed. Ironically enough, it is not only the materialist Hobbes, but also the great idealist Descartes, who contributed to this new enthusiasm for the machine. Descartes, as we are now going to see, turned over the whole material sphere to a mechanism that in essential spirit is not much different from that of his English contemporaries. Only there was still for Descartes another world above it.

VI 🏵

René Descartes

THE PHILOSOPHY of René Descartes cannot be rightly understood apart from his own person and life.[1] He himself has
deemed it useful to recount for the benefit of his readers the history
of his intellectual formation at the Jesuit college of La Flèche and the
sequence of reflections that led him to his final philosophical conclusions. Historical information has thrown light on some parts of his
narrative. It remains noteworthy, at least, that Descartes' philosophical
thought has come down to us inseparably tied up with what he once
called "the history of [his] own mind."

The Method

FRANCIS BACON had not been a very successful scientist; Descartes, on
the contrary, began his philosophical career as a very successful mathematician. Despite his exceptional merits, Viète had not clearly put
under the eyes of the public the idea of the new mathematical method
we now call analytical geometry. This is what Descartes did in his own
Geometry of 1637; but the main difference between Viète or the other
mathematicians like Fermat and Descartes was that mathematics was
never to Descartes other than the revelation of a universally applicable
method, which means that, over and above being a mathematician, Descartes was a philosopher. In its general notion and in its structure, the
whole philosophy of Descartes is conditioned by the fact that it was
born of the faith of its author in the universal validity of mathematical
reasoning.

The notion of "method" is therefore fundamental in the philosophy
of Descartes, not only in idea but in *feeling*. He felt convinced that,
once the true method was possessed, the inequalities among human

minds would lose much of their importance; the discovery of truth in all domains would become a question of "know-how." He himself never doubted that, equipped with his method, he would lay down at least the foundations of all sciences during his own lifetime, including even a scientifically founded medicine. His first philosophical publication was quite naturally devoted to this notion of "method." In his own mind, there was no difference between philosophy and methodical thinking. However, a first attempt to define and describe his method ended in failure. *The Rules for the Direction of the Mind* is unfinished. Descartes never said why he had not completed the treatise. But one likely reason is that he found it too long and too complicated as it had developed. A philosophical exposition of the true method had to be very short, or else it would not really itself be *methodical* in Descartes' sense. A second attempt resulted in the *Discourse on the Method of Rightly Conducting the Reason and Seeking for Truth in the Sciences.*[2] This time it was not a question of describing in a detailed manner the operations of a mind in quest of truth, but, in a more general way, the "principal rules regarding the method" which Descartes had discovered.

These rules are laid down in the second part of the *Discourse.*[3] They are four in number. The first is to accept nothing as true which the mind does not clearly see to be so. This abbreviated formula implies three stipulations: (a) carefully to avoid hasty and ready-made judgments (i.e., precipitation and prejudice); (b) in each judgment, to limit assent to that part of its object which the mind perceives clearly and distinctly to be true ("distinctly," that is, as being true of that object only); (c) to carry one's reflections in due order, the due order being that which, beginning with the simplest objects and the easiest to understand, progressively rises to the knowledge of the most complex and difficult to understand, this condition being so absolute that, even in cases when there does not seem to be an order of complexity between the objects, it is necessary to assume a fictitious one; (d) the last rule is, in each and every case, to make at the end of the demonstration a review so complete and so general that one can feel sure that nothing has been omitted.

These apparently simple formulae were laden with metaphysical implications, especially the first one. The decision only to assent to clearly and distinctly perceived objects of thought could not be extended beyond the boundaries of mathematics without assuming that all objects of knowledge could be so perceived. The assumption was all the bolder as, in Descartes' own terms, clear and distinct apprehensions should leave no room for doubt.

This difficulty has to be removed if one wants to understand the meaning of Cartesian philosophy, and the only way to remove it is to realize in what sense, in the mind of Descartes himself, its method is "mathematical." His discovery of analytical geometry had consisted in substituting algebraic symbols for lines and figures. The certitude and generality of the conclusions obtained by the new geometry were therefore due to the fact that, in it, understanding was operating on signs quite independently from the natures of the things such signs could represent. The only problem then left for the understanding to solve was that of finding the proper order between these signs, or the creation of one where none was found. Descartes knew for sure that this decision had been justified by success in the creation of analytical geometry. He also knew, from personal experience and from that of Galileo, that most arduous problems in astronomy and in physics could be successfully submitted to mathematical treatment. There was one more step to take; namely, to decide that the mind was to treat of all conceivable objects as mathematicians treat those of their own science. Descartes did not hesitate to make that decision. He knew it was a crucial one. At the beginning of his *Olympica* he has even dated it for us: "On the tenth of November 1619, as I was full of enthusiasm and finding the foundations of a marvelous science . . ." November 10, 1619, is the birth date of Cartesian philosophy.[4]

The nature of the admirable science should now be made clear. Descartes did not declare that the human mind is only able to know numbers and figures, as in arithmetic and in geometry; nor did he decide that henceforward all objects of knowledge could and should be given the forms of numbers and figures. Rather, he discovered that all objects should henceforward be handled as if they were mathematical objects, even if they were not so. This is the sense of the passage in the *Discourse*, II, where, right after laying down the four rules of the method, Descartes expressly adds that the "long chains of reasoning," by means of which the geometricians achieve the most difficult demonstrations, had caused him to think that, very likely, "all objects knowable to man" are mutually related in the same way as the terms of those long, but simple and easy, geometrical demonstrations.[5] So we know not only when Cartesianism was born, we also know how it was conceived in the mind of Descartes. It was brought about by those long chains of reasons which "gave [him] occasion to imagine that *toutes les choses qui peuvent tomber sous la connaissance des hommes* follow one another in the same way." *All things;* no exception is made; the order of all things is of the same nature as that of the terms of a mathematical demonstration. The only problem remaining is to find that order in each case and to avoid accepting any demonstration as true in which that order is not made evident.

The Tree of Knowledge

GIVEN THE CAUSE of the birth of Descartes' notion of science, then, it is evident that Descartes always held a global and unitary view of thought. Since all cognizable objects are knowable in the same way and follow an order similar to that of the terms in a mathematical demonstration, the whole body of human knowledge is necessarily one. To build up such an all-embracing philosophical expression of reality had been the ambition of Francis Bacon in his *Instauratio magna*—an ambition not fully realized; but Descartes thought he had found the proper way to accomplish it. Centuries before Bacon, the encyclopedia of Aristotle had looked like a fulfillment of that dream, but because he failed to realize the true nature of mathematical knowledge, the philosopher had followed an entirely wrong order, starting always from sense knowledge, and always impeded by it, as geometers were before the invention of geometrical analysis, when they hung on to sensations and images, instead of doing away with them to concentrate on the "order of the reasons."

All this entailed an entirely new departure in philosophy. As young Descartes had learned it from the Jesuits at La Flèche, the order of the philosophical disciplines imitated the order of acquisition of human knowledge. Because the mind goes up from sensations to concepts, so also according to the peripatetics the order of the sciences should rise from physics to metaphysics. In a philosophy that proceeds, instead, from clear and distinct notions to the knowledge of all its objects, the order was bound to be the reverse.

This consequence can be observed in the very important Preface added by Descartes to the French translation of his *Principles of Philosophy*.[6] Philosophy is the study of wisdom, which is the perfect

knowledge of all that which man can know in view of the conduct of
his life, of the preservation of his health, and of the invention of all the
arts and techniques. Such knowledge can only be "deduced from the
prime causes, so that, in order to acquire it, which is properly called
to philosophize, one must needs begin with the quest for those prime
causes, that is for the Principles." Now such principles must answer
two conditions: first, they should be so clear and evident that the human mind cannot doubt their truth (first rule of the method), and,
next, they should be such that the knowledge of all the rest is conditioned by them, while their own knowledge is conditioned by that of
nothing else (third rule of the method: order). After this, one must
strive to "deduce" from those principles the knowledge of the things
that depend on them, and this should be done in such a way that, in the
whole series of the deductions, there be nothing not wholly manifest.
True enough, only God is perfectly wise, for no one else thus owns
the entire knowledge of all things, "but men can be said to have more
or less wisdom, according as they have more or less knowledge of the
more important truths." In short, whereas the scholastics considered
philosophical wisdom as proceeding from things to their principle, and
theological wisdom as proceeding from the first principle to things,
Descartes conceived philosophical wisdom as an imperfect imitation of
theological wisdom, following the same course and proceeding in a
similar way.

Thus understood, "the whole philosophy is like unto a tree, of which
the roots are Metaphysics, the trunk is Physics and the limbs that spring
from that trunk are all the other sciences, which can be reduced to
three main ones, to wit: Medicine, Mechanics and Ethics, meaning
thereby the highest and most perfect Ethics which, as it presupposes
the entire knowledge of the other sciences, is the ultimate degree of
Wisdom."

Such a philosophy—one whose method is inspired by that of mathematics; which considers sense experience an impediment; and which,
doing away with imagination, undertakes to deduce the whole body
of human knowledge from a small number of self-evident principles
and, if possible, from a single one—such a philosophy marks a singular
turning point in the history of the human mind. The world, the structure of which Descartes intends to explain, is not to him a product of
his own mind; in this sense, his philosophy is a realism. On the other
hand, his interpretation of the universe goes from mind to things; it

does so of set purpose; to that extent, then, it shares in the nature of idealism. Those who like labels could perhaps call Cartesianism a methodological idealism, or an idealism of method.[7] Whether, in philosophy, an idealistic method can justify realistic conclusions is of course a problem beyond the competence of mere history. But the history of philosophy proves its usefulness just by raising such questions.

Prime Philosophy

THE MARKED PREFERENCE of Descartes for the name of "prime philosophy" is now easy to understand. The traditional appellation "metaphysics" was entirely justified because, in peripateticism, the discipline designated by that name really came "after" physics; in Cartesianism, on the contrary, it comes before physics as being the root of all the other disciplines; its properly Cartesian appellation is therefore justified.

Descartes has given four expositions of his prime philosophy: in the *Discourse*, in the *Meditations*, in the *Answers to the Second Objections*, and in the First Part of the *Principles of Philosophy*. The text of the *Meditations*[8] is the most perfect of the four. To follow the thought of Descartes through the six meditations, be it in a summary fashion, is the only possible way to form an idea of what, using the traditional language, we call his metaphysics.

THE METHODICAL DOUBT

THE METHOD requires (first rule) that we should accept in our judgments nothing that is not so clearly and distinctly understood that we can have no occasion to doubt it. The First Meditation is an application of that precept. It accumulates all the reasons and pretexts it is possible to find for revoking into doubt certain commonly received notions which philosophers sometimes use as principles in their doctrines.

In doing so, Descartes naturally draws on the supply of arguments heaped up by the skeptics from antiquity till his own day, but this is not because there is any trace of skepticism in his own mind. When he uses a skeptical argument such as, for instance: How do I know that I am not insane? or that I am not asleep and dreaming what I seem to see? he does not mean to tell us that he really is in doubt of those points. His aim is merely to make us realize that such certitudes as these are not, as they say, *beyond doubt*, so none of them can be the first principle. The usual objection, that Descartes cannot really pretend he does not know whether he is awake or not, is pointless. Of course he knows it; the only question is: Is that knowledge of such nature that its truth cannot possibly be questioned? The answer is, no. If a man looks for something in a basket full of miscellaneous objects, the best way to make sure whether the thing is there or not is for him to empty the basket and to sort its content until he finds what he is looking for. This does not mean that the rest is not good; if it is, it will have its turn, only just now it is not wanted.

The name "methodical doubt" well expresses this deliberate character of the operation. It also accounts for the "hyperbolic" nature of certain reasons of doubting invoked by Descartes; for instance: that I might have been created by some evil genius who employs his whole power in deceiving me (this is called the argument of the *Malin Génie* —the Great Deceiver). The question is not: "Is this true?" but "Granting that it is not true, how can I be sure (by natural reason) that it is not true, at a moment in my inquiry when, since it is its first moment, I have not even proved that there is a God?"

But why all this insistence on showing as doubtful conclusions that men particularly like to hold as certain, not to say sacred?

First, we are so prone to assent to uncriticized judgments that Descartes wants us to bend backward to lose the habit of assenting to prejudice, which is incompatible with philosophical and scientific inquiry. To get rid of it is to get rid of a vice; this cannot be done in a moment, nor without methodic effort.

Secondly, this training in the practice of scientific method is so different from skepticism that its ultimate aim is to eliminate, once and for all, the skeptical prejudice that certitude does not exist. If Descartes succeeds in his undertaking, Montaigne will have been beaten at his own game. The skeptics insist that sense knowledge is deceitful. They are right. The greatest single cause of errors in philosophy precisely is that we take the testimony of sense at its face value. The methodical doubt sets out for us a very effective way to detach our mind from the senses and thus to get it fit for a truly mathematical and philosophical speculation.

THE FIRST PRINCIPLE

DESCARTES IS LOOKING for the first principle. Such a principle must exhibit two properties: In order to be a principle, it must be self-evident, and in order to be first, it must be such that, without itself being deducible from anything else, it can lead to the knowledge of all the rest. The objection that the first principle is being as such is irrelevant from the point of view of Descartes. From the abstract notion of being, nothing at all can be inferred. What Descartes calls the first principle is the first known object of knowledge which, being known and dealt with according to the exigencies of order, will make possible the knowledge of all the rest. The principle to be found is that of a science of the real, not that of a logical deduction.

Is there anything I remain sure of even while doubting of all the rest? Yes, my own existence; for if I doubt, I think, and if I think, I am. At least this is what I say if I am asked how I know that I am. My answer to such a question necessarily assumes the form of a reasoning, but there is no reasoning in the judgment whereby I grasp my own existence in my very act of doubting. *Que sais-je?* (What do I know?) Montaigne asks. Montaigne knows at least this, that he is, otherwise he could not even ask the question.

Let us therefore start from this initial certitude: "I think, hence I am." Now this is for us the time to remember the first rule of the method: to accept nothing more in my judgment than what is presented to my mind so clearly and distinctly that I can find no occasion to doubt it. In the present case, what is there in my judgment that cannot possibly be doubted? There is this, and this only: that I am, and since I know I am because I know I think, the only kind of being I can claim for my own is that of a thinking thing. I therefore know that I am and, to some extent, what I am, but if I do not want to admit anything that is not necessarily true, I must confine myself to saying that "I am, precisely speaking, nothing else than a thing that thinks; that is to say, a spirit, an understanding or a reason." This is real knowledge, for indeed "I am a true thing, and a truly existing thing," but if I am asked what kind of thing I am, my only answer is: "I already said it: a thing that thinks."

Attention must be paid to the clause of Descartes' answer: as far as I know at present, I am but a thinking thing. It follows from there that

I am nothing else. At least, if I am anything else, I am not aware of the fact. Am I what is called a "human body"? Perhaps, but just now I know nothing about that. I know that I doubt, that I reason, that I will, that I imagine; I know all these things because to doubt, to reason, and to imagine is to think. But I do not know that I am a body, or that I have limbs, or that there is outside me such a thing as what they call extension according to the three dimensions of space. I am not denying the existence of those things; my only point is that, at the stage of my reflections I now have reached, I have no reason to judge that they belong to my nature, nor even that they actually exist. To conclude: I think, hence I am, is evident; I think, hence I have a body, is not evident; let us therefore affirm the first of these two propositions and refrain from affirming the second one.

Summing up this Second Meditation, Descartes himself says that it teaches us two things: First, that even if I make free to deny the existence of all those things of whose existence I have the least doubt, it nevertheless remains impossible for me not to recognize that I exist. Secondly—and this point is of great importance[9]—I have learned to draw a distinction between the things which pertain to the nature of a thinking thing—that is to say, to mind—and those which pertain to body. Even though I were the toy of some deceiving genius, he could not deceive me in this, for if I am deceived, I think, and if I think, I am an existing thinking thing, Q.E.D.

OF GOD: THAT HE EXISTS

SO FAR, the knowledge I have of myself as mind does not permit me to affirm the existence of another being besides myself. I do not know I have a body; I am not even certain there is such a thing in the world. On second thought, however, I realize that the knowledge I have of myself as mind necessarily implies another judgment; namely, that there is a God.[10]

Indeed, the thinking act that enabled me to grasp my own existence was an act of doubting. In order to know I was doubting, I must have had the notion of what my cognition was lacking for it to be a certitude; so I was discerning the imperfect from the perfect; now, in order to see this distinction, I must first have had the notion of perfection. Whence did that notion come to me? Since it is clear and distinct, it has an object in the mind, and although an object in the mind has not the same reality as the same object outside the mind, one cannot pretend it is nothing. This "objective reality" of the clear and distinct notions—that is to say, their reality as containing a real object of thought (which is not the case of obscure and confused ideas)—is the very basis of Descartes' proof of the existence of God from his effects.

For indeed, if our notion of perfection has any objective reality, it is something. According to the principle of causality, there is nothing without a cause; hence my notion of perfection has a cause. Moreover, it follows from the same principle that there cannot be more in the effect than there is in the cause (otherwise that supplement of reality would have no cause); the problem then is to discover a cause of the notion of perfection that contains as much reality as is represented by the notion. I cannot be that cause, since I am grasping my own existence in an act of doubting, which involves imperfection. Only a perfect being can be such a cause, and since God is the name we use in order to signify a perfect being, it is evident that God exists.

A first remark on this demonstration. Such as it is found in the Third Meditation, it offers a perfect sample of what Descartes called a chain of reasons similar to those used by the geometers. This can be shown by submitting it to the acid test of the fourth rule. Let us enumerate and review its moments. God exists; why? Because I can think of no other cause of the presence of the notion of "perfect" in my mind. How do I know that notion is there? Because I realize I am doubting. How does the notion of "doubt" involve that of perfection? Because to doubt is not to be certain, a fact I would not notice if I had not the notion of perfection in knowledge present to the mind. How am I sure I really am doubting? Because doubt was the very act of thought that propelled me to discover that if I think, I am. Going over the whole chain of reason, I finally grasp it, so to speak, as a simple intuition. At first I was saying: I think, hence I am; I can now say: I doubt, hence God is, which is tantamount to saying: I think, hence God is.

A second remark is that this first proof of the existence of God is calculated to fill up the place of the traditional proofs taken from the effects of God (the so-called *a posteriori* demonstrations). But, since Descartes cannot assume the existence of an external world, which he intends to prove in the Sixth Meditation only, he cannot base his demonstration on the fact that there is a material world subject to change. Nevertheless, it is his intention to comply with the teaching of St. Paul (*Rom.* 1:20), that God can be known *a creatura mundi;* that is to say, from the things he has created. For indeed man is such a creature; his mind is likewise a creature, and if there is in man's mind an objectively real notion of perfection, that objective reality, too, is a creature. This is what Descartes recalls to the theologians of the Sorbonne in the Dedicatory Letter prefixed to his *Meditations*. Moreover, he himself notes now, his very method complies with the injunction of the Apostle. Arguing as a theologian, from Scripture, Descartes adds: "Again, by what is said in the same passage, to wit: *That which is known of God, is manifest in them*, we seem to be warned, that all that which can be known of God can be shown by reasons which we need not seek outside of ourselves and which, taken in itself, our mind is able to provide to us." It seems, then, that Thomas Aquinas did not pay enough attention to this *in illis* of the Apostle. Just as Galileo in his *Letter to the Grand Duchess Christina*, Descartes is explaining Scripture to the theologians.

There is another—and very important—point. By establishing the existence of God as the cause of man's notion of perfection, and since there must be in the cause at least as much as there is in the effect, Descartes has proved that God is perfect. Now to deceive is a mark of imperfection. God therefore is not a deceiver. This eliminates the "hyperbolic" skeptical argument by the possibility of man being created and constantly misled by some "Great Deceiver." The last skeptical doubt as to the validity of rational knowledge has thus been removed.

OF THE TRUE AND THE FALSE

I AM NOT being deceived by God; still I am often deceived; how is this possible? God has not created man with such a nature that error be for him unavoidable (otherwise God would be a deceiver), but he should not have created him exposed to error. In short, man is not infallible; is not God responsible for the fact? The Fourth Meditation removes this difficulty.

God cannot be blamed for producing an imperfect creature, for the very nature of created being implies that it is finite and imperfect. The question is: Does the kind of imperfection proper to man on this point necessarily condemn him to commit errors? In order that there be error, there must be judgment. Taken in itself, an idea is neither true nor false; it becomes true or false when I affirm it or deny it of another one; thus to associate and dissociate ideas is to judge. To affirm or to deny is the proper act of judging. How are judgments possible?

Were understanding the only faculty of my mind, I still would perceive ideas, which is the very function of understanding; but I could not associate and dissociate them in order to form judgments. To account for the possibility of judgment, one must resort to a different faculty, which is the will. Every act of judging thus presupposes ideas perceived by understanding and a will that affirms them or denies them. When the will affirms only that which understanding evidently sees to be true, there can be no error; on the contrary, there always is error when the will affirms or denies that which understanding does not perceive clearly and distinctly. Things being so, man has nothing to complain about. His will is free; because it is free, it can judge in the absence of evidence and thus be mistaken, but the very same freedom enables it to avoid ever judging in the absence of clear and distinct knowledge, so that, if man does judge precipitously, he is, absolutely speaking, responsible for his errors.

This is actually in what man's liberty really consists. He has free choice, since his will is always able to will or not to will, but this always open possibility (liberty of indifference) is not itself liberty.[11] True liberty consists in using free choice only to affirm as true that which is true and to choose as good that which is good. Ethics is here at one with the first rule of the method: The perfection of liberty consists in never assenting to that which understanding does not clearly and distinctly perceive to be true. The responsibility for our errors therefore truly rests with ourselves; we are fallible because we are creatures, but it lies in our power never to be mistaken.

SECOND PROOF OF GOD'S EXISTENCE

THUS ASSURED that true judgments are possible in themselves and always in our power, the mind makes a first attempt to get out of itself and out of the realm of spiritual beings. Already in the Second Meditation the idea of body and that of extension offered themselves to the mind's examination. The conclusion then was that, in the last analysis, a piece of matter, such as, for instance, a piece of wax, is to my mind nothing else than what I know about it. Nevertheless, on reflection, I realize that, besides the clear and distinct ideas of mind and God, there is in me still a third one; namely, that of extension such as it is defined by geometers. It assuredly is clear and distinct, since thought can distinguish in it several figures endowed with necessary geometrical properties which we have no other choice than to attribute to them. Can it be proved that extension exists?

Descartes is here out to prove the existence of the external world of matter, but the very thought of geometrical extension causes him to change direction and to make tracks for a second demonstration of the existence of God.

What confers upon geometrical figures, such as triangle and circle, the character of certitude and necessity which geometers attribute to them? It is precisely that, in geometrical demonstrations, the mind affirms nothing of those diverse figures beyond that which it perceives as belonging to them with necessity. Now, if we examine the idea of God, which has been seen to be that of an absolutely perfect being, we shall realize that existence belongs to such a being as necessarily as their own properties belong to triangles or to cubes. And indeed there is contradiction in thinking of the supremely perfect being as deprived of such a perfection as actual existence; consequently, God is, or exists.

This argument calls for two remarks. First from the point of view of history. Just as the preceding proof of the existence of God was a reinterpretation of the traditional argument based on the principle of causality, this second one is a reinterpretation of the famous argument of St. Anselm in his *Proslogion*. The scholastics were divided in their preferences, some favoring the *a posteriori* way of Thomas Aquinas, others preferring the *a priori* way of Anselm, proceeding by an analysis of the notion of God; Descartes shows that his metaphysics justifies both methods, which, to him, was one more proof of its superiority.

The second remark is philosophical. The casual way in which Descartes introduces his second proof, as though it were on the occasion of an altogether different problem, that of the existence of matter, surprises at first in a philosophy where the order of the reasons reigns supreme. In point of fact, Descartes is here proceeding in an orderly way. The order of the reasons cannot be, in Descartes' doctrine, of the same nature as in a philosophy inspired by the logic of Aristotle. It does not deduce, in a linear way, from the general to the particular. The Cartesian order of the reasons is imposed by the very nature of its objects. In the present case, it is only natural that the metaphysician should be reminded of the existence and nature of geometrical objects at the very moment he turns to extension in order to ask the question of its existence.

Having reached this conclusion, Descartes feels at last free to proceed with the examination of an infinitude of objects that are neither God nor the mind; namely, material objects. But do such objects exist?

THE MATERIAL WORLD AND MAN

THE EXACT TITLE of the Sixth Meditation deserves attention: *Of the existence of Material Things, and of the real distinction between the Soul and Body of Man.* Descartes could not say more clearly and explicitly that the distinction of soul and body receives its complete demonstration in this meditation only. Moreover, it calls our attention to the fact that, in order to prove the *real* distinction of mind and body, one must first establish that material things exist.

There is something amazing in the confidence betrayed by the first sentence of the Sixth Meditation: "Nothing now further remains but to inquire whether material things exist." Is there, outside my mind, an actually existing extension answering to my idea of it? Here again the method forbids us to conclude the actual existence of the external world from any other thing than the content of our own thought. We started from the *I think*, we are still in it, and it is within it that we must find a way to get out of it. The moment is an important one for the history of philosophy. We are now witnessing the first attempt to *demonstrate* the existence of the world. Innumerable philosophical consequences will follow from it.

Extension first offers itself to the mind as an *idea*. It is the very same notion which provides geometry with its object. Insomuch as it is intelligible, that idea is not necessarily tied up with imagination. This can be seen from analytical geometry, which, doing away with images, appeals only to the mind. Now from the mere idea of extension nothing can be concluded as to the actual existence of its object. The idea of a non-existing God is an absurdity, and it is not absurd because the mind finds it to be so; on the contrary, I know that God exists because the intrinsic necessity of an existing God forces upon my own mind its own necessity. No such thing happens with extension. I find no contradiction in thinking of a non-existing extension. In fact, the extension which is the object of geometry does not actually exist, so its idea provides no way out of the mind.

The *image* of extension is also contained in my mind. The easiest way to account for its presence would be to suppose that my mind is united to a body so that, by applying itself to it, imagination could form its image. This is a possible explanation, but we decided (first rule) never to assent to any conclusion in which understanding could find the slightest occasion to doubt. Now it is not evident that, by itself and without a body, mind is not able to form such an image. Taken as the object of traditional geometry, the image of extension provides an excellent object for scientific knowledge. This is seen from the geometry of Euclid. Since it is not absolutely evident that mind cannot form images, the image of extension in it is no proof that extension exists outside it.

Nothing else now remains to be accounted for in the mind but *sensation*. Indeed, the sensations of color, heat, weight, etc., are likewise thoughts, so their existence in the mind demands to be explained. This time, however, the situation is different. Unlike our idea and our image of extension, sensations are confused and obscure. They exhibit no intelligible content to the mind. This would not be if they were produced by mind only. Taken in itself and apart from any other thing, thought should normally contain nothing that is not intelligible; that is to say, clear and distinct. That there is in thought obscurity and confusion can only come from the fact that its substance is altered by a substance foreign to its nature. It even must be tied up with that substance intimately enough to account for the deep modification its content undergoes in consequence of its union with it.

The mind then must be united to a body, because otherwise the existence of such thoughts as sensations could not be accounted for.

Now this union is a fact which is experienced as such. I know that sensations do not originate in the mind alone because, unlike ideas and even images, they are not in our power. They come unexpectedly and, when they do come, it does not rest with us to perceive them or not. Hence, in every man, an irresistible propensity to consider sensations as coming to us from actually existing external objects. This is not a belief; it is an immediately given experience, of which the evidence is such that, were we deceived in this, God could not be excused from the reproach of being a deceiver. Since he is not a deceiver, it is certain that God has so constituted man that the movements caused in our nerves by external objects modify definite portions of the brain by which, in virtue of its union with the brain, mind is so affected as to produce the kinds of thoughts we call sensations.

There is therefore, outside of mind, a world of matter with one particular portion of which it is united. This union is a substantial one, so that, in the last analysis, there are three diverse orders of substances: mind, extension, and the union of mind and body, which is man. It is noteworthy that, in this philosophy, the real distinction of soul and body cannot be demonstrated except through the demonstration of their substantial union. Sensation proves their union; for this union to be real, body must actually exist, since mind cannot be really united with a non-existent; consequently, the very demonstration of the substantial union of mind and body is, by the same token, the final proof of their real distinction. Thus is explained the otherwise paradoxical title of this Sixth Meditation, which I beg to recall: *Of the existence of Material Things, and of the real distinction between the Soul and Body of Man.*

The problem raised by this conclusion was to occupy some very great minds during the whole seventeenth century, and later.

Natural Philosophy

METAPHYSICS IS THE ROOT of the Tree of Wisdom. Physics is the trunk of the tree. How does the trunk grow out of the root?

The last conclusions of metaphysics, or prime philosophy, are the prime principles of physics. The latter studies the world of bodies; now metaphysics has just defined the object of physical research with perfect precision; nothing further remains for physics but to accept it.

Prime philosophy is loosely said to prove the existence of the external world; it only proves the existence of extension and nothing more. Without the union of mind and body, as well as the confused thoughts that follow from it, the actual existence of the world of bodies could not possibly be proved; but the only clear and distinct idea we can form of that world is that of extension, along with that of motion, which is but the series of places occupied in space by one and the same body. Now extension and its modes are the only things whose actual existence we have demonstrated; moreover, they are the only notions related to the external world which we can clearly and distinctly conceive; they are therefore the only things that can possibly be the objects of physics.

Hence three important consequences: [12]

In the first place, the physics of Aristotle is completely eliminated, because the foundation upon which it rests is overthrown. According to the peripatetics, every body is a substance composed of two elements: a form that defines its nature and confers upon it its specific properties, and a matter that provides for the form a subject in which to subsist. In order to account for the properties and operations of any being, the physics of Aristotle simply attributes to it a form that is supposed to be the cause of such operations and properties. This illusion of the Aristotelians can be accounted for; still it remains an illusion.

Descartes will admit in nature one case, and one only, of a body joined to a form with which it constitutes a substantial unity; it is that of our own body, of which the form is our soul. From early infancy, man experiences in himself what it is to be an animated body, which its form moves and directs in its operations; by a spontaneous, though illegitimate, extension of this human experience, men imagine that what is true of their own body is also true of all the other ones. Hence they supposed that there was in each and every body an internal principle of growth and motion, which is its "form." Hence the physics of Aristotle, in which all bodies are conceived as analogous to the human body, endowed with kinds of souls which we call "forms." Aristotelianism in physics is a barely disguised universal animism. What prime philosophy teaches us, on the contrary, is that soul is really distinct from body, so that, outside of thought, nothing exists but extension and its modes. The notion of substantial forms is thus destroyed; the traditional explanation of physical phenomena disappears along with it; the way is open to a purely mechanistic interpretation of the material universe. The world of modern science has now found its definition.[13]

The second consequence following from the new prime philosophy in the order of scientific knowledge is that, since the new universe is nothing but extension, it must possess all the attributes of extension, and no other ones. This completely transforms the traditionally received view of nature. In the first place, matter becomes an entirely intelligible notion. In the philosophies of Plato and Aristotle, the notion of matter represented what there is of the accidental and irrational in reality; it symbolized that which, in things, remains impervious to the mind. Henceforward, since it now is identical with extension in space, which is the object of conventional geometry, it becomes just as fully intelligible as space itself is; answering, as it now does, the more exacting demands of mathematical demonstration, physics, which has matter for its object, ceases thereby to be a dialectic that stops at probabilities.

As extended matter itself, it becomes the proper domain of necessity.

There is more. Because of this same identification of matter with extension, it will become possible to deduce *a priori* the main characteristics of the universe. Since the universe is extension in space according to the three dimensions, we can be sure that it exhibits all the essential properties of extension itself. Space is indefinite, since, in thought, space can be limited only by another space; hence, since it is space, the world is indefinitely extended. For the same reason, the world is full and there is no void in it; for indeed, space is a continuum, so an empty space would still be space. Again, space is indefinitely divisible, since there is no particle of space, however small, that we do not conceive as susceptible of being still further divided: hence matter is indefinitely divisible and there are no indivisible atoms like those imagined by Lucretius. Generally speaking, it suffices to know the propetries of geometrical extension in order to know those of space, and thereby of matter; since our only clear and distinct idea of it is that of geometrical extension, we can feel sure that the world of nature contains all that which is contained in it, and nothing else.

A third series of consequences following for physics from metaphysics is that the nature of physical laws is previsible from what we now know of the nature of God. The Supreme Being whose existence is demonstrated by prime philosophy is not a mere "author of nature," very powerful, yet finite. The Prime Being is a God worthy of the name; that is to say, a perfect being, truly all-powerful, creator not only of nature but of the very laws of nature, including those of mechanics and mathematics. There are no such things as the so-called eternal laws, which philosophers consider binding for God himself. That could not be. Our understanding is finite; all that which it comprehends is bound to be also finite; consequently, it cannot be binding for an infinite God. The contrary illusion comes from our habit of thinking of God as a sort of superman, more intelligent and more powerful than we are, but endowed as we are with an intelligence and a will. Hence the common temptation to guess the hidden reasons why he has made things such as they are. The naïve hunting for final causes, besides being useless, has no object. Since God is infinite, he is simple; there is in him no distinction, even of mere "reasoned reason," between what we call understanding and will. The universe is just what God made it to be; the physicist has not to ask himself any "why": his only task is to describe it such as it is.

The Cartesian World

LET US SUPPOSE a free and infinitely powerful God who is also a perfect God; we cannot ask *why* he is going to act thus rather than otherwise, but it is permitted to ask *how* he will act. One of the most obvious characters of his action will be immutability. God then can only have created an extended matter, endowed with a certain motion, of which the quantity remains constant, and which is continually transmitted from one part of extension to another according to laws themselves constant and simple.

This principle being admitted, the fundamental laws of nature can be deduced from it: (1) every thing remains in the state in which it is as long as nothing acts upon it to modify it; (2) every moving body always tends to continue its motion in a straight line; (3) when a body impels another, it cannot impart to it any quantity of motion without losing an equal quantity of its own, nor can it take from it any quantity of motion without its own being increased by so much. What is remarkable is that, according to Descartes himself, these rules evidently follow from the fact that, being immutable and acting always in the same way, God produces always the same effect. At any rate, it is possible to deduce from these three mechanical laws all the calculations that permit us to foresee how the motions of two bodies will be modified in consequence of their shocks. In other words, it is possible to deduce from the true notion of God all that which is intelligible in the reciprocal actions of natural bodies.

Let us then suppose that God has created one single sort of matter, indefinitely divisible, actually divided into a very great number of particles and quickened by a constant quantity of motion transmitting itself according to these three laws; all the parts of matter will be seen to take up certain figures. The principal of these figures are three in number: corpuscles of irregular and angular shape; corpuscles of round shape, remnants of the preceding ones progressively polished by countless shocks; then exceedingly thin and rare corpuscles, a kind of powder caused by the wearing of the preceding one and which fills up the intervals between the angular particles and the round ones. Such are the three elements of which the universe is composed and by which it is mechanically produced.[14]

In a universe where, because matter is pure extension, a void is impossible, the only possible form of motion is that of vortexes, no particle being able to move unless the immediately preceding one be moving in front of it. The third and powderlike element is animated by an extremely rapid vorticular motion, thereby producing the sun and the fixed stars. The round element, animated by a less rapid motion, produces the heavens. The angular and irregular element, moving more slowly, causes the earth, the planets, and the comets. All bodies observable in nature can be accounted for by these three elements and by the laws according to which they move in space; and not only inorganic bodies, such as minerals, but organized bodies as well, such as plants, and even those we wrongly call animated, such as animals. Descartes says "wrongly" because living organisms must be explained, like all the rest, by certain combinations of material particles following the laws of motion. The notion of "soul" has no part to play in this kind of explanation. Living organisms are automatons, mere machines similar to clocks with exceedingly complicated wheels. Naturally, this is also true of the human body, for all those of its functions that escape the control of will.

Thus the whole physics of heavenly bodies, of the terrestrial bodies as well as that of the living bodies is finally but a *mechanics*, whose fundamental laws are deduced from a *metaphysics* which itself is *mathematically* evident. The method remains the same from one extremity of human knowledge to the other. Nevertheless, when the question comes up of explaining the detail of phenomena, an auxiliary method is required: one must resort to experiment.

The reason given for this is eminently typical of the Cartesian spirit. In a physics that grows out of metaphysics and makes use of universal mathematical method, the principles are so ample and all-embracing that there is nothing that cannot be deduced from them. From extension and motion it is possible to deduce all that which is, plus all that which could be. The difficulty, then, is not to explain that which exists, but, rather, it is to know what does actually exist, before undertaking to explain it. Observation and experiment only can make us know, from among an infinite number of possible combinations, which ones have been actually realized. Nor is this all. Once we know that a certain combination has been realized, several diverse explanations of the being at stake remain possible, because we can then imagine several different mechanical combinations according to which the same effect could have been produced. The explanatory power of the method is such that it extends, beyond the real world, to possible ones. Experiment must therefore intervene again in order to determine, among the possible causes of a certain phenomenon, which is the real one. The only possible way to *explain* a fact is to deduce it from its causes; the scientist resorts to experiment in order to prove that, among different explanations equally possible, one is in fact true.

Ethics

THE CARTESIAN TREE of philosophy was to flower, according to the original plan, into a mechanics, a medicine, and a "morale." Descartes, before his rather early death, had made considerable contributions to the first; his contributions to the second, hampered, he always complained, by the lack of a National Science Foundation to provide funds for experimentation, were more quaint than truly helpful, even though he attached great importance to the search for ways to assure the body's health, on the grounds that the soul should not be encumbered in the pursuit of happiness by its illnesses. The ethics was to come last of all, as a crowning achievement. Their great absorption in study of the universe did not keep seventeenth-century thinkers from being equally concerned with the human character. If we are to judge by the dramas of Corneille and by the religious revival in the French Catholic Church,[15] Descartes lived in times that were morally earnest indeed. As for himself, he desired that his entire philosophical quest should result in illuminating our nature so that we might conduct ourselves surely and knowingly toward our true end. Descartes was only fifty-four when Queen Christina of Sweden called him out for the seventeenth-century equivalent of an eight o'clock class, resulting in his catching a fatal pneumonia. The formal moral treatise had not yet been written. But since the philosopher had been working toward this goal all his life, he has left important indications of what the main lines of such an ethics should be. With the help of letters to his royal patron, we can deduce its main principles from the true metaphysics and the physics. Then there is the code of "provisional morality," provided in the *Discourse* as a guide for life to be followed while the way is being made straight for the definitive scientific ethics. And finally, there is the important scientific study of the passions, the last work Descartes ever wrote.

MAXIMS FROM THE PROVISIONARY ETHICS

ETHICS is concerned with the detail of our judgments and of our acts. The maxims of the provisional ethics, despite the fact that they were included in the introductory *Discourse* and seemed destined to disappear when a definitive ethics was finally achieved, are enlightening in this regard. When we reread the four maxims in the light of Descartes' maturest thought, we see that they were in fact cleverly cast to retain a basic validity even for the final wisdom. The first maxim prescribes that one adhere to the laws of one's country and be guided by faith and the example of wise men. In this regard, it might help to add another remark. When Descartes opened the *Discourse* with the statement that, of all God's gifts, *le bon sens*—good sense—was the most universally distributed, he was not being ironic, even though the "proof" he offers for his declaration is clearly so; to wit, that no one ever complains that he has not enough of it! Those who accuse Descartes of conformism for having urged adherence to the laws and customs of one's country and to the "middle way" that skirts all apparent extremes are just as wrong as those commentators who think that because he was a revolutionary in philosophy Descartes must have also been a kind of forerunner of Robespierre. The remark made earlier in regard to the methodic doubt holds here. In setting aside all the truths that did not meet the acid test of absolute, mathematically conceived certitude, Descartes did not intend that they should be definitively junked. One often forgets that from the moment he decided as a young man upon his great enterprise of philosophical reconstruction Descartes set out on a search for varied experience among the great men and the courts of all Europe, a search that was to last nine years. It is not in fact untrue to say that Descartes espouses in detail the morality accepted on the grounds of common sense and religious faith by the majority of great men of his time.[16] He would ground that morality scientifically; he would nurture it from the deep roots of metaphysics and have it draw its strength through the solid trunk of the physics he has just elaborated. In a word, he would have the ancient wisdom flourish in new soil, not be uprooted and die. It is in this spirit that we should understand the first maxim.

There is one other essential point in the definitive ethics established in the provisional code; that is the need for *resoluteness*. To some it has seemed strange that the author of the methodic doubt should have counseled what almost appears to be a stubbornness in action precisely when we lack the light to know certainly what we are about. Actually, the counsel to resoluteness is a perfect pendant to Descartes' scientific attitude, if it is rightly understood. The philosopher was under no illusion about the impossibility of extending the reign of certain knowledge to every moment of our activity. Yet he realized that the same firmness of will had to be present throughout any course of action as throughout the course of theoretical inquiry. Even though we discover the limits and uncertainties of our lights, it still remains true that nothing can be accomplished in the order of action without *follow-through*. This resoluteness in no way invites stubbornness. Descartes is not suggesting that we persist in doubtful ideas, but in those actions which we must at any time launch according to the best lights then in our possession.

THE TREATISE ON THE PASSIONS

BY FAR the most extensive preparation for the ethics is that last great *Treatise on the Passions*. Descartes' purpose in scientifically studying the passions as the final preliminary to the formal study of ethics is quite simply stated. The soul may possess firmly its own province, but man is more than a soul; Providence has joined the soul to a body and placed man in a world of extended things in which he must make his way, find his food, avoid mortal dangers, and seek those pleasures that make this life bearable. The soul, acting as will, can move the body; but the body, too, can make its demands felt on the will.[17] The actions of the body are received in the soul in the form of passions. Although they elicit the will, it remains the will's task to be their master. In order to exercise full control, the will and reason need to know as much as possible of their subjects and of the arms at their disposal. The *Treatise on the Passions* is intended as a contribution to this end.

An example can help us understand the "movements" involved in a typical passional experience. If I suddenly see a hungry tiger on the loose, I grow tense, cold, and start to tremble, and I find, without any need on my part to send out specific voluntary commands, that my body, before I know it, is halfway up the nearest tree. As Descartes sees it, my reaction unfolds on the bodily level as automatically as the sheep's flight before the wolf, except that its reverberations are felt in the soul in a way that opens the possibility of a potential voluntary intervention in the midst of the process. In its bodily genesis, the fright is caused by an impression "having a close relationship with the things which have been formerly hurtful to the body," so that the imagination associates the image with the previously experienced pain. The reaction that is linked with this concrete sense estimation in the brain will not be the same in every human body; it will vary according to the different "temperaments" and depending on the different "strengths of soul" of the individuals affected. Through the notion of temperament Descartes wishes to introduce the element of different physiological constitutions and, through the notion of "strength of soul," the element of different habitual dispositions in the brain caused by varying degrees of command of the individual's will over the body in the past. Before the will has a chance to intervene, the brain will have been setting into motion the various physical changes in the body which accompany, according to temperament, the frightful apparition. The legs will perhaps be commanded to prepare for flight and the heart to pump to the brain the rarefied blood, or animal "spirits," which, coursing to the pineal gland directly in the middle of the brain, and being "adapted for the maintenance and strengthening of the passion of fear," will affect the soul, eliciting it to throw the weight of its command behind the mechanism of the fear reaction.[18] The will, however, cannot be constrained by this bodily, material elicitation; the will's desires remain "absolutely in its power, and can only be indirectly changed by the body," which makes it possible for the will to seek to countermand the movements of fear being sent from the brain.

If it seeks to do so, the will must carry out its countermanding on the passions' own level. The will has, as it were, to fight fire with fire. It must, by the originative action of its desires, cause a countermovement in the body, which it can do only by commanding the imagination center of the brain to present an image capable of provoking an equally strong, and contrary, movement in the body. "Thus, in order to excite courage in oneself and remove fear, it is not sufficient to have the will to do so, but we must apply ourselves to consider the reasons, the objects or examples which persuade us the peril is not great." [19]

If man were a disincarnated *cogito* this would of course not be necessary. But the whole point of the *Treatise on the Passions* is to deal with the fact that man is a composite of body and soul, that each is a real principle, each works on and through the other.

It is the body's job to present to the soul the demands of material existence, which means that it must hold before the mind's eye the material realities in a way that reproduces in the soul the duration that is characteristic of things in time.

> The utility of all the passions consists alone of their fortifying and perpetuating in the soul thoughts which it is good it should preserve, and which without that, might easily be effaced from it. And again all the harm which they can cause consists in the fact that they fortify and conserve these thoughts more than necessary, or that they fortify and conserve others on which it is not good to dwell.[20]

And again, "the customary mode of action of all the passions is simply this, that they dispose the soul to desire those things which nature tells us are of use, and to persist in this desire . . . disposing the body to the movement which serves for the carrying into effect of these things . . ." [21] When the body receives an impression and then magnifies it through all the movements of the bodily resonance, this keeps the reality present to the soul the time necessary to set into motion movements originating in the free desires of the will.

Composite man is then the seat of continual strife; but tradition was wrong to conceive of this strife as a fight between the higher and lower parts of the soul, for a simple, spiritual substance has no parts; nor even, properly speaking, between soul and body, *l'ange et la bête*, for what the good man does in this life is done in part through the body, and the body is the source of great and legitimate pleasures. Rather, the strife is a question of imposing the discipline of order among the parts of this composite. It is the problem of the soul to handle properly the bodily mechanism, through the use of the proper mechanical methods.

In its struggle to gain sure control, the soul enjoys excellent weapons. First, consider its right to command: Its great strength is its knowledge and, to employ the key word of the "provisionary morality," its *resolution,* to see that life will be employed to pursue what it knows to be ultimate goods, through "firm and determinate judgments respecting the knowledge of good and evil, in pursuance of which it has resolved to conduct the actions of its life." [22] It must exercise this right in a way that respects the realities of the body, and when it does so, many are its levers of control.

Certain objects have a natural propensity to incite certain passions. But already on this most primitive level of the body's operation the soul can intervene and separate the object, to some extent, from the passion it normally incites, attaching it through *habit* to another. Descartes illustrates this with the homely example of training a setter so that instead of obeying a passion to run upon sight of the quarry, he now will stand perfectly still and set. Habit is a powerful weapon of the will, a most effective way of playing the body off against itself. The first time the will forces the body, in the presence of a certain object, to consider a course of action other than the natural one, it may be very difficult and require much ingenuity of the imagination to produce the right "objects and examples." But once this is done, "traces of the passage of the animal spirits" associated with the desired dispositions are left in the brain,[23] fraying a path for a much easier association the next time.

The ultimate weapon, of course, is the simple fact already alluded to: the will cannot be coerced. So, failing all else, and while working to extend a more regular empire through gradual development of the virtuous habits, the will can still hold out against noxious "commotions" in the body.

> The most that the will can do while such a commotion is in its full strength is not to yield to its effects and to restrain many of the movements to which it disposes the body. For example, if anger causes us to lift our hand to strike, the will usually can hold it back.[24]

Descartes does not stop with these general considerations of the physiology of the passions and of the basic weapons the will can use in establishing and maintaining its control over the body; the more we know of the individual passions, their manifestations and elicitations, the more sure and subtle becomes the potential guidance of our lives. Consequently, in a Second Part of the *Treatise*, Descartes passes on to the definition of six genera of passions. While it lies beyond the scope of this history to enter into the truly marvelous details of these descriptions, we can at least consider rapidly the principal genera and then turn to one particular passion, "generosity," which assumes enormous importance as a key instrument of the will's general control.

The genera of passions are distinguished according to "the many diverse ways our senses can be moved by their objects." [25] The first, "wonder," is the reaction caused by the sudden appearance of something that strikes us as new; the next, "love and hate," arise from a kind of union by anticipation with the object; the mode of all three being fundamentally that of the present; "desire," on the other hand, is of the future mode, a drive to be joined to that from which we are separated; "joy and sadness," following upon a definitive possession of a pain or sorrow, rather look to the past of what is an accomplished fact. With this brief table of distinctions to guide us, let us consider each primitive emotion in its turn.

The appearance of "wonder" at the head of the list admirably reinforces our point that Descartes in the *Treatise* is arguing for a human nature quite different from a disincarnated *cogito*. "Wonder is a sudden surprise of the soul which causes it to apply itself to consider with attention the objects which seem to it rare and extraordinary." [26] A disincarnated *cogito*, all wrapped up in contemplation of its innate ideas, would have no reason to be interrupted by the phenomenon of the body's surprise at an impression coursing across the brain, fraying a new way, unprepared by previous experiences—especially when we remember that the great agitation which surprise can cause is due precisely to this newness of its *physiological* course (Descartes compares it to the effect obtained from gently tickling a foot that is not accustomed to it); it "affects the brain in certain parts in which it is not usually affected, and the fact that these parts are more tender than those which a frequent agitation has solidified, increases the effect of the movement they there excite." [27]

This grossly physiological explanation points up an important consideration. Because Descartes gives such a great part to the body in our knowing processes, the will, as we have been emphasizing, must fight out the battle of control to an important degree on the corporeal level. Now we are seeing very concretely, in the case of one of the primitive emotions, what this can mean. The phenomena of attention and memory, both implicit in the reaction of wonder, have their corporeal aspect which must be taken into consideration when the will seeks to command them. "Although a thing which was unknown to us presents itself anew to our understanding or to our senses, we do not for all that retain it in our memory, unless the idea we have of it is strengthened in our brain by some passion or else by the application of our understanding which our will determines to a particular attention and reflection." [28] Only attention can bring about retention of an object in the memory. This attention, or "strengthening" of the impression in the brain, can be commanded either by the will, working through the understanding, causing a motion in the brain, or by the movement of surprise. Without this latter, however, we could never learn anything new. If there were not provision for the body to react automatically— i.e., physiologically—when something new frays its path, the initial attention needed for retention, whether reinforced or not, would not occur, and we would be limited to learning only what our innate ideas could direct us to seek out.

On the other hand, the body must not be allowed to do the directing, so that we haphazardly follow all the vagaries of our wonder. To be without wonder is to be hopelessly "dull and stupid," that is true! But the most intelligent people are not necessarily those who are most disposed to "admiration"; those given to idle, unguided wonder are usually people who "have a fairly good supply of common sense, but at the same time have no high opinion as to their own sufficiency." [29] Descartes is not just calling attention to the sad case of the man of many hobbies, winner of quiz programs. He is applying ethically the metaphysics of ideas. If knowing is an active process, directed internally by the intimate resources of the understanding, then application to nature for knowledge must be judiciously structured by considerations drawn from the understanding itself. Parmenides had said it, in warning against getting too involved with the "many" and in insisting on absolute possession of the correct *hodos;* the Platonic epistemology is dominated by the same notion. In Bacon we found an echo of something similar when he recognizes that it is not enough to "observe" nature without a plan; rather, she must be made to yield up her secrets through being "vexed" by experiments. The Cartesian position is much more extreme than Bacon's. The real business of wisdom is with the clear and distinct innate ideas; observation and experiment help the soul take more explicit possession of its intimate resources, the innate ideas; these then direct subsequent inquiry. In the ethical realm, the same order prevails. Ultimate ends are to be sought among the innate ideas.

Wonder arising from practical experience can help us better discover them, but that experience itself must ultimately be directed by a knowledge higher than that yielded up by the senses.

Now that the passional presentation of the object has occurred, there arises attraction to or repulsion from it in the soul. "Love is an emotion of the soul caused by the movement of the spirits which incites it to join itself willingly to objects which appear to it agreeable." [30] Love, then, involves an estimate of suitability (which is of course not the same as wonder's estimate of novelty, but rather involves the anticipation of union) and a will to be one with the object. "By the word will I do not here intend to talk of desire, which is a passion apart, and one which relates to the future, but of the consent by which we consider ourselves from this time forward as united with what we love." [31] Being one by anticipation with its object, love is much calmer than desire, the great characteristic of which is precisely its aggressivity as it faces the future and attempts to overcome the gap separating the person from the desired object. "Desire agitates the heart more violently than any of the other passions and furnishes more spirits to the brain . . . which renders all the parts of the body more mobile." [32]

Ethics is above all concerned with the regulation of desire, not only because of its extremely explosive nature, but for a much more positive reason: It is through its intermediary that the other passions can move us. [33]

The most important distinction that can be made regarding the moral regulation of desire, declares Descartes, following Epictetus, [34] is that between desires whose accomplishment depends only on us and desires which depend only on other things. We cannot too much encourage the first, and we must strive diligently to dampen the second. The things that depend entirely on us constitute our true empire, that to which we should devote our attention exclusively. The vain desiring of that which depends on Providence, operating as a fate we cannot change, is nothing but an inauthentic distraction from our true pursuits. [35]

The key to this proper regulation lies in what we might call the great seventeenth-century virtue, "generosity." [36] Descartes again echoes Epictetus, "That true generosity which causes a man to esteem himself as highly as he legitimately can, consists partly in the fact that he knows that there is nothing that truly pertains to him but the free disposition of his will." [37] We recognize now that those individuals who give themselves up to idle and vain admirations and who, consequently, can be said "to have no high opinion of themselves" lack the just and true view of the human condition which alone can keep us from becoming the prey of dangerous and futile desires. A man who has this just view recognizes that all men possess the powers of self-determination, of free will, and are, therefore, like himself, called "to do great things." [38]

Generosity is the passional movement in the body incited by the soul's possession of a true view of things, which brings with it necessarily a high "estimation" of oneself. Estimation is likewise a feeling, a movement in the body, disposing the spirits to incite us to sentiments corresponding to our true state. The status of Cartesian man is a highly Stoic one. He takes possession of his own kingdom, the realm of the will, precisely because he renounces the vainglorious attempt to possess the shadow kingdom of the material world. This Stoic sentiment is at the base of Descartes' rather passive attitude regarding the political situation. Presuming a Christian king and a fundamentally tolerable regime, Descartes would have us move in harmony with it, freeing the attention of the soul to dedicate itself to that pursuit of wisdom and virtue which is properly the will's province. As a result, the Cartesian hero is free to concentrate on being *maître chez lui*. A good sign of his victory is his command over fear and anger. Having "confidence in his virtue," the generous man need never submit to that vague *angoisse* directed at no particular object, the great nemesis of the man who cannot be sure of himself. And should he encounter an all too concrete reason for fright, a real and immediate menace to his life, he will be practiced in restraining himself from flight and in summoning up those noble reasons that, if there is grounds for doing it, will move him to stand up to the danger. As to anger, what for him can be the point of it? "Esteeming very little all those things that depend on others, he never gives so much advantage to his enemies as to recognize that he is hurt by them." [39]

"Joy" and "sadness" arising from union with a good or an evil are logically the last primitive passions to be considered. They do not deserve an important place in Descartes' consideration. The body's satisfactions are something to enjoy when they are legitimate; but they can so easily be superficial and ephemeral that it is better not to accord them much place. Actually, sadness is the more important of the two, for it warns us of the presence of things noxious to the body's survival. The main reason that desire, the aggressive emotion *par excellence*, and generosity, the most important particular passion, occupy a much more important place than either joy or sadness is that our existence in this life is one of quest, not of final bliss. Descartes may have been very optimistic about the ultimate issue of the will's battle to control the passions. But he seems to have recognized that, even in the man of great and solid virtue, life would continue to issue new challenges calling for continued exercise of the greatest moral skill.

Conclusion

THE ENDEAVOR of Descartes has not been in vain. His remains a great name in the history of mathematics. His physics was of doubtful value in the order of science; in the philosophical order, however, Descartes has popularized and defined with precision the ideal of a physics practically identified with mechanics, and although physics is much more than that, it is that to a very large extent, so much so that its secret desire might well always be to remain just that. Descartes has been the spokesman of the spirit of his time on still another point: like Francis Bacon, though in a less crude way, he openly declared man's ambition to render himself "master and possessor of nature." Like Bacon, he would find himself quite at home in our mechanized world. One sometimes thinks of the joy it would be to take him through some modern industrial plant and to let him see his own dreamland come true. The point is directly relevant to the history of philosophy because of the part industrialism will occupy in the mind of early-nineteenth-century philosophers.

In the history of culture, Descartes is now considered by some of our own contemporaries as representing what they call an anti-Renaissance or anti-humanistic movement. There is a great deal of truth in that view. Descartes considered wasted the time spent in learning Latin and other classical languages. Science, not literature, was what he was interested in. As one blessed with a good classical education, he could afford to despise it.

In the field of philosophy, his influence has been enormous; whether or not it always was to the good is not a question this history will attempt to answer. One thing at least must be said in his favor: The complete failure of peripateticism to provide a philosophy for the new world of science made it necessary for somebody to attempt it. Unlike

Bacon, Descartes did not consider it necessary to do away with metaphysics properly so called; on the contrary, under the influence of his mathematicism, he attempted a general deduction of the whole body of knowledge from metaphysical principles. In doing so, he never lost sight of what was to him a most important point: to provide science with a notion of matter in which nothing would resist a purely mechanical explanation. In this sense, the main object of the six *Meditations* is to establish that matter is nothing but geometrical extension, motion itself being a mere mode of extension.

In science proper, this resulted in a mechanicism without dynamics. In metaphysics, the famous mind-body distinction left the successors of Descartes with a frightening problem to solve. In anthropology, if man is made up of two really distinct substances, what kind of unity is his? In general metaphysics, if mind and extension are radically separate, how can they communicate? Nay, how can any substance communicate with any other one? This Cartesian problem of the "communication of substances" will dominate the philosophies of Malebranche, Spinoza, and Leibniz.

3   CHRISTIAN PHILOSOPHY

WITH THE EXCEPTION of Benedictus Spinoza, all of the great seventeenth-century philosophers were Christians, or least had received a Christian education. But only two of them can be said to have philosophized as Christians, in the sense that the starting point of their meditations and the whole spirit thereof is considered, even as a philosophy, inseparable from Christian revelation—to wit, Blaise Pascal and Nicolas Malebranche. In this regard, their attitude resembled less that of Descartes than that of a thirteenth-century theologian. But neither is any more an Aristotelian scholastic than Descartes. What makes them interesting is the fact that they attempt, we might say, the Christian experiment within modern philosophy. Both were mathematicians, both were influenced by Descartes; however, these two statements apply to each very unequally. Malebranche was less than a great mathematician, and Pascal a very great, creative one. Pascal, though deeply influenced by Descartes, retains in his spirit a "free" quality that makes it impossible to think of him simply as a "Cartesian." But Malebranche is an enthusiastic Cartesian, and indeed deserves to be considered the greatest of a whole band of them.

VII

Nicolas Malebranche

DESCARTES lived long enough to realize that his philosophy would have to overcome stiff resistances before being generally accepted. As it actually evolved, the Cartesian school certainly would have surprised its founder. Nothing went as he had hoped. His analytical geometry was a positive contribution to science, but even during his own lifetime mathematics was entering the new ways of Pascal, Leibniz, and Newton, the ways of the infinitesimal calculus, which was something not at all Cartesian. In natural science, Descartes felt convinced he had laid down once and for all the principles of a true mechanistic explanation of all phenomena, but this corpuscular physics was not essentially different from that of Lucretius, of Gassendi, and of many others who contented themselves with accounting for facts by imagining plausible mechanical explanations. Leibniz' charge of scientific sterility lodged against the Cartesian school was not without reason.[1]

In metaphysics, the situation was somewhat different. Descartes himself had elaborated his own prime philosophy as a preamble to his physics. In his own mind, that part of philosophy had been completed. Nevertheless, it turned out to be the part of the doctrine which continued to live after the death of Descartes. The developments it took in Christian circles would have sometimes caused him great surprise, if not indignation.

Let us pass over the doctrines of those authors who contented themselves simply with borrowing from Cartesianism some elements they considered useful from the point of view of apologetics. There certainly are elements of Cartesian origin, for instance, in the philosophical treatises written by Bossuet.[2] The use he made of them permits us to observe a phenomenon visible in the works of practically all the Christian philosophers who fell under the influence of Descartes: All that is lost by Aristotle in their doctrines is gained by St. Augustine. This was to be expected: By separating mind from body, Descartes himself had been led to revive the philosophical method of introspection used by Augustine. Even the "I think" had Augustinian antecedents.³ This blending of Cartesianism and Augustinianism is typical of the evolution of the Cartesian school.

The Cartesians Move toward Occasionalism

DESCARTES had left his followers a very grave problem to solve: If mind and body are really distinct, how can they unite to form the substantial unity of man? More generally, if no immaterial elements such as forms are included in the structure of physical beings, how can there be any communication between these two radically separated substances, extension and thought? To these two problems, a third one was soon to be added. According to Descartes, mind and body are really distinct because they can be conceived apart, but if the same principle is applied to any two substances, since they can be conceived apart, it will become difficult to imagine how one of them can communicate with any other one. This difficulty became known as the problem of the "communication of substances." Malebranche was to do his best to solve it, he could not avoid it, as he inherited it as part of the Cartesian legacy; others before him and around him were asking themselves the same question.

The difficulty had not escaped Descartes himself. When he had to say that, in man, a certain modification of the nerves and organs is regularly attended by a definite type of sensation, he often resorted to the word "occasion." In modern language, we would say that a particular sensory excitation is, for the soul, an "occasion" to form a corresponding sensation.⁴ The first disciple of Descartes to use the expression of "occasional causes" seems to have been Louis de la Forge.⁵ Like Descartes himself, he simply meant thereby that, since mind is the cause of ideas, material objects and their action on our own body are, at most, *remote and occasional* causes for mind to form corresponding ideas in consequence of its union with body. As to the nature of this union, that remains a mystery. One cannot form any clear and distinct idea of how body can act upon mind and vice versa. God, who is all-powerful, has simply created man that way. So also, when a body moves another body, it does not cause anything in it; the moving body simply calls for God to apply his own force and moving power to the moved body according to the laws of motion he himself has established in the world.

A step farther in the same direction was made by Géraud de Cordemoy, in his treatise of 1666 on the distinction of soul and body: *Le discernement de l'âme et du corps.*[6] This author's "occasionalism" asserts itself in the Fourth of the six Discourses. The demonstration is simple and entirely Cartesian: A thing has not of itself that which it can lose without ceasing to be itself; now every body could lose all motion without ceasing to be a body; therefore, no body has of itself its own motion. On the other hand, one can conceive two kinds of substances only—mind and body. Consequently, since no body can cause motion in another body, the cause of its motion must be a mind. Lastly, a third axiom assures us that an action can be continued only by the same agent that caused it first; we must therefore conclude: "Only the same spirit that began to move bodies, can continue to move them." When we say that a certain body moves another body, then, we simply mistake the occasion of the motion for its cause.

The same reasoning still more obviously applies to cases when it seems that bodies are moving minds and vice versa; souls and bodies move one another in the same sense that bodies move other bodies. The problem is the same: "Just as one must acknowledge that the meeting of two bodies is, for the power that moved the first one, an occasion to move the second one, it should not be difficult for us to conceive that our will is, for the power already moving a body, an occasion to direct its movement toward a certain side answering that thought." Cordemoy finally lays down the general rule presiding over the phenomena of a thus conceived world: There must needs be a first mind who caused movement and preserves it; moreover, "having posited laws between bodies, following which he moves them diversely because of the diversity of their encounters, he has likewise posited between our souls and our bodies laws which he never infringes." According to these laws, this supreme mind "always directs certain movements [of our bodies] according to our desires."[7] Summing up the general tendency of Cordemoy's treatise, it has been rightly said that its six Discourses are inspired of the same idea—"to exclude all causality from the sensible world."[8]

In 1672, an anonymous book written by a Jesuit was published at

Paris under the title *Letter of a Philosopher to a Cartesian.* One of its articles declared that "according to the Cartesians only God can produce local motion." Stressing the paradoxical nature of their position, this critic observes that, in order to explain how the soul is united to the body, they begin by proving that no conceivable creature can act upon bodies so as to move them. When we see a wall wrecked by a cannon ball, we naturally imagine that the ruin of the wall is caused by the ball, but we are badly mistaken. No gun, no gunpowder, no cannon ball, no engine, no man, no angel, no imaginable creature can produce such an effect. It is God, and God only, who, on the occasion of the explosion, pushes the ball, and then, on the occasion of the ball meeting it, overthrows the wall which otherwise would remain unshakable. We do not move our finger; God moves it on the occasion of our will to move it. "In a word, it is God who produces all the motions that happen in the world, and the only thing creatures do in this, is to provide God with an occasion to execute what he has resolved to do under such and such circumstances." [9]

With great acumen, the same critic concluded by asking why the Cartesians should stop there. If souls have no efficacy to move bodies, why should they have any power to produce their own thoughts? Malebranche would not hesitate in this regard; he would finally draw that redoubtable conclusion. "Of its nature," Malebranche will say, "the mind is capable of movement and of ideas; I grant it. *But it does not move itself,* it does not enlighten itself; *it is God who does all that there is of physical in the minds* as well as in bodies." [10] This was not going to be the whole of Malebranche's philosophy, but it was to provide it with its metaphysical foundation.

One might well ask, why call "Cartesians" men who were upholding philosophical positions utterly foreign to the philosophy of Descartes? Impatient as he was with the slightest departure from his own conclusions, and even from the very way he himself was handling his own principles, one dares not imagine how he would have reacted to the principles of those alleged "Cartesians." If one remembers certain pages of the *Treatise of Human Nature*[11] he will not fail to see that such Cartesians were on the straight road to Hume, whose skepticism was exactly what Descartes had resolved to kill in its germ.

Still, there is a justification for calling those men "Cartesians," for Descartes had really laid down the principle from which they were drawing such unexpected consequences. According to the first precept of the method, one should accept in judgments nothing more than what is presented to the mind so clearly and distinctly that there is no occasion to doubt it. Hence, as an immediate consequence, we must never attribute to any thing what is not clearly and distinctly included in its notion. This leads us to what, in his sixth *Rule for the Direction of the Mind,* Descartes called "pure and simple essences." These are "absolutes"; few in number, each one of them provides the initial term of a series so that, when we reach one of them, we should stop short in our investigation. An excellent rule indeed, but if I grasp myself, clearly and distinctly, as a "thing that thinks," how shall I ever get out of thought, taken as a simple term, in order to reach extension, another simple term? The thing cannot easily be done. At any rate, this was the origin of the evolution that led the greatest of the Cartesians to erect an extraordinary metaphysical bridge to link mind and body through God.

The Christian Quest of Père Malebranche

THE ATTITUDE with which Père Malebranche[12] attacks the task of solving Cartesian problems is in marked contrast with the attitude Descartes has communicated to us about his own philosophizing. Descartes was concerned that his philosophy should serve the ends of Catholic orthodoxy, and he was convinced that indeed it did. But we cannot say of it, as we can of the philosophy of Malebranche, that it seems intended to exploit every opening it has made to the direct and explicit magnification of God's position in reality. It can be argued that, if Malebranche brought God so much into the picture, it was merely to solve problems left by Descartes' metaphysics. And this is in the main true. But we know that Malebranche was very concerned that the new philosophy be put to the work of justifying and *explaining* traditional Catholic dogmas. And we cannot ignore the fact that he took up his interest in philosophizing from within a congregation—the *Oratoire*—that was one of the pillars of the Catholic reform in seventeenth-century France, and that he did so at a time when it must have become evident that the new rationalism held threats as well as promises for traditional religion. So there is an air of urgency about the way Malebranche reduces everything to the action of God, almost as though any element left to itself might slip away from Godly auspices forever. And there is something pathetic about the way he would introduce universal Reason into the inner sanctums of Christian mystery. He not only wants to uphold doctrines of the centrality of grace, the necessity of the Blessed Trinity, the role of the angels, the Blessed Virgin, the sacraments, and the Church—he wants to explain them. The God to whom all is ascribed in Malebranche's philosophy does not remind one very much of that God of whom it is written, "dark and inscrutable are His ways." In reading Malebranche we are inclined rather to think, "illumined and regular is His causality." Malebranche seems awfully eighteenth-century in the way he intends this formula: *Il faut que la foi nous conduise à l'intelligence*, especially when we know the standards he has laid down for what constitutes intelligence!

Sentiments and Ideas

IT IS REVEALING to note what Malebranche considered to be the *positions acquises* of Cartesianism. To begin with, he accepted as indisputable the results of the application of the methodic doubt. Malebranche says very little about the doubt, simply because he is persuaded that Descartes' demonstrations in that regard were definitive and so have become a kind of starting point for all future philosophy. It can be taken for granted that *all we know are our own representations*, and of these, only our ideas can be considered true and objective. Descartes has shown that only our clear and distinct ideas possess internal grounds for being held as representative of something; as for all the other affections in the soul, all the confused representations, be they sensations, dreams, imaginings—the *sentiments*, as Malebranche calls all the affections that do not meet the criteria of the *ideas*—they surely exist in the soul, but what possible ground is there for affirming that they reveal something true about things lying outside consciousness? "Aristide, never mistake your own sentiments for our ideas, the modifications which touch your own individual soul for the ideas which illumine all spirits. That is the greatest principle for avoiding error!" [13]

For, after all, Descartes has reminded us that the Truth is universal, "illuminating all spirits," unchanging, eternal, because clear and certain. Sentiments, on the other hand, are individual (the fact that I feel queasy this morning touches no one but myself; its "truth" is individual and subjective); they change continually (now I feel fine, thank you); they are misleading (I am blue, so the world is gray!). Their role is purely practical, they teach us something about what is useful or dangerous for the body. The senses, declares Malebranche, "are faithful witnesses of that which concerns the good of the body and the conduct of life; as for all the rest, there is no exactitude, no truth in their disposition." And again, "Never judge by the senses of what things are in themselves, but only of the rapport that they have with our body, because in effect they are not given to us for knowing the truth of things in themselves, but only for the conservation of our body." [14]

Why, then, does everyone persist in attributing to objects existing in themselves sensations relative to what Descartes has termed "secondary qualities"—those having to do with other than the manifestations of extension and movement as such? When an object causes some movement in the fibers of my body, even though I know only the result and not the hidden cause, still, because the sensation comes to the soul without the soul's initiative, a strong prejudice pushes me to believe that my sensations must be contained in the cause that is felt to be their source.[15] But, in the final analysis, there is no *reason* why there has to be "heat" in the fire for me to feel it when I approach my hands to the blaze. That there *is* some kind of movement in some kind of extended substance, there are perhaps good grounds for believing; but objective assertions beyond that, and even the bare assertion that there is always something there, have no certain grounds.

For the very reason that they are not supposed to be objective, there can be no error in the senses, only in the judgments we persist in making about the supposed objective bearing of our perceptions.[16] If one cannot resist this temptation to objectivize sentiments, it will lead to two equally disastrous results, both rendered unnecessary in the light of Cartesian philosophy: in the theoretical order, it leads to belief in Aristotelian substantial forms, which throws one completely off the track of the true distinctions between things, distinctions which arise from different configurations of the parts of matter; in the moral order, it leads to making exterior objects the principle of our pleasures and pains.[17]

Because of their practical importance, the senses and the imagination tend to persuade us that only what they represent is real and that ideas are something far removed from the "real" world. Malebranche counterattacks this empirical realism with what he considers a major blow: Descartes has shown that it is much easier to demonstrate the reality

of ideas than the existence in itself of the material world! Perception
could not even occur if it were not for the existence in us of the idea
of extension. When I perceive a white marble column, the qualities of
whiteness and stoniness can disappear, rendering the column no longer
visible, but the idea of extension which determined in me its presence
will subsist and can still represent the column to me as modality of the
extended.[18] From this we can see that the sentiment, to the extent that
it participates in the perception, is grounded in the idea as its necessary
condition. If the spirit did not have as its object the idea of the extended, it could not dispose upon a given part of the extended those
colors which are the spirit's own modifications. The sentiment is joined
to the idea, but it is the idea which provokes it and furnishes it the
means to project itself "outside."

> What is called seeing bodies is nothing but having actually present
> to the spirit the idea of the extended which touches and modifies
> the spirit with diverse colors; for we cannot see them in themselves
> at all, either directly or indirectly. It is then certain that one sees
> bodies only in the intelligible and general extended rendered sensi-
> ble and particular by the color; and that the colors are only sensi-
> ble perceptions that the soul has of the extended, when the ex-
> tended acts on it and modifies it.[19]

It is obvious that Malebranche is introducing some very sharp, very
important distinctions here. "Introducing" is perhaps not the right
word, for the distinctions we are now going to consider were already
suggested by Descartes, but once again it remains to Malebranche to
draw out their radical implications.

The basic distinction to be made is one between our *pensées* and our
idées, "thoughts" being the very broad term for all the movements of
the soul, for all the sentiments, as we have been expressing it. What
distinguishes an idea, however, is precisely its *objectivity*. Now Malebranche has derived from his reading of the great geometer a very
strict notion of what constitutes "objectivity." He sees it to consist in
the idea's independence of the individual spirit, in the sense that the
clear and distinct, true idea presents itself as imposing its truth on me,
as common to all minds in all times and places. This is the essential note
—the note of transcendence—that we have seen Malebranche emphasize from the beginning. It only remains to him now to draw the implications from the presence of such ideas in us. What precisely are
those ideas? How are they in us? Can they answer the truly devastating

question of subjectivity that is raised by the Cartesian reduction; namely, how, as we know immediately only ourselves, can we know anything outside ourselves?

Vision of the Ideas in God

IN ADDRESSING HIMSELF to the first question—just what are those ideas? —Malebranche shows at once that he is not going to introduce God into the picture as guarantor of the ideas' validity in the same way Descartes did. To begin with, Malebranche denies flatly that the idea of God is among the clear and distinct ideas in our possession, nor, for that matter, is the idea of the soul. This is no mere detail. Malebranche objects to the Cartesian notion that we possess a clear and distinct idea of God on two grounds. First, he realizes that holding that the finite can conceive the essence of the infinite dangerously confuses the absolute and relative orders of things. Secondly, he appears to realize that the Cartesian proof of God from an analysis of the separate idea we are supposed to have of Him rather puts the question of God on one side and all the other ideas on the other. Malebranche proposes to integrate the presence of God more perfectly into the very nature of the clear and distinct ideas themselves, and in so doing better protect the distinctness of the finite and infinite orders. Malebranche will so integrate God as the mediator through whom *all* the ideas are made possible that he can truly say, as he does in the *Entretiens Métaphysiques*, that the reason God's existence is evident is that there is no idea of him.[20]

Malebranche's attack on the notion that we possess a clear and distinct idea of the soul has similar motives. We *feel* the presence of our soul, continuously, confusedly; we do not conceive of it. Malebranche would thus eliminate the danger of our being tempted to think of the clear and distinct idea of the *ego cogito* itself as the ultimate ground for the objectivity of the other clear and distinct ideas. Malebranche wishes to emphasize the superior ontological status of the ideas themselves, the very objectivity of which proves their independence, their transcendence of the individual *cogito* in which they happen to be found.

The only clear and distinct ideas we possess, then, are those grouped about the conception of the intelligible extended world. It is this universal, objective idea of the material extended that was being so carefully distinguished from the mere sentiments of color in the quotation cited above. There it was stated categorically that we cannot see bodies in themselves at all, but rather all we can do is have "present to the spirit the idea of the extended" which is rendered "sensible and particular" by the movement of the sentiment of color. That idea of extension is unique; we need no other idea, since all the particular bodies, with all their particular figures, are as many modifications of the intelligible notion of geometrical extension. Again, it is only the idea, not the sentiment, which is objective, because only the idea is *universal*. Malebranche carries the problem of finding an absolute ground for the validity of universals to its ultimate extreme. He begins by asking how can these ideas enjoying a truth which largely transcends our own particularity be present to us? It is in answering this question, and not by deduction from a fictitious clear and distinct idea of God, that Malebranche deduces the Creator as ground and light of all truth.

In the *Recherche de la vérité*, Malebranche examines and rejects in turn four classic explanations for the presence in us of universal truths. 1] He rejects the notion that the idea is produced in us by abstracting it from the real world on the grounds that the particular, material world could never be the cause of the infinitely superior universal, certain, spiritual idea. 2] The idea cannot, indeed, be produced by us in any way, for the simple reason that the understanding is a purely passive function which receives its objects and knows them as transcending the understanding itself. 3] Nor can we say that, in creating us, God puts all the ideas in us at the start, to be seized one by one as needed, for that would mean that he would have to create in each of us an infinity of ideas and sustain them in existence to be ready when the occasion arose. Malebranche refuses to accept a complicated explanation when a simpler will suffice. 4] Finally, Malebranche rejects Descartes' suggestion that maybe the soul, upon contemplating its own perfection, can deduce from it all the perfections of other things. The soul can only grasp in this way its own modifications, the sentiments; but the ideas, by nature, represent something outside the soul, and therefore can never be grasped in these subjective modifications.[31]

What, then, is the solution? When I consider, for example, that two and two make four, I am convinced that there is not a man in the world who cannot see this truth as well as I; how can this be so obvious to me, since I am just one particular person; it must be that I am illumined by a universal Reason, as unchanging as that truth is immutable, a

Reason that is infinite, for there is in the extended an infinitely infinite
number of figures and properties of figures. The Reason which illumines me can be no other than that of God himself, author of all things
who, through his infinite creative bounty, wills to let me see in the
ideas a part of the divine plan for things. Here indeed is an Augustinian
notion! [22] But, after all, the *Oratoire* considered itself in the tradition
of the great Platonic Father, and Malebranche, for his part, was proud
to be thought a follower of Augustine!

In the *Treatise on Morals,* our Augustinian identifies the universal
and unchanging Reason of God illuminating with the *Logos* of St.
John's gospel:

> The reason which illumines man is the Word or the Wisdom of
> God himself. For every creature is a particular being, and the rea-
> son which illumines the spirit of man is universal. If my own spirit
> were a Reason or a light, my spirit would have to be the Reason
> of all intelligences: for I am sure that my Reason, or the light that
> illumines me is common to all intelligences. No one can feel my
> own pain, but every man can see the truth that I contemplate.[23]

This last quotation lets the metaphysics underlying Malebranche's
epistemology show through very manifestly. "Every creature is a particular being, and the reason which illumines the spirit of man is universal." If we distinguish clearly the creature from the creator, the
finite from the infinite, we see at once the essential particularity of the
one and the all encompassing nature of the other. Consideration of the
universality of Reason simply leads us to discovery of the universal
source of all particularity. The moment any knowledge is "objective,"
then it must transcend the limits of my own spirit as particular, for it
enjoys a validity for spirits everywhere and at all times. What renders
a sentiment devoid of truth is its particularity—it has to do only with
me, now, this instant, in an individual encounter with other particulars.
If there were a grain of truth in the practical situation, that grain
would be the universalizable element in which we would recognize a
face of objective Being, and whose reality we would therefore see in
the light of the universal Order that reigns over the world. What permits us to *see* anything is its Being; that is, the moment in it by which
it joins the universal—the aspect of its being part of the divine whole.
"Thus we take away from man his liberty to think of all things if we
separate his spirit from Him who embraces all." [24] The intelligibility

contained in any movement of the soul moves us, when we contemplate it, toward the vision of the ideas in God.

For God is creator of all, mover of all. All things have their origin and their meaning in the idea God had of them from the beginning. When we speak of the things in the world, we must distinguish therefore their aspect as wisdom, light, perfection—that is, the aspect in which they constitute the divine substance as its idea—and their aspect as created, particular, as participations in the divine idea.[25] God is the necessary support of extended things—if there are any. But since God's creation is a free act, it cannot be concluded from his nature that there are in fact any things corresponding to the idea of the extended intelligible. Moreover, since what we ourselves know is only the idea of the extended intelligible in God, then we must rely for knowledge of the actual existence of bodies strictly upon revelation, which tells us of such creation and of God's concern for a world of bodies.[26] Since God is alone the mover of all things and therefore sole cause of the movements of knowledge and feeling in my soul, and since he has revealed the existence of bodies in an extended world, we can believe that, corresponding to the movements God causes in our souls, there are like movements, also caused by him, in the correlative bodies.

Descartes had already called in God to guarantee for the "objectivity" of our perceptions, in the sense that God made them so that they would report on the way things really are. But Malebranche has dispelled the last drop of equivocation from the Cartesian position and dissolves its still realistic aspirations into a thoroughgoing parallelism. My body and my spirit are distinct and cannot interact. But God, author of the movements of both, can, as part of the economy of creation, move my body and my spirit simultaneously so that the movements of the one will correspond perfectly with the affections of the other.

The Occasional Causes

BUT DOES NOT this doctrine, that God is the unique cause of all, mover of all, tend to make of the world a continual series of miracles, of direct divine interventions? The Christian conception of the created world must always be armed with some sort of doctrine of what St. Thomas called "secondary causality," the action proper to creatures. According to the Thomistic doctrine, in creation the creature is given an act of existence proportioned to the essence also accorded it by the same divine *fiat*. With this act of existence, the individual creature, although primarily moved by the divine *actus purus*, is nevertheless endowed with what we might term some "directional initiative"; in other words, it can decide, so to speak, when and which way the divine impulsion is going to be directed; it can do so because God, in creating the world, deigned to delegate a share of reality to each thing, even though the individual remains totally dependent for its act at every instance on the divine source.

Now Malebranche must work out his Cartesianized version of "secondary causality." It is most instructive for the student of St. Thomas' philosophy to see what happens when the all-seeing clear and distinct eye arranges everything neatly, dispelling all mystery, all equivocation, explaining away all the problems. God's efficient causality—his giving of that mysterious, ultimate actual principle, source of all qualities as well as quantities, the act of *esse*—is translated into the clear and distinct terms of the geometrized philosophy by making God simply the necessary and universal source of all movement. Movement is the only idea that will accord with the clear and distinct idea of extension. Yet, adds Malebranche, when we consider still closer, we see that there is nothing in the notion of extension that inevitably suggests motion. Not only cannot body act on spirit, nor spirit on body, but body cannot act on body, for there is nothing in the idea of material extension that would make it of its very nature possessed of motion. All motion must derive from the ultimate efficacious principle, God. Moreover, there is another reason for saying this, over and beyond the notional consideration of extension; namely, the fact that "every efficacity, no matter how small one suppose it, has something of the infinite and the divine." Only God is cause. To act is to produce a new being, something which did not yet exist; in other words, it is really to create. And creation is proper only to God.

Malebranche, then, would reduce all efficacity to movement and reabsorb all movement into the single-univocal source of all creativity, God. "There is only the Creator who can be the mover." But what about all the actions of nature going on about us? If movement is creative, and since only God can create, it might at first glance seem that the slightest trembling of a leaf or the least flicker of a sensation in a human body would require for its explanation a special divine *fiat*. Malebranche will not accept the scholastic notion of a creation of "natures" endowed with some efficacity of their own. This notion of a nature able to operate and cause by itself is good for the pagan Aristotle; it is a "philosophy of the Snake." Nevertheless, Malebranche will admit that creation is endowed with a certain structure. For God has deigned to move according to a series of general laws of motion, or *volontés générales*, covering every sphere of activity and eliminating the need for a special divine intervention at each moment. God has decreed that his activity proceed always in a manner "regulated, constant and uniform" (as befits a reasonable world); therefore he consents to act regularly, "as the occasion demands," we might say.[27] But what is the "occasion" that demands? Precisely the general laws set down for how each sphere of reality should act under certain circumstances. Just what this means will become clearer if we consider the various sorts of laws, or general kinds of occasions, that govern respective areas.

First, there are the general laws of the communications of movement, putting some structure into the movements of bodies. The "shocks" of bodies are the "occasions," in this area, according to which the divine power moves. Secondly, there are the laws governing the union of soul and body. A movement in the body is the "occasion" for God to create a corresponding movement in the soul; just as, reciprocally, my thought that I should like to move a leg provides the law according to which God will regularly send forth his efficacity to move a limb. A third sort of occasional relation exists between the human soul and the divine source of all universal Reason. Here the "occasion" is our attention; that is to say, on the occasion of my attention being brought to bear on an eternal truth God will move to present that truth to the soul. Movements of physical bodies, reciprocal movement of the human soul and its body, and the movements of the spirit are all regular, uniform, intelligible, because God has deigned to make of his all-englobing creative activity not an arbitrary chaos, but the orderly and reasonable movement of the Creator of a universe.

In addition to these general categories of occasions discovered by reason, there are two more that scriptural Revelation makes known to us. There are the laws by which Jesus Christ has received sovereign power over our bodies and our spirits for the distribution of interior grace, laws the "occasions" of which are the movements of the sacred soul of Jesus. The last category strikes us as a surprising one to place among the data of Revelation—until we reflect a moment on what we have already seen: that is, those general laws by which we have power over bodies in the world inferior to us—the occasions of which are our practical desires. Why do we need Revelation to know we have this power? It is not exactly that we need to be told that we have desires; rather, we need Revelation to know that there really are bodies to correspond to our practical impulses. Malebranche, we must remember, has cut the representational bridge to independent things by making all impressions movements only in the spirit that possesses them.

The central idea in this explanation is ORDER, the key to which is the banishment of any ontologic element that might be slightly incomprehensible. "God only communicates his power to creatures," declares Malebranche, "by establishing occasional causes in order to produce certain effects, as the result of laws which he makes to execute his designs in a uniform and constant manner, by the most simple ways, the most worthy of his wisdom and other attributes." [28] Only in the case of the last set of laws might mystery enter; for one cannot expect to know the whys and the wherefores of the movements of the soul of Jesus. But in all the others, it has no place.

Yet for all its dramatic metaphysical implications, and for all its neatly serving rationalist ends, Malebranche's doctrine is still fundamentally religious in intent. For this reason, considerations of Christ as occasional cause of the movements of grace should not be taken as a merely bizarre addition alongside the mainstream of an essentially epistemological-metaphysical development. A study of Malebranche's moral doctrine, fully and systematically presented in the *Traité de morale*, affords a particularly sensitive view of just what kind of world Malebranche imagined man to live in. From this vantage point we can better weigh Malebranche's religious vision, which helps counterbalance our principal view of him as a metaphysician.

Moral Doctrine

"THE LOVE OF ORDER is not only the principal moral virtue, it is the unique virtue: the fundamental, universal mother virtue." [29] There are other good habits, but in reality these are only parts of the essential virtue, aspects in the realization of its program. Before we see what they are and how they help realize the perfect moral program, let us first consider explicitly the metaphysical reasons for this rather bald declaration that the "Love of Order" is the unique virtue.

If God is the source of all movement, and if God moves all things through the system of occasional causes which are the regularized particularizations of his general will, then successful existence consists in moving in tune with this universal arrangement. The Love of Order is nothing more than the will to do just that, to respect the divinely ordained movement of the world. This requires of the individual an effort not to interfere with the operations of the divine impulsus, rather than a positive effort to contribute something himself.

That this last statement, Stoic as it may seem, is not an exaggeration of Malebranche's conception can be seen if we consider the conditions necessary for the soul to live according to Order. The first, according to our Oratorian, is *Force of Spirit*. Now God alone can distribute whatever light there is within the soul.

> But one must look nowhere else but in ourselves for the *occasional* cause which determines Him to communicate it [the light] to us. By a general law, which he follows constantly and all the consequences of which He has foreseen, God has attached the presence of the ideas to the attention of the spirit: for when one is master of his attention and uses it, light does not fail to spread in us in proportion to our work.[30]

God's purpose in establishing our own proper attention as the occasional cause of our light was to allow us to be masters of our will,[31] cooperating in the work of grace through the effort of our attention. The Force of the Spirit is then that habit of attention, inseparable from the Love of Order, and therefore the very center of the moral training of the character. "To acquire this veritable *force* by which the spirit supports the work of attention, it is necessary to put to work early. For naturally habits can only be acquired by acts: One can only fortify oneself by exercise." [32] The moral life essentially consists of a series of attentive acts of the intelligence, seeking to know the true order among things.

> Truth and order consist only in the rapports of grandeur and perfection things have among themselves. But how discover these rapports with absolute evidence, when one lacks clear ideas? How can one give to each thing its appropriate rank if he esteems everything only in relation to himself? [33]

Force of Spirit is the very opposite of egocentricity. It is a devotion to the Truth which drives us to look outside for the clear and distinct ideas of things, which alone should be allowed to satisfy us and which alone can reveal the proper order of things.

"The *force* of the spirit is to the search for the truth what the *liberty* of the spirit is to the possession of the same truth." [34] The Force of Spirit is the habit of attention that keeps us looking for the adequate idea; the Liberty of the Spirit is the virtue of refusing to accept as adequate all confused ideas. "He who is free enough to suspend always his consent, although he cannot deliver himself of his ignorance, a necessary evil in every finite spirit, can deliver himself from error and from sin which renders man worthy of disgust and subject to punishment." [35] A fantastically negative conception of liberty? Radical Stoicism? Yes, but remember the positive doctrine of which it is part. The light and love of God flow into us at all times. Our task is to avoid precipitous judgment so as not to succumb to unworthy desires which attach us to invalid moments of the divine Whole. He who can discipline himself to attend only the real Evidence, the clear and distinct idea, will be in possession of that light which alone, of life's gifts, is genuine. It is this perfect light and this alone which should become the object of one's practical desires.

Man's situation as body-soul is, after all, one of trial.[36] He must work to merit God. Since the horror of the original sin, the solicitations of the body, intended originally only for the necessary preservation of corporeal existence, are capable of getting a stranglehold on the spirit. The spirit now has to learn, through the work of hard discipline, to shun the suggestions of the body. "The body speaks to the spirit only to blind and corrupt it in its favor." [37] All concupiscence without exception is suspect, "that universal instrument of iniquity which has inundated the earth." [38] Man, "wishing invincibly to be happy, can heal his heart corrupted by sensible pleasures only through the unction of grace, the taste of the true goods." [39] The Force of the Spirit and Liberty are the cardinal virtues of a soul working to merit that grace. Through our liberty we cannot force grace to come, but we can make sure that no false idol is put in its way. Malebranche remarks elsewhere, "The power that we have to love different goods is a miserable power, a power of sin." [40] What is usually called free choice is then an abomination, an initiative taken on our part to decide without the presence of the true good, the evidence that compels—as Descartes already pointed out. There is no excuse for so doing, for the light is always there, if we are ready to cooperate with it. We can see that this is our

Augustinian's deepest conviction from the very way he defines the will: "The natural movement that God imprints without cease in the soul to bring it to love Him." [41]

Submission is the word then. Force to seek the evidence, liberty to retain us from precipitous judgment, submission to the step-by-step development of the Truth, such are the elements of Malebranche's formula for a holy life. Indeed, an ethics utterly consistent with the occasionalist solution to Descartes' metaphysical problems!

Conclusion

CRITICS SEEKING CAUSES for the breakdown of Faith in the eighteenth century are usually pretty hard on the good Father Malebranche, or rather on the Cartesianism which he mobilized in a defense of the Faith —a weapon that can truly be said to have backfired. The rationalistic spirit of the whole enterprise, its insistence on explaining everything with reason as the ultimate criterion, certainly did nothing to discourage the atmosphere in which a certain *libertinage* would soon be flourishing. The effort to reduce reality to the movement of God, although intended to reinforce belief in his dominion over things, tended to simplify the universe to such a pale reflection of its former stature that a natural reaction was invited, especially after Bishop Berkeley went to the ultimate extreme of denying matter altogether; as an antidote it was easy, once all efficacity was concentrated in God, either to deny the one great Principle, or to relocate it, for example, in the human mind itself.

But these are very general reactions to broad aspects of Malebranche's program. We can find evidences of the disastrous effects of his vulnerability in much more particular arguments. David Hume pointed out a particularly devastating weak point. Malebranche had insisted that it is the fact we have no adequate idea of the efficacy of material things that keeps us from attributing to the material extended world "any power by which it may produce, or continue, or communicate motion." But, asks Hume, have we any such notion in regard to God? "Since these philosophers, therefore, have concluded that matter cannot be endowed with any efficacious principle, because it is impossible to discover in it such a principle, the same course of reasoning should determine them to exclude it from the Supreme Being." [42] This makes it clear that what happens to physical causality in Hume's hands is a development of a physical skepticism already present in Malebranche.

Malebranche detested Spinozism and was outraged at the slightest suggestion that his doctrine tended toward pantheism. Yet he was so accused in his own day, and still is in ours.[43] Occasionalism does not satisfy either Spinoza or Leibniz or Hume. And today's critic would say that it does not leave the created order of secondary causality enough of an empire of its own. Malebranche's doctrine is not the thoroughgoing pantheism we are going to study when we turn to Spinoza; but any doctrine whose fundamental tools of analysis slice through the protections of analogy the way the Cartesian mathematical eye does, inevitably finds itself with far too little with which to resist Spinoza.

The second of our "Christian philosophers," Blaise Pascal, to whom we are now going to turn our attention, was from his earliest day enamored of the mathematical eye. But he never let it *obscure* (ironically, that *is* the word for it!) his feeling for the mystery of the human condition. The unsystematic nature of his endeavor may have cost him a place on the Olympus of great system philosophers. But his has been a secure throne in the hearts of Christians, in a way that Père Malebranche would surely envy.

VIII ❧

Blaise Pascal

IN PASCAL'S OWN COUNTRY[1] professors often begin their lectures on Pascal by quoting a celebrated page of Chateaubriand's *Génie du Christianisme*:

> There was a man who, at twelve, with lines and circles, had created mathematics;[2] who, at sixteen, had done the most learned Treatise on Conics ever seen since Antiquity; who, at nineteen, reduced to a machine a science that entirely exists in the understanding; who, at twenty-three, demonstrated the phenomena of the gravity of air and destroyed one of the great errors of ancient physics; who, at that age when other men hardly begin to be born, having gone the full circle of human sciences, realized their nothingness and turned his thoughts to religion; who, from that moment till his death arrived in his thirty-ninth year, always infirm and suffering, fixed the language spoken by Bossuet and Racine, gave the model of the most perfect wit as well as of the strongest reasoning; who, in fine, in the short intervals of his pains, solved, by way of distraction, one of the highest problems of geometry,[3] and threw on paper thoughts that smack of God more than of man. That frightening genius was named Blaise Pascal.

The Method of Geometry

To PASCAL as to Descartes, the true method in all domains of natural knowledge was that of mathematics, and to both of them mathematics was geometry; only, to Descartes, geometry meant his own *Geometry* of 1637, whereas to Pascal it meant his own *Essay on the Conics*, published by him in 1640, under the form of a simple sheet, when he was sixteen years old. Other mathematical works of the same period are now lost; we only know them from a summary made by Leibniz, and the intention of that summary was clear. It was "to pit a method against another method: pure geometry against pure algebra." [4] In other words, it was to oppose the algebraic geometry of Descartes, which uses mathematics as a sort of passkey for opening all problems, to the Pascalian mathematics, an instrument invented anew by the mind to solve each particular problem. Descartes was after a speculative science of nature, a theoretical physics such as that of his *Principles of Philosophy;* Pascal wanted to think mathematically *within* experienced physical reality.

This feature of Pascal's method expresses one of the deepest tendencies of his mind. He knew the geometry of Descartes, but he took no interest in it because he was not interested in obtaining the results it permitted one to achieve. What interested Pascal most in nature was that it was *not* deducible *a priori*. His main care was not to jump to conclusions. Take the case of his attitude toward the air-pressure experiments. What was at stake in Torricelli's experiments was to know if, after them, it still could be maintained with the Aristotelians that nature abhors a vacuum. Since there was a vacuum left at the top of the tubes, the answer seemed to be evidently in the negative. This Pascal himself was soon to agree with, but not at once. He first contented himself with saying that, from the experiments hitherto carried out, it only followed that nature abhors a vacuum up to a certain point, but perhaps not absolutely. Differently conceived experiments were required in order to prove that there actually is a vacuum in nature. Pascal performed them, and only then was his mind at rest. A mind proceeding step by step in its investigation of a fundamentally unpredictable nature, such was the exacting master the geometry of Pascal had to serve. It is small wonder that the servant did not give full satisfaction. [5]

The important fragment, *On the Spirit of Geometry,* well expresses Pascal's high ambitions in the matter of demonstration as well as his doubts about the possibility of fulfilling them.

There are three main objects in the study of truth: to discover it when seeking for it, to demonstrate it once found, to discern it from the false while examining it. Typically enough, Pascal will leave aside the first point, for indeed geometry, which excels in the three departments of this study of truth, has already found the answer to the question. Geometers call it "analysis," and there would be no point in discoursing about it after so many excellent writings on the question.

Directly or not, Pascal was here paying Descartes a deserved compliment.

His own considerations on method bear on the second point, which also really includes the third one, for if one knows how to prove truth, it will suffice to examine the proof in order to know if that truth is really demonstrated. So, in Pascal's own mind, the very core of the method consists in the art of demonstration. Be this as it may, Pascal himself seems reluctant to take the word *truth* seriously so long as it applies to something which, although found, has not yet been "demonstrated."

The truly convincing demonstration is geometrical demonstration, which to Pascal is synonymous with "methodical" and "perfect" demonstration as such. Nevertheless, there is a method still more perfect than that of geometry, but since "that which is above geometry is above us," that *ideal* method is beyond our power; "it is however necessary to say a few words about it, although it is impossible for us to practice it."

That "ideal" demonstration, which would constitute the most excellent conceivable method (if we could use it), would consist in two things: 1] defining all the terms, 2] never advancing any proposition without justifying it by already established truths; in short, defining all the terms and proving all the propositions. This is indeed a beautiful method; but why is it, alas, an impossible one? Because we *cannot* define *all* the terms. The definition of one term involves the use of other terms which likewise need to be defined, and these in turn involve others, and so on to infinity. Perfect demonstration, for this reason, is not possible.

Geometrical demonstration, however, is the nearest thing to it. In geometry, there are absolutely first terms, for the simple reason that the mind of the geometer makes them. He is free to start from any definition set up by him and to call its object any name, provided only he always uses the same name to signify the same thing. By sticking to this freely established set of signs, the geometer will avoid all equivocation.

The problem then is: How can geometrical method, in which all terms can be defined, be extended to the other fields of knowledge in which not all terms can be defined? The answer is that, absolutely speaking, it cannot be done. Still the situation is not totally hopeless;

we can proceed as far as possible, as long as we do not pretend to achieve an impossible ideal.

Even in geometry not all terms are defined. Far from it. The notions of odd and even numbers are perfectly definable, but that of number is far from clear. The same can be said of many others, such as space, time, motion, equality, and so on; geometry does not define them because their names so clearly point out the things they signify that any attempt to define them would obscure them. These, then, are "primitive names," understood by all and used by all in the same sense, provided precisely that no attempt be made to explain what they mean.

The same result would be obtained in all the other fields of knowledge if philosophers likewise accepted to philosophize from such primitive terms, whose meaning is known to all. There is nothing weaker than the philosophers' so-called definitions. What point can there be, for instance, in defining what is meant by the word *man*? Or by the word *time*? Or by the word *motion*? Left undefined, everybody understands the same things by their names; the reason they should be left undefined is not that their definitions are hard to find, but, rather, that they are indefinable, as can be seen in the case of the word *is*. Any conceivable definition of *is* will begin by saying that *it is* . . . this and that, which is to define it by itself.

Almost all controversies in philosophy arise from the common neglect of this precaution. To describe it with more precision, let us say that, as often as not, philosophers mistake plain propositions for definitions. Asked for a definition of movement, they answer that it is the act of what is in potency, only insofar as it is in potency. Now this is no definition; it is a proposition made up of several terms, each of which needs to be defined. The question is not to know if it is possible to define them; what matters is to realize that any attempt to define them will result in controversies, whereas if we take them at their face value they will be understood at once, by all and in the same way.[6]

Pascal thus conceives the possibility of extending the method of geometry to all fields of knowledge, exactly as Descartes was doing at practically the same time, but instead of making all knowledge as evident as mathematics, he was thereby imposing upon all knowledge the limitations suffered by geometry itself. All human knowledge can assume the certainty of geometry if it contents itself with strictly demonstrating consequences that are demonstrable, starting from principles naturally evident. In all orders of knowledge, the mind should stop when it gets there; everything held by it will then be certain, either because it is naturally evident or because it is correctly demonstrated.

Spirit of Finesse and Spirit of Geometry

THE HIGHEST QUALITY of the human mind is universality. Pascal's ideal of man is the perfect *honnête homme*. This is one of those terms that are better left undefined. Some people know a gentleman when they see one; so did a Frenchman of the seventeenth century know an *honnête homme* when he saw one. Such a man had one important feature in common with the "gentleman": He was not a professional, or, if it was his misfortune to be one, he did not look like one. This was true in social life; it also was true in intellectual life. A man of that sort was equally able to speak of mathematics, of literature, of ethics, and of theology, only he never made a show of his knowledge. You would not have thought he knew anything about mathematics or about poetry until some occasion naturally arose for him to express views on such matters. This Pascal calls a "universal" man.

He had not to go very far to find one, but he was impressed by the fact that not all men enjoy universality. On the contrary, they divide into two classes: those who are gifted for mathematics, and those who are gifted for the conduct of human affairs in everyday life. Usually they are not the same men. While the ones make themselves ridiculous by arguing in a mathematical way about the subtle problems of human conduct, the others are unable to grasp a mathematical reasoning. The first class possesses the spirit of geometry (*esprit de géométrie*); the second enjoys the spirit of finesse (*esprit de finesse*). Since the method of demonstration is everywhere the same, being but an extension of the geometrical method, the difference between these two classes of spirits must lie in their relation to principles and, ultimately, in the very nature of the principles themselves.

The so-called "geometric spirit" has slow views; it is hard and inflexible. Once it has grasped the principles, it sees them clearly, and they are so big that it would take a particularly distorted mind to go astray in reasoning about them. The difficulty is to see them first. The principles of geometry are tangible and visible, only they are so far removed from common use that many people find it hard to turn their attention to them. Think of people who cannot understand mathematics. They get lost from the very beginning because the meaning of the elementary notions escapes their mind.

The very reverse is true in the spirit of finesse. The principles are in common use. They are there for everybody to see, only they are so subtle and in such large number that it takes good eyes to see them. It is almost impossible not to miss some of them. Now, as has been said, to omit one principle leads inevitably to error. Who can flatter himself that he knows, for instance, all the motives that account for the behavior of any one man, be it himself, in a particular case? So one ought to possess a good sight to discern the principles in such a matter and a good mind to reason correctly about them. The best is to have both the spirit of geometry and the spirit of finesse; to have at least one is good; to have neither is to have no understanding at all.[7]

Pascal has left to us only fragments of a book he never wrote. In reading him, therefore, one should try to get the gist of what he says rather than stick to the terminology. He lacked the time to follow his own recommendation, always to use the same words in the same sense. Nevertheless, it is important to know the meaning of some of the words he used to signify the peculiar kind of spirit that enables man to discern the principles in the order of social intercourse. Man has only one mind, but it functions as reason in demonstrating conclusions from principles; whereas, inasmuch as it apprehends principles by a sort of simple and comprehensive sight, it functions differently—Pascal calls this "heart." This is almost exactly the classical distinction of intellect and reason, or the modern one between intuition and reason.

Of what Pascal calls "heart," two things at least are sure. First, it is the faculty whereby all principles are known, in geometry as in anything else. It may have to do with feeling, particularly in moral and religious problems, but not necessarily so. The principles of geometry are grasped by heart, at a glance, not as the conclusions of any reasoning; and certainly not by feeling.[8] Secondly, because its very essence is to be a simple sight, heart extends from notions to relations between them. This is the reason men endowed with the spirit of geometry, but lacking that of finesse, appear so clumsy in everyday life. They always want to prove, to demonstrate, and to deduce in matters where the main point is really *to see*.[9]

One of the most important consequences of this distinction is the difference it introduces between two main activities of the mind as well as between the men who represent them. The type of the man with *esprit de finesse* was a young friend of Pascal, the Chevalier de Méré; naturally, he had no *esprit de géométrie*. Pascal vainly tried to open his mind to the meaning of one of those principles of geometry so far removed from common use that some men never succeed in seeing them —the notion of infinite.[10] It will help us understand Pascal better (and perhaps to participate a bit in the *esprit de géométrie*) if we follow his discussion of this difficult principle.

Infinity is a fundamental notion, signifying a property common to all things in nature, its knowledge opening the mind to the most surprising marvels in the world. Its notion can only be grasped by the mind, not demonstrated; which is to say it is a principle perceived by the "heart." Still, many men gifted with an otherwise excellent mind fail to grasp it.

As soon as it is grasped, the concept of "infinite" is seen to divide into two infinities present in all things: infinity of magnitude, infinity of parvitude. Since infinity includes them both and is present in all things, these two kinds of infinitude are likewise present in all things.

Infinite magnitude is found in motion (however fast a motion, a faster one is conceivable); it is found in space (however large a space may be, it remains possible to think of a still larger one); it likewise belongs to time (however long a time, it still remains possible to add one moment to it). But infinite parvitude is likewise present everywhere: There is no speed, no extension, no duration that cannot be conceived by the mind as still smaller than it is. There are infinite degrees of slowness between any motion and absolute immobility; one can always think of a space smaller than a given space without ever reaching indivisibility. The same is true of time: no indivisible of duration is conceivable. Generally speaking, this twofold infinity belongs to all things because it belongs to number, which, according to Scripture, is found in all things: *Deus fecit omnia in pondere, in numero et mensura* (*Wis.*, 11:21).

> However great a number may be, one can conceive a greater one, and again another one greater than the latter, and so to infinity, without ever reaching one that cannot be increased. And, on the contrary, however small a number may be, say the hundredth or the thousandth part, one still can conceive a smaller one, and always so to infinity, without ever reaching a zero or nothingness.[11]

It can therefore be said that all things are found between nothingness and infinity and, which is more important, at an infinite distance
from these two extremes. These truths are the very foundations and
principles of geometry. They cannot be demonstrated; they must be
seen. In fact, nearly all men realize that there is no magnitude that
cannot be increased, and this whatever its actual size. The "infinity of
magnitude" is conceivable to almost all minds. Not so with the infinity
of parvitude. Some affirm they can think of a magnitude made up of
two indivisible parts; the chief reason is that, because they cannot picture to their minds a content divisible to infinity, they conclude it is
not actually divisible. This is a bad reason, or, more exactly, it is in
man "a natural disease" to believe that he always grasps truth directly,
so that he feels like denying all that which he cannot understand.
Whereupon, as if his very epistemology were tainted with his Jansenism,
Pascal remarks that man should conclude the reverse, for, in fact, "the
only thing man naturally knows is mendacity (*mensonge*), so that he
should consider true only the things of which the contrary look false
to him." Instead of denying a proposition because we cannot realize its
meaning, we should withhold judgment *and examine the contrary proposition carefully*. If its contrary is manifestly false, then the proposition
at stake, though unconceivable by the mind, is true.

Such is the case with the infinitude of smallness. It is absurd to hold
that, in always dividing a certain space, one eventually will obtain two
halves, each one of which is indivisible. For indeed, space is that which
has parts outside one another; now, if one half of a space is indivisible,
it has not parts; hence it is no space; indivisible space then is patently
absurd. Again, let two indivisibles be given, can we conceive them as
touching one the other? If they do so completely, they are one, but
then how can we still say that each makes up a distinct single indivisible? If they do not touch completely, they touch only in part, but then
they have parts, and how could they still be indivisibles? It is therefore
certain that all things are divisible to infinity, whether or not the mind
can picture to itself an infinitely small thing.[12]

These reflections impressed Pascal the more deeply as they were
bound up in his mind with his own mathematical discoveries, which
took him to the very threshold of infinitesimal calculus. Like that of
Descartes, his philosophy was an enlargement of his scientific view of
the world. Everything in it was intelligible, except the principles from

which is derived its very intelligibility. A clear instance of this is the apparently simple notion of the number one, which can be considered a number or not according to the definition of number adopted by the mathematician. Euclid and some early arithmeticians had found a definition of number that covered all numbers except unity. So they decided unity was no number. Still, since the same Euclid admits that, added to itself, unity can exceed any number, then unity must share in the nature of number, and thus it can be called a number if one decides to do so. At any rate, the adding of one to one makes up a number, because two is of the same nature as one, by the repetition of which it is obtained.

Not so in the case of those principles which some call the "indivisibles" and which are supposed to make up space. Were there such a thing as an indivisible, it would have no parts; on the contrary, the very definition of space is to have parts; so indivisibles added to indivisibles cannot produce space, because indivisibles have not the nature of space. In other words, you can add non-space to non-space as many times as you please; the sum will never be space. The only true indivisible of number is not one, it is zero; zero is a true indivisible of number, as an indivisible is a true zero of extension, or space. Which last remark leads Pascal to his metaphysical and properly Pascalian conclusion:

> The same proportion will be found between rest and motion, and between an instant and time; for all these things are heterogeneous with their respective magnitudes since, being multiplied an infinity of times, they only can produce indivisibles, just as the indivisibles of extension do, and for the same reason. Then a perfect correspondence will be found to obtain between all those things; for all those magnitudes are divisible to infinity without falling into their own indivisibles, *so that they all keep the middle between infinity and nothingness.*[13]

Between Pyrrhonism and Dogmatism

EVERYTHING LIES in the middle, between two opposite infinites. This is true of man himself and, above all, of his knowledge.

Two epistemologies claim the allegiance of philosophers. On the one hand there are the skeptics; on the other hand the dogmatists, who have no doubt that absolute certitude can be attained by human reason, and who, in fact, have no doubt that they have attained it. Both are wrong. Absolute skepticism is an error. It is simply not true that invincible certitude cannot be attained by man; only he does not attain it by means of reasoning; invincible certitudes are attained by "heart." The principles that are apprehended by "heart" are absolutely certain—and this is more than enough to overcome skepticism.

The contrary illusion arises from the failure of the skeptics to distinguish between the apprehension of the principles, either in matters of geometry or in those that require more finesse, and the apprehension of the conclusions at the end of rational demonstrations. The principles are certain when they are naturally evident. Their evidence is not that of a demonstrated conclusion; the mind does not see *why* they are true, but it sees *that* they are true. How does the mind see it? In trying to refuse them assent, for indeed, however hard one tries to do so, he fails. This is Pascal's answer to the "methodical doubt" of Descartes. Pascal has seen perfectly well that Descartes never really doubted whether he was awake or asleep, of sound mind or insane. The point Pascal wants to make is not simply that the doubt of Descartes was feigned, but rather that, even though he seriously tried, Descartes *could not* have doubted such truths. They come to us from nature; it is not in our power not to assent to them, which is precisely what is meant by their being evident.

This doctrine of the *natural* evidence of principles constitutes Pascal's idea of a decisive refutation of the "Pyrrhonians," or skeptics. Their chief arguments consist in showing that the principles we use in demonstrations are not demonstrable. And indeed they are not, but neither should they be, precisely because they are *principles*. Descartes asks how do I know I am not dreaming? What I know is that I do know it, and no argument in the world will cause me to doubt it. True enough, I wish I were able to prove everything I hold true, but that I cannot do so simply shows the weakness of my reason; it does in no way prove the uncertainty of all our cognitions, as the Pyrrhonians pretend it does.[14] Necessary consequences following from evident principles are necessarily true; skepticism easily triumphs in proving that principles are not demonstrable; but it simply forgets that principles should not be demonstrated.

The dogmatists make the same mistake. They make bold to demonstrate everything, including the principles; naturally they fail, and their failure goes a long way toward confirming the skeptics in their own error.

Descartes is one of those dogmatists. "Descartes," Pascal says, "useless and uncertain." [15] He is useless, since he goes to the trouble of demonstrating propositions whose truth is evident. He is uncertain, because his way of demonstrating them is so complicated that the mind feels rather shaken in its certitude after following them to the end. According to Descartes, I cannot be quite sure I am awake, or that there are other beings besides myself, until I have established my own existence in the Second Meditation, the existence of God in the Third and Fifth Meditations, his veracity in the Fourth Meditation, and the existence of the world of bodies (including my own) in the Sixth Meditation. Now I may well fail to understand that long chain of reasons, or to perceive their cogency; it may even be the case that they have no cogency at all. It does not matter much anyway, because I have not ceased one moment knowing that I am awake and not insane; in short, I have not doubted one moment the truth of what nature teaches me in a most convincing way. Principles are not lacking demonstration; their certitude is above demonstration.

Another field in which dogmatism is particularly harmful is that of juridical, social, and political philosophy. There again the skeptics have no difficulty in showing that most laws, social usages, and political constitutions are changing with time, different and sometimes opposed from country to country and, in fine, without decisive rational justifications. In this Montaigne is right; but he is wrong in imagining that such opinions *should be* rationally justified. For they are justifiable only from certain principles which are neither rationally demonstrable nor even naturally evident.

The origin of most codes of conduct is long-established usage, *la coutume;* and how customs came to be established is something seldom easy to see. Naturally, when asked to say why they follow certain rules of conduct, most men will answer: "Because they are just." If such were the true reason, all codes of conduct, all laws, all constitutions would be the same everywhere. Obviously, they are not; what is justice this side of a border is injustice on the other. In fact, the source of the authority enjoyed by laws is the force of the sovereign, in the case of a monarchy, or the force of a plurality in non-monarchical states. "Not being able to make that which is just be strong, they have made that which is strong be just." This is not to say that there is no justice.

The point is that, without force, justice could not make itself respected. So force contradicted justice and said that it itself was just. This way, at least, justice and force are together, which makes for peace, itself the sovereign good.[16]

The dogmatists are not satisfied with such a situation. They want to provide necessary demonstrations justifying the rules of human conduct, the laws and constitutions; which would be all to the good if laws and constitutions were what they should be. But to justify them such as they are is, most often, impossible. The dogmatists by these efforts bring about two results. On the one hand, by attempting to account by justice for rules the only justification of which is force, they give the skeptics occasion for an easy triumph; on the other hand, they foment social and political unrest by revealing to law-abiding citizens that what they are obeying is not justice but mere force without any moral justification.[17] Thus are occasioned revolutions, causes of great suffering for all concerned, and after which the source of authority still is not justice, but force. The difference is that force no longer is in the same hands.

To conclude, neither skepticism nor dogmatism is the truth. It is not true that all is uncertain and that nothing is known, since, in all domains, the principles are certain to the sight of those that have eyes to see them. But it is not correct, either, that every true proposition is rationally demonstrable, for the principles are not subject to demonstration and yet they are true. The wise man wants to be neither Montaigne nor Descartes, but he can make good use of Montaigne against those who share in the dogmatism of Descartes.[18] Pascal himself stands betwixt and between, a skeptic to the dogmatists and a dogmatist to the skeptics. But who knows but what this is not a faithful picture of the human condition?

Man in the Middle

God, the author of nature, is infinite; his works naturally bear the mark of his infinity. From what precedes it can be foreseen that their own infinity is a twofold one, of magnitude and of parvitude, man himself being in the middle, a finite being between two infinites that exceed him out of all proportion.

The universe is infinitely extended in space, our own solar system being but an imperceptible point as compared with the immensity of the firmament. "All this visible world is but a trace in the ample bosom of nature." However much we may try, we fail to picture to ourselves the immensity of things; what we call the universe is but an atom compared with the world, that sphere whose center is everywhere and whose circumference is nowhere. That our imagination loses itself in that contemplation is a perceptible mark of the all-powerfulness of God, but it is also for man an invitation to realize that he is lost in a small corner of nature. What is a man, swallowed up in infinity?

On the other hand, consider the smallest of known insects; you will find in it a prodigiously complex system of limbs, veins in the limbs, blood in the veins, drops in the blood, and so on. Nor is this all, for we should conceive each drop as another universe, itself containing other ones with their own firmaments, planets, earths, then on each earth more animals like the one now at stake, and so on to infinity. Now instead of appearing an atom as compared with the whole, man sees himself as a colossal giant; after being imperceptible to himself in the whole, man now sees himself as a whole in comparison with that nothingness which it is impossible to reach. He who considers himself that way will veritably frighten himself. Seeing himself, with the mass nature has imparted to him, suspended between those two abysses of infinity and nothingness, he will feel more like contemplating them silently than submitting them to the scrutiny of curiosity.

Man therefore finds himself situated in the middle of nature, caught between two infinitely distant extremities, and this in all orders of reality as well as of knowledge.

As a being, man is nothing compared with infinity, but he is a whole as compared with nothingness. As a knowing being, he is hanging between two inscrutable mysteries, that of the nothingness from which he was created and that of infinity in which he is drowned: both his origin and his end escape his sight. In the order of sciences, the same remarks apply, for each science goes to infinity in the number of its problems as well as in that of its principles; only these so-called principles just happen to be those beyond which we cannot go. There are others before them, and still others before these; the principles at which we stop are no more prime than the so-called "indivisibles" at which some geometers decide to stop. Could we push the consideration of one of these two infinites, we would meet the other. For indeed one of them depends on the other; but they meet only in the truly infinite being, in God.

Let man then know himself thus situated in the middle, with not enough being to grasp the infinity of magnitude and too much being to see the infinity of parvitude. In a striking sentence Pascal declares that "our intelligence holds, in the order of intelligible things, the same rank as our body in the order of nature." This remark becomes, in his thought, the source of countless psychological and moral observations. Our senses can perceive neither extreme in their objects: neither extreme heat nor extreme cold; neither too much light nor too little; too much pleasure finally displeases; even too much truth blinds the mind, and this is the reason the prime principles are so hard to grasp; being too young and being too old both impede the mind, just as having received too much instruction or too little. In short, all extremes are for us as though they were not, and with respect to them we are not. They escape us, or we escape them.

The practical conclusion of these reflections is decisive. Since nothing can stabilize the finite thing which is man, suspended between the two infinites, the wise thing for each one of us is to stay quietly in the very condition in which nature has placed us. Since this middle of ours always remains infinitely distant from the extremes, it does not matter much whether we have a little more or a little less of anything, even knowledge. If we know a little more, we start from a little higher in our demonstrations, but we remain as infinitely distant from the beginning as we ever were. From the point of view of those infinites, all finites are equal. This certitude should help us to keep our peace, fully convinced of the limitations inherent in human nature and sensible enough to live accordingly.

Man and God

Nowhere does man more clearly appear in the centrality of his position than in his very structure. Endowed with a body, like beasts, and with a mind, like angels, he is neither an angel nor a beast. He is a man, so much so that he cannot even try to play the angel without playing the beast.

This does not mean that the two component elements of his nature, body and soul, are equal in dignity. By his body, man is an exceedingly small thing in nature; but by his mind, he can encompass nature. As a material being, man is as frail as a reed, but he is a thinking reed. It takes very little to break it, but were man crushed by the universe, he still would be greater than what crushes him, for he knows at least this, that he is being crushed, whereas the universe itself knows nothing about it.[19]

The greatness of man lies in thought, which is both admirable and incomparable in its nature, but ridiculous in its defects. For this very reason the greatness of man can be seen from his misery, and vice versa. Man knows he is miserable, so he is miserable; but he is great also, *because* he knows his misery. As nature has endowed him with a great desire to be happy, he wants to rid himself of his misery. To achieve that result is the only motive behind all the actions of men. Some go to war in the hope of finding happiness there; others do not go to war for the very same reason. Even those who hang themselves do so for this motive. In fact, all men complain, princes and subjects, rich and poor, old and young, scholars and ignorant, healthy and sick, in all countries, at all ages and of all conditions; none finds himself satisfied with his own condition.

There must be a reason for the universality of this desire coupled with its inability to achieve fulfillment; it is that there once was in man a true happiness, of which he has nothing left now but the vestige and the empty place. All his efforts aim at filling up that vacuum and at recouping its loss. As often as not, man seeks in all sorts of pleasures, hobbies, and games means of diverting his attention from his empty feeling,[20] but nothing really helps. What man once possessed and now has lost was perfect happiness; the finite objects at his disposal do not compensate for the loss of the infinite good which alone could appease the infinite avidity of his desire. Himself changing and finite, man finds in his heart an infinitely deep cave which only an infinite and immutable object can fill up; that object is God.[21]

The problem raised by philosophy thus finds its answer in religion. Philosophers often refuse to listen to the answer because, among other things, they cannot find a good demonstration for God's existence. But the truth of God's existence is a principle, not a conclusion. That there is a God is one of those propositions that are perceptible by the "heart" or whatever we wish to call that faculty of the soul, inborn in us, by which nature reveals to us the fundamental truths without which human life is unbearable, not to say impossible. Because this feeling has become obscured in the heart of man, God has revealed himself. God perceptible to the heart of man, not to reason, such is faith.[22] This is how man knows with perfect certitude the existence and name of the good he has lost.[23]

At the same time, religion reveals to man how he has lost that good. The doctrine of original sin is the only satisfactory answer to the enigma of the present condition of man. Nothing else can account for the contradictions inherent in human nature as it is now. The greatness of man is the image of his Creator in him; his misery is in him the effect of sin. It is "an astounding thing that the mystery the farthest removed from our knowledge, which is that of the transmission of sin, be a thing without which we can have no knowledge of ourselves!" Indeed it is a *mystery*. For to know how the sin of Adam could have rendered guilty men so utterly foreign to it is certainly something reason finds hard to understand; still, supposing it to be true, the rest becomes clear: "Man is more inconceivable without this mystery, than this mystery is inconceivable to man." [24]

Last, not least, if the religion we accept is Christianity, we learn the remedy to our misery at the same time as its cause; Pascal intended to provide a complete Christian apologetics, including all the traditional arguments in favor of the divinity of the Christian religion: miracles, prophecies, and the like. The *Pensées* have preserved a great many of the arguments he would have used in his demonstration; but what we are here interested in is the impact of Christian faith on Pascal's philosophical positions. Now it must not be forgotten that the basic philosophical problem for Pascal is raised by the permanent opposition between skepticism and dogmatism. Their opposition is permanent because neither one has been able to win, and what surprises Pascal most, in this history, is that for no good reason skepticism, or Pyrrhonism, has never been able to win. Nay, there probably never was a thorough skeptic, for the simple reason that, were a skeptic to take his own arguments seriously, he would not be able to survive. The perpetuity of dogmatism, despite its inability to achieve truly demonstrated conclusions, is the sure sign that something remains in man of a state of perfection he has lost.

To have accounted for this position, however, does not eliminate it. It takes a last and supreme mystery to liberate man from this inner contradiction, source of many other ones. Jesus Christ and the grace of redemption are the only complete answer to the problem. Some men, the dogmatists of the Stoic family, considered nature incorrupted, so they could not avoid seeking refuge in pride; others, like the Pyrrhonians, or skeptics, considered the corruption of human nature as its normal condition, so they could not help a lazy surrendering to evil. Christian religion only was able to rid man of these two vices. It did not expel the one by means of the other, as the earthly wisdom of philosophers had vainly tried to do; it expelled both at once by the divine simplicity of the Gospel. The Christian religion alone "teaches the just, whom it raises up to participation in the divinity itself, that even in that sublime state, they carry with them the source of all the corruption which renders them, during their whole life, exposed to error, to misery, to death, to sin; while, at the same time, it loudly reminds the most impious of men that they are able to receive the grace of their Redeemer." [25] Whereupon Pascal confidently adds: "Who can refuse to believe and to adore these celestial lights?" Only the author of such a philosophy could write, along with his essays on the method of geometry, the sublime pages of the *Mystery of Jesus* and carry on himself, sewn in the lining of his garment, as a perpetual reminder of his greatest mystical experience, the *Mémorial*.[26]

4   THE GOLDEN AGE
OF METAPHYSICS

NO OTHER PERIOD since the Middle Ages, with the possible exception of the brief moment early in the nineteenth century when Fichte, Schelling, and Hegel were building their systems, has seen such grand metaphysical effort as the end of the seventeenth and the first decades of the eighteenth century. Without Leibniz and Wolff, Kant would never have come to be. Consequently, we must credit in part even the systems of the post-Kantians to the accomplishments of what we shall term "the Golden Age of Metaphysics."

Like all "golden ages," this one was a rich harvesting of fruits sown by fertile predecessors. Descartes is of course the father of all this invention; but all who contributed through science to the conviction that at last the human spirit had found the secret that would let it commune directly with the principles of the universe, and through its intuitions rule majestically over the world, can legitimately claim a participation in the crowning results: the metaphysical systems of Leibniz and Spinoza.

And, again like all golden ages, it begets the inevitable reaction; the attacks on idealist metaphysics launched by the *philosophes* toward the middle of the eighteenth century owe their violence and much of their importance to the greatness of the enterprises they will be combating. Like the *philosophes*, and strengthened by the new blood of English empiricism—especially the accomplishment of Newton— the critical thinkers of the German *Aufklärung*, in seeking to move beyond metaphysics (understand rationalist metaphysics), will be pushed to the heights of inventiveness in seeking out new realms of the human spirit to explore. They were forced far afield by the immensity of the obstacle left by Spinoza and Leibniz across what had become the traditional main road of continental philosophy.

IX

Benedictus Spinoza

Like hobbes, Benedictus Spinoza[1] frightened the philosophical wits out of many of his contemporaries; but out of no one more than the Cartesians of the Strict Observance. Imagine the impression made by this brilliant Jew, excommunicated by the Hebrew community of Amsterdam and thus beholden to no religious authority, quietly grinding optical lenses in a rented room while refusing all professorships, thus unbeholden to any civil authority, who consequently was free to turn the instruments of Cartesian analysis to the purposes that pleased him—which happened to be the erection of a system of thoroughgoing pantheism! Little was available to the general public beyond rumor by which to judge the monster's work—which only added to the fright and awe in which he was held. The philosopher's main systematic treatise, *Ethics Demonstrated According to the Geometrical Order,* was circulated in private manuscript and was finally published only after the author's early death in 1677. As long as the *Ethics* was not public, the Cartesians could content themselves with railing at it from afar, contending that any work that came to such a God-compromising conclusion could not possibly owe anything to Descartes, but rather must be simply using its "geometric method" as a vile subterfuge to put over a fundamentally anti-Cartesian enterprise.

Such was Père Malebranche's attitude, carefully nursed by ignorance of Spinoza's text. Yet a generation later, the *Ethics* now having become general property, we find Leibniz making a careful study of it, callously showing how very Cartesian is its inspiration, and heartily disassociating himself from this Cartesianism.[2]

When we attempt today to read Spinoza's *Ethics* with a bit of that objectivity which distance permits, we have to disagree with the Cartesians' estimate of it in two important respects: first, Spinozism does clearly grow directly out of the most serious intrinsic difficulties in the

Cartesian approach; to put it bluntly, Spinoza is just what the Cartesians had coming to them! Secondly, we are struck by the sincerity of Spinoza's purpose, which was to erect on the "scientific" basis of Cartesian geometric analysis an ethico-metaphysical view of reality that would make possible a good, though not a Christian, life. The Christian Cartesians of the end of the seventeenth century refused to believe there could be anything sincere about such ghastly intellectual *libertinage*!

From the first lines of the *Ethics*, it is clear that Spinoza means to take Descartes very much at his word. It is not the Euclidean form of his demonstration that makes it Cartesian (the whole work is laid out like a geometry text, with definitions, axioms, demonstrations, and scholia); critics had a point when they insisted such a form of presentation *could* possibly be just a front to hide an essentially un-Cartesian doctrine. But the whole order of exposition and the very nature of the definitions themselves give us fair warning that we are in the presence of an argument that can be more "Cartesian" than the text of Descartes himself.

The Unique Substance

ON THE THEORY that there must be one clear and distinct idea from which all other ideas can be deduced, Spinoza at once places the conception of God at the very center of his treatise. It is to function both as the principle of necessity for the whole logical order and as first, necessary cause in the order of being; this is quite in keeping with the main postulate—that the orders of thought and reality are one.[3] Spinoza quickly establishes that this one absolute clear and distinct idea must be infinite substance, the one reality that in the strict sense can "be in itself and conceived by itself." He does not feel called upon to prove this first principle; rather he presents it as simply a question of definition: it is clear that there must be a first reality *quod in se est, et per se concipitur.*[4] This first reality we call God.

The absolute, infinite substance must be unique. Descartes had already conceded that only God could be considered to exist in and by himself and that all other beings can be considered substances only in a derivative sense. Spinoza refuses categorically to tolerate in a philosophy aspiring to perfect rational clarity any such vestige of medieval analogy.

"Relative substance"—could any notion be less clear, more indistinct than that? If substance is to be conceived as a rationally acceptable notion (within Cartesian ground rules for what is "rational"), then the only logical solution to the one-many problem is the one Descartes has already discovered but refused to exploit. Reality is one substance; the many aspects of reality are its basic attributes[5] and its changing modes.

Now, an infinite substance must possess an infinity of attributes. Unfortunately, the finite human understanding's knowledge of the attributes of the divine substance is limited to the only two of which we have any experience, thought and extension. In defining the nature of these two known attributes of the divine substance, Spinoza "Cartesianizes" them thoroughly. We must not think of "extension" in terms of the length, width, and breadth, and divisibility into parts that characterize the material things of our experience. God can have no parts, and the infinite extension of the divine substance is no mere set of dimensions. Just what it is, Spinoza is at a loss to tell us; indeed he seems better able to suggest what it is not. But what he is driving at is clear enough. He wants essentially to leave the impression that the divine being, as ground of all existence, cannot be described in dimensional terms, for he grounds extension too: he enfolds extension itself in a general way and therefore is the explanation for all particular corporeal extended things. The attribute of thought is less difficult to generalize into the notion of infinite thinking as such. Although once again we are not told positively what "infinite thought" might be, it is not difficult to imagine some sort of universal intelligibility underlying and founding all particular thought content.

Locating both attributes in the one absolute substance is of high importance: the thorniest Cartesian problem is thereby solved—or rather *dissolved*—in a single move. The "clear-and-distinct-idea" analysis had introduced a tremendous cleavage between the spiritual activity of thought and the material attribute of extension. Both Descartes and Malebranche, each in his own way, had recourse to God to help get over the most annoying results of this circumstance. Spinoza's solution is more radical than either Descartes' appeal to the veracity of God or Malebranche's occasionalism. By making thought and extension attributes of a single, unique substance, Spinoza can explain their interaction in particular things by invoking the unity of their origin.

One serious difficulty, however, plagues Spinoza's solution: the way

he distinguishes the divine attribute of infinite extension and the finite
extension which we encounter as the property of corporeal things.
Positing them as being absolutely different is no answer; what relation
is there then between the infinite extension, attribute of the divine
substance, and the corporeal extension encountered in our experience?
Spinoza attempts to solve the difficulty by suggesting that the limiting
characteristics of corporeal extension really arise from the finite nature
of the human imagination which deals with extension on the modal
level. The reason, on the other hand, in contemplating the conception
of infinite extension encounters the primordial, the really-real extension. But in suggesting that the sense power is misleading and only the
reason always right, Spinoza runs the risk of abandoning one of the
major benefits of his proposed solution to the problem of unifying
extension and thought; namely, a justification of the experienced fact
of a mind-body coordination in the real world. The problem then is
not really solved.

However, if one agrees to overlook this difficulty—and the fact that
it is really impossible *to understand* the relationship of the Substance to
its modes—it must be admitted that Spinoza, in selling out to the
pantheism of the One Substance solution, has gained a means of presenting a convincing tableau of the world of our experience. There
are, it has been explained, an infinity of divine attributes, only two of
which fall within the ken of our human experience: thought and extension. But each attribute is in turn capable of being manifested in an
infinity of particularities or "modes." In the case of the two kinds of
attributes known to us, this means, concretely, that the divine extension
can be manifested in an infinity of concrete bodies, and the divine
attribute of thought, in an infinity of ideas. Now these ideas, being
ultimately emanations of the same divine substance as the bodies, can
be the ideas *of* those bodies—their manifestations in the realm of the
intelligible and, in the case of living things, their souls. Moreover,
Spinoza has gained a way of explaining the perfect harmony, the perfect intelligibility of the entire universe. Above the particular modes—
the many ideas, the many bodies—he puts a general mode, *facies totius
universi*, which, although not very elaborately explained, seems to mean
a kind of combination, on the level of the most universal consideration
of the created world, of thought and extension, forming the perfect
symmetrical view of the knowable material world. Science is not hanging in air, then, but is seeking, using as its starting point the perfect en-

chainment of ideas in the material world, to rise to a closer and more intuitive grasp of the unifying idea underlying the whole complexus.

The unique divine substance is cause of its attributes and its modes, but in just what sense? The substance is the real ontological cause of the being of the modal particularities, but this efficiency must be conceived in a way consonant with the rationalistic approach upon which the conception rests. The modes are not the result of a *fiat* of the divine will; rather they are a necessary emanation of the divine essence. Intellect and will are not, according to Spinoza, divine attributes at all, but are *modes* produced by the Godly nature under the attribute of thought. Hence they cannot be the root of the creation of things. Rather, God creates the world with the same necessity by which he himself is maintained in existence. As *causa sui*, God's essence is his existence, he cannot not be—and for the very same reason, because of this very necessity, God *must* issue himself forth in all the modal manifestations. Creation flows from the divine nature the way conclusions flow from their principles in a mathematical demonstration.

Is God then not free? We have been somewhat prepared by our study of Malebranche for the answer Spinoza gives to this question. Freedom, for the rationalist, can only mean one thing: capacity to fulfill the conditions for rational intelligibility. These are summed up in the famous formula for the criteria of truth: clarity, and distinctness. Neither the necessity, nor the immutability, nor the infinity of God is an obstacle to the fulfillment of such conditions; on the contrary, these properties are that fulfillment itself. God is free, then, simply because he is what he is. God's freedom is the self-necessitation of his existence. All other things are compelled in their being and operation from without and depend on something else for their intelligibility. Only God is self-necessitated and self-explanatory. That is why he alone can truly be said to be free.

God is, then, the necessary efficient cause of finite reality, efficiency being understood here as the kind of sequence from principle to effect that occurs in a logical demonstration. Spinoza does not, however, consider God the final cause of creation; the rationalistic preoccupation with intelligible necessity leaves little place for an order of causality foreign to idea. We can see the full impact of this in Spinoza's statement that God is an *immanent* rather than a transitive cause. By this Spinoza means that the only kind of transcendence enjoyed by the first cause is that belonging to absolute substance in regard to the

relative modes, which is very much the primacy of the whole in relation to the parts. Spinoza denies that God can be a *remote* cause, except
in the sense that sometimes his effects pass by way of other modes
before flowing into the outermost modes, but even in this case the
proper definition of the "outermost" (if we may so express it) modes
must also necessarily include a reference to the divine substance.

While all of reality, then, is one massive substance, the distinction
between attributes and modes of substance makes it possible to conceive
within the unity of reality a kind of bi-polarity, distinguishing and
uniting the creating and the created. The divine substance and its attributes, considered as the free cause of all else, constitute one pole,
which Spinoza terms (borrowing a medieval terminology) *natura
naturans*. The other pole, the created reality, the sphere of the infinite
and finite modes, is *natura naturata*. "Nature naturing" and "Nature
natured," the active and passive participles, find their primordial unity
in Nature itself; i.e., in God: *Deus sive Natura*, is Spinoza's famous
pantheistic expression for this unity.

Even on the level of our finite human experience we encounter something of this polarity. We have already seen the important distinction
Spinoza makes between knowledge grasped by the imagination and
knowledge intuited by the reason. Actually, this ability of man to look
two ways is due to the fact that from his modal position he can look,
with the imagination, toward the world of particular things, or, with
the reason (which is an emanation of the divine attribute of thought),
toward the unique substance, source of all, in which he can view the
unity of all reality in the *natura naturans*. When, as in the everyday
common-sense situation, men consider things in the isolation of their
individual essences, their imagination is what is at work. The resulting
view is not inherently erroneous, but it plays easily into the hands of
error by encouraging one to view each thing and each act as though
the world of manyness, the world of time and death, were its own
explanation. Imagination properly united to reason will not lead one
into this error, for reason will persist in seeing everything in its union
with every other thing; above all, it will keep one aware that the
"contingency" and "corruptibility" supposed by imagination are only
limitations of modal knowledge. When one grasps the unity of reality
in the necessity of the one substance, it becomes evident that everything has to be as it is and that no reality ever really passes away into
nothingness but merely goes through modal changes. *Sub specie aeterni-*

tatis, every isolated thing is quasi-divine; nothing is to be despised; everything is to be honored with an almost religious devotion, as emanations and modes of the divine substance.

Human Nature

Spinoza's radical metaphysical position, as we have already suggested, supplies him with an effective means of solving the Cartesian matter-idea problem. Furthermore, the notion that individual minds are modes of one substance provides a means of explaining the status of the Truth to be found in the individual mind in a way that is even more unequivocal than Malebranche's solution of the "vision of the ideas in God."

By positing thought and extension as attributes of a single divine substance, Spinoza is able to affirm the existence of a complete harmony between the individual modal manifestations of the two kinds of attributes. Our experience presents us with the fact of different sorts of material things enjoying various degrees of being. This hierarchy he conceives as emanating modally from the divine substance under the attribute of infinite extension. Complex individual bodies are actually built up from the coordination of many simpler units working together for a time toward a single end: that body's reality; in turn, the whole assembly of complex bodies cooperate to form a single material universe which is, in effect, one unified gigantic individual, the body of God. Corresponding to it under the attribute of thought is the *idea* of God, the "*facies totius mundi*" we met above. This is a single complex conception of the physical universe, formed by a whole chain of ideas which in turn corresponds to the whole complexus of bodies; each of these ideas being exactly parallel to one of the bodies, as they coincide as one single mode of the same substance. It is clear, then, that the idea corresponding to a given body does not actually animate it, in the sense of exerting a physical, causal influence on it, and that the body cannot affect in a physical way its corresponding idea; this would compromise the whole point of the perfect parallelism made possible by Spinoza's doctrine of the single substance-with-many-modes. The union between a body and its idea is metaphysically more intimate in this conception than it would be in a realistic animism; as simultaneous aspects of one discrete act of a single, infinite substance whose simplicity is absolute, there is no possibility of their enjoying even the remotest moment of existence independently of one another.[6]

Applied specifically to the problem of human unity, Spinoza's conception permits again a neat solution to the Cartesian difficulty. "Everything that happens to the object of the idea constituting the human soul," declares the philosopher in the Twelfth Proposition, "must be perceived by that soul; in other words an idea of it is necessarily given in the soul, which is to say that if the object of the idea constituting the soul is a body, nothing can happen in the body which is not conceived in the soul." Spinoza conceives this human body as itself so highly composite and therefore so tied up with all the rest of matter that the soul, in mirroring every aspect of every one of its constituents, is actually brought to mirror sympathetically the whole range of ideas corresponding to the material universe.

The soul is not made to know things directly in a vision either of itself or of the divine nature. Each human soul exactly coincides with its body, hence it must work through—or better, parallel to—sense, imagination, and memory in its struggle to encompass the world of things.[7] Although the soul can progress beyond bodies to come to know spiritual truths, by turning toward the All rather than its modes, it must begin its struggle toward the heights on a level parallel to that of the senses and imagination. Spinoza's insistence on the importance of the struggle in finite human knowledge underscores the reality of the divine modes as a proper, albeit a finite, part of reality.

Knowledge, Passion, and Survival

THE CONNECTION between all this and an "ethics" may seem remote. But knowledge itself, in Spinoza's conception, is not a shadowy abstraction from reality, but a mode of the life-force. All modal individuals, as emanations of the divine substance, are, in both their extended and their ideational aspects, a part of the primordial reality. As such, each is impelled by a primitive force, a *conatus*, which urges it to persevere in being; each according to its degree of reality instinctively turns its inherent forces to this end. What tradition called variously "will," "appetite," "desire" in man are so many particular ways the force of existence manifests itself in the human reality. Knowledge is the highest of these manifestations. Hobbes had affirmed the oneness of the human moral force with the life-force in all things; Spinoza takes up the same idea, only reversing it, so that the lowest manifestations are now considered the outer effulgences of a single, divine force.

Situated as he is, high on the scale of being, man possesses powerful weapons in the fight for survival. He needs them badly, for the myriad elements of which he is composed try in their own ways to survive independently and thus tend to drag man along their separatist, confusing courses. Under the attribute of thought, these base movements result for man in the phenomenon of confused knowledge.[8] This, the lowest of man's cognitions, Spinoza terms *opinion;* it is characterized by its contingency, its fortuitous nature, and by its close attachment to external causes, in the sense that such concrete knowledge always refers to something other than itself, and other than man himself, as its necessary and inescapable source and end.[9] Such confused knowledge affords no leverage for control of one's destiny; rather, it itself tends to control the individual, pulling him haphazardly, now this way, now that, attracting him to first one object, then to another without plan or reason, and in a way that seems to invite things to take control of man rather than man to take control of things. The reign of opinion is the reign of passion.

This analysis is an interesting example of the potentialities inherent in Spinoza's intuition into the unity of reality and into the way this unity manifests itself in the coordination of body and soul in the human complexus. Spinoza sees clearly that all human action of its very essence involves knowledge, for it is always action toward and for the sake of something. He sees, further, that all human knowledge involves both passivity and activity to some degree—we are not a bundle of clear and distinct ideas possessed by a self-sufficient *cogito,* but souls which are "ideas of a body," or modes of a substance under its attribute of thought. As "idea," the soul is of course "of the attribute of thought" and therefore has tendencies toward absolute self-possession, clearness, and distinctiveness, similar to the self-possession of the All; but as "of a body," as a mode partaking of the same multiplicity as the composite, extended modes, it is constantly beset by the resulting confused affections. When the soul is led to act on the basis of these particular, unclear ideas, then it can be said to be in the throes of a passion. When it manages to direct itself, however, by its own active effort, on the basis of a universal clear and distinct idea, then it is acting *virtuously*—that is, powerfully—and can hope to take the initiative in extending its domain over the multiplicity of treacherous currents set running by the confused ideas.

Man will always be in the throes of passion, at least to some extent. Given his body-soul composition, this is inevitable; he will always be necessarily attached to the physical world. Man's vocation, and his hope, lies in the progress that can always be made toward the institution of a greater rule of reason.

Science, the second kind of knowledge, is precisely the first step toward the institution of such a reign of reason, toward the domination of passion by the action of virtue. Out of the chaos, externality, and individuality of opinion, scientific reason begins to bring order and universality and to reveal these qualities as traits interior to the order of reality itself. Hence science, even more than its value as knowledge, has a great ethical importance: it is the first step in the human being's realization of himself through reason as an emanation of the divine attribute of infinite thought. Scientific reason seeks the clear and distinct ideas underlying the multiplicity of sensible effects;[10] in other words, underlying the movements in the soul corresponding to the perception of things. This opens the road to a possible control of the effects of these movements, and therefore to the domination and unification of the human complexus by the divine principle of reason.

Scientific reason itself, however, is not yet the realization of this ultimate goal, for, like opinion, it still remains dependent on external sources for its original data and therefore does not yet actuate the full potential of the reasonable principle for independent existence and ultimate self-possession. For this, the reason must come magnificently into its own; it must grasp itself as a manifestation of the divine attribute, at the same time understanding its body as a coordinated modal manifestation of the divine, under the attribute of extension. This third and highest kind of knowledge, *scientia intuitiva*, grasping the supreme clear and distinct ideas of the divine substance, its attributes and its modes, would put the soul in a position, viewing all of reality *sub specie aeternitatis*, to exercise adequate control over everything we do. The beatitude of perfect virtuous existence coincides exactly with the highest grasp of the highest ideas; the ultimate result of the Spinozistic method of progressive mounting to the philosophical summit is a fruition that is at once practical and theoretical, ethical and metaphysical.

We can see better now how the main traditional moral conceptions take on a quite distinctive meaning in such a theory. "Will" is nothing but the *conatus* itself, considered in relationship to mind as the guiding principle. *Appetite* is simply this same force considered in terms of the union of both soul and body, appetite then being the effort of any body-idea correlate to preserve its being. Appetite is found in all modal beings, but only man, because of the superior nature of his idea, or soul, is conscious of his appetite and can direct it rationally. When conscious as in man, this appetite is more particularly termed *desire*, which, as fundamental drive, is the source of all the other affects in man. Because of the mutability of our nature (a mutability which in turn is due to our being so composite and to the complexity of the body), desire goes through a series of constant dynamic changes. As the mind increases its effort toward order and unity and passes from a lesser to a greater perfection, we experience *laetitia*, or joy; when the reverse is happening and the mind moves toward a lesser perfection, it is accompanied by *tristitia*, sadness.[11] All other passional affects are just combinations of the three primitive passions—desire, joy, and sadness—this is true even of love and hate, which are simply joy and sadness accompanied by an idea of an external cause. Desire and joy, when they are leagued with a clear and distinct idea, are of course no longer passions at all, but actions, active affects, and, as such, manifestations of the powerful virtuous principle in man.[12] As such, they are much more meaningful and fundamental realities than what is traditionally termed *good* and *evil*. Good and evil are only relative terms, based on some anthropomorphic model of perfection we set before ourselves at a given stage of our ignorance of ourselves. The fully liberated, authentic human being has no need of such incomplete and confusing notions; they are replaced by the realization of what they represent; namely, what is harmful or useful to us in terms of the fundamental *conatus* in us, which is then really viewed as a single, unequivocal drive of our own reality, and needs no such objectivization.

The notion of "liberty" is an outgrowth of past confusion. The very idea of introducing a cleavage between the intellect and the will and then of suggesting that the will can arbitrarily "withhold judgment" or, conversely, thunder forth with a great *fiat* independently of the vision of the understanding is, in Spinoza's opinion, a monstrous misunderstanding. We can only will—that is, affirm and deny (judgment and willing being one and the same function)—to the extent that we know. Not all of our knowledge—in fact, very little of it—is clear and distinct. It is in the vast area of the confused judgment that the phenomena traditionally ascribed to "libera voluntas" occur. But neither suspension of judgment nor judgment about what is in fact confused can be said to constitute the operation of an arbitrary power. In the case of suspension of judgment, one has simply seen "that he does not perceive the thing adequately. The suspension of judgment is then in reality a perception and not an act of free will." [13] As to arbitrary judgment, it is simply inadequate, uncriticized knowledge. When a child imagines a shape to be a horse, he simply affirms that the horse is present, even though he is not certain of it, because he sees nothing that excludes its possibility of existence. Our imaginings as such are not of themselves erroneous. They are only more or less adequate. After all, it is proper to an idea as such to represent something; it is therefore natural and right for the spirit to believe in all of its ideas, even the confused ones. But only the primitive or infantile soul, moving in sympathy with the confused representations of its complex body, at once subscribes wholeheartedly and indiscriminately to the reality of the confused images begotten by the power of the imagination. The mature soul—and in this its maturity consists—recognizes that there is a hierarchy of adequacy. Among representations, the adult soul recognizes the need for a critique of our ideas, using as criteria of credibility those clear and distinct ideas which carry with them in their own evidence the mark of their necessity.

The keystone of Spinoza's critique is a metaphysical assumption it would be well to state boldly, for it is an assumption destined to receive the closest scrutiny in the *Critique of Pure Reason*. That is the assertion that truth and rational necessity are perfectly equivalent, which in turn is based on the assertion that rational necessity is a manifestation of an ultimate and necessary substantial ontological reality in which the mind participates when recognizing it, as an effect participates in its cause. All of this is just a more detailed way of explaining what Spinoza states with perfect simplicity when he writes, "The order and connection of ideas is the same as the order and connection of things." [14]

The need for the clear and distinct ideas to extend their province over the lesser, confused cognitions can of course now be easily stated in moral terms. A passion is a confused idea to which we seem to submit because we do not possess the means to dominate it. That "means" can only be a clear and distinct idea that unveils the real sense of the confused representation—an active affect counteracting the passive one.

"An affection which is a passion," reads the Third Proposition in Part V, "ceases to be a passion as soon as we form a clear and distinct idea of it." For to understand an affection clearly and distinctly is to replace it in its ontological background and recognize it as a modal moment of the divine attribute itself. Such an understanding permits the soul to see that "all things are necessary," [15] because determined by the *conatus* to play a part in the structuring of reality in and by "an infinite chain of causes." The necessity of each and of all things understood, the conflicting desires or the sadness that might otherwise accompany such things are eliminated.[16]

Knowledge and Love of God as Beatitude

OUR MORAL DUTY, then, is to come to know all our affections clearly and distinctly, which means, in other terms, "that all the affections of the body, i.e., all the images of things, must be related to the idea of God." [17] To form a clear and distinct conception is to know the thing in relation to the idea of God.[18] This alone is truly *beatitude*. "He who knows himself and knows his affections clearly and distinctly—and that with the accompaniment of the idea of God—is joyous," for he knows and loves God.[19]

But what more exactly does that mean, to know all things in God? Proposition XXX of the Last Part of the *Ethics* tells us.

> Our soul, to the extent that it knows itself and knows the body as things having a sort of eternity, has necessarily the knowledge of God and knows that it is in God and conceives itself by God. Eternity is the very essence of God insofar as it envelops necessary existence. To conceive things with a sort of eternity is then to conceive things insofar as they are real beings by the essence of God, that is to say insofar as in virtue of the essence of God they envelop existence.

What it means to be "a real being by the essence of God" should by now be relatively clear: it means to be what one is because *it has to be thus*, the essence of God being the supreme necessity structuring the rational order of reality. Spinoza nowhere makes this clearer, and it is nowhere more evident that he has completed the Cartesian work of turning God into nothing more than the principle of rational necessity, than in Proposition XVII of the First Part: "God acts by the laws of His nature." In support of this proposition Spinoza is obliged to reject the notion that God can create arbitrarily. He falls back on the old truth that God could not create a triangle in which the sum of the three angles would not equal two right angles. From this he concludes, "This is why the almighty power of God has been in act from all eternity and remains for eternity in the same actuality." [20] There is in God, Spinoza explains, neither intellect nor will—not as we usually understand them—for both of these faculties involve distinctions and process, neither of which is admissible in God. God, being cause of the human intellect and will, as well as of their objects, must be essentially other, supreme necessity from which proceeds the infinity of modal realities. God cannot not act, and he cannot act otherwise than he does.

The God of Spinoza is not a personal God, and the act by which we know and love him cannot, I believe, in any meaningful sense, be termed "religious." Spinoza makes it quite clear that our grasp of God is, rather, an intellectual love, the result of a successful *philosophical* endeavor. "From the third kind of knowledge is born necessarily an intellectual Love of God . . . not insofar as we imagine Him as present but insofar as we conceive that God is eternal, and it is that which I call intellectual Love of God." [21] Spinoza goes on to explain that the human soul's love is really an action by which God considers himself insofar as he manifests himself in that soul. The human soul is cause of the idea it has of God; this is made possible by the fact that God is at work in it, since it is a mode of the divine substance. "Thus that Love of the Soul is a part of the infinite love with which God loves Himself." [22] The soul's intellectual love of God and God's love for man, then, are one and the same.

Let there be no mistake: there is nothing providential, nothing personal in this relationship; "providence" and "personal" are notions that only ignorance could attach to the infinite and necessary nature of God. Even the eternity (let us not say "immortality") which Spinoza accords the soul in virtue of its possession of eternal and necessary ideas cannot be termed personal.

> We do not attribute to the human Soul any duration definable by time, except insofar as it expresses the actual existence of the Body, which is explained by duration and can be defined by time; in other words, we do not attribute duration to the Soul itself except during the duration of the Body. But as that which is conceived

with an eternal necessity in virtue of the very essence of God is nonetheless something, there will be necessarily something eternal that belongs to the essence of the soul.[23]

Let us make no mistake then; this eternity of the soul consists uniquely in its necessarily eternal connection with the eternal ideas it possesses in time through the understanding. "The eyes of the Soul by which it sees and observes are themselves demonstrations," [24] and thus are eternal. This existence can hardly be considered a personal one. Spinoza affirms that "it is impossible that we remember having existed before the Body, since there can be in the Body no vestige of that existence and because eternity cannot be defined by time nor have any relation with it." [25] Although he does not expressly so state, we cannot but conclude that the same holds true for *after* as for *before:* "Eternity can have no relation with time." The eternity of the soul is an expression of the necessity of the idea of the soul in the divine Substance and not the foundation for an everlasting personal life in the Elysian fields.

Spinoza's Impact on the Eighteenth Century

THE MOST significant philosophical result of Spinoza's rigorous development of the Cartesian experiment is his influence on the greatest of the minds who seriously read him—and understood, in the deepest sense of the word "understanding," what was really being said there: Gottfried Wilhelm Leibniz; and through him, on the climactic development of the *Critique of Pure Reason*. This result will be our major concern in the chapters devoted to Leibniz and Kant.

But Spinoza's works had a much wider, a more popular, and of course a more superficial influence on the entire intellectual climate of the young eighteenth century. Spinoza was seen by the anti-Christian rationalists as a triumph of reason over religion; he had "put God in his place," which was that of a necessary principle rather than a meddling old monarch; the eighteenth century understood Spinoza as affirming that the universe is a republic of law, in which every reasonable man is a citizen by right of the use of his mind, and capable by his own intelligent efforts of obtaining in this life a rationally based beatitude.

As a matter of fact, Spinoza had published anonymously in 1670 a seditious little volume entitled *Theologico-Political Treatise* in which he provided quite overtly ammunition to be used against not only revealed religion but also the monarchical state, attacking both with a violence almost without precedent. It took a serious and deep mind really to make something out of the *Ethics;* but one did not have to be a great student to follow every page of the *Tractatus.* And it was read avidly and condemned avidly, reprinted and further distributed avidly for two decades.

Spinoza in his quiet Latin tranquilly asserted there that it is necessary to wipe the slate clean of all past beliefs so as to begin the search for truth on new grounds. The old beliefs have so lost their hold on the world, anyway, that one can scarcely distinguish a Christian from a Turk or a Pagan. Religion in the corrupted modern soul has ceased to be an interior act, becoming instead an affair of cult, of mechanical obedience to the priestly power, almost a political matter. Ambitious individuals have taken over the priesthood for the power involved, hence the jealousies, disputes, and even wars racking Christendom. Christianity has snuffed out the reason with prejudices and superstitions. It is that reason which must be liberated to become the principle of a new wisdom. In its name, two great illogical and ruinous constructions must be laid low: the city of God and the city of the King.

All of these monstrosities are backed up by the authority of the Scriptures. But what are the Scriptures? There were no real prophets writing under God's dictation, but poor and simple men, using to the hilt their gift for metaphor to cover over the poverty of their thought, invoking imaginary miracles to bolster their authority. How could there be miracles when the infinite order of nature is immutable and necessary? Spinoza did not hesitate to apply the rules of "criticism" to the Bible, nor to contest the authorship of the Sacred Books, and to declare its origins purely and humbly human. Finally he concludes that the Christian religion is only a historical phenomenon, product of its time, enjoying only a relative, a transitory value.

Kings have exploited to their advantage the religious prejudice, adding the prestige of divine approbation to the already formidable political power with which the monarchy holds its subjects in subservience. At the price of their blood, the people fortify the power and exalt the pride of one man, who, for their trouble, treats them like means and, robbing them of their liberty, takes away their reason and, with it, the very sense of their existence. To get out of this predicament, man must begin to apply the same critical spirit to the examination of political constitutions as has been effective in combating religious superstition. Once he begins to think freely, he will understand that the state is not for the sake of the despot, that power is only a delegation freely consented to by the people, that democracy is the form of government closest to nature, and that the end of political institutions is to assure the individual liberty of belief, word, and action.

Strong medicine to stomach in 1670! Even Pierre Bayle,[26] freethinking author of the rationalist *Dictionnaire historique et critique*, although tremendously admirative of Spinoza's refusal to be constrained in conscience and of his simple philosopher's life, could not swallow Spinozism, especially its root position, that God, as Supreme Substance, is cause of all. Bayle's interpretation of Spinoza in the *Dictionnaire* is rather *simpliste*, but as a reaction from a responsible liberal of the end of the seventeenth century, it is a good sign that Spinoza was still ahead of the evolution in the general intellectual climate. How can anyone accept the notion that the Infinite Being produces in himself all the follies, all the vagaries, all the crimes of the human kind? God would have to be not only the efficient cause of all these things, but the passive subject as well. Bayle writes:

> That men hate one another, that they kill one another in a corner of the forest, that they assemble armies to kill one another, that the victors sometimes eat the victims, all that is comprehensible, because one assumes that they are distinct from one another, that these distinct realities produce between themselves contrary passions. But if men are only the modifications of the same being, there being consequently only God who acts; and if the same God who modifies himself into a Turk modifies himself into an Hungarian, so that there are wars and battles, *that* surpasses all the monsters and all the chimerical follies of the craziest heads that have ever been locked up in "little houses." [27]

We cannot deny Bayle the fact that the problem is there. What we can deny him, however, is any credit for having understood what was really at stake in the drama of Spinoza's uncompromising pantheism; namely, the death throes of a philosophical tradition. For in bringing out so radically what it meant *ontologically* to assert the criteria of essential rationality as the standard of being, Spinoza, more than any other Cartesian, had made necessary an ultimate critique of the unpronounced assumptions underlying all "mathematical" philosophy. This, much more than the fact that he advanced the rationalistic spirit in the last days of the seventeenth century, is the philosopher's contribution to the march of history. Spinoza was to drive Leibniz to the last limits of inventiveness in an effort to save rationalistic metaphysics from the fate of the great Jewish thinker's excessive monism. This will be the last flight of the clear-and-distinct-idea metaphysics. Given Descartes, Spinoza *had* to be; that he yielded utterly to this necessity is a measure of his insight.

X

Gottfried Wilhelm Leibniz

L EIBNIZ[1] WAS KNOWN to complain, "I am not a Cartesian."
After all, he had corrected Descartes on many an essential
point: "Extension" is not a clear and distinct idea, for it is complex;
universal doubt is not a necessary propaedeutic to true philosophy;
mechanism does not suffice as an ultimate explanation of the physical
universe, and so on and on. Even the mathematics which inspired
Leibniz—that "infinitesimal calculus" the paternity of which he was
to dispute with Newton—leaves the static Cartesian algebraic geometry
as far behind as life can leave an inert mass. For his was a mathematics
that could calculate the almost living progression of a curve in a most
simple way. Inspired by such a breakthrough, Leibniz moved toward
philosophy through inventions in a pioneer symbolic logic that itself
contrasted vividly with Descartes. Leibniz' logic seemed as capable of
accommodating subtle differences as Descartes' logic was at dissecting
them with its cutting distinctions.

But Leibniz was destined to remain attached to Descartes through
his deepest roots.[2] For Leibniz shared the great Frenchman's idealist
vocation and mathematicist prejudices: he set out in the search of
Truth in the fair form of a philosophy that would proceed deductively
from clear and distinct principles supposed somehow to enfold in their
logical expression the very fountainhead of Being itself. The key conceptions that reign over Leibniz' whole quest? *Necessity* and *absoluteness*. To know is to know absolutely; what else can "clear and distinct"
really mean? To know absolutely is to know what *has* to be; it is to
grasp the necessary as necessary. Leibniz' philosophy demands that
everything be understood in terms of the "first truths."

First Truths

LEIBNIZ ACTUALLY GAVE just that title to one of those concise opuscules into which he periodically condensed the essence of his vast vision. In *First Truths* he asks what criteria a judgment should meet in order to be absolutely true. It would obviously have to achieve in some way an absolute *conformitas* of the idea known with the thing. But absolute conformity can only be *identity;* identity is that exact coincidence of subject with predicate which alone is absolutely necessary. Identity, necessity, the absolute—these are three ways of expressing the same reality; they are the properties of the clear and distinct truth. Consider the opening lines of the opuscule:

> First *truths* are those which make a self-identical statement in themselves or deny the opposite statement of the very fact of its being opposite. As: A is A, or A is not non-A. If it is true that A is B, it is false that A is not B or that A is non-B. Again, anything whatsoever is similar to itself or equal to itself. Nothing is greater or less than itself. These and other propositions of this kind, which may indeed themselves have their grade of priority, can nevertheless all be included under the one name of identical propositions.[3]

It is amazing to watch Leibniz spin from such a gossamer logical stuff the web of a powerful philosophy, destined to catch like a helpless fly much of the Western philosophical tradition. From Leibniz' meditation on the principle of identity, on that judgment, *A is A,* will spring inspiration for much of future philosophy. As Leibniz himself has said, "From these things, insufficiently considered because of their too great simplicity, many matters of great moment follow." The consummation of Cartesianism, the Kantian critique, Hegel's absolute idealism, Marxism—even the Bolshevik revolution—are among the historical great matters that come in part from "these things"!

What did Leibniz see of such importance in the simple principle of identity?

THE PRINCIPLES OF IDENTITY AND SUFFICIENT REASON

THE PRINCIPLE OF IDENTITY expresses the essential unity of a concept with itself. Absolute certitude is assured in a judgment of which the subject and the predicate are the same, for such a judgment expresses the ultimate *reason* for the thing; namely, that it is what it is. No more perfect *conformitas* can be imagined. Note well the ambiguity here of the notion reason; it can answer both to the question *why* and *how;* the *reason* for something here means of course its formal cause, therefore its essential intelligibility, but it also suggests the efficient cause. The final cause also easily slips into the question, especially if the decision has been surreptitiously made that the intelligibility of something *is* its *raison d'être*. What is remarkable about a judgment of identity is that it needs no more explanation; it manifests its own *ground;* it is evidently *its own* ground. Leibniz made an important addition to Cartesian lore when he decided he had discovered why a truly clear and distinct idea is something divine, an absolute criterion by which the reality and the intelligibility of all things are to be measured. This is because a clear and distinct idea has to be a judgment of identity, and a judgment of identity answers perfectly the question of "sufficient reason"; it is its own explanation because what it announces is simply one with itself. The judgment of identity manifests the ultimate, the divine reality, because it states with perfect simplicity that the subject is what it is. Ultimately, every true judgment then must be reducible to a judgment of identity, if it is true, if what it states is real, for that is just what it means to be *real, to be one with oneself perfectly*.

> In identities, that connection and comprehension of the predicate in the subject is in fact expressed; in all remaining propositions it is implicit, or to be shown by the analysis of concepts, on which demonstration *a priori* is based. This is true, moreover, of every affirmative truth whether universal or singular, necessary or contingent, and as well in those called intrinsic as extrinsic. And here there is hidden a marvelous secret in which is contained the nature of contingency or the essential distinction between necessary and contingent truths, and by which also the difficulty concerning the fated necessity of free things is removed.[4]

Leibniz is not pretending that human science is in fact able to reduce all that we know to judgments of identity. He agrees with Locke that our knowledge of essences, making it possible to see the necessity of including the predicate in the idea of the subject's essence, is highly restricted, which is why so much of our knowledge takes the form of contingent judgments.[5] When I judge on the basis of experience that "gold is yellow," I cannot be absolutely sure that it is never brownish red, because I do not know the exact *reason* for the connection between "gold" and "yellow." God, its maker, knows the essence perfectly, and therefore he knows exactly under what circumstances and why gold is yellow. All of God's knowledge of gold—and of everything else as well—is clear and distinct; i.e., reducible to a judgment of necessity which expresses the absolute unity of the thing with itself. Here, then, is that "marvelous secret in which is contained the essential distinction between necessary and contingent truths": To know something necessarily—i.e., absolutely—is to know its *reason* for existing; to know its reason for existing is to know the thing in its essence, so that the essential connection of all the predicates—of all the qualities, past, present, and future, of everything that has and will happen to it—is reducible to an essential expression of what the thing itself is.

Now we have a glimpse of some of those "many matters of great moment" that follow upon the consideration of identity. Leibniz spells out the fundamental doctrine in the very next paragraph:

> From this source springs immediately the received axiom that nothing is without a reason, or that no effect is without a cause. Otherwise there might be a truth which could not be proved *a priori*, or which would not be resolved into identical truths; but that is contrary to the nature of truth, which is always, either expressly or implicitly, identical.[6]

No more dramatic reduction of the order of being to the order of logic can be imagined. The "cause" of anything is its "reason"; i.e., its essential intelligibility—the fact that its entire destiny can be reduced to a logical whole, "otherwise there might be a truth that could not be proved *a priori*"; i.e., otherwise there might be an irrational element in the best of possible worlds. Heavens forbid! There remains only to draw the main implications from these rationalistic principles.

And Leibniz is surely the man for drawing implications; in this regard he is at the other extreme from Locke. To illustrate how large these implications are going to prove to be—and how metaphysical —we shall interrupt our recital of the chain of arguments in the little essay, *First Truths*, to consider the way Leibniz interprets the significance of the "principle of sufficient reason" in another brief summary of his thought, *The Principles of Nature and Grace*. "We must advance to *metaphysics*," he says at one point in the latter work, "by making use of the *great principle*, little employed in general, which teaches that *nothing happens without a sufficient reason;* that is to say that nothing happens without its being possible for him who should sufficiently understand things, to give a reason sufficient to determine why it is so and not otherwise." [7] He who "sufficiently understands" is, of course, ultimately God; but Leibniz, as we shall see, is not averse to taking a crack himself at explaining the universe in terms of at least some long-range transcendental reasons "why it is so and not otherwise." He goes on, "This principle laid down, the first question which should rightly be asked, would be, *Why is there something rather than nothing?* For 'nothing' is simpler and easier than 'something.' Further, suppose that things must exist, we must be able to give a reason *why they must exist so* and not otherwise." [8] Could Leibniz have asked a more ultimate, a more metaphysical question?

Taken in itself, the question, Why is there something rather than nothing? is once again ambiguous. It could mean, What is the efficient cause that has made be all the things of our experience? But Leibniz introduces the question in a different context; he precedes it by the assertion of the *great principle* that "nothing happens without a sufficient cause" and spells it out for us as soon as it is posed: it is the search for "a reason why they must exist so and not otherwise." The reason why there is something, rather than nothing, lies in the reason why things are so and not otherwise. They are so and not otherwise, because they are what they are. Being is one with itself in the unity of identity, of essential necessity.

The contingent things of our experience, however, can furnish no such explanation for themselves. We have already seen from an epistemological standpoint why this is so: Not knowing the essences of these things, we cannot reduce their predicates to the subject. Now Leibniz gives a *physical* reason why they cannot be their own explanation:

> For matter being indifferent itself to motion and to rest and to this or another motion, we could not find the reason of motion in it, and still less of a certain motion. And although the present motion which is in matter, comes from the preceding motion, and that from still another preceding, yet in this way we should never make any progress, go as far as we might; for the same question would always remain. [9]

The conclusion is easy to draw. The sufficient reason, which has no
need of another reason, must be outside this series of contingent things;
it must be found in a substance which is its own cause; i.e., which is a
necessary being, carrying the reason of its existence within itself. Put
this way, it is not hard to see the ultimate metaphysical position peep-
ing out between the lines: Contingent things cannot be their own explanation, and contingent judgments about them cannot yield essential
certainty because they are expressions resulting from a partial and inadequate view of reality. The quest for the sufficient reason is the quest
for the ultimate ground of all things, for the answer to the question,
Why is there something and not nothing? Leibniz realizes such a question can be answered only *transcendentally;* that is, by an answer that
englobes everything once and for all and states definitively *what is the
being of the things that are.*

"SUFFICIENT REASON" AND "THE BEST OF POSSIBLE WORLDS"

THE VERY WAY Leibniz poses the essential question—Why is
there something rather than nothing?—already reveals the solution he
will propose. For Leibniz, to ask why is there something rather than
nothing is equivalent to inquiring "What is the ground and explanation
for the intelligibility of things?" The atmosphere is one of reason, logic,
essence, light, as opposed to will, affectivity, existence, impenetrability.
It is important to point this out, otherwise Hume and above all Kant
will never become comprehensible to us. The measure of this rationalism is Leibniz' description of the "final reason of things"—that God
who "must contain in itself eminently the perfections contained in the
derivative substances which are its effects." [10] "It will have," Leibniz
declares, "perfect power, knowledge and will, that is, it will have omnipotence and sovereign goodness." [11] So far, this seems to contradict
what we have just said. But permit the philosopher to continue:

> And as *justice*, taken generally, is only goodness conformed to wis-
> dom, there must too be sovereign justice in God. The reason which
> has caused things to exist by him, makes them still depend upon
> him in existing and in working: and they are continually receiv-
> ing from him that which gives them some perfection. . . . It fol-
> lows from the supreme perfection of God, that in creating the
> universe he has chosen the *best possible plan*, in which there is the

greatest variety together with the greatest order. . . . For since all the possibles in the understanding of God laid claim to existence in proportion to their perfections, the actual world, as the resultant of all these claims, must be the most perfect possible. And without this it would not be possible to give a reason why things have turned out so rather than otherwise.[18]

In the next paragraph, which we shall not follow here, Leibniz deduces the laws of motion from the above consideration, beginning, "The supreme wisdom of God compelled him to choose the *laws of movement* best adjusted and most suited to abstract or metaphysical reasons." The principle of "sufficient reason" and the notion that this must be "the best of all possible worlds" are strict corollaries. The human mind can conceive of only one *reason* why an infinitely good and wise God should have made things to be this way rather than another: the way he has chosen must be the "best." But what *is* "best"? Obviously, whatever we discover in our experience to be necessary and essential is *best* because God has made it to be the way it is, and he has chosen it because it is best. The argumentation is perfectly circular. A "vicious" circle? I do not believe Leibniz would consider such circularity "vicious"; rather, he would see in it a sure sign that the explanation is absolutely fundamental. The argument, "Things are as they are because they are best, and they are best because they are," is little more than a metaphysical translation of the necessity of identity into terms of being and the good. Kant will analyze brilliantly the nature and value of such a construction of "pure reason."

There is still, hidden in the above argumentation, one element to be understood if we are to follow Leibniz' deduction of the outlines of this best of possible worlds. We just saw that whatever we, in our experience, discover to be necessary and essential is *best* because God has made it to be the way it is. The role to be played by the *criterion* for determining what is necessary and essential is then obviously very crucial. It is only because the human mind has access to truths necessary and essential that it can hope to discourse on what is best. The necessary judgment, the judgment of identity, the clear and distinct idea, the absolute principle—these terms are equivalent—is this criterion: for it is the understanding's direct participation in the Truth; such judgments show up the incompleteness of the partial truth, the merely tendential nature of contingent judgments; i.e., of the vast majority of our experience. But we should not mistake them for merely logical criteria—

there is no "merely logical" in such an idealism; they are perforce also expressions of Being, for what such principles announce is the way Being fundamentally has to be. Thus, the principle of identity is not only a criterion for determining absolute truths; it is also an expression of the fact that any thing that is in process—i.e., any thing that manifests itself to us as a multiplicity instead of a perfect identity—is not ultimate, but rather depends on something One in its nature, toward which perfect Unity of Identity the thing in movement must be proceeding. Leibniz is not denying the significance in our experience of manyness, movement, the partial. On the contrary, he acknowledges that the whole of our experience is concerned with a dynamic world. Yet he is confident that this world forms a reasonable whole, that every partial aspect, everything in process, every contingent idea that may express some aspect of such a partial thing, has its place in the unity of the totality, a unity that only God can encompass, but the necessity and reality of which is evident *to any finite mind that has been led to discover within itself the ultimate sense of its own innate ideas.* This last, we shall see, is the key to Leibniz' conception of how we should lead our lives.

Armed with these indications of the metaphysical significance of the otherwise innocent-sounding principle of sufficient reason, we can return to the deduction in *First Truths* that follows swiftly and economically the announcement of "the great principle."

Individual Substances and How They Form a Universe

THE PRINCIPLE OF THE INDISCERNIBLES AND THE "CONTINUITY" OF THE WORLD

LEIBNIZ' INITIAL APPLICATION of the principle of sufficient reason at first seems very strange:

> It follows that *two individual things differing only in number cannot exist in nature.* For surely it would be possible to produce a reason why they are different—which reason must be sought for from some difference in the things themselves.[13]

Two blades of grass, two grains of sand, if similar in every way, would have to be one; if different, then their difference must be intelligible, at least to their Maker. This *principle of the indiscernibles* may indeed seem odd, but actually we have already been told what is the *reason* for it: In creating the world, God sought to express his infinity through making the greatest variety of beings possible. In *First Truths*, this discovery is stated most succinctly:

> Indeed *all individual created substances are different expressions of the same universe*, and of the same universal cause, that is, GOD; but the expressions vary in perfection like different representations or drawings in perspective of the same town seen from different points.[14]

It is not difficult to see lurking in this statement Leibniz' singularly important *principle of continuity*, nor is it hard to see the "reason" for it. The infinite variety of individual beings does not spill from the creative hand of God in a stream of meaningless chaos. The infinite justice, we recall, is goodness ordered by wisdom; that is, creation ordered by mathematical reason. The individuals that pour forth from the divine creation form a continuum of infinitesimally graduated perfections; there can be no missing point on the infinite curve; in the full panorama of the universal city there can be no missing projection, and in the universe filled with these beings there are no gaps and no empty holes. A break in the perfect, harmonious continuity of creation would indicate a lack in the divine perfection. That is also the reason Leibniz' "nature" "abhors a vacuum." Indeed, the vacuum can be disproved on the basis of the principle that individuals must vary in kind. If there were a vacuum, the different parts of empty space would be perfectly similar and congruous with one another; they would differ only in number, which is absurd. In the same way as space, time is also not "a thing," [15] but a matter of "point of view." This dereification of time and space will be seized upon by Kant as a matter of utmost significance.

Leibniz has already assured the continuity necessary so that the world can respond to his great mathematical discovery, the infinitesimal calculus, as assuredly as Descartes' universe was the perfect home for an algebraic geometry. But Leibniz, as we have seen, was not given to stopping short of the ultimate implications of a position. He sees that a perfectly full, perfectly graduated, perfectly unified world would have to involve an interconnection between individual substances much more intimate than a mere gradation of essential perfection. Moreover, an explanation only in terms of graduated essential perfection is insufficient in a dynamic world. Leibniz is determined to develop an explanation for the unity of the world that will respect not only the multiplicity of the things of our experience but also their *dynamism*. He wants to break out of the static mechanistic explanations of seventeenth-century Cartesianism, to achieve what we might term an eighteenth-century Cartesianism at least as dynamic as Newtonian physics, as tendential as the calculus, and as vital as the new life sciences.

THE WORLD MIRRORED IN EACH SUBSTANCE

THE GROUNDWORK for this further expansion of the theory is first laid on the level of the individual substance, which itself must be seen to be a unity-amidst-multiplicity. *"A complete or perfect concept of an individual substance involves all its predicates past, present and future."* [16] When God chooses from among the infinity of possible individuals those which he considers "more congenial to the supreme and secret ends of his wisdom," he knows every moment of the course of action that each individual will follow. From this declaration of the unity of the substance throughout the many moments of its existence, Leibniz advances to an even more startling declaration of unity—that between the individual substance and all the rest of the universe.

> *Every individual substance involves in its perfect concept the whole universe*, and all existences in it past, present and future. For there is nothing, on which some true denomination cannot be imposed from some other thing, at least by way of comparison or relation.[17]

But, the reader might protest, isn't Leibniz going a bit far? In an effort to support his undeniably poetic vision of the relation of all to all, has he not been reduced to seizing upon the merely *external* relation of comparison? How can a merely external relation ever bind together a universe? Such an objection ignores Leibniz' basic conceptions. Comparison and relation are essential—and perhaps more real than our notion of causality itself—because they reflect the link between two things as viewpoints on the absolutely unique reality of the universe. *"There are no purely extrinsic denominations* which have absolutely no foundation in the thing itself denominated," Leibniz firmly answers. "For the concept of the subject denominated must involve the concept of the predicate. Hence as often as the denomination of the thing is changed, some variation must occur in the thing itself." [18] From this statement, it is clear that the "comparison and relation" that bind all things is no mere accidental juxtaposition, but again an expression of the absolute unity of the world, the sufficient reason for which has already been invoked: Leibniz' world is full because reposing on a rock of necessity. The equation of necessity with logical identity, we are discovering, is indeed heavy with metaphysical consequences. If being is in its foundations necessary, and necessity is construed rationalistically as adequately expressed only in the judgment of identity, then ultimately being is such that every principal predicate is deducible from its subject. There are then no *real* extrinsic relations or denominations. Any extrinsic relation is only apparent, not fundamental, an error of judgment. If one is ready to accept the necessity of identity as the ground for certain truth, then he should not flinch when the implications are drawn from this necessity in terms of the experiential world of things.

We should now be able to see the connection between the principle that there is no purely extrinsic denomination and Leibniz' attack on the reality of empty space and on the notion of time as a thing. Time and space are relations of extrinsic denomination and, like all purely external comparisons, lack ultimate ontological significance because they are due only to the limitations of a finite point of view. What we call "time" and what we call "space," as well as all groupings of things into abstract categories, are justifiable in terms of a passing practical value, but they must be recognized as foreign to the ultimate nature of things and therefore as not real.

We are, however, getting closer to that ultimate nature, to that primordial unity of reality, when we realize, as Leibniz goes on to state in *First Truths*, that "*every individual created substance exercises physical action and passion on all others*. For when a change is made in one, some responding change follows in all others, since the denomination is altered." [19] Although Leibniz illustrates this principle with a physical example, such a principle is clearly not an experimental, but a logical, an *a priori* one. Change one factor in a formula, and all the other factors in the formula must also be changed if it is to remain identical; and the change in each of the factors is deducible from the change in the first.

Leibniz' full and continuous universe is in perfectly identical unity with itself, like such a formula. When in the past philosophers tried to conceive of the connections of things in terms of efficient causality, they failed to rise to consider the system of nature as a whole. Had they done so, they would have realized that there can be no isolated cases of causal action and passion. Carrying this "absolute point of view" on the universe a step farther, Leibniz declares, "In strictness it can be said that *no created substance exercises metaphysical action or influence on another*." [20] The preceding principle expressed the absolute unity of the universe; this one hastens to explain that it is not the "things" themselves which are responsible for it, but the infinite they reflect. The philosopher points to two solid reasons why causation among created substances would be unthinkable: 1] The impossibility of explaining how anything would pass over from one thing into the substance of another, for each substance is an essence, each is represented by its idea, each is a full reflection of one aspect of the absolute; the passing of something from one to the other would violate the unity and integrity of each and leave them other than they are, which is impossible, as it would make of them no thing: false reflections, for the absolute itself of course cannot change. 2] "From the concept of anything whatsoever all its future states already follow." A substance, after all, is that which can stand alone. In choosing to create this rather than another possible substance, God chooses the individual complete with his total being, meaning that all the happenings that are spread out through what, from our limited vantage point, appears to us as time are eternally included in the perfect substantiality of the individual. "What we call causes are (in metaphysical rigor) only required as concomitants." [21]

THE CONCORDANCE OF PRE-ESTABLISHED HARMONY

ALL OF THE CARTESIANS are haunted by the problem of the radical nature of the distinction between ideas. A triangle is not a circle. Matter is not spirit. The body is not the soul. Having accepted the Cartesian notion that the ultimate criterion of truth lies in the necessity of the clear and distinct idea, Leibniz is obliged to join Descartes, Malebranche, and Spinoza in finding a way to explain the *concomitance* of things, their apparent working together. Spinoza's pantheistic solution horrifies a good Christian, so Leibniz will not entertain it for a second. Malebranche's occasionalism, he finds, posits a mere *deus ex machina*.[22] Leibniz' objection is that Malebranche's God has to intervene at every moment to assure the action-reaction between substances. Leibniz proposes a solution he considers more worthy of the divine creator, and one, we might add, which installs the principle of harmony more inherently in the things themselves. He explains his theory in terms of the most difficult of all substance confrontations, the body and the soul. God has from the beginning so fashioned soul as well as body, with so much wisdom and so much artifice, that, from the first constitution or concept itself of either one, everything that happens in the one corresponds perfectly to everything that happens in the other. This *concomitance* is true in all the substances of the whole universe but is not perceptible in all, as it is in the case of soul and body.[23] Leibniz elsewhere calls this notion "the principle of pre-established harmony." To render it "intelligible for every sort of mind," Leibniz illustrates his theory in terms of the different ways two clocks might be made to run concomitantly. The explanation according to causal influence would have one clock influence the other. A second way might be to have a skillful workman always present to move the hands of one clock the moment the hands of the other were moved—Malebranche's occasionalistic solution. A third way "would be to make in the first place these two clocks with so much art and accuracy that we might be assured of their future concordance," [24] as both record correctly one and the same time. This last is the only one of the three that accords with the logical necessity of the identity of the subject with its predicates. In selecting to create an individual, God establishes its whole being, which his wisdom will have accord throughout the course of its existence with every other substance he has also chosen to create, to modulate, each in its own key, his perfection.

The Monads

EVERY SUBSTANCE, then, is a little world closed in upon itself, there being neither the need nor the possibility of its opening out onto other things. Leibniz has not only succeeded in bringing the *individual* being back to the center of attention, but he does so with a theory of individuality that manages to fulfill perfectly the requirements of rationality. To be an individual is to be *one with oneself*. To be *perfectly* one with oneself is to be necessarily what one is. To be *what* one is, is to be unlike any other thing. Hence, Leibniz concludes, each fundamental individual entity must have a different essence, each individual is as different a kind of thing as each angel would be in St. Thomas' spiritual world.[25] There is, then, an individual corresponding to every clear and distinct idea and an idea corresponding to every individual. The orders of idea and of concrete being are thus brought perfectly into line.

And at the same time Leibniz finds himself with a good solution to the hoary problem of the "atoms." The world, unless it were composed of such "real" individual entities, would be a pure figment of the mind, divisible *ad infinitum*, devoid of any objective substantial reality. To this ancient atomistic stand Leibniz' "monads" add a revolutionary new element which keeps his atomism from having to be a materialism. Leibniz' doctrine is like a materialism in that it is absolutely monistic; but instead of explaining the highest and most spiritual phenomena by compounding it out of the lower, Leibniz extends the most spiritual principle, as we shall see, down to the lowest monad. Leibniz' doctrine is an inverted materialism.

Each monad reflects, interior to itself and from its individual point of view, all the other monads. In so asserting, Leibniz would subsume the crude mechanical bonds of efficient causality that held together the world of the materialist atomists into a more comprehensive theory which explains the unity of all-in-all without recourse to any interaction between monads. Instead of interacting, each monad runs its own course, reflecting interior to itself the changes occurring inside all the other monads. All of these interior lives are, of course, harmonized since the beginning of creation, according to that plan of "pre-established harmony" which God decided upon in choosing to create the finite world that would best express his infinite perfection.

The complex substances of our experience are explained, then, as harmonized groupings of these simple monads, organized about a "core" or directing monad which can finalize the whole. So a "material" living thing would consist of a "soul" monad about which are grouped other spiritual monads arranged to produce infinitesimal point outside of infinitesimal point; i.e., the "extension" of the body. All monads are spiritual, the "material" being only that complex arrangement of monads finalized to form an extension. Hence, the deepest sense of Leibniz' objection against Descartes, that extension is not a simple idea.[26]

Given a world built of such radically distinct entities, each of which is a little world reflecting from its point of view all the others, every essential attribute in the cosmos must be discoverable in every monad. What this really means is that all the monads must be different embodiments of a single reality—Leibniz chooses to call it *force;* they are distinguishable according to the different degrees of force they manifest. When we see that a great complex substance like a tree "lives," we must realize that the fundamental life-force we see there is actually to be found in every monad in some degree. "All nature is full of life." [27] Leibniz has successfully broken down the rigid Cartesian separation of the world into the living-spiritual and mechanical-extended spheres. Instead of these abrupt separations, Leibniz would admit the infinitesimal gradations of force that distinguish the monads, there being no gaps in what must be considered the *continuous* gradations of his *full* world.

But if all monads, even those that arrange themselves to form extended bodies, are spiritual, does nothing then ever die? No monad could ever go out of existence, except by the *fiat* of a divine act of annihilation, just as no monad can come into existence except by divine creation. Consequently, what appears as "dying" is merely the passing of monads from one to another combination. The complex substances of our experience are continually attaching new monads which are assimilated to the harmonizing whole, and constantly detaching others. When the breakdown of a very complex substance into less complicated ones is serious enough so that the resulting compounds are of a markedly lower intensity of force, then we experience the phenomenon which traditionally is called death.

There are many different sorts of complex substances—mineral, vegetable, animal, human; but before we attempt to see what it is that differentiates them, we had better first understand something more of the nature of that "force" which they all have in common. The life of every monad, from the dimmest and most confused, to the greatest and clearest, consists in some degree of *perception* and *appetition*. To grasp what Leibniz means by this, we must seek to understand the dim and lowly manifestation of the life-force in the least endowed of the monads in terms of the high degree we discover in ourselves by reflection, which high degree we can know, as it were, from the inside.

Leibniz defines *perception* as "the representation of the compound, or of what is external, in the simple";[28] i.e., representation of the manifold, the extended, the unfolded in the "real" unity. In the case of the monad we are privileged to know "from the inside" that highly endowed spiritual substance, the human soul. We can easily see what this means: engraved in each soul, composing it, are the innate ideas of every representation this particular soul can have in conjunction with the monads that cooperate to form its body. Each soul perceives its destiny unfolding according to its own basic law. But what can this mean in the case of a lowly monad, destined never to enter into any combination more exalted than that of an inorganic molecule? No matter how primitive, the least of all material combinations takes place by a kind of internally oriented seeking of one element by another. To borrow an example from modern chemistry: inscribed in the internal law of a hydrogen atom is its destiny of harmonious cooperation with oxygen atoms in the society of water. This example helps us see that it is no more fantastic for Leibniz to extend the sort of internally oriented representation of the outside world we call *perception* down to the humblest units of the world than it is for the materialist to attempt to build a conscious, living compound substance out of dead elements.

Appetition is defined as the monad's "tendencies from one perception to another," and is declared to be "the principle of change." [29] Appetition provides the unity amidst changing perceptions—a unity of finality. To clarify this, Leibniz launches into an explanation of how a *monad* (termed elsewhere the "entelechy monad," from an Aristotelian expression for the form that holds the end—*telos*) functions as the center of a compound substance; i.e., as the principle of its unity, surrounded by a mass of cooperating monads forming the body proper of this central monad. Every affection of each of these bodily monads is reflected in the entelechy monad as a perceptual representation; in this way it can be said, like the lowly monads above described, "to represent things outside of itself." [30] Let us not be misled, however, by this realistic-sounding expression "outside of itself"; every possible affection of every one of the infinity of associated bodily monads is "engraved" in the entelechy monad from its creation as its particular "law," ready, when attention is brought to it, to appear in that monad as a representation when the universal harmony demands. The string of perceptions continually going on in this central monad is guided "by the law of appetites or by the final causes of *good and evil*," just as "the changes of bodies and external phenomena spring one from another, by the laws of *efficient causes,* that is of movements." [31] That is to say that the same universal *conatus* manifests itself both in the soul's movement seeking the good, and in what in the past was handled as the mere mechanical motion of physical bodies. All monads are moving within the universal harmony, but with very different degrees of self-awareness. So we must always interpret causal terms in keeping with Leibniz' metaphysical vision: both what is traditionally called the final and the efficient causes are the law, the essential destiny of entelechy and corporeal monads, respectively. Hence Leibniz can add: "Thus there is perfect *harmony* between the perceptions of the monad and the movements of bodies, *established at the beginning* between the system of efficient causes and that of final causes. And in this consists the accord and physical union of soul and body, although neither one can change the laws of the other." [32]

To sum up "perception" and "appetition" in a word: The monad as representative of the whole universe is *perceptive;* while the monad considered as an individual realizing itself in a unified way is *appetitive.* Now that we are assured with at least some notion of what Leibniz means in general when he declares the life-force to consist of degrees of "perception" and "appetition," we can address ourselves to the problem of understanding the different kinds of compound substances, and particularly the human kind.

The Different Sorts of Compound Substances

ALL COMPOUND SUBSTANCES enjoy perception, centered and finalized in the entelechy monad; what distinguishes the different orders of substance is the relative degree of clarity—i.e., of force—and therefore of reality of these perceptions. The simple animal, for instance, is distinguished from the plant by the fact that its organs are so adjusted that by means of them there is clearness and distinctness in the impressions which it receives and consequently in the perceptions which represent them.[33] When these impressions are concentrated with sufficient force, they can cause *feeling or sentiment*—a perception accompanied by memory, "a certain echo of which remains a long time to make itself heard upon occasion." [34] Below this level of distinctness, in those simple animals whose perceptions are not sufficiently distinct to be remembered, so that they are as though in a deep and dreamless sleep, there is only perception, but not apperception. Apperception, the highest degree of perception, can alone be said to be *conscious;* i.e., capable of some internal reflection. Even in the high creature that is man, apperception—full, reflexive consciousness—is not always and everywhere present. Our corporeal monads are full of dim perceptions, lacking the force to become conscious; a real subconscious is operative and effective, even though passing unnoticed by the center of conscious attention. "It is for want of this distinction that the Cartesians have failed, taking no account of the perceptions of which we are not conscious as people take no account of imperceptible bodies." [35] The conscious life has its unnoticed "microscopic" substructures too!

Leibniz' conviction that conscious life grows out of and is founded in "subconscious" confused perceptions accords perfectly with the metaphysical principle of the *law of continuity;* namely, that "nature never does anything by leaps." The philosopher expressly reminds us in the Introduction to the *New Essays on the Human Understanding* how reasonable it is to conceive of the mass of dense, confused perceptions exercising an influence on the higher developments of thought. In fact, he goes to considerable trouble in that Introduction to explain just how "the remarkable perceptions" come by degrees from those which are too little to be remarkable. This subtle psychological analysis is indeed important, not only as indispensable background for differentiating the higher activities of reason from those of a more brute-like nature in man, but also because hidden in these descriptions is the key for the will's control of the whole knowing process, and therefore an important part of Leibniz' theory of human freedom, which we shall have to develop later.

As the soul [36] is in harmony with an infinity of corporeal monads, every one of which is internally caught up in a chain of efficient causality, this central entelechy monad is constantly besieged deep inside by an inconceivable multiplicity of impressions arising from all of these reverberations of efficiency. How multiple? Actually, its extent is that of the physical universe itself—this is what it means to say that every monad dimly reflects from its point of view every other monad in the world. Naturally, the individual person cannot apperceive all of these impressions at once, any more than we can attend to every background noise entering our ears, for they are "too little," "too many," "too

united," insufficiently distinguished. Nevertheless, as an assemblage
they have their effect; this constant pounding of the waves of the infinite sea on the shores of our experience, a pounding that continues
even as we are plunged in the most untroubled sleep (for it is this continuity of unattended-to experience that explains how we can ever be
awakened!), actually forms our taste.

> These little perceptions are of a much greater efficacity than one
> thinks. It is they that form that "I don't know what"—those tastes,
> those images of qualities of sense, clear as an assemblage but con-
> fused in the parts; those impressions which the bodies surrounding
> make on us and which envelop the infinite; that liaison which each
> being has with all the rest of the universe. One can even say that
> as a consequence of those little perceptions the present is full of
> the future and charged with the past, that everything is conspiring,
> and that in the least of substances, eyes as piercing as those of God
> could read all the suite of the things of the universe: *Quae sint,
> quae fuerint, quae mox ventura trahantur* [which are, which were,
> and which are going to come].[37]

Marvelous passage, whose intuition into the rapport between time and
experience will greatly profit the attentive Immanuel Kant!

In these same pages, Leibniz hastens to explain the bearing of this
discovery of the "little perceptions" on the whole affective life—and
thus on the later question of liberty. These little perceptions are at
work in cases where the vulgar think themselves free by an "indifference of equilibrium," as though we could ever turn indifferently to
right or left. Actually, the weight of their presence makes itself felt as
"taste," and as that "inquiétude," a kind of minuscule pain which is
often at the root of our desire and even our pleasure. The implication
for morals is clear, even though Leibniz does not choose to express it
here: Our liberty, using its great weapon—the conscious attention—
must extend its reign over these influences when they are improper, by
counteracting them with the clear and distinct apperceptions of the
higher activity of reason. The term "improper" seems paradoxical here,
as all perceptions must reflect some substantial reality; to understand it,
we must consider the nature of that reason, and especially wherein lies
the difference between it and the *apperception* of the higher animals.
Leibniz admits that the "continuity in the perceptions of animals" does
bear some resemblance to reason, but it is founded only in the memory
of facts, while reason involves a knowledge of *causes*. In "three-

fourths" of their actions men act only as brutes; that is, like the dog who remembers the man with a big stick, they react to mere facts. For example, we expect that there will be daylight tomorrow, because we have always had the experience; only an astronomer foresees it by reason, and even this prediction will finally fail when the cause of day, which is not eternal, shall cease. But *true reasoning* depends upon necessary or eternal truths, such as those of logic, numbers, geometry, which establish an indubitable connection of ideas and unfailing consequences.[38] What distinguishes the human *spirit* from every other sort of perceiving monad is its ability to reflect, for it is in the unity of the reflective act that is seated the power to grasp necessary propositions—propositions of identity—in their unity.

Apperceptions of fact can never yield the kind of ultimate cause which, with a necessity born of identity, cannot be other than it is. Why is this? The answer to this question will not only help distinguish the empire of the brute's perception from the high causal knowledge of human reason, but will distinguish within human knowledge the province of certain science from a "science" of contingencies that is always pushing toward infinity without hope of arriving at a final resting place. In the opuscule *Necessary and Contingent Truths*, Leibniz explains the metaphysical reason for the difference. Contingent truths are truths in spatial and temporal extension; truths unfolded, truths of the sort that are true at a certain time and in a certain place, and they express not only what pertains to the possibility of things (as essential truths do), but also what actually does exist, or would exist contingently if certain things were supposed.[39] Now there is a reason for every contingent truth, and we can proceed from a given fact to its reason. But, alas, that reason presents itself to us also as a fact, so we must seek a reason for that reason. God, who can englobe the whole universe and all its infinity of chains of reasons, can alone perceive clearly and distinctly the whole affair. And even though every monad mirrors darkly the entirety of this vast structure, the finite mind, in seeking to apperceive a single line of causation, finds itself swept along infinitely in an unending quest. For there is no portion of matter which is not actually subdivided into parts—we can never arrive at the end of the analysis if we search for the mover causing the motion of any body whatsoever and again for the mover of this; for we shall always arrive at smaller bodies without end.[40] As in the calculus, we can divide and divide, approaching ever closer to infinity, but never reach it. For we move indefinitely toward the infinitesimal, spiritual monad, a point never attainable by the finite mind.

Not only are particular judgments about individual things contingent, but so also are universal judgments, even our knowledge of those laws of nature which enjoy a very high degree of probability. From the first essential laws of any series in nature we can derive subaltern laws possessing "physical necessity," but not metaphysical, for "one could never by any analysis come to the most universal laws nor to the perfect reasons for individual things; for this knowledge is necessarily appropriate only to God." [41] Moreover, even when we are permitted to know certain essential truths, upon which physical science depends, the very existence of such a so-called "necessary" series is itself dependent on the *fiat* of the divine will, and so, considered absolutely, is still contingent; "hypothetically, however, if the series is supposed, they are necessary and so far essential." [42]

In view of this, we cannot help wondering what makes the few "necessary" ideas we possess so unshakable and so certain. Consider the catalogue of such ideas furnished in the treatise *The Principles of Nature and Grace*. "True reasoning depends upon necessary or eternal truths, such as those of logic, numbers, geometry, which establish an indubitable connection of ideas and unfailing consequences. . . . Souls are capable of performing acts of reflection and of considering that which is called ego, substance, monad, soul, spirit, in a word, immaterial things and truths." The ideas of logic are discoverable in the spirit's reflection on its own operation; numbers are derivable from the primordial idea of unity, which again is available to the spirit contemplating its own identity. Ego, Substance, Monad, Soul, Spirit, likewise. Geometry alone might cause some difficulty, but we must remember the Cartesian presupposition that pure ideas of the circle, the triangle, etc., could be drawn from the soul's own resources. This problem apart, all the other ideas listed are obviously necessary for the same reason that Descartes' *Cogito, ergo sum* was necessary, and for the same reason that Locke turned to the same intuition of our own existence when he wanted to be sure that the human understanding enjoyed at least one immediate and unshakable contact with being: The ultimate source of certitude is shifted from the representation to the "representor," from things to the consciousness that makes present the things known. The "Copernican revolution" begins not with Kant, but with Descartes.

Such a revolution, reversing the dependency of consciousness upon experience, so that experience depends on the structure of consciousness, must clearly entail a new concept of freedom. Of the freedom of spirits, Leibniz has written that it is "something greatest and most marvelous in the direction of a certain imitation of God." The same could as well be said of our ability to reflect, and thus to know ourselves, in the unity of an intuition, as the activity of consciousness making experience possible. Human freedom must now be conceived as radiating in some fashion from this fundamental logical-ontological necessity of our participation in the ultimate ground of things. Just how this can be and what the implications of this notion of freedom are for moral conduct is clearly spelled out in the opuscule *Necessary and Contingent Truths.*

The Problem of Freedom

THE WORLD THAT GOD chose to create was the best of all possible worlds. The question arises: Did God *have* to create the *best,* and if he did have to, how can he then be said to be free? Leibniz' answer to this question furnishes the indispensable background for understanding his conception of human freedom.

Before God created the world there existed in the divine mind an infinity of conceptions of possible worlds that he could call into existence. All that *had* to be were those essential ideas whose non-being would involve a contradiction, like the principles of identity and contradiction, the mathematical principles, and God's own existence. "We must distinguish," writes Leibniz to Clarke, "between a *necessity,* which takes place because the opposite implies a contradiction; which necessity is called *logical, metaphysical,* or *mathematical;* and a *necessity* which is *moral,* whereby a wise being chooses the best, and every mind follows the strongest inclination." [43] There is, from eternity, an infinity of logically possible worlds. In choosing to create this world, it was God's liberty itself which impelled him, in his wisdom and goodness, to choose the *best* among the possibles. When a wise being, and especially God, who has supreme wisdom, chooses what is best, he is not the less free upon this account; on the contrary, it is the most perfect liberty *not to be hindered* from acting in the best manner. [44]

We have already discussed this choice of the "best of possible worlds" in terms of its sufficient reason and the sufficient reason of all the created things. We have seen what "best" means for Leibniz and that this criterion for what is best is ultimately conceived as a rational one—*rational* turning out, of course, suspiciously to involve the kind of necessity the mathematical human mind is most at home with. Now one of the grave inconveniences about rational criteria of this sort is that they have a habit of being very clear and very necessary. These are qualities that afford little of that existential leeway, so to speak, that leaves room for liberty. What Leibniz needs to do, then, is get a feeling of *possibility* back into the picture. He attempts to soften the glare of necessity by emphasizing that, in choosing the best of possible worlds, God chose a world to exist only contingently; and he points out that the other possibilities *remain possible;* which seems to suggest that the human will can somehow turn away from the divinely chosen scheme of things toward the other possibilities, which of course *are not.* It is in just this context that Leibniz suddenly stresses the fact that the goods of this created world *incline* the will but do not necessitate it.[45] Along with this goes a reminder that the things of this world inform the understanding without forcing upon it the absolute conviction of certitude.

Is this *suggestion* of possibility enough to save a sense of human liberty in the face of a philosophy of necessity and identity? Let us look into the matter a little further. It is obvious that we can be inclined only to what we know; now what determines what we actually know? Available as the "raw material" of knowledge is the flood of *petites perceptions* of the infinity of corporeal monads that are associated with and reflected in the "soul." If the soul were but carried along in the chains of these flows of perceptions, liberty would be out of the question, and the soul would simply be at the mercy of the impressions strongest at a given moment. But the soul does possess a means of breaking free a little from these chains of impressions (or chains of efficient causes, as Leibniz sometimes calls them). It is able to imitate God in this respect, that "by the intuition of some final cause, they can break the nexus and course" of these impressions. "For as the course of the universe is changed by the free will of God, so by the free will of the mind the course of its thoughts is changed."[46] By this act of intuition of a final cause, man mirrors in his little world "what God does in the large world."

What is it that God does in the large world that the soul is privileged to mirror in its microcosm? He orders, by choosing the better part, and he can choose the better part because his divine intuition lets him know the principles of all things. Now it is our privilege and duty to do something like that. The understanding represents confusedly the whole universe; now we must direct the reason, through the application of attention, to search out the principles underlying that act of representation. These principles, functioning as final causes—as ultimate goods—should then guide the consciousness as it wends its way through the current of half-conscious and confused experiences furnished the soul by the corporeal monads.[47] The mind, Leibniz assures us elsewhere, "can put off and suspend judgment till further deliberation and turn its attention to thinking of other things." [48] A great power this, a command of the present that keeps man from being tyrannized by the past working darkly, in the form of desire, on the present. Desire is formed of the massive influence of perceptions; in the beast, where there is no higher intuition to oppose and overcome it, desire rules all; it often does in man, too, but it does not have to be so. For the spirit, through the intuition of reason, can know of a final cause that surpasses all desires and that can therefore direct our future toward a pleasure and happiness beyond any invention of the body, tending as it does to lose in extension and the manifold a true concept of the real Good found in unity. It is toward God as object that reason must turn in search of that which "surpasses all of our desires." Revelation alone can tell us some details of the "great future" awaiting us, but reason suffices to assure us that it lies beyond the things of desire. But what is it that the reason intuits when it seeks beyond its impressions their very principle, if not the *cogito* itself as unity of all representations? The intuition of this superior principle is in the present a principle of freedom; the intuition of the principle of identity then becomes the standard, the end toward which all is to be directed. The contingent, the incomplete, the unclear are to be rejected in favor of the necessary, the total, the clear and certain principles which are attained in the *cogito's* intuition of itself. For Leibniz, as for all Cartesians, the quest for God becomes the *cogito's* quest to possess itself in perfect self-identity.

What is hardest to reconcile with the rest of Leibniz' thought in this explanation of liberty is all the talk of struggling to bring this about—struggling "to break the chains of impressions," to surpass desire, to suspend judgment and direct attention. How does this note of struggle, essential to a doctrine of finite liberty, fit with the "pre-established harmony" that was previously posited as essential to so "continuous" a rational universe? Are terms of struggle justified when we know that every moment of every monad's action has been pre-established by the divine *fiat?* Leibniz argues that God's foreknowledge does not compromise liberty, for *what* God foreknows is that the spirit monads will dominate the *petites perceptions* in a manner that is precisely in keeping with what we experience in enjoying our freedom.

No one would want to hold it against Leibniz that he was unable to *solve* the mystery of God's ordering the course of the world in a way that makes human freedom possible. What we can regret is that he sometimes sounds as though he thinks he is *explaining* it. If Leibniz really thinks he has, then he is indeed in this regard, as well as another we are now going to consider, the spiritual father of certain Catholic apologists in our own century!

The Problem of Evil

SINCE THE FAMOUS LISBON EARTHQUAKE and *Candide*, it is inevitable that one wag the problem of evil in the face of Leibniz and his "optimism." Actually, Leibniz was far from falling into the stupid optimism of Voltaire's philosopher. He did not deny the existence of a problem of evil. He recognized the validity of the medieval distinction of evils—metaphysical, physical, and moral—and admitted all of them into his universe, although his definitions of them are, as usual, subtly altered to fit his global vision.

Metaphysical evil is lack of unlimited essential perfection; suffering—the lack of total physical integrity (*physical evil*), and sin—the lack of absolutely adequate judgment and rectitude (*moral evil*)—can only exist because we do not—and the world does not—enjoy metaphysical perfection. God could not create a perfect world—only he himself can be perfect. In creating the best among the infinitude of possibles, God still had to create a world with limitations. The freedom of man operates within this context of finitude—that is why it is a "*libre arbitre*" and not like God's creation, destined to produce the best. Man's lack of constantly necessitating clear and distinct intuition in concrete circumstances means that he is not obliged to turn his attention always toward what is best. "The mind never chooses what now appears worse, still it does not always choose what now appears better, since it can put

off and suspend judgment till further deliberation and turn its attention
to thinking of other things." [49] We have just seen that we have to work
hard, under the right kind of final motivation, using our attention, to
discover clearly and distinctly what is here and now right, to overcome
dark desire, and to direct ourselves unfailingly toward the glorious end
reason can reveal to us, this end being to further and reflect the universal harmony. Custom, education, habit have their role in turning us
toward the natural light by making the innate ideas stand out strong
and clear. Failing this, we sin, and in sinning turn ourselves toward the
dumb sleep of animals whose confused "little perceptions" reign tyran-
nically over their souls. Leibniz would certainly agree that the wages of
sin is death: it is dissipation of one's unity into the manifold, and therefore time and change.

In attacking the problem of explaining the sense of the senseless
things in this, the best of possible worlds, Leibniz is possessed by a
strange zeal that deserves a special remark, not only for the light it
throws on the last developments of Cartesian idealism (and on Kant as
well as Leibniz), but because a note of the same thing has crept un-
invited into some later Catholic apology.

One of the most-read of Leibniz' works is entitled *Theodicy;* its
well-published purpose, to "justify the ways of God to man." Such an
enterprise is a natural consequence of the whole "sufficient reason" way
of arguing. The rationalist transformation of final causality into the
cogito's intuition of the divine necessity in itself, making possible for
it to rise above all desire, eliminates all need to probe among the dark
realities of experience for the sense of things. The effect of all this is to
create the attitude that we can pretty well understand what the real
sense of things must be. While the Leibnizian would never pretend to
know the reason for each thing's being the way it is, he cannot forgo
thinking that he must be able to pull from his intimate intuitions of the
foundations of being reliable answers to the principal questions of life.
A phenomenon like evil or sin is not a mystery; it needs only be examined in the light of what we know of the divine wisdom, and of
human freedom, to see why, in the best of possible worlds, it has been
allowed a place.

The reader should not imagine that Leibniz engaged in a desperate
defensive action on behalf of God in the face of the attacks of Hobbes.
The optimism of Leibniz is not a forced sentiment, but an exalted one.
In the face of the worst things in the world, he calmly recalls that a

finite creation cannot be perfect, and if God permitted imperfections to exist, they are for the sake of the incomparably greater good of his production. But Leibniz goes beyond such general declarations in an effort to show how some of the phenomena we consider unadulterated evils are really turned to good by God's wise use of them. Sin is perhaps the best example: Leibniz' explanation of how God turns sin to the general advantage of mankind instead of against it is very much in the spirit of the excellent qualification of Original Sin by the Good Friday liturgy as *felix culpa*, the happy fault that was the occasion for so generous a redemption. Sin is a by-product of our finite liberty, a result of an unfortunate use of that liberty. But God can put even this to use; it becomes an occasion for his mercy and forgiveness. The lesson is clear: we must see in everything, even in those things that are most imperfect, their positive reality; for it is this, and not the negative side, that is explicable in terms of a sufficient reason.

Voltaire's objections and the fist-wavings of others like him were motivated more by social and political concerns than by purely philosophical ones. Those who could not abide the Leibnizian sort of metaphysical optimism may have been intuitively right in rejecting idealist metaphysics altogether; but neither Diderot, nor d'Alembert, nor Voltaire, any more than their beloved John Locke, was possessed of very good reasons with which to neutralize it. Hume, who had had a brush with what is not far from the height of the idealistic, Bishop Berkeley's spiritualism, was forced by his knowledge of the shrewd bishop's system to seek some sound reasons for attacking "metaphysics." And Kant, who was to know Leibniz through a less subtle but still important Leibnizian, Professor Wolff, and was to be awakened from his personal "dogmatic slumber" by Hume, would complete this last thinker's work of undermining the metaphysical claims of such an optimism; but then, curious thing, he will try to keep the optimism without the metaphysics!

XI ✤

Christian Wolff

Leibniz Enters the Schools

IT HAS BEEN POINTED OUT that none of the great seventeenth-century philosophers was a professor, and in general it can be said that they were not especially concerned about establishing a school of disciples to cluster about their feet. Yet their works often got into the universities, and schools of followers were thus formed anyway. The manner of transmission could have a considerable influence on just how a philosopher's thought would come to influence young men for generations after his death. In Leibniz' case, the way his thought was injected into the scholastic bloodstream and, through it, into the brains of the *Aufklärung*—the German "enlightenment"—is especially decisive; for frequently, later manifestations of Leibnizian influence in an awakening Germany are really *Wolffian;* that is to say, the thought of Leibniz strained through the multifarious, immense, and determining manuals of Dr. Christian Wolff,[1] professor of mathematics and philosophy at Halle and Marburg from 1706 until 1754. A fanatic for rational clarity, Wolff wanted to eliminate the opaque elements from Leibniz' thought (and in the process, as we shall see, he succeeded in removing also much of its substantiality) and to order it in a series of rigorous arguments based on terms defined with great exactitude and clarity.

A mere glance at the titles of his writings reveals the importance of two words in the language of Wolff: all the German titles include the word *vernünftige* (rational); all the Latin titles include the words *scientifica methodo* (by a scientific method). Actually, the two expressions mean the same thing; everything has to be treated in a totally and purely rational way—that is to say, from the point of view of what natural reason alone is able to know—and the best way to make sure of the purely rational nature of a demonstration is to conceive it after the pattern of scientific demonstration, especially as it is found in mathematics. This aspect of his thought, continuing as it does the rationalistic tradition of Descartes, Spinoza, and Leibniz, accounts for the opposition of his more religiously minded colleagues.

But there is another side to his personality. Already before Wolff, Leibniz had shown himself anxious not to blow up the bridges connecting his own philosophy and the great tradition of scholastic Aristotelianism. Wolff exhibits the same tendency. He himself expressly says that, when it comes to defining being, nobody can compete with Suarez. Generally speaking, the mathematical garb in which he dresses his own doctrine ill conceals the scholastic origin of many of its notions. We may say then that we are confronted here with a rationalist scholasticism whose substance is borrowed from the metaphysics of Leibniz. Here, then, is, in other words, a Leibnizianism taught in schools and written up in books usable in schools by both professors and advanced students. This second aspect of Wolffism explains his extraordinary influence on the teaching of scholastic philosophy, especially natural theology, in the Catholic schools. The tendency to consider philosophy as an analytical knowledge; to deduce it from the principle of sufficient reason, itself reducible to the principle of contradiction; to distribute the whole body of philosophy into the very divisions imagined by Wolff or into similar ones conceived in the same spirit; all these features attest the deep and lasting influence exercised by Wolff on the mode of presentation adopted for philosophy in many nineteenth-century Catholic schools. Even in our own century, this phenomenon has been noted, not without some surprise, in representatives of the scholastic tradition.[2]

Wolff's Division of the Sciences

WHAT, THEN, is this famous Wolffian division of philosophy? First there is logic. Now logic is a discipline anterior to all knowledge without distinction.

Philosophy proper divides into speculative and practical, following the distinction of the two powers of the soul, intellect and will. Speculative philosophy is but another name for metaphysics. Practical philosophy includes ethics, economics, and politics.

Speculative philosophy, or metaphysics, divides into four main branches: ontology, whose object is being in general; rational psychology, whose object is the soul; cosmology, whose object is the world in general; and rational theology, whose object is the existence and nature of God. This division goes far in explaining Kant's assertion that the three main ideas of pure reason are the soul, the world, and God.

ONTOLOGY

THE OBJECT OF ONTOLOGY—namely, being—includes all that which is either real or possible. The possible is anything which, because it involves no contradiction, is thinkable. Every thinkable object then is a possible being. Such a being is determined by its essence; rather, it *is* an essence. An essence is made up of determinators that do not follow from another thing, nor from any one determination among them. The reason for this twofold condition is as follows. If, among the elements of an essence, some are determined by another thing, that thing is the true constituent of the essence and it should be substituted for the elements at stake in the definition of the essence; on the other hand, if one of the elements constitutive of an essence follows from another one included in the same essence, it suffices to include this other in the definition, as positing it automatically posits the first.

Thus constituted, an essence is made up only of non-contradictory elements, no one of which is determined by another one. These prime constitutive elements of essence Wolff terms its "essentials" (*essentialia*). Essence is that about a being which is first conceived. For instance, the being of an equilateral triangle is its essence; this essence, in turn, is made up of two elements that are both compatible and prime: the number three and equality of sides. Or, to borrow an example from ethics, the essence of virtue is made up of two elements: a habit of the will, and the conformity with natural law of the acts that follow from that habit. The presence of such *essentialia* is sufficient (and of course necessary) to define an essence. The properties inseparable from the essentials are called the "attributes" of the thing. So, just as a thing cannot be without its essentials, it cannot be without its attributes. Over and above attributes, a thing can have further determinations which, although they are not incompatible with it, are not *necessarily* tied up with its essence. These are called "modes." A thing is sometimes found without its modes; it never is found without its attributes. Hence the Wolffian definition of essence: "Essence can be defined as that which is first conceived of about being and in which is to be found the sufficient reason why all the rest either actually belongs to it or else may belong to it."

. The primary position accorded essence is a fundamental character-istic of the metaphysics of Wolff. Consequently, for Wolff, *possibility* is the key consideration. All that which exists is possible, for it would be contradictory to admit that the impossible exists. On the other hand, not all the possibles are actually existing. When an artisan conceives a possible machine, it does not follow from its possibility that the ma-chine actually exists. So far, it is but a possible machine, and the main point is that, considering its essentials, not a single one of them makes for its existence. The famous formula of Kant, that there is nothing more in the idea of one hundred possible dollars than in that of one hundred real dollars, finds here in Wolff its proximate source. The consequences of this observation in Wolff's own philosophy are far-reaching, for if existence is neither an essential of any being nor an attribute of it, it can be only one of its modes. The cause of existence, then, always lies outside the possible being; it adds itself to it as an ultimate determination. Hence, Wolff concludes, "I define existence as the complement of possibility." [3] The necessary consequence of this existenceless conception of being is that the science of being (ontology) does not take into account the problems concerned with any kind of existence, be it that of the world or that of God. On the other hand, since actual existence is the complement of possibility, it follows that all that which is fully determined exists, and that nothing exists that is not fully determined.[4]

When a being consists of one single essence, it is simple; when it consists of several different parts placed outside one another, it is extended. Space is the order of co-existence of simultaneous things; time is the order of the continuous succession of things. The essence of the composite is the simple. There are absolutely simple things, but these are not perceptible because they are indivisible, having neither extension nor form. Those simple beings are the substances; Wolff obviously conceives them after the pattern of the Leibnizian monads, although, as we shall see, he prefers to give them another name. Com-posite things are made up of such simple substances, each of which is endowed with an elementary force enabling it to operate within itself and upon itself. Composites as such have no active forces of their own; their seeming operations are, in fact, combinations of the forces of the simple substances of which they are made.

Ontology thus provides the foundations of cosmology.[5] The material world consists of composite and modifiable things. The "world," in fact, is the totality of such beings, bound together by laws and constituting a sort of huge machine, a colossal clock.[6] The elements of that machine are extended bodies endowed with a certain quantity of inertia and a certain quantity of moving force.[7] Underlying these physical and visible elements are the invisible and metaphysical elements of which it has been said that they are the true simple and active substances. Here again Wolff is returning to the universe of Leibniz' *monadology*, with this difference, however: he seems to conceive those ultimate elements of reality in a more realistic way. Wolff calls them "atoms of nature" (*atomi naturae*).[8] In deep agreement with Leibniz, Wolff observes that, since substances are invisible, the extended wholes given to us in space, along with space itself, are but appearances. On the other hand, Wolff seriously diverges from Leibniz on the problem of the "communication of substances." Wolff does not know how substances could communicate, but he does not see why they should not be naturally interrelated. The famous doctrine of pre-established harmony is for him merely a likely hypothesis; in fact, Wolff would uphold it as the most probable one.[9] In passing from Leibniz to Wolff, cosmology has lost some of its metaphysical density.

RATIONAL PSYCHOLOGY

IN RATIONAL PSYCHOLOGY, the Wolffian notion of soul remains faithful to its Leibnizian model. It is conceived as a simple substance distinguished from the others by its power to represent to itself both itself and the world. This power is the force proper to souls. By it, they are driven from knowledge to knowledge and from representations to representations according as they expect to find pleasure in them or to avoid the pain which others portend. So knowledge and desire are inseparably bound together. This provides a basis for ethics, because pleasure is conceived in a purely rationalist way as the "knowledge" of a perfection, while pain is the knowledge of an imperfection.[10] Psychology thus accounts in an intelligible way for the fundamental distinction of good and evil.

The problem of the union of soul and body is solved in a genuinely Leibnizian spirit, yet with the same loss of metaphysical weight already observed in Wolff's cosmology. If nature is formed of units, each of which is endowed with a force of its own, then a reciprocal action of soul and body becomes difficult to imagine, the atoms of nature enjoying too much internal initiative; the occasionalism might explain it, but that was much too theological a notion for Wolff's taste; there thus remained for him Leibniz' pre-established harmony as the only answer to the problem. As he neither affirmed nor denied it in cosmology, he could resort to it in natural psychology. But in doing so, he introduces an important restriction. As Wolff understands it, pre-established harmony should rather be called a "spontaneous natural harmony." [11] Things are so made that all modifications undergone by body find their counterpart in soul, and vice versa. Once more Wolff leaves us confronted with a Leibnizian answer to a metaphysical problem, minus the metaphysical notion by which Leibniz had been able to solve it.

NATURAL THEOLOGY

AFTER WORLD AND SOUL, God. Wolff's preferred proof of God's existence is the well-known argument *a contingentia mundi*. All contingent being requires a necessary being for its cause; this classical argument acquires a particular force in a doctrine where essence is completely neutral with respect to existence. Wolffian beings are eminently deprived of any sufficient reason for their actual existence; it is therefore necessary to posit as their cause a prime necessary being. Natural theology thus provides an answer to a problem of existence for which cosmology is not competent. [12]

But what about Necessary Being itself? To conceive it as deprived of any sufficient reason, and therefore of any cause, is to make it a metaphysical impossibility. The answer to the problem had already been hinted at by Descartes, but it found in the natural theology of Wolff its complete formulation. Since God is the only being that is by itself (*ens per se*), and since we call "being by itself" such a being as has in its essence the reason for its existence, God exists by his essence—*Deus per essentiam suam existit*. [13] No stronger formula of the primacy of essence over existence can be found than Wolff's definition of God as that being "from whose essence existence necessarily follows." [14] In this doctrine where being is one with possibility, God finds in his very possibility the reason for his existence: "The being by itself exists, because it is possible." [15] The argument of St. Anselm thus found in the philosophy of Wolff a formulation that was to leave its mark on the philosophy of Kant.[16] In the well-known passage where Kant observed that all proofs of the existence of God ultimately include the "ontological argument," he certainly was remembering the natural theology of Christian Wolff, to which indeed the remark correctly applies. The situation would be different in a natural theology arguing from the actual existence of things, not from their essences or from that of God.[17]

How does practical philosophy fit in with this speculative system? The end of practical life is happiness, but happiness itself consists in achieving perfection. To determine the nature of perfection and of the ways that lead to it is the proper function of practical reason. The perfection here at stake naturally is that of human nature such as it is found in each one of us as well in other men. This notion leads Wolff to an ideal of moral life which agrees with preoccupations shared in common by most of the representatives of the Enlightenment. The main rule of ethics, then, can be formulated as follows: Do whatever can render thine own condition, as well as that of all thy fellow men, more perfect than it is. In thus requiring a ceaseless striving toward more perfection, Wolff was clearly anticipating the philosophy of progress; not, however, of a progress mechanically achieved in consequence of a natural law, but rather a progress obtained as a result of the will of man to achieve more perfection in himself and in others.[18] Happiness is the result of a moral life thus understood. Note that its very essence is the virtuous pursuit of the perfection of man determined by the rule of reason.

What Wolff Achieved

THE PHILOSOPHY OF WOLFF occupies a place of its own in the history of metaphysics. He himself did not pretend he was doing something new; rather it was his desire to bring a certain philosophical tradition to its point of perfection. One may well wonder if he was not undertaking an impossible task in attempting to build up a philosophy in which all terms would be unequivocally defined and disposed according to an order as strict as that of mathematical demonstrations. Is it possible to achieve absolute conceptual necessity? This is a philosophical question beyond the limits of a mere historical account, but we can permit ourselves this historical observation: Scholasticism had always aimed more or less to bring conceptual definitions to the point of univocal precision where they could be used as terms of necessary demonstrations. Without question, Wolff had a genius for defining and ordering philosophical concepts; we know he was a highly successful professor, and even today one cannot read him without admiring the clarity of a mind that could not leave behind anything undefined. It is not certain, however, that clearness in notions and rational necessity in demonstrations are the most precious of metaphysical gifts. A certain tendency to stop short on the threshold of metaphysical problems courageously handled by Leibniz might well be in Wolff a counterpart of his very qualities. In a sense, Leibniz himself had tended to naturalize God and religion; still, be it at the metaphysical level only, the God of Leibniz remained the ultimate and necessary answer to all the main problems of ontology, of cosmology, of psychology, and of ethics. But Wolff, on the contrary, always attempted to conceive reality such as it would be even though there were no God. Substances do not communicate, but they naturally agree and harmonize without necessarily resorting to the supposition of a pre-established harmony. There seems to be a pre-established harmony between soul and body, and in a sense there is, but nothing in the world could prove wrong the philosopher who simply concluded that, in the last analysis, things just are the way they are! The same remark applies in ethics; of course, there is a supreme lawgiver, but the highest rule of moral conduct would remain the same even if there were no God. Good is what it is in virtue of itself, not because God wants it to be so. Do that which will make yourself, your condition, and that of all your fellow men more perfect than it is: this highest of all moral rules would remain exactly as valid as it is even if there were no God. Rationalism and naturalism go hand in hand in this most remarkable philosophical expression of the German *Aufklärung*.

Wolff, we saw, wrote some works in Latin, some in German. Despite a progressive invasion of the philosophical field by the German language, even Kant will still occasionally use Latin. It must nevertheless be observed that we are nearing the moment in history when it will become necessary to begin to speak of "French," "German," "English," and "Italian" philosophies. The community of language will henceforward tend to create a common line of speculation for those who use the same linguistic instrument. Intercommunications will never cease, of course; translations will remain possible; but the language problem will always cause a certain delay in the transmission of ideas and, not infrequently, it will create misunderstandings.

Partly for this reason, but still more certainly because of the nature of his philosophy, Wolff does not seem to have perceptibly influenced contemporary French thought. English philosophy also seems to have remained outside the sphere of Wolff's influence, but there was a decided and important Wolffian school in Germany, as we shall see when we study the *Aufklärung*. Above all, we must remember that, to Kant, metaphysics itself was from the very beginning identical with the metaphysical rationalism of Christian Wolff. There was an impressive greatness about Wolff's philosophical "dogmatism," and Kant felt it, but he had to say no to Wolff, and because to him Wolff was metaphysics itself, this amounted to rejecting metaphysics itself.

5 🙊 A GOLDEN AGE IN ENGLAND

IN *The Crisis of the European Conscience,* a study of the period 1680-1715, the historian Paul Hazard argues that there occurred "a renewal of that powerful and tenacious people," the English, at the end of the seventeenth century. To judge from the vantage point of philosophy, this is so; for two capital figures in the intellectual sector of that general renewal are certainly of the greatest possible importance to the history of European philosophy: John Locke and Isaac Newton. Both are empiricists, and there is certainly something very English about that; but they are empiricists in different ways, a matter that turns out to be of no little importance.

If we were writing a general cultural and intellectual history of the period we should have also to dwell at length, as someone like Hazard or like Basil Willey has done, on the literary achievements and on the religious quest. Despite the loss of Dryden in 1700, letters in the new decades of the eighteenth century remain brilliant in every genre: poets —Pope, Gray; moralists and essayists—Addison, Steele, Shaftesbury;

satirists *par excellence*—let us mention Pope again, and of course the incomparable Jonathan Swift. And the entire period is one of sincere, urgent quest for religious truth and moral enlightenment on the part of the English people. No country had excelled the British Isles in the violence of its passion for reform at the time of the religious revolt. But not only were English sentiments violent, they managed to be long-lived. The end of the seventeenth century and the early eighteenth find Puritanism still struggling with the established church, the Methodist reform solidly established and still spreading, and Deism rearing its head.

The Cambridge Platonists form but one current in this complex movement of religious thought. We are going to single that school out for brief attention because their effort was of such a nature that a brief *résumé* of it can somewhat offset the impression made by leaving the English stage too much to materialists like Bacon, Hobbes, and Hume and to empiricists like Locke and Newton.

There cannot be claimed for this *school* (for such it truly was in the strictest sense) any overpowering influence on the ultimate outcome of the English spirit's development, nor even any profoundly original discoveries within its own quiet precincts. But a moment's consideration of the so-called "Cambridge Platonists" will serve to remind us not to overschematize our picture of English philosophical development. Even though none of these people can be said to have created an original world unto himself—there is no English Pascal or Scotch Kierkegaard—the generous and sincere atmosphere into which the Cambridge thinkers guided their students was not without fruit for many individuals, and even provided liberation (from Puritanism) for the young Locke and deep inspiration for the moralist Shaftesbury.

XII

The Cambridge Platonists

THE CAMBRIDGE THINKERS[1] are so much of a mind that there is nothing to be lost by our considering together the great among them—Benjamin Whichcote,[2] John Smith,[3] Ralph Cudworth,[4] and Henry More[5]—as exponents of a single doctrine. All were at Cambridge at the middle of the seventeenth century; in fact, all but More were products of the Puritan college, Emmanuel, where they constituted the loyal opposition. All were swept by the fashion for learning Greek; all had read Plato and, even more, Plotinus (probably also the Florentine Renaissance Platonist, Marsilio Ficino), and they spent many a cold night heatedly discussing the ancient wisdom until the wee hours stole into an upper student's room. All were fed up with the spirit of chicanery and narrow sectism in which religious controversy was still being carried on, for they saw that the same insidious spiritual pride fed this obstinate bickering and the Puritanism in whose name it was carried on.

Each of them being endowed with his own forceful personality, the characteristics we are treating in common were to be found with varying accents in each of these men. Whichcote, for instance, is especially associated with the plea for Christian tolerance, emphasizing that how a man lives the truth, and not how violently he argues it, is what brings him to God. John Smith is the epitome of the movement's personal spirituality. Ralph Cudworth is its great moralist. And Henry More, the poet and the devotee of the bizarre. But all turned with equal firmness against Calvinistic predestination, against the Cartesian separation of the world into mechanical-material sphere and spirit, against the sensism and the anti-intellectualism of the materialists; all alike moved toward a doctrine that saw God everywhere in the world, and advocated finding truth through reasoning on a lived experience of Christian goodness.

The Reaction to Puritanism

THE CAMBRIDGE THINKERS had all been subjected to Puritan indoctrination in their youth, but each of them seemed from the depths of his own sensibility to react negatively to the vision of a tyrannical God, an unrelenting, arbitrarily predestining Will, with its corollary that many face inevitable eternal damnation because their being made low magnifies the divine justice. It is as though these young men had been touched with a lingering vestige of the liberal Christian humanism which had first touched Cambridge in the person of Bishop John Fisher (1459-1535), one-time chancellor and benefactor of the university, had flourished at Oxford in the person of John Colet (1467-1519), and had reached to the highest places in the person of the great Lord Chancellor, Thomas More, sainted martyr at the time of the Reform. The humanists had advocated reading the Scriptures in the integrity of the entire context; they were sure that if one would, he would find there a doctrine of hope and love, as well as justice and rigid moral demand. Just as the humanists had felt the need to undercut the sterile debates of a waning Aristotelian scholasticism, so now the young Cambridge group felt the need to undercut the Puritan dogmatism and return to the same living source, the Word of God.

Granted, passages can be found in Scripture that present the frightening power of God's justice. But the whole of the divine message in no way supports the notion that he is sheer Will. Cudworth sums up the Cambridge reaction: "Good and evil, just and unjust, honest and dishonest (if they be not mere names without any signification) cannot possibly be arbitrary things, made by will without nature. . . ." [6] Their reaction was a human, moral, religious one; they were deeply concerned with what the very atmosphere of the Puritan tyranny was doing to souls.

Religion is no sullen Stoicism or oppressing Melancholy [states John Smith in his discourse on "The Excellency and Nobleness of True Religion"], it is no enthralling tyranny exercised over those noble and vivacious affections of Love and Delight. . . . Those *Servile* spirits which are not acquainted with God and his Goodness, may be so haunted by the frightfull thoughts of a Deity as to scare and *terifie* them into some worship and observ-

ance of him . . . they are ready to paint him forth to themselves
in their own shape: and because they themselves are full of
Peevishness and *Self-will* . . . they are apt to represent the Divinity also to themselves in the same form. . . .[7]

The suggestion that one's God is as one himself is, Nietzschean as it
sounds, is actually rather deeply rooted in the Cambridge group's
outlook. Men can only taste of the goodness of God's truth by living
that wisdom in lives of sweetness and grace. "Nothing is *the true
improvement* of our rational faculties, but the exercise of the several
virtues of sobriety, modesty, gentleness, humility, obedience to God,
and charity to men." Thus Whichcote; John Smith puts it this way:

> The Divine Truth is better understood as it unfolds itself in the
> purity of men's hearts and lives, than in all those subtle nicetics
> into which curious wits may lay it forth . . . and therefore our
> Saviour's main scope was to promote a holy life, as the best and
> most compendious way to a right belief. He hands all true ac-
> quaintance with divinity upon doing God's will.[8]

John Smith's remark about the Puritan's frightful God touches a deep
nerve of this latter-day Platonism and shows it to be an effort to
reintegrate what seventeenth-century rationalism was tending to rend
asunder. Reason and will, the intellectual and the moral, are emanations
of one divine reality, and so they need to be united in the action of a
single life in order to be appreciated in their full actuality. The goodness in the life of a saint *is* the radiating reality of God.

> When nothing can to God's own self accrew,
> Who's infinitely happy; sure the end
> Of this creation simply was to shew
> His flowing goodnesse, which he doth out send
> Not for himself; for nought can him amend;
> But to his creature doth his good impart,
> This infinite *Good* through all the world doth wend
> To fill with heavenly blisse each willing heart,
> So the free Sunne doeth 'light and 'liven every part.[9]

This emphasis on discovering the goodness of God through living
our convictions is not intended, however, to depreciate in any way the
value of reason, that "candle of the Lord," as Lancelot Andrewes called
it. God in his goodness has given us a natural faculty to lead us to faith.
Original sin has dimmed but has not corrupted this light, which is one

of the ways the very light of the Lord shines in us. "As the sun giveth light to the body, so God hath provided light for the soul; and that is, first, the light of nature, which teaches us that this is a just thing, *ne alii facias quod tibi fieri non vis*: from this light we have this knowledge, that we are not of ourselves but of another, and of this light the Wise Man saith, 'The soul of man is the candle of the Lord.' " [10] Reason directs us to the moral life, which in turn is the threshold of faith—a conception not without distant premonitions of the *Critique of Practical Reason*. The Cambridge Christians are not about to abandon "reason" to the Cartesians, nor to oppose the materialists with a blind adherence to mysteries. Reason conducted rightly, might sum up their answer; but *conducted rightly* implies more than discovery of a right theoretical method; it means reason meditating on the substance of a morally rich life. Reason brings us up to the threshold of the things of God, but then only faith can take us beyond. We cannot be expected to believe what reason will refuse, but the actual intimacy with divine things takes us beyond mere reason. "Reason enables man," explains John Smith, "to work out for himself all those notions of God which are the true Groundwork of Love and Obedience to God and conformity to Him. . . . But, besides this *outward* revelation of God's will to men, there is also an *inward* impression of it on their minds and spirits, which is, in a more special manner, attributed to God. We cannot see Divine things but in a Divine light." [11]

This emphasis on the reasonable foundation of faith provides an important plank in the platform against Puritanism's picture of God as crushing Will. The Cambridge Platonists insist that we live in a world of law, that God being infinite Intelligence as well as Infinite Will, has created according to an order, of which we are a part, and to the knowledge of which our reasons are naturally ordained. A world of law, a world with a nature, is not a thing of brute tyranny, but a universe in which a creature of love and reason can hope to feel at home.

The Anti-materialism of the Cambridge Group

PERHAPS THE READER is wondering what is so Platonic about all this. There is obviously little in the doctrines we have been discussing that is not quite consonant with the Neo-Platonic spirit—the emphasis on the unity of reality radiating downward from the highest principle; the suggestion that one should turn inward to find the presence in us of that highest principle; the union of the practical and theoretical lives —of the *on* and the *agathon*—all of that is in perfect harmony with the Platonic vision. But we can see the "Platonism" of the Cambridge thinkers even more explicitly in the way they oppose the vigorous materialism accompanying the grand augurs of seventeenth-century mathematical physics. The Cambridge thinkers fell back on their enthusiastic reading of Plotinus to find a spiritual code to oppose, in the arena of reason, to the engaging rhapsodies of Francis Bacon and the threats bristling in the philosophy of the Malmesbury Monster. With Ralph Cudworth leading the attack, the Cambridge school is ready to fight philosophy with philosophy, knowing full well that not just good personal example but also theoretical countervision has to be presented to the seventeenth-century mind to prepare it for the consideration of the things of faith.

The great rationalist materialists were careful to throw a sop to faith; Bacon and Hobbes both argued, apparently sincerely enough, that faith has its rightful province. But then they went on to discuss the world philosophically as though nothing that faith taught was of the least bearing. The root error in their way of conceiving the world, according to the Cambridge critics, is the effort to derive the higher from the lower principle. How could the soul arise from matter; how could an idea ever be derived from mere material sensation? Rather that an angel should come forth from the brawn of an ape! And what can mechanism explain? Certainly not living things, and not even qualities among the lifeless. Quite in harmony with the central Platonic intuition, the Cambridge thinkers turn materialism upside down and derive the whole of their world from the other end of the scale: in short, there is spirit in everything, a world-soul, created by God, which inhabits and directs the destiny of the least realities.

> Onely that vitality,
> That doth extend this great Universall,
> And move th'inert Materiality
> Of great and little worlds, that keep in memory.[12]

Ralph Cudworth, the metaphysician of the group, worked the doctrine out in considerable Platonic detail. The divine law commanding the works of nature is not to be understood as a direct order; rather, in his

wisdom God has created a system of Immediate Agents and Execution-
ers provided for the producing of every Effect.

> Since neither all things are produced fortuitously [as the Puritan
> emphasis on will might lead to believe] or by the unguided
> Mechanism of Matter [as the empiricists would have it], not God
> himself may reasonably be thought to do all things Immediately
> and Miraculously [remember, Malebranche's occasionalism was
> being evolved at almost the same time Cudworth is writing *The
> True Intellectual System of the Universe*, published 1678], it may
> well be concluded, that there is a *Plastik Nature* under him, which
> as an Inferior and Subordinate Instrument doth drudgingly exe-
> cute that Part of his Providence which consists in the Regular and
> Orderly Motion of Matter: yet so as that there is also besides this
> a Higher Providence to be acknowledged, which presiding over it
> doth often supply the defects of it, and sometimes overrule it.[13]

Cudworth is here aware of what St. Thomas would call "secondary
causality," and even though he integrates this doctrine into a basic
Plotinian conception of the descent of all reality from a single, highest
Principle, it is clear from this quotation that he manages not quite to
lose the essence of a very sound notion.

The descent of lesser beings from the High Principle is not too well
clarified as to mode; what *is* clear is that the doctrine is conceived in a
strict anti-mechanistic context:

> . . . no Effect can possibly transcend the Power of its Cause.
> Wherefore it is certain that in the Universe, things did not thus
> *ascend* and mount, or Climb up from *Lower Perfection* to Higher,
> but on the contrary, *Descend* and *Slide* down from Higher to
> Lower, so that the first Original of all things, was not the most
> *Imperfect*, but the most *Perfect Being*. But . . . it is certain . . .
> that *Life* and *Sense* could never possibly spring, out of *Dead and
> Senseless* Matter. . . .

Cudworth describes the Immanation:

> A *Perfect* Understanding Being, is the *Beginning* and *Head* of the
> *Scale* of Entity; from whence things *Gradually* Descend down-
> ward; lower and lower, till they end in *Senseless Matter* . . .
> *Mind is the Oldest of all things,* Senior to the Elements, and the
> whole Corporeal World . . .

In the same context, Cudworth blasts at the materialist notion that ideas are derived from material sensory experience:

> . . . *Life* and *Sense* could never possibly spring, out of *Dead and Senseless Matter* . . . Much less could *Understanding* and *Reason* in men, ever have emerged out of *Stupid Matter,* devoid of all manner of *Life* . . .[14]

The two prongs of this position—the derivation of things from God and the origin of our intellectual notions from the same source—are organized into a theory of the intelligible ideas. From the infinite seat, the intelligible ideas pass into the finite world in two distinct but related ways; by an act of God's will, things are called into existence of which the ideas become the essences; concomitantly they pass as intuitions into finite centers of consciousness, there guiding us on the one hand to the true reading of the universe, and to the immediate sympathy of God on the other. The doctrine of innatism was very central to these Cambridge thinkers; in fact, it was against them that John Locke was to react directly in his empiricist attack against innate ideas. John Smith put all of this in a very ethical way, revealing quite exactly what it was the Platonists wanted us to feel. "Though every good man," he argues, "is not so logically subtle as to be able, by fit mediums, to demonstrate his own immortality, yet he *sees* it in a higher light. His soul, being purged and enlightened by true sanctity, is more capable of those Divine irradiations, whereby it feels itself in conjunction with God; and by the light of divine goodness, mixing itself with the light of its own reason, sees more clearly, not only that it may, if it please the supreme Deity, of its own nature exist eternally, but also that it *shall* do so." [15]

We shall look in vain if we seek in the writings of the Cambridge Platonists either very profound or very original arguments in support of these rather ancient positions. Most of their writings are exhortatory or, in the case of Henry More's poems, lyrical. An exception—and one of monumental dimensions—is Cudworth's 900 folio pages of twisting argument seeming to refute every conceivable attack against belief in God's existence, this whole great effluvium constituting only the "Propyleum" of the mighty temple he had hoped to erect. Of this huge work, Cassirer did not hesitate to write that its "tedious diffusion leads to disintegration of the central idea."

It was not only the archaic and rather ineffectual literary forms in which the Cambridge thinkers expressed themselves (their great, rambling sermons could not, in print, rival the trenchant works of a Descartes or the sharp essays of a Bacon) that account for their failure to exercise a deep and wide influence on the age. The basic reason is that they were seriously out of sympathy with it. Not that they opposed the new science—the very soul of the seventeenth-century intellectual movement; indeed there were those among them who encouraged experimentation and took a vital interest in it. But to a man, their training in mathematics was weak and their creative scientific ability non-existent. This made it hard for them to capture the imagination of the most creative spirits of the times. Wherever their personal example could radiate, it was of course a different story; but direct personal influence could hardly turn the great intellectual tide.

Their influence, however, was felt at least a bit through two thinkers whose works radiated far and wide. We mentioned that John Locke worked hard to refute innatism; but he was also the first to admit that the Cambridge Platonists liberated him from the narrowness of Puritanism and encouraged in him respect for a generous and charitable Christianity. He once wrote:

> If you desire a larger view of the parts of Morality, I know not where you will find them so well and distinctly explained, and so strongly enforced, as in the practical Divines of the Church of England. The sermons of Dr. Barrow, Archbishop Tillotson, and Dr. Whichcote, are masterpieces in this kind.

The other important person upon whom they exercised a considerable influence was the moralist Shaftesbury.[16] He was much influenced by their teachings on the goodness of God, a theme he went on to develop until he made not only goodness but *good humor* the very essence of true religion! [17]

A countercurrent, an interlude, but pure and touching, Cambridge Platonism can serve to remind us that our brief schematizing must of necessity leave out of account some of the breadth and richness of the movement of intellectual development in Europe in the centuries that are our concern. The undercurrents and the eddies, the efforts that either fail to appear on the surface or turn too narrowly upon themselves, are like those *petites perceptions* that Leibniz says enter into the formation of conscious movements of the soul, though we never are aware of them for themselves.

XIII

John Locke

Background, Method, and Importance of *An Essay Concerning Human Understanding*

IN JOHN LOCKE,[1] the English Golden Age produced a philosopher whose influence, like Newton's, was fundamental. His modestly titled *An Essay Concerning Human Understanding* was to become the basic point of reference for English empiricists and, through Pierre Coste's French translation (1700), to challenge the best minds of the Continent. Leibniz, for one, was inspired to write a 500-page essay paralleling Locke's topics. To the generation of *philosophes* he became a god. His *Two Treatises of Civil Government* (1690) gave expression to the dominant Whig Republican sentiments and thus became Holy Writ for a century of English and American liberal Democrats.

Locke's purportedly common-sense approach and empirical method made of the *Essay* a rallying point for all who were by nature or conviction tired of the rationalist-idealist metaphysical constructions. Here, in place of flights of metaphysical fancy, was, supposedly, a kind of natural science of the human soul, a *history* of what really goes on in us, following, as Locke calls it, "a plain method." European philosophy was destined never quite to get over the idea that somehow Locke achieved about all a "common-sense realism" could achieve; despite the devastating criticisms hurled at the work by Leibniz, Berkeley, Hume, and Kant, many of its assumptions were yet (and in some cases still are) taken for granted—even by these very critics—and its failures were largely charged against *realism* as such.

The intent and the nature of the work are clarified when we know something of its origin. Locke was the farthest thing from a professional school philosopher—a fact which helps explain an unfortunate imprecision and lack of analytic thoroughness in the work. Locke was a physician by training, although he practiced little; by vocation, a political secretary. (This seems to be the profession that produces English philosophers in our period!) Locke found his work leading him into earnest and continuing discussion with his friends of the religious-political problems confronting England. We have been considering the religious tensions that coursed through England throughout the period. The conversations that led to the *Essay* occurred at a moment when these tensions had reached an acute stage on the political scene: the years of the Glorious Revolution; that is, the successful opposition of the Protestants to the Catholic party of James II. Packed in the baggage of the expelled Catholic majesty went not only the divine-right theory of kings, but a whole conception of God. The constitutional monarchy was to be watched over by a Whig deity, father of that deist first principle who would do little more than assure the bourgeoisie that the cosmic watchworks would keep running properly.

When Locke and his friends started arguing about what sort of deity must see to the management of the empire, all this was yet to be accomplished. The pantheistic monster of Spinoza seems to have posed about as much direct threat to these English gentlemen as the Turkish Allah. But the Catholic Cartesian Deity whose prophet, Malebranche, was far more acceptable than the warlike Semite, was another proposition. Locke had been little impressed by either Oxford's Peripateticians or Cambridge's Platonists. The Baconian scientific tradition, with its emphasis on analysis down to the irreducible elements, did leave a mark on the young physician, and so did the Cartesian example of radical inquiry, high rational standards, and careful distinction. What the practical Locke could not constitutionally absorb were the metaphysical flights to which the Cartesian method immediately led. Unconvinced by the results in physics, he was equally unconfident in a system of occasionalism in which one must have recourse at once to God to explain anything and everything, especially those phenomena which to the common-sense everyday observer seem most capable of modestly explaining themselves. The success of Robert Boyle, the chemist with whom Locke had had the honor of working for a while, was largely due, after all, to his willingness to let the humble facts of modest chemical situations reveal their plain history without benefit of a pre-established system of metaphysical explanation to give them an absolute significance.

It occurred to Locke, when his friends pressed ever harder toward the foundations of belief in revelation and the grounds of morality, that the real depths of the problem lay beyond religious matters. Until one can ascertain the roots in our understanding of any act of assent—whether it be certain intuition, opinion, sensation, belief—disputes over particular truths float in air, devoid of any critical foundation. The day it occurred to Locke to ask *What can we know?* criticism was born into the modern tradition; and since criticism has continued to our own day to dominate Western thought, this is no mean claim to fame.

The Cartesian methodic doubt had made straight the way for Locke's inquiry and even can be said to have rendered it necessary. It had by then become rather suspected that Descartes had posed a crucial question without really meaning it; for in relating how he had doubted, he leaves the reader with the feeling it was inevitable that he should discover at the end of his inquiry a resurrection of certitude that was a bit too preassured. What is so different about Locke's inquiry—and this is why it made such a great impression on the experiment-avid, Newton- and Boyle-fed eighteenth-century mind—is that one is made to feel by the expressed method and the form of its actual execution that Locke is taking one on an adventure the end results of which are not so assured in advance.

Alongside the towering metaphysical structures of Spinoza and Malebranche, the declared object of *An Essay Concerning Human Understanding* seems modest and easily controllable. "It shall suffice to my present purpose, to consider the discerning faculties of a man, as they are employed about the objects which they have to do with: and I shall imagine I have not wholly misemployed myself in the thoughts I shall have on this occasion, if, in this historical, plain method, I can give any account of the ways whereby our understandings come to attain those notions of things we have, and can set down any measures of the certainty of our knowledge, or the grounds of those persuasions which are to be found amongst men, so various, different, and wholly contradictory," yet always asserted in some part of the world with absolute confidence.[2]

To the practical English gentleman, troubled sincerely by the high metaphysical-theological disputes raging in the Church of England, overwhelmed by the rumors of pantheistic gods and autocratic gods worthy of Louis le Grand, who must move a twig when I hear a sparrow jump, such words were the breath of a new spring. How simple, how unpretentious, how hopeful! Let us dispense with transcendental theories and absolute answers. Let us take in hand a *plain, historical method*—plain, meaning common sense (and what better to fall back upon, for after all, common sense was building a ruddy good empire!); and historical, suggesting we proceed descriptively from simple beginnings, step by step as the reality is built up, "This is my purpose, to inquire into the origin, certainty, and extent of human knowledge." [3] Instead of launching into great speculations about the ultimate nature of things based on the analysis of certain first principles, let us content ourselves with considering the discerning faculties of man—which after all are going to have to supply whatever it is we may turn out to know—considering them as they are when they are hard at work. Let us not imagine that we are going to turn up miraculous new visions, but rather let us be thankful for little results: criteria of our certitude and how we arrive at it; some help perhaps in threading our way through the diversity of tenaciously held conflicting opinions. How refreshing it is to encounter at last someone who recognizes this diversity and wants to find a critical basis for handling oneself in the face of it, instead of zooming straight to the absolute answers all men are supposed to be able to pull from the resources of their common reason!

So far does Locke go in renouncing the intention of supplying absolute answers to ultimate problems that he even devotes a good part of the Introduction to the declaration that human understanding has its limitations, that we must come to recognize what they are, and thus protect ourselves against "meddling with things exceeding its comprehension." [4] To this he adds privately a touching note about the imperfections peculiar to this particular work, developed slowly amidst hectic times, and "written by incoherent parcels," so that there is strong possibility "that too little and too much may have been said in it." [5] Unfortunately, the letter in which he admits this was not used as a preface to the *Essay*. The impression left by the Introduction is still a very confident one, despite the strong note about the limitations of our understanding which is calculated perfectly to take away the appetite for ambitious metaphysical constructions. For our limited knowledge is yet "far above all the rest of the inhabitants of this our mansion," and proportioned by the bountiful Author of our being to the necessary obtaining of "the conveniences of life and information of virtue." ⁶ "The candle that is set up in us," we are assured—on what grounds is not revealed—"shines bright enough for all our purposes." When you really think about it, that is not too much less assuring than Descartes' universal distribution of *bon sens.* A good estimate of our powers will reveal grounds for avoiding the temptation to give up trying because we think we cannot know anything, or to go around perpetually questioning everything.

Locke sounds peacefully a note that Hume will swell and Kant thunder forth with full diapason. "Men, extending their inquiries beyond their capacities, and letting their thoughts wander into those depths where they can find no sure footing, it is no wonder that they raise questions, and multiply disputes, which, never coming to any clear resolution, are proper only to continue and increase their doubts, and to confirm them at last in perfect scepticism." ⁷ The contemporary student, who has lived through the experience not only of Kant but of the critical endeavor of Husserl's "philosophy without presupposition" and with the example of Descartes to back up the experience, knows how redoubtable is the enterprise of being "critical." However, the historical perspectives must be kept straight, if we want to be just: This is the first experiment in critical epistemology, born of a sincere and pressing religious necessity, in a time and atmosphere that had long forgotten, for example, the balanced realism of a St. Thomas. Locke could not know, before trying, the perils and pitfalls of the endeavor to "search out the bounds between opinion and knowledge." Once he had assembled his "incoherent parcels," Locke put no store by their being definitive. This Englishman's modesty was that of a true gentleman.

But, on the other hand, the *Essay* still says what it says, and fails to say some other things. First and greatest of its kind, its influence was immediate and enormous; writing in 1729 in the Introduction to the second edition of his French translation of the *Essay,* Pierre Coste attests, "Adopted in some way at Oxford and Cambridge, this masterpiece is read and explained to young people as the work most suited to form the spirit, to regulate and extend their knowledge, so that Locke presently holds the place of Aristotle and his most famous commentators in these famous universities." Today it still stands straddling the highway of history, challenging all comers to bring it down. In the incomparably difficult enterprise of reflective discovery of the ways and means of the human understanding, Locke's work has ever since captured groping imaginations with its definite declarations. These foundations still need to be contended with as they did two hundred years ago.

Innate Clear and Distinct Ideas Refused

THE FIRST THING for an empiricist to do is to get rid of the idealists' clear and distinct innate ideas. The main part of such a program will obviously consist in the positive effort of replacing the innate ideas with a successful "plain history," accounting for all of our knowledge with nothing but an original *tabula rasa* (or, as Locke says, "a blank piece of paper") and the elements of experience which will get engraved on it. We shall wait to evaluate this part of Locke's program until we have seen how he builds up his "history" of our experience.

The most important thing to do in the way of a purely negative attack on innate ideas is to cast doubt on their universality: Does everyone actually possess any such innate ideas? Locke devotes all of Chapter Two in the First Book to this attack. In view of the subsequent rebuttals of Leibniz and the analyses of Kant, it must be said bluntly that his arguments are not effective. He considers the epicenter of the innatist argument to reside in a claim that there is "universal consent" to certain fundamental propositions, like the principle of causality, for example. Locke's counterargument consists in pointing to the absence of such ideas in "children, idiots, etc." He even goes to the extent of claiming that the propositions that most deserve consent—namely, the principles of identity and contradiction—"are so far from having a universal assent, that there are a great part of mankind to whom they are not so much as known." He claims that a child cannot be made to assent to the principle of contradiction because he cannot grasp the large, comprehensive, and abstract names it involves. Our empiricist makes it painfully evident that the only thing "innate idea" means to him is an explicitly reflected upon, determinate, ideational content. He attempts to counter the idealist argument to the effect that, as Locke puts it, "the understanding hath an implicit knowledge of these principles, but not an explicit, before this first hearing," by answering, "It will be hard to conceive what is meant by a principle imprinted on the understanding . . . unless it be this; that the mind is capable of understanding and assenting firmly to such propositions." [8] In other words, there are no universal innate ideas in the sense of explicitly held principles, but there is a sort of universal readiness to assent to such principles when experience gives rise to them. But Locke is playing right into Leibniz' hands. In his essay on the *Essay*, Leibniz will have only to point out that the deep sense of "innate idea" is just this disposition of mind to assent to first principles, it being understood, of course, that the reason for this is that the mind itself, like those principles, is a manifestation of the underlying reality of all experience.

In addition to doing something about their innateness, the empiricist must transform the criterion of the fundamental ideas from "clarity and distinctness," which leads right to an absoluteness he rejects, into something that will retain the ideal of a rational standard but recognize the finite aspect of all the mind's determinations. On the negative side of this task, Locke has had his work done for him already by the Cartesians. For they had by then already made it clear that the "clear" ideas are not clear at all, which disposes one to look for different criteria. Descartes had found nothing clearer than the ideas we possess of God and of our own souls. Nothing so unclear, objects Malebranche, and he supports his argument well. What, asked Descartes, could be so clear as the innate idea of extension? Anyone who had pondered the problem of relating Spinoza's infinite divine attribute of extension with the extension possessed by the modal entities could honestly reply, "Almost anything must be clearer than that!" What is more, Leibniz challenged the very fundamentality of the idea of extension on the grounds of its complexity—the extended being the idea of parts outside of parts. And confusion was welling up about the whole problem of the primary and secondary qualities, and about the "clear and distinct" idea of substance.

Locke does not need to bring these things up when he proposes a new criterion for his version of a fundamental idea. His contemporaries were aware of the problems besetting the Cartesians, and so they were ready to show enthusiasm for a fresh approach to the problem of founding rational certitude. Locke's ideas are not the innate grasp of the ultimate clear and distinct principles of reality and consciousness. Rather they are sensations and complex combinations built up from sensation, as well as reflections on our conscious acts. Consequently, they need to be "determinate and determined," rather than clear and distinct. To say that an idea is determinate simply means that it is present, definite, and primary.[9] The quality of being *determined* applies to complex ideas. When a name is attached to a complexus, this idea is determined if its various parts are articulated in regard to one another in a way that is definite and makes sense. From the way Locke presents this, it seems that the clearness and definiteness of a complex idea—using these terms in a popular, not a Cartesian, sense—are then something to be worked for: a voluntary effort of thought and language construction. In other words, the empiricist would have us strive to forge complex ideas that can serve as adequate principles in thought, rather than think, as the Cartesian idealist did, that we can discover in ourselves principles which, if adequately known, would in themselves have to be utterly clear and distinct.[10] What the criteria "determined and determinate" really mean, however, we cannot decide until we know better what our ideas are and whence they originate.

The Origin and Nature of Our Ideas

IF THERE ARE NO INNATE IDEAS, it follows that everything we know must come from "experience." The burden now falls on Locke to show how everything we know can indeed be accounted for by an empirical description.[11]

SIMPLE IDEAS

THE STARTING POINT seems neat enough: all our ideas are derived from experience. Locke gives the same broad meaning to "idea" as Descartes did, meaning *whatever* is in our mind, be it "phantasm, notion, or species." But what is *experience?* It is, he says, "our observation, employed either about external sense objects, or about the internal operations of our minds, perceived and reflected on by ourselves." [12] Note this well: sensation is not the only original source of the content of our experience. There are "two fountains of knowledge"—sensation *and reflection*—"that notice which the mind takes of its own operations, and the manner of them." [13]

Locke's description of this "first fountain" begins with a note of confident realism:

First, our senses, conversant about particular sensible objects, do convey into the mind several distinct perceptions of things, according to those various ways in which those objects do affect them . . . when I say the senses convey into the mind, I mean, they from external objects convey into the mind what produces there those perceptions.[14]

"Conversant about particular sensible objects" . . . "from external objects"—music to a realist's ears; but what does he mean by "several *distinct* perceptions"? Locke tells us exactly what he means:

Though the qualities that affect our senses are, in the things themselves, so united and blended that there is no separation, no distance between them, yet it is plain that the ideas they produce in the mind enter by the senses simple and unmixed . . . and there is nothing that can be plainer to a man than the clear and distinct perception he has of those simple ideas, which, being each in itself uncompounded, contains in it nothing but *one uniform appearance or conception in the mind*, and is not distinguishable into different ideas.[15]

Each simple idea yielded by sense then is utterly simple and unmixed; it is *one uniform appearance*, not distinguishable into parts. Indeed Locke goes so far as to declare that the feel of cold and the feel of hardness when I touch a piece of ice are as distinct as the odor and the softness of a lily.[16] These *distinct* simple ideas of sense are *atoms* of consciousness (Locke himself uses the term), a kind of stable building block out of which, along with that other source of original "simple ideas," reflection on our mental operations, Locke will build the edifice of consciousness. It is in this sense that the criterion of all ideas being "determined" must be understood.

There are four genera of simple ideas. Two of the genera we might have expected anyway are: 1] discrete sense data (what we have just been talking about), and 2] discrete reflections on the mind's own operations. But two others are introduced, and they at once pose problems: 3] qualities discovered through the cooperation of several senses, and 4] ideas derived from a cooperation of sense and reflection.

Locke lists as ideas discovered through the cooperation of several senses: extension, figure, rest and motion—the qualities termed by the Cartesians "primary." The problem is this: the Cartesians claimed that the "secondary" qualities—color, sound, taste, etc.—are subjective, relative, unreliable, but that the *primary* qualities are just the opposite. The primary qualities are common to all our experiences of extended things, and they are everywhere the same. The big rub for an empiricist

is the Cartesians' explanation for this fact. The reason the primary
qualities are found in no one sense by itself (they are not "proper objects" of an individual sense, but "common sensible objects," as the
medieval philosopher would say) is that their root is not really sense
at all but the mind's intuition of the clear and distinct idea of extension
which is innate to it. Now the intuition of innate ideas is one aspect of
Cartesian philosophy that we know Locke is dead set against. He has no
qualms about accepting the notion that the secondary qualities are subjective and relative. But he *must* find some explanation for the primary
qualities that is more down to earth than innatism.

To this end he makes two moves. One is to reinstate something close
to the medieval "common sensible," a sensible object grasped by the cooperation of two or more senses. The other is to add a new quality to
the list, one that not only is not explicable in terms of extension as such
(and therefore is clearly anti-mathematical!) but also carries with it
the strongest suggestion that there is really something "out there" that
opposes itself to me—to wit, *solidity*—a quality that feels as though it
might resist being reduced to an innate condition. When it is a question
of dealing with ideas derived from both sensation and reflection, it
becomes even more evident that Locke is trying to handle problems
conceived idealistically with an empiricism unable to solve them. In
this fourth category of "simple ideas" (that is, ideas apprehended by
a simple act of perception) we find *existence* and *unity*, *power* and
succession. These are ideas with long records of idealistic interpretation. Locke makes two significant remarks about them: first, he says
that they are "suggested to the understanding by every object without
and by every object within." Then he says that they are particularly
easy to derive from *reflection* on our own inner acts of thought and
volition.[17] Take the idea of "existence and unity," for instance. This
idea can be found as well in any one of our own thoughts as in any
given thing: "When ideas are in our minds, we consider them as being
actually there, as well as we consider things to be actually without us:
which is, that they exist, or have existence: and whatever we can consider as one thing, whether a real being or idea, suggests to the understanding the idea of unity." [18] The same could as well be said for
"power": we can perfectly well discover this idea by reflection on
the way one thought gives rise to another—we do not have to have
recourse to real things in order to discover "cause and effect." As to
"succession," it also is perfectly accessible interiorly.

It is quite clear what Locke is preparing us for. Once it is said that our sensations are not the real grasp of things such as they are in themselves, but effects caused in us by the things, then one must be prepared to build the whole structure of consciousness out of whatever simple ideas the senses have stored up in the soul. Consequently, the work of establishing connections to tie together this structure has to be carried out among ideas. But where are we to find the connectors? Cold, sweet, loud, red, acid, tepid, pink are discrete atoms of sensations, so they cannot connect. But there remains "that other source" of ideas—reflection on our own conscious activities. Apparently what Locke has done is to reflect on our thinking and willing activities and from these derive the ideas of *succession, cause and effect,* and even the notion of *endurance within the flow of experience*; i.e., a certain kind of unity of continued self-identity, which is what he seems to mean by "existence." So in addition to reifying impressions, Locke also reifies functions of consciousness in order to provide connections for a united world.

The last group of simple ideas common to all objects and attained by reflection and sense together is that of pleasure and pain; i.e., the whole order of the affective, "whether we call it satisfaction, delight, pleasure, happiness, etc. on the one side; or uneasiness, trouble, pain, torment, anguish, misery, etc. on the other." [19] These simple ideas have been "annexed to several objects, and to the ideas we receive from them, as also to several of our thoughts" by "our wise Creator" so that we shall not be indifferent to what we need and to what we must avoid.[20] Clearly Locke has to provide some basis in our knowledge at the most fundamental level for an ethics. Pleasure and pain can be considered *sensations* without much difficulty, but what sort of sensations? There is no room for them among either the primary or the secondary qualities, and they are certainly not the product of a simple reflection on our thought and will. The fourth category seems established to take care of just such difficult cases.

COMPLEX IDEAS

THE SIMPLE IDEAS are received by a relatively passive sensory system. The compounding of simple ideas into complex ones, however, requires a very active role on the part of the mind; these basic activities of the mind are activities of *combining, comparing,* and *separating.* The results of these activities are complex ideas that fall into three general categories: *substances, modes,* and *relations.* "The ideas of *substances* are such combinations of simple ideas as are taken to represent distinct particular things subsisting by themselves; in which the supposed or confused idea of substance itself is always the first and chief"—obviously a point which deserves closer scrutiny. "*Modes* I call such complex ideas which, however compounded, contain not in them the supposition of subsisting by themselves, but are considered as dependences on, or affections of substances." [21] Finally, *relation,* "which consists in the consideration and comparing one idea with another." [22]

Ideas of substances are of two sorts: single and collective. For example, man is a single substance and an army is a collective substance. This poses no problem and is of little importance, but the same cannot be said of Locke's effort to explain the origin and nature of the idea of substance as such. From our reading of history since Bacon and Descartes, we have learned that conceptions of substance are one of the most significant indexes to the metaphysics of an author. Locke's conception could not be more significant.

The empiricist's description of how the ideas of substances are concocted seems to make Hume's eventual position—and that of Kant—absolutely inevitable.

> The mind being furnished with a great number of the simple ideas conveyed in by the senses, as they are found in exterior things, or by reflection on its own operations, takes notice also, that a certain number of these simple ideas go constantly together; which being presumed to belong to one thing, and words being suited to common apprehensions, and made use of for quick dispatch, are called, so united in one subject, by one name; which, by inadvertency, we are apt afterward to talk of and consider as one simple idea, which indeed is a complication of many ideas together: because, as I have said, not imagining how these simple ideas can subsist by themselves, we accustom ourselves to suppose some *substratum* wherein they do subsist, and from which they do result, which therefore we call *substance.*[23]

Descartes had suggested that the various qualities are welded into a single thing by the clear and distinct idea of substance which the mind "intuits." As part of his program of criticizing what he considers the illusory innate ideas, Locke is led to show that there is no such "clear and distinct idea" of substance at all, but only "a supposition of one knows not what support of such qualities," [24] a supposition produced by the imagination to give body to the *accustomed* "going constantly together" of a number of simple ideas. Much of what Hume and then Kant will have to say of the problem is here quite clearly stated by Locke. Hume's argument that the association of ideas, whether it be the grouping of accidents about the core of a "substance," or whether it be the effect's always following a cause, are creatures of habitual juxtapositions of ideas, only explicates the fact that, upon seeing a number of simple ideas regularly together, we gather them under a single word and "accustom ourselves to supposing some substratum wherein they do subsist." Locke then had clearly seen that the thing in itself, or substance, is not an idea that adds anything to the qualities, but is only an *Etwas ueberhaupt* or X, as Kant will say in the first edition of the *Critique of Pure Reason,* which, because it adds nothing essentially to the content of impressions, can be said to be, as Kant bluntly puts it, *Nichts.*

How true it is that Locke's basic conceptions cannot hold out against idealism at the critical points, we shall see by tracing further his efforts to give unity to the intentionally isolated psychological world he has set up. We shall trace this effort in three areas: Locke's analysis of the formation of general ideas, his analysis of cause and effect, and the problem of personal identity.

The Formation of General Ideas

The analysis of the abstraction of general ideas fulfills the program of considering the different kinds of activity of the mind—the combining, comparing, and separating which occur in the formation of complex ideas. Actually, the philosopher has presupposed through the previous analysis the operation of *separation*—the formation of general ideas by "separating" the universal from the particular elements—as a natural accompaniment of the comparing and combining that go on in the formation of modes, substances, and relations. But before turning to his final analysis of the structure of human knowledge, he realizes it is important to go into the question of abstraction in its own right; for without a theory of the formation of general ideas, there can be elaborated no theory of language; and a philosophy of the understanding that explained neither generalization nor language would be drastically incomplete.

Locke's theory of abstraction shows all the scars of his early brush with both Cartesian thought and Platonic realism. Against the Platonists he directs the sound remark that only individuals exist, and consequently "general universals are creatures of the understanding." [25] Such a statement is, however, ambiguous. To the Thomistic moderate realist this would mean that, while only concrete individuals exist, there can be many individuals each possessing the same essence. The understanding, intuiting through the sensible presence of these things the structure they possess in common, is thus able to form universal conceptions. To the extreme "nominalist" it can mean that, there being no principles in things capable of being common to several individuals, all "universals" are nothing but words, fabricated by the mind to stand for any gratuitous resemblance.

Now, Locke is obviously sensitive to the idea of giving universals any kind of real status of their own. Still, his common sense tells him that the radical nominalist position is to be avoided. But will the principles of his philosophy permit a delicate middle solution? Locke likes to make realistic remarks about the real essences of things, but his initial position forces him to conclude that we cannot know the real essences of things. No "complex idea," fabricated out of the atoms of sensation, could ever be that "foundation of all those qualities," which is the real essence. The "simple ideas" are impressions too discrete and external ever to combine into something we could possibly take for the thing itself. So, he must conclude, we cannot "rank and sort things, and consequently denominate them, by their real essences, because we know them not. Our faculties carry us no farther toward the knowledge and distinction of substances, than a collection of those sensible ideas we observe in them, which [collection of sensible ideas], however made with the greatest diligence and exactness we are capable of, yet it is more remote from the true constitution from which these qualities flow than, as I said, a countryman's idea of that famous clock of Strasburgh, whereof he only sees the outward figure and motions [instead of knowing all the springs and wheels as the maker does]." [26]

In the concrete examples he furnishes of the process of forming from our complex ideas those "nominal essences" which are so inadequate to the real nature and so external, Locke shows that he is making no distinction between the kind of constructed notion science uses as a guide and a natural, reliable, though partial grasp of a universalizable structure in things. Locke's way of jumping from the fact that we *do* construct many would-be "universals" on the basis of evidence that is far from approaching any essential intuition and in the process are very susceptible to error, to the conclusion that we can *never* know, even partially, a real essence, is reminiscent of the way cruder empiricists will leap from the fact of an occasional sense error to the conclusion that the senses yield no truth.[27] Chemists, says Locke in support of his stand, will classify together as "sulphur" substances which, upon closer examination, "betray qualities so different from one another, as to frustrate the expectation and labor of very wary chemists."[28]

It is very understandable that Locke wished to caution against the impression, left by Cambridge Platonists and continental Cartesians alike, that the mind can plunge readily to the ultimate foundations of reality and there grasp at once the deepest secrets of its being. Against such unfounded rationalism, Locke urges the fact that "there is not so contemptible a plant or animal that does not confound the most enlarged understanding. . . . What makes lead and iron malleable; antimony and stones not?"[29] But the very way Locke poses the objection proves he has failed to make some very important distinctions. In the very act of asserting that we do not know essences, he blandly declares that iron *is* malleable and that stones *are not*. The ultimate *why* is indeed one question, but our knowing *that* all stones of their essences are not, at normal temperatures, malleable is quite another. He never did, nor will Leibniz, Berkeley, Hume, or Kant, give serious thought to the possibility that the awareness that the concrete realities we call "stones" are always immalleable at normal temperatures might constitute a knowledge of a universal sort which is neither constructed nor at all uncertain.

Locke's sketchy psychological analysis of how a child supposedly forms a general notion of "man" is a not untypical example of the sort of descriptive basis upon which the philosophical arguments over "abstraction" usually rest. I shall quote the description *in toto*, for without knowing the sort of "evidence" upon which the tradition depends, the student will never understand why it developed as it did.

> The ideas of the nurse and the mother are well-framed in the children's minds; and, like pictures of them there, represent only those individuals; and the names of nurse and mamma the child uses, determine themselves to those persons. Afterwards, when time and a larger acquaintance have made them observe, that

there are a great many other things in the world, that in some common agreements of shape, and several other qualities, resemble their father and mother, and those persons they have been used to, they frame an idea, which they find those many particulars do partake in; and to that they give, with others, the name man for example. And thus they come to have a general name and a general idea. Wherein they make nothing new, but only leave out of the complex ideas they had of Peter and James, Mary and Jane, that which is peculiar to each, and retain only what is common to them all.[30]

Anyone who has observed a child abstracting, symbolizing, relating, knows that this description is as suspect as it is sketchy. The modern reader might wonder why the eighteenth-century "empiricist" was not more dedicated to analyzing the full complications of a real phenomenon like this.[31] Two centuries of research work were to be required to provide an adequate method for such an undertaking.

Ideas of Cause and Effect

The same mixture of common-sense realistic conviction and of phenomenalism characterizes Locke's analysis of causality, with results similar to those obtained by his analysis of abstraction.

For Locke there can be only one type of causality, efficient causality (formal and final causality are already outdated and can obviously not be deduced from the fragmentary impressions and reflections that constitute the "simple ideas"). Can one, in fact, even speak of efficient causality? The simple ideas we have of bodies, derived from sensation, yield no experience of bodily motion actually beginning. In Locke's seventeenth-century mechanistic world, the only admissible sort of motion and thus of causality is the kind that occurs when a rolling billiard ball collides with another to start it rolling; we can experience a whole chain of such shocks without knowing anything about how the series begins. Such experience is limited to a knowledge of "passive power"; i.e., to the ability to receive change. But Locke is hesitant to pay the price of such a concept: in such a world there can be absolutely no freedom nor real activity. He must reinstate them; but not in the mechanistically conceived "outer world" where they obviously do not fit. Active power, the ability to cause change, can only be truly experienced by exploring the mind.[32] We can infer from the "obscure" experience of passive power in bodies that there must be an active

power at work there, but when we turn to reflect on the operations
of our minds, there is no need to infer, for there we encounter the
"active power" of the will originatively moving the body to action,
and the causality of "thinking" actively combining simple ideas into
complex ideas, which are then real effects of a real mental activity.[33]
It is reflection, then, that "affords us a clear and distinct idea of active
power."

Locke's intention in this analysis is not to undermine our confidence
in the sensible experience of causality, but rather, and more positively,
to secure in our experience an unquestionable basis for our grasp on
the reality of causality. His purpose is not to accentuate the "confusion
surrounding the sensible experience of causality," but merely to underscore the clarity and adequacy of the notion to be obtained internally
by reflection. However, while Locke is not interested in pressing the
implications of his remarks, others will be only too willing to do so.
Leibniz will suggest that reflection must constitute an independent
source of objectively valid ideas if we are able to draw out of ourselves
something we cannot secure in external experience. Hume will jump
on the suggestion that cause is traceable to mental conditions and suggest that it is merely the imagination's way of structuring experience.
A passing remark Locke had made about the tendency of the *fancy*
or the imaginative association of ideas to join together inadvertently
such ideas as mode and support, beginning of change and active power,
without the benefit of experience to justify it, is all Hume will need.
Whereas Locke considered such association of ideas without the basis
of the "natural order of connections" to be the beginning of bad reasoning and even insanity, Hume will see in the habitual association of
ideas this very same "order of natural connection," the source in the
mind of that structuring of experience which makes good reasoning
and sanity possible.

Personal Identity

Because Locke refuses to accept innate ideas and because therefore the mind itself must be considered prior to our first empirical
experience a *tabula rasa*, it becomes necessary to replace the Cartesian
notion of the self as clear and distinct idea with a new explanation of
our kind of identity. We must reject not only the *cogito* explanation
but also any solution in terms of substance. Locke is keenly aware of
the limitations of the idealist conception of substance, which tends to

equate each clear and distinct idea with a corresponding substantial unity, so that man is quickly slit into *two* substances, one material, one spiritual. Now, Locke must seek interior to consciousness for the principle of personal unity; obviously his phenomenalism gives no grounds for seeking it in some kind of objective essence, *man*.[34] To be the same person means to be one and the same "thinking intelligent being, that has reason and reflection, and considers itself as itself, the same thinking thing, in different times and places; which it does only by that consciousness which is inseparable from thinking . . . it being impossible for anyone to perceive without perceiving that he perceives." [35] Here, then, is the *cogito* psychologized; that is, conceived as the psychic function of thinking. Personal identity consists merely in this "sameness of a rational being"; hence it extends only so far as memory can provide the outer limits of my grasp of my own acts.[36]

This is an important discovery in the history of modern philosophy. Locke does little with it. Perhaps he instinctively feels that probing might lead him face to face with solutions that shock common sense, like the psychological cement provided by habit in the philosophy of Hume, or like the transcendental unity of apperception in Kant. His successors will prove less hesitant about developing explicitly what Locke is satisfied to suggest. We must credit Locke in part for these accomplishments, at least to the extent that he set inquiry on the psychological trail that led ultimately to the deeper transcendental viewpoint of Kant.

By rejecting the clear and distinct idea-substance formulation of the problem of man's unity, Locke cleared away all obstacles to conceiving of man in terms of a single principle. He sees quite clearly that if personal unity is to be found in the conscious stream of a psyche, there is really no reason within such a conception for not considering the consciousness and the body as one. Man could be simply a material complexus endowed by God with the attribute of thinking. But, Locke quickly adds, since the idea of *the man* includes the ideas both of bodily structure and of a thinking principle, it is *probable* that the latter is a distinct, immaterial complexus of its own rather than merely a function of the material complexus.

The materialists in the next century—the Diderots, d'Alemberts and d'Holbachs—were not going to let so wonderful a suggestion as that *thinking matter* slip by insufficiently exploited. Nor did Locke's hesitations—the soul is *probably* distinct from the body—make the going any easier for the defenders of an orthodox Christian point of view. About Locke's personal religious conviction in these matters, there is no doubt. But his *philosophy* was driving him to admit, in all honesty, the possibility of a materialist solution; in fact, his formulation of an empiricism of sensory atoms positively encouraged such a view.

The Reality and Extent of Our Knowledge

BUT SUCH CONSIDERATIONS, important as they are, can cause us to lose sight of the central question of the *Essay on the Human Understanding*; namely, that of the reality of our knowledge. It is as preamble to this study that the question of identity takes on its main significance. In the last book of his *magnum opus,* Locke is finally willing to face up to this question, and reversing the analytic movement of the preceding chapters, he turns toward the synthetic task of explaining how all of our ideas compose to form a knowledge representative of a real world.

IDENTITY AS GROUND OF JUDGMENT AND AGREEMENT

THE FIRST STEP in this reassembling is to assert that knowledge, properly speaking, is not to be found yet on the level of the ideas taken in isolation, but in "the perception of the connection of and agreement, or disagreement and repugnancy, of any of our ideas." [37] It is only when the mind composes, divides, and reflects; it is only when the principle of personal identity is at work, that an enduring entity or principle of knowledge can be said to be present before the spirit. Locke does not, as the transcendental idealists later will, explicitly underscore the assembling activity of the spirit as the making-come-to-be-in-time that accounts for the being of the representation; but in locating knowledge in the *activity* of seeking agreement and disagreement among ideas, and in the details of his descriptions of the sorts and import of these agreements, he will definitely foreshadow this development. As we just said above: Locke's psychologism is father to the more fundamental transcendentalism of Kant.

The agreement and disagreement of ideas can be of four sorts: 1] identity, or diversity; 2] relation; 3] co-existence, or necessary connection of qualities in a subject;   4] real existence. The first Locke declares to be the foundation of all knowledge and the font of all certitude. In discussing intuition—the act by which the mind grasps the identity of an idea with itself—Locke explains:

> It is on this intuition that depends all the certainty and evidence of all our knowledge, which certainty everyone finds to be so great, that he cannot imagine, and therefore not require, a greater: for a man cannot conceive himself capable of a greater certainty, than to know that any idea in his mind is such as he perceives it to be; and that two ideas, wherein he perceives a difference, are different and not precisely the same.[38]

Locke is thoroughly Cartesian in insisting first on the certitude of the intuition of the identity of an idea, rather than on its relevance to existence, and in making any certitude we may have as to the real existence of an object depend on the prior certitude of the identity of the idea, rather than showing that the identity of the idea with itself in the mind derives from the necessity inherent in the existence of the real things which the ideas represent. The moment the simple ideas were conceived as fragments of real substances, they could carry no such existential necessity in themselves; there remained only the essential necessity of the identity of an idea; that is, the necessity of the idea to be *what* it is. Truth is then separate from existence and can rejoin it only in the fleeting instant of the factual contact, and then in a way which the empiricist is at a loss to explain.

THE VALIDITY OF THE MIND'S ASSEMBLINGS

BY WHAT CRITERIA, then, are we to know whether what is put together or separated by the mind is really so, *outside* the mind? This question, inevitably raised by the approach Locke has taken—an approach which subordinates existential fact to the rational conditions of identity—is the major concern with which Locke finds himself confronted in his concluding chapters. In order to answer it Locke takes us back over the process by which our knowledge grows from simple ideas to complex ones, tracing step by step the kind of claim each sort of knowledge has to being considered real and at the same time showing the *extent* of such claims; that is, what we can legitimately affirm we know.

First he tries to show that the *simple ideas* are necessarily valid because they simply represent what they represent, and so cannot be erroneous. "They represent to us things under those appearances which they are fitted to produce in us, whereby we are enabled to distinguish the sorts of particular substances, to discern the states they are in, and so to take them for our necessities, and apply them to our uses." [39] Note that the accent here is on the *practical* sufficiency of the simple ideas: here is particular experience about the concrete presence and existence of this or that, presented in a way fitted to produce in us what we need to know to survive in the real world.

But such experience, in its primitive state, cannot be termed *science*, for the simple ideas as such have no universality and therefore do not extend in themselves as simple ideas beyond the moment of the sensory experience. Science must do something to extend our knowledge beyond the moment; true knowledge in the full sense of the word begins only with the complex ideas. Still, the ideal of certitude that we must seek among true complex ideas will find its model in the mind's intuition of the identity of its simple ideas; truth, as we have just seen, has its foundation in the intuition of identity, "This is what it is" and "That is different from this." A position fraught with idealist propensities! We have seen what Leibniz can do with such a conception of ideal "necessity."

Mathematical and Moral Complex Ideas

How can certitude be realized among the complex ideas? In broaching the subject, Locke divides the problem, considering first *all complex ideas except those of substances*, and secondly the problem, so absolutely critical for the future of natural philosophy, of a scientific knowledge of *substances*.

"All our complex ideas except those of substances, being archetypes of the mind's own making, not intended to be copies of anything, not referred to the existence of anything, as to their originals, cannot want any conformity necessary to real knowledge." [40] Locke is thinking here first of mathematical knowledge, but he also quickly extends this archetypal validity to morals.

For the mathematical complex idea, the criterion of truth is the compatibility or incompatibility of its components, "and things are not otherwise regarded but as they are conformable to them." So, whether we intuit the connection of one idea with another directly,

or indirectly, by *demonstration* working mediately through inter-
vening steps, the result is absolutely certain. And the resulting complex
ideas are "nevertheless true and certain even of real things existing;
because real things are no farther concerned, nor intended to be
meant by any such propositions, than as things really agree to those
archetypes in the mind." [41] General propositions, we are told a moment
later, are not concerned with existence; it does not matter whether
there really is any such thing as an equilateral triangle in the world,
the principles concerning equilateral triangles will be true; and if there
are things in the world which realize concretely the truth about equilateral triangles in general, then those things can be said to be true
to the extent that they are conformable to our ideas. The same holds
for moral ideas.

> The truth and certainty of moral discourses abstracts from the
> lives of men, and the existence of those virtues in the world
> whereof they treat; nor are Tully's *Offices* less true because there
> is nobody in the world that exactly practices his rules. . . . If it
> is true in speculation, i.e., in idea, that murder deserves death, it
> will also be true in reality of any action that exists conformable
> to that idea of murder.[42]

What is never explained is why it happens that such complex ideas
do often manage to have an applicability to reality. Of the mathematical ideas, Locke asserts with qualification that "they are nonetheless true and certain even of real things existing," [43] even though
they do not pretend to pronounce concerning the nature of things-in-
themselves, but of things *only so far as they conform to our ideas.* The
suggestion is that the simple ideas carry with them, even into the
universal combinations of the complex mathematical ideas, some stamp
of real things, and thus, even if it is evident that the necessity of complex ideas lies in the mind, where idea is connected with idea on the
basis of their internal intelligibility, such universal ideas, when applied
to reality, turn out to be relevant and helpful in the practical order.

Complex Ideas of Natural Substances

There is a lot of wisdom in the sentiments behind *le sage* Locke's
remarks about our knowledge of natural substances. Like Newton, the
philosopher wanted to deal a death blow to the cherished Cartesian
notion that it is possible to deduce logically a science of material objects.
Such a deductive physics was incompatible with his decision to

oppose the innate-idea theory and to derive knowledge of material substances from the simple ideas. Science should not try to meddle with the archetypes of material substances. These archetypes lie without us and cannot be known in themselves. Our only contact with them is through the complexus of simple ideas "supposed taken from the works of nature," but which "may yet vary from them, by having more or different ideas united in them than are to be found united in the things themselves." [44] For, unfortunately, our simple ideas generally "carry with them in their nature, no visible necessary connection or inconsistency with any other simple ideas, whose co-existence with them we would inform ourselves about." [45] Our concern in material sciences is with the secondary qualities; as these are rooted in the primary qualities "in their minute and insensible parts," or in something yet more remote from our comprehension, "it is impossible we should know which have a necessary union or inconsistency one with another." [46] So sciences must of necessity be experimental and stop looking for absolute knowledge. Passages like the following signed the death warrant of alchemy and heralded Boyle's research and with it modern chemistry: ". . . for, not knowing the roots they spring from, not knowing what size, figure and texture of parts they are on which depend and from which result those qualities which make our complex idea of gold, it is impossible we should know what other qualities result from or are incompatible with the same constitution of the insensible parts of gold." [47]

Actually, Locke's skepticism toward science's capacity to discover the absolute explanation of the world and the true essence of things is rooted in a deeper and more serious difficulty, one rendered especially acute by his own philosophy: "There is no discoverable connection between any secondary quality and those primary qualities it depends on." [48] Even if we were to discover the "size, figure, or motion of those invisible parts which produce them," [49] we would still see no necessary connection between these minutiae and the primary qualities themselves. The trouble is, suggests Locke, that primary qualities—size, figure, motion are the ones he mentions here—just do not seem to have anything to do with our sensations of yellow color, sweet taste, etc.; "there is no conceivable connection between the one and the other."

The conclusion Locke must draw concerning the conduct of natural philosophy is clear: Although some necessary dependence and necessary connection can be known between a few of the primary qualities, for example, that figure necessarily supposes extension, "yet there are so few of our ideas that have a visible connection one with another, that we can by intuition or demonstration discover the co-existence of very few of the qualities that are to be found united in substances; and we are left only to the assistance of our senses to make known to us what qualities they contain." [50] We know that the yellow color, weight, malleableness, fusibility and fixedness of gold go together because we see and feel them in the same substance; and we can be fairly sure that, were we to find any four of these qualities together in some thing, the fifth would also be there. "But the highest probability amounts not to certainty, without which there can be no true knowledge." [51] Locke thus accepts a Cartesian notion of what it is to know, on the basis of philosophic reasons he considers irrefutable, and concludes that we can enjoy no such knowledge of substances outside us. In this way, he hopes to block natural scientists from vainly pursuing a deceptive course toward the deduction of essences.

> In these we can go no further than particular experience informs us of matter of fact, and by analogy to guess what effects the like bodies are, upon other trials, like to produce. But as to a perfect science of natural bodies (not to mention spiritual beings), we are, I think, so far from being capable of any such thing, that I conclude it lost labor to seek after it. [52]

Locke's vision of the science of the future has proved in one essential respect far more exact than the Cartesian prediction: Science is to be a never-ending, by nature never-satisfied quest, its conclusions always tenuous, always subject to revision as experimentation advances and experimental tools improve. Yet science can be said to acquire some truths "once and for all." Only the realistic position, which admits the possibility of a grasp of certain truth short of a perfect knowledge of being, can explain the actual evolution of a science that is neither deductive nor absolutely uncertain.

THE KNOWLEDGE OF EXISTENCE

IF THE OUTLOOK for our knowledge of essences is a bit dark, what about our knowledge of particular existence? "Hitherto we have only considered the essences of things, which, being only abstract ideas, and thereby removed in our thoughts from particular existence, give us no knowledge of real existence at all." [53] Locke has repeatedly made it clear that general ideas have nothing to do with existence. What kind of knowledge do we have then of this principle of "particularity"? The philosopher discovers an access to existence corresponding to each of the degrees of knowledge of which we are capable: an *intuitive* knowledge of our own existence; a *deductive-demonstrative* knowledge of the existence of God; and a *sensible* knowledge of "other things."

That Locke should anchor our knowledge of existence in an internal intuition of our own being, completely divorced from any embarrassing questions about the existence and nature of other things, comes as no surprise. Whatever problems may arise around our sensible knowledge of the existence of material things, at least a fundamental knowledge of something real is thus secured, and in the best Cartesian fashion.

Nor is it surprising or any the less Cartesian the way Locke demonstrates God's existence, beginning with the certain intuition of one's own existence and proceeding deductively to demonstrate that there must exist a Creator who made me. However, Locke is not inclined to accept the Cartesian proof based on the idea of a Perfect Being, for such a way too obviously involves a leap from the order of idea to the order of existence, and what Locke wants to show is that we have a sound knowledge of existence independently of any logical analysis of our ideas.

In exposing his proof, Locke invokes a strange kind of ontological intuition for which there is absolutely no preparation in any of his positions up to this point. After recalling that we enjoy a direct intuition of the fact of our existence, Locke goes on: "In the next place, man knows by an intuitive certainty that bare nothing can no more produce any real being, than it can be equal to two right angles." [54] The question might be raised: On what grounds do we know that some being has been produced? By an intuition of our own internal operations we can know that some being *is;* and Locke might even argue that in those operations we see new impressions beginning to exist; from which we might conclude to the productive effort of our consciousness, but not to any genuinely original creative act. Be this as it may, Locke is nevertheless quite certain what *kind* of a God he wants to prove; namely, an all-powerful, intelligent being, wholly immaterial, the providential origin of the unity and perfection of the visible world . . . the traditional God "proven" with the ruins of what was once a very profound argument, the proof from causality. A feeble proof for the traditional God will always turn into an invitation for his "destruction" at the hands of later thinkers.

Locke argues hard for the reality and suitability of our sensory knowledge of material things. While we can only be sure of what we are sensing right now—our past knowledge of things being only as strong as our memory, and our knowledge of the future being only probable—the present sensation, while not as absolutely certain as either the intuition of our existence or the deduction of the existence of God, is "yet an assurance that deserves the name knowledge." [55]

> This evidence is as great as we can desire, being as certain to us as our pleasure and pain, i.e., happiness or misery; beyond which we have no concernment either of knowing or being. Such an assurance of the things without us, is sufficient to direct us in the attaining the good and avoiding the evil which is caused by them, which is the important concernment we have of being made acquainted with them.[56]

Sensory knowledge is adequate, then, to the practical end of avoiding pain and seeking pleasure. Its debilities in the theoretical order—the fact that it cannot found a universally valid science of the natures of material things—in no way takes away from the efficacity of this candle's flame to tell me when I touch it that I would be better off somewhere else.

To bolster confidence in this principle of practical knowledge of concrete existences, Locke points to a number of sound indications that sensation has to do with real beings. First there is the fact that those who are wanting an organ are devoid of a sense, which indicates that the sensations are of external origin, passing by the channels of the different senses. Then there is the fact that a real and present sensation is a very different affair from a mere memory of the same sort of sensation. This is even more striking in the case of the pleasure or pain that accompanies a given sensation: the dentist's intervention is always even worse than my memory of it, accompanied as it is by exquisite overtones of dolor that I always forget. Finally, the very good point that our senses assist one another's testimony of the existence of outward things.[57]

This analysis of the practical reliability of sensation, coupled with the previous pessimistic remarks about the possibility of a certain science of material things, tends to point up the importance in man's life of the feel-your-way-along world of practical affairs. Not an ideal basis for the sciences of nature, his *Essay on the Human Understanding* is highly consistent with the fact that John Locke is remembered as one of the great political philosophers of the eighteenth century, and as the philosopher of political common sense at that.

Locke's Political Philosophy

LOCKE BEGAN PHILOSOPHIZING, we recall, because he wanted to find a solid base upon which to rest the arguments about practical religious and political problems he had been having with his friends. Locke's later influence as a moralist was not very great; but his *Two Treatises of Civil Government* evolved a political and social philosophy that had a lasting effect on the destinies of England and the United States.

Locke believes in the existence of a natural law, based in the will of God. Human moral and political conduct needs ultimately to be grounded in this law. Unfortunately, men often do not know this well enough; consequently, the law has to be made to appeal to them through motives closer to their self-interest. God has so created man and so willed the law that there is some correlation between what brings happiness to men and what they should indeed seek. Thus when men are motivated politically by the desire to preserve their lives, to appropriate the goods they need for life, and to pursue happiness, these things are not at all out of keeping with God's law. Given men's limitations, it is on this level of the search for self-preservation that Locke feels political philosophy is most meaningfully discussed.

The state of nature[58] was not quite so terrifying as Hobbes made it out to be. After all, men had their reason to guide them—the very reason that eventually brought them to the conviction that a higher form of political organization would advance the common ends of preserving life and property. In the state of nature, all men were equal; this does not mean that all men were the same, only that each was the master of his own destiny, and each was left to forage for the goods he needed to preserve his life. All had the right so to seek; all, in other words, were *free*. Primitive freedom was not license, but simply a natural inborn right of self-determination in the business of securing life and happiness.

Private property[59] grows out of the exercise of this right. What man fundamentally possesses is his own person and his own labor. In the process of acquiring what he needs, he works on the things of the earth, transforming them, mixing his labor with them, and therefore making them in some way his own. Long before the nineteenth-century labor-value theory of the Marxists, Locke contended that almost all the value of a thing came from the labor bestowed upon it; that labor Locke considered individual, rather than belonging to the group. In the state of nature, this right of possession is limited to what a man can produce and consume before it spoils. As one moves toward a more complicated society and money is introduced, it seems tacitly accepted that a man possesses much more than he can personally either produce or consume. The movement from the state of nature to civil society generally accompanies a movement from an almost hand-to-mouth existence to one in which production is sufficiently organized to provide a surplus above pressing needs, a surplus that can be amassed in the form of riches.

The state of nature is by no means idyllic. The appeal to reason and to the natural law does not suffice to restrain men from accumulating more than their fair share of the world's goods. Where there is no clear law defining the proper bounds, there is no one to settle the disputes that inevitably arise through the conflict of interests, and there is no one to enforce just decisions, even if there were someone to make them.[60] This situation compels men to seek a higher social organization than that which the natural law provides. The independent individual must now agree to give up some of his natural right to pursue his preservation and happiness precisely as he alone sees fit, and he must agree to cease altogether serving as his own settler of disputes by being his own judge and executioner. This agreement to alienate some of one's freedom constitutes the *social contract* which establishes the state.[61]

The notion of government that Locke wants to support with his social-contract theory is a moderate one, removed from either the divine-right-of-kings theory or Hobbes' crushing *Leviathan* state. Locke is in fact the spokesman for the Whig settlement, which, in an aura of good common sense, established the English monarchy within severe constitutional limits. Locke stresses the point that the people do not hand over their liberty to the state lock, stock, and barrel, but only enough of it to help them achieve the natural end of preservation of life and pursuit of happiness through possession of needed property. The people remain the possessors of the real ground of all power. If the government abuses its power and goes beyond merely assuring the "better preservation of property," then its legitimacy is forfeited, power reverts to the people, who are then in their right in establishing another government. Revolution in such a case is just.

Political power in Locke's commonwealth clearly resides, then, in the will of the majority. Locke apparently believes that reason will persuade most men to pursue a course of enlightened self-interest. They will be motivated by "the common good," a conception that remains extremely vague in Locke's *Treatise*. The possibility that the majority might turn tyrannous is gingerly avoided. But of course no one has an answer for those cases where a whole people seems to renounce the restraints of reason. Where, however, we might wish for better definition of "common good" is in regard to the state's role as uniquely defender of property. Locke did make it clear that property was intended to assure the individual liberty and happiness. But a richer analysis of the end of the civil society might have helped prevent his teachings from becoming so associated with the *laissez-faire* attitude fostered by the nineteenth-century bourgeoisie. Had Locke been able to see what would be made of his doctrine, he might have felt more inclined to more careful definition.

XIV

The Influence of Newton

JOHN LOCKE's junior contemporary, Isaac Newton,[1] influenced the course of philosophy as much as the wise Locke. In him, English science, already renowned,[2] achieved its Golden Age. It was not the content of his new revelations of the physical world that caused the impact. Their importance was, of course, very great, and their effect on science enormous. But the nature of Newton's contribution in science was not so much the addition of new truths; actually, all the basic elements of the theory of universal gravitation had been discovered long before Newton. Descartes had propagated the laws of inertia, Kepler's three laws of the motions of planets formed an important part of it, Huyghens had worked out for terrestrial bodies the mathematics for expressing the stone's staying in the sling, etc.[3] It was the way Newton, through a few incredibly simple intuitions, pulled all of this together into a clear and uncomplicated synthesis that amazed his contemporaries and convinced them that the method by which he accomplished this must be *IT*. Newton's influence on philosophy is not due to his properly philosophical and theological writings (about which we shall say something below), nor to the *doctrines*, so to speak, encompassed in the great theory, but rather to the impression he gave of achieving the perfect marriage of empirical and rational elements—or, as Kant would say, of the *a posteriori* and the *a priori*.

What really convinced those of an anti-idealist turn of mind that Newton had found *the* way to tap the truth was the fact that he had been able to soar from phenomena observed on this earth out to the ends of the solar system, and there apply them mathematically, after which he could observe these things and discover that what he projected as probably the case actually turned out to be just as he foretold. See the wonderful movement of thought: from empirical observation of phenomena one rises by induction to principles expressive of the general nature of the relationships involved. Then, through the medium of a mathematical formulation of these relationships, one deduces the results one should obtain when applying these formulae to the gross phenomena of the planetary system. Whereupon one returns to empirical observation to verify the conclusions; i.e., to see if the planets show up where they should if everything really works as projected. Newton himself emphasized in the *Principia philosophiae naturalis mathematica* the extreme importance of the final empirical checking because he felt there was nothing anywhere in this process so necessary as a Cartesian deduction. The world, he felt, is not simply a mathematical entity. And Newton was a man who did not like to be hurried into ill-founded absolutization of his conclusions. When, for instance, Cartesian critics got very upset about his reintroducing an "occult power" which they thought they had banished—namely, "attraction" between bodies separated by an empty space—Newton quickly pointed out that he was indicating a function, not pretending to reveal the essence of the things involved and the innermost secret of their relationship, hence the whole thing should be taken in the spirit of a mathematical relationship.[4]

Newtonian enthusiasts were not always successful in following the master's cautious example. Those who, like Fontenelle, form the bridge from Newton to the eighteenth-century *philosophes,* and who are responsible for first having decided what the general philosophical implications of Newton's achievement must be, like to leave the impression that the whole world is a machine and that Newton's method is perfectly proportioned to the mechanism. Since Galileo, Kepler, and Descartes, men had suspected that the world was a machine. Now, by showing that a comprehension of the working of the smallest part here on earth can become a steppingstone to an understanding of the whole universe and, moreover, by having shown how the parts of the mechanism go together, Newton had confirmed belief in the Great Machine. Better yet, all of this confirms belief in the illimited power of human reason once rightly conducted! The enthusiasm that accompanied the popularization of this scientific breakthrough mounted swiftly until one can speak of a kind of second wave of enthusiasm for science as the answer to man's problems—provided this is not taken to imply that, beyond the reservations of a Pascal, there had been in the second half of the seventeenth century any slackening in interest. Simply, what was before the passion of a few became now the folly of almost the whole upper bourgeoisie, especially in France, where that class was strong and given to intellectual pursuits. Again let us say, we cannot blame Newton for that.

Newton himself was a religious man; in fact, he was more interested in his theological speculations than in his mathematical studies. Newton's theological conceptions tended to be rather poetic, despite the fact that they were take-offs on his physical discoveries, which poetic attitude befits someone who admired the thought of the Cambridge poet, Henry More. So the Great Machine was read by Newton as the very presence of God. Whence comes it that Nature does nothing in vain and always chooses the simplest ways? Whence all the order in the world? The most elegant compaction (*elegantissima compages*) of our solar system? These things cannot be explained by merely mechanical laws, nor could they have come about by a purely natural development. The delicate balance of masses, distances, velocities, and densities could have been arranged only by a supernatural force—to say nothing of the wonders of the animals. Newton is one of the fathers of the favorite eighteenth-century proof for the existence of a watchmaker to explain the wonderful clockwork of the universe. He introduces an element, however, that pleases neither deist nor rationalistic materialist: he points to imperfections in the universe (Newton's favorite example of an imperfection is the confounded comets that come wandering across those *cieux que Newton s'est soumis*, as Voltaire adoringly put it),[5] which require regulation from God. If this were not the case, and the universe could function without God's supervision, God would then seem rather superfluous.[6]

Coupled with this is Newton's view that space, far from being just another phenomenon, is as the very organ of God's presence in the world. This "unlimited and homogeneous sensorium" is an absolute reality not determined by a relation to anything external. In this absolute space are absolute points of reference—absolute places— which, though not sensible, are the points in relation to which all things move. This last position obviously involves an objectification of conditions necessary to render possible the mathematical conception of the universe Newton had proposed. In the *Principia* he seems to waver between his common-sense attitude, that the real space is the space people (*vulgus*) conceive as inseparable from things, and the notion that space must really be as mathematics conceives it. Newton

seems to have become tempted to uphold this last hypothesis by reasons
of natural theology, after having so long resisted for reasons of scientific
truth![7] But on the notion that it is in and through space that God
is in the world, there is no hesitation.

Obviously, if Newton owed his place in the history of philosophy
to his natural theology, one could relegate him to a footnote. But
in Newton's physical doctrine and method "lay a deeper philosophy
than he himself was able to extract from it," as one historian has put
it, and this is why his presence will be so strongly felt in the pages
to come. It was because others—the *philosophes,* David Hume, and
above all Kant—were able to see in the results of the Newtonian
physics epistemological implications Newton was never able to grasp
explicitly that he remains as great an influence as any metaphysician
of the eighteenth century.

6 ⚘ THE PHILOSOPHIES OF THE HUMAN MIND

OUT OF THE COLLISIONS of spiritualism and materialism, innatism and empiricism, was generated the need, if solutions to these problems were ever to be found, to plunge deeper into the workings of the human soul. And indeed the eighteenth century is the century of *psychology*. Two of the figures we shall discuss in this chapter—Berkeley and Hume—are main actors in the drama of the *Götterdämmerung* of idealist metaphysics. But the most important common contribution of all the thinkers we are going to discuss is not their metaphysical insights, but the new horizons they opened in psychology. Not surprisingly, however, it is again those who came most squarely to grips with the deepest metaphysical problems of the tradition who made the most revolutionary advances in psychology too. Berkeley's insistence that the object of knowledge be grasped as an unfolding, living whole enjoying the unity of a style grows directly out of his metaphysical concern: he wanted to explain the objectivity of the object in terms of the dynamic interconnections of ideas rather than through recourse to "matter" as a resisting, objective stuff. Hume's discovery of the mind's active structuring of a received datum through its habits was a key step in the elaboration of the theory of transcendental synthesis which Kant will advance. Neither Condillac nor the thinkers of the anti-Locke reaction we have grouped about Thomas Reid are such monumental philosophers. But their influence on the century—especially that of Condillac—was tremendous. The French were already *psychologues* by nature, but no one in that country did more, since Pascal, to give weight and importance to matters of psychological concern than Condillac.

XV

George Berkeley

$\mathbf{A}$T TRINITY COLLEGE, Dublin, the young George Berkeley[1] had evidently read the modern philosophers carefully. From Descartes he retained the conviction that there is nothing more certain than my own act of thinking. From Malebranche he learned that the objectivity and reality of those thoughts that I find populating my mind are fundamentally dependent on the ultimate, infinite Mind, the creative source of all intelligibility and all being. From Locke he discovered that an empiricist, devoted to serving the cause of common sense, could also conclude that what I know are first of all ideas and that the problem of their objectivity has to be solved from within the starting point of a mind thinking its own thoughts. From all of them he learned that there is a problem in relating my representations to that inert, mysterious material substance, that "something" lying behind these impressions, that has for so long now been supposed as the ground and source of unity of all sensations.

Berkeley had also read the Monster of Malmesbury—the redoubtable materialist, Hobbes, who had convinced him of the danger of according any independent existence in itself to a resistant material principle; for this invites subordination of all human spiritual activities to the mechanism of matter. Berkeley seems to have been convinced from an early age that either "matter" has to be entirely reabsorbed into the perceptive operations of spirit, or spirit will risk being explained away in terms of a materialist psychology whose one basic concept is the notion of an extended reality that functions mechanically.

The young divine saw that, regardless of what may or may not really be outside us, we know only what is "actually imprinted on the senses," or what we can recall in the memory of what was once so imprinted, with the exception, of course, of what we can know by reflecting on the operations of the mind itself. Since it is *ideas,* and only ideas, that we know, what then is the point of supposing that there must be *behind* the impressions a no-one-knows-what supporting them, a mysterious something which, by definition, can never be known in itself by a finite mind? Might it not be possible to undercut all of the violent and apparently futile arguments about the nature of substance as such simply by concluding that what is meant when we speak of something being *real* is the fact that it is *really represented in our senses?*

The simplicity of such a solution is overwhelming. Things *are* just their *being perceived*—their *esse* is *percipi.* Swept away with one blow are all problems of bridging the subject-object gap; gone are all suspicions that what we perceive in things is at best a surface and subjective foam on an unfathomable ontologic deep. Yet the subject-object opposition retains its most basic and helpful sense, that of the opposition of knower and known: the activity of the mind as *percipere* is clearly distinguishable from the received impression, the *percipi.* To insure the objectivity of the thing perceived—its otherness—there is no need to posit in it an impenetrable principle which past philosophers mistakenly considered necessary to establish, that the object was not an arbitrary product of the mind's activity. There do exist, as a matter of fact, such arbitrary products—the figments of the imagination. But even a moment's reflection will establish the essential contrast between the passively received sense impression, which comes to me almost against my will, and the product of an active imagination, which product is willed and fabricated according to the dictates of whimsy. Moreover, the products of the imagination themselves bring out vividly our essential dependence on the receptivity of objective sensation: our wildest images can be compounded only of material furnished by the senses; the imagination cannot extend the empire of our knowledge a single iota.

A radical experiment, this immaterialism of the young Irish philosopher! Could it be made to work? The advantages were evident, if it could: conceptual simplicity, an end to the serious "thing-in-itself" problem that plagued modern philosophy ever since Descartes convinced his contemporaries that philosophizing had to begin with ideas, a reinterpretation of "extension" that could remove the last bit of tension between this fundamental physical notion and the spirituality of the order of knowledge. Above all, there were incontestable apologetic advantages to be gained: the most important of these become evident only as the argument develops; but it is already obvious from the start that spirit will become all-important and that God is going to have to be called in as principal support for the intersubjective objectivity of the "real" world, thus making himself too indispensable to be tampered with. This positive goal, the magnification of God's role, was Berkeley's keenest desire.

But a host of difficulties will have to be overcome first. Berkeley is a significant philosopher, not because he was able to cope with all of them and thus assure the triumphs of immaterialism, but rather because he managed to overlook no serious objection: he confronted all honestly, if not always successfully, and in the process, because of the brilliant way he pursued his radical idea, succeeded, as perhaps no one else has, by his very failure, to show that traditional philosophy had perhaps been right after all in having recourse to a principle "other" than idea and resistant to it, a receptacle in its own right of a deposit of the divine creativity. In other words, by default, Berkeley helps re-establish the need for a certain dualism including a principle that is what Aristotle would call "potential." Kant will be haunted by this realization, although he in his turn will have grave difficulties dealing with it. Finally, where his positive successes are greatest— especially in calling attention to psychological phenomena previously overlooked—he becomes a power to reckon with, a genuine influence on the whole eighteenth century.

Berkeley makes no secret of what he considers the most serious problems facing what we might call his "spiritual empiricism." In the attempt to make "objective reality" synonymous with our perceptions, two correlative steps have to be taken to assure that the totality of our experience will constitute a homogeneous, subjectively possessed reality: 1] He must show that all our experience is concrete and intuited sensibly; 2] he must show that every element of that concrete experience must be sustained by the knowing subject. For there are two remnants of realism in Locke's otherwise thoroughly idealized analysis, and Berkeley must neutralize both of them: the suggestion that there are universals ("abstract absolute natures," Berkeley calls them), and the suggestion of transcendence that still hangs around the notion of the "primary qualities." What we are going to see Berkeley do now is directed at eliminating any chance that such realistic elements might ambiguously survive.

An Attack against Abstraction

IF THERE REALLY were such a thing as an "absolute nature" shared by many concrete individual things (the existence of which Locke was certainly persuaded of but did little to explain), then there would be introduced into the very heart of our *subjective* knowledge an element the essence of which is to belong *objectively* to things existing in themselves. An "absolute nature" could never be reduced to *this* peculiar concrete set of sensations—this individual glint of color, combined with this shape, this pungent odor, and this slimy feeling. One would have to maintain that there must be "something more" to it—a reality that could manifest itself through a whole series of different sets of sensory impressions of the same individual, and could appear in sensory impressions representing many different individuals of the same type. We would therefore have to believe in some principle "behind" and supporting the sensory impressions as source of their structure and sense. But what could this "something" be? All the explanations Berkeley had read in the modern tradition slunk wearily every time into the bogs of "substratums" that were not perceptible and yet accounted for every series of perceptions. That was the beginning of all the trouble he hoped to eliminate.

Yet George Berkeley could not for a minute toy with the temptation of utter nominalism—not in an age of science,[2] when science depends on some sort of generalities for its success, certainly not in the face of Locke's long descriptions of "general" terms, the importance of which could hardly be denied. "Here it is to be noted," writes our author in the Introduction to his main treatise, *The Principles of Human Knowledge*, "that I do not deny absolutely that there are general ideas, but only that there are any *abstract* general ideas." How can an idea become general without being abstract? Simply by representing a number of similar "particulars" in things that resemble one another, but without pretending to be the intuition of their absolute nature. We can separate particularities from particularities in order to leave out certain differences between individuals, as when I drop all that is peculiar only to John, to note only those particularities about John which also apply to Peter. John may be very tall, and Peter very short; fine, let us leave aside these considerations if we want to consider what they have in common; namely, the possession of some bulk quite within the normal range particular to all human beings. I can leave behind that which is particular to all men and form a general idea of animal; this idea does not somehow mysteriously transcend all the particularities represented in concrete sensations, but is itself still a group of particularities which I can sense in this concrete slinking leopard, that lazy old cow, and this mustached cowherd.

In opposing the false notion of abstraction, Berkeley would have us bear in mind two points: 1] First, the fact that, whenever we call to mind an "abstract" idea, we are obliged to represent it to ourselves by means of a concrete image. I cannot *imagine* a triangle that is neither isosceles, scalene, nor equilateral, for when I attempt to think of a triangle, I must always put before the mind's eye a definite image. The Cartesians would reply that this necessity results from a limitation of the imagination, which does not affect the understanding. Berkeley does not push his point very far; he is content to leave us with the impression that even the most general ideas are still compounded of positive, particular traits, and hence are always rather concretely representable. 2] The other point is the preposterousness, whatever Locke might have thought, of the suggestion that things can be separated which in fact cannot exist apart. Motion cannot really be conceived apart from a concrete body that moves; color cannot really be separated from extension, and extension from a determinate concrete entity.

The Nature of the Concrete Thing

WHAT IS BEHIND THIS LAST OBJECTION is nothing less than an important new conception of the nature and presence in knowledge of the concrete thing, one which Berkeley is convinced faithfully adheres to the givens of common sense and even to Locke's own basic premises. Locke has written, "Sensible things are those only which are immediately perceived by sense. . . . Sensible things therefore are nothing else but so many sensible qualities, or combinations of sensible qualities." [3] Such a definition accords perfectly with common sense, if we only understand what "our sensible experience" really means. I smell an odor; that really means there is interior to my perception an odoriferous impression. I see a horse; to me, a real horse is a perceived horse, perceived either actually by me, or formerly by me, or actually by some other spirit. To think of a horse "existing" without being perceived is nothing short of a contradiction, for what can that possibly mean? Certainly, I can imagine a closed closet filled with books actually perceived by no one—I can imagine it, because I simply separate arbitrarily the books from a perceiver, although in reality books that are utterly unperceived by any mind—even the mind of God—just simply would not be.

When Locke asserts that sensible things possess "a real absolute being, distinct from, and without any relation to their being perceived," he asserts something perfectly gratuitous in terms of his own most fundamental descriptions of perception. What is worse, such an "absolute" existence would be something that would inevitably escape our perception, since its only particularity is that it exists over and beyond our sensations.

This conception of the sensible thing as *percipi* requires Berkeley to take a stand in regard to the hoary dispute over the primary and secondary qualities. He is glad to step into the arena and clear up this confused business once and for all. Berkeley accepts with gratitude Locke's neat job of showing how the secondary qualities—colors, sounds, tastes, etc.—are not "the resemblances of anything existing without the mind." [4] This leaves only half of the job yet to do: Berkeley will have little trouble extending this subjectivization to the primary qualities. "They will have our idea of the primary qualities [extension, figure, motion, rest, solidity—Berkeley accepts Locke's innovation—and number] to be patterns or images of things which exist without the mind, in an unthinking substance which they call matter." But extension, figure, etc., are only ideas, just like any other ideas; and, like all ideas, they must by definition exist in the mind. Locke had argued that the difference between primary and secondary qualities is that the secondary qualities cannot be conceived apart from other sensible qualities. But the same is true of all of the primary qualities: there is no "motion" existing all by itself; rather, there is movement of a colored, tangible, extended thing. "It is not in my power to frame an idea of a body extended and moving, but I must withal give it some color or other sensible quality which is acknowledged to exist only in the mind." [5] Thus endeth the story of the seventeenth century's cherished notion, born of Galileo's effort to secure a mathematical analysis of the material world, that primary and secondary qualities should be distinguished. The ever-increasing subjectivization of our grasp of qualities as the criticism of the later thinkers continued, very justifiably brought Berkeley to throw the whole affair into radical question. Subsequent to Berkeley's attack, the problem fades in importance, as principles of interpreting our experience of the world in a non-mathematical but a more psychological way come to the fore.

The bishop-to-be has a field day, then, with every opening Locke left for subjectivism. We have already seen several. There are still others. For instance, Berkeley latches onto Locke's analysis of relative notions, "great and small, swift and slow," etc., "changing as the frame or position of the organs of sense varies." [6] With the help of a bit of careful description of our real experience, he is quickly able to show that the sphere of the relative (and therefore, he concludes, the subjective) is much greater than at first suspected—in fact, it is, we might say, using Kant's word, transcendental; i.e., a characteristic of all our knowledge. "Extension" as such, "motion" as such are abstractions, because all motion falls under the regime of "fast and slow," all extension under "big and small," and these are terms relative to the perceiver's position. Let Berkeley say it: "Thus we see how much of the tenet of extended movable substances existing without the mind depends on the strange doctrine of *abstract ideas*." [7] Try to pin down any of those supposedly rock-solid primary qualities to a real, concrete, perceptual experience and you will find that they are very different "in real life" from the trumped-up lifeless abstractions Locke has tried to make of them. Such abstractions are pure fantasies.

We have been stressing the negative aspect of Berkeley's attack on the notion that things exist independently of the mind and in so doing possess characteristics that seem to transcend the level of experience. And we are not finished with the negative side of our story yet—there is still the final blast against the incoherence of the notion of "material substance" to be considered. But before we enter into this supreme moment of annihilation, let us pause along the way to remind ourselves that the ultimate goal of all this is positive, and that at least one very real gain for the future of philosophy has already been reaped as a kind of by-product of this attack on Locke.

This is Berkeley's insistence that consciousness has to be considered more as a living whole than as a mere sum of lifeless parts. Because he wishes to eliminate an inert, mysterious material substance as "support" of a series of impressions, he is required to ground the various impressions we have of one and the same thing in the dynamic spirit itself instead. It would be an exaggeration to suggest that Berkeley realized very fully the implications of such a position; we cannot even say that he had turned his back definitively on the empiricist "atomism" of his predecessors, for he still talks as though the fundamental building blocks of all experiences are isolated sensations of color, sound, etc. Still, he does show that no sensation of any quality ever stands alone; that each implies others in its very sense; that all work together to present "things"; and that all are relative, not only to the knower himself, but, he suggests, to one another. Berkeley draws a spiritualist conclusion from all this: The various impressions owe their reality to the spirit that sustains them. A later philosophy will push the description farther and show that their implication of one another is a manifestation of their intentional reality. As we shall see in a moment, in attempting to explain that our ideas are real and objective, Berkeley skirts close to such a discovery.

The Attack on "Material Substance"

WE CAN APPRECIATE THE NUANCES of the bishop's positive position better if we try to understand more sensitively what it is about the notion of "material substances," conceived as the Cartesians thought of it, that repels him, much as a generation of phenomenologists two hundred years later will be repelled by the notion of a "thing-in-itself" hiding behind the perceived phenomena of our experience.

The philosopher bears down hard on the notion that matter is a substratum *supporting* accidents.

> If we inquire into what the most accurate philosophers declare themselves to mean by *material substance*, we shall find them acknowledge they have no other meaning annexed to those sounds but the idea of *Being in general*, together with the relative notion of its supporting accidents. The general idea of Being appeareth to me the most abstract and incomprehensible of all other; and as for its supporting accidents, this cannot be understood in the common sense of those words (as when we say that

pillars support a building); it must therefore be taken in some
other sense, but what that is they do not explain.[8]

We know what Berkeley thinks of abstraction! That "abstractest"
of all conceptions, Being, is, then, just nothing. With this conclusion, one cannot hesitate to agree: the notion of Being of which
Berkeley is thinking is not what the Thomist means by its analogy,
but the general idea of that bare "something" remaining after all
particularities are separated from our experiential notions. What remains in the way of a "clear and distinct idea" of Being, is really
nothing at all. And in attacking the non-sense of the much-abused
notion of the "support" furnished by the Cartesians' substratum,
Berkeley is again justified within the limits of his own philosophical
tradition. The whole business of support had been gratuitously assumed by Cartesians and empiricists alike, without any acceptable
"clear and distinct" or "common sense" ontological explanation. Given
their chosen starting points, neither the Cartesians nor Locke could
ever offer this explanation. Descartes cannot, for he has so thoroughly
"interiorized" substance by making it a clear and distinct idea that
already in the famous analysis of the melting piece of wax the reader
can hardly keep from thinking of Berkeley: it sounds for all the
world as though the *support* of all those changing qualities—the smell,
the feel, the taste of the wax—was the spiritual act of the *ego cogito*
itself rather than anything existing outside. Similar impressions follow
our reading of Malebranche, Spinoza, and Leibniz—in every case, the
final principle of unity for the row of qualities manifested by a thing
seems much more a knowing *spirit* than an inert thing-in-itself. In the
case of Locke, whose personal belief in the existence, independent of
all mind, of material substances was as firm as Aristotle's, there is no
hope for him, given the chosen starting point of his analysis of our
experience, ever to make any sense of the notion. For once it is
granted that what we are presented with in sensation are separate
impressions whose fundamental reality is to be ideas, then the joining
of these images becomes purely an affair of ideas, exactly in the spirit
of Berkeley's famous dictum, *"an idea can be like nothing but an
idea."* [9] The knowledge of substance seems equated in Locke to the
compounding of complex ideas from simple ideas, the subjectivity of
which process, despite Locke's objectivist faith, never ceased to strike
us.

Even if we grant philosophers their "material bodies," he points out, that won't advance anything, "since they own themselves unable to comprehend in what manner body can act upon spirit, or how it is possible it should imprint any idea in the mind." [10] Without such an explanation, the concept of "matter" adds nothing to our understanding. "If therefore it were possible for bodies to exist without the mind, yet to hold they do so, must needs be a very precarious opinion; since it is to suppose, without any reason at all, that God has created innumerable beings that are entirely useless, and serve to no manner of purpose." [11] Obviously, the only purpose a created thing can have is to be an idea in a spiritual mind.

Useless, worse than useless, this notion of "matter" as support of "qualities" which are really the ideas we have of those qualities; for it involves a couple of terrible contradictions. Material substance is said to be *inert*, and still at the same time we are supposed to believe that it is the *cause* of ideas in us. It is supposed to be *unperceiving*, and still it is supposed to possess qualities whose mode of existence, according to Berkeley, is *to be perceived* by the spirit. If there is a tragic flaw in the philosopher's whole attack, it is right there in his acceptance of Locke's supposition that, because the only qualities in our experience are known ones, they must simply be nothing but *ideas*.

Defense of the Reality of the Sensible World

PRECISELY to the extent Berkeley feels he has succeeded in disclosing the confusing meaninglessness of "material substance," he has generated for himself another, this time a more positive, problem: that of defending the "reality" of a sensible world unsupported by material substance, a world existing only in the spirit.

Berkeley has no desire to dissolve the world into subjectivism. He has been repeatedly so interpreted, today as well as in his own time; against such an interpretation he has struggled valiantly. The main prong of his argument has to be, of course, a new interpretation of what it means for something to be "real." Berkeley approaches the problem through the savant use of a telling contrast. I notice that I can excite ideas in my mind at pleasure, varying and shifting the scene as often as I wish, simply by *willing*.[12] Such ideas are fanciful and arbitrary. But, whatever may be the power I have over my own thoughts, I find the ideas actually perceived by *sense* do not depend in this way on my will. When I open my eyes in broad daylight, it is not in my power to choose whether I shall see or not, or to determine what particular objects will present themselves to my view. "The ideas imprinted on [my senses] are not creatures of my will. There is therefore some other will or spirit that produces them." [13]

This receptivity of the ideas of sense, in contrast to the activity that characterizes ideas called up by the will in the imagination, is accompanied by other indications of their "reality." "The ideas of sense are more strong, lively and distinct than those of the imagination; they have likewise a steadiness, order and coherence, and are not excited at random, as those which are the effects of human wills are, but in a regular train or series, the admirable connection whereof sufficiently testifies the wisdom and benevolence of its Author." [14] Many decades later, Edmund Husserl, also seeking from within an analysis of the givens of consciousness, to awaken in his readers a feeling for the reality of that stream of experience, will likewise fall back on the consistency, the order, the sense of a temporal flow of representations. The phenomenologists will push their analyses much further than Berkeley in search of details of that logic, that "unity of style," which provides so much internal evidence of the fact that our experience has a meaning far transcending the mere fact of its appearance-in-consciousness. Berkeley indeed at once gives a characteristically eighteenth-century turn to what we have called his encouraging discovery of the fact that experience really needs to be considered as a sense-bearing whole if we are ever to understand its ontologic significance. He immediately thinks of this unity of style, if we may so term it, as a "set of rules" or "established methods" which he hastens to label *the laws of nature*. These we learn by experience, which teaches us that such and such ideas are attended with such and such other ideas, in the ordinary course of things. Berkeley is obviously in a rush to turn his discovery into a quick guarantee for the usefulness of some sort of science. This regularity with which idea follows idea (how Humean a way of putting it!) gives us, he announces, "a sort of foresight which enables us to regulate our actions for the benefit of life." [15]

Admitting even this much regularity in the way one idea follows another risks reintroducing into the ideas themselves, precisely as *other*, a certain independence, a certain causal necessity, as though one idea worked upon another. Berkeley will not permit such a dangerous opening in his anti-materialist offensive line; but in closing it, he leaves his flank utterly unprotected against Hume. We must not attribute "power and agency" to the ideas themselves, he says, as though one were the cause of another, "than which nothing can be more absurd and unintelligible." [16] Berkeley does not go to the trouble of elaborating in this text a non-causal explanation for the phenomenon of this regularity. The suggestion from the whole context seems to be that the will of the Infinite Spirit is responsible for the regularity. Hume will provide a much less metaphysical, indeed a thoroughly *psychological*, explanation for this regularity, as we shall in due course see.

Berkeley's next move is to underscore the distinction between the mind and its sensory ideas. For one thing, he attacked the notion that ideas are "modes" in a subject-mind. He wanted us to see that the ideas are *objects* in the mind, not properties flowing from it.[17] The point is, as he goes on to explain, that the world is really distinct from the perceiver, in the sense that there is a real distinction between the mind and the objects of the mind. That is why the things of our experience manifest themselves as depending only accidentally on the human understanding. We do not know their innermost secrets; we are not a party to *why* one idea follows another. God surely knows, because he is their Creator and absolute Sustainer. As they are presented to us, what we know will form a perfectly coherent story, but an incomplete and always growing one.

This last emphasis on the fact that it is in the divine Spirit that the ideas ultimately lodge, and only accidentally in this or that particular mind, provides great help in forestalling an objection Hume was quick to see: the problem of what happens to the world when my mind is turned off, or worse yet, of whether things cease to exist when nobody at all is perceiving them. Of course, he could argue like Leibniz that the mind, being of its very nature a willing and perceiving activity, never completely stops as long as it exists—and he will so argue; but that does not really touch the gist of the affair. For no matter how continuous my and everybody else's perception may be, neither I alone, nor all of us together, always have the same objects in view, and often many things must be under the actual consideration of no finite spirit. Berkeley is clearly reluctant in *The Principles of Human Knowledge* to call too overtly upon the actual existence of things in

God's mind as the ultimate support of their reality. But that is clearly the implication. For we read:

> Though we hold indeed the objects of sense to be nothing else but ideas which cannot exist unperceived; yet we may not hence conclude that they have no existence except only while they are perceived by us, since there may be some other spirit that perceives them though we do not. Wherever bodies are said to have no existence without the mind, I would not be understood to mean this or that particular mind, but all minds whatsoever. It does not therefore follow from the foregoing principles that bodies are annihilated and created every moment, or exist not at all during the intervals between our perception of them.[18]

The bishop was too thorough a thinker to overlook the fact that no quantity of finite minds would ever suffice to forestall the possibility that nobody would happen to be perceiving this thing right this moment; only an infinite mind can provide the all-encompassing perception, the ultimate, stable spiritual support for the things of our experience.

The Existence of God and the Problem of Intersubjectivity

ONE REASON WHY BERKELEY, although knowing that he must ultimately fall back upon God as support of the reality of the world, is hesitant in his basic work to invoke the divine principle too explicitly is that in attempting a proof for God's existence he is obliged to use as his main arguing point his initial position, that *esse* is *percipi*. When one is playing with a circular argument, it is often best to expose the two semicircles in contexts that remain as distant from each other as possible.

Berkeley's way of approaching the question of God's existence is a peculiar one, as we might expect, given the unusual nature of his immaterialist doctrine. After again recalling the distinction between those ideas which we can call up at will in the imagination and those perceived ideas which occur in the senses without our willing it, the philosopher describes how we know that we are in the presence of another finite spirit. From this he passes to the fact that we can know from the passive way in which we receive all of our perceived ideas that they mark the presence of an infinite spirit. How, then, do we know that we are at a given moment in the presence of another human spirit? "When we see the color, size, figure and motions of a man, we perceive only certain sensations or ideas excited in our own minds . . . we do not see a man—if by *man* is meant that which lives, moves, perceives, and thinks as we do—but only such a certain collection of ideas as directs us to think there is a distinct principle of thought and motion, like to ourselves, accompanying and represented by it." [19] Similarly, we cannot say that we *see* God. But just as we know that the human manifestations received in our sensibility are not caused by us, but by another, so too must we realize that indeed all our passively received perceptions are caused in us by another spirit, "since it is repugnant that they should subsist by themselves." "But if we attentively consider the constant regularity, order and concatenation of natural things, the surprising magnificence, beauty and perfection of the larger, and the exquisite contrivance of the smaller parts of creation, together with the exact harmony and correspondence of the whole," then we must realize what sort of spirit is responsible for this unfailing regularity. It is this spirit, "intimately present to our minds, producing in them all that variety of ideas or sensations which continually affect us, on whom we have an absolute and entire dependence, in short 'in whom we live, and move, and have our being.' " [20]

So the risk of *solipsism*—the risk of arguing to a position that leaves my spirit *solus ipse*, all alone by itself—has to be run. Even though I perceive bodily motions, lips moving, gestures being made, and conclude from them that since I experience myself causing like motions when I talk, these must be produced by a spirit like myself, still, strictly speaking, such an inference does not constitute a proof with the validity of the argument for God's existence. For this problem remains: it has been established, in terms of the most fundamental principles of this philosophy, that ideas are inert, that they cannot themselves cause. So even though I have ideas that seem to emanate from a body like my own, still only God can be the cause of those ideas of motion and speech in me. This is what Berkeley means when he frankly states that God alone can "maintain that intercourse between spirits, whereby they are able to perceive the existence of each other." [21] Conversely, God has to create in other minds the ideas that will correspond with my intentions in moving my body. Here is occasionalism carried to the last extreme. We keep saying that I move my body. Actually, with my will I intend what used to be meant, when men still thought in terms of material substance, by "body." But we have eliminated all that. So now the occasionalism becomes spiritual substantialism: the only mediation between spirits is through the great Substance, the all-encompassing Spirit of God.

Still, when we think of three men standing in a field looking at the same cherry tree, we feel that all of this is highly inadequate. Each of these men, according to Berkeley's principles, would have a different idea of the tree, and what is worse, there isn't any *Baum an sich*! The colonial American philosopher, Samuel Johnson, brandished this problem at Berkeley,[22] and Berkeley did his best to answer it in the *Third Dialogue between Hylas and Philonus*. Berkeley's answer was this: If the word "same" be taken in the everyday sense of the term, then different persons can perceive the same thing, meaning that the ideas in each of the minds of three men have the same reference. Even though this reference is not to a material thing external to them, it is to "an external archetype . . . supposed to exist in that mind which comprehends all things." Is this explanation sufficient to ground an objective truth and a universal science of nature?

A Spiritually Grounded Science of Nature

ACTUALLY THE PROBLEM of grounding a universal science is less of a problem for an idealism than *solipsism*. We have already seen a suggestion of how Berkeley will approach this problem, and that he will lean heavily on the order of *praxis*, that is, the "practical," for help.

Berkeley's task here is more complex than a mere regrounding of contemporary science in his epistemological-metaphysical principles. In view of his ultimate religious program of securing the place of God and of the spirit in modern speculations, he ambitioned nothing less than a critique of the way the seventeenth century mixed mathematical and philosophical demonstration. Berkeley had become thoroughly disenchanted with arguments such as those based on the possibility of dividing to infinity. Such reasonings will be anathema, once we recognize the true limits and validity of mathematical demonstrations.

That the principles laid down by mathematicians are true, and their way of deduction from these principles clear and incontestable, we do not deny; but we hold there may be certain erroneous maxims of greater extent than the object of mathematics, and for that reason not expressly mentioned, though tacitly supposed throughout the whole progress of that science; and that the ill effects of those secret unexamined errors are diffused through all the branches thereof. To be plain, we suspect the mathematicians are as well as other men concerned in the errors arising from the doctrine of abstract general ideas, and the existence of objects outside the mind.[23]

Such a passage as this is evidence that the star of mathematicism is waning. Criticism is advancing; Berkeley's immaterialism is not the product of a personal whim, but of strong arguments against the deficient positions previous philosophers had taken with regard to extension and material substance. What he wants now is that mathematics be brought back under practical control and cease being the source of wild flights of metaphysical fancy. His contribution to this deflation of mathematicism was an effort to undermine the speculative importance of both *numbers* and that conception of *extension* from which the worse pretenses of geometrizing philosophers grow.

The attack against the value of numbers as absolute knowledge begins with an attack on the basic notion of "unity." "Unity" is an abstract idea; there are things that are concretely identified, but there is no "unity" as such. "We say one book, one page, one line; all of these are equally units, though some contain several of the others." [24] Yet numbers are defined as a "collection" of units; so, "if there be no such thing as unity or unit in the abstract, there are no ideas of number in the abstract denoted by the numeral names and figures. The theories therefore in arithmetic, if they are abstracted from the names and figures, as likewise from all use and practice as well as from the particular things numbered, can be supposed to have nothing at all for their object; hence we may see how entirely the science of numbers is subordinate to practice, and how jejune and trifling it becomes when considered as a matter of mere speculation." [25] Elsewhere Berkeley speaks of the "obvious relativity" of numbers; for example, the same extension is one, or three, or thirty-six, according as the mind considers it with reference to a yard, a foot, or an inch. "Number is so visibly relative, and dependent on man's understanding, that it is strange how anyone should give it an absolute existence without the mind." Berkeley could not foresee what would be done with these numbers in modern mathematics. Our young divine wrote only shortly after the invention of the calculus, with an eye to what was past, more than to what was on its way, and his complaint was a rather narrow philosophical one, aimed at those who jump from mathematical speculations to philosophical conclusions. He wished to despoil mathematics of any pretense to enjoy access to a deep layer of reality.

Berkeley's attack on the notion of the infinite divisibility of a line shows this even more clearly. If he is upset at the notion that there are supposed to be, as he puts it, "infinitesimals of infinitesimals of infinitesimals, etc., without ever coming to an end," [26] it is not because he is seeking to undermine the validity of that exercise which is the new calculus—on the contrary, "whatever is useful in geometry, and promotes the benefit of human life, does still remain firm and unshaken on our principles; that science considered as practical will rather receive advantage than any prejudice" from the kind of criticisms Berkeley is offering.[27] But all of this talk about *infinite* divisibility leads easily to the illusion—which the geometers have little desire to dissipate—that one has some special access, through speculations on matter, to the infinite. It is an oversimplification to state Berkeley's grief just this way, but it might help indicate what he is driving at: he approves of Newton's modest restriction of the significance of his explanations, while he would most surely disapprove of the metaphysical conclusions Leibniz draws from his mathematical visions. Of Sir Isaac's method he writes, "This mechanical philosophy does not assign or support any one *natural efficient cause* in the strict and proper sense; nor is it, as to its use, concerned about *matter*; nor is matter connected therewith; nor does it infer the being of matter." [28]

Our philosopher's dispatch of infinite divisibility is carried out very cleverly. The legitimate ideas of extension we have are not abstract but concrete. I do not know "extended line in general" but this line here, one inch long, every part of which I must actually perceive. Now if I do not actually perceive an infinity of parts within this inch —and of course I never can—that is simply because there is no such "infinity of parts," for what cannot be perceived—that is, what has no existence in the mind—has no existence at all. Period.[29]

From the remark about Newton quoted above, we can gather an excellent notion of what Berkeley considered the real limits of mathematical physics to be. That a physics has to be more than concretely descriptive, he was the first to admit, for if it remains concrete, it will get nowhere. Generalization through mathematical tools is perfectly acceptable, so long as the bogus pretenses made for it—for example, by certain zealous followers of Newton—are rejected firmly, whether they happen to seem to advance or to prejudice the cause of religion. Explanations in terms of mathematically formulable "causes" are perfectly all right so long as they instruct and work practically. We must simply realize, however, that such formulae do not touch the *real* causes of things in nature; to wit, minds or spirits. Moreover, the regularity of the laws of nature is not absolutely necessary. God could, if he wanted, make the dials of a clock turn without there being any mechanism behind the face; "but yet, if He will act agreeably to the rules of the mechanism, by Him for wise ends established and maintained in the creation, it is necessary that those actions of the watchmaker, whereby he makes the movements and rightly adjusts them, precede the production of the aforesaid motions." [30] The natural regularity is conditionally necessary—it is regular so long as God in his wisdom so ordains. In the *Dialogues*, Berkeley even refers to it as a *relative* or *hypothetical existence*.

Why does God will such a regularity? That we may know "what to expect from such and such actions, and what methods are proper to be taken for the exciting such and such ideas," [31] not that we might revel in the theoretical knowledge of causes and effects. We must not mistake the connections in nature for causes; "the connection of ideas does not imply the relation of *cause and effect*, but only of a mark or *sign* with the thing *signified*. The fire which I see is not the cause of the pain I suffer upon my approaching it, but the mark that forewarns me of it." [32]

The objection we have just suggested is unavoidable; indeed, it must be said that Berkeley seems to be inviting the full blast of Humean skepticism. What Berkeley is *trying* to tell us, as we have been saying all along, is that we should see in things the sustaining action of God. The bishop does not mean that we see things in God, as Malebranche had taught, but that we can learn to see in all things God's supporting presence—see God in things.

> As in reading other books a wise man will choose to fix his thoughts on the sense and apply it to use, rather than lay them out in grammatical remarks on the language; so, in perusing the

volume of nature, it seems beneath the dignity of the mind to affect an exactness in reducing each particular phenomenon to general rules, or showing how it follows from them. We should propose to ourselves nobler views, namely, to recreate and exalt the mind with the prospect of the beauty, order, extent, and variety of natural things: hence, by proper inferences, to enlarge our notions of the grandeur, wisdom, and beneficence of the Creator; and lastly, to make the several parts of the creation, so far as in us lies, subservient to the ends they were designed for, God's glory, and the sustenation and comfort of ourselves and fellow-creatures.[33]

If there are any "atheists or Manicheans" it is merely "for want of attention and comprehensiveness" on their part. Indeed, for those who want to see, it is evident that " 'the eyes of the Lord are in every place beholding the evil and the good,' that He is present and conscious to our innermost thoughts, and that we have a most absolute and immediate dependence on him." [34] Berkeley does not in his early treatise develop the metaphysics of participation which his position implies, although he will do so in a much later work, the *Siris*. It is clear that the human spirit is sustained by God, and as an active, knowing, willing principle, is somehow halfway between the infinite activity of God and the inertness of the purely passive ideas he causes in us. Human *passivity* is manifest in our dependence on the reception of ideas through the senses; human *activity* consists in our ability to call up and recombine ideas through will. This "in between" nature of man is the key to understanding the nature of his duty.

The Vocation and Duty of Man

How SHOULD MAN command his active nature in a way best suiting his nature and status as a finite spirit? Let us recall first in what Berkeley makes our activity consist. The understanding is passive, in the sense that it must receive its ideas through God's causation. However, the actual act of understanding is something we ourselves must *do*. Most of the philosophers we have been studying, having closed the mind in on itself, and being thus obliged to draw a doctrine of being from the resultant purely idealistic resources, have given great importance to *attention*. Berkeley must obviously be no exception to this: how else explain the nature of the understanding's activity? We have just seen that the great fault of the atheists is essentially their "want of attention." This is accompanied by a want of "comprehensiveness": they err not only by failing to attend to the deep sense of each experience, but also to the whole scope and range of reality. We have emphasized the importance Berkeley attaches to the interpretation of reality as a whole, so preferable to trying to reweave it out of separated strands once they have been extracted, string by string, from the fabric of experience. The importance of this can be illustrated by the need, when interpreting the moral significance of a pain or a pleasure, to project its significance against the backdrop of all that we can know of the divine design of the universe.

> Our prospects are too narrow. We take for instance the idea of some one particular pain into our thoughts and account it *evil*; whereas, if we enlarge our view, so as to comprehend the various ends, connections, and dependencies of things, on what occasions and in what proportions we are affected with pain and pleasure, the nature of human freedom, and the design with which we are put into the world; we shall be forced to acknowledge that these particular things which, considered in themselves, appear to be evil, have the nature of good, when considered as linked with the whole system of beings.[35]

The comprehensiveness of our view must depend then on our willingness to attend to the whole magnificent scope of the ideas the Creator is ready to share with us—that is, with the whole of the natural world.[36] Berkeley's view of the substantial dependence of all things on God's creative support has thus immediate moral consequences. "The apprehension of a distant Deity," he declares in the last *Dialogue*, "naturally disposes men to a negligence of their *moral* actions, which they would be more cautious of, in case they thought him immediately present, and acting on their minds without the interposition of matter, or unthinking second causes." [37] Once again, for the idealist the key to moral rectitude is a correct and comprehensive view of things.

Berkeley's Influence

BERKELEY'S CRUSADE, religious in intent, ironically enough seems to have had a greater influence on the scientifically inclined psychologists of the eighteenth century than it did on the reform of pious souls. What Diderot would later say of the French psychologist Condillac, seems to be valid for the century as a whole: he says that Condillac adopted Berkeley's principles but tried to avoid their consequences—he accepted the psychology of Berkeley's early analysis, *An Essay towards a New Theory of Vision*, without wanting to accept the metaphysics of *The Principles of Human Nature*. It was with the psychological problems, especially the problem of space, that the whole of the Enlightenment, from Fontenelle and Maupertuis, through Voltaire and Condillac, to Kant himself, was to struggle, trying to conquer the central problem of idealism, "a system which, to the shame of the human mind," writes Diderot, "is the most difficult to combat, though the most absurd of all." [38] To understand this development, especially its culmination in Kant, we shall give the last word to a more technical review of what was in fact Berkeley's starting point, both doctrinally and chronologically, in the form in which it will most influence future developments.

If we think of a single ray of light impressing itself on the eye, we cannot imagine that it will be able to tell us anything about an object's distance or its shape—certainly not taken by itself, as a single impression of just *this* ray. It would seem logical that the distance, position, and magnitude of a thing would not be visible; in fact, that there should be structural elements, if we may so put it, which are by nature imperceptible. Yet, in the whole of our experience, spatial perceptions are perfectly united with sensory data; ". . . distance," writes Berkeley, "is in its own nature imperceptible and yet it is perceived by sight." [39] How can this be?

Berkeley's answer is to reconceive perception, not as something to be comprehended in its isolated elements, but as a representational whole, a spectrum of equivalent signs indicating to us the course of action God wishes us to take. Throughout our analysis of Berkeley we have stressed this point repeatedly; the ultimate significance of it will become evident only when we have studied Kant's laicized doctrine of the "transcendental unity of apperception," and of judgment as cohesive agent of a living experience. But it is already in this direction that Berkeley has turned his influence, an influence to be felt throughout the psychology of the century. Every sense impression possesses a reference to other sensations; it is not just its own specific content, but implies other impressions as well. The strong and regular bonds of experience are neither causal nor mathematical-conceptual; this reciprocal play of impressions is a part of experience itself, is the very way we grasp God's will through our five senses at once; the deciphering of which is molded somehow by habit and practice. Our ideas as such belong to no particular sense, no more to sight than to touch. That is why space, to take a crucial example, is not originally given as a color any more than as a tone, but rather is to be found in the relationship among the various sense data. Consciousness has learned to relate tactile to visual data; it is this recognition of equivalence, this unification, which is the true root of the ultimate structures of experience, including space. The habitual, rapid, and smooth nature of this process of unification causes us to overlook it in our reflection; we don't even notice that it involves successive steps. Later psychologists will emphasize these steps, though, and will seize on the experience resulting from the surgeon Cheselden's successful operation in 1728 on a fourteen-year-old boy blind since birth. It was discovered that the youth could not at once correlate his newly acquired visual experience with his long-familiar tactile knowledge, but rather had to learn gradually and laboriously to distinguish between the corporeal forms presented to his vision. Voltaire likened the process whereby sense resides in the whole rather than in its parts to our learning to read.

> We learn to see just as we learn to speak and read. . . . The quick and almost uniform judgments which all our minds form at a certain age with regard to distances, magnitudes and positions make us think that we need only open our eyes in order to see things as we actually do perceive them. This is an illusion. . . . If all men spoke the same language, we should always be inclined to believe that there is a necessary connection between words and ideas. But all men speak the same language with respect to the imagination [Voltaire does seem to wonder why]. Nature says to all: When you have seen colors for a certain length of time, your imagination will represent to you in the same manner the bodies to which these colors seem to belong. The prompt and involuntary judgment which you will form, will be useful to you in the course of your life.[40]

Give the last word in a chapter on Bishop Berkeley to the irreligious Voltaire? It is indeed another of those supreme and all too frequent ironies with which the history of philosophy is liberally sown. But just count all the elements in the last quotation that smack freshly of the text of Berkeley. The Bishop may have spread the cause of a certain subjectivity and even a certain relativism in experience for pious reasons. All through this chapter we have been threatening Hume; after that, a little threat like Voltaire is almost nothing!

The impression made by this notion, that the sense of the whole of experience is relative to the way the experience is put together, had an effect on the age that went far beyond philosophy. In *Gulliver's Travels*, Swift uses the relativism suggested by Berkeley's theory of optics to shrink and enlarge the scale of the universe as one passes from Lilliput to the land of the Brobdingnagians. Voltaire played with the idea in *Micromégas*. It is true, Berkeley had no real immediate successor. But the whole Enlightenment absorbed him, with results surely far from his liking. But who can help it if it is the inner sense of one's doctrines and not one's apologetic aspirations that ultimately prevail?

XVI ❧

David Hume

IN THE INTRODUCTION to *A Treatise of Human Nature*, David Hume[1] wastes no time getting to the spirit of modern criticism: There is confusion in the great science of philosophy, and only criticism can clear it up. Indeed, there is so much confusion within the noble house of philosophy that the rabble standing outside are beginning to wonder if all is well with their captains disputing inside. Obviously, the time has really come to get at the roots of things.

But, we might ask, isn't this just what Descartes had said in those years of disillusionment and skepticism which plagued early-seventeenth-century thought? It is indeed, but the measure of what has since occurred is to be found in the contrasting solutions offered by the two thinkers; Descartes proposed a new science grounded in the certainty of a method inspired by mathematics; but Hume's answer has to take into consideration the vicissitudes of the Cartesian conceptions of extension, matter, and substance under the blows of later thinkers, culminating in Berkeley's attack on the philosophical significance of all mathematics in the name of a deeper analysis of human knowledge than any before attained. A still more fundamental critique of the nature of this knowledge is obviously needed. So, instead of battling peripheral problems, Hume marches directly to what he considers the problem central to all the sciences, human nature itself. "There is no question of importance," states the Introduction, "whose decision is not compriz'd in the science of man; and there is none which can be decided with any certainty, before we become acquainted with that science." The movement started when Descartes located the source of truth in the representational power of the *ego cogito* has now come almost full circle: There can be no truth without criticism, there can be no criticism prior to the elaboration of a psychology of the knowing processes.

Hume launches forthwith into a psychological analysis of human cognition. What follows may in its turn be characterized as the reaping of the whirlwind. We are not sure just what text of Hume fell into the hands of the great sage of Königsberg, but whatever it was, its effect on Kant was, by his own admission, tremendous: "I was awakened from my dogmatic slumber." This slumber was the soporific state brought on by nothing less than the decline of the whole tradition we have been studying. Hume refreshingly opens fire on the mistakes of the whole row of great thinkers from Descartes to Berkeley. He takes his predecessors at their word, accepting their traditional descriptions of how our knowledge is put together from fragments of sensory impression, and then proceeds to show what the *ultimate conclusions* concerning the limits and validity of a knowledge so constructed would have to be; those conclusions are shocking enough to awaken a philosopher from his sleep even in Ostpreussen!

The Nature of Our Ideas

HUME IS DETERMINED to introduce into the fundamental study of man the method that had achieved such resounding success in natural philosophy, Newton's experimental approach. In fact, the *Treatise of Human Nature* is subtitled "An Attempt to Introduce the Experimental Method of Reasoning into Moral Subjects." But how does one apply "the Experimental Method" to an analysis of human nature? Negatively, it means avoiding rationalistic hypotheses about the constitution "in themselves" of material and spiritual substances, and great *a priori* pronouncements about the nature of our reasoning power. Positively, as we shall now see, it means reducing the whole structure of our comportment to its sensory, empirical, "experimental" beginnings. And the old "essences" or "natures," already rejected by the natural philosophers, must be replaced in "moral"—i.e., human—studies by "experimental" descriptions of a more functional nature.[1]

Hume reduces all knowledge to its elements with a grand and simple sweep worthy of Locke; indeed, he accepts as starting point Locke's dust of impressions; his first major distinction he borrows from Berkeley: the contrast of ideas of sense and ideas of imagination. In both cases, however, he has his own purpose in mind and freely changes the traditional terminology to fit it. Sense perceptions he insists should be termed *impressions*, and what is remembered and regurgitated by the imagination, *ideas*, the essential contrast being one of *vividness*: the impressions of sense strike us with a living force, while all ideas, even though they may frequently be very adequate copies, are nonetheless derivative and therefore by nature pale in comparison.[3] Hume chooses this terminology to make as unequivocal as possible the reduction of every element of cognition to a single subjective source; he is not going to run the risk of falling into the ambiguities caused by Locke's distinction between ideas of sense and ideas of reflection, and between the way we know primary and secondary qualities. Hume is not perfectly satisfied with his new terminology—he especially wants to avoid giving the idea that "impressions" are stamped in us by some external cause. But, like Berkeley and Locke, while criticizing realism, he is nevertheless not above leaving the feeling that somehow our ideas do have something to do with the way things are after all.

Are our ideas always simply weak copies of our vivid impressions? Yes, but all ideas do not necessarily correspond directly to a real impression. Some of our impressions are simple, others complex; the same thing is true of our ideas. Now some of our complex ideas do not have corresponding to them directly any complex impression. I can summon up a complex idea like "The New Jerusalem" to which there will correspond in my experience no direct complex impression. One can also add that not all complex impressions can be perfectly translated in ideas: When I am receiving directly the complex impression of the whole city of Paris as I look from the Butte Montmartre, I cannot reproduce with my eyes closed, try as I will, the whole rich complexity of the scene. Both considerations reinforce our realization that it is the impressions which count, and above all, the basic, simple impressions. This does not really complicate our problem. When we break down our complex ideas into their simple components, we find a universal one-to-one agreement: corresponding to every simple idea there is (or was) a simple impression at its origin, and from every simple impression, there follows a simple idea, for if the impression was vivid enough, we can surely remember it, at least potentially. This much is the minimum required if Hume is to be able to argue that philosophical and scientific ideas must be traced back critically to their empirical origin (or, in the case of spurious ideas, their lack of it).

There is one exception to all this—Hume considers it no more than a trifling curiosity, but later philosophers are not so sure that it is not important. If one were to spread before us a spectrum of colors in which one shade—say a light blue between a lighter and a deeper blue —was missing, we could interpolate the missing color. A later philosopher could argue, as Alfred North Whitehead did, that such an example suggests the tendential nature of a knowledge always in process. It is always well to be wary of the "insignificant" exceptions in philosophy!

Not all of our *impressions* have their origin in sensation. There are also *impressions of reflection*—desires, emotions, passions, etc.—which can actually follow upon an idea, as well as upon an impression of sensation. For instance, upon remembering a fine Chinese meal I enjoyed last night, there follows a new impression of desire.[4] This being the case, it is not the temporal priority of the sense impression that gives it its privileged position in Hume's analysis as the *source* and sinew of all knowledge and consequently of all action—it cannot be, since it has just been admitted that some impressions can actually follow upon certain ideas. No, what gives them their unique importance is that impressions do not have to refer back to something else, the way ideas do. We might say that the importance of impressions derives from the fact that they are original, while *ideas* are not. Consequently, since the pursuit of truth, whether in mathematics, natural philosophy, metaphysics, ethics, or anything else, is an affair involving *ideas*, it becomes clear at once that the faculty responsible for the *elaboration* of ideas (let us for the moment stick to a vague word) is going to be the key to all criteria of truth. Now the faculty that can freely combine, separate, recombine, compound, and construct complex ideas out of impressions and out of simple ideas is the *imagination*.

The Role of the Imagination

WE HAVE BEEN WITNESSING throughout this survey the progressive movement of the imagination to center stage. Of course no philosopher of our concern, from Descartes on, has ever wished to deny its importance; but there is something more afoot in the new glorification of this faculty than any mere giving of the devil his due. Locke seemed to realize that the faculty that could build from the simple material of sensations the complex noetic structures with which all learning and science are concerned, somehow held a key to the very meaning of truth. But Hume is much more conscious of his direction than Locke and is therefore ready not only to stress the imagination's position, but to theorize on the very nature, sense, and validity of its combinings. Judging from the central position accorded the *Einbildungskraft* in the *Critique of Pure Reason* as *the* principle of explanation for the "transcendental synthesis," we can venture to say that it was this, as much as anything in Hume, that awoke Kant from his "dogmatic slumber."

What has caused the imagination to be pushed into the role of central cognitive faculty? Very simply, the Lockian theory of sensation. Once it is assumed that sensations present us with distinctly separate "impressions" and that it is from these that all complex notions are built, then obviously the imagination, the faculty that can at will disassemble and reassemble these distinct units, is going to be of primordial importance. That it really is, no one would deny. But the question is, what is this imagination? How is it supposed to go about its work? What is the basis for the legitimacy of its fabrications and the criterion for their truth? Obviously, the answers to these decisive questions will depend upon, and will reveal, the philosopher's most secret convictions about the nature of the original sensible "stuff" of experience. This is the point to watch closely, then, for it is going to make all the difference between a Humean empiricism tending toward skepticism, a Kantian transcendental idealism, a Husserlian phenomenology, or a Thomistic realism. Moreover, each philosopher's description of the combinations and separations of the imagination helps reveal further what has been lurking only half-consciously understood in the modern tradition's fundamental notion of primitive experience.[5]

In the Appendix to *A Treatise of Human Nature*, Hume comes as close as he ever did to telling us in the frankest terms the underlying principle of his conception of our knowledge.

> Whatever is distinct, is distinguishable; and whatever is distinguishable, is separable by the thought or imagination. All perceptions are distinct. They are, therefore, distinguishable, and separable, and may be conceived as separately existent, and may exist separately, without any contradiction or absurdity.

This paragraph alone could justify the assertion that in Hume we are witnessing the *dénouement* of the Cartesian drama. The notion of distinction is still haunting the tradition; the clear unit is still the foundation of all knowledge; analysis down to this unit is still the road to philosophical knowledge. And the assumption that each of these distinctly intuited building blocks is—indeed, *must* be—the really-real itself, that each *impression* must constitute a kind of ultimate, a kind of thing-in-itself, just as in Descartes each clear and distinct idea had to be accepted as representing an aspect of being itself, this assumption, which actually affirms the ultimate possibility to conceive of whatever "reality" itself might be, remains utterly unquestioned. And of course *the* rational criterion remains *contradiction,* and the conception of "contradiction," both static and naïve. All mystery is anathema, even the most common mysteries of existence, process, and limit.

This much, then, remains commonly accepted from Descartes to Hume. But something has obviously been changing; to wit, the metaphysical climate in which these assumptions are expected to mature. The inherently disintegrating nature of Hume's theory of sensation was kept in check and amply compensated in the Cartesians by the marvelous unification given the world by an infinite God. Remember how Malebranche's God could coordinate a world the individual pieces of which never could touch one another. Or think of Leibniz' miraculously harmonized clocks, so carefully kept parallel by the divine Clockmaker, who can establish them to run simultaneously without any causal connection between them.

But we are now in 1740, and the atmosphere is no more that in which the pious Oratorian worked confidently to bolster the omnipotence of God in the 1660's. We have surveyed the damage wrought by Locke and witnessed the extremities of the metaphysical efforts of Leibniz and Berkeley to counteract it. We have watched the unrelenting progress of psychologism in the eighteenth century—we have even seen how Berkeley played into its hands. We know that in 1740 Voltaire had already behind him two visits to the Bastille and, what is more important, one to England; the climate which was to spawn the project of the *Encyclopedia,* the first volume of which would be in subscribers' hands eleven years later, was indeed well installed. The efforts of a Berkeley had by no means assured that God was to remain permanently in his heaven and that all was well with the world. The vicissitudes through which the great cohesive notions—cause and effect, substance, material extension—had passed, and the growing withdrawal of a harmonizing, unifying, miraculously directing God had left the way open for the disintegrating forces of psychological assumptions common to the entire tradition from Descartes on to work complete havoc. It is Hume's intention to profit from this havoc to destroy the old metaphysics and to glorify the new psychology which is now to step squarely in the world of our normal experience, to provide the cohesion necessary to explain all of that experience.

Hume could have centered his attack on any of the central cohesive notions, and in fact none is altogether neglected by his critique. But he chose to concentrate his effort on cause and effect. The main reason for this is probably the fact that post-Newton, when a sense of process and time was beginning to stir, it was very wise to show that all the problems recently raised around this typically temporal combination could be accounted for adequately by a new theory of imagination. Had not Malebranche (to whom Hume expressly refers on this point) hastened to prove that no philosopher had ever been able to explain the so-called "secret force and energy of causes"? Malebranche's position amounts to saying, declares Hume, "that the ultimate force and efficacy of nature is perfectly unknown to us, and that it is in vain that we search for it in all the known qualities of matter." The fault goes back to the Cartesian notion of matter; "as the essence of matter consists in extension, and as extension implies not actual motion, but only mobility; they [the Cartesians] conclude that the energy which produces the motion cannot be in the extension." [6] The Cartesian way of getting around this was of course, as we suggested a moment ago in a more general context, to bring in God as source of all the motion. But Hume is ready for this argument: Why, if the notion of efficacy seems to them inapplicable to matter, do the Cartesians think such a notion will apply to God? [7]

If, then, the Cartesians have fixed it so that causality can no longer be considered as the transportation of a thing by another thing, or as the transportation of a thing by the power of God, how is it to be conceived? What remains, after the searching criticisms of the last decades, out of which to mold some explanation for the phenomena formerly explained as cause and effect?

There are the impressions, and there is the principle with which we began this consideration of the theory of the imagination: "All perceptions are distinct . . . and may be conceived as separately existent, etc." Out of this a new explanation of causality—a psychological, an anti-metaphysical, a basically skeptical explanation—will be built. With it, the Cartesian world, the last vestige of real causality washed out of it, dissolves into the night.

The whole problem is translated into a quest for principles governing the "association of ideas."

> As all simple ideas may be separated by the imagination, and may be united again in what form it pleases, nothing would be more unaccountable than the operations of that faculty, were it not guided by some universal principles, which render it, in some measure, uniform with itself in all times and places. Were ideas entirely loose and unconnected, chance alone would join them.[8]

These principles must not be thought of as necessary connections—there is no reason why one idea absolutely has to follow another, nor does the imagination always have to follow such a principle in order to join two ideas, "for nothing is more free than that faculty." Rather, we should think of it as "a gentle force, which commonly prevails . . . nature pointing out to everyone those simple ideas, which are most proper to be united in a complex one." [9] There are three sorts of such association: resemblance, contiguity in time and place, and cause and effect . . . but the greatest of these is cause and effect; we shall examine it "to the bottom," for it produces a stronger connection in the fancy than any of the others.

Hume distinguishes two broad genera of relations underlying all the acts of the imagination's coupling of ideas: (1) *natural relations,* in which ideas are connected by the force of *association* just mentioned, one idea introducing the other *"naturally"*; that is, customarily. All the relations involved in association—namely, resemblance, contiguity in time and place, and cause and effect—have this natural quality; i.e., they seem to force people's minds gently from one idea to another. (2) *Philosophical relations* are mere *comparisons* of objects where no connecting principle is implied, but rather where the connections are made *arbitrarily* by the imagination. Hume lists certain comparisons which are *only* "philosophical"; namely, identity, quantity or number, degrees of quality, and contrariety.[10] Moreover, all the kinds of relations that occur in some instances "naturally" can be made arbitrarily also, where the natural compunction is absent.

The philosophical relations, which all have their root in some resemblance, can be further divided into two classes: those depending entirely on the ideas compared, and those that are completed independently of any idea but rooted in fact. Resemblance, contrariety, degrees in quality and proportions in quantity or number are relations of the first sort, relations involving ideas, and therefore enjoying a certain constancy. The mind is able to *intuit* when objects resemble one another, or when two ideas are contrary, or when two things stand in a relationship of degree, like a warm and a very hot day. In the case of relationship of number, the mind is even capable of *demonstration*, of passing along a chain of relations tying together a series of proportions and numerical relationships. Such intuitions and demonstrations actually permit a certain "science." "We are possessed of a precise standard, by which we can judge of the equality and proportion of numbers; and according as they correspond or not to that standard, we determine their relations without any possibility of error."

But the situation is altogether different in the case of those relations which are not rooted in a constancy of idea—those relations that can even be changed without a corresponding change of idea. These are of three sorts: *situations in time and place, identity*, and *causation*.[11] The first two actually depend on the third, for whenever we conclude to such relations over and beyond the actual sensory perception of the connection of two objects, it is always by sneaking in cause and effect that we do so. If we conclude, beyond direct experience, that the presence of one thing in time must bring about a phenomenon that always follows it, there is no intellectual necessity forcing us to do so, but only the assumption that some secret cause must be operative, cause that will always bring about the expected sequence. Similarly in the case of *identity:* When an object comes in and out of the range of our experience repeatedly, we suppose that it remains in existence even when we do not see it and that it is thus one with itself; we suppose this, because we are ready to assume a unity of cause underlying this presence. "Of these three relations, the only one that can be traced beyond our senses, and informs us of existences and objects, which we do not see or feel, is *causation*." [12]

Relations of ideas and *relations of fact*, as Locke had already named them, are very different affairs then, the first being the foundations of mathematics, but the second, the basis of most of our efforts to extend our conclusions beyond the ken of our here and now perception of the co-existence of two objects over and above mathematics. If all

our efforts to extend our conclusions beyond experience are grounded
in the relation of cause and effect, it is apparent that upon the nature
of this relationship depends most of our speculative and even practical
knowledge outside of mathematical physics. How will Hume approach
the analysis of this "nature"?

> 'Tis impossible to reason justly, without understanding perfectly
> the idea concerning which we reason; and 'tis impossible perfectly
> to understand any idea, without tracing it up to its origin, and
> examining that primary impression, from which it arises. The
> examination of the impression bestows a clearness on the idea; and
> the examination of the idea bestows a like clearness on all our
> reasoning.[13]

He will, therefore, reduce causation "experimentally" to the play of
impressions giving rise to it.

"Cause and Effect"·

HUME'S FIRST CONCLUSION is a negative one: Neither cause nor effect
can be qualities, since any thing can on occasion be considered either
as cause or as effect, depending on the point of view. This notion must
be rather understood as a relation. The first thing we notice about
such a relation is that whatever objects are considered as causes or
effects are always *contiguous*, and "that nothing can operate in a time
or place, which is ever so little removed from those of its existence." [14]
Secondly, we notice that they are related successively; i.e., the cause
always precedes the effect in time. A cause co-temporal with its
effect would of necessity exert its causal influence and would always
have to, having no reason to come into causation—i.e., having itself
no cause to begin or end causing—which would reduce the world,
argues Hume, to one great a-temporal necessity. Time would be annihilated and our experience of succession rendered meaningless. "For
if one cause were co-temporary with its effect, and this effect with
its effect, and so on, 'tis plain there would be no such thing as succession, and all objects must be co-existent." [15] This emphasis on
temporal succession helps preserve, to Hume's satisfaction, the distinction of the two impressions that enter into this relation; he wants no
mysterious "power" crossing over from one to the other.

It is for this same reason that Hume quickly attacks the emptiness of the notion that the effect is a *production* of the cause. Such an expression, he argues, really says nothing, it simply repeats the notion "cause" without explaining it. In fact, all we can add to the notes of contiguity and succession characterizing this relationship is that of *necessary connection*. Two objects may be contiguous, and one may precede the other in time without their being considered related to one another as cause and effect. For this relationship to be in force, there must be some connection, considered in some way necessary, between the two impressions.

What grounds this supposed necessity? We find a prime example of belief in causal necessity immortalized in the principle, presumed intuitively certain, that whatever begins to exist must have a cause. But is this principle really *necessary*; is it, as claimed, intuitively certain? Actually, the imagination can perfectly well separate the notion "beginning to exist" from the notion "having a cause." "The separation of the idea of a cause from that of a beginning of existence, is plainly possible for the imagination; and consequently the actual separation of these objects is so far possible, that it implies no contradiction nor absurdity; and is therefore incapable of being refuted by any reasoning from mere ideas; without which 'tis impossible to demonstrate the necessity of a cause." [16]

Once satisfied he has exploded the belief in ideal necessary connections, Hume inquires whether there might not be another kind of ground for making such a union, an *experiential* one this time. The way to approach this possibility, declares our philosopher, is to inquire most generally into the grounds of our ever being able to conclude "that such particular causes must necessarily have such particular effects, and why we form an inference from one to another." [17]

Of course we can experience the following of one thing upon another. The point is, though, how from this experience, or from many such experiences, even should we see it repeated to infinity, we can infer its later repetition. Because I have witnessed B following upon A some three thousand times, I presume that this time, when I see A, I can infer from these past experiences that B is going to follow fast upon it. Or if I encounter B, without seeing A about anywhere, I can infer that A must have been operative there just a moment before as the cause of B.

Your appeal to past experience decides nothing in the present case; and at the utmost can only prove, that that very object, which produced any other, was at that very instant endowed with such a power; but can never prove, that the same power must continue in the same object or collection of sensible qualities. Should it be said, that we have experience, that the same power continues united to the same object, and that like objects are endowed with like powers, I would renew my question, *why from this experience we form any conclusion beyond those past instances, of which we have had experience.*[18]

Radical skepticism? Yes, as far as drawing certain implications, binding in the case of existential judgments, on the basis of past empirical experience. But don't blame Hume for these conclusions; blame an entire tradition whose conception of our fundamental experience has become unable to support one iota more of universal and necessary inference than just that allowed by Hume. "Reason," he says flatly, "can *never* show us the connexion of one object with another, tho' aided by experience, and the observation of their constant conjunction in all past instances." And, if reason is such as Hume conceives it, that is perfectly correct. The conjunction of one impression with another, their contiguity and succession in time and space, whether repeated in our experience thrice or three million times, can never justify the least leap beyond experience and beyond time. Science is thus reduced by empiricism, and by all those who would substitute a dust of sensory impressions for the living whole of our real experience, to a play of ideas devoid of existential significance the moment it strays beyond the limits of concrete sensible verification.

Belief in Existence

IF, THEN, we have cast such doubt on the common belief in inference by appeal to causality, must we not raise the very general question of belief in general: In what consists our belief in various objects? What are the grounds and the legitimate limits of such belief in existence?

Do I add anything to the concept of an object—that is, to its idea— when I think of the object as existing and believe in its existence? Existence and belief in existence are nothing over and beyond the affirmation of the idea of the object. Yet there is obviously a difference between the idea of an object, the simple conception of its existence, and genuine belief in it, a difference which, if it does not lie in the composition of the idea, must lie in the *manner* in which we conceive it.[19] What distinguishes the idea in which we believe from one in which we do not is that we conceive the first more vividly, " 'tis only a strong and steady conception of any idea, and such as approaches in some measure to an immediate impression." [20] We do not have to "believe" in an impression, for the vividness of its presence precludes the necessity of belief. But an *idea* is precisely a perception that must rely on memory or imagination; belief in an idea therefore arises only when the vividness of an impression is communicated to the corresponding idea by its being associated with a present impression. The imagination itself is not the source of belief, for belief is a *feeling* that gives a reality more weight than a fiction.

Hume admits that it is difficult to find the right words to express what comes over us in the presence of the real and what is missing when we are only toying with air castles. But he is nevertheless sure of one thing: When taking the question of belief in existence out of the realm of logic; when penetrating beyond the notion that truth resides in the judgment's composing and dividing of concepts; when attempting to suggest that belief in reality involves some sort of primordial, prelogical contact with things, he is on the right track to a revitalization of philosophy. As we read a passage such as the following, we are convinced that Hume himself indeed *felt* very deeply that the real world had somehow to break through the dried crust of categories in which the philosophers of Europe had been trying to fit their thought:

> If one person sits down to read a book as a romance, and another as a true history, they plainly receive the same ideas, and in the same order; nor does the incredulity of the one, and the belief of the other hinder them from putting the very same ideas in both; tho' his testimony has not the same influence on them. The latter has a more lively conception of all the incidents. He enters deeper into the concerns of the persons: represents to himself their actions, and characters, and friendships, and enmities: he even goes so far as to form a notion of their features, and air, and person. While the former, who gives no credit to the testi-

mony of the author, has a more faint and languid conception of all these particulars.[21]

Hume shares with the romantics a desire to break out of intellectualist limits and to give the world of feeling and action its due. If with all these thinkers the liberation of the existential takes place at the expense of the logical and rational, it is not because the intelligible itself is somehow at odds with the world of sentiment and will; it is simply that the narrow and finally poverty-stricken conceptions of sensible and intellectual experience which they inherited could afford no basis for a balanced, unified doctrine of a human nature embracing sense, intellect, will, and feeling in one defensible structure.

Now that some description of belief, sketchy as it is, has been attempted, we must inquire into its causes: Under what circumstances do we believe? What "bestows vivacity on the idea"? The question really concerns the junction between the present impression and the idea which enjoys an animation from it. It is not a demonstrative or reasoned connection that instantly and without reflection transfers the firmness of the impression to the associated idea, but the bond of *custom*. In the past, an association has been made repeatedly between the present impression and the idea it summons up. If in the present instant I am not obliged to have recourse to conscious liaison of ideas, but find rather that in an "insensible manner," before there is time for reflection, the idea is summoned up and receives the glow of the impression, it is because the habit of the association is already formed from past experiences. It is the very automaticity of the process, its timelessness and ease, its "insensible nature," which permits the glow of reality to spread from a group of present sensations to a whole realm of ideas derived from past experience.

> Thus all probable reasoning is nothing but a species of sensation. 'Tis not solely in poetry and music, we must follow of taste and sentiment, but likewise in philosophy. When I am convinced of any principle, 'tis only an idea which strikes more strongly upon me. When I give the preference to one set of arguments . . . it is custom operating upon imagination . . .[22]

The accumulation of experience then carries its weight into every department of our noetic life and, like the *petites perceptions* of Leibniz, adds up insensibly to a constant, subtle, but determining influence.

This doctrine has two aims. For one, it strives to restore the unity of man split by Descartes into body and mind, intellect and will, judgment and sentiment, etc. To say that we *feel* the truth of things, and that that feeling is educated in us by the whole weight of all our past experience, is to reintegrate man into a living unit, so permeated by the reality received in every impression that he can no longer account for his decisions and actions in terms of clear and distinct ideas followed by necessary judgments. Secondly, this explanation of human comportment gives full importance to individual education and to the influence of particular environment.

Its great shortcoming is that it lacks a means of giving any kind of base to objectivity; everything is absorbed into the organism, culminating in subjective feeling; and even though Hume would leave us with the impression that the intensity of a sentiment is due to an accumulation of ideas that must represent *something* real, there is within the doctrine, strictly speaking, no ground for such an assumption. This will throw on his shoulders the burden of showing how the new doctrine can be made to suffice as a guide to human conduct; but meantime he can gloat at having ruined traditional metaphysics. Hume realizes that he has undermined the pretense of traditional philosophy to prove the existence of any supratemporal object, be it the "world," the personal self, or God. Not that he would have us doubt there is such a unity as the "world," or the "self," or "God"; it is just that the pretended demonstrations of the metaphysicians can no longer be considered the privileged avenue of access to "reality"; instead, Hume would shift this privilege to the order of *praxis*, to the order of action and the "practical." Let us see how the analysis of causality just completed can be used against the traditional positions in each of these regards.

The Attack on the Metaphysical Unities

WHAT ARE THE GROUNDS for the common man's belief in the separate existence of things in a world outside the mind? Berkeley's challenge of Locke's insistence that behind our ideas there were also things is now in turn ready to be challenged, as Hume shows that no appeal to God as spiritual support of our images can save the situation, but only the realization that the imagination is what provides the continuity necessary for such a belief. When we say that we believe in the real existence of bodies, we ordinarily mean, according to Hume, that they enjoy a continued existence when we are not sensing them, and that their existence is distinct from our ideas.[23] Obviously we cannot *perceive* that things continue to exist beyond our perceptions of them, nor can we reason to their possessing an existence distinct from the impressions we have of them. For if reason identifies the perception and the object, it is meaningless to talk of inferring anything from one to the other; if it distinguishes them, it can never proceed from the existence of the perception to that of an independent object. All of that is quite evident. Whence, then, the common belief in both the continuity and distinct existence of material objects?

Enter . . . the imagination, of course. The imagination passes insensibly from awareness of the coherence and constancy of certain impressions to an affirmation of the coherence and constancy—and therefore the continued existence—of their supposed bodily counterparts; once supposed to exist continuously, beyond the interruptions of my perceptions, they are of course held to exist distinct from my impressions of them. Hume strikes a pragmatic note in suggesting why we fall into this habit: It is necessary for life.

> There is a great difference betwixt such opinions as we form after a calm and profound reflection, and such as we embrace by a kind of instinct or natural impulse, on account of their suitableness and conformity to the mind. If these opinions become contrary, 'tis not difficult to foresee which of them will have the advantage. As long as our attention is bent upon the subject, the philosophical and study'd principle may prevail; but the moment we relax our thoughts, nature will display herself, and draw us back to our former opinion. . . . Thus tho' we clearly perceive the dependence and interruption of our perceptions, we stop short in our career, and never upon that account reject the notion of an independent and continued existence.[24]

Hume does not pursue the subject very far; he probes neither into the reasons for our postulating the distinct existence of things nor into our belief that they form the unity of a world; he does not develop a full-fledged pragmatic doctrine. But Kant will absorb his suggestions and pursue them much further, not only toward a more thorough and fundamental criticism of the roots of metaphysics in these common beliefs, but toward a systematic moral doctrine consistent with the findings of Hume's critique.

The doctrine of personal identity of the self undergoes the same treatment. If the foundation of conscious life consists in the possession of discrete impressions, then mind must be "nothing but a heap or collection of different perceptions, united together by certain relations, and supposed, though falsely, to be endowed with a perfect simplicity and identity." [25] If the mind really enjoyed simplicity and identity, then we should be able to discover some impression that remains through the whole suite of our experiences, linking all sensations and ideas with one another. Once again the imagination is up to its tricks. There is no such unifying impression, but the imagination can borrow from our experience of the way one impression leads to another the notion that all our experiences must do likewise. Memory helps by recalling past perceptions resembling our present ones, suggesting some sort of causal bridge between moments of our experience. And passion, with its propensity for anticipating, gets into the act by suggesting that there must be some continuity toward the future, otherwise my present desires would never receive fulfillment.

But let the imagination borrow all it wants from such "experiences" of causal connection: We have already examined *au fond* the pretenses of "cause and effect." What we are seeing here is nothing more than a particular example of the critically unacceptable general tendency of the mind to forge a unity for itself. Hume does admit that we experience a certain feeling that all our perceptions *belong* to us, and in the Appendix to the *Treatise* he even goes so far as to admit that he cannot reconcile this phenomenon with the fact that "all our distinct perceptions are distinct existences." As usual, our philosopher is ready to acknowledge that he is directing this attack against a philosophical tradition and not against the real existence of the thing he is showing difficult to "prove" theoretically. In the present instance what he is really after is the Cartesian substantial soul and all its religious implications, as developed by Berkeley and all "metaphysical" immortalists. He rails at "the curious reasonings concerning the material or immaterial substances, in which they suppose our perceptions to inhere," and he confesses that it is "to put a stop to these endless cavils" that he asks "what they mean by substance and inhesion." [26] It is in this context that he attacks the problem of personal identity.

After this no time need be wasted on the questions of the immortality or immateriality of the soul. All such problems have been
undercut by throwing doubt on whether the soul is a substance at
all; whether indeed there is any ground for the common feeling that
the mind is a unity.

The third stronghold of unity in traditional philosophy—namely,
God—is battered in a later work, *Dialogues concerning Natural Religion,* which Hume thought it prudent to withhold from publication
until 1779—not that it would have taken much acumen for the readers
of the *Treatise* to work out the main lines of the coming attack on
the old arguments for God's existence. Even then, Hume avoided
personally attacking the idea and the existence of God through a
complicated interplay of the three principles in the *Dialogues.* But the
main lines of critique are quite clear: Hume takes out after an *a
posteriori* and an *a priori* proof, both quite typical of the lamentably
lame theological arguments current in the middle of the eighteenth
century. Against an *a priori* argument from the idea of God to the
necessity of his existence, Hume opposes the principle that "whatever we conceive as existent we can also conceive as non-existent"; in
other words, he refuses absolutely (as does St. Thomas) to admit the
legitimacy of a transition from the order of idea to the order of
existence.[27] If one is going to start interjecting this "necessary being"
business into the question, why cannot the material universe be
chosen just as well for the honor? We do not know God very well,
but neither do we know material things so well either. "We dare not
affirm that we know all the qualities of matter; and for aught we can
determine, it may contain some qualities, which, were they known,
would make its non-existence appear as great a contradiction as that
twice two is five."[28] The point is that we neither know God well
enough to say that he is absolutely such and such, nor matter well
enough to say that it is not. As for the argument beginning, "Everything that comes to be must have a cause," we have seen quite
enough already in the *Treatise* to know what must happen to that!

The *a posteriori* argument—the typical eighteenth-century argument for the existence of God based on the marvelous design of the
universe—engages Hume's attention a bit longer, perhaps because it
was so current and favored at the time—and such a wonderful wind-
mill to tilt with! So it remains today, too many simple souls still confusing this fraud with the very complex and subtle argument from

finality developed by the Thomists. It is not Hume's intention to deny that our contemplation of the complicated structures of things does persuade us to argue that there must be an analogy between what we see here and the phenomenon of human artistic creation. He is not about to jump on the atheist bandwagon. But he does want to put this kind of persuasiveness in its right place: he wants us to realize that we are confronted here with a probability, not a dogmatic certainty,[29] and he wants us to know that such an argument does not advance us very far in our knowledge of God's nature. Once again the movement of the mind when confronted with this analogy is a natural one, like our belief in the separate existence of things or the substantial soul. As to what it proves, given the incommensurable distance that separates the divine grandeur from our frail and miserable selves, it is certain that the argument from an analogy with human intelligence must yield a modest result. In fact, asks Hume, are the atheists and the theists so far apart? The atheists admit that there is some principle bearing an analogy to our intelligence, at the root of the world's organization, while the theists admit that God is very different from our finite selves. Are the two not really locked in an argument over *degrees* where neither can ever claim the least certitude? [30]

The Guidance of Human Affairs

WE HAVE REPEATEDLY POINTED OUT that Hume has been subtly shifting the grounds for traditional philosophical "beliefs" from "dogmatic" to practical ones. Let us by way of conclusion now survey the sort of ethical possibility that would be consonant with the critique we have been following.

There is one thing to be gotten out of the way at once: *liberty*. People believe, as we have seen at length, that the constant conjunction of material phenomena is to be explained by the necessary conjunction of a cause with its effect. But when they turn inward to reflect on the constant conjunction of their motives and their actions, they fail to *feel* any such necessity. Ah! they conclude, that is because material things operate under a regime of necessity, while we spirits enjoy the reign of liberty! But we have shown the strange, imaginative origin of the feeling of causal connection; and consequently we know that the failure to *feel* any such necessity when we turn to our own motives and actions is simply part of the general lack of any real experiential grounds for such a belief. This failure to feel necessity, however, in no way proves that human actions are under any regime different from that affecting material objects. Let us then proceed to the consideration of human actions without getting bogged down by the confused idea of "liberty."

The key to our actions lies rather in the *passions*, the complications of which Hume proposes to reduce to a few simple principles. Our impressions, it will be remembered, are characterized by their vivacity and their passive nature. Up to now, working as we have been in an epistemological context, we have spoken of our *primary impressions* largely in terms of 1] sensations; but now it is important to note that our sensations are accompanied by another sort of primary impression, namely 2] bodily pleasures and pains. We must similarly expand our consideration of the *secondary impressions*, based on primary ones, which include 1] our reflections of causal inference among sensations, but also 2] *passions*, which follow upon the primary impressions of pleasure and pain. They follow upon primary impressions, yet they are themselves "original"—not representative of something else, but having a complete sense in themselves. Hume distinguishes two sorts of passions: the *direct*, which follow directly upon the feelings of pleasure and pain, and the *indirect*, which involve other qualities as well. It is to the latter that he devotes the most attention, yet even a moment's consideration will show that the *direct* passions are of very great importance to the conduct of our life.

Desire and aversion, grief and joy, hope and fear, are direct passions, original instincts that move us directly to action. Their asserted importance notwithstanding, Hume does not analyze them at great length. Perhaps they are a little too direct, a little too simple, while the indirect passions, as we shall see in a moment, offer the prospect of a complication Hume is able to twist nicely into line with his general epistemological theories; the direct passions, if examined too carefully, might raise some embarrassing questions of intentionality; Hume is already obliged to admit to their ranks, in order to assure the ethics in which he wants us to believe, the passion of desire for a friend's happiness or an enemy's punishment. This he considers an original impulse, not dependent on any feeling of pleasure or pain, although it may be accompanied by it. Hume is obliged to posit such a primitive direct "natural impulse," even though it is "perfectly unaccountable," and to make it independent of a feeling of pain, so that he can explain the fact of sacrifice for others.[31]

Of course Hume's presentation of the indirect passions raises its problems too, when we try to understand it in the light of the analyses completed in Book I of the *Treatise*. Hume divides the indirect passions according to their object, which can be either the self or another. It should be noted that the idea that arouses a passion and the object to which it is directed are not the same, but it is the object toward which the passion is directed that most distinguishes it. Pride and humility, as self-regarding indirect passions, are to be distinguished from love and hatred, which are other-regarding. To cause a passion, an object must 1] produce pleasure or pain, and 2] have a reference either to ourselves or to another person. And, it so happens, the passion itself must consist essentially in a pleasant or painful feeling and must of its essence be oriented toward another person or toward the self. Even though Hume repeats his phenomenalistic description of the "self" at this point, as though to warn us that the lessons of Book I have not been forgotten, no other explanation for all this causal influence and for these happy parallels between the causes of passions and the passions themselves is forthcoming. Instead, we sail at once into a description of a system of passions sufficient to found an ethics. Hume's critique may have achieved its negative objectives effectively, but its deficiencies on the positive side become more evident the more detailed and positive the context in which we are working. Philosophers rarely hesitate to plow right ahead and do what is obviously necessary to elaborate an ethics even when their previous epistemological critique leaves no sound theoretical foundation for what they now feel has to be accomplished.

The great upshot for ethics of Hume's original analysis of the passions was to liberate morality from the dominance of pure reason. Something of the kind had to happen; the deficiency of the rationalist-inspired eighteenth-century notion of an abstract intellect to carry out the existential role of a true "practical intellect" is certainly evident in retrospect. Someone had to achieve a breakthrough, letting in the contingent and particular and their representatives, sentiment and feeling; someone had to do away with the vain pretense of being able to deduce a code of moral conduct from a few intuitively held, absolutely certain principles, and clear away the illusion that it suffices, in order to be good, that one come to know scientifically this handful of dicta.

With great insight, Hume saw that *morality* could be neither an affair having to do only with things nor an affair having to do only with ideas. "As moral good and evil belong only to the actions of the mind, and are derived from our situation with regard to external objects; the relations from which these moral distinctions arise must lie only betwixt internal actions, and external objects, and must not be applicable either to internal actions, compared among themselves, or to external objects, when placed in opposition to other external objects." [32] Today we would say, in a less satisfactory terminology, morality raises the issue of a conduct that is neither objective nor subjective, but cuts across this distinction. In an effort to show that moral considerations are not reducible to ideas, Hume had insisted that reason as such has nothing to do with action, that only another action could affect a passion: "Morals excite passions, and produce or prevent actions. Reason of itself is utterly impotent in this particular. The rules of morality therefore are not conclusions of our reason." [33] Not that judgments have no effect on moral conduct; of course they do; but the goodness or badness of an act is never reducible to the truth or falseness of whatever judgments may be associated with it. I may judge wrongly that this thing is good for me; I may again judge incorrectly that this means will be effective in obtaining that thing. I am doubly mistaken, and doubly frustrated. I may be silly, but no one is going to say that I am guilty of viciousness for my error. We must look elsewhere, beyond judgments, for the good and evil and efficacity, for benefit or harm, of human actions.

But where? What is the essence of good and evil, if morality cannot be a matter for reason, nor even a "matter of fact"? What does our experience then tell us it is? If you examine a hideous act of murder, you will find, as long as you examine the object, only certain passions, motives, volitions, and thoughts. There is no other matter of fact in the case. The vice entirely escapes you, as long as you consider the object. You never can find it, till you turn your reflection into your own breast and find a sentiment of disapprobation, which arises in you, toward this action. Here is a matter of fact; but it is the object of feeling, not of reason. It lies in yourself, not in the object.[34] What could be more inevitable than such a solution? Hume keenly recognized what sort of reason would have to function in morality, and that Cartesian-Lockian reason, chimeric as it had proven, could never fulfill the requirements. Knowing of no way around his own destruction of "metaphysical" reason, which has no material to build with but phenomenalistic sensations, Hume simply rules out reason altogether as source of moral conviction. In its place, following Hutcheson and the English Moral Sense school, he substitutes a *feeling* which has the merit of suggesting that the moral reaction is somehow concrete and existential. "When you pronounce any action or character to be vicious, you mean nothing, but that from the constitution of your nature you have a feeling or sentiment of blame from the contemplation of it." [35] But whereas these moralists had seemed to suggest a sort of sixth sense common to all men (Hume too must agree that this sense is roughly the same in all men), Hume integrates the sentiment into his general position on the passions. Pride and humility, love and hatred were seen to be passions excited "when there is anything presented to us, that both bears a relation to the object of the passion, and produces a separate sensation related to the sensation of the passion." [36] The feelings of virtue and vice arise in just such circumstances. These feelings resemble the more general category of feelings of pleasure and pain but have the particularity of having as their object either ourselves or some other person: they give rise to any one of those four "indirect" passions: pride, humility, love, or hate.[37] "To have the sense of virtue," explains Hume, "is nothing but to *feel* a satisfaction of a particular kind from the contemplation of a character. The very *feeling* constitutes our praise or admiration." In other words, the good is what awakes in us a feeling of approval—the bad of disapproval. It is well for Hume to underline *feeling*, but does that really explain anything—above all, how will he answer the inevitable question, *why the feeling*—and you may take *why* in any of its possible meanings. Let Hume continue: "We go no farther; nor do we inquire into the cause of the satisfaction. We do not infer a character to be virtuous because it pleases: But in feeling that it pleases after such a particular manner, we in effect feel that it is virtuous." [38] *We go no farther* because, as badly as it is needed now, inquiry into the *cause of the satisfaction* is no longer possible. We blew up our bridges in Book I!

This is typical of Hume's whole philosophical undertaking. In clearing the path for the future, he often blows up the good with the bad. To do him justice, we should remember that, a philosopher, he also was a historian and a remarkable essayist whose psychological and moral observations often are valuable in themselves independently of the general trend of the system. To the new movement to recognize the significance of history, Hume offered new reasons for recognizing the importance of the concrete and for giving a new and central role to custom and habit, to the temporal. To the growing concern of the thinkers of the Enlightenment for aesthetics, Hume offered the suggestion that the concreteness and particularity of aesthetic appreciation is not a weakness—a sign of its scientific anemia—but its forte; applied to aesthetics, Hume's general position ("All sentiment is right; because sentiment has a reference to nothing beyond itself, and is always real, wherever a man is conscious of it") suggests that every appreciation of beauty, not despite but because of its variance in every mind, is desirable ("Beauty is no quality in things themselves: it exists merely in the mind which contemplates them, and each mind perceives a different beauty").[39] A radical subjectivism indeed, left without any foundation in reality but, from another point of view, a sound reaction against a false rationalistic objectivism, equally out of touch with the true ontological roots of beauty.

By and large, however, the influence of Hume was mainly destructive. It was to be felt as such by the eighteenth-century philosophers who, coming after him, saw in his skepticism the ultimate conclusion of a movement initiated by Descartes and ending in a sort of desperate nihilism redeemed by good intellectual manners and an inborn respect for philosophical decencies. The "common sense" school of Reid will attempt to stem the threatening invasion of universal skepticism; Kant, of course, will take stock of the philosophical situation and assess it with much deeper insight. Kantism will conceive itself as the decisive philosophical reply to the skepticism of Hume; and indeed, Kantian criticism is the fruit of Humean skepticism; this even is the reason why the worm is in the fruit.

XVII

Condillac

THE FIRST SENTENCE ever published by Condillac was in praise of metaphysics. No science, he says, has done as much as metaphysics to give the human mind clarity, precision, and amplitude. It seems, therefore, that this science should be used in order to train the mind for the study of other sciences; yet "today metaphysics is so neglected in France that this remark will no doubt sound paradoxical to many readers." This opening sentence of the *Essay on the Origin of Human Knowledges* suggests a philosophical climate very different from that of the seventeenth century.[1]

Two main influences had contributed to bring about that striking change on the Continent. Newton had not only substituted for the cosmology imagined by Descartes a solidly demonstrated one, he also had laid down the precepts of the only method capable of achieving solidly demonstrated knowledge in astronomy and physics. On this point the doctrine of Newton was as explicit as it was clear. In his *Mathematical Principles of Natural Philosophy* (1687) Newton had announced his decision "not to feign hypotheses"—*hypotheses non fingo*—for indeed "whatever is not deduced from phenomena, must be called a hypothesis, and whether they be metaphysical or physical, of occult qualities or mechanical, hypotheses have no place in experimental philosophy."[2]

The second influence at work in France around 1740 was that of John Locke. The *Essay* had been translated into French[3] and the book had been widely read. Its "plain historical method" had created a favorable impression. As Voltaire was to say, after so many reasoners had told the romance of the soul, "a wise man came who told us its history."[4] In eighteenth-century French, *le sage Locke* was as hackneyed a formula as, in scholastic Latin, *Philosophus* had once been to designate Aristotle. And those who used it, mentally contrasted the "wise Locke" with the less wise Descartes. In all this, Condillac was a child of the century, but he was not giving up metaphysics as a lost cause. On the contrary, convinced that Locke had given the proof that a sound metaphysics was possible, he only wanted to improve it.[5]

Critique of the Systems

A PERIOD of intense metaphysical productivity is usually followed by one of critical examination and judgment. After Platonism and the flowering of Greek systems came the skepticism of the New Academy; at the end of its golden age scholasticism had heard the objections of Ockham, Montaigne, and Sanchez to overconfidence in the demonstrating power of reason; Condillac comes to play a similar role at the end of the seventeenth-century metaphysical flowering. Still he himself is in no way a skeptic; the proof of this can be found in the fact that, having decided to criticize systems, he undertakes in a positive spirit to find the cause of their errors.

Condillac does not say "the causes," for he thinks that a true philosopher should be able to detect the cause of causes that lies at the origin of all such errors. His criticism of systems is part of his general design, which is the study of the human power of knowing (*l'esprit humain*) not in order to know its nature (an impossible undertaking indeed) but in order to know the way it operates. This can be done, and it is a helpful knowledge to acquire because it can found an art of directing these operations so as to acquire all the knowledge of which man is capable. Avoiding error is part of the problem of knowing truth.

Systems are not to be condemned as such, but there are good and bad ones. It is important to remember that there is a good way to systematize, for the whole doctrine of Condillac will aim at realizing this ideal, in which regard at least it will differ from the plain historical method of Locke. Good systems, the only ones that should lay claim to the title, are identical with science: they start from observed facts. The wrong systems are of two sorts. First, there are the "abstract systems." Instead of starting from ascertained facts, these begin by laying down abstract principles. Others start from some supposition. This second kind of system can be called "hypothetical": their principle being a supposition, they themselves are mere suppositions. "In all true system, there is a prime fact, a fact that is its beginning and which, for this very reason, should be called *principle*, for *principle* and *beginning* are two words that primarily mean the same thing. Suppositions are but suspicions, and if we need to make some, we are doomed to grope our way. Since suppositions are but suspicions, they are not observed facts; so they cannot be the principle or the beginning of a system, for then the whole system would reduce itself to a suspicion." [6]

Suspicions, or suppositions, cannot become principles of any true system, but they have their part to play in the quest for truth, for they are the principle, or beginning, of the means at our disposal to find the beginning, or principle, of the system.

A similar remark accounts for the multiplication of "abstract systems." Abstraction is indeed a necessary operation of the mind. Rightly used, it enables us to gather particular facts into classes, and since these classes themselves can be ordered according to their respective degrees of generality, we find there an abridged way to take stock of our cognitions; the more general the abstraction, the more abridged the summary. For instance, *being* is a short way to signify all that which is. But here again a common mistake must be avoided: One should not mistake the principles of the representation of acquired knowledge for the principles of the acquisition of knowledge; they are two different things. [7]

Abstract systems rest upon the belief that God, in creating our minds, endowed them with certain principles, and that the whole of human knowledge can be deduced from them. In fact, nothing can be deduced from such principles. Suppose we start from a principle like *all that which is, is;* or from *it is impossible for a thing to be and not to be at the same time;* where do we go from there? No knowledge has ever been acquired from such beginnings. In order to give such principles some appearance of usefulness, one often starts from a proposition true in some cases and to which one ascribes universal validity. For instance, it is often true that "one can affirm of a thing what is included in the idea we have of the thing"; so the Cartesians lay it down as a principle; still, this is not always true, for most of our ideas are only partial ideas, and what is "true" of such ideas may turn out to have no validity at all. The Cartesians made great use of this principle, and it led them to costly mistakes. [8]

All abstract systems have in common one terrible defect: their uselessness. If a man is lost in a labyrinth, will he lay down general principles concerning what to do in such cases if he wants out? Such is precisely our human lot.

> We are born in the middle of a labyrinth wherein a thousand turns and returns are indicated only to lead us to error; if there is a way to truth, it does not show first; it often least looks like the one to be trusted. We could not be too cautious. Let us go slowly. Let us carefully examine all our steps, and know them so well that we always be able to retrace them. It is more important for us to find ourselves back where we were at first than too lightly to imagine ourselves out of the labyrinth.[9]

The Cartesian precept that one always is better off anywhere else than in the middle of a forest meets here with rebuke. Condillac knows something worse than merely to be in the middle of a forest; it is believing oneself out of it when still there.

Judged on the strength of these principles, the great systems of the seventeenth century became for Condillac an easy target. Their main errors followed from the common prejudice that there are innate ideas. This notion is particularly harmful because it makes it so easy to justify any so-called principle of human knowledge; for example, the erroneous Cartesian principle already mentioned, that *all that which is included in the clear and distinct idea of a thing can be truthfully affirmed of it;* for example again, Malebranche's peculiar way of distinguishing understanding and will by resorting to the abstract principle that *ideas and inclinations are to the soul as figures and motion are to matter.*[10]

Generally speaking, there are two perils to avoid in a system: the one is to assume the phenomena one intends to explain; the other is to explain them by means of principles that are not clearer than the phenomena themselves. If Descartes made the first mistake, Leibniz has made the second. Such is clearly the case when he accounted for extended substance by describing it as composed of inextended substances, without clearly saying what an inextended substance actually is. Leibniz does clearly say what his "monads" are not, but he fails to say what they are. They are not extended, that is clear; but when he adds they are "forces," this is not clear. He does not clearly say what such forces are, nor why they should have perceptions, nor what such perceptions should be, nor why there should be in each monad an infinity of perceptions representing the universe.[11]

If one wants to give a tangible example of the way abstract systems

are made and of the errors to which they lead, "no work is better
calculated for it than that of Spinoza." The title of his *Ethics* announces that the work is "geometrically demonstrated." Two conditions are required for that kind of demonstration, clarity of the ideas
and precision in the meaning of the words. Not one of Spinoza's
definitions meets these requirements. What is it, for a thing, to be
causa sui? No thing can be cause of itself, for the reason that, in
order to cause, a cause has to be distinct from its effect. Since
Spinoza intends to prove that there is only one single substance, it
would seem important to define exactly the meaning of the word, but
that is something neither Spinoza nor any other philosopher will ever
be able to do. Let them try. "Substance" is *that which* is in itself; or
that which subsists by itself (as the scholastics would say); or *that
which* can be conceived independently from any other thing (this
would be Descartes); or again, *that which* preserves essential determinations and essential attributes while its modes vary and succeed one
another (this is in Wolff's style); in all these definitions, do not the
words *that which* point out some unknown and indeterminate subject? Whoever heard a geometer say: A circle is *that which* is this and
that? They say at least this much, that a circle *is a figure* which is
such, or which has such and such properties. In defining substance as
he does, Spinoza merely acknowledges that he does not know what
is the subject of the properties he attributes to it.[12]

Condillac has well observed that the famous words of Newton,
hypotheses non fingo, cannot be taken absolutely. In seeking after truth,
the mind cannot avoid making suppositions, but suppositions should be
of such nature that their verification be possible, and in no case
should any of them be used as a principle until it is verified. On this
problem, Chapter XII of Condillac's *Essay,* "On Hypotheses," and the
following one, "On the Genius of Those who in Order to Reach up
to the Nature of Things, Make Abstract Systems or Gratuitous
Hypotheses," are a condemnation of the arbitrariness of Cartesian
physics as contrasted with the solidity of the science of Newton; in
common with the whole French eighteenth century, Condillac sides
with Newton against Descartes.

To conclude, let it be recalled that Condillac is not condemning
systems as such. On the contrary, his point is that "abstract systems"
(i.e., systems whose principles are mere abstractions) do not properly
deserve the title of systems. The essential requirement for constructing

systems is sufficient observation to grasp the way phenomena condition one another. In no case can we hope to start from absolutely unconditioned conditions; in the last analysis, "the best principles one can have in physics, are phenomena that explain other phenomena, but which themselves hang on causes unknown." [13]

Beyond Locke: the *Essay*

CONDILLAC'S OWN AMBITION was to achieve a system of metaphysics whose object would be "to go to the origin of our ideas, to observe the way they combine and how we should conduct them in order to acquire all the intelligence of which we are capable." So the "nature" of understanding is not at stake. On the other hand, and in this Condillac shows himself a disciple of Descartes more than of his beloved Locke, his "design is *to reduce to one single principle all that concerns human understanding.*" That principle will be neither a vague proposition nor an abstract maxim, but rather a duly ascertained experience, of which all the consequences will be confirmed by new experiences.[14]

That initial fact (beginning; i.e., principle) is sensation. This is of course no new discovery. Aristotle had said that all knowledge comes through the senses, but then he immediately proceeded to describe an entirely different source of knowledge which he called intellect. In modern times, Bacon had seen the importance of the principle; the Cartesians scorned it because they could see in it only the use the Peripatetics had made of it; at last Locke grasped it and, says Condillac, was the first to *demonstrate* it. For Condillac this statement has a very precise meaning. It signifies that, to his perpetual honor, Locke has been the first philosopher to demonstrate that *there are no such things as innate ideas.* The point was of capital importance, for to prove that there are no innate ideas is, by the same token, to prove that all knowledge indeed comes from sense.

The *Essay* of Locke nevertheless suffers from serious defects. It is the intention of Condillac to remedy the most serious of all. In his own *Essay on the Origin of Human Knowledges,* Condillac points out, from the very title, the point neglected by Locke and which he himself intends to clear up: How do all our cognitions arise from sense knowledge?

In saying that all knowledge comes from sense, Locke meant to say that there was nothing in understanding that had not first been in sense, yet he never doubted the distinction between sense and understanding. This is so true that he emphasizes that these constitute *two sources* of human knowledge. This belief in the initial duality of our knowing powers is what made it impossible for Locke to achieve a really unified "system" of human knowledge; the aim and scope of Condillac's own philosophy will be to remove that duality. When Locke said that all comes to intellect from sense, Leibniz answered yes, except intellect itself. In the light of his own principles, Locke really could offer no reply. The doctrine of Condillac will avoid this pitfall, for he intends to prove that intellect itself comes from sense; for what comes from sense is sensation, and intellect is nothing but *transformed sensation*. In other words, in showing that "the origin of human knowledge" is sensation, and sensation *alone*, Condillac was to wipe out intellect as a distinct power of the soul; his aim was to bring to completion the task Locke had left incomplete.[15]

Condillac has often stressed the difference between his method and that of Descartes. The two doctrines, he says, diverge from their very beginnings. Descartes begins by the methodical doubt; that is to say, by deliberately holding for uncertain or false all his previous cognitions, but he does not really ask himself of what they are made up. The result is that, at the end of his doubt, his ideas themselves have been left uncriticized. For instance, Descartes doubts that two and two are four or that man is a rational animal, but though he doubts those propositions, he does not question the ideas they correlate: two, four, man, animal, and rational. Since error mostly arises from badly formed ideas, the method of Descartes does not permit us to redress them. On the contrary, Condillac's method makes it possible to decompose ideas into their elements. These elements are sensations, so, instead of saying with Descartes that he will reduce our knowledge to the ideas that are the simplest, he contents himself with starting from the simplest ideas *transmitted to us by sense*. These are no abstract notions; each sensation is a particular fact.[16] They are, so to speak, the materials out of which human knowledge is made.

Since they are facts, sensations should be taken at their face value. Judgments about sensations may be erroneous. I may err in saying that a tower is round, while it simply appears to be round; but these errors of attribution can be corrected. In themselves, sensations are sound material for the building up of knowledge. In themselves, and despite what Cartesians say to the contrary, sensations are clear and distinct; our ideas of extension, lines, angles, figures—in short, all those that constitute the object of geometry—contain nothing deceptive; in themselves, they deserve to be trusted. They likewise deserve to be trusted as witnesses to the existence of a world distinct from us.[17] Condillac posits the existence of the external world as an immediate datum of sense perception.

What is sensation? Condillac seems to use the words "sensation" and "perception" indiscriminately. Both words mean to him that which is immediately grasped by sense. Some perceptions are stronger, others less strong, and a large number of them are so weak that they are immediately forgotten, but none of them is unconscious. Condillac will have nothing to do with Leibniz' *petites perceptions*. The notion of an unperceived perception is a contradiction in terms.

Starting from any such sensation or perception, the genealogy of the operations of the mind can be reconstructed.[18]

At the beginning there is in the soul one single perception which is but an impression received from the presence of some object. Considered as warning the soul of its presence, this sensation is called *consciousness*. Perception and consciousness are one and the same operation called by two names. Sensations are more or less intense; if my perception of one of them is such that it seems to be the only one of which I am conscious at the moment, *attention* comes into action. Such strong impressions usually reappear later on in the soul; a thus-reappearing sensation is called *reminiscence*. "Consciousness so to speak says to the soul: here is a perception; attention says, here is a perception which is the only one you have; reminiscence says: here is a perception you have already had."

The first effect of attention is to cause perceptions to subsist in the mind even in the absence of the objects which caused them. Sensations are usually preserved in the same order in which they have been perceived. Hence a sort of bond (later called "association") between perceptions, and this bond becomes the origin of other operations.

These later operations are three: The first is *imagination*, which takes place when, by the force alone of the bond established between a perception and its object, this perception reappears at the sight of its object. In other cases, the perception itself does not reappear whole, but only its name and the abstract notion that it refers to a perceived object seen somewhere, say a "flower"; such an operation is *memory*. A third operation follows from the bond established by attention between our ideas;[19] it consists in uninterruptedly keeping present to the mind the perception, or the name, or the circumstances of a sensation whose object has just disappeared. This is called *contemplation*. It is related either to imagination, if it preserves perception itself; or to memory, if it preserves the name or the circumstances only.

Having reached this point, Condillac finds himself confronted with his hardest problem. So far, all the operations of the soul have been accounted for by a kind of mental atomism consisting in the spontaneous associations of simple elements, the sensations. No active power, or faculty of the soul, has been brought into play. One might feel tempted to say that Condillac conceives the operations that take place in the soul, if not as resulting from a downright passivity, which would sound absurd, at least as manifesting a non-reflexive spontaneity. From sensation to contemplation, everything follows its natural course without requiring the slightest collaboration on the part of the knowing subject. Since he acknowledged the existence of a soul endowed with active powers of its own, Locke could easily proceed beyond this point. For Condillac, the problem was to account for the possibility of reasoning, searching for more knowledge, forming new conclusions and demonstrating them, without resorting, beyond self-transforming sensation itself, to any other principle of explanation.

He found an answer to the difficulty in a personal theory of signs and of the part they play in the life of the mind.

There are three kinds of signs: (1) accidental signs; that is, any object accidentally tied up with one of our ideas and apt to revive it (the sight of a man reminds me of a place where I chanced upon him); (2) natural signs established by nature to signify some feelings (groans, tears, laughter, etc.); (3) arbitrary signs, or institutional signs; that is, those which were freely chosen and have no natural relationship with the ideas which they signify.[20]

When arbitrary signs were first attached to different ideas in order to signify them, this was a progress of decisive importance. In the first place, it liberated the mind from the necessary relations between ideas created by chance or by nature. Condillac considers as one of the more essential elements in the quest for truth "the operation whereby we give signs to our ideas," but, he says, it is among the least recognized. One might wonder how that operation is possible. In a doctrine where all so-called faculties of the soul are but transformed sensations, how can arbitrary signs "choose" themselves in order to attach themselves to certain classes of objects?

One looks in vain to the *Essay* for an answer to the question. On second thought, one should not expect it to be there. The *Essay* is built along different lines. Condillac is bringing the work of Locke to completion. He *knows* that it is possible to reduce the operations of the human mind into a system by decomposing them into their simplest elements and then recomposing them from there. The only thing one can expect from the philosopher is a truthful description of what, in fact, is happening in the human mind. All the operations of the mind *cannot be* anything else than sensation variously transformed; consequently, the question of the possibility of such transformations does not arise; they simply have to be observed. This is what Condillac undertakes to do.

Before the institution of arbitrarily chosen signs, he tells us, the exercise of "contemplation" (i.e., dwelling on a certain idea) is impossible to him, but

> . . . as soon as a man begins to attach ideas to signs he himself has chosen, memory develops in him. He then begins to dispose by himself of his imagination and to give it a new exercise; for, by means of the signs which he can recall at will, he revives, or at least he *can* revive, the ideas that are bound to them. Later on, he acquires more power over his imagination as he invents more signs, hence a larger number of means of exercising this imagination.[21]

Here is where one begins to discern the superiority of our soul over that of the beasts. Their body does not prevent them from speaking; in fact, some of them actually do pronounce some of our own words. So the cause for their inability to think must rest with their souls: these are unable to attach their ideas to conventional signs. In beasts, therefore, sensation cannot transform itself by reflection.

By "reflection," Condillac understands the aptitude of the soul to recall whatever ideas it chooses and, dismissing the others, to associate or to dissociate them at will.

> That way ourselves to apply our attention, by turns, to diverse objects or to diverse parts of one and the same object, is what is

called *to reflect*. This shows so to speak tangibly, how reflection is born of imagination and memory.[22]

After all this, one shares in the feeling of relief experienced by Condillac when he says: "We have at last developed what was hardest to discern in the progress of the operations of the soul." [23] And indeed, once endowed with the ability to apply reflection to a system of institutional signs which it can combine at will, there is no "human knowledge" of which a mind is not capable. Still, if one remembers that Condillac himself does not hesitate to speak of the degrees of "effort" required from attention according to the different classes of objects with which it deals, cannot one help wondering of what kind of effort purely passive sensations are capable? Obviously, Condillac's "sensations" belong to a soul, and the "soul" belongs to a man—all notions this clever analyst seems to take for granted. One cannot help wondering whether, while he professed to follow the method of Locke against that of Descartes, it was not the spirit of system so powerful in Descartes that was carrying Condillac beyond Locke. Let us recall the way Condillac himself had defined the aim and scope of this philosophical inquiry: "to explain the generation of the operations of the soul by deriving them from one simple perception." He knew full well that this was an entirely new design, and he admitted it. He also knew, and said, "Locke does not seem to have thought of it." He might perhaps have added that the "long chains of reasons" so dear to Descartes, and so mistrusted by Locke, still exercised on his mind their power of seduction.

Beyond Berkeley: the *Treatise*

Condillac was never to go back on the positions developed in his *Essay on the Origin of Human Knowledges*. Far from it, and one might rather wonder at the remarkable unity and continuity of his thought. One reason for it was his extraordinary aptitude not even to see problems when he could not do them justice without going out of his way. One cannot read the opening chapters of his *Essay*, where he deals with the essential veracity of senses, without wondering why he should bother about their objects. This is particularly striking in the passage of Chapter I, 1, 2, where he calmly declares that there is neither error nor obscurity, nor confusion in our way to relate sensations to something outside us. How could one justify such a certitude *on the strength of sensations alone?* For a philosopher writing in 1746, this shows a callous disregard of the warning Berkeley had issued many years before.[24]

The problem was placed under the eyes of Condillac by Denis Diderot in his *Letter on Blindmen for the Use of Those Who See* (1749). Diderot defined the *idealists* as those philosophers who, having awareness of nothing else beyond their own existence and their sensations, refuse to recognize anything else. An extravagant system indeed, and one which, to the greater shame of the human mind, is both the most absurd and the hardest of all to refute. Then he added that Condillac's idealism should be pointed out to its author; it would be no doubt most interesting to watch him try to refute it on the strength of his own principles, "for these are precisely the same as those of Berkeley." Does not the author of the *Essay on the Origin of Human Knowledges* expressly declare that, wherever we may go, "we never get out of ourselves, and it is only our own thought that we apprehend: now this is the result of the first Dialogue of Berkeley and the foundation of his whole system"? [25]

This was to Condillac a challenge to vindicate himself of the charge of teaching principles from which an idealism such as that of Berkeley necessarily followed. He did so in his *Treatise of Sensations* (1754). Written with faultless elegance, this work begins by restating the doctrine already taught in the *Essay*. "Immediately after Aristotle came Locke, for one must not take into account the others who wrote on the same subject." [26] Still faithful to Locke, he remains firm in his design to go beyond him:

> Locke distinguishes two sources of our ideas, senses and reflection. It would be more exact to acknowledge only one, either because, in its principle, reflection is but sensation itself, or because it is less the source of ideas than the channel through which ideas flow from senses.[27]

As could be expected, there were many improvements in the new presentation of the doctrine, and in the Second Part of the *Treatise* the dangerous question asked by Diderot was faced and received an answer.[28]

Condillac was clearly aware of the nature of the problem: On the one hand, all our cognitions come from sense; on the other hand, our sensations are but our own modes of being. How, then, can we see objects outside us? "Indeed, it seems that we only should see our soul differently modified." In the Second Part of the *Treatise*, the title of Chapter IV bluntly defined the question: "How we pass from our sensations to the knowledge of bodies." [29] Now, since one can make extension out of extension only, and bodies out of bodies only, "it is evident that we shall pass from our sensations to the knowledge of bodies, only to the extent that our sensations will produce the phenomenon of extension. . . ." A carefully guarded statement indeed, since Condillac does not say: "to the extent that they will produce *extension*" but, simply, "*the phenomenon* of extension." But his very prudence was making it impossible for him to refute Berkeley on the strength of his own sensism: however hard we may try, the sensed phenomenon of extension will never be more than one particular modification of our mind.

His answer to the problem is none the less interesting to follow. Condillac first shows that the perception of a continuum answering all the conditions of space is possible by means of touch only. Next, well aware that all our senses seem likewise to perceive external objects, he proceeds to show that touch "teaches the other senses to judge of external objects." [30] The conclusion of this demonstration, then, is that the sense which perceives extension is touch, all the other senses perceiving it indirectly by reason of their association with it.

The successive redactions of Condillac's *Treatise* prove that the problem is exceedingly hard to solve, be it only to his own satisfaction. "Questions well asked are questions already answered," Condillac once said on the occasion of this difficulty. To which he added that the remark was particularly true in metaphysics, where it is hard to speak with simplicity. From this point of view, the Second Part of the *Treatise* does great honor to Condillac. Imagine a statue coming to life gradually, he challenges us. Its senses open successively. So long as it only has sensations of smelling, hearing, tasting, and seeing colors, the statue cannot take cognizance of external objects. Even with the sense of touch, it would remain in the same ignorance, if it *remained immobile*. Unless it moves, the statue can only perceive the sensations produced in it by the air around it; it can feel cold or warm, and it can experience pleasure or pain, but in such a case it perceives itself only.

In order to make a man judge that there are bodies, three conditions must be fulfilled: 1] His limbs must be determined to move themselves;   2] his hand, the main organ of tact, must touch him as well as what is around him;   3] among the sensations he experiences, there must be one that necessarily represents bodies.

This latter requirement is of decisive importance. Extension is a continuum constituted by the contiguity of other bodies, and, generally speaking, all continuum is formed by the contiguity of other continuums. Consequently, even touch will give us no knowledge of bodies "unless, among the sensations it gives us, there be one that we shall not perceive as a mode of our own being (*une manière d'être de nous-mêmes*) but, rather, as a mode of being of a continuum formed by the contiguity of other continuums. It is necessary that we be forced to judge this sensation itself to be extended."

In other words, our knowledge of an external world can be accounted for only by a certain type of sensation, and that sensation must be such that it necessitates our mind to affirm the existence of its object. I am perceiving extension as an actually existing non-ego. To come back to our supposed statue, we should not imagine that it would pass from itself to bodies by means of some reasoning. In a statement of decisive importance, Condillac observes that "there is no reasoning that could make it to effect that passage." With exemplary constancy in his views, Condillac insists that the judgment "bodies exist" should be given in a sensation.

But how could this be? At the moment the statue of Condillac receives the sense of touch, it has not yet begun to reason. Yes, Condillac replies, "but nature has reasoned for the statue; nature has organized it so that it would be moved, that it would touch and that it would have, in touching, a sensation that causes it to judge that there is, outside of its feeling being, continuums formed by the contiguity of other continuums, that is to say extension and bodies." The demonstration of this thesis fills up the Second Part of the *Treatise of Sensations*.[31]

A simple sketch of what is central in the philosophy of Condillac does not do him justice. As a philosopher, Condillac is at his best in the detail of his subtle demonstrations. Moreover, his effort to solve metaphysical problems by the lone resources of psychological introspection, with occasional appeals to recently made medical observations, has been rewarded, if not in the field of metaphysics, at least in that of psychology. Artificial as it may be, his method of mental reconstruction of the operations of the mind has at least helped impart precision to problems in which vagueness was prevailing.

It may be that the ideal of scientific knowledge entertained by Condillac did not fit him for the kinds of problems he wanted to handle. A passionate love for clarity and lineal order cannot hope to find much satisfaction in the analysis of the human mind such as we now know it. Condillac hated obscurity, confusion, and disorder in all domains. An *Art of Writing*, followed by an *Art of Reasoning*, then by an *Art of Thinking* and by a *Logic*, of which he himself declared that it was unlike any logic ever written, are as many titles witnessing to what was uppermost in his mind. To him, logic was one with analysis; analysis itself was a method taught to man by nature and served by an art of reasoning which Condillac promised to "bring down to a well made language." [32] This philosophy of *homo loquens* had its limitations; nature refused to display the simplicity Condillac had hoped to find there; the results of his philosophy failed to be convincing, but an extraordinary number of other philosophers felt tempted to take up after him the task he had not successfully achieved. Condillac had a large posterity, which naturally blended with that of Locke,[33] in Italy as well as in France. Associationism, which Bergson will still have to oppose in the philosophy of Taine, found its origin in Condillac's *Treatise of Sensations*.

XVIII

The Reaction
Against Locke

THE ESTABLISHED TRADITION that found in Locke its proximate origin did not reign unchallenged. Countless refutations attended the publication of the new interpretations of man and the world. That controversial literature has not been seriously studied; it should be, for a mere glance at it reveals a great wealth of worthy material. By and large, however, it resorted to the kind of "refutation" whose main preoccupation is to denounce error. A true philosophical reaction to error consists in going to its root, in exposing it, and, above all, in substituting truth for it. Nothing is destroyed until it has been replaced—this remark of Comte is a great truth.

The properly philosophical reaction to the movement represented by Locke, and partially at least caused by him, assumed a twofold form. First, there was what is now called the Scottish School of Philosophy. Its founder was Thomas Reid and he remains its greatest name. The other form of reaction borrowed its inspiration from the classics of modern Christian philosophy; it was initiated in Savoia by the now unjustly forgotten Cardinal Gerdil.

The Philosophical Reaction: Thomas Reid

THE INTELLECTUAL EVOLUTION of Thomas Reid [1] is known to us from his own narrative of it. He himself has described his attitude as a reaction. That reaction was not directed against the "eighteenth century": he himself was part of it. Nor was he opposing the French movement born of Locke: Reid's philosophical horizon does not include contemporary France. His major philosophical merit was to recognize the organic continuity of a long chain of thoughts beginning with Descartes' dogmaticism and ending with the skepticism of Hume, all of which looked to him like a huge collective error.

THE ADVERSARY

FROM THE VERY BEGINNING, Reid presented himself as writing *against* a certain philosophy. He also knew that the representatives of that philosophy had become the leaders of public philosophical opinion. Consequently, he himself was not rating his chances of success very high. Immediately prior to himself, he could see Descartes, Malebranche, Locke, Berkeley, and Hume. Who was he to oppose such great names? "A view of the human understanding so different from that which they have exhibited, will, no doubt, be condemned by many without examination, as proceeding from temerity and vanity." Still, it had to be done. Not indeed in a spirit of blind negativism; on the contrary, Reid openly proclaimed his indebtedness to the very man he was opposing, and in this also he showed himself a true philosopher; but in the course of time the initial error had brought forth such evil fruit that something had to be done about it. There have always been skeptics, but until Hume nobody had really doubted the *principles* themselves.[2] The situation obviously could not be permitted to last.

Let us look at the history of the movement at stake. At the beginning, Descartes began by revoking everything into doubt, including his own existence. True enough, he never *really* doubted that he was a thinking substance, but the method had been applied for the first time, and its effects were to develop in due course. Then came Locke, who doubted that thought implied a mind; he suggested the possibility of a thought without any "I" that thinks; that is, without any thinking thing. Then Malebranche established that, in fact, things do not cause my own ideas; God causes them in me. From this, Berkeley correctly inferred that there was no reason to affirm the existence of external and material objects. It is important to note, with respect to Berkeley, that what makes his case significant is that he has really demonstrated his conclusion; namely, that there is no external world answering my own perceptions of it. In short, Berkeley "has proved by unanswerable arguments what no man in his senses can believe." The more recent comer, David Hume, has then dissolved man just as Berkeley had eliminated the world. With sensations and two or three laws of association, he has fabricated a puppet which he calls man. So, while

Berkeley has eliminated matter in the hope to save the world of spirits, Hume was now eliminating spirits. Nothing was left but complete skepticism.[3]

The main point in this philosophical analysis of the history of recent philosophy was its conclusion; namely, that the system of all these authors is the same and leads to skepticism.[4] Its germ is the decision made by Descartes, *that the immediate objects of man's knowledge are his ideas*. Starting from there, the rest is bound to follow. For if there are ideas, the question arises: How can I go from ideas to things? Of course I cannot. If you begin with Descartes, you will go on with Locke and end with Hume.

There is no reason for despairing, for there is a remedy, if one only: It is to deny ideas, belief in which is necessarily the source of skepticism.[5] The whole body of philosophical speculation founded on this error, Reid begs leave to call *the ideal system*, a close approximation of the term "idealism" soon to be invented.

At the bottom of this global philosophical reaction, there is, as usual, an emotional feeling: a reaction against ridiculous disproportion between the infinitely rich concreteness of given reality, be it that of man or of the world, and the poverty-stricken images of it proposed by the famous exponents of "the ideal system."[6] Reid could have found an ally in Pascal, but his own great man was Francis Bacon, less for the detail of his doctrine than for his insistence on the primacy of observation as a method of knowledge. This preference is important to know for a correct interpretation and appreciation of the work of Reid; he himself once said he felt quite capable of rating the intelligence of a man from his opinion of Francis Bacon.

CRITICISM OF THE IDEAL SYSTEM

AGAINST THE "IDEAL SYSTEM" or the "system of Descartes," Reid posits that "no solid proof has ever been advanced of the existence of ideas." He himself holds them to be a mere fiction of the mind, contrived in order to solve problems it cannot solve and opening the way to skepticism.

As Reid conceives it, the "hypothesis of ideas" consists in holding, with Descartes, that "external things must be perceived by means of images of them in the mind." This notion looks quite simple, satisfactory, and, at any rate, innocuous. In fact, once it is admitted that there are such ideas, they become the only immediate object of knowledge. From then onward, what we call the external world is something made up of objects inferred, signified, or pointed out by ideas in the mind. Immediate contact with it being lost, its very existence becomes hypothetical. Hence the unanswerable argument of Berkeley that, *since the only things we know are ideas,* there is no ground for affirming the existence of anything beyond them. Reid always is careful to observe that this "hypothesis" is the principle from which all the absurdities of idealism and skepticism have been *correctly* deduced. Far from being harmless, "the theory of ideas, like the Trojan horse, had a specious appearance both of innocence and beauty; but if those philosophers (Descartes, Locke, Malebranche, and Berkeley) had known that it carried in its belly death and destruction to all science and common sense, they would not have broken their walls to give it admittance." [7]

The reason why this retrogression had to take place is that, as soon as they began to interject ideas between objects and us, philosophers began to realize that those ideas were most unlike the objects they were supposed to represent. From Descartes to Locke, Malebranche, Berkeley, and Hume there has been a gradual discovery of an important truth, which is "the dissimilitude between the *sensations* of our minds and the *qualities* or attributes of an insentient, inert substance, such as we conceive matter to be." [8] Hence, the just conclusion drawn by Berkeley, "that extension, and figure, and hardness and motion; that land, and sea, and houses, and our own bodies, as well as those of our wives, and children, and friends, are nothing but ideas in the mind; and that there is nothing existing in nature but minds and ideas." But Reid never tires of repeating that, after Berkeley, the worst still was to come:

> The progeny that followed is still more frightful; so that it is surprising that one could be found who had the courage to act the midwife, to rear it up, and to usher it into the world. No causes nor effects; no substances, material or spiritual; no evidence even in mathematical demonstration; no liberty nor active power; nothing existing in nature, but impressions and ideas, following each other without time, place, or subject. Surely no age ever produced such a system of opinions, justly deduced with great acuteness, perspicacity and elegance from a principle universally received. The hypothesis we have mentioned is the father of them all. The

dissimilitude of our sensations and feelings to eternal things is the innocent mother of most of them.⁹

The proper object of the *Inquiry into the Human Mind* was to substitute another interpretation of its faculties for that which had led to such dreadful consequences. Let it be noted, however, that in Reid's own mind this did not mean imagining a more satisfactory answer to the questions asked by Descartes and his successors; to avert their errors it was necessary to provide a *truer* description of what takes place in the mind, following Francis Bacon's principle: Observe. For there are two ways to proceed in such questions. The more commonly followed one is that of imagination; it mainly consists in reasoning by analogy from more to less familiar, and its conclusions are far from safe; the second one is that of observation, following "the strict and *severe method of induction*"; this method, since delineated by Bacon, had been successfully applied to the study of nature but, for no visible reasons, hardly to anything else.

COMMON SENSE AND REALITY

REID THEN PROCEEDS to describe correctly sensation and the formation of ideas.

What is the mind conscious of when we smell a rose or a lily? Following common usage, we call it a *smell* or an *odor*. But what relation is there between the smell and the thing that causes it? Feeling affected in a new way, he who smells such an odor is conscious that it comes to him from outside; but though he realizes he himself is not the cause of that smell, he cannot form any hypothesis as to the nature of that cause. Is it a body or a spirit; is it near or at a distance? The smell itself, considered "abstractly," as Reid would say (i.e., as unrelated to all that which it is not, such as it is being experienced), can be defined as an "original affection," undergone by the mind; it is evidently ridiculous to ascribe to it any quality pertaining to bodies; a smell occupies no more place than melancholy or joy; it has no existence except while it is being smelled. In short, this "original affection" is a simple feeling of the mind; it cannot possibly be in any body; "it is a sensation and a sensation can only be in a sentient thing." ¹⁰

This point needs to be stressed, for the whole doctrine rests upon

it. Reid is trying to make his reader realize that sensation, if it is carefully observed in itself, is strictly nothing else than such an original
affection of the mind, unrelated to any "thing." What it is immediately
related to, however, is judgment; not to judgments in general, but
rather to definite judgments from which it cannot be separated. Such
judgments do not stand in need of being justified by abstract reasoning. Man is so constituted that, as soon as he has sensations, he cannot
help forming the judgments at stake. What are those judgments?

Any sensation, "a smell for instance, may be presented to the mind
in three different ways; it may be smelled, it may be remembered, it
may be imagined or thought of."

In the first case, I cannot not apprehend "that the sensation really
exists." "This is common to all sensations, that as they cannot exist but
in being perceived, so they cannot be perceived but they must exist."
In Reid's doctrine, the judgment "things are" is as evident and necessary as the "I am" of Descartes. And let us not call to Berkeley for
objections, for indeed the Bishop of Cloyne never denied the existence
of sensations; on the contrary, he preferred to "let them stand upon
their own bottom, stript of a subject, rather than to call in question
the reality of their existence." [11]

Reid describes the judgment "this smell is" as simply the expression
of an unshakable *belief* in the existence of that smell. In the same way,
when the sensation is presented to the mind as remembered, "it is
accompanied with a belief of its past existence." Only in the third case
is there no judgment; consequently, there is no assent given by the
mind to anything; in the language of the logicians, it is a "simple
apprehension." Of course this is the very point where the reader is
hoping for an explanation on the part of Reid, but he is headed for
disappointment, for indeed Reid's doctrine precisely rests upon the
fact that such judgments are primitive, so that they must not, indeed
they cannot, be accounted for.[12] Again:

> If you ask me why I believe that it existed yesterday, I can give
> no other reason but that I remember it. Sensations and memory,
> therefore, are simple, *original* and perfectly distinct *operations of
> the mind,* and both of them are original principles of belief.[13]

What Reid is about should now become apparent: he is denying the
existence of primitive ideas conceived apart from the primitive judgments by which they are naturally and necessarily accompanied. Fail-

ure to recognize this is precisely where the "ideal system" is wrong. It teaches that the first operation of the mind is a "simple apprehension" unaccompanied by any judgment; later on, after comparing such simple apprehensions, we would perceive agreements or disagreements between some of them, and our expression of that perception would be judgment. In other words, the tenets of that system maintain first that there are simple apprehensions without judgments; next, that, in point of fact, simple apprehensions always precede judgments. All this is fiction unfounded in reality, for indeed the very reverse is true. From what was said above, it follows on the contrary that, since sensation always goes before memory and imagination, "apprehension, accompanied with belief and knowledge must go before simple apprehension, at least in the matters we are now speaking of," [14] which all are related to the fundamental belief of men in actually existing external reality. What Reid is attacking is, of course, the Lockian theory of belief conceived as "a perception of the agreement or disagreement of ideas," in which he sees "one of the main pillars of skepticism." By making judgment and belief precede ideas,[15] he himself radically eliminates the very possibility of such an error.

The real difficulty with Reid is to take him at his word, for his refusal to answer certain questions is for him the very truth to be grasped. If I say that a sensation exists, I understand myself; but if you want me to say that there is an agreement between my idea of any sensation and that of existence, I find myself confused. I know what belief is, just as I know what it is to hear and to see. If a man does not know these things, let him expect no help from logic or metaphysics. To conclude: "it is no less a part of the human constitution to believe the present existence of our sensations, and to believe the past existence of what we remember, than it is to believe that twice two make four. . . . To reason against any kind of these sorts of evidence is absurd; nay, to reason for them is absurd. They are first principles; and such fall not within the province of reason but of common sense." [16]

As Reid understands it, then, common sense is the power with which nature has endowed man to conceive at once certain beliefs concerning given reality. There is no innateness about such principles; what is inborn in us is the power to conceive them. What is true of the first judgment of existence is likewise true of many other immediate beliefs on which hangs the possibility for us to form demonstrated knowledge in the field of speculation as well as in that of action. Reid carefully avoids listing the first principles of common sense. In the *Inquiry*, he contents himself with "taking notice" of several original principles of belief. Substance, causality are such primary beliefs, but there are many others since, in perceiving a tree, sight gives us not only a simple apprehension of the tree but a belief of its existence, of its figure, of its distance and magnitude, "and this judgment or belief is not got by comparing ideas, it is included in the very nature of the perception." [17]

The proper object of Reid's inquiry was to ascertain the nature of common sense rather than to undertake a systematic exploration of its contents.[18] From this point of view, his thought cannot be more clearly expressed than it is in the Conclusion of his treatise:

> Such original natural judgments are therefore a part of that furniture which nature has given to the human understanding. They are the inspiration of the Almighty, no less than our notions or simple apprehensions. They serve to direct us in the common affairs of life, where our reasoning faculty would leave us in the dark. They are a part of our constitution, and all the discoveries of our reason are founded upon them. They make up what is called *the common sense of mankind;* and what is manifestly contrary to any of those first principles, is what we call *absurd*. The strength of them is *good sense*, which is often found in those who are not acute in reasoning. A remarkable deviation from them arising from a disorder in the constitution, is what we call *lunacy*; as when a man believes that he is made of glass. When a man suffers himself to be reasoned out of the principles of common sense by metaphysical arguments, we may call this *metaphysical lunacy*; which differs from the other species of the distemper in this, that it is not continued, but intermittent; it is apt to seize the patient in solitary and speculative moments; but when he enters into society common sense recovers her authority. A clear explication and enumeration of the principles of common sense, is one of the chief desiderata in logic. We have only considered such of them as occurred in the examination of the five senses.

Clearly enough, Reid was interested in vindicating and restoring the rights of metaphysical knowledge. Whereas everybody in England and in France was following in the footsteps of Locke and, every time, going one better, Reid was simply breaking relations with all that school and returning to philosophical positions anterior to the time when Descartes had ill-advisedly decided that they stood in need of rational justification. In this respect he can be said to advocate a return to the pre-Cartesian condition of philosophy.[19] On the other hand, it can be wondered if this attempt to restore metaphysics was not doomed to failure before it got under way. It was suffering of the very disease it intended to cure; namely, empiricism. Francis Bacon was right in advocating observation as a scientific method, but, if no other method is added to it, observation will never lead to metaphysical conclusions. This very shortcoming insured the success of the doctrine. It offered an irresistible temptation to all apologetics. The philosophy of common sense thus was welcomed everywhere there were men looking for metaphysical conclusions without having to resort to truly metaphysical speculation. It was low-priced metaphysics; there always is a market for that useful commodity.

For the same reason, the followers of Reid did not improve on his philosophy. His doctrine suffered from two major defects. As has been seen, Reid never succeeded in setting up a satisfactory table of his first principles; moreover, he does not seem to have thought of a method to distinguish the kind of evidence proper to truth from the pseudo-evidence enjoyed by firmly rooted prejudice. In consequence, all he could do when he wanted to maintain a conclusion against the conjoined forces of Locke, Berkeley, and Hume was to appeal to common sense. If asked how he knew that a certain conclusion was supported by common sense, he could only answer: Because it was justifiable neither by experience nor by rational demonstration. His followers could not go much further than Reid himself had gone by means of the same method and on the same way.

James Beattie[20] repeated the attacks of Reid against the skepticism of Hume, always using the evidence of common sense as his preferred weapon. However, being somewhat younger, he took on new adversaries besides those chosen by Reid. Beattie indulged in violent attacks against Voltaire and Rousseau, whom he opposed on religious grounds. Toward the end of his life he likewise denounced the French Revolution on account of its atrocities. In philosophy proper, Beattie toned down the rather loose psychology of Reid. He distinguished perceptive faculties from active powers (which roughly corresponded to the two series of Reid's essays and, incidentally, to the titles of the chairs of philosophy traditionally maintained in Scottish universities: psychology and morals). The "perceptive faculties" divided into speech, perceptions of external senses, reflection, memory, imagination, sympathy, taste. The active powers divide into instinct, habit, appetite or

desire, passions and affections, moral principles. The second part of
Beattie's *Elements of Moral Science* is devoted to natural theology.
According to him, the proofs of the existence of God are innumerable
and evident. They are either *a priori,* as when one shows that the non-
existence of God is unthinkable, for it is an absurd and impossible
proposition; or else they are *a posteriori,* such as the arguments proving a cause of the existence and order of the world. On the whole, the
more valuable contribution of Beattie to philosophy might well be his
interesting essay on poetry and music. He himself was a poet whose
poems went through many editions; so he then was speaking from personal experience, and the reader feels it.

A better-known exponent of the philosophy of common sense,
Dugald Stewart[21] was not noticeably more successful than Beattie.
Reid was already lacking in force and in organizing power; Stewart,
alas, even more so. A very brilliant mind, as can be seen from his remarkable academic career, he contented himself with indulging in the
kind of superficial observation of the mind to which there is nothing
to object precisely because it says so little. His widespread influence,
first in England, then in France at the time of Cousin's eclecticism, can
only be explained by the low level of philosophical thought in the
last years of the eighteenth century. The common-sense school of
philosophy never yielded valuable fruit until, in the first half of the
nineteenth century, William Hamilton established contact between the
tradition of Reid and the young metaphysical ambitions of German
idealism. By that time, however, the philosophy of the Enlightenment
had become a thing of the past.

Gerdil's Christian Reaction

REID HIMSELF WAS CONSCIOUS of returning to the traditional attitude
of the pre-Cartesian philosophers; he himself expressly said so,[22] only
he never realized the peril involved in attempting to overthrow the
conclusions of Humean empiricism by means of such an empiricism
as that of Francis Bacon. In France, there was no metaphysical spirit
alive that could counter the triumphant progress of the method and
doctrine of Locke. Malebranche had lost much of his influence even
among Christian philosophers. One could almost say of his doctrine of

the "vision of ideas in God" that, in France as in Scotland, it remained "as a foreigner never naturalized in this land." [23] The long and short of the story might well be that de-Christianized countries have no use for Malebranche, and in the eighteenth century, French society was certainly that.

Strangely enough, however, there still remained in Europe a sort of sanctuary where Catholic-minded thinkers still hung on. As a political entity, it remained a rather fluctuating and undetermined affair, neither Italian nor French. For convenience's sake, let us call it Savoia with Torino for its capital.[24] The more determined metaphysical reactions against empiricism, skepticism, and, generally speaking, the spirit of the *Encyclopedia*, will originate there.[25]

GERDIL'S CHRISTIAN METAPHYSICS

SIGISMOND GERDIL'S[26] DOCTRINE is a clear case of Christian philosophy, but it witnesses to the rupture of the Christian philosophical tradition caused by Descartes and the rise of modern philosophy. When he lists the men who "restored" philosophy, Gerdil finds it natural to quote "Galileo, Bacon, Grotius, Descartes, Gassendi, Leibniz, Newton, Bossuet, Nicole," all good names indeed, but which explain why scholasticism was the reason that, at the beginning of the seventeenth century, philosophy needed restoring. Gerdil certainly had some such idea in mind. A Cartesian, he considered outdated the philosophy of Aristotle and, by a necessary consequence, all scholasticism inasmuch as it was Aristotelian. On the other hand, having realized that Locke and his school were responsible for the low state of metaphysics in his own time, Gerdil turned to the classics of Christian philosophy for a remedy. Blending together St. Augustine and St. Thomas Aquinas, he decided that Malebranche had brought the essential truth of the two doctrines to its point of perfection. The result was amazing. It is hardly possible to exaggerate the influence of Gerdil's doctrine on the later development of Christian philosophy in Italy, in Belgium, and in France.

What is at stake can be seen at once from the very first sentence of his admirable *Metaphysical Principles of Christian Morals*. Laying down the first principle of his philosophy, Gerdil calmly declares: "The first and only object of our cognitions is being." That sweeping statement discourages criticism. Even granting that being is the prime object of our knowledge, how are we to understand that it is its only object?

Gerdil is very far from objecting to the notion that knowledge presupposes ideas, or intelligible species (the name does not matter), mediating between the object and the mind. In this respect his criticism of Locke has nothing in common with that of Reid. On the contrary, Gerdil affirms (1) the necessity of such intermediaries between mind and things, and he adds (2) that, in order to cause knowledge, such an idea, or intelligible species, must contain in itself or, rather, must *be* the resemblance, the act, the reality of the object. Finally (3), and this is of capital importance in the doctrine, no finite being can contain in itself the reality of another being. Each particular thing can only be itself, otherwise things would be found to be in two different genres at the same time, which is absurd. It is therefore impossible that the idea or resemblance by which the object is known to us be found either in our soul or in an angel—in short, in any finite being. So the only possible answer is that the species or idea by which we know other finite beings be found in an infinite being; that is, in God.

Gerdil is here encountering the doctrine of the vision in God, but his metaphysical path to it is not identically that of Malebranche. His main argument, that no finite being can contain another one, is borrowed from an ontology the depth of which cannot be denied. What this precisely comes to is a reduction of epistemology and noetics to ontology. Gerdil is asking all questions about knowledge in terms of being, and the strange thing about his undertaking is that, having to look for a notion capable of justifying it, he can think of no better one than the notion of God in the doctrine of St. Thomas Aquinas. Gerdil needs an infinite being who, because of his very infinity, can act for us as the idea or intelligible species of all finite things; and indeed St. Thomas says in his *Summa Theologiae*, I, 84, 2, 3m: "The essence of God is the perfect resemblance of all things, as to all that which we find in things as being the universal principle of all."

The secret of the operation here discloses itself. Gerdil is turning the ontological notion of St. Thomas, that the essence of God, conceived as infinite being, is the perfect idea of all things, into a noetic principle; to wit, that the divine essence is the only idea, intelligible species, or resemblance in which we can know all other beings. This explosive metaphysical combination is obtained by adding to an Augustinian metaphysics of truth an adequate dose of the Thomistic metaphysics of being.

Seldom was a philosopher more lucidly aware of what he was doing: watch him go on. The essence of God is alone unrestricted being. As such, it contains eminently the reality and perfection of all possible things. Consequently, to use the language of St. Thomas, God contains the archetypes of all things, or, in other words, he is the archetype of all things.

On the other hand, since God is spirit (as perfect and immaterial), the divine essence is the only one we can conceive as able to unite itself to all spirits, intimately and in an intelligible way. Consequently, nothing is simpler and more agreeable to reason than to say that it is by this union to the intelligible archetypes in God that one perceives all that which one knows by idea, and not by confused feeling.

To conclude, since our perceiving power is passive, as has been acknowledged by all philosophers, including Locke and even the Peripatetics—for although the latter made up an active intellect to fabricate the species, they also have admitted a passive intellect to receive them—"We can conceive no other efficient and exemplary cause of our perceptions besides the divine essence which, by acting upon our understanding, can by its efficacy represent to it the archetypal ideas it contains, and, by that means, let it know the nature and the properties of the beings, which were all created after the resemblance of those Ideas."

The doctrine then consists in saying two things: first, the relation between our idea of being and our notion of the various species of beings is analogous to the relation in God, between his essence and his archetypal ideas; next, it is God who, by causing in us the idea of being, represents the various beings to our understanding. It is important to note that, in Gerdil's own doctrine, this intimate relationship of the human mind to God is not one of seeing power to seen object. Gerdil does not say that we see God; he even avoids Malebranche's language, that we see everything *in* God; on the contrary, he expressly and forcefully specifies that God actively produces cognitions in us as an efficient and exemplary cause; all we contribute to the operation is our passive reception of the notions caused in us by God.[27]

Gerdil had no intention to innovate. When he thought of it, that "so simple and so beautiful" conception of our way of knowing had behind it the highest authorities in the past: Plato and St. Augustine have likewise believed that immutable truths cannot be seen otherwise (see Augustine's *De Magistro, De Libero arbitrio, De Trinitate,* and *Retractationes*), and other doctors have upheld the same doctrine; in fine, "Father Malebranche has carried it to its ultimate perfection by explaining it as clearly as possible in all his writings, by proving it in the most solid way and by no less solidly answering all the objections that ignorance can form against a system whose truth is as clearly demonstrated to attentive minds as that of the propositions of Geometry." [28]

However one may feel about the doctrine, it must be conceded that it was a radical destruction of the very principles of Locke. Gerdil was not reinstating the notion of innate ideas, he was substituting for it the doctrine of the illumination of all minds by the light of God.

GERDIL'S CHRISTIAN EPISTEMOLOGY

HAVING THUS ASCERTAINED the principle of the doctrine, it remains for us to see it at work in its development.

The first object of human knowledge is being. This object is given to us under the form of beings. Each being is known to us by its idea. Beings, or their ideas, have relations. These relations between beings are therefore for us relations between ideas. One calls *truths* the relations between ideas thus perceived by our minds.

All such relations divide into relations of quantity and relations of perfection. In other words, beings are given to the mind as more or less great and as more or less good. The first class of relations constitutes scientific knowledge, the second class of relations constitutes moral and religious knowledge.

Taken together, the relations of perfection make up our very knowledge of *order*. The idea of order consists in this, that certain objects are known to us as more or less perfect than others. To the notion of order must be joined that of the relation of means to end, for indeed means are there in view of ends just as the less perfect is in view of the more perfect.[29]

Of the objects outside, some have with us relations of convenience; some, on the contrary, of inconvenience or unsuitableness. The first ones give us pleasure, the others are for us occasions of pain. Sensations of pleasure and pain are modifications of our soul. For that very reason, it is absurd to suppose that they resemble their causes. Pain, a spiritual fact, cannot resemble the object extended in space by which it is caused. Sensations, then, are *feelings*, not *ideas*. This must be firmly maintained against Locke.[30] As to the origin of sensations, only an infinitely wise law can let us perceive those confused feelings that discover to us no truth but inform us of the present condition of our bodies, of their relations with other bodies as well as of all that which it is necessary for us to know in view of self-preservation.

At this point we find ourselves brought back to the problem of the actual cause of our cognitions. As was said, we have a clear idea that only God can act upon the mind and cause in it both ideas and feelings. That idea is clear because it is comprehensible that a mind should act upon another mind. On the contrary, no other explanation of the origin of ideas and feelings in us makes sense. Their cause cannot be sensations: senses can discern objects, they cannot discern relations and order between objects. Nor can their cause be the other source of knowledge assigned by Locke, reflection, for indeed Locke himself grants that reflection only lets us know the operations of our own soul. All it does is to take notice. The epistemology of Gerdil thus confirms the conclusions of his metaphysics. The whole body of human knowledge, including even sensations, is caused in us by the efficacy of God acting according to the laws he himself has established, or, rather, which he himself is.

NATURAL THEOLOGY

THUS FAR, the existence of God has been taken for granted. In a way, it has to be. Since God has to be posited as the very cause of human knowledge, any reflection on the nature of knowledge unavoidably leads the mind to the notion of God. Besides, universal consent witnesses in favor of that truth. Only Locke pretends there are some savage tribes ignorant of the existence of God, but even Voltaire, Locke's great admirer, disagrees with him on that point. In fine, the existence of God is known from the consideration of things around us. There are so many of them that it is hardly necessary to relate them. However, here is one to which Gerdil seems to attach particular value. As will be seen, it is the classical proof by the contingency of finite beings.

Possibles may not have actual existence; nay, since one of them cannot be another one, the actual existence of one of them is incompatible with the actual formal existence of the others.—All those possibles are finite beings which, as finite, cannot exist without some limitation.— Those beings, then, although actually existing, can without contradiction be supposed not to exist.—Those beings therefore, not being by themselves determined to be, must be determined to actual existence by the Supreme Being that contains them all eminently. The world, then, has received its existence from that Supreme Being. The conclusion is the more satisfactory as it more perfectly fits the notion of God defined by St. Thomas Aquinas: God is the very act of Being in its absolute perfection.[31]

However we prove it, the problem is not to establish the existence of God, but to purify our notion of him. The universal consent about God's existence does not extend to his nature. Only by fighting imagination do we succeed in conceiving God as absolute Being, superior to all others, most perfect and all-powerful.

The very necessity there is for us to fight imagination in thinking of God sufficiently proves that his notion does not come to us from sense. Locke pretends that it is an "idea of reflection"; that is to say, composed by the human understanding. Exactly, it is a "mixed mode," or a complex idea composed of several simple ideas such as existence, power, duration, felicity, etc. But Locke does not say after what model we gather those simple ideas together in order to form the composite idea of God. He should have said it. According to himself, such "mixed modes" are formed in three different ways: 1] from observation—that is, from seeing certain simple ideas given together in experience—but no man ever perceived such an actually existing infinite and all-powerful being;   2] by inventing them, but, precisely, there is no reason why such simple ideas should be gathered together one way rather than another;   3] by enumerating its elements, but, for the same reason, this is impossible unless the idea be already there.[32] The idea of God, then, is neither empirically given nor formed by the mind.

The only explication for its origin is to admit that "the idea of God is no other than the idea of unrestricted Being, of Being that contains all reality, the idea, in a word, of the sovereign perfection." In the light of what precedes, this is evident. There is being: Now being is the same thing as reality, and reality always is a certain perfection. Inversely, all perfection, all reality has and implies being. There are relations of perfection: An alarm clock is more perfect than a simple clock; a horse is more perfect than a tree, etc. On the other hand, no given being is the whole being: It always is such and such a being. If, therefore, there is a being that is nothing else than being, he must needs be all-perfection at once: "And this really is the idea of God. God is Being and it is under that magnificent notion, which in one single word comprises everything, that God has wanted us to know Him, when he said: He Who Is has sent me unto you." [33]

A simple inspection of that notion of being reveals that, like the notion of God of which it is but another name, it originates neither in sense nor in reflection. It is acquired by a reflection, not of the mind upon itself, but of the mind upon finite beings. As was shown above, it can be established by considering the contingency of finite beings; or else, following the method of St. Thomas in the *Quarta via*, by arguing from the degrees of perfection found in empirically given beings. Here again, Gerdil does not make our knowledge of God himself a direct intuition. Everything we know of him, including his very existence, needs to be proved *a posteriori*, but all the demonstrations about God are carried out in the light of the first object of human understanding, the notion of being, a notion which reveals in us the very presence of its cause, Being. [34]

CHRISTIAN MORALS

IT IS A COMMON FEATURE of all Augustinianisms that, in them, epistemology and ethics are indiscernible from metaphysics. Gerdil will therefore continue to fight empiricism in ethics exactly as he had done in epistemology, and on the strength of the same principles. It is not without some justification that his two treatises on the immateriality of the soul and on the theory and practice of education now are respectively called his anti-Locke and his anti-Rousseau.

Natural law is the natural knowledge of the difference there is between just and unjust. Such a knowledge does not come to us from sense; sensations only let us know objects, facts, and acts between which relations of justice and injustice obtain, but neither justice nor injustice is perceptible to sight. Neither are they notions of formation, which we make up by combining other simple notions as Locke vainly pretends. Here, as in the case of our notion of God, there is no empirically given model after which that complete notion could be formed. One would vainly maintain that the notion of justice comes to us from education: Where did the educators themselves find it? Gerdil cannot approve of the simplified and fanciful views of education developed in Rousseau's *Emile*.[35] The mind knows natural law in the same way as it knows all other truths; namely, by its union with the wisdom of God.[36]

This is for Gerdil's reader one more occasion to watch him blend Augustine, Malebranche, and Thomas Aquinas. Applying to the notion of "natural law" what Thomas Aquinas says of the natural light of reason (a legitimate move indeed), Gerdil goes on to say that natural law is in us an impression, an emanation, a reflected light beam of the eternal law in God. Even those who deny the existence of innate ideas acknowledge the agreement of minds on some notions. There seems to be in men a disposition to form the same notions of the same objects. Now this can be understood only by taking literally the opinion of St. Augustine, that our understanding shares in the knowledge of eternal truths, and that in the practical as well as in the speculative order. We are indebted to Father Malebranche for having removed all the difficulties which ignorance and prejudice never fail to find in that doctrine.[37] There is no reason, therefore, to follow Locke in his assertion that the rule of our actions is usefulness, either our own or that of society; the true rule of human acts is the light of God.

Granting this, there still remains to explain how, from the knowledge of that universal rule, we can derive the precepts concerning the immense variety of particular acts. The answer is provided by the notion of the relations of perfection that obtain between beings. Each being occupies a certain place between more perfect and less perfect ones; in order to act as it should, every thing must act according to that which it is. All our operations then should regulate themselves after the relations of perfection obtaining between us and the objects of our operations. This implies that man know the kind of being he is and the kind of beings objects are. Since that knowledge is the work of reason, man must act according to reason in order to act according to that which he is. By thus acting in every occasion as he should act, given his own nature and that of his objects, man finds himself in spontaneous agreement with other men who, having the same nature and dealing with similar objects, follow the same rule. Thus is established, by common agreement in the same light of reason, a society between all intelligent beings and, since their common light is that of

God, between those beings and God.[38] The doctrine of Hobbes, according to whom the natural condition of men is war, finds itself refuted by the Christian and true notion of a universal communion of all spirits in the same divine light.

This union of our mind with the supreme reason is the foundation of the cult we owe to God. It is a cult rationally founded in spirit and in truth. At the same time, since it rests upon the common love of man for the same good, it inspires them with mutual love, which is the very bond of their society. Gerdil therefore finds himself at the very antipodes of the doctrines that identify social order with a self-establishing order or with some convention freely decreed by its members. God is the only true bond there is between men, and this is the reason everything that reinforces the union and society of men with God strengthens by the same token the social bond between men.[39] Indeed, there is more perfection in that which binds us to God than in that which binds us to men.

One would look in vain on the French philosophical scene for anything like this solemn vindication of the rights of metaphysical thought in the middle of an all-destroying anti-metaphysical and anti-religious hurricane. The fact should be kept in mind in attempting an appreciation of the doctrine; the case of Cardinal Gerdil is a fruitful subject of reflections. He wanted to bring a remedy to the situation of metaphysics, be it only because the teaching of Christian truth in the modern world of philosophers and scientists is impossible without a minimum of metaphysical speculation. To appeal to the traditional philosophy of the scholastics was impossible for him. He was convinced that the metaphysics of Aristotle had been superseded by that of Descartes, itself brought to perfection by Malebranche. The Aristotelian notion of substance, for instance, was to Gerdil a thing of the past.[40] All he expected from St. Thomas Aquinas was his truly admirable notion of God, of which he himself was to make a very personal use. By and large, Gerdil could find no better help than Malebranche, the man of whom it had been said that one could not become acquainted with his doctrine without becoming a better philosopher and a better Christian.

Theoretically speaking, bigger and better things could have been done, but more than one hundred years were still to pass before the revival of Christian philosophy by Pope Leo XIII. The situation was nearly desperate. The sensism of the Encyclopedists, the materialism of d'Holbach, the naturalism of Rousseau were deadly perils to which some metaphysics had to be opposed. It is amazing to see with what indulgence, and almost sympathy, the good cardinal speaks of that charming M. de Voltaire, whose theism, as compared with the brutal negations of Diderot, offered at least some possibilities of mutual understanding.[41]

The result was the peculiar brand of Augustinianism circulated under Gerdil's authority. His *Defence of the Sentiments of Fr. Malebranche*, which today he probably would not be permitted to print because its language smacks of ontologism, was published in 1748 with the three *approbationes* of his ecclesiastical censors: Giovanni Marchetti, President of the Gesù; Ignazio Filippo Perini, of the Congregation of the Oratory; and Thomas Vincent Pani, O.P., Master of the Sacred Palace. What Gerdil was doing must have looked natural to them as well as to him, and he must have felt still more completely justified in his attitude when, in later years, he was appointed President of the Sacred Congregation of the Index. Without Austria's veto, Malebranche would have ascended with him to the Holy See. At least it must have been for Gerdil a great satisfaction to hear himself hailed by Pope Benedict XIV as the *ripurgatore della buona filosofia*.[42] Even in philosophy, to come at the right time is important.

7 🌀 THE AGE OF THE PHILOSOPHERS

WHEN OLD Christian Wolff was permitted by Frederick the Great, upon that illustrious monarch's accession to the throne, to return to Prussia, there to die honorably in 1751, it was to a kind of historical monument that honor was being done. For Wolff had decidedly outlived the era of metaphysics. By the midpoint of the century English empiricism had conquered the Continent. The great systems rooted in Descartes were already looked upon as relics—respected relics, to be sure, but relics nonetheless. Toland in religion, Newton in science and epistemology, Locke for psychology and political philosophy, these were the new patron saints of an energetic and worldly group of thinkers who did not hesitate for a moment to assume for themselves the glorious title of *philosopher*. Feeling themselves called to the mission of spreading the liberating and illuminating message of the role of empirically founded reason, the "philosophers" set out to bring the sciences to practical fruition, to turn the method of empirical inquiry against the forces of dark superstition, to probe the mysteries of the human soul with the instruments of a kind of Newtonian psychology, and to point the way politically to a reign of the enlightened bourgeoisie which would let technology command the destinies of men. *Aufklärung,* the Germans called it; "the Enlightenment," in English; *"l'âge des lumières,"* in Paris, spiritual center of this international movement. All three names trumpet forth the essential idea of the movement: Light is to be brought into every corner of man's activity—the light of empirical reason, illuminating for the first time the sense of human history, the rights of man, the nature of his intelligence, the nature of true government, the spirit of laws.

So the "philosophers" we are now going to study are not metaphysicians in the old sense; they are moved by a new ideal of what constitutes "wisdom." In the present chapter we shall consider the loosely knit group gathered about the great "philosophical" institution of the *Encyclopedia;* this is the group that actually called themselves *philosophes.* In subsequent chapters we shall study other thinkers who shared their enthusiasm for spreading the light and who actually contributed more to the real illumination of areas previously neglected in the modern tradition. Finally we shall turn to the *Aufklärung* in an awakening Germany. That will quite naturally bring us to the climactic figure of eighteenth-century philosophy, Immanuel Kant, who is as much the beginning of a new chapter in history as the closing of an old one.

Fortunately one of the important "philosophers" himself has attempted to picture for us the aspirations of the Enlightenment. In this regard, the *Preliminary Discourse* written by d'Alembert[1] as an introduction to the *Encyclopedia* is an irreplaceable document. Let us now leave him the floor.

XIX

D'Alembert and the Idea
of an Encyclopedia

THE *Encyclopedia* was born of the desire to do over again, but much better, the *Cyclopaedia or Dictionary of Arts and Sciences,* published in England by Ephraïm Chambers in 1728. A French publisher had asked Diderot to translate it; Diderot found there an occasion to plan and to publish an immensely more ambitious work in which no less than the sum total of human knowledge would be summarized for presentation to a large public. In 1751 at Paris was published, with the concurrence of d'Alembert, Rousseau, Voltaire, and a host of distinguished experts, the first volume of the *Encyclopedia or Reasoned Dictionary of Sciences, Arts and Crafts;*[2] the last volume was to be published in 1758. In the meantime, d'Alembert had discreetly withdrawn; Voltaire had practically done the same thing on account of the active opposition of the religious and political authorities, and Rousseau had pulled out in one of his characteristic huffs. Not that these gentlemen were any less anti-religious than the director, but d'Alembert thought there was nothing to be gained by openly attacking established churches and religious beliefs. Voltaire was busy elsewhere. And Rousseau had withdrawn to dwell in solitude with benign Nature. Diderot would carry on the great enterprise alone.

But d'Alembert was still enthusiastic about the project when he penned the general introduction. The *Preliminary Discourse* is a review of the principal sciences, each one of which provides d'Alembert with opportunities for stating his own views. He always does this with great moderation and discretion, and never more so than when he is treading on thin ice. It is not impossible, however, to extract from this cagey introduction precise information on his views, which are so expressive of the spirit of the Enlightenment as a whole, and of the motivational force behind the *Encyclopedia* in particular.

"Philosophy forms the dominant taste of our century."[3] This statement neatly establishes the general tone. In the thirteenth century, the dominant taste among intellectuals had been theology. In the seventeenth century, up to and including Malebranche, many an intellectual would have felt pulled between theology and a reason-go-it-alone philosophy. By 1750 no hesitation is possible. The thing to do is to be a "philosopher." According to the same witness, the gratifying progress recently achieved by philosophy suggests its decision to make up for lost time.

When did that progress take place? Bacon and Descartes had prepared the ground for it. Had he been more of a metaphysician, Newton would have himself achieved it. But "what Newton had not dared to do, or perhaps, what he had not been able to do, Locke undertook and successfully completed. One can say that Locke created authentic metaphysics much as Newton created physics." After condemning abstractions, Locke did not study books, he rather looked at himself for a long time; then he wrote up in his *Essay on Human Understanding* the description of what he had seen. "In one word, he brought down metaphysics to that which, in fact, it ought to be: *the experimental physics of the soul;* a physics very different from that of bodies, not only in its object, but also in its way of envisaging it." In physics, one often discovers new facts, because its object is exterior to man; in metaphysics, all the facts are in man; they are as ancient as the world, and since they have always been known, there is no hope of discovering new ones. "Reasonable metaphysics can only consist, as experimental physics, in carefully collecting all those facts, in turning them into one body, in explaining the ones by the others, in distinguishing those that must come first and serve as a base."

The reflections suggested to d'Alembert by his own definition of metaphysics are very instructive. The slowness of metaphysics' progress shows how hard men find it to apply their attention to simple elements of human knowledge. "The title of 'metaphysician,' even of 'great metaphysician' is still common enough in our century, for we like to be lavish in all domains: but how rare are the persons truly deserving that name!" Those who call themselves metaphysicians simply obscure clear ideas by their subtleties. No wonder such men despise one another: "I do not doubt that this title will soon be resented by good minds as an insult, just as the name 'sophist,' which means 'wise,' dishonored in Greece by those who bore it, was rejected by true philosophers." [4]

To sum up, the age in which d'Alembert lived was that of "philosophy"; philosophy is "metaphysics"; but metaphysics is now defined as the physics of the soul; its founder is Locke, its progress is slow, and d'Alembert fears for the good renown of the name. Thirty years later, in 1781, the Preface to the first edition of Kant's *Critique of Pure Reason* will show that d'Alembert's prophecy was fulfilled.

What are the nature and limits of knowledge? The time of systems is past.

"The spirit of system is in physics what metaphysics is in geometry," for it is a spirit of hypothesis and conjecture which can set us on the way to truth but cannot lead us to it. The observation of nature suggests possible explanations, but only calculus can establish the existence of those supposed causes "by exactly determining the effects they can produce, and comparing these effects with those that experiment reveals to us." [5]

So much for the *nature* of knowledge; as to its *limits*, they are two: all the objects we can know are comprised between two extremities, both of which escape our understanding.

Take for example the first object that offers itself to the mind: our own existence. The desire to protect his own existence invites man to establish relations with other men; inequalities bring about oppression, and along with it come the acquired notions of justice and injustice. In examining the possible cause of such notions and of our moral actions, we acknowledge that it cannot be our body "since the properties we observe in matter have nothing in common with the power to think and to will; whence it follows that the being we call *we* is formed of two principles of different nature united in such manner that there obtains between the movement of the one and the affections of the other a correspondence which we can neither suspend nor alter, and which keeps them both in a reciprocal subjection. This enslavement, so independent of us, joined to the reflections we are forced to make on the nature of the two principles and on their imperfection, elevates us to the contemplation of an all-powerful Intelligence to whom we owe all that which we are, and which, consequently, demands our worship. In order to be acknowledged, his existence would only need our inner feeling, even though the universal testimony of other men, and that of the whole nature, did not confirm it." [6]

Certain as they are, these conclusions nevertheless constitute the *upper limit* of human knowledge. "The nature of man, whose study is so necessary, is a mystery impenetrable to man himself when he is enlightened by reason only. . . . The same can be said of our existence, present and future, of the essence of the Being to whom we owe it, and of the kind of worship he requires from us." Hence the necessity of a revealed religion, destined to supplement natural knowledge and uncovering to us some part of what escapes our sight.

If we investigate the nature of our body instead of that of our soul, we are led to the consideration of extension, which is the object of mathematics and constitutes the *lower limit* of knowledge. True enough, mathematical sciences are certain, but we should not let ourselves be awed by their certitude. They chiefly owe it to the simplicity of their objects, and because their objects are not equally simple, the various branches of mathematics are not equally certain. The only truly exact sciences are algebra, geometry, and mechanics; and, because its object is the simplest of all, the principles of the first are clearer than those of the other two. The more concrete its object, the less clear the principles of a science. Extension is really mysterious; motion is an enigma to philosophers; the metaphysical principle of the laws of impact is not clear. What d'Alembert seems to retain of the discussions of the metaphysicians about the problem of the communication of motion is that "the more deeply they scrutinize their idea of matter and of the properties that represent it, the darker that idea becomes and the more it looks as though it wanted to escape them." [7]

D'Alembert carries this critical examination of the lower limit of human knowledge further. Leaving aside the different levels of certitude attainable by the various mathematical sciences, he examines mathematical knowledge itself. At first sight, it seems that its conclusions are without number and, so to speak, inexhaustible, but if, after taking stock of them, one looks at them with a philosophical eye, their number does not look so great; "one realizes that one is, in effect, much less rich than one imagined." The axioms of geometry consist in expressing one simple notion in two different ways; to say that two and two are four adds nothing to saying that two and two are two and two. The notions of whole, part, greater, and smaller are, in fact, one single notion, since one could not have one of them without having the others. The same can be said of theorems. Look at a series of geometrical propositions, deduced in such a way that each one of them implies the next one, "you will realize that they all are but the first proposition deforming itself, so to speak, successively and little by little, in passing from a consequence to the next one; it has not been really multiplied by the chain of consequences, the first proposition has but received different forms." [8]

As represented by d'Alembert, the rationalism of the Encyclopedists is therefore very different from the gloating self-satisfaction of a reason unaware of its limits. There is more than a touch of Pascal in the way this eminent scientist pictures to himself the world he is striving to understand. Unfortunately there will be enthusiasts who are not this sensitive. As d'Alembert sees it, there is between the upper and the lower limits of knowledge an immense interval in which the supreme Intelligence seems to deride our efforts to understand, for it is full of clouds that, here and there, a few light beams seem to pierce as if to excite our curiosity: "One could liken the universe to certain works of a sublime obscurity, whose author, by coming down to the level of his reader, tries to make him believe that he understands nearly all." [9] In physics, we understand different fragments of the whole and we explain them by means of different principles, as if, being detached from the rest, they were different truths. The apparently different properties of electricity would appear to us as explicable by one single cause "if we could reach up to the prime cause. For him who could embrace it all from one single point of view, the universe would be, so to speak, one single fact and one great truth." [10]

D'Alembert himself was a good example of the best type of man the *Aufklärung* could produce. A first-class scientist, well informed of the history of philosophy since Descartes and Bacon, he judges the systems in the light of what the word "science" represents to him. We saw that the empiricism of Bacon and Locke come first in his esteem, but he is too great an algebraist not to appreciate the point of view of Descartes; finding both experience and mathematics perfectly associated in Newton, he sets up Newtonian physics as the very model of a really founded human knowledge. On the other hand, he approves in Leibniz the feeling for the continuity observable from one domain of reality to another and, like Pascal, he finds science moving with variable degrees of certitude between two extremes that seem destined to remain for man two inscrutable mysteries. A man of his own times, he trusts nothing but reason; limited as it is, reason is the best we have. But he decidedly does not like to see ratiocination overdone. For example, should it invade the fine arts?

> One makes abuse of the best things. That philosophical spirit, so much the fashion today, that wants to see everything and to suppose nothing, has invaded even literature. Some say it is harmful to its progress, and one cannot easily pretend not to see it. Inclined to combination and analysis, our century seems decided to introduce cold and didactic discussions into the affairs of sentiment. Passions and taste have a logic of their own, and that logic has principles wholly different from those of ordinary logic.

This last-stated conviction, that passions and tastes have a logic of their own, with the suggestion that this is a logic quite different from that of Cartesian rational analysis, becomes an important theme of the *Aufklärer*. Rousseau's explorations of the affairs of the heart, Vico's assertion that history has its own sort of significance, Montesquieu's analysis of the peculiar spirit of law, and the contributions of Diderot, Lessing, and others to a new spirit of criticism in art and literature are so many manifestations of the *Aufklärung's* desire to study the human phenomenon for its own sake and not just as an appendage to the analysis of the divine *Logos* coming to be through the *ego cogito*. The literature of the period of Louis XV is worse than that written under Louis XIV, feels d'Alembert, because it is less sensitive to this other logic—the language of sentiment and passion—and it expresses a much less realistic feeling for life.

Moderation also characterizes d'Alembert's attitude with respect to religion. Himself a confirmed deist, decidedly hostile to all established religions as well as to all belief in any supernatural revelation, he does not feel inclined to carry on a political activity directed against any church.[11] He does not want to fight in the open, like Diderot, unless, of course, he finds churchmen invading themselves the political field.

These various points of view are expressed in the *Preliminary Discourse* as occasion arises within the framework of a general classification of sciences or, more exactly, of a general division of philosophy. Intended to provide some order for the material which the *Encyclopedia* will present alphabetically, d'Alembert's division follows Bacon's closely. Departures from the order set up by the model are generally announced. The results are summarized in a diagram under the title of "Figured System of Human Knowledges." [12] The supreme faculty is Understanding (*entendement*), which divides into Memory, Reason, and Imagination.

Reason includes philosophy, and nothing else, but philosophy itself includes everything: the Science of Being in general (metaphysics); the Science of God (theology, first natural, then revealed); [13] the Science of Spirits (good or evil); the Science of Soul (pneumatology; science of rational soul and of sensitive soul); the Science of Man (logic and ethics); the Science of Number (mathematics, either pure or mixed, and physico-mathematics); the Science of Nature (zoology, astronomy, cosmology, botany, mineralogy, and chemistry).

Just as philosophy includes all the sciences produced by reason, history includes all those produced by memory. This part of the division does not run as smoothly as the preceding one. It includes Sacred History, Civil History, Natural History (normal and pathological), and even (a particularly large section in view of an *Encyclopedia of Sciences, Arts and Crafts*), under the separate headline of "Uses of Nature," "the Arts" (other than fine arts), "the Crafts and Manufacturing Techniques." D'Alembert naïvely believes that history is a matter of memory, as if it were not the art whereby understanding produces something for memory to remember. Like Descartes, he despises erudition, as if erudition found a ready-made material which the scholar only has to learn and remember. D'Alembert little realizes that to ascertain any historical fact requires an intellectual activity identical with that of the physicist (observation, hypothesis, demonstration). In this regard he is peculiarly behind the times, for Vico, Wincklemann, and the histories of Voltaire are an essential part of the *Aufklärung's* broader inquiry into human reality. [14]

He is more felicitous and original in dealing with crafts, although, in view of their ceaseless progress, one does not see why they should be listed under the general headline of Memory. D'Alembert feels somewhat embarrassed by the problem of the kind of dignity (or lack of dignity) one should attribute to manual arts. Up to a certain point, and more or less according to cases, all arts are handicrafts. Manual labor has been too long unreasonably despised. This should come to an end and d'Alembert formally says so; on the other hand, he lacks the sincere enthusiasm which was then leading Diderot himself to learn the crafts he had to describe and to plan the remarkable collection of plates illustrating their tools in the *Encyclopedia*. Here

again, he keeps a middle course and, as always, he does so in an ir-
reproachable sentence: "While respecting with justice the great
geniuses that enlighten it, society should not humiliate the hands that
serve it." [15]

The third panel of the triptych, devoted to Fine Arts, under the
general heading of Imagination, is about what one would expect in a
doctrine where the Fine Arts are included in a general classification of
"human knowledges." D'Alembert is helped by the Aristotelian notion
that arts are chiefly "imitation," for to imitate is to represent acquired knowledge. But here d'Alembert lets his intelligent imagination
run away with him; after doing his best with painting and sculpture,
which he describes as typical "of those knowledges which consist in
imitation," he acknowledges that, with architecture, "the imitation of
beautiful Nature" is less striking and restricted between narrower
limits than it is in other arts, and when he comes to music, which
speaks to both imagination and sense, d'Alembert frankly confesses
that it comes last in the order of imitation. Whereupon he begs leave
to add a few remarks. "Music which, in its origin, was perhaps
destined to represent nothing but noise, has little by little become a
kind of discourse, even a language, wherewith to express the different
sentiments of the soul, or rather, its different passions." Why not
extend that language to sensations themselves? Having to picture a
frightening object, the musician could look in nature for the kind
of noise that can produce in us the emotion the more closely resembling that which the object itself would cause. True enough, such a
music would demand a rare power to discern between the subtlest
shades of sensations: "Perceived by the man of genius, felt by the
man of taste, discerned by the clever man, such nuances are wasted
on the multitude"; thus conceived, music has to carry some meaning:
"All music that depicts nothing, is but noise." Whereupon d'Alembert
goes on to say, as if carried by some secret inspiration: " 'Tis true a
musician careful to depict everything, would sometimes offer to us
harmony pictures not calculated to please vulgar sensibilities; but of
this one should only conclude that, after setting up an art of learning
music, one should also devise an art of listening to it." [16]

With men like d'Alembert, even an error is never a total loss.
Nevertheless, history has not retained an affectionate memory of him.
Resolutely hostile to any religion that went beyond mere Deism,
d'Alembert cannot have many Christian friends; on the other hand,

being no less resolutely hostile to meddling in politics, he preferred personal peace to the notoriety of the reformer, so he was charged with duplicity by people like his disciple Condorcet for not coming up frankly against what he himself called "superstition." He thought, Condorcet said, that "instead of fronting dangerous prejudices, it is better to set up by their side truths from which the falsity of those opinions is a consequence easy to deduce." This is of course not meant in praise of d'Alembert!

But explosive religious and political revolutions were destined to be later fruits of the Enlightenment's spirit of wide-ranging inquiry. And, despite his withdrawal, d'Alembert remains the best summary of the movement. In an essay on "The Elements of Philosophy" he summed it up in one unsurpassable statement:

> The discovery and application of a new method of philosophizing, the kind of enthusiasm which accompanies discoveries, a certain exaltation of ideas which the spectacle of the universe produces in us—all these causes have brought about a lively fermentation of minds. Spreading through nature in all directions like a river which has burst its dams, this fermentation has swept along with it with a sort of violence everything which stood in the way. Thus, from the principles of the secular sciences to the foundations of religious revelation, from metaphysics to matters of taste, from music to morals, from the scholastic disputes of theologians to matters of trade, from the laws of princes to those of peoples, from natural law to the arbitrary laws of nations . . . everything has been discussed and analyzed, or at least mentioned. The fruit or sequel of this general effervescence of minds has been to cast new light on some matters and new shadows on others, just as the effect of the ebb and flow of the tides is to leave some things on the shore and to wash others away.[17]

A nice d'Alembert touch, the recognition that the *Aufklärung* has not everywhere brought light! And a perfect phrase to describe the period with which we are now concerned, *a general effervescence of minds*. That effervescence's most characteristic creation was Diderot's *Encyclopedia*. Who was this Denis Diderot? And what was the *Encyclopedia*?

XX

Diderot, the Soul of
the *Encyclopedia*

IT IS NOT EASY to state exactly the philosophy underlying the many volumes of the *Encyclopedia*. D'Alembert's division and description of the sciences and his analysis of the role of reason are certainly part of it. But Diderot is the real soul of the *Encyclopedia;* his own philosophical writings hold the key to the philosophical successes and failures of the work as a whole. It is not just that Diderot was gradually abandoned by his more eminent confreres, and therefore forced to take on more of the actual writing himself; from the beginning his was the unifying stamp, recognizable in all the lesser articles which he took it upon himself to write. The overriding enthusiasm for mechanical techniques, the accent, we might say, on *technology* as much as science, can be laid at his doorstep. So, too, can the fact that the *Encyclopedia* was destined never to become itself an important original source of truth. It was not Diderot's fault that at the end he found himself without the powerful aid of a d'Alembert, a Voltaire, a Rousseau, even without much help from the Baron d'Holbach, and therefore forced to turn more and more to second-rate collaborators who largely just condensed into their assigned articles the content of already existing studies. But this state of affairs is somehow curiously consonant with Diderot's whole personal intellectual life. He was full of original ideas, but not good either at demonstrating them or at following them up systematically. His works are full of the problems of the time and contain many flashes of things to come, but they themselves do not provide the firm new horizons of a fresh chapter of history; such is the *Encyclopedia*. Despite its immense size and its countless brilliant moments, it fails to congeal into a new world, for Diderot, its soul, was not a world-founder, even though he had recognized the opportunity when it presented itself.[1]

The Letter on Blindmen

DIDEROT'S OWN PHILOSOPHICAL IDEAS are scattered through short essays on typical contemporary philosophical problems. He attacked, for example, the so-called "problem of Molyneux," [2] which ran as follows: Given a man born blind, but trained to distinguish by touch between a cube and a sphere of about the same size and of the same metal, if he is given his sight, and the sphere and cube are placed in front of him, will he be able to distinguish them by sight alone? Locke had offered his solution to this by now classical problem, so had Berkeley, then Condillac; the testimony of blind men operated for cataracts had been sought by philosophers who wanted to be present at the time of the operation and to interview the patient right after it. Diderot had tried to attend one of those *expériences* but, failing to be admitted, he had consoled himself with interviewing blind-born persons and writing about the question.

The *Letter on Blindmen for the Use of Those Who See* shows Diderot making good use of simple observations. The blind-born man he examines suggests by his answers that sight is but a particular kind of touch, which, Diderot observes, is exactly what Descartes has demonstrated in his *Dioptrics*. This can be ascertained by merely glancing at the plates illustrating the *Letter;* they are full of men busy seeing by means of sticks. Diderot's description of the psychology of the blind remains worth consulting even today. He particularly stresses the fact that a geometrical notion of space is possible for a man entirely deprived of visual images and unable to imagine any color. What interests him in such observations is that they teach us the relativity of what we consider properties inseparable from reality. Depending on touch alone, the totally blind man has only tactile images, but he can combine them, and since he will perceive things in a more abstract way than we do, he might even be less liable to be mistaken than we are in matters of pure speculation. The example of Nicholas Saunderson (1682-1739), the blind English geometer whose methods of calculating Diderot describes, shows that blind men can not only practice geometry for themselves, but also talk about it, and even teach mathematics with astounding success. [3]

When attacking the "problem of Molyneux," Diderot begins by comparing the answers and reasons offered by Locke, Condillac, and Molyneux himself, all of whom, with some reservations on the part of Condillac, concluded that the blind man could not, at first sight, distinguish between the two figures. He then added that the question asked by Molyneux included in fact two other queries: 1] Would the man born blind see at all immediately after the operation? 2] In case he could see, would he see well enough to discern figures and to apply to them with certitude the names he used to give to objects which, up to then, he knew only by touch? These hesitations led Diderot to set up a program of precautions to be observed in the future by those who will carry out similar observations. He himself is of the opinion that, the first time his eyes will be opened to sight, the newly operated man will see nothing at all; then his eyes will begin to experiment, but the eyes only, without the man at first resorting to touch. This will progressively enable him roughly to discern the limits of objects. Whether or not the man will be able to discern by sight alone the objects he used to discern by touch will depend on the individual. The answer cannot be the same in the case of a wholly uneducated man and in that of persons used to distinguish between their ideas and to reason about them. A metaphysician would probably start reasoning as soon as he distinctly saw objects, then he would say:

> I feel very much inclined to believe that this is the body I always called a circle, while that one is the body I always called a square; but I shall refrain from deciding that things are really so. Who can assure me that, were I to approach them, they would not vanish from under my hand? How do I know whether the objects of my sight are also destined to be objects of my touch? . . . Gentlemen, he would add, this body here seems to me to be the square, and that one, the circle, but I have no scientific certitude that they are to touch such as they are to sight.

How distrustful Diderot is of *a priori* reasoning! As he himself has put it in his *Thoughts on the Interpretation of Nature*, "We are nearing the time of a great revolution in sciences. Judging from the present leaning of minds towards ethics, literature, and experimental physics, I would almost dare to affirm that, before a century is over, there will not be left three great geometers in Europe." Diderot was not lacking scientific imagination, far from it; only, as will presently be seen, his imagination was running along other ways.

Already in the *Letter on Blindmen,* Diderot had taken a few flutters in the field of cosmology. Now taking advantage of the publication of the *Life and Character of Dr. Nicholas Saunderson . . . ,* by his disciple and friend William Inchlif, Diderot feigned a deathbed conversation between the blind geometer and a worthy minister, Holmes by name, on the subject of the existence of God. As could be expected, Saunderson comes off rather brilliantly, the more so as he evidently is but the mouthpiece of Diderot himself.

Holmes having argued from the marvelous order of nature (as if Saunderson could see it), the dying geometer answered that he felt quite willing to admit the present existence of a universal order, but he begged leave to feel free to think differently about the primitive condition of the world, a state of things, he remarked to Holmes, "on which you are not less blind than I am." He then sketches a wild theory according to which, "in the first instant of the formation of animals," some had no heads, others no feet, and still others no stomachs or no intestines. His hypothesis is that, in such a condition, all the vicious combinations of matter would have successively disappeared, leaving only those "in which mechanism suffered no major contradiction, so that they could subsist and perpetuate themselves." Had man been such a misfit, there simply would be today no mankind. As it is, there still appears from time to time a being deprived of some important organ; blind men are such beings; nature itself is responsible for their existence as well as for that of clear-sighted men.[4] And why not say of worlds themselves what can be said of animals? We do not know how many worlds unfit to last are even now being formed and dissolved in remote corners of the universe, combinations being tried until some enduring arrangement is found. Time, matter, and space are perhaps but one point; what we call wise purposiveness is perhaps nothing more than the haphazard consequence of blind motion.

The Dream of d'Alembert

THIS KIND OF SCIENCE FICTION would be of no interest but for two of its features. Historically speaking, it marks the moment when Deism as well as Theism come to an end.[5] Diderot expressly bids farewell to Locke, Clarke, Leibniz, and Condillac; let us add to Voltaire and to his friend d'Alembert as well. Secondly, these wild suppositions, so far removed from positive verifications, contained the seeds of scientific theories, some of which are still under consideration—for example, reduction of time, space, and matter to one and the same point.

Three other opuscules also show Diderot's aptitude for philosophical daydreaming: *A Conversation between d'Alembert and Diderot*; *The Dream of d'Alembert*; and *A Sequel to the Conversation*. These being some of the pages in which as a writer Diderot is at his best, we cannot hope to reconstitute their intellectual and social atmosphere, so we shall limit ourselves to their philosophical content.

The conversation with d'Alembert, strictly speaking, probably never took place; yet, in a perhaps more real way, it did. In his *Preliminary Discourse*, d'Alembert had taken it as evident that "the properties we observe in matter have nothing in common with the faculty to will and to think." What we call *I*[6] is formed of two principles of different nature, united in such guise that there is perfect and necessary correspondence between the movements of the one and those of the other. This fact alone would suffice to attest to the existence of an all-powerful Intelligence.

Diderot could not accept such a way of posing the question, let alone its answer. His own view of a self-organizing world of matter required a cosmogony in which no supreme Intelligence would be at work, no distinction of soul and body required, nothing beyond mechanical action needed as explanation. The *Conversation with d'Alembert* is a direct answer to this mathematician's traditional views upholding the distinction of soul and body and the existence of a supreme Wisdom, author of the world order.[7] What Diderot wanted to do, as we have seen, was to account for everything by means of matter moved mechanically and haphazardly. The ambiguity of Condillac's method here offered some tantalizing suggestions. Straight idealism was one of them: if external reality totally agrees with what sensations teach us about it, how can one distinguish between sensations and things? Perhaps sensations are the things themselves, and vice versa. Straight materialism was another. At the beginning of the third part of the *Reasoned Abstract from the Treatise of Sensations*, Condillac had made this rather bold supposition: "Let us forget for one moment all our habits, let us transport ourselves to the creation of the world and let us suppose that God should tell us: *I am about to produce a soul to which I shall give certain sensations that will be but modifications of its own substance. . . .*" A faithful reader of Locke and Condillac, Diderot merely shuffles the question a little. Let us suppose that God said: "I am about to produce a body to which I shall give certain sensations that shall be but modifications of its own substance," what would happen?

The answer is: exactly the same thing as in the philosophy of Condillac. If the whole structure of human knowledge is either sensation or some transformation of sensation, it makes no difference whether that which feels be called soul or body. Here indeed is the latent peril behind Condillac. If the soul's operations are conceived after the pattern of material operations, spiritualism is, in fact, nothing but materialism. In other words, there is no point in affirming the distinction of soul and body if souls are conceived as operating after the manner of bodies. D'Alembert, as we have seen, maintained the dualism of Condillac; Diderot simply realized what his friend had not, that under such circumstances, soul could be eliminated by a very simple operation. There was no need to attribute reason and intelligence to body; let us suppose that body *feels*, all the rest is clear.

Strangely enough, this assumption of Diderot's brings him back to certain positions of Telesio and Campanella (whom he does not seem to have read) about things sensing. If I assume that my own body feels, then matter is able to feel and, consequently, everything feels: "If sensibility is a general and essential quality of matter, then stones must needs feel." But is there a reason to assume this? Simply that, otherwise, there is no way to account for the possibility of reasoning beings arising from matter alone: Listen, Diderot says to d'Alembert, and you will pity yourself; you will realize that, for not admitting a simple and all-explaining supposition, that is to say sensibility conceived as a general property of matter or a product of organization, you are renouncing common sense and plunging headlong into an abyss of mysteries, of contradictions, and of absurdities.

To d'Alembert's objection that feeling is essentially incompatible with matter, Diderot rejoins: "How do you know that sensibility is essentially incompatible with matter, since you know neither what matter is, nor what sensibility is?"[8] There is only one substance left in the universe, in man, in animals. The union of soul and body, at which d'Alembert marvels, is but the union of an organized body with another similarly organized body. Similarly built harpsichords will naturally be attuned and give the same sounds when submitted to similar excitations. In short, where there is only one substance, there is no problem of the communication of substances, and where all beings are similarly constituted, there is no difficulty in understanding how it is that their cognitions agree. The invincible objection of Berkeley to the existence of bodies simply does not make sense. There just was a moment when one of the feeling harpsichords went mad; "it thought that it was the only harpsichord in the world and that the whole harmony of the world was taking place in itself."

D'Alembert observes that there still are difficulties. It is hard to see, in such a system, how we form syllogisms and how we draw consequences; to which Diderot replies that, precisely, "we do not draw consequences, they all are drawn by nature." In the true vein of Condillac's associationism, he goes on to say: "We only enunciate conjoined phenomena whose bond is either necessary or contingent. In all cases these are phenomena known to us by experience, necessary in mathematics, physics, and other exact sciences, contingent in ethics, in politics, and other conjectural sciences." And what about analogy? d'Alembert asks. "Analogy in the more complex cases, is but a rule of three effecting itself in the feeling instrument." If it is known that in nature a given phenomenon is attended by a second given one, what will the fourth phenomenon be if a third one is given similar to the first? Whereupon d'Alembert quits: "I am sleepy, good night."

After such a discussion he naturally has a bad night. He dreams and talks in his sleep; having nothing better to do, a friend has jotted notes of what he was saying and reads them the next morning to the physician Bordeu. This reading, along with the remarks of Bordeu, constitute *The Dream of d'Alembert*. In it, Diderot has his dreaming friend describe an organic universe, an animal that is one and, at the same time, is made up of a multitude of smaller animals, our own organs themselves being distinct animals of which our body is made up, and which the law of continuity keeps together, united by a general sympathy or, rather, by a general identity. Our world is made up of smaller worlds, and since the elements are everywhere the same, it is always possible to pass from one to the other, by addition or subtraction of elements without discontinuity.[9] Everything comes from the fermentation of one vast sediment and everything will return to it. And who knows what may yet arise out of it? Where there is sense, there is *need:* "Organs produce needs and, reciprocally, needs produce organs." Whatever they are, all organisms will ultimately consist of other organisms, carried away with the rest of the world in the universal flux.[10] Man has no other continuity in time than that of his memory—and thus goes on and on what is really a conversation of Diderot with himself. The *Sequel to the Conversation* takes place between the physician and Mlle. de l'Espinasse, "after the servants are gone." And indeed it is one of those conversations which "enlightened" persons could hold between themselves but not in the presence of common people. In it Diderot provides himself with an opportunity to air his naturist views on human conduct. He also exposes there the then popular theme of the "good savage" corrupted by his contact with the depravities of allegedly "civilized" people. He will insist on the theme in his *Supplement to the Voyage of Bougainville* (*c.* 1772); and of course we shall find it handled in a deeper and more philosophical vein by Rousseau.

Of all the men found in that loosely knit group of "philosophers," Diderot is the only one who gave signs of a creative imagination in the field of ideas—but he never follows things up. With a great gift for affirming and repeating affirmations until they sound true, he never bothered too much about demonstrating anything. Hence, these curious "conversations" in which the philosopher who had never made any scientific discovery, nor even tried to make one, uncovers the secrets of nature for the benefit of a patient and discreet d'Alembert, who at least could claim to have solved the problem of the Precession of the Equinoxes. On the other hand, there are few subjects about which, in the middle of tiresome, disordered, and at times gratuitously vulgar ramblings, Diderot does not occasionally hit upon surprisingly original and fecund ideas. His essays on art particularly deserve attention for their originality.[11] In that field again, Diderot could speak with the authority born of inexperience, for he was in no way a trained artist, and he had fallen into the role of critic quite by accident; but here again he proves himself full of felicitous insights. The secret of the man's power[12] might well be found in the very title he himself gave to his *Encyclopedia* when he presented it as the work of a "societé de gens de lettres." He would make a good patriarch for that curious race of men whose proper function it is to "write about things." [13] But of course there is another contender for the title; with at least as much talent, and with a duplicity wholly foreign to the character of "le bon Diderot"; to wit, the Old Fox, Voltaire.

XXI

Voltaire

It is equally difficult either to leave Voltaire out of a history of eighteenth-century philosophy or to include him. Had there been no Voltaire, the world would not be the poorer by a single idea, philosophical or otherwise; on the other hand, Voltaire was, and still remains, typical of a widespread attitude toward philosophical and religious problems. To most of his own enlightened contemporaries, he was the very embodiment of Enlightenment; were it for this reason alone, the history of ideas could not let his name pass unnoticed.

Another difficulty arises from the intense presence of the man in his works. There are too many cases in which it is hard to form an opinion as to what he really means without at the same time wondering about the kind of man he was. Had he been a different man he might have said pretty much the same things, but his tone would have been different, his influence considerably diminished, and nobody would today mention the name of Voltaire. As a first approach to his work, and with all conceivable reservations, let us then meet the man who, at a time when there were no newspapers to speak of, managed to become the king of columnists and in the process to turn himself into a star of European magnitude.

The "Philosophic Spirit"

Voltaire[1] was one of the more versatile creatures ever to pick up a quill. In a Dewey-decimal catalogue you will find some of his books in practically every section. He wrote a great deal of verse (one hesitates to call most of it poetry), an epic, novels, histories (he was in fact a pioneer modern historian), treatises in science, in philosophy, and in theology; and he carried on an immense correspondence with many outstanding personalities—all this in a clear, easy-flowing, graceful, witty, and very often amusing style. He knew how to flatter, but he also knew how to hurt. Voltaire possessed an unsurpassed, perhaps an unequaled, mastery in the art of destroying adversaries by ridiculing them. Any pretext would do. Two unfortunate Jesuits have not to this day recovered from having been afflicted with, to French ears, most comical names—Nonotte and Patouillet. One of the very few men who courageously stood up to him, and whom now nobody reads, Fréron,[2] is in our own day classified, thanks to Voltaire, as an "immortal sot" (Verlaine) by men who could not mention the title of any one of his writings. Here is a sample of how Voltaire immortalized his victims:

> L'autre jour au fond d'un vallon
> Un serpent mordit Jean Fréron.
> Que pensez-vous qu'il arriva?
> Ce fut le serpent qui creva.

To deserve this, poor Fréron had simply felt free to write about Voltaire as Voltaire himself felt free to write about everything; in such cases, posterity always sides with Voltaire, one of the first "untouchables" produced by modern times.

Besides his literary talent, perfect in all respects this side of genius, there was another reason Voltaire attracted such a large audience. Not gifted for abstract speculation, he felt intensely interested in problems of human conduct at the personal, social, and political levels. This is also why he still keeps that audience. Voltaire asks questions which no thinking being can fail to ask, and he asks them in terms intelligible to all.

What Voltaire wants before anything else is to be happy. Everyman's ultimate end is, he affirms, the "pursuit of happiness." Nothing, therefore, that stands between Voltaire and his personal happiness is sacred; every such obstacle must be destroyed. Even if not necessarily such as it should be, everything else can be allowed to remain untouched so long as it does not hurt him, or can be turned to his own advantage. This trait needs to be mentioned because it accounts for Voltaire's remarkable indulgence toward social and political inequalities. Himself a prosperous speculator, a self-appointed nobleman careful always to live in style, surrounded by vassals, and ladies of wit, while at the same time spiritually assisted by a personal chaplain, he could permit himself occasionally to poke fun at the established order of things, but he certainly had no intention of shaking it, much less of destroying it. To the extent that his personal happiness was tied up with what was soon to become the *ancien régime,* that social order deserved in his eyes to be respected by all men.

Voltaire's enemies were of a different sort: all generally received ideas, or traditions, or beliefs, that pretended to force upon him certain ways of life he did not like or to forbid him certain ways of life he did like. This was natural enough; the only difficulty is that, to Voltaire, the ways of life conducive to his own happiness were, by the same token, universally valid as conducive to all men's happiness in general. For instance, if religion were true, at least under the form it had taken in Christianity, Voltaire could not do many of the things he wanted to do, while on the contrary, he would have to comply with many obligations he did not want to recognize. So Christianity was an evil. This must apply for all men as well as for Voltaire; consequently, it should be destroyed. One should not interpret Voltaire's attitude as one of impatience with religious interdicts or prescriptions only. Of course he did resent these. One could fill a volume with the fuss he made about poor people being forbidden to eat cheap mutton on Fridays; but his main target was the religious dogmas that pretended to justify their interference with free action by a previous interference with free thinking. Voltaire is a model of "free thinking," and he can be hailed as the patriarch of the so-called "free thinkers"; that is, those who refuse assent to all impediments to the free use of their own power of judging. As will be seen, such men are not necessarily anti-religious. So long as they are left free to conceive religion as they please, they have no objection to it, but they decidedly are against all *revealed* religions. Voltaire opposes all so-called "revelations" at whatever moment of history and in any country on earth (although he does not oppose every revealed tenet, as we shall see). Along with revelations, he naturally opposes sacred books of all denominations, all religious dogmas, all churches, all clergies, all religious ways of life, and, more than any other one, monastic life, which is the very type of life Voltaire does not want to live. In Voltaire's own country and during his own lifetime, religion means Christianity, along with the Christian Church, be it that of Geneva or that of Rome,[3] along with Christian dogmas, Christian practices, and Christian ways of feeling and thinking. The fact that, in Voltaire's France, the power of the state was trying to turn religious belief into a legal obligation, occasionally enforced by the police, was bound to make things worse. Formulated in its entire generality, the aim of Voltaire was to destroy all "dogma," first in religion, next in philosophy, and last in any domain where it might happen to assert itself—the definition of "dogma" simply being any proposition that demands to be unconditionally accepted as true and exempted from the duty of justifying itself in the sight of reason. The very essence of the "philosophical spirit," on the contrary, is to exact from all dogmas either their rational justification or else the admission that they have none.[4] In matters of metaphysics and natural theology, the personal contribution of Voltaire to philosophy was just that kind of effort, but nothing beyond that.

What method did Voltaire use in order to achieve his purpose? Since he had to deal with irrational positions, he could not easily oppose to them philosophical objections. The dogmas he intended to ruin proclaimed themselves as belonging to a higher order than reason; reason therefore was powerless against them. Voltaire thought of two weapons perfectly suited to his own literary gifts; what could not be refuted could be reviled and ridiculed. The bulk of the *Philosophical Dictionary* consists of nothing else, for indeed dogmatism breeds superstition, which in turn breeds fanaticism, and the only remedy to this disease "is the philosophic spirit which, progressively gaining ground, softens men's behavior and prevents the spreading of the disease."[5]

A "Philosopher's" World

VOLTAIRE HIMSELF never set about unraveling metaphysical difficulties, but he had very definite ideas how men should handle philosophical conclusions; on which ground he had formed personal opinions about most of the great metaphysics of the preceding centuries. Taken together, these opinions make up a good picture of what must have been a common view of the world in the enlightened circles during the reign of Louis XV.

His deepest conviction is that in no case should a man be arrested, jailed, tried, and condemned for holding any philosophical opinion. Fanaticism is no more justified in matters of philosophy than in matters of "superstition." Tolerance is the healthy condition of a normal human mind, as befitting the limits of the certitude accessible to man. Voltairian toleration rests upon this genuinely Voltairian ground: "What is tolerance? It is the lot of mankind. Weaknesses and errors are the stuff we all are made of; let us mutually forgive one another our foolishnesses, that is the law of nature." [6]

The causes of our ignorance can be more precisely defined. We lack the clear knowledge of the principles, beginnings, or first and last terms of knowledge.

> The nature of nearly all the principles of things is the secret of the Creator. How does air carry sound? How are animals formed? How do some of our limbs constantly obey our wills? What assigns to ideas a place in our memory, keeps them there as in a file and extracts them at will, sometimes even against our will? Our own nature, that of the universe, that of the humblest plant, everything is, for us, plunged in an abyss of obscurity. [7]

Voltaire remembers Montaigne and does not hesitate to quote him. His predecessor's motto, *What do I know?* suits him perfectly. [8]

This accounts for Voltaire's mistrust toward the all-embracing systems. Matter is one of the principles, and some think they can account for everything by means of material principles only. Voltaire knows their doctrines quite well, but he cannot picture to himself the notion of a thinking body. In fact, the very notion of matter *qua* matter is obscure. We cannot conceive it otherwise than as extended in space and divisible, but it cannot be divided unless it is subjected to motion, and, precisely, while matter cannot be conceived without extension in space, it can be conceived without motion. On the other hand, if it has motion, matter cannot, at the same time, have impenetrability. Moreover, if it is divisible into parts, are the parts themselves divisible? That unknown being called matter, is it eternal? Some philosophers thought so; are the others right in denying it? Many professors, and even pupils, have answers to all those questions, but "wise men are more cautious." "Asked what the soul is, they answer they don't know. Asked what matter is, they give the same answer." [9] After all, the question is of no importance; whatever the nature and origin of matter may be, the rules of human conduct must remain the same. What we say about it is forgotten as soon as it is said, like table talk.

Knowing neither what matter is nor what soul is, Voltaire does not see how matter could think, but he cannot see either why matter could not think. On this point, he never tired of quoting the passage of Locke's *Essay* [10] where it is said that "without revelation" we probably shall never know whether God has given to some portions of organized matter the power to think or if, rather, he has not joined to thus organized matter an immaterial substance that thinks.[11] A wise man will affirm neither. He may feel inclined in favor of the second solution, but he will not exclude the first possibility.

Such being our ignorance of the nature of the soul, its immortality cannot be a certitude, but this is a point on which Voltaire does not like to trifle. His position on the question is bound up with his attitude concerning revelation. Voltaire, it must be remembered, is not opposed to all revelation; to him, revelation is true and useful when it uncovers to men sensible conclusions of which reason can approve, especially if it contributes to order in society that such conclusions should be known and accepted by all.

The immortality of the soul is one of these truths. One should bless its revelation the more heartily, as well as that of the rewards and punishments after death, as "the vain philosophy of men has always doubted it." Nothing better shows "the need of a revelation." For indeed, if we are not certain that the soul is immortal, we are not certain either that it is not immortal. In the *Chinese Catechism* of Voltaire, the philosophers Kou and Cusu exchange the following remarks: "And who tells you there is another life?—In doubt of it, you must behave as if there were one.—But what if I am sure there is none?—I dare you to be sure of that." Voltaire does not wish to live in a society which doubts the immortality of the soul and the afterlife of rewards and punishments. To believe those things "is good for the people and for the princes." [12]

The same attitude is recommended by Voltaire with respect to the problem of God, and for the same reason. As late as 1765, thirteen years before the end of a long life, he proclaimed himself a "theist." According to his definition of it, "a theist is a man firmly persuaded of the existence of a supreme Being as good as he is powerful, who has formed all beings, be they extended, vegetating, feeling or reflecting; who perpetuates their species, punishes crimes without cruelty and bountifully rewards virtuous acts." [13] How God rewards and punishes, he does not know, but he does know that God is just, and that is enough for him. This is the whole of his religion, and if they are carefully weighed, the terms of his profession of faith will reveal the limits of his beliefs. Voltaire believes in an author of nature, cause of the general order of the universe; he does not speak of creation; he hopes for indeterminate rewards and wants other people to fear bearable punishments. No hell of course, that is superstition[14] but a place bad enough to frighten people away from crime. If this cannot be proved to be true, it cannot be proved to be false, and since it is profitable for society that it should be thought to be true, philosophers should not fail to teach it.[15] In his own famous words: "If God had not existed, He should have had to be invented."

Voltaire and the Encyclopedists

IF HE IS GRANTED a "religion without superstition," Voltaire feels free to uphold positive conclusions on a small number of points. He does think there is a God. His evidence in favor of this conclusion is the order of the world. There is no watch without a watchmaker. The watchmaker does not create the watch from nothing, but he fabricates it and makes it tick. Final causality found in Voltaire a decided supporter.[16] It is all a question of common sense. A man must be crazy to deny that stomachs are made to digest, eyes to see and ears to hear; on the other hand, one must be quite taken up with final causes to maintain that stones were made for men to build houses. Noses have not been made to wear spectacles as eyes were made to see. The difference is clear: "When effects are invariably the same in all places and at all times, when those uniform effects are independent from the beings to which they belong, then there visibly is a final cause." [17] All animals have eyes, and see; they all have ears, and they hear, so these are final causes; but not all houses are built out of stones, not all noses wear spectacles, not all fingers have a ring, not all legs are covered with silk stockings; silkworms therefore were not made to clothe our legs in the same way as nature made our mouth to eat. All effects, however, happen according to laws established by God. In short, "a final cause is absolutely invariable in all places and at all times." [18] With these precisions, he considered himself a "cause-finalier." [19]

There is even much to be said in favor of optimism, but it is going too far to argue, as Leibniz did, that "all is for the best in the best of all possible worlds." Voltaire attacked the metaphysical optimism of Leibniz in verse and prose. One of his novels, *Candide* (1759), pokes fun at a certain Dr. Pangloss for obstinately (and not very intelligently) upholding Voltaire's version of Leibnizian optimism. Voltaire fails to find any consolation in the thought that the pain suffered by one being is the pleasure of another one: "The question of good and evil remains a hopeless chaos for those who investigate it in good faith; for those who dispute about it, it is an intellectual pastime: they are convicts playing with their chains. As to the non-thinking crowd, they are pretty much like fishes transferred from a river to a fish pond: they do not suspect they are there to be eaten in Lent; by ourselves, therefore, we know absolutely nothing of the causes of our destiny." [20] Note the careful "by ourselves," which reserves the rights of revelation.

Here, for once, Voltaire has a philosophical reason to oppose a philosophical conclusion. He believes in a God, cause of order, but who leaves room for a good deal of disorder. Chance, accident, hazard are important elements in the making of the world. In the *Dictionary*, the two articles "Chain of the Created Beings" and "Chain in the Events" show him persuaded that there is a good deal of discontinuity in the world of history as well as in that of nature. This conviction has found its expression in the celebrated *Essai sur les moeurs* (1756), which has rightly been considered as opposing the providentialist view of history represented by the *City of God* of St. Augustine and the *Discourse on Universal History* of Bossuet. The *Essai* develops an accidentalist view of history, or more exactly, perhaps, a discontinuous view of it. Voltaire likes to proceed by pictures of periods, epochs, and global views of typical moments. He was a master at this sort of thing. His *Le siècle de Louis XIV* (1751; final redaction 1768) is the finest example of modern historical writing seen up to then. The feeling in this kind of history is rather the opposite of Montesquieu's feeling for the presence of "laws" at work behind the apparent discontinuity of peoples, constitutions, and civilizations. Voltaire rather sees in history human wills at work, along with passions and superstitions ceaselessly opposed by reason, but never wholly overcome by it.

Voltaire's attitude toward the materialism of some of his contemporaries is harder to describe. For all sorts of reasons, including his personal temper, he would have liked to be a straight materialist. However, when he looked at the systems of Helvetius or d'Holbach, he could not really bring himself to subscribe to their conclusions. He felt the somewhat clumsy brutality of d'Holbach's *System of the World*.[21] Voltaire did not mind thinking of himself as a more or less well-regulated machine; but then there were moments when he preferred to feel otherwise; so that, generally speaking, he found it more convenient to think of the world as a universal necessity tempered by a bit of disorder and chance.

Voltaire was the living antithesis of Pascal, and he knew it. Pascal stood for all that Voltaire detested: the divine revelation laid down in the Bible, the Jewish revelation on miracles,[22] religious rites, asceticism, religious mysteries as well as the mysterious side of nature and man. Even their Pyrrhonism differed, for Pascal used skeptic arguments as a way to faith, whereas Voltaire used them as a way to incredulity. Both recognized that man is caught between two infinites, but Pascal considered it a duty for man to explore them, whereas Voltaire warned us to keep away from them. It would have been easy for Voltaire to dismiss Pascal as one more case of religious and philosophical fanaticism, were it not for the fact that, both as a master of French prose and as a mathematical genius, Pascal could simply not be ignored. Voltaire's *Remarks on Pascal*,[23] a devastating denunciation of Christianity, could not turn out to be anything but a hopeless misunderstanding.

Voltaire is the best vantage point from which to survey the group of the Encyclopedists and their work. Like Voltaire himself, the group had a loose, but still real, unity. It included spiritualists and materialists, a few good priests and many poor Christians, supporters of a mechanistic view of the world and believers in purposiveness as well as in a kind of wholesale providence; still they had a more or less common purpose, which was to bring down all doctrines, ideas, and feelings to the level of sober reason.

With the exception of a few misled fellow travelers of no importance, all the Encyclopedists were anti-Christians, as well as opposed to any established church. They spread the simplest opinion, still popular on account of its very simplicity, that all religions have been invented by priests who, secretly allied with political powers, have helped the rulers keep men in a state of ignorance and slavery. Not that the other Encyclopedists, any more than Voltaire, saw any harm in maintaining poor people in a state of economic inequality;[24] in fact, they probably failed to see how things could be otherwise; but they did resent what today the Marxists denounce as the economic "alienation" of man from himself under the pressure of established religions.

In the field of philosophy, all the Encyclopedists inclined toward an associationist conception of the human mind, a materialist notion of the human soul, and, with notable hesitations, toward a materialistic interpretation of nature and societies.

The very fact that they were fighting religion made it necessary for the *Encyclopedia* writers to stress the importance of ethics. But since, on account of their metaphysical skepticism, they were left without any foundation for it, they all tended to believe that, in fact, this was no problem. Societies, manners, social and political situations are just given; at each moment of history, they simply happen to be what they are. At every moment, too, it is up to reason to keep under control fanaticism and prejudice and to make the best possible use of the data of the situation in order to promote the welfare and happiness of all.[25] So, while on the one hand declaring the highest precepts of ethics to be "Enjoy yourselves without fear; be happy" (d'Holbach) or else: "Do everything you please" (La Mettrie), they could not on the other hand ignore the existence of selfishness, brutality, cruelty; in short, of the sources of the very inequalities they were busy denouncing every day in their own writings. They thus were led to the notion, vague but intensely felt, of an ethics without benefit of religion or metaphysics, empirically felt on the level of facts—a sort of art of living well. A wise legislation could do much to bring men nearer to that goal. In point of fact, modern societies are seldom more clear on the principles of their respective legislations than the Encyclopedists themselves ever were. Most of them would agree with d'Holbach that a well-organized society should be an *Ethocracy;* like the Encyclopedists again, they still are on the lookout for any principle, notion, or social science that could provide a foundation for it.

8 ❦ THE PHILOSOPHIES
OF SOCIETY

ALTHOUGH THE PHILOSOPHERS of antiquity and the thinkers of the Middle Ages considered society an important object of philosophical speculation, Descartes was prevented by the mathematical method from easily including it among his concerns. Hobbes had courageously tackled the problem, but without realizing that any branch of the philosophy of man would require principles and methods distinct from those of the philosophy of nature. It is not until the middle of the eighteenth century that we witness a new flowering of doctrines centered upon the problem of man as a social animal. But suddenly, there they were—three masterpieces of social philosophy: The *Scienza nuova* was published in final form right after the death of Giambattista Vico in 1744; *L'esprit des lois* of Montesquieu in 1748; and the *Discours* of Rousseau on sciences and arts in 1750. Of course practically all the Encyclopedists were interested in problems related to man as living in society; but what was really new about Vico, Montesquieu, and Rousseau was that they made man-the-social-animal the very center of their philosophical speculation.

XXII

Vico and the New Science

IT IS IN RETROSPECT that we recognize in Vico's work a turning point. A solitary thinker, entering new ways and writing a rather obscure language, Vico[1] was largely unknown in the
eighteenth century. He was one of those true originators who are
remembered long after for their inherent worth, not for their influence
on contemporaries. A poorly paid professor of rhetoric in Naples, he
was not exactly at the Anglo-French center of things; but he had interesting things to say, as we finally came to recognize.

Humanism versus Cartesianism

DESCARTES HAD EXPRESSED CONTEMPT for the traditional form of intellectual culture represented by the Latinists, Hellenists, and all those
who considered eloquence and its auxiliary disciplines as providing a
complete and truly "human" intellectual formation. Naturally, there
had been humanist protests against the Cartesians before, but these
shared in the vagueness which sometimes seems the essence of eloquence. Vico's own protest was much more articulate. The Italian and
Neapolitan tradition of Boccaccio found there its authentic expression.
Poetry as an important form of intellectual culture, the "genealogies
of the gods" and the whole body of classical mythology, already exploited by Boccaccio and many other humanists, were expressly set up
as sources of philosophical knowledge, instead of being reduced to
the condition of documents for the erudition of grammarians. The
stock of knowledge Vico himself had to exploit consisted basically of
jurisprudence and of what he knew of general history, including its
mythological origins. The plate printed on the front page of the *New
Science* represented Metaphysics receiving from divine wisdom an

illuminating beam which it reflects upon a statue of Homer. Poetry thus becomes a necessary moment of the science of historical and social man.

The fundamental reason for Vico's opposition to Cartesianism is well put in his early *Program of Studies for Our Own Times* (1709). As he himself defined it, the problem was this: Which is better, our own method of study or that of the ancients? What he opposed in the modern method of study was of course its Cartesianism (i.e., reliance upon the cultivation of critical reason) as opposed to the formation of judgment in view of reaching, not the *true*, which so often escapes us, but the *likely*, with which we must usually rest content in human affairs. Common sense[2] is the power of the soul that should be developed, for in it we find the rule of prudence as well as of eloquence, which itself is wisdom, as everyone has known since the time of Cicero. Whom should we rather trust, Cicero or the Cartesian Arnauld with his *Logique de Port-Royal*? Back to classical eloquence! could be Vico's motto. In his own terminology, let us say: Common sense should be formed before educating the critical spirit born of science; *topics* should come before *dialectics*.

Vico invokes pedagogical reasons in favor of his thesis. Old age is the age of reason; youth is the age of memory and imagination. Vico is not against reason, nor against science, which is excellent in its proper place; but neither reason nor science should be permitted to sterilize the other powers of the mind, making them unfit "for arts in which fancy, or memory, or both predominate, such as painting, poetry, oratory, and jurisprudence; critique, our common instrument in all the arts and sciences, should be an impediment to none of them."

Vico's deepest objection by far to the universal mathematicism of Descartes appears already in the same treatise, lost among many other considerations, as though he himself were not clearly aware yet of its philosophical importance. It is found in Vico's considerations on "the geometric method applied by our moderns to physics." It is of the essence of Cartesian physics that nothing in it can be denied without jeopardizing the very principle from which it flows. Being geometrical, it is either all true or all false. Now, the Cartesians do not propound their physics as an interpretation of nature or as an instrument for its investigation; "they say that their very physics, along with the method with which they teach it, is nature itself, so much so that, whichever side you may turn to contemplate the universe, you will meet that same physics." If their pretension is well founded, all is for the best; but if things are different, "if one single law of motion is false (not to recall that more than one has already been declared false) let them look out, and look well, lest, probing too confidently into nature and too anxious about the external aspect of things, they should overlook the foundations."

The main error of the Cartesians is to apply geometry to matters it does not fit. Excellent in its own domain, mathematics is a vicious mode of reasoning in matters not susceptible of demonstration. Used out of place, it fails, and its failure breeds skepticism. Because of the geometric method they use in the form of exposition, the conclusions of the Cartesian physics everywhere supersede the true ones. Still, "they are merely probable, for indeed they have the method of geometry, but not the demonstration. *Geometrical truth can be demonstrated because we make it;* could we demonstrate physics, we would be its makers. But the fact is that only in God exist the true forms of things, forms after the pattern of which the nature of things themselves is moulded."

This remark expresses a deep-seated conviction in the mind of Vico. To know a thing is to be able to produce it. For him, *verum et factum convertuntur*; since we did not make nature, there is little hope for us to reconstruct it as if its laws necessarily coincided with those of our minds.

Respectful of the complexity of reality, Vico was also convinced that man should cultivate the qualities which enable him to express it. Subtleness is not the same thing as acuteness; subtle people follow one single line, acute people follow two. The geometers do not want discourses about nature to be ornate; they want them merely to be true. This is the reason they content themselves with being subtle, their minds always following one single line of reasoning and deducing the like from the like. A true philosophical mind acts otherwise; it tries to grasp at a single glance identical causes in dissimilar things. This suppleness of mind is akin to the results of a good rhetorical education. The Latin ideal of the eloquent man, able to clear up a question for those whose minds are slow, and even to make it seem clear when it is not, is also the ideal of our Neapolitan professor of rhetoric. Physicists like to order their discourses methodically, starting from the prime truths, whereas a good orator leaves out these truths which are known to all; only, while talking about the consequences, he manages to make his auditors remember the principles and thus feel as if they themselves were forming his arguments.

Answering his initial question at the end of the treatise, Vico concludes that we should be able to integrate both in a type of culture which did not allow the knowledge acquired by the moderns to shove the knowledge possessed by the ancients into oblivion. But the main interest of the work is not there. It lies in the vindication of history and law as necessary disciplines of the mind. Looking at the body of existing sciences, Vico realizes that the study of nature far outweighs that of man. A new science is required to restore the balance, and he himself will found it.

The *New Science*

THE *New Science* is preceded by an allegorical plate for which Vico furnished a detailed explanation; among other things, it represents "the globe, that is the physical or natural world, supported only in part by the altar." The reason is that, thus far, the philosophers have contemplated Divine Providence in the world of nature only; this is a most partial understanding of It: they forget to recognize that the same Providence also acts in the world of man, and therefore in the mode of existence most proper to man: society. The aim and scope of the book is to map out a way to fill this gap.

Though he shows little sympathy for rationalism, Vico nevertheless starts from principles similar to those of many an Encyclopedist. Man was created by God in a state of justice; having lost it in consequence of original sin, he would now live in complete disorder if God had not seen to it that "utility itself should bring men to live justly, to conserve themselves in society and thereby to manifest their sociable nature." Now, sociability is the true civil virtue of man. In this sense, the new science intends to be a "reasoned civil theology of the divine providence."

The work is divided into five books, the first of which is devoted to laying down the basis on which the rest will be built. It begins by a chronological table, with commentaries, in which are compared the testimonies of various peoples concerning the origin of humanity. This first effort to extract from mythology valid data for the history of man is naturally out of date, but Vico was doing pioneer work when he attempted it. The rest of the book describes the Axioms, then the Principles, last the Method. It is curious that, opposed as he was to an undue extension of the geometric method, Vico himself seems to have succumbed to it in the end.

Among his many axioms (or postulates), some are particularly significant for a correct interpretation of his work. Axiom x is one of these: "Philosophy contemplates reason, from which comes the *science of the true;* philology observes the authority of the human will, and from it comes *the awareness of the certain.*" This distinction between the *true* and the *certain* is made clear in the same article. The "true," of course, is the domain of all universal knowledge as accessible to reason; the "certain" defines the domain of philology—that is, the learning of the grammarians, historians, and critics who busied themselves with the study of the languages and ways of life of the various peoples. The area of knowledge Vico had in mind was exactly what is called today the "sciences of man." Then comes this important remark: the philosophers were wrong in not confirming their reason by the authority of the philologians, just as the philologians were wrong in not caring to verify their authority by the reason of the philosophers. It is remarkable that Vico, in going back to the Ciceronian ideal of *eloquentia,* spontaneously revives the medieval tradition of the "Wedding of Mercury and Philology": *de nuptiis Mercurii et Philologiae.* This is a clear case of what we shall see Vico call a *ricorso.*

Another important axiom concerns the *senso commune.* What is unusual in Vico's philosophy is that commonly admitted notions are not to him necessarily universal. There is a different kind of "common sense" proper to each social group, be it a class, a people, or a nation. There is even one kind proper to all of humanity (Axiom xii).

Uniform ideas found in whole peoples not knowing one another must have a common ground. "This axiom is a great principle; it establishes that the common sense of the human kind is the criterion taught to the nations by divine Providence to determine what is certain[3] concerning the natural Law of the Nations (*al diritto natural delle genti*). Peoples make sure of it by ascertaining the substantial unity of that Law on which, with some modifications, they all agree" (Axiom xiii). One of the main objects of the *New Science* is to show that the natural law of nations was spontaneously born in diverse peoples who did not know one another.

This axiom leads to a no less important one which provides an instructive contrast with what we shall soon read in Montesquieu: "The nature of things is nothing else than their being born in certain times and with certain characters (*con certe guise*), which are always such; hence things are always born such and not other" (Axiom xiv). This compact sentence implies that there are, in the course of history, *certi tempi*—that is, times—or historical moments, such that things born in one of them will always present similar characters. In modern philosophical parlance, Vico suggests that, in its very essence, *nature* is *historicity*. Hence another major task of the new science; namely, to rediscover the ends to which were born popular traditions, preserved by whole nations during long spaces of time and now become unrecognizable because of changing languages and usages (Axiom xvi).

Languages are the most important witnesses to the customs obtaining at the time when they themselves were formed. But ascending from social group to social group, and observing larger zones of "common sense" as the groups themselves grow in size, one realizes that, in the nature of human affairs, there must be "a mental language common to all nations." This language uniformly expresses the substance of what is required for human social life. Proverbs are a case in point, for indeed they are maxims of wisdom that reappear, substantially the same, among many different peoples (Axiom xxii).

Traits common to different civilizations follow certain regular patterns comparable to laws of the evolution of societies; for instance, the succession, in the history of one and the same people, the Egyptians for example, of three ages: the age of the gods, that of the heroes, and that of men, each with a corresponding language (Axiom xxviii). In loose aphorisms, Vico thus suggests the foundation of many "human sciences" such as comparative mythology, comparative linguistics, and, above all, comparative law and jurisprudence, in which he sees, in a spirit entirely opposed to that of Montesquieu, one of the surest proofs in favor of the divine origin of natural law: Natural law is born of the "common sense" of mankind, without any reflection, without any mutual consultation or imitation, simply because it was thus ordained by Providence, which holds sway over human affairs (Axiom cv).

Founders of new sciences are apt to let their imaginations run ahead of their reasons; they start legislating universally long before they have gathered enough evidence. Vico falls into this temptation, describing the law of succession of all dominant human characters in the history of the world. "The nature of peoples is first cruel, next severe, then benign, then again delicate and finally dissolute" (Axiom lxii). History, he claims, bears out this view, for in the human race giants, like Polyphemus, came first; next great souls and proud, like Achilles; then brave men and true, like Aristides and Scipio the African; nearer our time appear men with great semblances of virtue attended by great vices, and these are hailed by the crowd as noisily as though they deserved true glory; such are, for instance, Caesar and Alexander; then come the sadly brooding dreamers, like Tiberius and, finally, the furious, dissolute, and corrupt, like Caligula, Nero, and Domitian. "The first of these classes of men was needed in order to get man used to obeying other men within families, thus preparing him to obey the laws when there would be cities; the second class, who would yield to no one, was needed to establish, over the families, aristocratic republics; the third class paved the way for popular liberties; the fourth class introduced the monarchies; the fifth stabilized them; the sixth overthrew them. This axiom, together with the preceding one, yields part of the principles of the eternal ideal history whose course all nations follow in their rise, progress, steadiness, decline, and end" (Axiom lxviii).

The *storia ideale eterna* of which Vico was here dreaming has not yet been written, but the modest professor of rhetoric had his own reasons to hope for it. In the section of his book devoted to the *Principles*, Vico notes that, though men did not make the world of nature, which they boast to know so well, they certainly did make the human world. This is the main foundation for Vico's assurance that the "new science" is possible. Here is a truth impossible to doubt, "that this civic world has certainly been made by men, so that its principles can, nay, they must, likewise be found within the modifications of our very own human soul. In fact, it is amazing that philosophers always seriously strived to gain the knowledge of that world of nature of which only God, since He made it, has the science, while they neglected to meditate upon that world of nations, or the civil world of which, since men made it, they can acquire the science." [4] But human minds are so buried in their bodies that they lack the courage it takes to look at themselves. They resemble the eye, which sees all other objects directly, but cannot see itself without a mirror.

The most remarkable feature of Vico's doctrine is his justification for the use he makes of mythology and of ancient poetry. In this respect, the second part of the book has lost nothing of its suggestive power, for although its information is out of date, the thesis itself still deserves attention.[5]

Vico recalls one of his Axioms, that all the histories of the pagan peoples had fabulous beginnings. Those fables constitute for him a "poetic wisdom." True human wisdom is metaphysics; but men need a metaphysics from the very beginning, long before they are ready to acquire it by the light of reason. Poetic imagination provides men with a kind of rough approximation of metaphysics, a kind of natural theology. But this is not enough. From that poetic metaphysics, as from a common trunk, the ancient theologian-poets have derived, on the one hand, a whole series of practical disciplines (logic, ethics, economics, and politics: the moral sciences), and on the other, the complete series of speculative sciences (physics, cosmography, astronomy, chronology, and geography). All these sciences are "poetic," as we see them in Homer and the other great poets. Reflection conducted men from these poetic observations to philosophy as it conducted them from poetic theology to natural theology, which transcends sense, thus preparing them to receive revealed theology by faith, this latter transcending not only sense but human reason itself. The *New Science* thereby becomes history at once of the "ideas, customs and deeds of the human kind." Vico's "discovery of the true Homer" situates the Blind Sage at the very peak of poetic wisdom.

In his masterpiece *On the Recurrence of Human Affairs in the Resurrections of the Nations*, the philosopher's description of the course followed by the nations in their respective histories adheres to an *a priori* tripartite scheme: three kinds of nature, of customs, of natural law, of governments, of languages, etc. Of all this, Vico, too, was anticipating the science to come by a sort of provisory scheme. But his creative dream takes an unexpected turn in the fifth and last book of the work. After noting so many correspondences between situations and events happening in diverse nations and in different centuries, Vico makes it clear that history is made of *corsi* and *ricorsi*. Vico does not think that all human events are doomed eternally to reproduce themselves, at set intervals and in identically the same order. There is no "law of eternal return" in his philosophy. He does think, however, that history is self-repetitious, in this sense at least: that, in it, similar circumstances bring about the return of similar events. In a doctrine which defines the nature of things by their being born "in certain times and with certain characters," and which adds that, these remaining the same, things are born the same (Axiom xiv), a measure of repetition can be expected. If it is so, God has willed it to be so, for in the last analysis, the infinite wisdom of God is the source of all events as it is the cause of all things. He who is not pious cannot truly be wise.

XXIII

Montesquieu

THE FIFTH VOLUME OF THE *Encyclopedia* opened with an *Eloge du Président de Montesquieu*[1] by d'Alembert. The document is still well worth reading. D'Alembert had added to it an extensive *Analysis of the Spirit of Laws*, intended to facilitate the reading of the book for persons liable to get lost in its wealth of details. Montesquieu, d'Alembert said, had opened new ways. "He was among us what Descartes had been for philosophy, enlightening often, blundering sometimes but, even in his errors, instructive for those who can read." Of course d'Alembert would not pass up the opportunity to annex Montesquieu to the loose federation of "Encyclopedists." But he did have some justification for doing so. Montesquieu had promised the *Encyclopedia* an article on "Taste." The work was found unfinished among his papers and published in the same fifth volume. He was at best a marginal member of the group, and much closer to d'Alembert than to Diderot.

The Nature of Law

THE PHILOSOPHICAL SUBSTANCE of Montesquieu's great work, the *Spirit of Laws*, is wholly contained in the first six of its thirty books. Of course the meaning of the doctrine becomes clearer in its countless particular applications, but its essence remains unaffected by them.

Montesquieu begins by defining the nature of law. Each thing in the world has its own necessary nature; brought together, things react on each other, and, just as their respective natures are necessary, so are their mutual relations. These relations are what we call "laws." Hence laws may be defined as "the necessary relations that derive from the nature of things." [2]

In this sense of the word everything has its laws because everything has a nature. The Deity has its laws; the material world has its laws; Intelligences above man have their laws; brutes have their laws; man has his laws. Some have said that everything is the work of blind necessity, but this is absurd, for there are intelligent beings such as men, and how could blind fatality produce intelligent beings? Since there is reason in man, reason must be found at the origin of things, and so, too, of laws: "There is a primitive reason, and the laws are the relations that obtain between that reason and the various beings, as well as the relations of those various beings with one another."

The problem for Montesquieu is to find for human laws their own place within this framework. Faithful to theological tradition, he subordinates natural law to divine law. God is related to the world as both creating and conserving it, the laws following which he has created it being also those according to which he is conserving it. In terse and packed sentences, Montesquieu adds: "God acts according to those rules, because He knows them; He knows them because He made them; He made them because they have relation to His wisdom and to His power." Montesquieu used to say that skipping intermediate ideas is one of the secrets of style; he himself, obviously, could pull the trick!

Two classes of beings exhibit permanent relations to God. First, the world of material objects. Deprived of intelligence, that world nevertheless exhibits regularity in its operations and stability in its existence. Consequently, it must obey invariable laws. Far from favoring the notion of a world arbitrarily produced and preserved, the notion of creation entails that of a world ruled by God as invariably as it would be by the fatality of the atheists. The skipped intermediate idea here is that, since no world can subsist without laws, God cannot possibly create and conserve one without, by the same token, creating its laws and conserving it through them. Owing to such laws as, for instance, those of motion, each diversity is seen to be a *uniformity*, each change a *constancy*.

The second world, that of intelligent beings, is likewise subject to laws, but here the difference is that some of the laws are made by the intelligent beings themselves, and some are not.

Before intelligent beings actually existed, they were possible; so there were possible relations between them, and thereby they enjoyed in their state of possibility possible laws. Before laws were made, there were possible relations of justice. This leads Montesquieu to oppose the doctrines, as he says, "of Hobbes and Spinoza," according to whom there are no relations of justice and equity prior to the establishment of positive laws.[3] "To say that there is nothing just or unjust except that which positive laws prescribe or prohibit, is to say that, before a circle was drawn, all the rays were not equal."

One must therefore recognize relations of equity anterior to the positive laws that actually establish them. Such relations are valid for any possible society. For instance: supposing there were societies of men, it would be just to obey their laws. Again: supposing there were intelligent beings and they had received benefits from another being, they should feel grateful. Again: had an intelligent being created an intelligent being, the created one should remain in the same state of dependency wherein he found himself at his very origin; or suppose that an intelligent being harms another intelligent being, he would deserve to receive the same harm, and so on.

As a physical being, man, like the other animals, is ruled by invariable laws, but the intelligent world is not so well regulated as the physical world. Human reason is limited by man's very nature; he is consequently liable to err. Moreover, since it is his nature to act on his own, there is not in his operations the regularity observable in the way the physical world obeys its own laws. Man does not constantly follow the primitive laws, not even those he gives to himself. "Such a being was capable of forgetting his creator any time, so God recalled him to Himself by giving him the laws of religion; such a being could at every moment forget himself, so the philosophers warned him by the laws of ethics; made to live in society, that being was susceptible of forgetting the others, so the lawgivers brought him back to his duties by political and social laws."[4]

Natural and Positive Laws

FROM WHAT WE HAVE JUST SEEN, it follows that men are ruled at one and the same time by *natural laws*, so named because they exclusively derive from the constitution of his being; and by *positive laws*, decreed by legislators. Montesquieu wishes to describe both kinds in due order, which leaves him confronted with a perhaps unanswerable question: What would man be in a pure state of nature, prior to the establishment of societies? "The laws of nature are those which men would receive in such a state."

It is not uncommon to see philosophers defining man as a "social animal," then wondering what man looked like before there were societies. Some of them openly declare their intention of ignoring history and imagining what the "state of nature" must have been like; others, among whom we find Montesquieu, seem convinced that a mere inspection of human nature permits us to infer, from what man now is, what kind of being he may have been before the era of civilization.

The first of natural laws impressed in the mind of man by his Creator is that which reminds him of his dependence on Him. Still, Montesquieu observes, although this is the first of all natural laws by its importance, it is not the first law man discovers in time. In the "state of nature," man would have knowledge potentialities rather than actual knowledges. His first ideas would certainly not be speculative; "he would think of preserving his being before investigating its origin." In short, Montesquieu concludes, in such a condition man would at first be conscious of nothing but his weakness. Montesquieu's primitive savage is an extremely shy man. In proof of this, he cites the case of the savage found in the Hanoverian woods and who was shown in England during the reign of George I. He was afraid of everything; anything makes wild men run away.

In accordance with this view, Montesquieu imagines that, until he lives under social laws, every man feels himself inferior to other men; "he does not think of attacking others; the first natural law is peace." This position constitutes a flat denial of Hobbes' contention that men desire to subjugate one another. In keeping with the analytical method dear to the Encyclopedists, Montesquieu objects that "the idea of domination and of dominion is so complex, and it depends on so many other ones that it cannot be the first one such a man would have." When Hobbes asks why men never go unarmed, and why they have keys to lock their houses, he is forgetting that, in the state of nature, men have neither arms nor houses. Weakness and fear, then, are the source of man's first natural law.

The second source of natural laws would be man's feelings of need, especially that of food. Seeking satisfaction of these primitive needs naturally follows. Now, according to the first law, men would avoid one another; "but the signs of a mutual fear would soon invite them to meet." Animals take pleasure in encountering animals of their own kind. "Moreover, the charm which both sexes find in experiencing their differences would increase that pleasure, and the call they always address to one another would make up a third law." [5]

Finally, it should be remembered that, although in the beginning deprived of knowledge, men still are able to know from the very start. They begin at once to store up cognitions. So over and above the animal feelings that impel them to seek the company of other men, their desire to communicate and their need to exchange ideas provide another strong motive to unite. This desire to live in society Montesquieu considers a fourth natural law. Notice that Montesquieu does not consider sociability to be an absolutely primitive mark of human nature. Man first is a timorous being, next a hungry being, then a friendly being, last an intelligent and, by the same token, a sociable one. (The moments of this decomposition of the primitive laws of nature should not be understood as following each other in chronological succession; they are so many moments of a conceptual analysis of human nature in the course of which its fundamental laws are successively revealed.)

We are now about to meet the most curious turning point in this ideal history of mankind. In losing fear, men lose peace. The common feeling of their individual weakness established between them a kind of equality; when men lose that equality, they begin to fight. In a word, society means war.

War is a catching disease. As each particular society comes to experience its force, a state of war between nations sets in. Likewise, within every given society, each particular person begins to feel his force; every man attempts to make the most of that society, and this causes another state of war. To remedy these two kinds of disorders, laws had to be established. These are called positive laws because they were set up by men, rather than being the work of nature.

As the planet earth is so large, there are bound to be different peoples and, by the same token, laws established in order to regulate their relations. Such laws constitute the Law of Nations (now called International Law; that is to say, a code of principles regarded as binding for all nations). This *jus gentium* rests upon the principle that the diverse nations should, in peacetime, help one another as much as possible and, in war, harm one another as little as possible. From this twofold truth, all the laws forming the Law of Nations should normally follow.

Besides that law common to all societies, each individual society has a law of its own, for no society can endure without a government. The union of all particular forces within a given human group constitutes what is called the "political state." The laws thus uniting men into one single body politic are called "political law." This definition of the "political state" as the "reunion of all the particular forces" is attributed by Montesquieu to Gravina, the contemporary Roman scholar of jurisprudence.[6]

Particular forces cannot unite unless individual wills agree. This union of wills, still according to Gravina, constitutes "the Civil State," which is regulated by Civil Law. Taken in general, law is but human reason governing all the peoples of the earth, but the "political laws" and the "civil laws" of each nation must be but the particular cases to which that human reason applies itself. This indeed is the only strictly universal principle of those laws. Montesquieu lays it down as the very justification for the extensive study his book will make of many different legislations. The Political Law (or constitution) and the Civil Law of each particular people should be so perfectly adapted to that nation that, with perhaps a rare exception, the laws befitting one nation should not befit another. Whether the laws form the nation as do the political laws, or whether they preserve it as do the civil laws, they all must be adapted to the climate of the country; to its size and to the nature of its soil; to the kind of life of its inhabitants (plowmen, hunters, herdsmen); to the degree of liberty a particular constitution can bear; to the religion of the inhabitants, to their inclinations, their wealth, their number, their trade, their habits, and their manners. Above all, the laws of a country should harmonize with each other and with their origin, as well as with the intention of the lawgiver, and with the order of things about which they are concerned.

Montesquieu intended to consider all known political and civil legislations under all these aspects. Defining the aim and scope of his work, he declared: "I shall examine all these relations; taken all together, they constitute what is called L'ESPRIT DES LOIS." This is the exact meaning of the formula in Montesquieu's own doctrine, and it accounts for the plan followed in it. For it does not deal with the laws themselves, as a jurist would do, but rather with their spirit, and since this "spirit of laws consists of the relations which laws may have with diverse things," Montesquieu has followed less the natural order of the laws than that of the things and of the relations of the laws to things.

Governments, Their Natures and Principles

THERE ARE THREE KINDS OF GOVERNMENT: *republican, monarchic,* and *despotic.* In a republican government, the body politic collectively wields the supreme power; in the monarchic government, one single man exercises power and governs by means of fundamental laws; in the despotic government, there is no other law than the will of the master or, more exactly, of the tyrant. This is not to say that there are no other types of government in the world. It even is probable that one would not find one single pure case of republican, monarchic, or despotic constitution. This remark of d'Alembert is justified, the more so as Montesquieu himself suggests it, but it should not obscure for us the aim and scope of Montesquieu's effort. What he intended was to disengage from the endless multiplicity of particular legislations the fundamental forms in which, in different degrees, all participate.

This tripartite division corresponds to the nature of the fundamental forms of governments. Montesquieu here introduces a distinction of great importance in his doctrine, that between the *nature* of a form of government and its *principle.* The nature of a type of state is that which constitutes it as such. We have just defined the respective natures of the republican, monarchic, and despotic states. The principle of each state, or type of government, is that which keeps it alive and makes it work. Whatever their particular form may happen to be, all laws should be related to the *nature* as well as to the *principle* of the fundamental type of government of the nation.[7] Let us briefly summarize the main laws that follow, first from the nature, then from the principle of the three fundamental types of constitutions.

It is of the *nature* of a democracy (or republic) that the people be in one sense sovereign and in another sense subject. The people of a republic obeys, as subject, the laws that, as monarch, it has made. Being monarch by his vote only, and his vote expressing his will, the will of the monarch (i.e., the people) is the monarch himself. The electoral laws, then, are fundamental in a republican constitution or form of government. Like all sovereigns, the people of a republic must do by itself all that which it can do well, particularly choose its representatives and magistrates. The people have a natural gift for discerning merit and picking out the men who will serve them best. They may make mistakes but, by and large, their choices are good. Whatever the people cannot do directly and by itself should be delegated to a senate. Such is the case for the making of laws, for indeed, though it is a fundamental rule of democracy that the people alone should make the laws, there are a great many cases when a senate should pronounce for the people.[8]

In a monarchy the supreme power is in the hands of a single man, but the nature of this form of government demands that there should also be many intermediate powers and ranks between the monarch and the people. Availing himself of this opportunity to express his personal preference for a constitutional monarchy, Montesquieu stresses the need of a constituted body, keeper of the laws and mediating between the monarch and his subjects; in other words, a parliament.

By contrast, despotism demands that the tyrant should himself exercise power, if not alone, then at most through one single man who represents him. It is in fact of the nature of such a form of government that the despot should finally delegate his power to some grand vizier, his first slave, through whom, without personal effort, he can sway all the others.

So much for the *nature* of the three types of government; now, what about their *principle*? The active force by virtue of which a democracy (or republic) efficaciously operates is "virtue." Nothing else can substitute for it. In a monarchy or under a despot, the will and power of the sovereign suffice to keep together the body politic and to insure the respect of laws. But in a republic, besides all the powers required by other political regimes (for, as monarch, the people also must be obeyed), virtue also is necessary. So virtue is the principle proper to democracy. Observe that its principle is consonant with its nature: If virtue alone can bind a democracy to the observance of its own laws, it is because in a democracy the body politic possesses the political power. Reciprocally, the body politic can possess the political power, as virtue will bind it to the observance of its own laws.

The principle of monarchy is bound to be different. Such a state subsists independently of virtue, of the love of the country and of true glory. A monarch's politics is to strive to obtain that great things be done with the minimum of virtue. The spring on which he plays is "honor." Each and every citizen is prompted to act by the ambition to climb the social ladder, to attain a higher rank and to secure the esteem of the monarch. Here again, the principle and the nature of monarchy are consonant: The many degrees of intermediate powers and ranks between the king and the people provide the social ladder to be climbed, and thus a motive to act for all.

Perhaps we should interrupt this analysis for a moment in order to recall the nature of the problem at stake. Montesquieu is not a historian, because he does not intend to picture any one political constitution in particular. He is not thinking as a jurist (although he himself is one), because he does not aim to describe any particular type of legislation. What he is, is a philosopher endeavoring to disengage from complex facts the idea or essence of each fundamental type of political society. Every real society is definable in terms of its particular degree of participation in these political ideas. It is irrelevant to object to Montesquieu that, in fact, there is honor in democracies and virtue in monarchies. He knows that, but his point is that democracy does not live fundamentally by honor nor monarchy by virtue. The proof of it is that well-conducted democracies mistrust honors and intelligent monarchs prefer not to be served by too virtuous men. Cardinal de Richelieu must have had something like this in mind when he wrote in his *Memoirs:* "One must never employ men of low birth; they are too austere and too difficult."

Nor is honor the principle of despotic states. Under tyranny all men are equal in slavery. Honor and virtue have rules of their own; despots obey no rule. The only principle on which a despot can rely to keep the state together is sheer fear. Men acting by honor or by virtue are deadly perils to such a regime. Any man the despot cannot destroy at will is a threat to his power. One cannot speak without horror of such monstrous governments; in monarchic states the power of the prince is limited by honor and its laws; in despotic states, the power of the prince is limited by nothing.

As if anxious to avoid all unnecessary misunderstandings, Montesquieu adds these concluding remarks:

Such are the principles of the three governments: which does not mean that, in a given republic, men are virtuous, but that they should be. This does not prove either that, in a given monarchy, men have honor; and that, in a particular despotic state, men have fear; it only proves that one should have honor and fear, failing which the government will be imperfect.[9]

The laws set up by the legislator must agree with the principle of each form of government. In a republic their aim should be to foster virtue; that is, the love of the commonwealth (or "republic"). "The love of the commonwealth in a democracy is the love of democracy; the love of democracy is that of equality." By the same token, it is the love of frugality. The love of equality limits the ambition of citizens to the sole desire of serving the country better than the other citizens; the love of frugality limits the "desire to have" to what is necessary for the family, all the surplus going to the country. The aim and scope of all laws in a democracy is to promote this two-fold ideal of frugality and equality.[10] In a monarchy the object of well-conceived laws is to support the nobility without crushing common people. In a despotic government the purpose of the laws is to reduce men of all conditions to complete silence. Starting from there, Montesquieu goes on to show how criminal and penal legislations should be understood under each of the three types of government, thus pursuing his immense inquiry with admirable verbal economy.

Among the many problems handled by Montesquieu in the remaining sections of the book, three at least deserve special mention. First, his description of the ways each of the three forms of government gets corrupted by the corruption of its principle, despotism alone proving it is already corrupt of its very nature.[11]

Secondly, his remarks on political liberty. Montesquieu opposes the preconceived idea that liberty cannot exist under a monarchy and that it inevitably flourishes in democracies because in democracies the people can do what it pleases. This, Montesquieu remarks, is to confuse the *power* of the people with the *liberty* of the people. True liberty consists in being able to do what one should want to do and in not being constrained to do what one must not want to do.[12] Such a state of affairs can exist in a monarchy and does not necessarily have to in every democracy.

The third point is one of the highlights of Montesquieu's doctrine.

It concerns the problem of knowing "what laws form political liberty in its relation to the citizen." Among his many remarks on this important question, what Montesquieu says about the division of the fundamental powers in the state deserves particular attention, especially because of its influence on the American Constitution.

Aristotle had distinguished three powers in the state, the legislative, the executive, and the judiciary.[13] Locke had taken up that same distinction and stressed its importance with respect to the executive and the legislative powers. In agreement with the general trend of his work, Montesquieu shows this distinction to be the fundamental condition for the possibility of political liberty. The passage in which he develops this view is a classic. It must be read just as Montesquieu himself wrote it:

> In a citizen, political liberty is the tranquility of mind that arises from the opinion every one has of his security; in order to obtain that liberty there must be such a government that no citizen can fear another citizen.
>
> When, in the same person or in the same body of magistrates, legislative power is united with executive power, there is no liberty; because it is to be feared that the same monarch, or the same senate, might make tyrannical laws in order to execute them tyrannically.
>
> There still is no liberty if the power to judge is not separated from the legislative and from the executive power. Were it joined to the legislative power, the power on the life and on the liberty of the citizens would be arbitrary; because the judge then would be legislator. Were it joined to the executive power, the judge could have the force of an oppressor.
>
> All would be lost, if the same man, or the same body of notables, or of nobles, or of the people, did exercise those three powers, that of making laws, that of implementing public resolutions, and that of judging the crimes and the lawsuits of private persons.[14]

Some readers of the *Esprit des lois* feel disappointed because, when all is said and done, Montesquieu does not say which form of government is best. But one of his objects had been to make clear that if there is a "spirit of the laws" it should consist in the ceaselessly renewed effort to devise constitutions adapted to the countless particular circumstances under which, at different times and in different places, diverse countries have to live. The circumstances are so many that no two legislations are interchangeable in place or time; nevertheless, given a law, it is always possible to account for it by relating it to some cause and, taken all together, this multitude of varied facts seems to distribute itself according to a small number of basic patterns. In fact, these are, as we have seen, three in number, and knowledge of them simply provides observers with centers of intelligibility.

Montesquieu has obtained some important positive results. Before him, there was a tendency to oppose the world of nature, subject to laws, to the world of human societies, subject to the human will. Montesquieu is very far from cutting off social facts from the human will. Man does make laws, and laws are causes; however, he thinks that, even in the making of laws, human liberty is conditioned by facts and by necessary relations between facts. It is important for us to know those facts and those laws. The very focus of Montesquieu's thought is the consideration of the organic correlation in each basic form of society between its nature and its principle; between these two and the laws that follow from them, whether these be criminal or civil laws; then again the organic correlation between basic forms of government and their systems of education and of taxation, their conceptions of national defense, their trade and the form of their industry. In discussing the circumstances independent of the form of government, such as the nature of the soil, the climate, etc., Montesquieu shows how well-calculated laws can remedy some of their harmful effects or, on the contrary, insure countries the full benefit of such physical advantages. In short, Montesquieu has left us a prototype of that science of political and juridical facts which the modern "sciences of man" are still trying to constitute. To find the "reasons" for every one of those facts was his great ambition. He himself said so in his Preface: "I am not writing in order to censure the order established in any country whatsoever. Every nation will find here the reasons of its own maxims." And he wishes to reach this knowledge for most practical purposes. It is important that citizens should be informed of the reasons they have for liking what pleases them in the political regime to which they are subjected. It is likewise important that rulers should know what to do and what to avoid in order to preserve, to improve, or to modify a given political regime according to its own nature and possibilities. "If I could bring rulers to increase their knowledge as to what they must prescribe, and those that obey to find a new pleasure in obeying, I would think myself the most fortunate of mortals."

XXIV

Jean-Jacques Rousseau

THE VERY NAME OF ROUSSEAU[1] can alone start a controversy. It would be wise to leave his person out of an appraisal of his doctrine were it not for the fact that they were inseparable in his own mind. In a sense, the philosophy of Rousseau is a series of commentaries about his personal case as a human being. His hardly readable dialogues about himself, *Rousseau as a Judge of Jean-Jacques*, show him lost in the maze of his own feelings and, of course, possessed by an intense desire for self-justification. It is so true that Rousseau's more abstract and general ideas spring from an acute awareness of his personal problems that we cannot introduce his very first work without taking them into account, for Rousseau himself stresses the importance of its origin.

The Discourse on Sciences and Arts

IN THE FIRST DAYS OF OCTOBER 1749, Rousseau, so he tells us, was walking from Paris to the dungeon of Vincennes, where Diderot was being detained after having published his *Letter on Blindmen*. He had in his pocket a copy of a then well-known literary magazine, the *Mercure de France* and, while leafing it, he chanced upon a question posed by the Academy of Dijon in view of an open essay competition: *Did the restoration of Sciences and Arts contribute to purify morality?* "If there ever was anything like a sudden inspiration, it was the commotion that took place in me when I read this; all of a sudden, I felt my mind dazzled by a thousand lights." Full of vivid ideas that plunge him into utter confusion, he falls prey to a sort of intellectual drunkenness. A violent palpitation of the heart obliges him to stop; he sits down under a tree alongside the road and stays there for half an hour in such a state of agitation that, when he got up, he realized he had been shedding abundant tears without even knowing it.[2]

Before criticizing this narrative as unlikely or as trumped up, some facts should be taken into account. First, Rousseau's age: he then was thirty-five years old and had not yet published a single book. Next that, being very sensitive and painfully aware of his social inferiority in a world where he was intellectually superior, he found himself a full-grown adult in a state of moral rebellion against society, or rather, against the two societies he had been trying to join and in both of which he had failed to make the grade. On the one hand was the smart set of noble men and women who prided themselves on protecting arts and letters and liked to play hosts to writers. Intellectuals despise such protectors, but they envy their fortune, and when Rousseau realized that one cannot be at once protected and free, he deeply resented the situation. On the other hand, there also was another smart set, that of the intellectuals themselves with their tacit, yet very strict conventions of mutual adulation, at least in words. Wherever there is such a jungle of "gens de lettres," you can be sure it has its laws. The citizen of Geneva still had a lot to learn about those things when he read the question asked by the Academy of Dijon, but he knew enough to form an instantaneous opinion. Had the restoration of arts and sciences improved morality? The answer was, no. Rousseau suddenly realized he had all the elements of the answer, only he had not thought explicitly of asking the question.

There is another piece of data necessary to appreciate the situation. At thirty-five, Rousseau had learned to be dissatisfied with society, but he also was dissatisfied with himself. A jack of all trades, he had tried a little of everything, even some of the less honorable ways of making a living. But he always had a divided conscience, except on one point about which he could never entertain any doubt; namely, that whatever he might do, he remained fundamentally good. But how, being a fundamentally good, just, and upright man, could he do the things he was doing? The answer is one that today has grown familiar: Society is responsible for the situation: "Having discovered, or at least thinking I had discovered, in the false opinions of men the source of their miseries and of their cussedness, I felt that those very same opinions were what had made me unhappy, and that my evils and my vices came from my situation much more than from myself." [3] A good case in point is his abandoning all his illegitimate children.

Had he undertaken their education, society would have taught them to hate their parents, even perhaps to betray them; Jean-Jacques is all right, it's society that is to blame.[4]

A last feature of his character must be kept in mind: When denied by nature or society the objects of his desires, Rousseau seeks compensation in imagination. He dreams of what reality refuses him, and, being a born artist, he finds an intense consolation in picturing for others as well as for himself the object of his dream. He himself has noted the fact with respect to his novel, *La nouvelle Héloïse*: not finding in reality the women he would have liked to love, he made them up. True, it was against his principles to write novels and thus contribute to the corruption of society; but the society in which he lived was already so corrupt that one more novel would make little difference: "Corrupt peoples need novels: I saw the present way of life, and I published these letters; ah, that I had lived in a century where I should have burnt them!" [5] Once again, the fault rests with society.

This constant trait had to be noted because it accounts for most of Rousseau's thought. Emile Faguet once said that Rousseau "never saw any thing such as it was." It would be more exact to say that, because he so often did not like things such as they were, Rousseau frequently substituted for them imaginary beings made to his own liking, which Faguet later aptly expressed:

> His works are himself and, what is less common, they are nothing else but him. Before anything else, he is a man of imagination: All his works are novels. He made the novel of humanity, and it is the *Inequality*; the novel of sociology, and it is the *Contract*; the novel of education, and it is *Emile*; a novel of sentiments, and it it is the *New Héloïse*; the novel of his own life, and it is the *Confessions*.[6]

True as this is, it leaves one thing unexplained. Rated as novels, many other works of the period make better reading than the philosophical writings of Rousseau; yet Rousseau's works were widely read, their influence was very deep—so deep that it still is impossible to write a history of philosophy without taking them into account. The reason is to be found in the depth of human experience from which they spring. Rousseau is a choice witness to the permanence in human nature of a feeling of nostalgia for a lost earthly paradise. Rousseau neither knows why man lost it nor even that he lost it. How paradise lost became paradise regained is even more foreign to his view of the world and of history. But the homesickness is there, and the obscure longing, and because all men confusedly feel that things are not what they should be, many put up with Rousseau's extravagant sophistry. He did not believe in the earthly paradise, but at least he was intelligent enough not to pretend that we are now in it, or on the way to it.

Ideas of this sort had been accumulating inside him for many years when Rousseau read the question asked by the Academy of Dijon, and that is why as soon as he had read it he knew the answer to it as well as to an infinity of others. When on the same day Rousseau asked Diderot to guess which side he was going to take, his friend answered: "The side you are going to take is that which nobody else will take." "You are right," Rousseau replied; whereupon he wrote his answer, which today is known as the *Discours sur les sciences et les arts*.

As a matter of fact, the *Discourse on the Sciences and Arts* did not actually answer the question, which really was whether the flowering of sciences and arts we now call the Renaissance (the word was then not yet in use) had raised the general level of morality. Rousseau answered that, *ever since the origins of mankind* (which certainly broadened the question!) sciences and arts had been a cause of moral decadence. After recalling in a few lines the change brought about by the revival of arts in Italy and their introduction into France, Rousseau simply indulges in a satire of the society life he knew and hated. The simple and natural ways proper to rural life have yielded to affected ones; the easy relationship once obtaining among men has been superseded by a conventional, yet exacting, code of behavior. "Politeness demands, decency prescribes; one always follows usages, never one's own genius." This uniformity of manners makes it impossible ever to know what kind of man one is dealing with. Hence a universal insincerity. Not knowing the true nature of the men one meets, sincere friendship becomes impossible. Suspicions, fears, jealousies, coldness, hatred, and betrayal come to hide behind the veil of good manners. We owe all this to the lights of our own century. "Where there is no effect, there is no point in looking for a cause, but here the effect is certain, the depravation is real and our souls were corrupted in proportion as our sciences and our arts were gaining in perfection."

All of this is not an accident proper to modern Europe. The fate of morality and probity is as tied to the progress of the sciences and the arts as are the tides to the phases of the moon. Rousseau shows that such was the case first with Greece, then with Rome. Luxury, depravation, and slavery have always and everywhere attended and punished the efforts of men "to get out of the blessed ignorance in which eternal wisdom had placed them." Here again Rousseau seems to remember the Bible's warning on the peril there would be in tasting of the fruit of the Tree of Science, but his own protest is directed against the arrogant self-satisfaction the men of his time were taking in the accumulation of learning. Rousseau is resolutely against science. "The thick veil under which eternal wisdom has concealed all its operations seemed a sufficient warning that it had not destined us to vain research." But is there a single one of those divine lessons that was not overlooked or neglected? "People do know once and for all that nature intended to preserve us from science, as a mother takes away a dangerous weapon from the hands of her child; all the secrets nature hides from us are so many evils from which it protects us, and the very trouble you find in learning is not the least of its favors."

With typical inconsequence, Rousseau concludes by an eloquent invitation addressed to kings to welcome at their courts scientists of the first order and to let them find there the only reward worthy of them, "that of contributing by their credit to the happiness of the peoples to whom they will have taught wisdom." How this jives with his contention that, of its nature, science makes for the depravation of nations and the misery of man, Rousseau does not explain. He contents himself with a hopeful sentence on "virtue, science and authority working in harmony for the felicity of the human kind." Still there was a meaning in this inconsequence. The *Social Contract* would someday disclose it.

The Origin of Inequalities

ROUSSEAU MET WITH BEGINNER'S LUCK. To his great surprise, the Academy of Dijon crowned his *Discourse*. This unexpected success gave him confidence in himself and revealed to him that he had possibilities as a writer. In 1753 the same academy proposed a second question well calculated to attract Rousseau's attention: "What is the origin of inequality among men, and is it authorized by natural law?" Rousseau had touched upon the point in the *Discourse*, but with discretion; he felt surprised that the Academy had dared to raise the problem and he thought that, since they had had the courage to ask it, he himself should have enough to answer it.

The *Discourse on the Sciences and Arts,* which was, after all, a first effort, was not too well written; there was too much rhetoric in it, which explains why the Academy had given it first prize. The *Discourse on the Origin of Inequality Among Men* was a model of sobriety in style and was incomparably deeper in thought. So in 1754 Rousseau did not get the prize.[7] But by then he knew who he was and what he was worth. So he published the second *Discourse* and at once found many readers.

In the beginning, the *Discourse* asserts— that is, in the state of nature —there was little inequality. What does Rousseau mean by that assertion? Not that science will discover this to have been the primitive condition of man: science can know only his present condition; the state of nature is past and lost, no experiment can restore it so as to teach us what it was; yet, deeply buried under more recent layers of usages and institutions, the original nature of man must still be present. An attentive inspection of man as he now is should therefore enable us to distinguish in him the old from the new, the natural from the artificial; that is to say, that which man was at first in his primitive condition from that which later developments have superadded to it. It is noteworthy that Rousseau identifies the natural with the primitive, gratuitously assuming that what did not come first could never belong to the true nature of things.

"Let us begin by discarding all facts, for they are irrelevant to the question." This astounding statement must not be misunderstood. Rousseau does not mean to say that his answer to the question will be unreal, but simply that its truth will not be that which belongs to historical facts. Starting from man such as he is, and attentively considering his nature, we shall form "hypothetical and conditional reasonings, more proper to clear up the *nature* of things than to show their veritable origin." Rousseau wanted to make it clear that he had no intention of contradicting the revealed teaching of *Genesis* on the origins of mankind, but he also wanted to rid himself of all scholarly research in a discussion to be conducted by philosophical reflection alone.

In this respect, one should read his apostrophe to man at the end of the Introduction: "O man, to whatever country thou mayest belong, and whatever thy opinions may be, listen; this is thy history, such as I thought I was reading it, not in the books of thy fellow men, who are liars, *but in nature,* which never lies." Times have changed and man now is very different from the being he used to be; nevertheless, Rousseau tells him in a statement, every word of which counts, "It is, so to speak, the life of thy species that I am about to describe, from the qualities thou hast received, which thy education and thy own habits may well have depraved, but which they cannot have destroyed." What Rousseau intends to do is to describe the life of the species; this accounts for the fact that his discourse reads like a history. But he will not turn to dusty manuscripts for information; he will write it in the light of what he can guess about the state of nature from the vestiges of that state still discernible in civilized man. And what criterion will he use? Of course, he himself, Rousseau. Man in the state of nature is man in the state where Rousseau himself would like to be. In no less extraordinary a sentence, Rousseau adds: "There is, I feel, an age at which individual man would like to stop; ask yourselves at what age you wish your species had stopped." In short, the state of nature is the state of mankind in which you dream to live.

The method is simple, but it is not absurd. There is nothing unlikely about the idea that man can discover in himself the remnants of an older, better, and happier condition than his present one; the question is to know whether Rousseau is better qualified than other men to say what that state once was. He, at least, has no misgivings on this point, and since he dislikes nothing more than inequality, he feels perfectly certain that, in the primitive state of nature, there were few or no inequalities.

Working on that assumption, he first describes physical man in his primitive condition, endowed with all manner of qualities since then lost. Considered from "the metaphysical and moral point of view," primitive man differed from other animals only by his will. The specific difference between man and brutes is due much less to his understanding than to his quality as a free agent. "Nature issues commands to all animals, and the brute obeys. Man feels the same impression, but he recognizes himself as free either to comply or else to resist; and it is chiefly in his awareness of that liberty that the spirituality of his soul shows itself; for indeed physics somehow explains the mechanism of senses and the formation of ideas, but in the power to will, or rather to choose, and in the feeling of that power, originate only spiritual

acts, of which nothing can be explained by the laws of mechanics."
The difference between the history of animal species and that of the
human species is thereby made clear: Having no choice, the brutes
never change; being free to choose between several possible courses
of action, human beings are perfectible. Perfectibility is a character
proper to the human kind.

In his primitive condition, man lives in the present; being provided
by nature with the necessities of life, man has no more need of another man than a wild beast of other beasts of the same species. He
has only two fundamental and necessary instincts: first, the instinct
of self-preservation, without which man could not survive and which
everyone still experiences within himself; next, the dislike of seeing
other living beings suffer and, still worse, perish. Apart from these
simple motives, primitive man has no reason to fret. Having no mutual
relations, he knows neither vanity nor consideration, neither esteem
nor scorn; the notions of mine and thine are foreign to him. So is the
notion of justice. If he fights, it is as dogs fight; little harm is done
and, when done, is soon mended. No arts, of course; neither education
given nor progress made. Every invention perishing with its author,
there could be among men no perceptible inequalities.

Differences first appeared when men began to feel the need to look
to other men for help. As soon as reciprocal needs united them, men
found themselves in a first state of servitude: To need another man is
to be dependent on him. The history of mankind is that of the successive efforts made by men to organize a system of exchanges in consequence of which they all finally found themselves in a state of almost complete mutual dependence.

"The first man who, having fenced in a piece of ground imagined:
This is mine, and found people simple enough to believe him, was the
true founder of civil society." All evils come from having forgotten
that fruits belong to all and that the soil belongs to nobody. With
private property, relations of justice and injustice set in, equality disappeared, the necessity of making tools and of enslaving other men in
order to cultivate large estates progressively imposed itself. Poets say
that silver and gold are the first causes of our present misery, but "to
the philosopher, it is iron and wheat that civilized men and lost the
human kind."

Rousseau realizes there are objections to this interpretation. Some
observe that savages, as we now know them, are far from being the

meek and passive beings he describes. But today's savages are not primitive men; they do not represent the state of nature; they are far too civilized. Let us skip an incredible wealth of imaginary, though not unlikely, history, which all boils down to a single law: the continuous increase of inequality between nations and nations, then between persons and persons, leading eventually to the kind of social and political oppression under which we now suffer.

At the end of his memoir, Rousseau excellently sums up the content of the work:

> I tried to expound the progression of inequality, the establishment and the abuse of political societies, as fully as those things can be deduced from the nature of man by the sole lights of reason and independently of the sacred dogmas which confer upon the supreme authority [Rousseau means that of the king] the sanction of divine law. From what was said it follows that, being almost null in the state of nature, inequality derives its force and its increase from the development of our faculties and from the progress of the human mind, until it finally becomes stable and legitimate owing to the establishing of property and of laws. It still follows that moral inequality, authorized by positive law only, is contrary to natural law every time it does not at the same time answer a proportional physical inequality; this distinction sufficiently determines how one must feel towards the kind of inequality which obtains among all civilized peoples, since it is manifestly against the law of nature, however you may define it, that a child should rule over an old man, that a stupid man should lead a wise man, and that a handful of people should have a surfeit of superfluities, while the hungry multitude lack necessary things.

These last remarks constituted a direct attack against the personal power of kings and, at the same time, against excessive inequalities in economic conditions. Rousseau's was not a merely speculative rebellion. In writing his second *Discourse*, he had in mind other projects and other problems. He was dreaming of writing a *Political Institutions* in which, as in an anti-*Esprit des lois*, "he would have weighed the advantages and the disadvantages of all government with respect to the rights of the state of nature, and in which would be disclosed all the different faces under which inequality has shown itself till today, as well as all those under which it is liable to show itself in future centuries, along with the revolutions which time will necessarily cause in them." Of that colossal program, only one part was to be fulfilled, the *Social Contract*.

The *Social Contract*

THE PUBLICATION of the *Contrat social* was a great literary event,[8] and of all the philosophical writings of Rousseau it remains the most frequently commented and republished.[9] Wholly misunderstood at first, it seems to be now at last viewed in a truer perspective. For one thing, nobody would now uphold the once popular point of view that, in the *Contrat social*, Rousseau contradicted all his preceding works.

The idea of the *Contrat* first appears in the *Discourse on the Origin of Inequality*, where Rousseau stipulates that, for the time being, he will argue "following the common opinion." That opinion was that the establishment of the body politic is a true contract between the people and the leaders it chooses for itself. According to such a contract, both parties pledge themselves to observe the laws stipulated in it and which form the bonds of their union. In writing these things, Rousseau was making all due reservations as to what his own answer to the question would be "after research still to be done concerning the nature *of the fundamental pact of all government*."

Rousseau had not written on the origin of inequality with the idea that mankind should return to its primitive state and, in Voltaire's own words, "go on all fours." Let us remember what he disliked most in social life, and thus what he was writing about: inequality arising from the power exercised by man over man. All the minor limitations of personal liberty caused by life in society finally arose from that first and fundamental one. Society had to be reformed, not destroyed, be it only for the reason that to destroy it would prove an impossible undertaking. There is no returning to the golden age when man was living alone in nature. Even then, he had to undergo the pressure of the physical world. But social pressure under the form it had taken in the course of centuries—to wit, the oppression of man by man—this is much more unacceptable. By "oppression" Rousseau does not necessarily mean enslavement; *any* dependency on other men is unbearable to him. Since society is here to stay, the only remedy to the situation seems to be *to turn society itself into a sort of nature*. If this can be done, social life will assume an entirely new aspect; this is the aim of the *Contrat social*.

The first lines of the *Contrat social* clearly define its object and its method: "Man was born free, and everywhere he is in chains. He believes himself the master of others, who nonetheless is more of a slave than they.[10] How that change did happen, I know not. What can make it legitimate? That question I think I can answer."

Rousseau once more dismisses history. Starting from its result—that is, the universal state of slavery in which all men now find themselves on account of society—he will look for a way to render social bonds legitimate and therefore bearable. Force is no answer to the question, for indeed force is a *physical* bond, not a *social* one. Nature is no answer either, for the *Discourse on the Origin of Inequality* has shown that society was not the primitive condition of man. Social order then can rest on conventions only. The problem is, what conventions?

The relation of father and son and that of master and slave are irrelevant to the problem. Children are bound to parents so long as they cannot provide for themselves; from then onward, children should be free. Slaves obey masters so long as they cannot do differently—i.e., slavery is a relation of force; slaves cannot turn their submission into a contract, because nobody can, by contract, totally alienate himself, which would amount to agreeing to cease to be. But the relation of king and subjects does rest upon a contract, some sort of *magna charta*; this presupposes, however, that there is a people. Since, before choosing to itself a king, a people is a people, what made it such, if not the social contract? The social contract then is the base of all civil society, and it is in the nature of that contract that one must look for that of the society which it constitutes.[11]

Let us suppose men have reached the point where the obstacles to survival in the state of nature have become too much for the personal resistance of isolated individuals. The primitive state of man then ceases to remain possible. Rousseau fully realizes that the birth of society did answer a need. Had it not changed its way of life, the human kind would have perished. Quite possibly there was no choice; Rousseau's only point is that, avoidable or not, the birth of society was for the human condition the beginning of a decadence.

In such a condition what can mankind do in order to survive? Not being able to create new forces, it can only unite to direct the existing ones. These forces are the strength and liberty of each individual. But our own strength and our own liberty are, for every one of us, the only instruments of survival. How can we engage them without neglecting the duties we have toward ourselves? The problem then is to find a form of association protecting, by the force of all, the person and the goods of each associate. The thing should be done in such a way that, "while uniting himself to all, each and every one nevertheless obeys but himself and so remains as free as he was before."

All the clauses of such a contract boil down really to the total alienation of each and every associate, along with all his rights, to the community as a whole. Should a single man make any reservation in his own favor, equality would not obtain. But, if everybody alienates everything he owns, including himself, he alienates himself to nobody in particular. The force to which he will be submitted will not be somebody (and this is the main point), rather it will be *something*.

The formula of the social pact, then, should run as follows: "Each and every one of us sets in common his person and all his might under the supreme direction of the general will; and we all receive, in a body, each and every member as a part undividable from the whole."

The effects of such a pact are many. The public person thus formed by the union of all private persons used to be called a *City*; now it is called a *Republic*, or *body politic*; considered as *passive*, the public person's members call it *State*; considered as active, *Sovereign*; with respect to its like, *Power*. The belonging associates collectively take the name of *People*; each particular one is both a *Citizen*, as sharing in the supreme authority, and a *Subject*, as submitted to the laws of the State.[12]

Why does this answer to the problem give Rousseau satisfaction? Because, in such a society, as the sovereign consists of the united wills of all, it cannot have any other will than a common and general will. Consequently, the acts of the sovereign can only be directed to general and common objects. Hence this consequence, which is to Rousseau of first importance, that no private citizen can be harmed by the sovereign without all the others being harmed at the same time,[13] a thing which cannot happen since, for the sovereign, it would amount to hurting itself. From this point of view, the citizens being subjected to the sovereign only (and not to any particular citizen), and the supreme authority being nothing else than the general will, it follows that, in obeying the sovereign, each particular man obeys but himself. No such guarantee existed in the state of nature because, however small, there were then inequalities. After the pact, no inequalities at all can possibly subsist; thus, in the last analysis, "one is more free in the social pact than in the state of nature." [14]

The social pact marks a turning point in the (ideal) history of mankind. Whenever and wherever men decide to live under the social pact, a decisive change in their condition is bound to follow. Man in the state of nature had no other rules than instinctive ones; under the pact, *justice* replaces instinct and, with justice, *morality* in actions appears. Other changes flow from these. In the state of nature, man obeyed physical impulses; from now on he will obey *the voice of duty*; instead of being carried away by appetites, man will now obey *law*. This is what Rousseau meant by saying that after the pact man is freer than ever before. True enough, he now must deny himself some of the advantages he held from nature, but his faculties begin to exert themselves, his ideas grow wider, his feelings become nobler; in short, "if the abuses of his new condition did not often debase him beneath that which he has just left, man ought never to cease blessing the happy moment when he got out of it, and which, out of a stupid and narrowly limited being, made an intelligent being and a man." [15] Civil liberty far excels natural liberty because it is moral liberty.

Such are the principles from which Rousseau deduces the general structure of the ideal state in which all citizens would be strictly governed, yet supremely free. Strictly governed because, the law being the impersonal expression of the body politic, purely private interests could not be taken into account: such a law binds like a man-instituted nature, as indifferent to personal preferences as physical nature always was, and is. On the other hand, hard as it is, that law is never tyrannical, precisely because, operating with the impersonality of a nature, it is the same for all. [16]

This supposes that, over and above the institution of the body politic, there was instituted a legislative power to enact the laws and an executive power to enforce them. Against Montesquieu, the desire to emulate whom is obvious throughout the *Contrat social*, and in consequence of his very notion of the social pact, Rousseau rejects the notion of a division of the political and the legislative powers. By essence, political power is indivisible. As a legislator the people determines what is for the body politic the objects of its *will*. Besides *will*, the body politic has *power*; it has both *legislative power* and *executive power*. Now all decisions of the executive power are concerned with particular objects, and since both the sovereign and the legislative power always have general objects, the executive power can belong to neither one. It belongs to *Government*, which is "an intermediate body established between the subjects and the sovereign in view of their mutual correspondence, entrusted with the execution of the laws and with the preservation of liberty, civil as well as politic." [17] It can be a one-man government or a college; its size should be proportioned to the form of the government (democracy, the whole people; aristocracy, a small number of men; monarchy, one single man); hence the conclusion: Since, in the various states, the number of the supreme magistrates should be in inverse ratio to that of the citizens, "it follows that, in general, the Democratic Government begets smaller states; the Aristocratic Government, the middle sized ones, and the Monarchic the larger ones. This rule immediately follows from the principle, but how can one enumerate the multitude of circumstances that can occasion exceptions?" [18]

Rousseau develops the details of his political philosophy with a mind divided between the pleasure of indulging in dreams and the effort of preparing a new and better form of reality. The book is signed: "J.-J. Rousseau, Citoyen de Genève," and he is certainly thinking of a similar, though more perfect, type of society when he describes the democracy of his dreams; only, the more he thinks of it, the less he believes in its possibility. All the powers flowing in that society from the same source, the danger of their becoming confused is great, as Rousseau is well aware. Is there a people virtuous enough to control itself and to respect, as subject, the laws it enacts and enforces in its capacity as sovereign? There never was a true democracy in the proper acceptation of the word, nor will there ever be one. "It is against the natural order that the larger number should govern and the smaller one be governed." Think of all the conditions required for such a regime: First, a very small state in which the whole population can easily assemble and where each citizen can easily know all the others; secondly, a great simplicity of life, so as to avoid the multitude of affairs and the thorny discussion they breed; then a great equality in rank and fortune, for otherwise equality would not last long in rights and authority; lastly, little or no luxury, for luxury either comes from wealth or makes it necessary. Let us add that, because of its shifting nature, no government is more exposed than democracy to the peril of civil wars; no other form of society requires from its citizens more vigilance and more courage in order to maintain it. "Were there a people of gods, it would govern itself democratically. So perfect a government is not suitable for men." [19]

Education

EVERYTHING WAS FINE as it came from the hands of God; everything deteriorates at the hands of man. The trouble is that man cannot leave well enough alone. He cannot accept nature as its Author made it. Elements, plants, animals, man changes all; he transforms all and mutilates all. He seems to like monsters. In short, man "will have nothing such as nature made it, not even man." This is manifest in our corrupt system of education. Normally, man should be educated in view of himself; i.e., to make a man out of him. But what do we do instead? We educate future men and women in view of society. Hence the great importance attributed to the kinds of studies that will enable a man to exercise a profession and the emphasis on teaching the child good manners. In its present state, education aims at preparing future members of the body politic; at its best, it aims to turn out citizens, not men.

The intimate connection of this problem with Rousseau's other positions is clear enough. Once more he proposes "to imagine" a possible dream remedy. The result is *Emile*, the case history of a fictional pupil raised by an ideal tutor. Once again the whole structure will be fantastic but consistent, and in its detail even abundant in sound suggestions.

That his whole educational program is unrealistic seems evident even to Rousseau himself. The end in view is to provide the child with a "natural education." "I am showing the goal one should keep in mind; I am not saying one can reach it; but I do say that he who will get nearer to it, will be better than other men." Here are some of the conditions required for the education of Emile. Neither school nor college, needless to say; we are not educating Emile for society but, rather, we are protecting him from it. So we shall have to find a preceptor, young in years yet old in wisdom, single and prepared to devote twenty-five years of his life to the education of one child. Still worse, how could he know what to do unless he were Rousseau himself? So really, there is only one possible preceptor for him, Rousseau:

"I therefore resolved to give myself an imaginary pupil, to suppose I had the age, the health, the knowledge and all the talents required for attempting his education, and to conduct him from the very moment of his birth till the time when, a grown-up man, he will need no other guide than himself."

But now that the problem of finding a preceptor is settled, how is the preceptor going to find a child? He will not take the first one he happens to be offered. The child must be a boy—much later, Providence will supply for Emile a suitable Sophie. He must live in a country of temperate climate, not too far north nor too far south; the boy should be wealthy—"the poor child needs no education": he could do nothing with it. He has no choice—Emile had best be of noble parentage; that will make at least "one victim of prejudice liberated from it." Emile should honor his father and mother; but Rousseau specifies, "he shall obey only me; this is my first or, rather, my only condition"; in other words, his father and mother might as well be dead, and this is the reason Emile is often thought to be an orphan. Nor does Rousseau care for a sickly and brooding child; so Emile will be robust and in good health. He will need "neither physicians with their prescriptions, nor philosophers with their precepts, nor priests with their exhortations"; in short, once in charge, Rousseau will have nobody else around. They would only spoil his good work.

Such an ideal situation is the matter of *Emile*. As Rousseau himself says, "not being able to perform the more useful task, I shall at least attempt the easier one; following the example of so many others, I shall not take the work in hand, but the pen; and instead of doing what should be done, I shall attempt to say it." [20]

In the state of nature, man was not exactly happy, but at least he was not unhappy, because he was subject not to men, but to nature only. He took his condition as it was, for the simple reason that he could do nothing about it. Now education should train man to react to society, the man-made "nature," as he would to physical nature. Man feels before he knows and reasons; he is, so to speak, molded from without by the impressions he undergoes from soil, food, climate and weather, parents, nurses, and, generally speaking, people of all denominations. This is the kind of reality the child will be up against during all his life. Even to educate him as a man, and not as a professional man or as a man of his own class, it is necessary to adapt him to the kind of external reality society will always remain for him. [21]

The preceptor should avoid an elemental mistake, which is to treat the child as if he already were a grown-up man. Rousseau has strongly insisted on the specificity of the psychology of the child as distinct from that of the adult. In this he was a pioneer: "Childhood has ways of seeing, of thinking, of feeling that are proper to it; nothing is less sensible than to will to substitute our own for them." To do so is simply to corrupt children and produce fruit that will rot before ripening.

His preceptor, then, should not appeal to Emile's reason. Let us teach him nothing of what he is naturally taught by nature (standing up, walking, etc.); above all, let us not argue with him and attempt to explain to him why certain things should be done and others not. To reason with children was a great maxim with Locke and, Rousseau adds, it is very much in practice today, but this is to put the cart before the horse. If they could use their reason, children would not need to be educated. The problem is to treat the child according to his age: "Put him first in his place, and keep him there so well that he does not try to get out of it. Thus, before knowing what wisdom is, he will practice its most important lesson."

Here again, as is so often the case with Rousseau, there is danger for us to miss a decisive, and yet an almost invisible, turning point. You must see to it that the child knows his place and stays there; don't argue with him, *not even to tell him things.* "Never order him in any regard, none whatsoever, absolutely none. Do not even let him imagine that you pretend to any authority over him. Let him only know that he is weak and that you are strong." The reason for this is obvious: the child must *feel* upon his proud head "the hard yoke nature imposes upon man, the heavy yoke of necessity, to which, ultimately, every finite being must submit; let him see that necessity in things, never in human caprice; let his rein and bridle be *force*, not *authority*." By so doing, you will render him patient, resigned, and quiet, even when he does not get what he wants. The important point is to submit him to a human rule as impersonal as that of a nature. Everything new in Rousseau's pedagogical methods follows from that principle.

First of all, the celebrated method which consists in staging incidents and situations in which the child will learn by himself why certain things must be done while others should rather be avoided. "Never give your pupil any kind of verbal lesson; he must receive lessons from experience only." If the course of events does not provide the necessary lessons, just make them up. For instance, do not try to explain to him the abstract notion of property; rather, let him sow a few beans, water them, take pleasure in seeing them grow and, above all, in thinking that they are *his;* since he himself made them grow, there is in them something of his work, of his person, so that he can claim them as his own against anybody who might pretend to take them away from him. Then, one day, wreck the little garden in his absence. Naturally, the boy will be in despair; then the gardener arrives, duly coached, and he explains that he himself had first sown melons at the very same place where the boy was growing beans. "All right," the preceptor says, "we shall buy you more melon seeds, and we shall never more cultivate any ground without first making sure that nobody else has tilled it before us." Finally, the gardener concedes to the boy a corner of the garden for him to cultivate, adding this last piece of advice: "Do not forget that if you touch my melons I shall go and plow up your beans." Why this complicated method? Because it is not a "verbal" lesson. The word "property" has not been pronounced. Nor would there have been any point in punishing the child for doing something wrong: "Innocent of all morality in his actions, he cannot do anything morally evil and deserving punishment or blame." Even to bid him to apologize is a waste of time; he does not know what it is to be wrong.

The general problem, therefore, is to place the child in an environment that will bring him spontaneously to react in the proper way. The main difficulty will be with the preceptor, not with the child. There are a few things he should first be convinced of before undertaking his noble task.

First, "let us lay down as an uncontrovertible maxim that the first movements of nature are always right; there is no original perversity in the human heart." The only primitive passion is the love of self. In itself, such self-love is sound so long as the actions it inspires are related to the subject only, not to other men. Pending the time when he will be able to reason, let him follow the inspiration of nature; he will do nothing wrong.

Secondly—and this is the most important of all the rules in education—what matters is not to gain time, but rather to waste it. The danger zone in human life is from birth to twelve, because we are appealing to the child's reason at an age when it is still asleep. "The first education should therefore be purely negative; it consists, not in teaching either virtue or truth, but in protecting the heart from vice and the mind from error." Here, do give the boy's body due exercise, train his organs, his senses, his strength, "but keep his soul idle as long as possible." Only thus will he be the pupil, not of the preceptor, but of nature, which is the main point.[22] When in doubt, act contrary to received usage and you will almost always be right.

Rousseau accompanies the child through adolescence; Emile has by now already added ideas to the sensations he had as a child. What does he know? He has, if not extensive knowledge, at least "a mind truly universal, not by its lights, but by its aptitude to acquire them." [23] The notion of *usefulness* becomes the main motive in his formation; the sacred word is *what is this good for?* The first book Emile will read, and the one that will constitute the whole of his library for a long time, is neither Aristotle, nor Pliny, nor Buffon; no, it is *Robinson Crusoe!* No more a children's book to the eighteenth century than *Gulliver's Travels,* Defoe's novel is a serious attempt at the return to nature. Rousseau must have envied the condition of Robinson on his deserted island; it is small wonder that he thought of exploiting it for the formation of his pupil.

The more useful an art, the nobler it is. Emile will therefore learn an art, or a craft, or a trade. As he proceeds in his work, following Emile through the stages of his sentimental education, as he learns to react to beings others than himself, Rousseau realizes that his pupil will very little resemble his well-to-do and noble parents. And the socialites of the court will look at Emile with surprise, for indeed "he is not the man of man, he is the man of nature. Surely, he must look very strange to their eyes." Emile is no savage; simply, caught as he must needs be in the social whirlpool, he refuses to let himself be dragged under by it. Besides, that "man of nature" will have one powerful guide to tell him how to conduct himself in the middle of social life. Emile will have religion.

Rousseau's *Profession of Faith*

THE FOURTH BOOK OF *Emile* contains the famous *Profession of Faith of the Savoyard Curate.* Cleverly presented as part of a narrative, partly true and partly fictional, it provided Rousseau with an opportunity to express his own views on the natural theology of a "man of nature."

The preceptor of Emile was Rousseau as a teacher; the Savoyard vicar is Rousseau as a preacher, a function for which he was eminently fitted. It is, however, impossible to read his *Profession of Faith* without perceiving behind it a real philosophical reflection on the problem of God.[24]

Man cannot live in a state of permanent and universal doubt; moreover, there really are absolute certitudes. I am, I feel. Whether I am something distinct from my sensations is not clear; but I know at least this, that the cause of my sensations is exterior to me; there are other beings; namely, the causes and objects of my sensations. All that which is outside myself I call matter, and all portions of matter joined together I call bodies. So idealists and materialists are equally wrong.

Reflecting upon the objects of my sensations, I find myself able to compare them. This is the capacity to judge. Unlike sense, it is an active power. Tacitly but effectively arguing against Condillac, Rousseau concludes from the presence in man of the power of judging that, since I am exercising it, "I am not merely a feeling and passive being, but an active and intelligent one." I also know, however, that since truth is in things and not just in the mind that judges them, the less I introduce of my own into my judgments about things, the nearer to truth I shall get: "so my rule to entrust myself to feeling rather than to reason is confirmed by reason itself."

Man now knows that he is; that he is not simply his sensations; that there are, outside himself, other beings called bodies and that those non-feeling and non-thinking bodies are made up of matter. We perceive matter to be sometimes in motion, sometimes at rest; so neither motion nor rest is essential to matter; but since rest is simply the absence of motion, it can be surmised that the natural condition of matter is to be at rest.

Motion is of two kinds: some of it is communicated and received, some is spontaneous or voluntary. I know there are spontaneous motions because I feel them. I myself can move my arm and I know this motion has no other immediate cause than my will. Obviously opposing Diderot, d'Holbach, and La Mettrie, Rousseau absolutely refuses to admit "the idea of a non-organized matter moving itself or producing any action." The world therefore is not a vast self-moving animal; there is a cause of its motions outside it; the fact that matter moves according to laws is irrelevant to the problem, for laws tell *how* the world moves, they do not account for the fact *that* it is in motion. One cannot imagine an infinity of causes, for to posit such a progress to infinity in the series of causes would amount to positing no cause at all; so there must be a first cause; and since only a will can cause motion, a will must move the universe and animate nature. "And this is my first dogma or my first article of faith."

If moved matter points to a will, matter moved according to certain laws points to an intelligence; hence Rousseau's second article of faith. The well-known argument drawn from the presence of purposiveness in the world is invoked in favor of this conclusion.

The world then is governed by a powerful and wise will. Many other questions can be asked about that prime cause, but most of them are idle questions, useless for my conduct and surpassing my reason. So let us content ourselves with this certitude and with calling this prime cause God.

Turning attention now to myself, and wondering what is *my* place in the universe, I realize that, of all known beings, man is the only one that adds to self-knowledge the knowledge of all the rest. So man must be the king of the earth he inhabits. It is silly on his part to wonder whether or not he is superior to animals. This is no occasion for pride; it is, rather, an invitation to admire God and to thank him for his gifts.

Here, however, a difficulty arises: while considering and admiring the divine Providence, the thought occurs that, nevertheless, there is evil on earth. How is that possible?

The answer is found in the twofold nature of man. There are in him two opposite principles, the one that elevates him to the consideration of eternal truths, the other that brings him down to himself and submits him to the tyrannic domination of his sensibility: "No, man is not one; I will and I will not; I feel myself both enslaved and free; I see good, I like it, and I do evil; I am active when I listen to reason, passive when my passions carry me away, and my worst torment, when I succumb, is to know that I could have resisted." Man himself then is the author of evil. Rousseau knows, of course, how man has brought evil into the world. It was by substituting civilization for nature: "Take away our finest progress, take away our errors and our vices; take away the work of man, and all is well."

Still, even in the present condition of man, happiness remains possible for him. The more deeply we inquire into ourselves, the more clearly we read these words written in our souls: *Be just, and you will be happy.* Those who argue the contrary on the ground that some virtuous men lead a miserable life simply forget that, "if soul is immaterial, it can survive body, and if it does, then Providence is justified." This very thought is itself such a solid proof of the immortality of the soul that it justifies the scandal of wickedness triumphant in this world. When, freed from the humiliations and disgraces by which our enemies make us buy the right to practice virtue in this world, we shall "enjoy the contemplation of the supreme being and of the eternal truths whose source He is, when the beauty of order will impress all the powers of our soul, and when we shall be uniquely occupied with comparing what we have done with what we ought to have done, then the voice of conscience will regain its force and its dominion over us, then also will pure voluptuousness born of the approval of oneself, and the bitter regret of having debased oneself, mark off by inexhaustible feelings the destiny which each and every man will have prepared for himself." The good will thus be rewarded and the wicked will be punished. How long will they be punished? This is one more idle question. As a matter of fact, Rousseau doubts that their punishment will last forever, but he does not know, nor does he worry about it: "What does it matter to me what will become of the wicked? I little care for their fate."

By studying God in his works, we progressively enlarge our notion of his nature and of his justice; when all is said, however, exaggerated striving to contemplate God's infinite essence is a sign one little realizes what he is; he does exist, and that is enough for us. The less I try to conceive of him, the more I shall worship him. "I humiliate myself and I tell Him, Being of beings, I am because Thou art: ceaselessly to meditate upon Thee is for me to rise up to my own source. The worthiest usage of reason I can make is to annihilate myself in Thy presence; this is the delight of my mind, the charm of my weakness, to feel myself overwhelmed by Thy greatness."

Once assured of those speculative certitudes, it remains for us to see what practical consequences follow from them for the conduct of life. Following his own method, Rousseau will not have to deduce moral rules from abstract principles; in his own words, he "will find them at the bottom of his heart written by nature in indelible characters." Then he goes on to say: "I have but to consult myself on what I want to do: all that which I feel to be good, is good, all that which I feel to be bad, is bad; the best of all guides is, conscience, and it is only when one is bargaining with it that one resorts to the subtleties of reasoning."

This is one of the better-known parts of Rousseau's doctrine because, duly transformed, it will leave a trace in the practical philosophy of Kant. The twofold nature of man and the inner opposition it begets find in this doctrine their explanation: "Conscience is the voice of the soul, passions are the voice of the body; is it to be wondered that often these two languages contradict one another? Too often reason deceives us, we have but too many grounds to challenge it; on the contrary, conscience is never wrong; it is the true guide of man: it is to the soul what instinct is to the body; who follows it, follows nature and does not fear to go astray."

> Conscience! Conscience! divine instinct, immortal and heavenly voice; trustworthy guide of a being ignorant and limited, yet intelligent and free; infallible judge of good and evil which renderest man similar to God, thou makest the excellence of his nature and the morality of his action; without thee, I feel in myself nothing that elevates me above the brutes, except the sad privilege of going astray from error to error by means of an understanding without rule and of a reason without principle.[25]

In this conclusion of his *Profession of Faith,* Rousseau seems to muster, as in a supreme effort, all the main principles of his philosophy. There is something pathetic in the sight of a man desperately clinging to remnants of Christianity and trying to justify them, in his own sight, by means of flatly naturalistic arguments.[26] Still, as compared with the crowd of materialists he was courageously opposing, Rousseau shows stature. When he described conscience as "an innate principle of justice and virtue by which, despite our own maxims, we judge our actions and those of others as good or bad," he was greeted by the clamors of the sensists: "Errors of childhood! Prejudices of infancy!" But he stood his ground. To those who mistook moral principles for prejudices, he aptly answered that "the acts of conscience are not judgments, they are feelings." For human beings, to be is to feel. "Our sensibility is undoubtedly anterior to our intelligence, and we had feelings before having ideas." Conscience is such a feeling. In the final analysis, it is small wonder that Voltaire, Grimm, and Diderot hated him so. How else could the "philosophers" react to such a passionate and irrational "confessor" of the type of God they were trying to destroy?[27]

XXV

Condorcet

T HE MAIN REPRESENTATIVES of the "philosophy of lights" died before that French Revolution which, not without some oversimplification, is often seen as the result of their work. The young Condorcet had sometimes expressed his surprise at the political prudence of such men as Diderot. He himself was young enough to see the Revolution and to share in it.[1] It was even the cause of his death, but with exemplary courage and fidelity to his own principles, he managed first to write a sort of philosophical profession of faith. In Condorcet, the spirit of the philosophy of light proved itself capable of inspiring a man with heroic courage, even within the narrow limitations of its anti-religious rationalism. Condorcet is the spirit of the *Encyclopedia* at its very best.

Written in the shadow of impending death, Condorcet's contribution to social philosophy, *Prospectus of a Historical Picture of the Progress of the Human Mind,* is resolutely optimistic. When reading it, one should remember that it is not the work of a professional philosopher, historian, or jurist, but of a mathematician like d'Alembert. Condorcet here simply wishes to state his personal view on the future of human knowledge and civilization, to the extent that it can be inferred from a consideration of the past.

The object of the work is therefore both limited and wide. It is a history of the progress achieved by man in his conquest of science, a progress both in the knowledge of truth and in the application of practical means of relieving man's needs. Progress itself is a fact. There was progress from the first notions about numeration to the invention of integral calculus, from hourglasses to modern chronometers, from the vague maxims of the early Greeks concerning the mind, ethics, and legislation to the deep analyses of Locke and Adam Smith. The object of the book is to describe the way followed by the human mind in achieving such progress.

By and large, Condorcet starts from the notion of man developed by Condillac: that of a being endowed by nature with the power to undergo sensations, to compose them, to compare them, and finally to attach to notions signs whereby their communication is made possible and their combination facilitated. "If one contents oneself with observing and knowing the general facts as well as the constant laws presented by the development of these faculties in that which individual men have in common, such a science bears the name of *metaphysics*." The same development, if considered in various individuals living together in the same country, or in different countries and at different times, becomes a history of progress. If it is followed from generation to generation, such history is a picture of the progress of the human mind.

The general conclusion Condorcet aims to establish is that "nature has set no limits to the perfecting of human faculties; that the perfectibility of man really is indefinite; that the progress of that perfectibility, henceforward independent of all power that might pretend to stop it, has no other term than the duration of the globe on which we were thrown by nature." Condorcet does not consider human progress automatic; its speed is not regular; progress can be more or less rapid; the point is that the march of the human mind never is retrogressive. The doctrine of Condorcet can be called a gospel of progress, and in this it admirably expresses the implicit confidence placed in the happy future of mankind by the representatives of the philosophy of lights. To them, men are socially united for the common pursuit of happiness, and not only this, but it is a sure thing that they will ultimately reach it.

As could be expected, Condorcet does no more than imagine what the early beginnings of progress must have been. Ethnography was hardly born and human paleontology did not exist at all when Condorcet's *Tableau* was written; the method he follows is that of *likelihood*: Since all that mankind now knows must once have been invented, we are invited to witness a succession of strokes of good luck which all result in felicitous inventions. As an example of the method, here is how Condorcet accounts for the invention of alphabetic writing (italics ours):

Men of genius, eternal benefactors of humanity whose names and even countries are forever sunk in oblivion, *observed that* all the words of a language were but so many combinations of a very limited quantity of primary articulations, *and that* the number of these, very limited as it is, sufficed to form an almost infinite number of diverse combinations. *They imagined* to designate, by means of visible signs, not the ideas or their corresponding words, but those simple elements of which words are composed. *From that time,* alphabetic writing was invented . . .

Of course there was a drawback to that marvelous invention of writing; at first, it served "to prolong ignorance." A new written language should now be invented, exclusively reserved for the use of sciences, consisting of simple and perfectly defined notions in view of strictly calculated operations of understanding. Such a language would be common to the whole of mankind and greatly promote the propagation of knowledge as well as the improvement of scientific methods.

With the invention of writing, the picture of the progress of the human mind can become really historical. Written records tell the story of how the more enlightened countries of Europe have reached their present state of civilization. In this part of the work, "there is nothing left for philosophy to guess"; on the contrary, the concluding part of the picture must be entirely scientific and philosophical. Its object would be to establish "a science enabling one to foresee the progress of the human kind, to direct it, to accelerate it." It is noteworthy that Condorcet clearly anticipates the modern ambition to build up a physics of social facts whereby it would become possible to engineer the political conduct of the nations and their social as well as their economic legislation.[2] Only, his own objective is more limited; Condorcet merely desires to facilitate the birth of a general science of the progress of humanity and to base a technique of their future on a history of their past.

In his "hypothetical history of one single people," Condorcet finds himself at grips with a regrettable fact: prejudice. Even in a world thus devoted to final light, there is darkness. Progress can be achieved only through countless incidents and accidents, some of which actually constitute momentary and local regressions. These are temporary obstacles unable to stop the over-all forward march of mankind. Condorcet sees very well that, in a sense, the discovery of every new truth is, by the same token, the origin of a new prejudice. Error, as much as truth, is part and parcel of the history of the human mind. The fact that errors oppose everywhere and at all times the progress of truth originates in the general laws of the development of our faculties. At each period of progress, new prejudices arise from the simple fact that recently acquired cognitions outlive the time during which they are true: "Men still preserve the prejudices of their infancy, of their country and of their century, a long time after recognizing all the truths necessary to destroy them." Moreover, in all countries and at all times there are prejudices proper to each class of citizen, to each profession as well as to the various levels of instruction. This can be seen at work in universal history: The prejudices of the philosophers slow down the discovery of new truths; those of the ignorant part of the population slow down the propagation of the already acquired truths; those of certain influential and powerful professions put stumbling blocks in the way of economic progress. Condorcet sees the history of mankind as a permanent battle between good and evil, i.e., reason and prejudice[3] under the threefold form of those enemies which reason is obliged ceaselessly to fight. Divided into nine periods, or epochs, Condorcet's philosophy of history deals therefore at length with "the rise, triumph and fall of the prejudices." On the whole, errors are doomed to be defeated, because they are both self-defeating and mutually opposed, whereas truth is sure to carry a lasting and universal victory, nature having indissolubly united the progress of the lights to those of liberty, virtue, and the respect for the natural rights of man.

The "Tenth Epoch" constitutes the most original part of the work. It rests upon the hypothesis that, since the future state of the physical world is predictable from our knowledge of its laws, the future destinies of mankind should be likewise predictable from the knowledge of its past. Condorcet simply neglects to prove that our *historical* knowledge of the human past consists of general laws in any sense comparable with our *scientific* knowledge of the physical present. Still, we shall concede him what he demands, lest his picture of the future progress of human societies be rendered impossible.

Condorcet's hopes for the coming condition of mankind can be reduced to three main points: 1] the destruction of inequality between nations; 2] the progress of equality within each particular people; 3] the real improvement of man. On these three points, our philosopher naturally reasons as a European and as a Frenchman. To

establish equality between nations means to him to raise them all to
the then present level of the French and of the Anglo-Americans. This
is the only concrete foundation for his hopes, but it was a real one.
From his place of hiding, Condorcet was already witnessing the political independence of the New World as an accomplished fact; an immense increase in its population would insure the triumph of civilization over all its territories, since this was bound "either to civilize,
or else to wipe out, even without conquest, the savage populations that
still cover large sections of its territories." As to Asia and Africa,
speaking in a mood of resolute anti-colonialism, Condorcet foresees
the moment when, instead of finding in Europeans tyrants and ex-
ploiters, their peoples will find in them true brothers ready to help
them to achieve progress in independence. Condorcet sees all this as
"infallibly" following from the liberty already achieved by the French
Republic and by that of North America.

Generally speaking, inequalities arise from the discrepancy between
the rights which law grants to citizens and those they actually enjoy.
In other words, there is a wide distance between the equality decreed
by the political institutions and that which actually exists between
individuals. Individual differences arise from three main causes: inequality in wealth; inequality of conditions between those who inherit
a fortune and those whose survival depends uniquely on the part of
their life during which they are fit to work; lastly, the inequality in
instruction. These three sources of inequality have natural causes, so
they cannot be expected to disappear; one cannot hope "to wipe them
out without opening still more fecund sources of inequalities, without
putting the rights of men still more dangerously in jeopardy," but
intelligent social laws can insure old-age pensions, generalize credit,
and put instruction at the disposal of all citizens.

Just as prejudices accumulate, progressive movements confirm one
another and multiply with a geometrical progression. The advantages
resulting for men will have no other limits than those of the perfectibility of the human mind. For science is the perfection of the mind,
and in a universe where equality of instruction will reign in countries
themselves equal, no limits can be set to the development of scientific
knowledge.[4] This is particularly true of the sciences of man, on which
will ultimately depend the "social art" whereby societies will safely
be directed to their ends. Even the moral goodness of man can be
"indefinitely improved," since nature binds together, as by an un-

breakable chain, "truth, virtue and happiness." The destruction of prejudices will naturally go hand in hand with intellectual and social progress.

While thus depicting the better society of the future, Condorcet feels his heart full of such a joy that he finds in it

> . . . the reward of his efforts towards the progress of reason and the defence of liberty. . . . That contemplation is for him a sanctuary wherein the memory of his persecutors cannot follow him; there, living in thought with man reestablished in his rights as well as in the dignity of his nature, he forgets those whom avidity, fear and envy torment and corrupt: there does he truly abide with his own likes, in an Elysium which his reason has known how to create for itself, and which his love for humanity embellishes with the purest joys.

This was the swan song of the philosophy of lights; its mixture of generous truth and of unconscious prejudice is disconcerting; yet it is the more moving as the swan was waiting for the butcher's knife and knew it.

9 ❧ GERMANY, FROM *AUFKLÄRUNG* TO CRITICISM

GERMAN WRITERS characteristically speak of the eighteenth century as a time of awakening national consciousness in the lands north of the Rhine. It is perfectly true that there is a chasm between the period with which we are now concerned and that German Renaissance which had seen Dürer a figure of European scope, Luther remaking the German language, Melanchthon giving a new turn to its religious thought, the Fuggers reigning from Augsburg over an immense commercial empire; the two eras are separated by a century of misfortune, disaggregation, and bloodletting. Something approaching a miniature dark ages descended on Germany. Take just the example afforded by the history of architecture. The first quarter of the sixteenth century saw a brief flourish of German Renaissance structures, like the Michaelskirche in Munich and the Augsburg Rathaus. Then nothing, nearly absolutely nothing until the beginnings of German baroque, which does not appear until almost the end of the seventeenth century.

By the middle of the eighteenth century, Germany is bursting into a second spring. German music, from Schütz, Lübeck, and Buxtehude, has begotten not only the greatest German musician but perhaps the greatest musician of all times, J. S. Bach, who died in 1750. By the middle of the century the new German baroque has welled up in a plethora of palaces, chapels, and great pilgrimage churches, with a vitality and a personality that far transcended mere imitation of Bernini and begot a German rococo which for fantasy and lightsome joy can hardly be equaled; the names of the great architects of the first half of the century—Fischer von Erlach, the Brothers Asam, Johann Michel Fisher, Balthasar Neumann, the Brothers Zimmermann—deserve an honorable place in the history of art. In the difficult world of politics, a Friedrich Wilhelm, though called by his enemies the Sergeant-King because of his defense policies and laughed at for his pfennig-pinching, laid the foundations for a strong Prussia, establishing a model state, tightly run and stable, and succeeded in begetting and educating the most extraordinary political specimen of the *Aufklärung*, Frederick the Great.

In philosophy, this latter-day German Renaissance dramatically opened in the person of the great Leibniz. The middle of the eighteenth century is not, however, dominated by Leibnizian philosophy but by the *Aufklärung*; that is, by an effort to clear away old orthodoxies with the light of reason; this is still in large part an imported commodity, made available on the German market by Voltaire, Diderot and company from France, and by Locke, Newton, and associates from England. Leibniz' influence itself was felt in a "cleared-up" version, suitably sieved through Reason and somewhat diluted to fit the tastes of the time, thanks to the efforts of Universitäts Professor Wolff. But in the second half of the century, the intellectual scene becomes very vital and very original indeed. Like their French and English counterparts, the German thinkers of the "Enlightenment" distrusted what they considered sterile metaphysical speculation; instead they turned their minds loose on areas of human experience that had not been explored by the rationalist philosophers. Hand in hand with this effort to open new horizons of thought arose a desire to be independent of French literature and to find true expression for the German spirit. Soon German thought is operating quite independently of the French and becomes rapidly by far the more vital and original. Aesthetic theory, philosophy of history, and literary criticism are the strong points. We shall see these things at work in the thought of two of the most influential of the German thinkers in the last half of the century, Lessing and Herder.

Immanuel Kant is a product of these times too; but he is also, like

Goethe and Hegel, one of the truly world-historical creative figures that one does not like to treat as just a product of their time. With such as these it is more comprehensible to consider rather the times that ensue as *their* product! It is true, Kant is understandable only when we realize that the metaphysics he is criticizing is Wolffian, that the physics he describes is Newtonian, and that his theories of the beautiful and the sublime need to be projected against the background of what his contemporaries were writing. This is not sufficient, however, to explain why he succeeded in creating a vantage point from which much of the nineteenth and twentieth centuries will seek to view the world. We shall save Kant for last and seek then to bring out what is new in that critical transcendental idealist point of view; for here is the portal through which we must approach the great philosophers of the beginning of the next century.

XXVI

Gotthold Ephraim Lessing

A HISTORY OF GERMAN LITERATURE would have to devote an important space to Gotthold Ephraim Lessing.[1] More brilliantly than any other person before the arrival on the scene of the two giants, Schiller and Goethe, he battled for the ideal of a truly German literature, for a theater that would break free of the arbitrary shackles imposed by the imitation of the French classics, and for a view of aesthetics based on the realities of our perception rather than on artificial rationalist norms. Lessing's efforts to help found a German theater may not have been successful, yet his best plays stirred the imaginations of young writers by suggesting the possibilities of a native drama. But his dynamic personality, much more than anything he did or any one philosophical position he may have held, is what generated the feeling that a new quest for national expression was under way and that the new generation possessed different and more sensitive methods of inquiry than its predecessors. His works throb with the passion and excitement that begot what the Germans dramatically call their *Sturm und Drang*. To study Lessing just for his theoretical positions, as we shall have to limit ourselves to doing in this history of philosophy, is to miss his essential personality. This great creator of style, this personal and passionate writer, cannot be reduced to the restricted role of being a philosophical "influence."

Lessing's Aesthetic Theory

USING AS AN EXAMPLE the renowned *Laokoön*—a Hellenistic sculpture group unearthed in 1506 and since then in the Vatican collection, showing the Trojan priest Laokoön and his two sons ensnarled in the coils of great snakes sent by Athena or Apollo to punish the priest for helping Troy—Lessing unfolds a masterful description of the essential differences between the ways poetry and *malerei,* in this instance meaning all the plastic arts, handle the same subject. The tendency among the rationalists of the seventeenth century had been to treat all arts as basically the same and to consider them in function of their pictorial clarity in communicating an idea. But *beauty,* Lessing will now assert, is the end of art, and it is realized in each art quite differently.

Lessing chooses Laokoön as his example, because this statue had been the core of a controversy among art historians who argued its relationship in time with Vergil's *Aeneid;* which of the two works had inspired which? A minute comparison enables Lessing to reach the conclusion we would expect: if one did influence the other, it must have been the poet and not the sculptor, for poetry permits complex possibilities which are forbidden plastic artists by the very essence of their art. Why? Because poetry exists in time, of its very nature: its materials, words, cannot co-exist in the instant; the plastic arts, by contrast, exist in space alone. The implications of this obvious but far too often forgotten fact are many and highly important: the poet is allowed a wider and more intense range of emotions; the old classical tenet that Greek artists never depict exasperated states of emotion because they reveal unheroic lack of dignity is simply erroneous—true of Greek statuary, it is absolutely false of Homer, the poet of poets. Why, then, this discrepancy? Simply because of the essential difference between the two arts. The poet can permit Laokoön to scream in agony, as Vergil has done, because ugliness is not forbidden matter to the poet: he does not place in front of us an actual representation of the ugly instant, which thus has no chance to act directly on our senses and cause feelings of repugnance which would destroy the "beauty" of the artifact; moreover, the very suggestion he makes of the scream does not endure and cannot built up in us emotionally to the point of becoming unbearable. Finally, every art object must give free rein to the imagination, so important in building up the aesthetic emotion. Imagination is poetry's realm; no problem there; but the sculptor must provide for it.

> When Laokoön thus sighs, the imagination can hear him scream; but when he screams, then this representation cannot proceed either a step higher or a step deeper without leading the imagination into a vehement and therefore uninteresting condition.

So the plastic artist should seek to represent the instant immediately preceding or following the emotional climax.[2]

From these remarks, Lessing draws up an aesthetics which will inspire a whole generation of poets. He first reminds them of the aim and scope of their own form of art:

> Objects that exist side by side, or whose parts exist side by side, are called bodies. Hence bodies with their visible properties are the proper objects of painting. Objects that exist one after the other, or whose parts follow in succession, are called actions (*Handlungen*). Hence actions are the proper object of poetry.[3]

Of course, since bodies exist not only in space but also in time, the sculptor or painter is also confronted with the problem of seizing an action. To handle this in terms of a body in space, he must choose to represent the one moment that will permit the viewer best to conclude to what preceded and what will follow (Lessing speaks of this as the *fruchtbarer Augenblick*, the fruitful instant). Reciprocally, the poet is confronted with the converse problem. Actions cannot exist except in bodies; but unfortunately the most exact verbal description of a body cannot bring its concrete reality any nearer the reader. Haller can describe a particular Alpen flower in his poem "Die Alpen," until pedantry gets almost ridiculous; still, if the reader has never seen an "Enzian," this will not make him visualize it; but if the reader does know the flower, then what is the use of all this:

> Der Blumen helles Gold, in Strahlen ungeborgen,
> Türmt sich am Stengel auf und krönt sein grau Gewand,
> Der Blätter glattes Weiss, mit tiefem Grün durchzogen,
> Strahlt von dem bunten Blitz von feuchtem Diamant, etc., etc.

> The light gold of the flowers, basking in the sunrays
> Rise aloft on their stems, crowning their gray garment
> The glossy white of their leaves, interlaced with deep green
> Flashes with the multicolored lightning of fiery diamant, etc.

Haller strings qualities one after another; but this catalogue makes neither for action nor for real extension. The ear cannot replace the eye. When the poet violates that principle and lets action languish, his public languishes too.

How, then, should the poet deal with bodies? Homer can give us the answer. He will outline an object with rarely more than one or

two descriptive terms (*Epitheta*) which present concisely the impression this person would make on another man. Thus, even in descriptions he remembers that the realm of the poet is action; i.e., "a series
of movements directed to a single end." [4] The poetic gift consists in
taking static, bodily beauty and setting it into motion, thus producing
that transitory beauty we call "charm" (*Reiz*), which appeals, not to
sense directly, but to that higher faculty already mentioned above:
the imagination.

The effect of all this on the painters and sculptors was apparently
minimal. But its effect on the German poets was tremendous. In the
Eighth Book of *Dichtung und Wahrheit*, Goethe describes the effect
of *Laokoön*:

> One would have to be a youngster to realize what an effect
> Lessing's *Laokoön* had on us, in that this work helped us break
> out of the region of servile observation to the open spaces of
> thought. The so-long misunderstood "ut pictura poesis" was at
> once set aside, the distinction between pictorial and poetic art
> made clear, the summits of both now appearing separate, how-
> ever near their bases may be. The pictorial artist shall stay
> within the bounds of the beautiful, while the discursive art,
> which cannot forego any kind of significance, is permitted to
> ramble beyond those limits. The one works for the exterior sense
> that can only be pleased by the Beautiful; the other, for the
> imagination which can be satisfied with the ugly. All the conse-
> quences of this wonderful thought were illumined for us in a
> flash, and all previous directing and judging critique was thrown
> away like an old coat.

To understand why Lessing's effect was so great, we must realize
what an innovation—what a desperately needed innovation—he was.
Goethe makes it clear that the poets were already *feeling* a truth like
that to which Lessing now gave clear and forceful expression. They
were ready to revolt against the aesthetic conceptions of the era of
the great systems, whose logic disparaged the "confused" cognitions
of sensation, and whose ideal of scientific clarity had inspired the
moral analyses of Corneille and Racine, that French dramatic tradition which Lessing, calling Shakespeare, Diderot, and Aristotle re-
discovered to the rescue, had so violently attacked in order to free
the German theater forever from its desiccating and artificial influence. The "misunderstood" dictum, *ut pictura poesis*, which had been

taken to mean that poetry should seek to achieve the pictorial clarity of a classical painting, had actually already been formally and intelligently attacked before Lessing, by, of all people, Wolff's greatest disciple, Baumgarten.[5] This philosopher, in a rather scientific, text-bookish sort of way, had argued that aesthetic experience had a logic of its own, that its goal is beauty, not scientific, rational clarity. "The goal of aesthetics is the perfection of sensory cognition as such. And this is beauty," [6] and "the perfect language of sense is poetry." [7] Most of Lessing's basic insights are there, and even as great a critic as Herder has spoken of the "subtle simplicity" and "charming little points that escape ordinary eyes" which "grace" Baumgarten's *Aesthetica*, a great favorite of his.[8] But the philosopher did not have Lessing's personal breadth, that combination E. Cassirer observes in him, of "the elements of richness, magnitude, truth, clarity, assurance, abundance and nobility which Baumgarten demanded of the genuine aesthetician." [9] Lessing could take in hand the aesthetic ideas of his contemporaries and give them expression in those concrete terms we have just been witnessing in the *Laokoön*, opening new horizons to the efforts of men like Schiller and Goethe.

Religious-Philosophical Views

FROM HIS FIRST EFFORTS at independent thought, Lessing showed little instinctive sympathy for orthodox Lutheranism. Already in 1750 he wrote against North German orthodoxy a defense of the Sect of the *Herrnhuter* from the standpoint of current Deism. When he was at Wolfenbüttel, he found an opportunity to deal a colossal blow (judging from the frenzy of the reaction) by issuing the papers of the recently dead professor of Oriental languages, Hermann Samuel Reimarus. This most-illumined product of the *Aufklärung* attacked all "revealed" religion in general and the Old and New Testaments in particular (a pack of lies, a deliberate trick of the Apostles, the Old Testament was not written with the intention of revealing a religion, etc., etc.). When a flood of literature was stirred up by the light emanating from the Herzog's Bibliothek in Wolfenbüttel (more than thirty opposing pieces were thrown into the breach opened by the Reimarus papers in little over two years), Lessing decided he had better help lead the discussion back to a more inquiring and scientific plane. In the *Gegensätze*, then, it is Lessing and not Reimarus speaking. The tone is much milder, but not much more orthodox. Christianity, viewed historically, was a necessary step in the evolution of mankind. Lessing emphasizes its ethical worth, although he is not agreed that these ethics need be presented as a revelation. As to the contradictions in the gospels which Reimarus took to betray priestly deception, Lessing attributes these to accidents in the transmission of the text and to difficulties inherent in the way they came into existence in the first place. In one of these polemical pieces, called *Eine Duplik*, Lessing expressed in a way that has never been forgotten that feeling, so characteristic not only of his effervescent spirit but of that of contemporary Germany, that the excitement of the quest for truth is perhaps greater than the possession of the truth itself. "If God held tight in his right hand all truth and in his left the impulse to truth, although with the consequence of my having always and forever to wander, and He said to me, 'Choose!' I would touch his left hand with humility and say, 'Father, give! For the pure truth is indeed for thee alone!' " But it must be remembered that such a passage is not meant as a presentation of the excitement of the quest, but as an effective appeal for the tolerance with which those attacking orthodoxy were anxious to be met.

It is at the very end of his career that Lessing's two most important works on the subject of religion were completed. The one is the important poetic drama, *Nathan the Wise*; the other is the treatise, *The Education of Humanity*. Set during the Third Crusade, *Nathan the Wise* presents in the person of the hero the contrast between this Jew's great personal wisdom and the narrow world-view of the Christians, both Eastern and Western, and Mohammedans with whom he must contend; though they are not all bad sorts, all of these people become menaces because they insist that each possesses *the* one, sole, solitary vision of THE TRUTH. Nathan's wisdom springs not from books but from knowledge of himself and of all men; he is wise because he will not allow prejudices, religious or national, to block his recognition of real human worth in whomever it manifests itself. *Ich weiss, wie gute Menschen denken, weiss, Dass alle Länder gute Menschen tragen* (I know how good men think, know that all lands bear good men).

The message of *Nathan* is developed philosophically in *Die Erzie-*

hung des Menschengeschlechts. In this work Lessing distinguished three stages in the realization of humanity. In its childhood (corresponding to the Jewish, Old Testament age), man is brought to moral action less through the presentation of serious arguments than through the promise of punishments and rewards of a kind that appeal directly to the senses. Christianity represents a second, higher stage, *das Knabenzeitalter,* the youthful age, when men are moved toward higher ends which they expect to achieve in the world beyond; they no longer expect fire to rain down on their heads or to be turned into pillars of salt; but they do expect to enjoy the reward of a heavenly life after death. Lessing now announces the dawn of a new era, *das Zeitalter der Aufklärung* we might as well name it, and it is, of course, the age of the mature man. The self-centeredness (*Eigennützigkeit*) of the preceding eras is at last uprooted from the human heart, good is no longer done with a view to avoiding punishment or obtaining a reward; rather, when this time is fulfilled, "then Good will be done because it is Good."

Only that can be educed from man which is really in him; in this regard, the superimposition of a "Revelation" would be of no avail as a supplement to reason; but it can play, and did play, an important role within the perfectly rational enterprise of bringing up mankind: it accelerated and lightened the process. "Revelation offered nothing to mankind that the human reason, left to itself, could not have gotten to; but it gave, and gives, the most important of these things earlier." Because of their educational role, the various revelations each take a form proper to the development of the people they are intended for. With the dawn of the "new eternal testament," the language of reason must from now on be the form of our revelation, which is to say that we need no more revelation, no more Jewish folk tales nor New Testament parables. Our great task is now to find the reasonable counterpart of the revelations of the great past religions. "Where before man's reason was led by revelation, now revelation must once and for all be illumined by reason." The future task of philosophy, then, is to inquire into the ideas of religion in order to discover their historical significance, and thus put them at the service of the knowledge of man.

The idea that philosophy should somehow be an inquiry into the sense of history was to achieve its greatest development in the *Phe-*

nomenology of the Spirit of Hegel. Between Lessing and Hegel, however, there came another thinker who contributed to spreading this concept. This was Kant's contemporary and student, the professor and later in turn student of Goethe, Johann Gottfried Herder.

XXVII

Johann Gottfried Herder

A LESS MONUMENTAL FIGURE than Lessing but nonetheless original, versatile and influential, Johann Gottfried Herder,[1] variously teacher, theologian, writer, stands at the intersection of influences: himself a student of the younger Kant (though Rousseau was his greatest hero), he in turn, while still in his twenties, comes to exercise the greatest influence on a young Frankfurt poet, Wolfgang Goethe.

Aesthetic Theory

THE INFLUENCES molding Herder's aesthetic theory were very similar to those operative on Lessing's thought: Winckelmann had served to awaken a feeling for the importance of classical sculpture; and his extreme stand—to wit, that only the classical forms invented by the ancients are worthy of the artist's efforts—was bound to provoke a growing sensitivity to the historical range of differences in European art; Baumgarten's emphasis on the importance of studying the senses in their own right and for their own "logic," coupled with Diderot's remarkable discrimination of the senses of touch and sight, suggested the need for basing important aesthetic distinctions on distinctions in sense powers; finally, there was, of course, Lessing's contribution. Where the *Laokoön* leaves off, Herder takes over.

Lessing had successfully opposed his famous distinction between poetry and the plastic arts against the seventeenth-century tendency to consider all art as one; moreover, he had effectively combated the rationalist idea that the success of any art is to be measured by its ability to communicate ideas clearly. Herder accepts as a given Lessing's insistence that *beauty* is the concern of art, and that, as Baumgarten

had shown, beauty is an affair of the senses, the rules of which are not
the same in the time-centered unfolding of poetry as they are in the
space-centered creation of the *malerei*. Herder will now introduce two
further distinctions: the one based on the different senses to which the
plastic arts appeal; the other, on the variation of conceptions of beauty
in different ages.

It may seem incredible to the contemporary reader that either of
these "discoveries" should ever have had to be made. But anyone who
has seen to what an extent modern thought was born under the star of
mathematics-inspired rationalist idealism will appreciate that the various efforts to wrench the European mind away from the hold of that
exciting ideal of achieving absolute rational unity, clarity, and necessity
were so many triumphs, even though they must have looked and look
at times, not only to the eighteenth-century exponents of rationalist
idealism, but even to us today, as victories of darkness over light. For
if wider, richer, and more adequate horizons were opened, it was at
a price. The exponents of religious orthodoxy had embraced rationalist
idealism as the modern vehicle for religious thought. Malebranche and
Bossuet had made that identification very strongly for Catholicism;
Berkeley was considered a spokesman for what was most conservative
in English religious thought; Leibniz and Wolff were clasped to the
breast of many a right-wing Lutheran divine in Germany. Spinoza was
alone among the great idealists to help weaken the feeling that Cartesianism was sent by God to replace Thomism. But suddenly consider
the anti-idealists: John Locke, as far as religion is concerned, is not
too bad; but Thomas Hobbes! but David Hume! but Voltaire, Diderot,
d'Alembert! All of these are leading the fight to wrest from idealism
the banner of philosophical initiative. The battle against rationalist
idealism and toward a broader and richer interest in all aspects of the
historical human phenomenon is tending, then, to become a struggle
with a modern scholasticism, and therefore feels obliged to take on
the onus of battling all of Christendom itself.

This is the perspective in which the accomplishment of someone
like Lessing, more effective than Diderot's but in the same spirit, stands
out clearly as revolutionary. But with Herder, with the young Goethe
and Schiller, and, I think we can say, with the Kant of the great
Critiques, still another era in the struggle is upon us. The general commanding the new division that now enters the field is none other than
Jean-Jacques Rousseau. We do not wish to exaggerate his importance;

to say that Herder or Kant or Goethe is a Rousseauvian would be to overstate the case grotesquely. But Rousseau did introduce a new dimension without which any of the aforementioned would be unthinkable: the feeling that there are deeper levels to the human spirit's struggle to assert itself than the by now rather tired opposition *rationalist idealism* vs. *an anti-religious empiricism*. In plunging headlong into the exploration of *the history of a soul* (*Emile*), in giving great weight to the study of *sentiments* (*La nouvelle Héloïse*), in suggesting the importance of a development in mankind (*Du contrat social*), Rousseau invented nothing that had not already been suggested by others. But he stamped each of these things with the unforgettable passion of his personality, and, thing most wonderful to behold, he presented the whole as an enterprise in the service of religion, not against it. A funny sort of religion, to be sure, to a modern Catholic's taste; but that in the depths of the soul are to be found the remains of man's original goodness pointing to some sort of ultimate, non-rational union with the divine principle, such a romantic feeling was just what the late eighteenth century was looking for after the sterile battles of *philosophes* versus rationalist-metaphysical defenders of orthodoxies.[2]

It is in this context that Herder's discoveries must be appreciated. His classification of the plastic arts according to the senses is a continuation of the work of Diderot's generation; it puts the finishing touches on Lessing's *Laokoön*. But his historical studies, first in aesthetics, then more generally working toward a philosophy of history, are true post-Rousseauvian phenomena. Let us consider each briefly in turn.

"Aesthetics should be a natural history of the beautiful." Since the beautiful is perceived by the senses, the study of the beautiful should begin by properly discriminating between the various senses. It is in the spirit of Diderot's principle, stated in the *Letters on the Deaf and Dumb*, that Herder proceeds: "My idea would be, so to speak, to decompose a man and to consider what he acquires from each of his senses."[3] The sense of sight has so monopolized the attention of man, and the sense of hearing is so different, we could almost say hostile to it, that men's attention has not turned sufficiently to the subtle distinctions that really count in discriminating between the plastic arts, failing even to note the capital distinction between touch and sight. The studies of those philosophers, among them Diderot, who confronted the "problem of Molyneux"[4] contributed to showing that each of the senses has its own "world," as the contemporary phenomenologist would say. Herder does not hesitate to assign the exact limit to the object of each of these senses; touch and sight are to one another what a body is to its surface or what form is to figure. "All that is the beauty of a form, of a body, is not at all a visible idea but a tangible one; it is in the sense of touch that one must originally look for each of its beauties. The eye is neither the source nor the judge of them." [5] The art that corresponds to vision is painting, which plays on the surface of things with its essential material, color; but sculpture is the art of the sense of touch, giving as it does mass to things. [6] The art that belongs to the sense of hearing—namely, music—is so different from the two others that there has never been any problem distinguishing it from the others. But there has been a continuous struggle going on between sculpture and painting. After the great flowering of painting in the sixteenth century, there was a tendency to approach sculpture in a painterly way, while just before Herder's time the enthusiasm of Wincklemann and Raphaël Mengs for the sculpture of antiquity became an invitation for painting to be dominated by sculptural conceptions. Herder would put an end to such confusion once and for all. There is hardly a rule valid for one of those arts, he declares in his essay *Plastik*, that will apply without serious modification to another. Elsewhere again:

> In painting art consists principally in spreading life out on a surface, and the ideal here has to do with arranging many figures, which, thanks to their positions and to the distribution of light and color, compose on that surface a magic and living world, as fantastic as it may be. . . . Nothing could be more different than the fundamental law of sculpture. The most numerous group of statues could never form a whole the way a painted group of figures can. Each figure on its base encloses the center and sensible origin of its beauty and the effect it produces; it must then, according to the very rule of art, be treated as something isolated. [7]

Sculpture is truth; painting is dream. [8] We should be able to feel the statue live; we should be seized by the statue as though by the living presence of a friend; but the painting is like a romantic novel, "it is the dream of a dream," it can present what the statue cannot—shade, the dawn, lightning, the water flowing in a brook. Herder speaks out strongly for painting as representative of the whole spectacle of nature, and in the process turns attention to the landscape, which both Winckle-

mann and Lessing had either ignored or viewed with hostility as insufficiently *ideal*. "Painting is a magic table as great as the world and
history, on which each figure without question cannot and must not
be a statue." [9] The ideal of a Poussin in the seventeenth century and
a Louis David in the eighteenth century is definitively rejected! [10]

The other important contribution of Herder to aesthetic theory
grows out of his major contribution to the century, his feeling for
history. Applied to art, Herder's historic sensibility made him bristle
against the narrow classic ideal being advanced by the Wincklemanns
and the Mengs. There cannot be one set of forms ideal for all mankind
in all times.

> Human nature, insofar as it is sensible, is not in all climates every-
> where absolutely the same; the chords of sentiment form another
> tissue, there is another world of objects and sounds which set cer-
> tain chords into vibration more than others. Nations, centuries,
> individuals do not attain the same degree of aesthetic culture, and
> that puts the seal on the differences in their tastes.[11]

The beauties of Greek sculpture are certainly exemplary; they form
"a light on a stormy sea," but being guided by them in a way that
permits us to remain faithful to our own time and people as well as
to each artist's own individual genius is one thing, being enslaved by
such an ideal is quite another.[12]

Herder, Philosopher of History

IT WOULD NOT BE AN EXAGGERATION to say that Herder's central intuition was just this feeling for historical diversity. He underscored and
developed its significance, not only for art, but for almost every realm
of the spirit—for poetry, for taste in general, even for religions, which
he treated as expressions of a people's ideological development at given
stages of their historical situation. In his celebrated *On the Spirit of
Hebraic Poetry*, Herder's attitude finds its most characteristic expression when he treats the *Book of Genesis* as a wonderfully simple and
majestic old poetry—the oldest poetry extant—but just poetry nonetheless.

The master work in which Herder synthesizes the various elements
of his thought—a feeling for the living God's providential rule over

human destiny, Lessing's dream of educating mankind, Shaftesbury's conception that it is in aesthetic expressions that the deepest currents of man's reality are to be found, the Spinozistic notion that God is the unity of the world, and the Leibnizian conception of the unity of history and nature—is his *Ideas for a Philosophy of the History of Mankind.* Everything else seems to have its philosophy and its science except that which is nearest to us: the history of mankind. Can God, who has ordered everything in nature with such wisdom and set the course of the stars, of the development of things, of the growth even of our own bodies, can this wonderful, all-wise God have failed to establish a *plan* for the development of mankind? Do we constitute a herd without a shepherd? Wherein lies our happiness? Is it the same for all men? How are we to follow the threads of its sense through all the ages, all the climates, all the nations that divide mankind? "Are you to carry on like fishes in the sea and worms in the earth, without a Lord?—Or need you not rather to know the Plan?" [13]

Herder delights in elaborating a view of the physical world as an ensemble of forces struggling upward toward higher and better things. The plants and animals, even the human bodies we experience, are as the outward instruments, the *organs*, fashioned for their use by these forces. The human soul is the highest, the most successful accomplishment of nature, and the conviction we enjoy of being immortal is simply the expression of the fact that all the forces in reality, as aspects of the creative power of God, have a sense, a destiny, a kind of eternity.

Within our own experience we can discover both the primordial force and evidence that we are but the highest manifestation of a reality that reaches all the way down into the earth: the force we feel in our desire to stand alone, to achieve our own self-construction independently of any outward assistance, to stand free and creative above all things. "Man is thus an artful machine, possessed of genetic dispositions and full of life . . . but . . ." But we forget the long years of infantile tutoring, of having to learn what we are to do and how to do it; man takes possession of himself only through a painful repetition of all that history has learned; hence the rest of the sentence, ". . . the machine does not play itself, and even the readiest man has to learn how to play it. The Reason is an aggregate of observations and repetitions (in the sense of practising) on the part of our soul; the sum of the education of our kind. . . ." [14] It is only through education that each person becomes a man. Mankind is nothing but the collectivity of individuals that makes this education possible.

This note of radical individualism Herder maintains as a good Leibnizian throughout his treatise. Speaking of the end of mankind, he points out that that end must lie in the individual, for the *Gattung*—the species—is only an abstraction. God loves each of his creatures and feels toward it like a father, as though each were the only thing in the world. All his means are ends, and his ends are made into means for greater ends in which the Infinite-All-Fulfilling reveals Himself.

> Thus what each man is and can be is the end of mankind; and what is that? Humanity and blissfulness to this particular degree, in this particular place, and particular to this and no other member in the great chain which runs through the whole of our kind. *Wo and wer du geboren bist, o Mensch, da bist du, der du sein solltest, verlass die Kette nicht, noch setze dich über sich hinaus, sondern schlinge dich an sie.* Only in your connections, in what you receive and give but in both cases factually are, only there dwells for you life and joy.[15]

The chain to which we must hold fast is called Tradition, *die fortpflanzenden Mutter*, which consists of one's language, one's culture, and even one's religion and holy practices. The religion and the language are closely bound up with one another as systems of signs and symbols to store the fruit of the past for reason. Herder gives great emphasis to the ordered way in which these possibilities are accumulated and passed on, evidently wishing to support the notion that history is an intelligible story of an unfolding education of humanity, the laws of which we can discover; in fact, the sense of which he himself has already discovered. Is the forward movement of this historical process always a progress? Individuals and whole peoples can become static, perhaps even regress; but because the whole of history is, after all, the foremost manifestation of the divine creative impulse, it is evident that the ultimate sum result must be toward higher ends.[16] Just as some individuals sin against the spirit and thus do not participate adequately in the movement toward progress, so too are other individuals the prime motive forces in great civilizations' finest realizations. There is no contradiction between Herder's call for one to accept his position in the chain of tradition and his admiration for the great creators; just as Nietzsche would later acknowledge, the really original creators are successful because they create from out of the deep sense of their time.

In the *Ideen*, Herder traces the development that has led to the greatness of Europe and explores the causes for the rise and fall of other civilizations. His genius for forging elements drawn from religions, literatures, economics, political history, etc., into a single, plausible explanation of the historical destiny of a folk is amazing—and a good preparation for the phenomenon of Hegel, who is about to appear on the scene.

The way Herder involves God in the very movement of history, the way he makes him the very substance of its movement, so to speak, shows his sympathy for Spinoza's central intuition. To Jacobi, who had a horror of Spinoza, Herder once wrote that if he reduced the deepest, highest, and all-comprehensive concept to a mere name, he, and not Spinoza, was the real atheist. Herder, we have seen, shared with Kant, Hamann, and Goethe a hatred for empty abstract distinctions, but he goes exceptionally far in wanting to combine all in all. His search for a philosophy for the whole man, and the way he runs together religion, poetry, aesthetics, and philosophy, makes him a loyal son of Rousseau and forerunner of nineteenth-century Romanticism.

XXVIII

Immanuel Kant

M ETAPHYSICS IN EAST PRUSSIA when Immanuel Kant[1] went
to school simply meant, as we have seen, what the
Wolffians were concocting. There were in Königsberg Wolffians of
the Strict Observance, but then there was no lack either of bright
young men to question the master's deductions. After all, Newton was
making a big impression—even that far away—and what was menac-
ing about Newtonianism was its evident success in integrating observational data into a necessary conceptual scheme. A critical young man
like Professor Martin Knutzen (who was only twenty-one when he
began teaching in Königsberg) never doubted for a moment the rationalist tenets that reality is completely knowable in itself and that
the human mind is capable of discovering its necessary principles. The
Aufklärer were of one mind with the great metaphysicians in these
matters. But he did feel that Newton had shown the way to truth to
lead through the things of our experience, rather than through deductions from a few principles grasped innately.

Throughout his years of youthful scientific inquiry, Knutzen's favorite student showed himself concerned to understand in terms of
method the success of Newtonian physics. Kant was not yet so extreme as he was to become on the question of the frustration of metaphysics. But with the passage of time he began to see the sterility of
traditional disputes about "substance" and "cause," of the ontological
proof for the existence of God, of wishful-thinking proofs of immortality. Hume helped him to see these things, and Rousseau played
also an important role in his development;[2] not, indeed, so much by
attacking idealist metaphysics, but by showing in *Emile* and the *Social
Contract* how important a vital moral philosophy can be, and how
far removed from life, by contrast, metaphysical speculation really

is! Already fifteen years before the *Critique of Pure Reason*, Kant's position had hardened to the point where he was saying, in effect, *modern physics works and Leibnizian metaphysics does not.*

Physics "works." It is not bogged down in perpetual arguments, repeatedly foundering in the same contradictions; instead, physics progresses, each generation building new knowledge on the universal principles already established. It works because, whatever may be the ultimate ontological status of its principles, they are completely oriented toward experience; they declare nothing that cannot be put to a sensible test, which test becomes the ultimate control of the universal pronouncements of the physicists, no matter how pretentious.

Metaphysics does not work. It brings forth no new knowledge, but instead leads the philosophers to contradict one another absolutely and hopelessly; absolutely, because the pronouncements of metaphysics purport to reveal the ultimate nature of reality taken as a whole, and thus contradictions among metaphysicians are absolute and permit no compromise; hopelessly, because the pronouncements of both sides in every metaphysical dispute are of their very nature beyond the sum total of experience itself, and hence incapable of sensible verification. Kant had lost hope that there would ever be a definitive resolution to problems like that of the true nature of substance, or of the necessity of causal connections, or the validity of the ontologic proof for God's existence, unless the whole plane on which metaphysical arguments unroll be undercut by someone pursuing the question Hume was really asking: What is the nature and validity of metaphysical inquiry as such?

In a mature work, the very title of which spells out the radical nature of Kant's re-examination of the science, *Prolegomena to Any Future Metaphysics*, the philosopher tells us the meaning Hume's inquiry held for him.

> The question was not whether the concept of cause was right, useful and even indispensable for our knowledge of nature, for this Hume had never doubted; but whether that concept could be thought *a priori*, and consequently whether it possessed an inner truth, independent of all experience, implying a wider application than merely to the objects of experience. This was Hume's problem. It was a question concerning the *origin*, not concerning the *indispensable need* of the concept.[3]

No one can deny the usefulness, indeed the indispensable nature, of the notion of cause and effect; but the problem is that in metaphysics we argue on the basis of such a "necessary" connection to conclusions that transcend any possible empirical verification—namely, to conclusions of an absolute universality which can never be put to the test because we can never examine sensibly that *everything* about which they so confidently pronounce; even to conclusions about God and the soul, the object of which precludes empirical verification by its very nature. Kant is raising a question *de jure*; in his precise logical terminology he puts it this way: How are *synthetic judgments a priori* possible; i.e., on what grounds can we pronounce, prior to experiencing *everything*, concerning the nature of an entire class, or even of all being as such? Such *a priori* judgments pretend to possess "an inner truth, independent of all experience, implying a wider application than merely to the objects of experience." [4] The very notion seems madly ambitious.

What troubled Kant about such judgments is not only that they seemed to go beyond "all possible experience," but that they do so because they pretend to pronounce on the ultimate nature of all reality as it is *in itself* (*an sich*). We should recall that Kant's immediate predecessors had failed to provide any foundation for a valid theory of abstraction, nor had they done anything to explain how the mind might form through experience a judgment that would legitimately pronounce on being itself. To do so has always been a most difficult undertaking, but recently it had not been undertaken at all. Kant was confronted with this spectacle: on the one hand, Hume utterly undermining the possibility of forming from experience a valid principle of being; and on the other, Leibniz blandly assuring that all judgments can be reduced to a judgment of identity, that there exists a sufficient reason for everything (unknown to us, of course; but how reassuring merely to know that such a reason exists and that everything has to be just as it is, and, *as* it is, is perfectly *rational!*). Hume and Leibniz are violent extremes. Kant will seek to find a way between them. He will not free himself from Hume to the extent of seeking a ground for universal judgments *in sensible experience*. There the skepticism of Humean empiricism is allowed to remain in possession of the field. But Kant will criticize the ontological pretensions of those universal judgments which, however, he will accord, do have their ground *in the subjectivity*. How can such judgments reveal anything "objective" about the "thing-in-itself," the "*Ding an sich*," when applied to the data of experience? Kant waves off the pretense of the metaphysicians ever to reach knowledge that transcends "appearances."

Transcendental Aesthetic

THE *Critique of Pure Reason* is divided into two parts (very unevenly as to number of pages—in a typical edition, four hundred pages for the first and only eighty for the second part)—A Transcendental Doctrine of Elements, which analyzes the sources of human knowledge; and a Transcendental Doctrine of Method, which criticizes the use of "pure reason"; that is, the use of reason beyond sensible experience. Both are entitled "transcendental" because they examine the roots of all knowledge as such and hence what is exposed there goes beyond (transcends) all the categories and divisions of things to pronounce concerning Being itself as we know it.

The Transcendental Doctrine of Elements is further divided into two parts, reflecting the "two sources of human knowledge (which probably spring from a common, but to us unknown root), namely, sense and understanding." [5] By the sense, objects are *given* to us; by the understanding, they are *thought* by us. The first part of the *Critique*, the "Transcendental Aesthetic," studies, then, the way things are *given* to us within the forms of space and time, which Kant believes can and must be studied before we can study the conditions under which they are *thought* by the understanding.

All objects are originally given to us through an intuition, in the receptivity of the sensibility. In the phenomenon so given we must distinguish the *matter*—i.e., that which corresponds to the sensation —from the *form*, which is what causes the manifold matter of the phenomenon to be perceived as arranged in a certain order, and which, since it is a question of a proper arrangement of the sensation, cannot itself be again a sensation. [6] The matter alone is given us *a posteriori*, while the form has to antedate the receptivity of the matter; it must be present *a priori*, ready to receive the matter, for it functions as the very formal possibility of such a reception. Kant thus distinguishes the faculty from what the faculty receives; the activity of sensing according to a certain nature proper to a finite knower, from that which is sensed and must be received by the *Vorstellungsfähigkeit*. [7] Kant recognizes that the object known, the "phenomenon," will be known in a way that is in keeping with the nature of the knower as well as of the object received; all empirical knowledge will be received according to the *form* of a human sensibility. How should one construe this incontestable fact that we know according to "our manner"? To a realist, it simply means that the kind of knowledge man is capable of is perforce partial, progressive, from a point of view; this does not necessarily keep it from being a faithful and real grasp of the thing; as long as we do not jump to conclusions, not authorized by our humble data, we can be certain nothing learned subsequently will in any way contradict essentially what little we already know. When Kant insists that the *form* of receptivity cannot itself be "another sensation" —in other words, that it adds no extraneous content to the received matter—he would seem to be working in this spirit, just as he certainly is in the text of the *Prolegomena*, in which he will say that the representation is an "appearance" but not therefore any the less "actual." [8] However, though not a sensation, sensitivity is still conceived by Kant as something *added to* the sensations to form with them the object known (phenomenon). "Their form must be ready for them in the mind *a priori*, and must therefore be capable of being considered as separate from all sensations." This is where the two ways part. Kant, for reasons connected with his theory of the origin of necessity in mathematics, goes so far as to think that we can have pure intuitions of representation that do not involve any empirical matter, just by intuiting directly and alone the forms of the sensibility. "I call all representations in which there is nothing that belongs to sensation, *pure* (in a transcendental sense). The pure form therefore of all sensuous intuitions, that form in which the manifold elements of the phenomenon are seen in a certain order, must be found in the mind *a priori*." To make of this "form" something that can be itself an object of intuition apart from an actual sensation objectivizes what for the realist would remain (and what Kant himself often sees must be) a mere *function*, never an element of content. Kant wants to feel he can extract the organizing element and hold it up for examination like a thing, while the realist feels that the functions of the receptivity are so teleologically ordered to the knowledge of the thing that they can only, and even then with great difficulty, be discovered in each act of perception.

But then Kant is still working with an unquestioned assumption, passed from Master to Disciple throughout the modern tradition, and exercising so tyrannical a hold that not a single soul for this entire period ever peered beyond it: that sensations are fragments of sound, color, touch, etc., requiring to be cemented together. This contention appears in the very text we are considering, and in a way that amply illustrates the need, if that were the case, for the subjectivity to add *content* to this arid dust of matter.

> Thus, if we deduct from the representation of a body what belongs to the thinking of the understanding, viz. substance, force, divisibility, etc., and likewise what belongs to sensation, viz. impermeability, hardness, color, etc., there still remains something of that empirical intuition, viz. extension and form. These belong to pure intuition, which *a priori*, and even without a real object of the senses or of sensation, exists in the mind as a mere form of sensibility.[9]

Kant is thus led into serious difficulty: If sensation is reduced to yielding only the "proper sensibles," then why shouldn't the "common sensibles" also be placed in the faculty of the sensibility *a priori*, just as every other unifying conception will have to be innate in the understanding, even though these conceptions will now be considered as dynamic functions?

It is then against this background of empiricism we must try to understand the transcendental aesthetic. If one were to select a key phrase to preface Kant's analysis of the pure forms of the sensibility, it would surely have to be this one, several times repeated: "An empirical proposition cannot possess the qualities of necessity and absolute universality, which, nevertheless, are the characteristics of all geometrical propositions."[10] The strength of the theory that time and space are forms of the subjectivity itself and are therefore subject to pure intuition, independent of any empirical experience, is that it can explain, among other things, how geometry can be founded on "apodeictic," certain, universal synthetic *a priori* judgments, which are pronounced prior to our experiencing all the objects of which they are predicated. If space is not something inhering in things, but rather is the condition in the subject for all experience of phenomena, and if this form of the sensibility can be immediately intuited by the mind, then obviously it must be the source *a priori* of the apodeictic certainty of those universal judgments of the geometers. The embarrassment of empiricism—its lack of a credible theory of abstraction and consequently its failure to explain universality and necessity—is overcome, and Hume's theory of association is subsumed into a "transcendental" explanation: The strand of necessity is not mere habit but is rooted in the very nature of the sensibility (and the understanding) as such. What more could we ask? Kant integrates mathematics and mathematical physics, saving his own philosophy from the skeptical breakdown of those who espoused in common the phenomenal-dust theory of sensation.

The universality and necessity of mathematics and mathematical physics are not derived from the data of sensation but from the form of the sensibility according to the conditions under which these data are received. This much being secured, Kant can feel free to join in the modern indoor sport of pointing up the relativity of individual sensations: "Color, taste, etc.," he affirms in this context, "must be contemplated not as properties of things, but only as changes in the subject, changes which may be different in different men." [11] A rose, for example, may be commonly taken as a thing in itself, but in respect to its color it is different to every eye, while its spatiality will manifest qualities (also commonly supposed to belong to the thing-in-itself) which all must acknowledge to be the same. This is because space, being the *a priori* form of the sensibility as such—i.e., unquestionably a property of the subjectivity itself—is, ironically, *more objective* than those sense data that will vary with the different sense organs of various individuals. Understand now what Kant means by *objective:* that which is certain, universal, necessary; and that can only be, we have just discovered, something *a priori*—namely, a property of consciousness itself.

Once again this does not mean that the sense data—the color, the feel, etc.—of the rose, however relative and "subjective" they may be, are useless and illusory.[12] It is precisely because mathematics and physics remain oriented toward the organizing of empirical data that they do not get bogged into the contradictions attending the "pure" use of the ideas of the understanding—but that is something to be considered in due course.

Is the contention that Kant surreptitiously transforms *function* into *content*, thanks to the indefiniteness of the term "form," borne out by anything in this text? When the philosopher says, "Geometrical principles are always apodeictic, that is, united with the consciousness of their necessity, as 'Space has only three dimensions,'" I think we can see that our charge is justified. The three-dimensionality of space is a determination, a whatness, a content, of an abstract something in which all the objects of our experience participate; it is certainly impossible to consider such a judgment a contentless function of receptivity; space, as three-dimensional, receives and adds to the thing the essential note of "having three dimensions." Nor can we hold that the three dimensions are known by the senses, the universality and necessity only being added by the subjectivity, for "three-dimensionality" cannot be the subject of either sight or hearing or taste, but is rather the *a priori* form of all of them. Against the contention that this "three-dimensionality" is only the expression of a relation imposed by the subjectivity on its data as condition of their reception, it should be pointed out that there is more implied in the predication of three-dimensionality applied to the object than its being "over there," "higher," "lower" with respect to a knowing subject. The colors, the impermeability, the texture, etc., of a house are, so to speak, strung out on a frame of objective spatiality which the phenomenal house appears itself to possess. Is it inexact to say that the great length and extreme narrowness of the Jones's house is any less a part of its appearance than its white color? That there is a subjective transcendental function according to which all our experiences are afforded a space in which to occur, and the assertion that material objects possess a certain spatial thickness and therefore dimensions are two statements which are not mutually exclusive but are indeed readily confused.

There is no science founded in the form of "time" the way geometry and mathematical physics are grounded in the form of "space." So Kant has an easier task making time sound more like a function than a content added to the givens of the senses.

> Time cannot be any determination of outward phenomena. It has to do neither with shape nor position; on the contrary, it determines the relation of representations to our internal state. And precisely because this internal intuition presents to us no shape or form, we endeavor to supply this want by analogies, and represent the course of time by a line progressing to infinity, the content of which constitutes a series which is only of one dimension.[13]

Taken in itself—that is, in abstraction from all the content of sensuous experience—time is *nothing*. This nothingness is indeed the true sign of its transcendentality, that it *is* function, that it is the subject's active receptivity. We are going to see, in the pages to come, that Kant returns a number of times, in the most significant passages, to this *Nichts* which is at the very root of the possibility of the finite knower's being able to experience being, to re-present things. "All in our cognition that belongs to intuition contains nothing more than mere relations . . . to wit, of place in an intuition (extension), change of place (motion), and laws according to which this change is determined (moving forces)," [14] all of which, as far as content is concerned, adds up to *nothing*. In the case of time—i.e., the internal intuition—the relations are succession, co-existence, permanence, which are "nothing else than the mode in which the mind is affected by its own activity, to wit its presenting to itself representations." [15] "That which as representation can antecede every exercise of thought (of an object), is intuition; and when it contains nothing but relations, it is the form of the intuition." [16] But how can there be a science of these mere functions *a priori* when they are in themselves "nothing"? We see a little better now why Kant will continue to be torn between conceiving the forms now as contentless, now as though they had a content.

So the activity of the sensibility's receptivity is a unification of the manifold of sense through the means of a subjectively accomplished relation according to the rule of space and time. But what we must see now is that this unification by the sensibility according to the forms of time and space is only part of the whole process of cognitive unification carried out by the finite knower. There is more to the process of our forging the unity of a world and of a single spirit out of the manifold sense impressions than just this temporal-spatial organization, although the organization of experience by time is, indeed, as we shall see, the very center of the whole affair. But, as Kant says, while the object is *given* to us through the sensibility, still it is only through the understanding that it can be *thought*. The understanding is the ultimate cognitive *act*, the *activity* of representing the representation, the "spontaneity" of a center of knowledge, but a "spontaneity" that is tied to a dependence on receptivity for its contents: "Thoughts without content are void; intuitions (of the sensibility) without conceptions (of the understanding) are blind." [17] It is quite evident that the real sense of the aesthetic intuition's unification of the manifold of sense according to the forms of time and space will not become evident until we have explored a little closer to its source that "spontaneous" activity of unification by the ultimate act of understanding.

The Concepts of the Understanding

WE HAVE ALREADY SEEN that the unification of the manifold in the sensibility is carried out by an intuition which is *relational* in nature. Since human cognition is ultimately a unity (Kant refers to the unity of the *cogito* as "the transcendental unity of apperception," a phrase to which we shall later devote our attention), we would suppose that the unification carried out by the "spontaneity" of thought should also be relational, the relations established by the conceptions of the understanding being parallel to the reception-oriented form of time, but now functioning actively at the center of the cognitive act. That is why these more spontaneous conceptions of the understanding reach out to embrace a span of time; for example, think of the way a "substance" will endure throughout a very long series of "accidental changes." Hence their tendency to appear supra-temporal, which appearance becomes an invitation for the reason to use the conception in a "pure" way, without regard for its essential function as unifier of the manifold of experience, and thereby to reify the conception as an a-temporal reality in itself, standing above the whole level of sensible experience. This metaphysicizing tendency, as we shall see, becomes the major target of the *Critique's* criticism. For the moment, however, let us concentrate on the understanding's legitimate activity as unifier of empirical experience.

The act of understanding is an act of *judgment*, and judging is a function consisting in "arranging diverse representations under one common representation." [18] Kant conceives the act of subsuming the particular under the more general as an activity of unification rather than as an act of abstraction, extracting the more general form from the particular. Any cognitive act implies essentially the mind's activity of holding things before the attention through a multiplicity of experiential moments. A conception like "body" is applicable to a piece of iron, a cat, and a planet because the mind can assemble through various moments these particulars under the one conception, body.[19] "All judgments, accordingly, are functions of unity in our representation, inasmuch as, instead of an immediate, a higher representation, which comprises this and various others, is used for our cognition of the object, and thereby many possible cognitions are collected into one." [20] Since all of our more particular conceptions can be brought under those most general conceptions which apply to all experience (like body, divisible, etc.), it is clear that the analysis of the understanding should proceed at once to the center of spontaneity in an effort to grasp in its purest form the act of unification that ties together all knowledge of reality into the world of a single *cogito*. ". . . Because these conceptions spring pure and unmixed out of the understanding as an absolute unity, and therefore must be connected with one another according to one conception or idea," they must form "a system to be determined by and comprised under an idea"; an analysis of the understanding must uncover this system—this ultimate unity—and see it as a complete whole, as a "unity of apperception," as the act of *an* understanding.

The process of joining different representations to each other and of comprehending their diversity in one cognition Kant terms *synthesis*. He introduces this term, instead of simply calling the process "understanding," to point to the fact that the act of understanding is part of a whole process of synthesizing, which is indeed the very essence of cognition. In considering the sensibility, we saw that already before the conceptions of the understanding are thought the data of the senses are primordially organized temporally and spatially. We must then distinguish within the cognitive unity of our apperception three levels: (1) the diversity of the pure intuition, and two levels of synthesis; (2) the synthesis of this diversity by means of the imagination, which yields as yet no cognition; and (3) the synthesis carried out by the conceptions of the understanding, the ultimate unity of the cognition, in virtue of which the imagination's synthesizing is made possible. [21] Although he in fact employs dozens of pages to explain their unity in one consciousness in terms of the "transcendental unity of apperception," Kant is quite capable of summing the whole thing up in a single breath-taking sentence like this:

> The pure form of intuition in time, merely as an intuition, which contains a given manifold, is subject to the original unity of consciousness, and that solely by means of the necessary relation of the manifold in intuition to the *I think*, consequently by means of the pure synthesis of the understanding, which lies *a priori* at the foundation of all empirical synthesis. [22]

In simpler terms, the unification of many sensations into one experience in time is an act of a single *cogito*. No unity of the knower, no time. But there is a reverse side to the coin: namely, that any unity achieved by human thought must be a unity *in time;* i.e., it must be oriented toward a manifold in experience, or it gets into metaphysical trouble. The true nature of the conceptions of the understanding, according to Kant, the empiricist, is to unify a sensible experience temporally. Consequently the conceptions of the understanding are all explicable in terms of their temporal function of unifying a manifold of sense into one cognition.

What, then, are those primordial conceptions of the understanding —those "categories" as Kant calls them? They correspond to all the possible kinds of judgment. Here is Kant's list of judgments and categories:[23]

Judgments	*Categories*
a) Quantity	a) Quantity
(1) Universal	(1) Unity
(2) Particular	(2) Plurality
(3) Singular	(3) Totality
b) Quality	b) Quality
(4) Affirmative	(4) Reality
(5) Negative	(5) Negation
(6) Infinite	(6) Limitation
c) Relation	c) Relation
(7) Categorical	(7) Inherence and subsistence (substance and accident)
(8) Hypothetical	(8) Causality and dependence (cause and effect)
(9) Disjunctive	(9) Community (reciprocity between agent and patient)
d) Modality	d) Modality
(10) Problematic	(10) Possibility-impossibility
(11) Assertoric	(11) Existence-nonexistence
(12) Apodeictic	(12) Necessity-contingency

Now what does all this represent? It purports to be a complete enumeration of the whole system of possible judgments and the fundamental conceptions (categories) of the understanding corresponding to them. In other words, we should be able to see the *cogito's* power of unification threading through all these functions of bringing together representations. With this list Kant felt he had replaced the categories of Aristotle, exchanging for the Stagirite's list of possible objective *forms* a system of intentional functions on the part of the subject, so that the "being" of the things of our experience is seen to reside, not in principles within them, but in the power of representation on the part of a subject making them *to be for us*.

Having just read the history of modern philosophy, we should recognize some old friends in that list; "substance" and "cause and effect" should especially jump to our attention. Let us see, as a means of understanding something of the "Copernican revolution" Kant effected in philosophy, what he has done with these troublesome notions.

He has identified them as two among twelve kinds of unifying conceptions; i.e., as two of the functions of the understanding that make thought possible by unifying representations. Now let us recall Descartes' exact words when he sought to describe how the substance remains the same throughout the transformation of all the accidents of a piece of wax as it grows warm.

> Abstracting from all that does not belong to the wax, let us see what remains. Certainly nothing remains excepting a certain extended thing which is flexible and movable. But what is the meaning of flexible and movable? Is it not that I imagine that this piece of wax being round is capable of becoming square and of passing from a square to a triangular figure? No, certainly it is not that, since I imagine that it admits of an infinitude of similar changes, and I nevertheless do not know how to encompass this infinitude by my imagination, and consequently this conception which I have of the wax is not brought about by the imagination. . . . We must then grant that I could not even understand through the imagination what this piece of wax is, and that it is my understanding alone which perceives it. . . . It is certainly the same that I see, touch, imagine, and finally it is the same which I have always believed it to be from the beginning. But what must particularly be observed is that its perception is neither an act of vision, nor of touch, nor of imagination, and has never been so even though it may have formerly appeared to be so, but only an intuition (*inspectio*) of the mind, which may be imperfect and confused as it was formerly, or clear and distinct as it is at present, according as my attention is more or less directed to the elements which are found in it, and of which it is composed.[24]

Through what long travails has the Cartesian idealist conception of substance passed before finally, in the *Critique of Pure Reason,* coming into its own! All the elements of Kant's solution are there in the *Second Meditation:* sensibility, imagination, understanding; but the greatest of these, when it comes to understanding the substantial unity that endures throughout the changes of accidents, is the intuition of the understanding. Moreover, there is already a suggestion of *critique* lurking at the end of the passage: Before being explicitly analyzed, the unity of apperception functions, to be sure, but confusedly; now that we have discovered the intuition of the understanding at work, "substance" becomes a clear and distinct idea. I quote Kant—the text is the one introducing the table of categories: "The synthesis of a diversity is the first requisite for the production of a cognition, which in its beginning, indeed, may be crude and confused, and therefore in need of analysis." [25]

All that remained for Kant to do was to effect the final translation of "substance" into terms of time, so that it could accord with his exposition of experience as essentially temporal.

> All phenomena exist in time, wherein alone as substratum, that is, as the permanent form of the internal intuition, co-existence and succession can be represented. Consequently time, in which all changes of phenomena must be cogitated, remains and changes not, because it is that in which succession and co-existence can be represented only as determinations thereof. Now time in itself cannot be an object of perception. It follows that in objects of perception, that is, in phenomena, there must be found a substratum which represents time in general.[26]

Kant goes on to explain that this "substance" is the "real" in the world of phenomena, that which does not change, and which, therefore, is subject in itself to no increase or diminution—a neat explanation of the truth of Leibniz' metaphysical assertion that the quantity of substances always remains the same!

"Causality" presents the same spectacle: Hume explicated transcendentally and translated in terms of time. In the synthesis of phenomena, the manifold of our representations is always successive, the present representation implying the preceding and necessarily following it. Why is this?

> For all experience and for the possibility of experience, understanding is indispensable, and the first step which it takes in this

sphere is not to render the representation of objects clear, but to render the representation of an object in general, possible. It does this by applying the order of time to phenomena, and their existence. In other words, it assigns to each phenomenon, as a consequence, a place in relation to preceding phenomena, determined *a priori* in time, without which it could not harmonize with time itself, which determines a place *a priori* to all its parts.[27]

Kant explains that this determination of place is not derived from the relation of phenomena to *absolute* time, which cannot be an object of perception, but rather that the phenomena must reciprocally determine the places in time of one another, and render these necessary in order of time.

Whatever follows or happens must follow in conformity with a universal rule upon that which was contained in the foregoing state. Hence arises a series of phenomena, which, by means of the understanding, produces and renders necessary exactly the same order and continuous connection in the series of our possible perceptions, as is found *a priori* in the form of internal intuition (time), in which all our perceptions must place.[28]

Kant has not only brought out the last drop of temporality inherent in Hume's doctrine, but he has succeeded in explaining in idealist terms the grounds for whatever necessity there may be in our perceptions of causality; and he has done so in a way that, far from turning traitor to Hume's empiricism, not only accepts it as an indispensable condition for valid experience, but lays the ground for showing why every effort to transcend the empirical plane must fail. Consider carefully the exquisite nuance of this declaration: "Whatever follows or happens must follow in conformity with a universal rule upon that which was contained in the foregoing state." It suggests that the *necessity* in any such connection is due to sensible experience, and without it the rule, or any application of it, would simply be devoid of sense; yet the whole matter is so phrased that we can see at once the temptation to extend the rule beyond this empirical usage!

The Mediating Function of the Imagination

THAT KANT HAS "SET UP" this explanation very carefully for the sake of the killing—the grand slaughter of "metaphysics" that is to follow—is, then, perfectly evident. However, before we proceed to within eye-sight of the critical guillotine, let us double back for a look at the centerpiece of Kant's whole construction, the temporal synthesizing function of the imagination. The question of how the "rule" of the understanding is made one with the multiplicity of sensible ex-periences can receive its answer—and thus Kant's whole doctrine be made into a unity—only through a doctrine of the imagination. Kant attacks this problem in a chapter of which he wrote, "I hold this chap-ter to be one of the most important," a chapter which a famous Kantian commentator has called *the pivotal piece* of the whole *Kritik*, the First Chapter of the transcendental doctrine of judgment, entitled "Of the Schematism of the Pure Conceptions of the Understanding." Why is the imagination—and this chapter on its function as *"Schematismus"*—so important?

In a doctrine like Kant's, the fundamental principle of which might be stated in Leibniz' words, "There is nothing in the intellect that is not first in the senses—except intellection itself," the key to the doc-trine of cognition lies in the faculty that can mediate between the pure rules of the unifying apperception and the multiplicity of sensible data—between the active principle and the received material, between the one and the many. The central cognitive faculty must then reflect somehow the unity of the *cogito* and the manyness of our experience; it must turn a face both ways and succeed in bridging the gulf sepa-rating unity and multiplicity by achieving a unity-within-many; i.e., a dynamic unity according to *time*. In the chapter on the "Schematism," here is what Kant has to say of this two-faced talent of *time* as dynamic unity of many into one:

> A Transcendental determination of time is so far homogeneous with the *category*, which constitutes the unity thereof, that it is universal, and rests upon a rule *a priori*. On the other hand, it is so far homogeneous with the phenomenon, inasmuch as time is con-tained in every empirical representation of the manifold.[29]

The details of this mediation between the universal and the particular are worked out in this chapter in terms of "images" and "schema" in recognition of the fact that our experience is no mere succession of points but a collection of qualitative, essential, formal determinations. Let us see what this all means.

First, consider well the problem: What Kant has to do is explain what was once explained in terms of abstraction in such a way that the generality of universal concepts is imposed from the center of apperceptive unity rather than extracted from the "stuff" of sensation. He does this in the following manner: The image (*Bild*) of a given triangle must always be either isosceles, scalene, or right-angled; yet I can form a conception of "triangle in general" which will apply to all of these, and to which no one image could ever be adequate. Obviously such a conception (which Kant calls a *schema* of the imagination, to differentiate it from the absolutely concretely determined *image* on the one hand and the very general *categories* on the other) must exist in thought rather than in the concrete sensibility; such a *schema* "indicates a rule of the synthesis of the imagination in regard to pure figures of space": i.e., its greater unity (generality) must be due to the understanding's ability to be present successively to every sort of image of every sort of triangle, and to keep the relation between these particular images straight.

> This schematism of our understanding in regard to phenomena and their mere form, is an art, hidden in the depths of the human soul, whose true modes of action we shall only with difficulty discover and unveil.[30]

What a vista of possibilities that simple statement seems to open—an *art* of according concrete experience and universal necessity—an art (*eine verborgene Kunst in den Tiefen der menschlichen Seele*). What a word! It suggests that Hume was right in underscoring the element of *praxis* in the formation of our knowledge, of habit, experience, and even cunning; it repurchases Leibniz' marvelous suggestion, that all is not clear calculation in the human spirit, that the *petites perceptions* effect a great subterranean work on those most conscious and clear. Yet, incredible thing! Kant seems to consider it unnecessary to "enter upon a dry and tedious analysis of the essential requisites of the transcendental schemata." He prefers to leave the matter after explaining only that the schema is "a transcendental product of the imagination, a product which concerns the determination of the internal sense, according to conditions of its form (time) in respect to all representations, in so far as the representations must be conjoined *a priori* in one conception, conformably to the unity of apperception." [31]

It is not at all sure that an analysis of the "essential requisites of the transcendental schemata" would have been so "dry and tedious." But

Kant tarries not—he rushes ahead to show how all schemata ultimately manifest the temporal unity of the oneness of apperception, how schemata according to number, substance, cause and effect, relation, necessity, etc., are all comprehensible in terms of the primordial possibility of experience in time. The question of quality, the question of according the content of experience to the conditions of universality—in other words, the question that was once handled by the doctrine of the abstraction of essential and accidental forms—is glossed over with a few remarks, the kernel of which we have just cited. Kant seems to want to leave to others the task of unveiling that "art" hidden deep in the soul, by which are imposed conditions of universality and necessity on sensible experience. Could Kant have probed very far into this *art* without encountering evidence that accords poorly with the phenomalistic, powdered-dust theory of sensation? We do not think so. Perhaps this is the reason that subsequent philosophers in this tradition have also left to someone else the "dry and tedious" task of describing the details of that art so essential to all human knowledge.

The Metaphysical Use of the Categories

THE PREVIOUS ANALYSES have been working toward this important critical conclusion about the "categories" of the understanding: Their function being that of the organization of empirical data into a unified knowledge, their sense must be subordinated to this end; yet these categories (so Kant has been working hard to make us believe) are not devoid of a certain logical content of their own; they can, therefore, become the object of a kind of formal knowledge, lacking, to be sure, any rich content (which only sense can supply), but more than making up for it (as far as *allure* is concerned) by a great show of unity and interiorly based certainty. Independent of sensuous intuition, the categories, when they thus pose as *pure ideas* of reason, pass themselves off, for that very reason, as superior to knowledge dependent on a passive reception of data. How can the human reason be expected to resist the temptation these pure ideas present—why, here is obviously *une sagesse toute faite*, a ready-made wisdom, available to all comers, not requiring the pain of long experience. All we have to do is turn inward, grasp the divine principles of our reason in themselves, and behold! we have seized the principle of all unity underlying experience, the *cause* of there being any being (in the sense that it is the unifying activity of our understanding which makes possible the *Vorstellen des Vorstellungens*, the re-presenting of the representation), as well as its ultimate sense, *because* it is the ultimate unity! "Metaphysics," concludes Kant wearily, is inevitable, it can even be useful, if we can just come to realize the real status of its claims, if we can just come, through our critique, to realize that it is not scientific, that it is a guide and not a fulfilled and genuine wisdom.

Kant's way of showing up the pretensions of metaphysics is markedly superior to his predecessors' (even to Hume, the most important of the previous critics). Instead of resting content to mention the fact of divergent metaphysical positions and their constant war, Kant explains, not only precisely why, in terms of a deep epistemology, they *must* war, but the exact sense of that war. In fact, he ranges the warring positions into a system of oppositions (antinomies), explaining these sets of contraries each as a dialectic that occurs when any category is used as a pure idea in itself. Then, as though that were not already a sufficiently final and glorious funeral for the innate clear and distinct ideas, Kant goes on to assign a perennial, non-scientific, practical value to this effort on the part of the mind's ultimate structuring functions to guide man toward wisdom. It is impossible to imagine a more thorough job of burying Caesar. With it, a new era came to philosophy, a new cycle of history opened for the world. Let us see how this dialectical destruction of metaphysics works, and just what the practical value or "pure reason's" elucubrations are supposed to be.

Kant explains thus the beginning of all the trouble: "Although the rules of the understanding are not only *a priori* true, but the very source of all truth, that is, of the accordance of our cognition with objects, and although on this ground, they contain the basis of the possibility of experience, as the *ensemble* of all cognition, it seems to us not enough to propound what is true—we desire also to be told what we want to know." [32] If we take away all sensible intuition from our thoughts, there still remains the form of thought.

Thus the categories do in some measure really extend further than sensuous intuition, inasmuch as they think objects in general, without regard to the mode of sensibility in which these objects are given. But they do not for this reason apply to and determine a wider sphere of objects, because we cannot assume that such can be given without presupposing the possibility of another than the sensuous mode of intuition, a supposition we are not justified in making.[35]

Such a notion is not at all self-contradictory—it *could* be that there exist objects very much like what the categories of our understanding suggest, and it is quite dogmatic of the materialists and the empiricists to assert absolutely that only sensible objects exist. For while we have positive evidence only of those objects that we intuit through the one intuition we in fact enjoy—namely, sensory intuition; and while therefore the categories of our understanding enjoy their rightful sense only when filled up by such data in the knowing of *phenomena*; still "the conception of a *noumenon*, that is, of a thing which must be cogitated not as an object of sense, but as a thing in itself (solely through the pure understanding) is not self-contradictory," for we have no right to assert dogmatically that sensibility is the only possible mode of intuition. It may be *for us*, but we have no grounds for asserting that we are the only knowers in the universe.

So the *transcendental* use of the categories might apply well enough to a "possible experience," but it is one of which we can have no actual knowledge. This realization, the finest product of the "transcendental analytic," has only just occurred, so long after the beginning of philosophy, in this very book. Even this great achievement will not suffice, as perhaps it should, to dissuade future generations from proceeding to an "ideal," that is, a *pure*, an *a priori* projection of the categories as metaphysical ideas. The mind can never be discouraged from making these anticipations of experience, nor should it be altogether. Kant would accord a certain reality to this natural movement of the mind toward an ideal unity of all its knowledge into a metaphysical wisdom —namely, the reality of a suggestion, of a natural tendency—which is all to the good, once we have been made to realize critically that such procedures do not constitute *proofs* of anything. Kant speaks of them as "regulative," meaning that they guide and urge on the understanding toward ever more comprehensive and unified syntheses of phenomena by holding up models of unity for the direction of scientific inquiry. This only becomes wrong when the use of them is *transcendent* instead of merely *transcendental;* i.e., when the mind thinks that the ideas can themselves become the object of an intuitive knowledge of a "something" lying beyond all sensible experience.

The three general ideas of reason grow out of the correspondence between the three forms of syllogistic reasoning (categorical, hypothetical, and disjunctive) with the categories of relation (substance, cause, and community). Reason, in seeking the unconditioned principle of categorical reasoning, posits the unity of substance as the thinking subject—i.e., the *soul*; it seeks the absolute principle underlying hypothetical reasoning in the totality of the causal series of appearances—i.e., the idea of the *world*; and that of disjunctive reasoning, in the unity of all perfections—i.e., *God*. The attribution of a real existence to these objects produced by the mind for its own satisfaction is what Kant calls "the transcendental illusion." The climactic part of the *Kritik*, the "Dialectic," is to expose this "natural illusion," and thus to unseat the pretensions of the three branches of traditional (i.e., Wolffian) philosophy that grow from the abuse of these three transcendent ideas: rational psychology, based on the transcendent use of the pure idea of the soul; rational cosmology, based on that of the world; and rational theology, based on the idea of God.

The rational psychology Kant has in mind is one that would deduce conclusions *a priori* from the *cogito*. The psychology that attempts to draw knowledge out of the thinking subject runs into a series of "paralogisms." [34] One of these, to take but a single example from the four Kant discusses, the "paralogism of substantiality," consists in posing the soul as a simple substance, which is, of course, what Descartes did in substantializing the *cogito*. What is wrong with this is simply that the notion of substance is not supposed to be itself the subject of an intuition, but only to serve as a unifying function. The *cogito*, declares Kant, cannot be for itself the subject of an intuition, whatever Descartes may have thought. We know only an *empirical consciousness*, entirely dominated by the form of time, attaining only to the knowledge of successive phenomena, and a *pure consciousness*, which is only a logical subject, the pure function of transcendental unification, not a thing, therefore not the object of an intuition of a thing-in-itself. Thus neither the materialist nor the spiritualist philosophies are right in asserting, respectively, that there is no soul or that there is a substantial soul, for neither has a legitimate basis for making such assertions. The soul remains an idea, of which it is impossible to know whether it exists or not; in any event, the reason is led to it necessarily, and there is nothing about it that suggests that it is impossible for it to exist. [35]

The effort to hold that the "world" exists independently of our experience leads to insoluble "antinomies," that is to opposed, contradictory positions, both the thesis and its antithesis being supported by equally impressive arguments. There are four sets of such cosmological antinomies, according to whether the world is envisaged from the point of view of quantity, of quality, of relation, or of modality.

1] Thesis: The world is limited in space and time.
Antithesis: The world has no limit either in space or time.

2] Thesis: Matter is composed of simple and indivisible elements.
Antithesis: There are no simple elements, and matter can be divided to infinity.

3] Thesis: There is in the world a free causality.
Antithesis: There is no liberty, rather everything happens in the world according to necessary laws.

4] Thesis: The world implies the existence of a necessary being.
Antithesis: There is no necessary being which is cause of the world.

These antinomies represent the gamut of possible rapports of the finite and the infinite. Now Kant claims that arguments can be found to support both sides of every one of these antinomies. Such a situation leaves the mind in suspense, a position it does not like to be in, and therefore invites skepticism. Is there any way out? The critical attitude shows there is one.

Kant divides for consideration the first two from the other antinomies. The thesis and antithesis of the two "mathematical" antinomies contradict one another. Neither can be held truly, as we can have no intuition of the world as a totality, because our intuitions all take place *in* time and space, so it is impossible to think truly of the world in terms of finite or infinite. As to the other two antinomies—Kant terms them "dynamic"—their theses and antitheses can be true together: the theses can be true of "the things in themselves," the antitheses true of the phenomena; we can admit liberty in the order of the thing-in-itself, and necessity in the order of phenomena, just as we can maintain that while the world of phenomena requires no necessary being, a necessary being can be held to exist outside this world. Not that either liberty or God is proven for all that. Kant simply wishes to indicate that they are not impossible, that there is logically a place for them, even though the reason is not graced with any intuition of either of them.[36]

The most influential part of this critique of the transcendent application of the pure ideas of reason is certainly Kant's attack on the proofs for God's existence. Kant believes that all the traditional arguments are reducible to three types: an "ontological" proof, which proceeds *a priori*; a "cosmological" proof, founded on the principle of causality; and a "physico-theological" proof, which works from the idea of the order of the world.

Kant's attack on the ontological proof is strikingly similar to St. Thomas': We cannot find the existence of an object—even God—by analyzing its concept, for "every judgment of existence is synthetic." Granted, if we deny of a subject a predicate that is identical with it, a contradiction results; for example, we must not assert "God is not all-powerful." But if one denies the subject as well as its predicates, then "there is no longer contradiction, since there is no longer anything that the contradiction can affect." So the judgment "God is not" involves no contradiction; the subject is simply suppressed. Kant invokes another example (become famous as the outstanding case of a great philosopher's recognizing that existence is not essence, without recognizing that it is nevertheless significant). There is no difference in idea, proceeds the example, between a hundred real and a hundred imaginary thalers; the difference residing "only" in the brute fact that the real ones exist and the imaginary do not. Existence has no idea-value, we might say. The real gist of the ontologic argument, then, lies in its illegitimate passage from the logical to the real order, a transition which no *idea* as such can ever authorize.[37]

The cosmological argument would proceed by way of causality to prove the existence of a necessary being from our experience of contingent beings. But this involves an abuse of the idea of cause similar to the abuse of the idea of substance that occurs in rational psychology. The idea of cause can serve to link phenomena within our sensible experience, but in the cosmological proof, it is projected beyond all possible experience to prove the existence of a necessary being, whereupon it becomes quite simply empty of all sense. Moreover, the cosmological proof really implies the ontological proof, for in effect what the proof attempts to do is deduce the existence of a necessary being from its idea. "What is necessary has to exist; God is necessary, therefore, etc." [38]

Kant protests his respect for the third proof, the physico-theological, the proof that argues from the order in the world. "That argument deserves to be mentioned always with respect. It is the most venerable, the clearest and the best proportioned to common reason." [39] But as a strict proof, it is no more valid than the others, first of all because it would leap beyond experience with the aid of a principle of finality that has no validity when used transcendentally; secondly, because it can only lead to an "architect of the world," to an organizing intelligence and not to a creator. In an effort to pass beyond the "architect" to a creator, the advocates of the physico-theological proof surreptitiously introduce the cosmological proof (which in turn has hidden in it the ontologic argument). [40]

The same can be said, then, of the idea of God as was said of the idea of a soul-substance: Reason cannot demonstrate His existence, but neither can it demonstrate the contrary; rather, as it had for the soul and for liberty, the critique has prepared for God a place, but that place remains experientially unfilled.

This, in a very summary way, is how the critique of pure speculative reason carries out its task of putting "dogmatic" metaphysics in its place. It is not difficult to see that Kant's critique is indeed successful in putting an end to the deductive pretenses of a long line of metaphysics issued from Descartes. Nor need we hesitate when the question is raised whether the *Critique of Pure Reason* has really achieved what it claimed; namely, to show the impossibility of a legitimate proof *a priori* in metaphysics. We must agree that it has . . . if one grants the starting point of the *Kritik*: that analysis of sensible experience which the "Transcendental Aesthetic" accepts from the modern tradition and puts into a climactic form. From such an experience, nothing like what Kant meant by a "synthetic *a priori* judgment" can ever legitimately follow. The *Prolegomena to Any Future Metaphysics* that Kant wrote as a kind of distillation of the central message of his great work fully deserves its title: In the future, no metaphysician should proceed without heeding its warning . . . *in full*. If there is one lesson our present reading of the history of philosophy from Descartes to Kant should have burned into our consciousness it is this: Any future metaphysics must build from real experiential grounds that resemble in no way the notions of empirical experience that have dominated this tradition. It is only because in fact the human consciousness enjoys a real communion with real things as *they are in themselves*, a sensuous-intellectual-affective-lived knowledge of things that is at once partial and rich; always from a point of view, yet manifesting within every individual point of view an objective core shared alike by every knower; it is because we can know things as they are in themselves *partially* (a possibility definitively rejected by the mathematicizing philosophers of the seventeenth century and never again, in the period of our concern, to be even for a moment entertained); it is because, in a word, human consciousness is part of a real world, and is proportioned and intentionally oriented to our survival in that world, that we can affirm confidently that the Kantian critique has not been the final word on the limits of our possible knowledge.

The *Critique of Practical Reason*

WHEN WE TURN to the practical order, to the world of moral conduct, we might well begin to wonder about the results of the *Critique of Pure Reason*. Is it not after all *atheistic*? Has not Kant, in delimiting the theoretical validity of the pure ideas of God, the Soul, and the World, neatly undermined the very foundations of traditional morality? And does not the Copernican revolution, which makes things in experience depend on the determinations of knowledge rather than knowledge being determined by things, open the way for a voluntaristic doctrine of morals; that is, for the notion that good and evil are what the dictates of the will impose on "things" as we form them?

Some commentators, indeed already in Kant's own day, upon reading the *Critique of Practical Reason* in which Kant not only works to restore an important practical role to the ideas of God, soul, and the world, but especially to establish a morality founded on a transcendental notion of *duty* very obviously intended to shelter morality from the cold winds of voluntarism, concluded that old Kant simply could not bear the onus of the first *Kritik*'s conclusions. Having weakened to the demands of traditional religion and bourgeois morality, he is now hard at work, they claim, to get God, the soul, and a stable order of things back into the picture. It is perfectly true that Kant was a bourgeois Christian and that he in no way wished to weaken the structures upon which rested the Protestant Prussian state. However, even in our brief synopsis of the last part of the *Critique of Pure Reason* we have seen enough to realize that already in that work, when Kant was pointing to the speculative limits under which the ideas of pure reason operate, it was not merely to criticize traditional metaphysics (which, after all, had already for a long time been under devastating fire), but to show that what was wrong with it was philosophy's failure to take account of the true operative order of things. Man has to live, man is a practical animal—Hume was right when he probed among the secrets of life as it is lived in customs and habit in his search for wisdom—it is in the practical order that we shall find the ultimate sense of the theoretical, and not vice versa. Kant, however, wishes to resist the anarchical suggestion advanced by Hume, that it is merely the accidents of custom, the way habits have happened to be built up, that govern in the practical order. He would establish a universal rule at the foundation of all morality, capable of supporting an ethics of an absolute sort. In so doing, and in exposing the practical reality of the pure ideas of reason, he is not "propping up a hastily erected building," but rather exposing "the true members making the structure of the system plain and letting the concepts, which were previously thought of only in a problematic way, be clearly seen as real." [41]

The two-page Introduction to the *Critique of Practical Reason* informs us at once that perspectives are now different, that condemnation of pure reason is not what is afoot, but rather practical justification of its ideas!

> The critique of practical reason as such has the obligation to prevent the empirically conditioned reason from presuming to be the only ground of determination of the will. The use of pure reason, if it is shown that there is such a reason, is alone immanent; the empirically conditioned use of reason, which presumes to be sovereign, is, on the contrary, transcendent, expressing itself in demands and precepts which go far beyond its own sphere. This is precisely the opposite situation from that of pure reason in its speculative use. [42]

Materialist empiricism, with its deterministic doctrines, makes assertions which nothing in the experience of the empirically conditioned use of reason can justify; it pompously asserts that there can be no life of the "spirit"; i.e., no *freedom*. Pure reason, on the other hand, points the way *practically* to just such an autonomy of self-origination as is necessary to ground a freedom. The positive task of the practical critique will be to bring out even more strongly than the *Critique of Pure Reason* the significance of these implications for a doctrine of freedom.

Just as Kant subsumed the empiricist and idealist metaphysical positions into his criticism of pure reason, so now does he begin by circumscribing the legitimate and limited place of materialist and hedonist ethics on the one hand, and idealistic ethics on the other. We do indeed desire certain objects because they cause pleasure and flee others because they cause pain; in this the materialists are quite right. Such determinations are empirical, and any rules of conduct that might be derived from them are themselves empirically based, reason being not so much a law-giver in such a case as a law-finder. In these instances "pleasure must be presupposed as the condition of the possibility of the determination of choice. But we cannot know, *a priori*, of the idea of any object, whatever the nature of this idea, whether it will be associated with pleasure or displeasure or will be merely indifferent. Thus any such determining ground of choice must always be empirical. . . ." [43] The rules of conduct that grow out of such experience are not, then, the morally binding laws that can found a universal code of conduct; they lack "objective necessity," not only varying from individual to individual, but even being capable of variation for the same person. [44] These maxims, then, are basically subjective, while an "imperative"—i.e., a rule characterized by an "ought"—is objective and universal. That is what the idealists saw so well. They understood that the objective grounds of a universal morality could not reside in empirical experience. Reason must enter in to determine the will by showing that if such and such is to result, then such and such will have to be ("ought to be") done. Reason alone can furnish the formal universality of an ethical "imperative."

"Imperatives" are of two sorts: There are those that determine the will in regard to a particular effect which it may be desirable to bring about, in which case they are only universal, necessary "precepts of skill," valid always when the special conditions with which they are concerned happen to be in play; hence Kant terms them *"hypothetical"*: given *this* desired effect, *that* will have to be done. But a moral *law* is still more, for it binds all men at all times. This universality will in fact be the basic criterion by which one can distinguish what is morally binding from what is not. A moral law is a *categorical* [45] *imperative* "completely determining the will as will, even before I ask whether I am capable of achieving a desired effect or what should be done to realize it." [46] It is with the ground of the *categorical imperative* that the "metaphysics of ethics" is primarily concerned. What are the conditions grounding such a transcendentally determining practical law?

For one thing, it must be the "form" and not the "matter" of the categorical imperative that gives it its transcendental necessity. When the will is subject to a material condition, then the will's object is what determines it. Hence a practical maxim or even a hypothetical imperative does not show the fundamental freedom of the will at work. "The mere legislative *form* of maxims alone can be the sufficient determining ground of a will." [47] No "events in nature" can determine the will; it functions outside the chains of causality because it is determined by reason which functions above the phenomenal level, the level of mere appearances. The will is a transcendental faculty—that is the true meaning of its *freedom*: It must legislate for the whole order of appearances, not be determined by moments of that experience. The reason is the "formal supreme determining ground of the will regardless of any subjective differences among men," providing "a law for all rational beings insofar as they have a will"; that is, insofar as they are competent to determine their actions according to principles. Note that man is not absolutely forced to act according to reason; he can let sensuous wants attract the empirical will away from the direction legislated by pure will. That is why the imperative takes for him, instead of the form of "holy will," as it does for God, the form of an "obligation," an "ought"; that is why it is exercised as a psychological event, a *duty*. "Such a will (i.e., the human practical will) is in need of the moral constraint of the resistance offered by the practical reason, which may be called an inner but intellectual compulsion." [48] We can only strive in this life to bring all of our maxims more consistently into line with the ultimate moral imperative, and to carry out our willed causal acts in keeping with this light as much as possible.

The formula Kant gives to the categorical imperative has become justly famous and, like many famous sayings, is usually misunderstood: "So act that the maxim of your will could always hold at the same time as a principle establishing universal law." [49] This is most often taken to mean simply that we can apply a good common-sense criterion to all of our proposed actions and, by projecting them on a cosmic scale, see if the intended act would dissolve society or not. This superficial interpretation is not altogether wrong. Like Descartes and Aristotle before him, Kant would like to elicit common opinion on his side. Most moralists prefer to show that their principles are really only the profound grounds of common beliefs, rather than throw the field open to revolution. [50] But the whole point of this formulation of the categorical imperative resides in the criterion that distinguishes universal and necessarily obligating principles of willful action: They are grounded in *reason*, the *form* of all experience residing in the unity of consciousness itself. The ethical doctrine of the categorical imperative has to be understood in terms of the positive discoveries of the *Critique of Pure Reason*.

A moment ago we saw that Kant envisioned the effort to attain a holy will as a struggle in which pure practical reason would play the central role of offering "resistance" to the "empirical" will. Here is where those "pure ideas" of reason which proved chimeric in the theoretical order come to ultimate practical fruition. Take for instance this question of the need to progress indefinitely toward the holiness of will.

> Complete fitness of the will to the moral law is holiness, which is a perfection of which no rational being in the world of sense is at any time capable. But since it is required as practically necessary, it can be found only in an endless progress toward that complete fitness; on principles of pure practical reason, it is necessary *to assume* [italics ours] such a practical progress as the real object of our will.[51]

The idea of the substantial, immortal soul, for which there was no corresponding intuition in the speculative order, finds a place now as a postulate of practical reason. So, too, do the other two pure ideas. The existence of God is postulated as necessary, because only the infinite, divine knower could ever encompass the whole sweep of our finite moral strivings and recognize (and validate) it as the human equivalent of holiness. We have already seen how the third postulate, freedom, furnishes the very atmosphere of morality; without presupposing that the will can in its self-determination stand free of the chains of causal mechanism in the world, the "ought" of practical reason would be devoid of sense.

Practical reason's need of these postulates "assertorically assures" the existence of the objects postulated, thus justifying theoretical reason for having assumed them. This "extension" of theoretical reason, however, is not an extension of speculation—a positive use cannot be made of those objects for theoretical purposes. "For nothing more has been accomplished by practical reason than to show that those concepts are real and actually have (possible) objects, but no intuitions of these objects are thereby given." Kant further explains, "knowledge is compelled to concede that there are such objects without more exactly defining them." [52] Rather than an extension of knowledge, this permits a purification of it, for reason can now reject, on the one hand, the "anthropomorphism" of the materialists who would deny freedom, immortality, and God, and on the other, the "superstition and fanaticism" of the idealists who promise an extension of knowledge "through supersensuous intuitions and feelings." [53]

Kant's Copernican revolution is complete—or almost so. Morality does not so much depend on God as God depends on moral experience. Needless to say, such an outlook can be accompanied by nothing loftier than a natural, rationalistic religion, one which goes no farther than what can be interpolated on the grounds of the practical postulates. We say that the Copernican revolution was *almost* completed, for it remained to Fichte to make the unqualified identification of the reality of God with the immanent moral law. Kant had wanted to suggest that God was more than a postulate of moral experience, but he provided no grounds for resisting the absolute identification of the one with the other; Fichte made it. Future exploration of the grounds of morality will have only one direction to follow, without breaking free of this tradition altogether: glorification of the will as ground of all "reality" in our representations. Schopenhauer and Nietzsche will push this possibility to its extreme.

The *Critique of Judgment*

IN KANT'S ORIGINAL PLAN for the critical philosophy, only the two *Critiques* of the theoretical and the practical orders were foreseen.[54] Kant quite early accepted the eighteenth-century division of our faculties into understanding, feeling, and will, but he had esteemed feeling to have little to do with the ultimate philosophical principles; feelings, he thought, are simply too empirical to be critically significant.

But the way the two *Critiques* evolved convinced Kant that the critical philosophy *needed* a third principle to save itself. For the two *Critiques*, as finally developed, seemed to have an effect very different from what Kant desired: they tended to leave the impression that man is split between two worlds: the phenomenal world of the theoretical understanding and the noumenal, practical world of will. Could a synthesizing principle be found between reason and will, somewhat the way imagination proved the perfect mediator between sensibility and understanding in the first *Critique*? Could the third faculty of mind—feeling—perhaps play such a mediating role?

Actually, the hope of showing the deep-down unity of the theoretical and practical faculties in the same human existence is not so difficult as might seem at first glance. Both theoretical and practical reason had been shown to furnish a structuring unity. In the theoretical order, the ideas of reason guide the understanding in the unification of a manifold of experience under its concepts; what is more, the reason moves inevitably toward the ideal of an absolute unification of all knowledge under its ideas. While this ideal unification has been shown to have objective limitations in the phenomenal order, it found a sense in the noumenal, practical order of will. There, too, there is initiative of unification; to wit, the unifying legislation of freedom. For this freedom, the ideas of reason were discovered to possess the necessity of practical postulates.

What a third *Critique* can do, then, is bring to light the common principle of these two sorts of unifying activity; a proper criticism of such activity should reveal the ultimate nature and limits of our grasp of the world. The principle common to both theoretical and practical reason is *judgment*, which is properly the act of unifying experience and idea, whether the experience is subsumed under concepts of the understanding, as it is in the theoretical order, or whether freedom is seeking to impose an order guided by the ideas of reason, as is the case in the practical sphere. In the activity of judgment in either order, there is operative what we might for the moment call a *supposition*, the critical examination of which should prove very revealing of the ultimate sense of our cognition. That supposition is the *teleological idea*—the supposition that nature meets the requirements of our knowledge by obligingly being in itself *a system*. It is very obvious that science's quest for a unity of conception presupposes that its object— nature—is in itself a unity. Now that the two *Critiques* have brought to light the ground of the real principle of unity, and it is discovered to be the consciousness itself, it would appear that the idea of the world as a teleological unity, then, is only just that, *an idea*. Given their phenomenality, we cannot intuit objectively a purposiveness and order in things themselves. But in *feelings* of the *beautiful* and the *sublime* we experience a harmony of our faculties, a union of the ideas of reason and the freedom of will which suggests through the phe-

nomenal itself a deeper reality. It is this sort of experience, so emphasized by the Lessings and the Baumgartens[55] of the last half of the
eighteenth century, that Kant wants to scrutinize in its ground through
the Third *Critique*.

THE FEELING OF THE BEAUTIFUL

THE JUDGMENT that an object is beautiful involves a feeling of
pleasure, but is "disinterested," because the pleasure involved does not
come from possession of a good—it is not a moral or practical consideration; rather the pleasure comes from "the state of the mind which
goes along with the relation of our faculties with one another." The
pleasure is the enjoyment of the free play of our faculties. What produces this in such an experience, and what is its significance?

What happens in an experience of the beautiful is that the imagination puts together a manifold of perception, with understanding supplying the unity of the conception connecting the elements of the
idea, but in such a way that these faculties are not tied down to a
strict rule, as they would be in, for example, a mathematical operation.
The object is simply concrete; the form involved is aesthetic, so that
the center of the experience is not an abstract conception, but a concrete unification of a manifold. Yet the object enjoys a certain
necessity; when I experience the beautiful I feel as though this beauty
ought to be felt by everyone the same way. I cannot *argue* the point,
for there is no universal conception upon which to argue it; but I cannot help feeling that anyone else who would experience this object
would also find it beautiful. The judgment of beauty really expresses
the relationship of the object to a knowing subject, not the relationship
of this object to other objects; hence the feeling it produces is subjective, and its universality is based in the universality of the subjectivity in
all knowers; that is to say, when I experience in my grasp of this thing
that *proportionirte Stimmung*, that feeling of something being wonderfully adapted to an end, what I am experiencing is not a thing-in-itself
perfectly functioning toward an objective end, but my faculties themselves working together perfectly toward their end, which end is that
very act of unification constituted by knowledge in action, and which
makes being come to be.[56]

The judgment of beauty is so intimately associated with a certain pleasure in the elements of the beautiful thing, or again with an emotion accompanying perception of some perfection, that it is often confused with one or the other of these. The *Reiz* (charm, attractiveness) of a pure color or a pure tone is something that accompanies the *matter* of an experience of beauty—but only the matter; while the judgment itself has to do with the form—the actual interplay of powers that brings about the *formal* unification which alone constitutes the knowledge. The appreciation of the perfection of a kind—e.g., of a "perfect man"—involves more than the beautiful; it brings in the *Good* as well; that is, conformity with an objective standard. The beautiful combined with the Good can affect us powerfully, to be sure, but it must be critically recognized that such an experience involves more than the beautiful as such.

Kant sums up his analysis of the judgment of the beautiful in this formula, "Taste or the sense of beauty is a faculty for judging an object in relation to that *free agreement with law* which is characteristic of the imagination." [57] Freedom and law might at first seem opposed, just as the structuring carried out by the conceptions of the understanding in the theoretical order at first seems difficult to relate to the spontaneity of freedom; which in turn, until the Second *Critique* had done its work, seemed difficult to reconcile with the need to be beholden to a necessary and objective law. But now the sense of all these moments of our experience is converging; they all reveal the fundamental nature of human existence as *legislating*; they all reveal the guiding role of the *noumenal* as ultimate substratum for the unity of the *phenomenal*. That is why the critical inquiry always comes back to the same fundamental question: What is the validity of this legislation as far as relations with the thing-in-itself are concerned?

THE SENTIMENT OF THE SUBLIME

THE MUCH RARER ENCOUNTER of the "sublime" is particularly suggestive of the ultimate nature of our cognition. Like the feeling of beauty, it is a singular judgment which yet claims universal assent. But in many another way it is very different from the judgment of beauty.

The feeling of beauty implies form and limitation. But the sublime, the formless and unlimited, or rather the self-limited, whole, utterly escapes our ability to grasp it by the imagination; we cannot *picture* it, we only *think* it absolutely. When I experience the beauty of the pattern of filigree and jewels that constitutes a Carolingian bracelet, the conception of the understanding is to the fore in the grasp of that form; but when I stand on the shore of a storm-wrenched ocean, I feel that this is beyond the comprehension of the imagination or of any conception, I feel momentarily overwhelmed; but then I realize that I am not really engulfed by it, rather that my mind is after all capable of encompassing it in *idea*. From the moment of temporary *échec* I surge forward to the realization of the ultimacy of the reason which can stand up to such things. The resultant feeling is the sentiment of the sublime. The beautiful seems to reinforce the life that is in us, while the sublime seems to challenge it, but then we realize that we are masters of the challenge. The sublime objects "raise the energies of the soul above their accustomed height, and discover in us a faculty of resistance of a quite different kind, which gives us courage to measure ourselves against the apparent almightiness of nature." [58] Its moral importance is obvious: "It calls up in us that power of regarding as small the things about which we are solicitous (goods, health and life), and of regarding its might as without any domination over us and our personality. . . . Nature is here called sublime merely because it elevates the imagination to a presentation of those cases in which the mind can make felt the proper sublimity of its destination, in comparison with nature itself." [59]

All of which will sound like mere moral exhortation if we lose sight of the deep critical sense of what Kant is here bringing to light. The experience of the sublime is the privilege of cultured souls with a capacity for Ideas and a developed moral character. "The mind must already be filled with manifold Ideas if it is to be determined by such an intuition to a feeling itself sublime, as it is incited to abandon sensibility and to busy itself with Ideas that involve higher purposiveness." [60] The sublime is the immeasurably great. In confronting an experience which the imagination cannot encompass by simply adding on the units by which we normally judge quantitative greatness, we are thrown back on the resources of reason to think a properly inconceivable infinite. The very fact that the reason can think this infinite (even though it cannot be represented sensibly) shows that the human mind is itself a supersensible faculty. "It is only by means of this faculty and its Idea of a noumenon—which admits of no intuition, but which yet serves as the substrate for the intuition of the world, as a mere phenomenon—that the infinite of the world of sense, in the pure intellectual estimation of magnitude, can be completely comprehended under one concept, although in the mathematical estimation of magnitude by means of concepts of number it can never be completely thought." [61] The feeling of the sublime is, then, the occasion for the reason to discover itself as noumenal substratum of the phenomenal world; the formlessness and the immensity of the "infinite" sublimity is nothing but the consciousness' confrontation of itself.

The sentiment of the sublime is indeed dramatic, but actually Kant does not consider it "nearly so important or rich in consequences" as the concept of the beautiful. "In what we are accustomed to call the sublime there is nothing at all that leads to particular objective principles and forms of nature corresponding to them; so far from it that for the most part nature excites the ideas of the sublime in its chaos or in its wildest and most irregular disorder and desolation, provided size and might are perceived." [62] On the other hand, when we encounter "independent natural beauty" we discover a "technique of nature" which represents it as a system in accordance with laws, the principle of which seems to transcend our faculty of understanding; we are brought to think of nature more as an affair of art than as a mere mechanism. "This leads to profound investigations as to the possibility of such a form." [63] Because it leads us to the very fruitful idea that the thing-in-itself might be structured teleologically just as our phenomenal grasp of it must be, the experience of the beautiful is of the greatest significance. But let us state once again (in the Third *Critique* it is stated many times, in many different contexts) the gist of that significance: It is not objective; i.e., it does not reveal to us that nature has fashioned its forms for our satisfaction; rather the purposiveness there encountered is a subjective purposiveness depending upon the play of the imagination in its freedom, "where it is we who receive nature with favor, not nature which shows us favor." [64] It is its *subjectivity* which gives it validity for everyone. So to state is but to rediscover in the heart of the aesthetic experience the First *Critique*'s great revelation: that the ground of all universal necessity (i.e., the ground of the objectivity of scientific judgments) is in the transcendental subjectivity. [65]

THE CRITIQUE OF TELEOLOGICAL JUDGMENT

THE OTHER ASPECT of the Third *Critique*'s quest of indications of the noumenal in the phenomenal is an inquiry into the supposition of a teleological order in nature. Does nature "really" unfold according to a plan? Is nature "really" an artifact and not just a mechanism? The presence of organic things strongly suggests that there really are ends pursued in nature. And it is evident that scientists are in some way successful in proceeding according to the supposition that there is such a design in the objects they study.

But Kant is not ready to budge an inch beyond the critical position that was leveled in 1781 against the "teleological argument." We will recall that this argument was found to be perfectly respectable but not objectively valid. The same may now be said of Kant's final judgment concerning design in nature. He explains the reason *why* the mind is led to seek design there. It is because, when the mind proceeds from the universal to the particular, the particular takes on the position of an accident in relation to the universal. Thus, if the accidental could be seen to conform to law, our experience would gain in necessity all the way to its perceptual extremes. Now the conformity of the accidental to law means its adaptation to an end; hence, declares Kant, the idea of a design of nature in its products is necessary to us, not as a conception which determines objects, but as a principle to regulate our reflection upon them. The only way our finite minds can conceive of a reality that would form a necessary whole is to think of the form and connection of the parts as dependent on the *conception* of the whole, on a super-design. Thus our reason uses the idea of design to bridge the gap between the particular and the universal; but, in so doing, it is acting on a subjective principle, one which need not hold good for the divine intelligence, and hence need not hold true for the things-in-themselves. The conception of design thus has only a *"heuristic"* value; that is, it aids us in putting questions to nature. But it itself cannot answer anything.

It is then simply due to the nature of our knowledge that, in trying to think of the relationship of the parts to the whole in nature we must fall back on conceiving it after the model of our own purposive activity; i.e., teleologically. The mind thus rejects the notion that nature is just a working juxtaposition of parts. To us the teleological and mechanical conceptions of nature will always seem radically opposed. But Kant leaves us with the thought that in the thing-in-itself it may be that the mechanical and the teleological are reconciled in some kind of organization we cannot possibly conceive of.

What, then, has the *Critique of Judgment* accomplished? It has certainly not reversed the *Critique of Pure Reason*'s verdict against all metaphysical pretense of transcending the limits of empirical knowledge and pronouncing on the thing-in-itself. On the contrary, after examining the experiences most likely to carry with them a feeling of "the ultimate," the last *Critique* reconfirms that such a contact with the depths is really nothing but the experience of our faculty of knowledge enjoying its own legislating activity. The *Critique of Judgment* not only points up the deepest sense of the two preceding *Critiques* by bringing out in full relief the ultimate, law-giving nature of the judgment; but (and this is of greatest importance for its effect on the whole of German intellectual culture) it also brings explicitly within the ken of the transcendental critique the whole sphere of the aesthetic and the teleological. In so doing, it became the first subsumption of the German *Aufklärung*'s very original poetic insights into the horizons of a fundamental and radically new philosophy—a system of thought working explicitly from the transcendental point of view. The *Critique of Judgment* was heavy with implications for that extraordinary generation of philosophers who were to follow Kant in the early years of the next century; Fichte, Schelling, and Hegel could see in this book a hint that the exploration of phenomena from the point of view Kant had inaugurated had tremendous possibilities. Fichte will then seek to tighten the unity of the whole enterprise, as he works toward a system of identity; Schelling will begin an expansion of its consideration to cover history, religion, the state—in fact, the whole vast field of culture; a process Hegel will complete in a towering synthesis that completes the task of putting Being under the seal of time. The subjectivization of the philosophical enterprise begun by Montaigne and Descartes will come to a climax, in the writings of the post-Kantians, as Being is made one with the historical march of the Spirit unveiling reality through the interpretation of time.

But practical necessity dictates that we punctuate our story somewhere. There are no breaks in the history of philosophy as neat as the slice of Robespierre's guillotine. Kant is equally the climax of the tradition we have been studying and the beginning of the story we shall tell in the next volume. He is the necessary rendezvous of the whole historical destiny of European philosophy and science since the Middle Ages. Kant's three *Kritiks* form the post and lintel of the Great Door into the era of temporality, relativity, and *Ek-sistenz*.

Conclusion

THE SIXTEENTH CENTURY had witnessed the end of a philosophical age—not just that of scholasticism—rather, it was really the end of the age of Greek philosophy. All the technical material used by the Christian philosophers and theologians, from Augustine to Marsilio Ficino, had been dug out of Plato, Aristotle, and Plotinus. The earlier sixteenth-century philosophers had turned to Epicureanism, to Stoicism, and to Greek skepticism; that is, they were still living on the philosophical heritage bequeathed by antiquity. But during the same century, science was entering new ways and making startling progress. Mathematics, astronomy, physics, biology progressively assumed the modern form under which they are still developing.

That birth of modern science was the decisive factor in the rise of modern philosophy. The scientific sterility of Aristotle's logical method contrasted unfavorably with the extraordinary fecundity of the new methods developed by Copernicus, Galileo, and Kepler. In consequence, philosophy underwent a twofold change. First, it detached itself from theology because, under its scholastic form, it had become entangled with the now-abandoned Aristotelian physics; secondly, it asked from the newly founded or reformed sciences of nature new methods of philosophical investigation similar to their own.

Science itself was proceeding in two different ways, according as scientists were stressing the mathematical method or the empirical methods of observation. Scientists have always known that both are necessary for an intelligible formulation of positively established facts, but some men are more gifted for mathematical deduction, others for factual observation. Hence two distinct interpretations of the "true" philosophical method; the one, following the pattern of the mathematicism of Descartes, is exemplified by the *Discourse on Method*; the other, inspired by the empiricism of the sciences of nature, by the *De Augmentis Scientiarum* of Francis Bacon.

To the influence of Descartes' mathematicism is due the metaphysical geniuses who dominate the second half of the seventeenth century and the first half of the eighteenth: after Descartes himself, Malebranche, Spinoza, Leibniz, and Wolff. All metaphysicians, they were nonetheless deeply versed in mathematics, some of them in a creative way (Descartes, Leibniz), the others, at least capable of sharing competently in a critical discussion of scientific results. Malebranche was a fellow of the French Academy of Sciences, and two volumes of his mathematical works are now being published for the first time. When Christian Wolff addressed his works to his French peers, he used to send them, not to the French Academy, the traditional seat of literary culture, but to the Academy of Sciences. The dictionaries still label Christian Wolff "a philosopher and mathematician."

In the beginning, the empirical tradition was overshadowed by the metaphysical pyrotechnics of the Cartesian school of thought, but the application of the biological method of observation to the structure and operations of the human mind finally reversed the situation. Owing to John Locke, Baconian empiricism was to become the driving force of the eighteenth century as visibly as the mathematicism of Descartes had been the dominant influence in the philosophy of the seventeenth. The conflict between those two forces came to a head in the *New Essays* directed by Leibniz against the *Essay* of Locke. As a philosopher, Locke did not compare with Leibniz, but he was working in the direction of history, and he carried the day. Consistently applied by Hume, the method reduced the human mind to an agglomeration of sensations and of associated images innocent of all intellectual necessity. When the Scottish school of common sense reacted against the generalized skepticism begotten by the doctrine, its founder vainly attempted to cure the psychologism of Locke by one more dose of psychologism. In France, Condillac tried to systematize the method of Locke in order to turn its results into a well-ordered whole. The success of the doctrine was to be prodigious. In fact, we shall see it dominate French and Italian ideology during the first third of the nineteenth century, although the method could lead neither to a legitimate metaphysics nor to a truly scientific psychology. Still, it is found everywhere at work in the French and English eighteenth century, truly the century of "the wise Locke." The reason for his triumph was simply, as Condillac put it, that "Locke was greater than Descartes, Malebranche and Leibniz precisely because he was the only one of them who was *not* a mathematician."

On one point, however, the two schools of thought were in deep agreement, their worship of reason. How could it be otherwise, since all these philosophers agreed that the method of philosophy and that of the sciences of nature were one and the same? The result was the kind of diffused rationalism typical of the eighteenth century, a rationalism that termed itself the *Philosophie des Lumières, Aufklärung,* or *Enlightenment.* The Goddess Reason was to be worshiped by the French revolutionaries of 1784; and it already was the object of a cult in the mind of the so-called *philosophes,* and the *Encyclopédie* of Diderot already formed the sacred book of the new cult. The elimination of all the non-rational elements in thought and in life—in short of all that Voltaire detested under the hated names of "superstition" and "fanaticism"—was but the negative and often blind aspect of a much nobler feeling which he shared in common with the "encyclopedists": the quasi-religious expectation of a new era of knowledge, of progress, and of happiness, when all men would enjoy the pleasures of an enlightened rational life. With, of course, differences owing to their various educations, times, and personal dispositions, Descartes, Leibniz, Spinoza, Wolff, and many others were of one mind with d'Alembert and Voltaire. The times were indeed ripe for the programmatic treatise of Kant *On Religion within the Limits of Reason.*

Kant's significance cannot be exaggerated. His philosophy makes no sense apart from the two centuries of speculation which it brings to a climactic conclusion. From Descartes to Wolff, the modern philosophers had remained convinced that, although they themselves were following methods inspired by those of the positive sciences, they still could uphold and justify metaphysical conclusions. They all proved the existence of God and at least the possibility of the immortality of the soul. In short, they all maintained the validity of metaphysical knowledge as properly "scientific" in its own right. But Kant's lucid insight led him to the realization that, starting from the methods of science, one could not hope to obtain anything else than scientific cognitions. Physics cannot beget metaphysics.

In his philosophical rationalism, Kant is a typical representative of the Enlightenment, and by far the greatest; but it was his privilege, without sinning against his own rationalism, to include in his ample doctrinal synthesis another aspect of the spiritual aspirations of his time. For Kant composed Hume with Rousseau.

The poet Heinrich Heine has represented Kant as very much put out at the thought that, as a result of the *Critique of Pure Reason*, his faithful manservant, Lampe, would be left without either soul or God. Hence he wrote the *Critique of Practical Reason*, so that poor Lampe could be compensated for the loss. This of course is another of Heine's witticisms, but still a grain of truth is hidden in it. In the second *Critique*, Kant attempted a rational justification of Rousseau's faith in the absolute value of the human person, and even perhaps of his deep-seated anti-rationalism. What Rousseau had called the "immortal and heavenly voice of conscience" would henceforward be called "moral obligation" and "voice of duty." In making that decision, Kant was doing much more than showing a sense of expediency; he was rightly doing justice to the ardent aspirations of so many *âmes sensibles* whom the dry purity of the Enlightenment could not wholly satisfy. Even the *Critique of Judgment*, in a sense the most original of the three *Critiques*, was helping to complete the *summa philosophiae* wherein Kant was including and ordering the leading tendencies of his own century. In all those domains, and at a philosophical level reached by no one else since the death of Leibniz, he was concluding the debate opened by the mathematical rationalism of Descartes. In his own sight, at least, such was the meaning of his work.

The eighteenth century was too rich in conflicting tendencies for any single doctrine to include them all adequately. Often developing on the periphery of the technical philosophical world—and sometimes even quite outside it—these forces are destined nevertheless to affect it in its deepest soul. Take the case of romanticism, for instance. To rationalize Rousseau was, ultimately, to betray him. Already at work in the sentimental novels of the English writers, the energies of affectivity had suddenly exploded in Rousseau's *Nouvelle Héloïse*. One cannot write the history of philosophy in the age of romanticism, in Germany as well as in France, without tracing it to its eighteenth-century origins.

A second force at work in the last years of the century was nationalism. In many ways, it was a new feeling. Men have always loved their own city and their own country, but cosmopolitanism was traditionally the normal attitude of writers, philosophers, and scientists. To be an Encyclopedist was to be a "citizen of the world." In Germany, Goethe and even Schiller did not feel differently. This is so true that, today, German historians are at a loss to account for the amazing statements made by Goethe on that point.[1] Nationalism, a feeling very different from patriotism, consisted precisely in attributing to the nation an absolute value in itself. To be "national," either as a feeling or as a product, whether intellectual, agricultural, or industrial, is by the same token to be good. To a large extent, the French Revolution of 1789 was a rebellion of the feeling of loyalty to France as a nation against the feeling of loyalty to the French king as a person. Propagated by the armies of Napoleon I throughout Europe, nationalism begot the "principle of nationalities," the consequences of which are still developing in our own day. Germany, still in the eighteenth century a political chaos of uncoordinated local tyrannies, began to move toward political unity, while the *risorgimento* was likewise driving divided Italy toward a unified monarchy. In both cases romanticism and nationalism joined forces to bring about a post-revolutionary era in European culture, especially in the field of philosophical speculation. At the same moment, America was entering the field of philosophical speculation in conjunction with the Encyclopedists and beginning to add a new branch to the old tree of Western culture. The nineteenth and twentieth centuries will witness its full growth.

The birth of the social sciences, under their modern form, is a third element of continuity between the eighteenth and the nineteenth century. With Vico's *New Science*, Montesquieu's *Esprit des lois*, and Voltaire's *Essai sur les moeurs*, a new field of research had been opened to scientific investigation. With Comte and his successors, modern sociology was to grow from that seed. Still more important, perhaps, political economy was defining its own field and methods at the same time that Great Britain was experiencing an industrial revolution that was soon to migrate to northern America and that was probably more significant than the political revolution in France. Karl Marx is surely an offspring of both the industrial revolution and the eighteenth-century political economy. Without Adam Smith, there would have been no Karl Marx. In short, the nineteenth century was to witness no new departure in any way comparable with the radical breaking away from scholasticism at the time of Bacon and Descartes, but a distinctly new era was about to begin within the modern age itself. We ourselves still are in that new era. Only a prophet could say how far we are from its end.

NOTES
AND
REFERENCES

GENERAL BIBLIOGRAPHY

M. Frischeisen-Köhler and Willy Moog, *Die Philosophie der Neuzeit bis zum Ende des XVIII. Jahrhunderts*, 14 ed., Basel/Stuttgart, Benno Schwabe, 1957. This is the Third Part of Friedrich Ueberweg's *Grundriss der Geschichte der Philosophie;* fundamental.

Wilhelm Windelband, *Die Geschichte der neueren Philosophie in ihrem Zusammenhang mit der allgemeinen Kultur und den besonderen Wissenschaften.* Vol. I, Von der Renaissance bis Kant, 5 ed., Leipzig, 1911; Vol. II, Die Blütezeit der deutschen Philosophie, 4 ed., Leipzig, 1907. English translation by J. H. Tufts, *A History of Philosophy*, New York, 1952.

Harald Höffding, *A History of Modern Philosophy*, translated by B. E. Meyer, London, Macmillan and Company, 1900, 2 vols.; New York, Dover Publications Inc., 1955, 2 vols.

Émile Bréhier, *Histoire de la philosophie*, II, La philosophie moderne, première partie, XVIIe et XVIIIe siècles, Paris, F. Alcan, n.d.; revised edition in preparation.

James Collins, *A History of Modern European Philosophy*, Milwaukee, The Bruce Publishing Co., 1954.

Frederick Copleston, S.J., *A History of Philosophy*, vol. IV, Descartes to Leibniz; vol. V, Hobbes to Hume; vol. VI, Wolff to Kant, Westminster, Maryland, The Newman Press, 1959-1960.

Jacques Chevalier, *Histoire de la Pensée*, vol. III, De Descartes à Kant, Paris, Flammarion, 1961.

On the general evolution of ideas in the seventeenth and eighteenth centuries: Bernard Fay, *L'esprit révolutionnaire en France et aux Etats Unis au dixhuitième siècle*, Paris, Champion, 1925.—Paul Hazard, *La crise de la conscience européenne, 1680-1715*, Paris, Boivin, 1935, 3 vols.—Same author, *La pensée européenne au dixhuitième siècle*, Paris, Boivin, 1946, 3 vols.

Notes

PART 1   THE DAWN OF MODERN TIMES

1. The Breakdown of Aristotelianism

1. GIORDANO BRUNO, b. Nola (Italy), 1548; d. Rome, 1600. Entered the Dominican Order; left it in 1575, then led a wandering life from city to city and was unwelcome everywhere on account of his unusual opinions. In 1580 at Geneva, he embraced Calvinism, but being unable to put up with Calvin, he went to Lyon, to Toulouse, and to Paris (1582-1583); then to London (1584) and to Paris again (1585). From France he went to Germany and Bohemia. In 1592 he was heedless enough to return to Italy, where he lived in comparative peace until 1598, when he was arrested, sentenced to death, and burnt at the stake in 1600 after refusing to retract his opinions.

All his works were published within ten years, from 1582 to 1591. His doctrine is not easy to systematize, as he borrows from many different sources. Still it has a loose unity of its own, owing chiefly to the predominance of a Platonist and Neo-platonist influence, but since he feels free to speak the language of several different philosophies in order to express one and the same notion, one is liable to get lost in trying to follow him. Thus, in one single verse of his *De immenso*, describing the first cause of being and first source of all forms, superior to all things and yet more intimate to each one of them than itself is to itself, Bruno calls it, at once, "Mind, God, Being, One, True, Fate, Word, Order." Whatever its name, this first principle and cause, unknowable for us such as it is in itself, is attained by us as inner life of the universe, which itself is a living being. Because God is infinite, his created image, the world, must needs also be infinite. Bruno conceives it as made up of elementary units which can be called atoms, provided we understand them as indivisible points of energy which it is hard not to compare with the "monads" of Leibniz. Two tendencies very active in the minds of the sixteenth century thus combine in Bruno's view of the world (as they do in that of several of his contemporaries): animism and a metaphysical atomism. A table, a garment is not animate as table or garment, but it is made up of elements that themselves live an obscure, but real, elementary life. Since everything is ultimately permeated by the same life (world-soul), a sort of natural magic is possible; all things may be produced from all because the same soul exists in all entities.

Among Bruno's main works, besides those devoted to the doctrine of Ramon Lull (Great Art): *Della causa, principio ed uno* (London, 1584). *Dell'infinito, dell'universo e dei mondi* (London, 1584). *De monade, numero et figura* (1591). *La cena delle ceneri*, ed. G. Aquilecchia (Torino: Einaudi, 1955). *Due dialoghi sconosciuti e due dialoghi noti: Idiota triumphans, De somnii interpretatione, Mordentius, De mordentii circino*, ed. G. Aquilecchia (Roma: Edizioni di Storia e Litteratura, 1957).

Collective editions: *Opera latine conscripta* (3 vols.; Naples, 1879-1891). *Opere italiane*, ed. Giovanni Gentile (3 vols.; Bari, 1907-1909). *Dialoghi italiani. Dialoghi metafisici e dialoghi morali* . . . con note da Giovanni Gentile, 3d ed., by G. Aquilecchia (Firenze: Sansoni, 1958).

Doctrinal: D. W. Singer, *Giordano Bruno: His Life and Thought* (New York: Schuman, 1950). L. Cicuttini, *Giordano Bruno* (Milan: Vita e Pensiero, 1950). Niccola Badaloni, *La filosofia di Giordano Bruno* (Firenze: Parenti, 1955). Ernesto Baldi, *Giordano Bruno* (Firenze: L. Gonnelli, 1955). John C. Nelson, *Renaissance Theory of Love. The Context of Giordano Bruno's Eroici Furori* (New York: Columbia University Press, 1958).

Bibliographical: V. Salvestrini, *Bibliografia di Giordano Bruno, 1582-1958*, 2d ed., by Luigi Firpo (Firenze: Sansoni Antiquariato, 1958).

2. BERNARDINO TELESIO, b. and d. Cosenza (Italy), 1509-1588. Studied at the University of Padua, then the most flourishing center of philosophical and scientific studies. Nev-

ertheless, Telesio escaped the domineering influence of the various branches of Peripateticism taught at that university. He himself taught at Naples, but he got himself in trouble when he began to publish his first works. Telesio conceives nature as mainly consisting of two elements: a passive one, matter, and an active one, of corporeal nature, capable of expansion and of contraction. Expanding, it is heat; contracting, it is cold. All corporeal qualities can be accounted for by this twofold motion. The more subtle and refined part of that active force is the spirit that causes in man sensations and discursive reasoning. The spirit then is corporeal in nature. On the contrary, mind (*mens*) is immaterial; it is the immortal element in man. Telesio has influenced his successors in his capacity as representative of a reaction against the *a priori* and abstract method followed by the Peripatetics in interpreting nature. In accordance with his own philosophy he himself favors an empirical method of observation: "One should not investigate the structure of the world, nor the dimensions and nature of the bodies it contains by means of reason, as was done by the Ancients (*non ratione, quod antiquioribus factum est*), but one should perceive it by means of sense; it must be obtained from things themselves (*et ab ipsis habendum esse rebus*)." It is this aspect of his philosophy which has interested Francis Bacon in his *De principiis atque originibus secundum fabulas Cupidinis et Coeli: sive Parmenidis et Telesii et praecipue Democriti philosophi tractata in fabula de Cupidine* (Fr. Bacon, *Philosophical Works*, ed. Ellis and Spedding, Vol. III, pp. 63-118).

The main work of Telesio is his

De rerum natura iuxta propria principia, 1565. New edition by Spampanato, in the collection "Filosofi Italiani" (Modena, 1910).

Doctrinal: Giovanni Gentile, *Bernardino Telesio* (Bari, 1911).

3. TOMMASO CAMPANELLA, b. Stilo (Calabria, Italy), 1568; d. Paris, 1639. Entered the Dominican Order, read the works of Telesio and fell under his influence; wrote a book in defense of the empiricism of Telesio: *Philosophia sensibus demonstrata*, 1590; finding life difficult for him in Dominican convents, wandered throughout Italy. Haunted by his dream of a universal society and actively engaged in the task of promoting it, he was arrested for political conspiracy and put in jail, where he spent twenty-seven years. Pope Urban VIII set him free on grounds of incomplete mental responsibility. Still full of his reformatory projects in the political as well as the philosophical orders, Campanella sought refuge in France, where he was pensioned by Richelieu and spent the last years of his life in a peace he had never known. These last years (1626-1639) were years of intense literary activity.

Campanella kept up the distinction introduced by Telesio between spirit (corporeal) and mind (incorporeal). Sensation is an alteration of sense by its object. No other faculty of the soul is required in order to account for the whole of knowledge; the same "spirit" feels, remembers, imagines, understands, and generalizes. Contrary to commonly received notions, general knowledge is inferior to particular knowledge, of which it is a weakened echo. On the other hand, having inherited and preserved the universal animism of Telesio, Campanella is led by his empiricism to see the world of science as full of secret influences and correspondences. One may well wonder how a philosophy in which all knowledge is sense knowledge ends in a kind of phantasmagoria. The answer is that to reason is to perceive the like in the like, and all things are like one another since they all resemble their common author, God. This law of universal analogy enables Campanella to build up a theology—a more classical one than might be imagined. Its main point: all that which is not the Trinity, is an image of the Trinity.

Leaving aside the political writings of Campanella, the following ones will be found typical of his philosophical outlook as distinct from that of Telesio: *Prodromus philosophiae instaurandae* (Frankfort, 1618); *De sensu rerum et magis*, 1620 (very important); *Realis philosophiae epilogisticae partes IV* (Frankfort, 1623) (this volume includes the famous utopia, *Civitas Solis* [the City of the Sun] in its Latin redaction). Several parts of the *Theologicorum* have recently been published by Romano Amerio in Rome: *Theologicorum liber XIV* (Magia e grazia) (Roma, 1957). *Theologicorum liber II* (De sancta triade) (Roma, 1958). *Theologicorum liber XVIII* (Cristologia) (Roma, 1958). *Theologicorum liber XVI* (Il peccato originale) (Roma: Centro Internazionale di Studi Umanistici, 1960).

Bibliography: Luigi Firpo, "Cinquant'anni di studi sul Campanella 1901-1950," in *Rinascimento*, 1955, pp. 209-348. To be supplemented by Francesco Gullo, "Tommaso Campanella in America" (New York: S. F. Vanni, 1957).

Biographical, Doctrinal: Léon Blanchet, *Campanella* (Paris, 1920). E. Gilson, "Le raisonnement par analogie chez Campanella," in *Etudes de philosophie médiévale* (Strasbourg, 1921), pp. 125-145. G. di Napoli, *Tommaso Campanella: Filosofo della restaurazione Cattolica* (Padua: Cedam, 1947). L. Firpo, *Ricerche campanelliane* (Firenze: Sansoni, 1947). Bernardino M. Bonansea, O.F.M., "Campanella as a Forerunner of Descartes," in *Franciscan Studies*, 1956, pp. 37-59. Same author, "The Concept of Being and Non-Being in the Philosophy of Campanella," in *New Scholasticism*, 1957, pp. 34-67.

4. GUILLAUME DU VAIR, b. Paris, 1556; d. Toneins, 1621. After a brilliant and agitated political career, Du Vair became President of the Parliament of Provence, chancellor of the kingdom in 1615, a position he occupied, except for the time of a short disgrace, until his death in 1621. The chronology of his works is uncertain because several of their first editions are lost. At an unknown date, he had been ordained a priest, then he had become Bishop of Marseille (1603) and later of Lisieux. Leaving aside his purely religious works, Du Vair wrote *La Sainte Philosophie* (c. 1580), first book written in French to put ancient philosophy at the service of Christianity; then the translation of the *Enchiridion* of Epictetus and *La philosophie morale des stoïques*, both c. 1585. His best-known work is *Traité de la constance et consolation ès calamités publiques*, 1590, new edition by J. Flach and Franz Funck-Brentano (Paris, 1915). He himself says in it he is not a stoic but a Christian; he only wants to make Christians feel ashamed of themselves by placing the virtues of the pagans under their very eyes. Several collective editions of his works, the best one being the posthumous edition of 1625. René Radouant, *Guillaume Du Vair, l'homme et l'orateur* (Paris, 1908). Léontine Zanta, *La renaissance du stoicisme au XVIe siècle* (Paris: Champion, 1914). An early English translation of Du Vair has recently been re-edited: *The Moral Philosophie of the Stoicks, Written in French by Guillaume Du Vair. Englished by Thomas James*, edited with introduction and notes by R. Kirk (New Brunswick: Rutgers University Press, 1951).

5. PIERRE CHARRON, b. and d. Paris, 1541-1603. First a successful barrister, then a priest and a famous preacher. Met Montaigne in Bordeaux, became his friend and disciple. A vicar-general of the cathedral of Condom (hence the often-used name, "the *théologal* of Condom"). A moralist, Charron used his gifts to elaborate a sort of apologetics; the materials of which he found in the Christian tradition, in Stoicism and in the skepticism of Montaigne. He published *Les trois vérités* (1593) in which he maintains against atheists that there is a God and a Providence; against deists, Jews, and Moslems that the true religion is the Christian religion; against the Protestants that the true church is the Catholic Church. Bossuet will avail himself of the material collected by Charron. Charron published *Discours chrétiens* in 1600 and *De la sagesse* (Bordeaux, 1601). There were objections; Charron revised the book, and the revised edition was published in 1604, one year after the author's death (November 6, 1603). Last reprint by Amaury-Duval (3 vols.; Paris, 1827).

In *De la sagesse*, Book I describes man, his faculties, passions, and conditions. This is done in the spirit of Montaigne (Charron had written on his own door: "Je ne sais").

In his own mind, the enemy was dogmatic scientism; but the weapon against it could be turned against religion, as in fact it often was in the first third of the seventeenth century. Book II lays down the general rules of wisdom. Book III defines particular rules for the practice of the four cardinal virtues. Charron's *Les trois vérités* had exposed religious truth, *La sagesse* had exposed philosophical truth; the seventeenth-century "libertines" read the second of these works only and, in it, they saw only the skeptical arguments. In Book II, chap. v., where Charron describes the frightening diversity of the known religions, all using similar arguments to justify different conclusions, the reader tends not to remember the arguments set forth by *Les trois vérités* in favor of Christianity. His impression is that all religions are equally false. This is the reason sound theologians do not consider skepticism good apologetics.

See Sabrié, *De l'humanisme au rationalisme, Pierre Charron* (Paris, 1913); also G. Lanson, "Charron" (art.), in *La Grande Encyclopédie*.

6. AGRIPPA OF NETTESHEIM (CORNELIUS), b. Cologne, 1486; d. Grenoble, 1533. Successively, or at the same time, a soldier, a professor, and a physician, also interested in occultism; he was jailed for a year in Brussels under an accusation of practicing magical arts. He took up the traditional position of the Christian apologist: Science and philoso-

phy are uncertain; besides, they are useless, since we have religion, which alone can lead man to beatitude (*De incertitudine et vanitate scientiarum declamatio invectiva*, 1527; French translation, 1582).

7. OMER TALON, author of *Audomari Talaei Academia . . .* (Paris, 1548). The attack of Talon's *Academia* against the uncertainty of natural knowledge freely draws on the well-known *Academica* of Cicero. The book is written in support of Ramus, who was attacking Aristotle. Talon objects to the Peripateticians who considered that to oppose Aristotle was the same as to oppose nature, truth, and God. Cf. W. Ong, S.J., *A Talon Inventory* (Cambridge: Harvard University Press, 1959).

RAMUS (Pierre de la Ramée), a professor at the present Collège de France, was attacking the peripatecians of all denominations, mainly, as it seems, because of the opposition he saw between the doctrine of Aristotle and Christian faith: *Scholarum metaphysicarum libri quatuordecim*, 1566. *Commentariorum de Religione Christiana libri IV*, 1576, etc.—On Ramus: Waddington, *Ramus et ses écrits* (Paris, 1856). W. Ong, S.J., *Ramus* (Cambridge: Harvard University Press, 1959).

8. FRANÇOIS SANCHEZ, b. Tuy (Spain), *c.* 1550; d. Toulouse, 1622: *Quod nil scitur*, 1581. *Opera philosophica*, ed. by J. de Carvalho (Coimbra, 1955).

II. Michel Eyquem de Montaigne

1. MICHEL DE MONTAIGNE, b. 1533, castle of Montaigne in Périgord; d. 1592, at the moment of elevation during a Mass said in his presence. Of a noble family, he himself lived the life of a nobleman, at times

holding public offices, among which the then heavy and dangerous one (religious wars) of mayor of Bordeaux. Translated into French *La théologie naturelle de Raymond Sebonde*, 1569. The first two books of the *Essays* were published at Bordeaux in 1580; Montaigne never ceased to revise and complete his work. When he died, he was preparing a sixth and enlarged edition by adding corrections and additions on a copy of the edition of 1588. Photostatic reproduction of that copy, 3 vols., 1912. Edition of the text of same, with all the additions and variants, by F. Strowski, F. Gebelin, and Pierre Villey, *Les Essais* (5 vols.; Bordeaux, 1906-1933) (three vols. of text, one vol. of notes by Pierre Villey, one vol. of lexicon by Grace Norton). An easily accessible edition in one volume is that of Albert Thibaudet (Paris: La Pléiade, 1933). English translation: *Complete Works. Essays, Travel Journal, Letters,* by Donald M. Frame (Stanford University Press, 1957). Same author, the *Essays* only (3 vols.; New York: Doubleday Anchor Books, 1960).

Biographical: Paul Bonnerot, *Montaigne et ses amis,* ed. (Paris: Colin, 1928).

Doctrinal: Fortunat Strowski, *Montaigne* (Paris, 1931). A. Cresson, *Montaigne* (Paris: Presses universitaires de France, 1947). D. M. Frame, *Montaigne's Discovery of Man* (New York: Columbia University Press, 1955).

2. *The Apology of Raymond Sebond,* p. 10.

3. Nietzsche's famous expression was already used by Montaigne.

4. *Essays,* III, 13.

5. A few days before his death, Montaigne's father asked him to translate a book of the Spanish theologian Sebond into French, which Montaigne did later with the more pleasure as, the book of Sebond being so badly written, he had nothing else to attend to but the meaning. We still have that translation (1569) and, along with it, his essay, Book II, chap. xii, entitled *An Apology for Raymond Sebond,* which he began in 1576 right after reading the *Pyrrhonian Hypotyposes* of Sextus Empiricus. The very same year he had a medal cast after his own project—on one side of it, his family crest; on the other side, a balance with its two scales perfectly level, the date 1576; his age, 42; and the Pyrrhonian motto: *Hepekho* (I abstain). Under the pretext of defending Sebond's natural theology, the leading theme of his *Apology* was that, since our intellect is so incapable of truly judging anything, there is no reason we should refuse to believe revelation, though its defenders fail to give valid proof of its truth. In order supposedly to justify religion, he revels in trampling rationalistic pride, to make pedants and professional thinkers feel the nothingness of human reason. This Montaigne achieves by showing the smallness of man in nature, how surrounded on all sides with natural mysteries the explanation of which escapes us. After contrasting the conclusions of the various philosophical sects, Montaigne concludes in favor of those who abstain from judging in such matters. As he says elsewhere: I do not know, is still too positive. True doubt carries itself away. Its best formula is: *Que sais-je?* I do not even know for sure that I do not know.

6. III, 13.

7. *Ibid.*

8. *Ibid.*

9. *Apology,* p. 156.

10. *Ibid.,* p. 187.

11. "I saw in Germany that Luther had left as many divisions and altercations on the doubt of his opinions and more than ever there were about the Holy Scripture" (III, 13).

12. I, 11.
13. I, 10.
14. Ibid.
15. Apology II, 12.
16. I, 25.
17. Ibid.
18. III, 13.
19. I, 36.
20. III, 13.
21. Ibid.

22. II, 11.
23. III, 12.
24. III, 13.
25. I, 40.
26. Ibid.
27. II, 11.
28. III, 13.
29. Ibid.
30. Ibid.

III. New Ways to Knowledge

1. GALILEO GALILEI, b. Pisa, 1564; d. Arcetri (near Florence), 1642. Educated in Florence and Pisa; met Christopher Clavius in Rome, 1587; taught at the University of Pisa, 1589; taught mathematics at the University of Padua; law of falling bodies, 1604; construction of telescope and first telescopic discoveries, 1609/10; tried and condemned by Inquisition, 1633; died in retirement.

Main works of philosophical interest: *Sidereus nuncius* (Venice, 1610). *Dialogo sopra i due Massimi Sistemi del Mondo: Tolemaico e Copernicano* (Florence, 1632) (translation by Giorgio de Santillana [Chicago, 1953], and by Stilman Drake [Berkeley, 1953]). *Nova-antiqua sanctissimorum patrum doctrina, de sacrae scripturae testimoniis in conclusionibus mere naturalibus* . . . (Strasbourg, 1635) (translated as *Letter to the Grand Duchess Christina*, in Stilman Drake, *Discoveries and Opinions of Galileo* [New York: Doubleday Anchor Books, 1957], pp. 145-171 [Introduction] and pp. 175-216 [text, essential; Galileo's views concerning "the use of Biblical quotations in matters of science"]). *Discorsi e dimostrazioni matematiche intorno a due nuove scienze* . . . (Leyden, 1638) (translation by H.

Crew and Alfonso De Salvio: *Dialogues Concerning Two New Sciences* [New York, 1914]). The volume of selections published by Stilman Drake, listed above, is an excellent introduction to the study of Galileo.

A comprehensive study: A. Aliotta and C. Carbonara, *Galileo* (Milan: Bocca, 1949). See also A. Koyré, *Etudes Galiléennes* (Paris: Hermann, 1939). E. Levinger, *Galileo, First Observer of Marvelous Things* (New York: Messner, 1952). Santillana has written, on Galileo's troubles, *The Crime of Galileo* (Chicago: University of Chicago Press, 1955).

2. FRANÇOIS VIÈTE, b. Fontenay-le-Comte, 1540; d. Paris, 1603. First a lawyer, then a counselor at the Parliament of Britanny and a member of King Henry IV's privy council (1580).

Collective edition: *Opera* (Leyden, 1646).

3. PIERRE DE FERMAT, b. Beaumont-de-Lomagre, 1601; d. Toulouse, 1665. A counselor at the Parliament of Toulouse with a passion for mathematics. This was a purely personal interest; Fermat seldom published his discoveries and, as often as not, he did not even write up their demonstrations. Pascal called him "the first man in the

world," but found him hard to follow, and no wonder, since some of the theories left by Fermat without their solutions have not yet been demonstrated. Collective edition by his son, Samuel de Fermat: *Varia opera mathematica* (Toulouse, 1679).

The attitude of this mathematical genius toward mathematics, which was to him a "pastime," can be matched with that of Pascal in his letter to Fermat, August 10, 1660: "For indeed, to speak of geometry frankly, I find it the highest exercise of the mind; but at the same time I know it to be so useless, that I make little difference between a man that only is a geometer and a skillful artisan. So I call it the most beautiful craft in the world, still, after all, it is but a craft." Blaise Pascal, *Pensées et opuscules*, ed. Léon Brunschvicg (4th ed.; Paris, 1907), p. 229. Those were the times when the great mathematicians were no more professors of mathematics than the great philosophers were professors of philosophy.

4. Thomas Aquinas, *In Boethium de Trinitate*, q. VI, art. 1, quoting Ptolemy, *Almagest*, Book I, chap. i: "Let us call the other two kinds of theoretical knowledge *opinion* rather than *science*; (natural) theology indeed on account of its obscurity and incomprehensibility, physics on the other hand because of the instability and obscurity of matter. Mathematics alone will give the inquirer firm and unshaken certitude, namely, demonstrations carried out with unquestionable methods"; ed. A. Maurer, C.S.B., p. 55.

5. CHRISTOPHER CLAVIUS, S.J., b. Bamberg (Germany), 1537; d. Rome, 1617. Collective edition: *Opera mathematica* (Moguntiae, 1612), Vol. I, p. 6, Prolegomena.

PART 2   THE BEGINNINGS OF MODERN PHILOSOPHY

IV. Francis Bacon

1. FRANCIS BACON, b. London, 1560; d. Highgate, 1626. Studies at Trinity College, Cambridge; a Bencher of Gray's Inn, 1586; first edition of the *Essays*, 1597; published the *Advancement of Learning*, 1605; returned Member for Cambridge University, 1614; created Baron Verulam, 1618, and Viscount of St. Alban, 1620; tried and sentenced by the House of Lords for accepting bribes, 1621; retired to Gorhambury, 1621; published the *De augmentis*, 1623; died April 9, 1626.

Main philosophical writings: *Of the Proficience and Advancement of Learning Divine and Human*, 1605 (in English); the Latin *De dignitate et augmentis scientiarum libri IX*, 1623, is a translation of *The Advancement*, with some additions. *Novum organum sive indicia vera de interpretatione naturae*, 1620; this "new organon," or new logic, and practically all the unfinished works left by Bacon were intended, as well as the *De augmentis*, to be included in a vast encyclopedia, the *Great Instauration* (*Instauratio Magna*), which he could not bring to completion.

Collected works: *The Works of Francis Bacon* by J. Spedding, R. L. Ellis, and D. Heath (7 vols.; London, 1861); reprinted 1887. J. Spedding, *The Letters and the Life of*

Francis Bacon Including All His Occasional Works (7 vols.; London, 1861); reprinted 1890.

On the doctrine a little-known but valuable study is included in G. Sortais, S.J., *La philosophie moderne depuis Bacon jusqu'à Leibniz* (Paris, 1930), Vol. I, pp. 99-278; also F. H. Anderson, *The Philosophy of Francis Bacon* (Chicago: University of Chicago Press, 1948); A. Cresson, *Francis Bacon* (Paris: Presses Universitaires de France, 1948); A. W. Green, *Sir Francis Bacon* (Denver: Swallow, 1952).

For references left in the text, the following abbreviations will be used: *OAL* for *Of the Advancement of Learning; DAS* for *De augmentis scientiarum; NO* for *Novum Organum.*

2. *DAS*, II, 2.
3. *OAL*, II, 2.
4. *Ibid.*, II, vi, 1.
5. *Ibid.*, II, vii, 3.
6. *Ibid.*, 5.
7. *Ibid.*, II, 7, vii, 7.
8. *Ibid.*, II, viii, 1.
9. *Ibid.*, II, xii, 3.
10. *Ibid.*, II, xiii, 1.
11. *Ibid.*, II, xx, 1.
12. *Ibid.*, II, xxii, 1-17.

13. *Ibid.*, II, xxiii, 5-7.
14. *Ibid.*, 49.
15. *Ibid.*, II, xxv, 6.
16. *Ibid.*, II, xiv, 9-12.
17. *NO*, I, i.
18. *Ibid.*, I, 41.
19. *Ibid.*, 49.
20. *Ibid.*, 51.
21. *Ibid.*, 50.
22. *Ibid.*, 53.
23. *Ibid.*, 54-55.
24. *Ibid.*, 59.
25. *Ibid.*, 60.
26. *Ibid.*, 61.
27. *Ibid.*, 64.
28. *Ibid.*, 65.
29. *OAL*, I, 15.
30. *DAS*, I, 5.
31. *NO*, I, 98.
32. *Ibid.*, 98.
33. *Ibid.*, 99.
34. *OAL*, II, xiii, 1.
35. Aristotle, *Metaphysics*, I, 6, 987b, 1-6.
36. *NO*, II, aph., ii-15.
37. *Ibid.*, I, 104.
38. *Ibid.*
39. *Ibid.*, II, 2.
40. *Ibid.*, 4 and 5.
41. *DAS*, III, chap. iv.
42. *Ibid.*

v. Thomas Hobbes

1. Descartes, Letter to Isaac Beeckman, October 17, 1630; AT, Vol. I, p. 159.
2. LUCILIO VANINI, b. Taurisano (prov. of Lecce, Italy), 1585; d. Toulouse, 1619. Ordained a priest at Padua; visited different countries; jailed in England for attacking the established church; the title of his last book is telling: *De admirandis naturae, reginae deaeque mortalium, arcanis libri IV*, 1616. Arrested and tried at Toulouse, he was condemned and burned at the stake as libertine and declared atheist. The

origin of the libertine movement was old. As Renan said, there is not one impiety ever said in the sixteenth century that was not already said in the thirteenth. No one of those men was philosophically important, but their presence has affected the philosophy of the seventeenth century. On account of the moral laxity of some of them, they were called "esprits forts." Attempts have been made at writing the history of that polymorphous movement: Henri Busson, *La rationalisme dans la littérature fran-*

çaise de la Renaissance (*1553-1601*) (Paris: J. Vrin, 2d ed., 1957); René Pintard, *Le libertinage érudit dans la première moitié du XVIIe siècle* (Paris, 1943). On Vanini: Luigi Corvaglia, *Le opere di Giulio Cesare Vanini e le loro fonti* (2 vols.; Società anonima editrice Dante Alighieri, 1935).

Pascal will have the existence of such men always before his mind. Descartes specified, in the Preface to his *Meditationes*, that nothing more useful could be done than to demonstrate the existence of God and the distinction of mind and body, which impious men refused to believe ("plerosque impios," AT, Vol. VII, p. 3, lines 9-21). When one disagreed with a philosopher on the way to conceive metaphysics, the shortest way was to accuse him of being one of those unbelievers. This was done to Descartes himself, who did not like it. See his protests against the accusation of secretly teaching atheism after the example of Vanini, who was burned at Toulouse: "ad exemplum Vanini qui Tholosae combustus est" (letter, January 22, 1644; AT, IV, p. 86, l.7-9); cf. p. 89, l.19-20: "mehic, tanquam alterum Vaninum, Tholosae combustum, subdole et admodum occulte atheismum docere . . ."

3. PETRUS GASSENDI, or PIERRE GASSEND, b. Champtercier (near Digne, France), 1592; d. Paris, 1655. Theol. doct. Avignon, 1616; ordained a priest, 1617; taught philosophy at the University of Aix, 1617-1622; professor of mathematics at the Collège de France, 1645-1648. Collective editions: *Opera omnia* (6 vols.; Lyon: Anisson, 1658); (6 vols.; Florence, 1727).

Main writings: *Exercitationum paradoxicarum adversus Aristoteleos libri septem* . . . (Grenoble: Verdier, 1624): "Paradoxical dis-

cussions against the Aristotelians in which the chief principles of the whole peripatetic and dialectical doctrine are scrutinized, while opinions either new or ancient but obsolete, are established." Only two books were written; they were recently edited by Bernard Rochot, *Dissertations en forme de paradoxes contre les aristotéliciens* (Paris: Librairie Philosophique J. Vrin, 1959). *Cinquièmes objections* (contre les *Meditationes de prima philosophia* de Descartes) in *Oeuvres de Descartes*, AT, Vol. VII, pp. 256-346; enlarged edition: *Petri Gassendi Disquisitio Metaphysica, seu dubitationes et instantiae adversus Renati Cartesii Metaphysicam et responsa* (Amsterdam: Joh. Blaev, 1644). *De Vita, moribus et doctrina Epicuri*, 1647. *Syntagma philosophicum*, 1658 (his main work, posthumously published).

Claims to revive the corpuscular philosophy of Epicurus, which, however, he caps with a Christian philosophy and natural theology. The question, did he believe in this spiritualistic supplement, or did he merely want to get out of trouble, is a matter of opinion. Like that of Descartes, his corpuscular physics consists in imagining structures of atoms that provide likely explanations for the figures and operations of observable bodies.

Doctrinal: Bernard Rochot, *Lettres familières de Gassendi à François Luillier pendant l'hiver* (*1632-1633*) (Paris: Librairie Philosophique J. Vrin, 1959). Same author: *Les travaux de Gassendi sur Epicure et l'atomisme* (*1619-1658*) (same publisher, 1944). The *Syntagma* being very long and diffuse, one still can use an old abridgment: François Bernier, *Abrégé de la philosophie de Gassendi* (Lyon, 1678). Bernier (b. *c.* 1625; d. 1688), a globetrotter, collaborated in Boileau's *Arrêt burlesque* rendered by the masters and professors of the University of Stagyra (in Chimeraland) in favor of the doctrine of Aristotle (*Oeuvres complètes de Boileau* [Paris: Les Belles-Lettres, 1942], pp. 31-35); the *Exercitationes . . . adversus Aristoteleos* is expressly denounced, p. 33. Despite his success, Gassendi does not seem to have left any philosophical posterity.

On his thought, see G. S. Brett, *The Philosophy of Gassendi* (New York, 1908); and the essays in *Pierre Gassendi, 1592-1655*, published by the Centre National de la Recherche Scientifique (Paris: A. Michel, 1955).

4. THOMAS HOBBES, b. Malmesbury, 1588; d. 1679. Was the son of a clergyman, went to Oxford at fourteen; in 1608 became tutor to the Devonshires, traveling several times to France with this great family; became interested in mathematics there; during third voyage (1634-1637) visited Mersenne and, in Italy, Galileo. During Long Parliament, found refuge in Paris for sixteen years, during which time he wrote his objections to the *Meditations* of Descartes, which came to be published along with them. He returned to England at the Restoration, 1651. For the latter part of his life he was in the service of the Cavendish family. Hobbes' first work, *The Elements of Law, Natural and Politic*, was written in 1640 but not published until ten years later. The *Leviathan* was written in Paris and published in 1652. Already in Paris he had conceived of a trilogy, to deal with the body, human nature, and the social body, the whole to be called *Elements of Philosophy*. He had already published the third part, *On the Citi-*

zen, long before returning from his self-imposed exile. Then in 1655 he published the first part, *On Body*, and three years later the second part, *On Man*. He spent much of his last years in polemic uproars over his views, his translation of Homer being one of the few truly fruitful endeavors in the last decades of his long life. He was ninety-one when he died.

Collected works: There are two collections, both edited by Molesworth: *Opera philosophica quae latine scripsit* (5 vols.; London: Bohn, and Longman, 1839-1845), and *The English Works of Thomas Hobbes* (11 vols.; London: Bohn, and Longman, 1839-1845).

Bibliographical: H. Macdonald, *Thomas Hobbes; a Bibliography* (London: Bibliographical Society, 1952).

Biographical and doctrinal: J. Laird, *Hobbes* (London: Benn, 1934); G. C. Robertson, *Hobbes* (Edinburgh: Blackwood, 1886); F. Tönnies, *Thomas Hobbes: Leben und Lehre* (3d ed.; Stuttgart: Frommann, 1925); F. Brandt, *Thomas Hobbes' Mechanical Conception of Nature* (Paris: Hachette, 1928); R. Polin, *Politique et philosophie chez Thomas Hobbes* (Paris: Presses Universitaires, 1952); H. Warrender, *The Political Philosophy of Hobbes* (Oxford: Clarendon, 1957).

5. *Leviathan*, Introduction.
6. *Concerning Body*, I, vi, 10.
7. *Leviathan*, Introduction.
8. *Concerning Body*, IV, xxv, 2.
9. *Leviathan*, I, c. 2.
10. *Ibid.*
11. *Ibid.*, c. 3.
12. *Ibid.*
13. *Ibid.*
14. *Ibid.*, I, 4.
15. *Ibid.*
16. *Ibid.*

17. *Ibid.*, I, 5.
18. *Ibid.*, 6.
19. *Ibid.*
20. *Ibid.*, I, 14.

21. *Ibid.*
22. *Ibid.*, II, 17.
23. *Ibid.*

vi. René Descartes

1. RENÉ DESCARTES, b. La Haye (in Touraine, France), 1596; d. Stockholm, 1650. Studied scholastic philosophy and some mathematics at the Jesuit College of La Flèche; studied law at the University of Poitiers and took service (without drawing a salary) in the Dutch army under Maurice of Nassau (1618); first personal reflections on geometry and the use of mathematics in physics; left Holland for Denmark and Germany (1619). In November of the same year, being in winter quarters, after successfully solving some problems in geometry, he conceived the possibility of finding a general method permitting to solve all geometrical problems, then that of a still more general one permitting to solve all the problems which the human mind can ask. All the sciences then appeared to him as branches of one and the same tree and constituting all together one single body of knowledge. Finding himself too young for such an undertaking, being only twenty-three years old, he wrote up his geometry. About the middle of 1628, feeling ready for the great task, he retired to Holland and devoted nine months to his metaphysics; he then worked on his physics: *Le Monde*. In 1633, as the book was nearing completion, he learned of the condemnation of Galileo, and as the motion of the earth was part of his own physics, he decided not to complete it. Hoping to create more favorable conditions for its future publication, he published three samples of it

destined to prove the fecundity of his method (*Dioptrics, Meteors, Geometry*), the three treatises being preceded by a Preface, the *Discourse on Method* (1637). Hoping thus to pave the way to his physics, he then published his *Meditations on Prime Philosophy* (1641) along with objections directed against them and his answers. Having found a way to present his physics without seeming to uphold the motion of the earth, he published it; the title, *Principles of Philosophy* (1644), announced a treatise covering the whole field of philosophy (metaphysics and physics). In 1649, a French translation of the *Principles* appeared, revised, completed, and with an important Preface where his philosophy presented itself as a wisdom both speculative and practical. Pursuing the execution of his plan, he turned his attention to ethics (*Les passions de l'âme*, 1649). Invited by Queen Christina of Sweden, he went to Stockholm, where, suffering cruelly from the cold and his constitution being rather weak, he died on February 11, 1650, not yet fifty-four years old.

Main works: *Discourse on the Method of Rightly Conducting the Reason and Seeking for Truth in the Sciences* (*Discours de la méthode pour bien conduire sa raison et rechercher la vérité dans les sciences, plus Le Dioptrique, Les Météores et La Géométrie qui sont des essais de cette méthode* [Leyden, 1637]). *Meditations on First Philosophy* (*Meditationes de prima philosophia* [Paris, 1641]; translated into French under the title *Méditations métaphysiques touchant la première philosophie, dans lesquelles l'existence de Dieu et la distinction réelle entre l'âme et le corps sont démontrées* [Paris, 1647]). *Principles of Philosophy* (*Principia philosophiae* [Amsterdam, 1644]); translated into French with a new Preface: *Les Principes de la Philosophie* (Paris, 1647). *The Passions of the Soul* (*Les Passions de l'âme* [Paris, 1649]).

Among the posthumous works, the more important one is the unfinished treatise, *Rules for the Direction of the Mind* (*Regulae ad directionem ingenii*), probably written before the *Discourse*. The correspondence is often important, especially the three exchanges of letters with: M. Mersenne, his Parisian correspondent; Huyghens, chiefly on scientific matters; and Princess Elizabeth, who succeeded in extracting from Descartes information on ethics.

Collective edition: *Oeuvres de Descartes*, ed. Charles Adam and Paul Tannery (11 vols.; Paris: Cerf [now Librairie Philosophique J. Vrin], 1897-1909; plus a Supplement, 1913). *Correspondence of Descartes and Constantin Huyghens, 1635-1647*, ed. Leon Roth (Oxford: Clarendon Press, 1926).

Collective translation of the main works: *The Philosophical Works of Descartes*, rendered into English by E. S. Haldane and G. R. T. Ross (2 vols.; Cambridge University Press, 1911), corrected edition, 1931. Paperback edition in 2 vols. (New York: Dover, 1955).

Biographical: A. Baillet, *La vie de M. Descartes* (2 vols.; Paris, 1691). Charles Adam, *Vie et oeuvres de Descartes. Etude historique*, published as a supplement to the collective edition, Vol. XII of same. Gustave Cohen, *Ecrivains français en Hollande dans la première moitié du XVIIe siècle* (Paris: E. Champion, 1920).

Doctrinal: O. Hamelin, *Le système de Descartes* (Paris: Alcan, 1911). A. B. Gibson, *The Philosophy of Descartes* (London: Methuen, 1932). H. Gouhier, *Essais sur Descartes* (Paris: Librairie Philosophique J. Vrin, 1937). Ernst Cassirer, *Descartes, Lehre, Persönlichkeit, Wirkung* (Stockholm: Bermann-Fischer Verlag, 1939). Martial Guéroult, *Descartes selon l'ordre des raisons. I. L'âme et Dieu* (Paris: Aubier, 1953); *II. L'âme et le corps* (Paris: Aubier, 1953). H. Gouhier, *La pensée métaphysique de Descartes* (Paris: J. Vrin, 1962).

Bibliographical: J. Boorsch, *Etat présent des études sur Descartes* (Paris: Les Belles-Lettres, 1937). Geneviève Lewis, "Cinquante ans d'études cartésiennes," *Revue philosophique*, April-June, 1951.

2. The *Discourse* is found in *Oeuvres de Descartes*, ed. Adam Tannery (henceforward quoted as AT), Vol. VI. Countless reprints in all scientific languages, among which E. Gilson's, with running commentary (Paris: Librairie Philosophique J. Vrin, 1925). English translation of Part II in Ralph M. Eaton, *Descartes Selections* (New York: Charles Scribner's Sons, 1927), pp. 10-20. The same volume contains in translation the *Rules for the Direction of the Mind*, Rules I-XII, with some abridgment. L. J. Beck, *The Method of Descartes. A Study of the Regulae* (Oxford: Clarendon Press, 1952).

3. *Discourse on the Method, II*; Eaton, *Descartes Selections*, pp. 16-17.

4. On the younger years of Descartes and the formation of his phi-

losophy: J. Sirven, *Les Années d'apprentissage de Descartes (1596-1628)* (Paris: Librairie Philosophique J. Vrin, 1928). Henri Gouhier, *Les premières pensées de Descartes. Contribution à l'histoire de l'Anti-Renaissance* (Paris: Librairie Philosophique J. Vrin, 1958). On the passage of the *Olympica* under consideration and the "scientia mirabilis," see the excellent interpretation, p. 49, note 1 included.

5. *Discourse on the Method, II,* in *Descartes Selections,* p. 17.

6. French text in AT, pp. 1-20. The exact title is "Lettre de l'auteur à celui qui a traduit le livre laquelle peut ici servir de Préface." The translator was Abbé Claude Picot.

7. Latin text, AT, Vol. VII. French translation, AT, Vol. IX. In Eaton, *Descartes Selections,* pp. 84-165; extracts from the *Objections and Replies,* pp. 166-266.

8. The title of the Second Meditation runs as follows: "Of the Nature of the Human Mind; and that it is more easily known than the body." The words "more easily known" translate the scholastic Latin *notior*. A thing is "more known" than another one when its knowledge precedes and conditions that of the other. This will be shown to be the case. I do not need to know body in order to know mind, whereas I cannot know body unless I first know mind. What is proper to Cartesianism is that, in it, if a notion is "more known" than another one, it is (in consequence of the first rule of method) really distinct from it.

9. The Second Meditation establishes (following the first rule of the method) that I know myself as mind without knowing myself as body. Hence my knowledge of self as mind precedes and conditions my knowledge of self as body. The effect of the Second Meditation is described by Descartes himself (in his own *Abridgment,* AT, IX, p. 9), as follows: It helps the mind "to make the distinction between the things that belong to itself, that is to intellectual nature, and those that belong to body." In this sense, it prepares the real distinction of mind and body, which will be completed in the Sixth Meditation, when the real existence of body is proved. These are the words of Descartes himself. The Second Meditation concludes that mind and body are clearly and distinctly conceived to be different substances; but it remains to be proved that "those things which we conceive clearly and distinctly to be diverse substances, as we conceive Mind and Body, are substances effectively diverse and really distinct one from the other; *and this is the conclusion of the Sixth Meditation.*" (AT, IX, p. 10; cf. "atque ex his debere concludi ea omnia quae clare et distincte *concipiuntur* ut substantiae diversae, sicuti concipiuntur mens et corpus, *esse revera substantias realiter a se mutuo distinctas, hocque in sexta concludi,*" AT, VII, p. 13, lines 15-19). In the abridgment of the Sixth Meditation: "I here show that the mind of man is really distinct from the body" (AT, IX, p. 88). The contrary thesis, that the proof of the real distinction is already completed in the Second Meditation, runs counter to these invincible texts.

10. A. Koyré, *L'idée de Dieu et les preuves de son existence chez Descartes* (Paris: Leroux, 1922). H. Gouhier, "Le malin génie et le bon Dieu," in *Essais sur Descartes,* pp. 143-196.

11. On the theological antecedents of the doctrine: E. Gilson, *La doctrine cartésienne de la liberté et la théologie* (Paris: F. Alcan, 1913), deuxième partie.

12. Descartes, *Principes de philosophie*, p. 11, *Des principes des choses matérielles;* AT, Vol. IX, pp. 63-102.

13. E. Gilson, *Etudes sur le rôle de la pensée médiévale dans la formation du système cartésien* (Paris: Librairie Philosophique J. Vrin, 1930), Part II, chaps. 2-7.

14. Descartes, *Principes de philosophie*, P. IV, *De la Terre;* AT, Vol. IX, pp. 201-325. A particularly illuminating exposition of Descartes' cosmogony is his unfinished treatise, *Le Monde;* AT, Vol. X, pp. 1-118; translated extracts in Eaton's *Descartes Selections*, pp. 312-349.

15. Descartes lived during an era of religious revival within the Catholic Church of France. Cf. Daniel Rops, *L'église des temps classiques* (Paris: Arthème Fayard, 1958), for a convincing review of all the manifestations of this vitality. St. Vincent de Paul, whose efforts to reform the diocesan clergy reached to the remotest villages of France and whose Daughters of Charity soon took themselves off to the remotest ends of the earth, was a contemporary. St. Jean Baptiste de la Salle was working during Descartes' lifetime for the establishment of modern Catholic schools. In 1611 Père de Bérulle had founded, following the prescriptions of Philip Neri, the influential and noble institution of the *Oratoire*, which in the first century of its existence was to count among its members the Fathers Bourgoing, Massillon, Mascaron, and, most famous of all, Malebranche. Descartes presaged the age of the great preachers: Bossuet, Fénelon, and Massillon derived from him not a little of the inspiration for the clarity and rigor with which they presented the picture and exalted the glory of high moral existence. We shall presently see what happens when Malebranche puts Cartesianism to an unabashedly theological use.

16. Gustave Lanson, in comparing the characters of *Corneille* with the *Treatise on the Passions*, and after showing how closely the works coincide, concludes that both the tragedian and the philosopher took as their common model the real aspirations of the great men of the time. Cf. G. Lanson, *Corneille*.

17. The later Cartesians were to worry about the problem of how spirit could be acted on by matter. Descartes, himself, however, did not hesitate much on this score.

18. *Treatise on the Passions*, I, Art. XXXVI.

19. *Ibid.*, Art. XLV.

20. *Ibid.*, II, Art. LXXIV.

21. *Ibid.*, Art. LII.

22. *Ibid.*, I, Art. L.

23. *Ibid.*, Art. XLII.

24. *Ibid.*, Art. XLVI.

25. *Ibid.*, II, Art. LII.

26. *Ibid.*, Art. LXX.

27. *Ibid.*, Art. LXXII.

28. *Ibid.*, Art. LXXV.

29. *Ibid.*, Art. LXXVII.

30. *Ibid.*, Art. LXXIX.

31. *Ibid.*, Art. LXXX.

32. *Ibid.*, Art. CI.

33. *Ibid.*, Art. CXLIV.

34. Compare Articles CXLV and CXLVI of the *Treatise* with Epictetus' *Manual*, I.

35. *Treatise on the Passions*, Arts. CXLV and CXLVI.

36. "Generosity" runs through Corneille like a *leitmotiv*. To cite only two among a hundred possible examples, "Sire, dans la chaleur d'un

premier mouvement, un coeur si
généreux se rend malaisément" (*Le
Cid*, II, vi.). "Toute excuse est
honteuse aux esprits généreux"
(*ibid.*, III, iii).

37. Treatise on the Passions, Art.
CLIII.
38. Ibid., Art. CLVI.
39. Ibid.

PART 3   CHRISTIAN PHILOSOPHY

VII. Nicolas Malebranche

1. The only Cartesian to carry on
scientific research according to the
principles of the master was
JACQUES ROHAULT, b. Amiens, 1620;
d. Paris, 1675. He married the
daughter of Clerselier, the editor
of Descartes' works. Rohault tried
to justify by experiments the conclusions of Descartes. He published
a *Traité de physique*, 1671, and
Entretiens sur la philosophie, 1671.
He was thereby trying to fulfill
one of Descartes' cherished desires:
to substitute the physics of Descartes for that of Aristotle in the
teaching of the schools. Rohault
had to give assurances of the orthodoxy of the chapter on man's
body. This body being conceived
as a machine, the man of Descartes
accomplished through this machine
many operations traditionally attributed to mind.

2. JACQUES-BÉNIGNE BOSSUET, b. Dijon, 1627; d. Paris, 1704. Entrusted
by Louis XIV with the education
of the Dauphin, he wrote for his
pupils some of his major works.
Among them: *Introduction à la
philosophie* (1677), published in
1722, from a copy and anonymously, under the title *De la connaissance de Dieu et de soi-même*;
under the same title, but from the
original manuscript, in 1722. Often
reprinted under the same title,
sometimes with other philosophical works likewise written for the
Dauphin: Bossuet, *Ecrits philo-*

sophiques, ed. J. Brisbarre (Paris:
Dezobry, 1861); includes, besides
De la connaissance de Dieu . . . ,
the *Traité du libre arbitre* and *La
logique*. In his letter to Pope Innocent XI, *De institutione Del-
phini*, Bossuet had noted that "here,
in order to be a perfect philosopher, man needs not study anything else than himself; and without perusing so many books,
without laboriously collecting the
opinions of philosophers, without
seeking very far for experiments,
but merely by observing what is
to be found in himself, he will
thereby recognize the Author of
his being." Three things are to be
considered in man: the soul apart,
the body apart, the union of soul
and body. The proofs of the existence of God are borrowed from
St. Augustine: There are necessary
and immutable truths; it is not in
me (a fleeting and changing being)
that I can see such objects of
knowledge; it is in God that I see
those eternal truths, and to turn
my mind to them is to turn it to
him: *De la connaissance . . . :*
chap. iv, 5. From the imperfection
of its intelligence the soul knows
there is a perfect one: iv, 6. God
is being itself (*Exod.* 3:14), so he
cannot possibly not be: iv, 7. Made
after the resemblance of God, the
soul receives in itself a divine impression each time it understands a
truth; in seeking for truth and find-

ing it man is seeking for God and finding God: iv, 9. In his *Logic*, Book I, chap. 41, Bossuet goes out of his way to deny the real distinction of essence and existence.

3. Augustine, *De Libero Arbitrio*, II, 3, 7: Migne, Latin Patrology, Vol. XXXII, col. 1243. L. Blanchet, *Les antécédents historiques du "Je pense donc je suis"* (Paris: 1920).

4. Henri Gouhier, *La vocation de Malebranche* (Paris: Librairie Philosophique J. Vrin, 1926; chap. iii: "Le principe des cartésiens." On the language used by Descartes, its reasons and its interpretation, 1 and 2, pp. 80-88).

5. Gouhier, *op. cit.*, iii, pp. 88-95.

6. *Ibid.*, iv, pp. 95-101. The philosophical benefit to be derived from the study of this doctrinal evolution is to show that the consequences of a principle usually follow from it with a sort of metaphysical necessity.

7. *Ibid.*, v, "Le principe des cartésiens," pp. 101-107.

8. *Ibid.*, p. 101.

9. *Ibid.*, pp. 103-104.

10. Malebranche, *De la recherche de la vérité*, Éclaircissement X, Obj. I, Answer.

11. D. Hume, *A Treatise of Human Nature*, Book I, Part III, sec. 14, "Of the Idea of Necessary Connection." In this passage, Hume expressly refers to the "Cartesians," whose conclusion he sums up with accuracy: " 'Tis the deity, therefore, who is the prime mover of the universe . . . and successively bestows on it all those motions, and configurations, and qualities, with which it is endowed." Of course Hume will reject that explanation of the "idea of necessary connection," and as he will find no satisfactory one, he will content himself with doubting there is such a thing in the world.

12. NICOLAS MALEBRANCHE, b. Paris, 1638; d. Paris, 1715. A novice at the Oratory, 1660; ordained a priest, 1664; according to tradition, discovered the doctrine of Descartes in reading his *Traité de l'homme* recently published by Louis de la Forge (1664); after the publication of his *Treatise of Nature and Grace* (1680) he was attacked by Arnauld and Bossuet; the work was put on the Index in 1690; a geometer, a mathematician, and a physicist, he became a Fellow of the French Academy of Sciences, 1699; he died at Paris, October 13, 1715.

Main works: *De la recherche de la vérité où l'on traite de la nature de l'esprit de l'homme et de l'usage qu'il en doit faire pour éviter l'erreur dans les sciences* (Paris, Vol. I, 1674; Vol. II, 1675 [often reprinted]); be sure Vol. II includes the priceless *Eclaircissements*; early English translations: Richard Sault (London, 1692); T. Taylor (2 vols.; Oxford, 1694); reprinted in 1712, 1720. *Conversations chrétiennes dans lesquelles on justifie la vérité de la religion et de la morale de Jésus-Christ* (Paris, 1675). *Traité de la nature et de la grâce* (Amsterdam, 1680). *Eclaircissement ou la suite du Traité de la nature et de la grâce* (Amsterdam, 1681). *Méditations chrétiennes* (Cologne, 1683). *Traité de morale* (Cologne, 1683). *Entretiens sur la métaphysique et sur la religion* (Rotterdam, 1688). *Traité de l'amour de Dieu, en quel sens il doit être désintéressé*, in a new edition of the *Traité de Morale* (Lyon, 1697). *Entretien d'un philosophe chrétien avec un philosophe chinois sur l'existence et la nature de Dieu* (Paris, 1708). *Recueil de toutes les réponses du P. Malebranche, prêtre de l'Oratoire, à M.*

Arnauld, docteur de Sorbonne (Paris, 1709). *Réflexions sur la prémotion physique* (Paris, 1715).

Collective edition: *Oeuvres complètes de Malebranche* by various editors under the direction of A. Robinet (Paris: Librairie J. Vrin, in course of publication); 20 volumes foreseen. This edition will include hitherto unprinted mathematical and other scientific works. Eight volumes published to date.

Biographical: Fontenelle, "Eloge de Malebranche," *Oeuvres complètes* (Paris, 1790); Vol. VI. André (of the Oratory), *La Vie de Malebranche*, written soon after the death of Malebranche, only published by Ingold, *Bibliothèque oratorienne*, Vol. VIII, 1886. Vol. XX of the *Oeuvres complètes* will be made up of biographical and bibliographical information.

Doctrinal: L. Ollé-Laprune, *La philosophie de Malebranche* (Paris, 1870). V. Delbos, *Etude de la philosophie de Malebranche* (Paris: Bloud, 1924). Henri Gouhier, *La vocation de Malebranche* (Paris: Librairie Philosophique J. Vrin, 1926). Same author, same place and date, *La philosophie de Malebranche et son expérience religieuse*, 2d ed., 1928. Martial Guéroult, *Malebranche* (3 vols.; Paris: Aubier; Vol. I, *La vision en Dieu*, 1955; Vol. II, *Les cinq abîmes de la Providence: l'ordre et l'occasionalisme*, 1959; Vol. III, *Les cinq abîmes de la Providence: la nature et la grâce*, 1959). André Robinet, *Malebranche et Leibniz, relations personnelles, présentées avec les textes complets des auteurs et de leurs correspondants, revus, corrigés et inédits* (Paris: Librairie Philosophique J. Vrin, 1955). P. Blanchard, *L'attention à Dieu selon Malebranche, méthode et doctrine* (Paris: Desclée de Brouwer, 1956).

R. W. Church, *A Study in the Philosophy of Malebranche* (London: Allen and Unwin, 1931). A. Cuvillier, *Essai sur la mystique de Malebranche* (Paris: J. Vrin, 1954). G. Dreyfus, *La volonté selon Malebranche* (Paris: J. Vrin, 1958).

13. *Entretiens métaphysiques*, III, i. The ultimate meaning of the distinction is that an idea is the intellectual sight of an object presented to the mind, whereas a "sentiment" (feeling, sensation) is the awareness of a modification caused in the soul by an object. In "sentiment," the known object is *the soul itself as modified in its very substance* by some acting cause.

14. *Recherche de la vérité*, L.i, chap. v, No. III.

15. *Ibid.*, chaps. xi and xiv. L.i.

16. *Ibid.*, I, chap. xiv.

17. *Ibid.*, chaps. xvii and xviii.

18. *Réponse au livre des vraies et des fausses idées*, chap. xiii.

19. *Réponse à M. Régis*, chap. ii.

20. *Entretiens métaphysiques*, ii, 5.

21. *Récherche de la vérité*, L.iii, Part II.

22. *Recherche de la vérité*, Eclaircissement X.—This influence of St. Augustine was due to two main causes. First, the fact that Cartesianism, by placing the "I think" at the beginning of philosophy, was favoring a return to the Augustinian method of going directly from soul to God; next, the fact that the decline of the Aristotelian scholasticism in theology was inviting a revival of the Christian philosophy of St. Augustine as the first stage of a revival of the theology of the saint. The Oratory was from the start an active center of that twofold revival. Louis Thomassin, b. Aix-en-Provence, 1618; d. Paris, 1695, having spent sixty-three years in the Congregation of the Oratory, is an extremely

important connecting link in the history of modern Augustinianism. Essentially a theologian (see particularly his *Dogmatum theologicorum*, Vol. II, "De Deo, Deique proprietatibus" [Paris, 1684]), Thomassin has nevertheless developed a complete system of prime philosophy in the spirit of St. Augustine.—Innate and natural knowledge of the existence of God in all men (Book I, chaps. i-viii); all men have, in some degree, a vision of God; although obscure and confused, that knowledge of God is in us more intimate than our knowledge of other men, because, between our inner light and that of God, nothing is interposited. Book III, chap. vii, is an inexhaustible mine of quotations of St. Augustine, selected among the really provoking ones on the subject of the "vision in God." A careful study of that part of Thomassin's doctrine will throw light on the apparently excessive aspects of the epistemology, not only of Malebranche, but also of Cardinal Gerdil and of Rosmini. For an introduction to the life and doctrine, see A. Molien, "Thomassin," art. in *Dictionnaire de Théologie Catholique*, 15 (1946), col. 787-823; bibliography, col. 823.

23. *Treatise on Morals*, Introduction.
24. *Entretiens métaphysiques*, II, 4 and 9.
25. *Réponse à M. Arnauld*, chap. XVI.
26. *VIe Entretien sur la métaphysique*.
27. *Traité de la nature et de la grâce*, 2ème discours, Part I, art. 3.
28. *Méditations chrétiennes*, V, 17.
29. *Traité de la morale*, I, c. 2.
30. *Traité*, I, c. 5.
31. *Ibid*.
32. *Ibid*.

33. *Traité*, I, c. 5.
34. *Traité de la morale*, I, c. 6.
35. *Ibid*.
36. *Traité*, I, c. 10.
37. *Ibid*. This is one of the vantage points from which the doctrine reveals its unity. The Preface to *De la recherche de la vérité* throws a vivid light on the general inspiration of the doctrine. It is frankly anti-scholastic, because scholasticism rests upon the acceptance of the philosophy of Aristotle, which is an essentially *pagan* philosophy. In it, man is a soul intimately united with a body; in a Christian philosophy, man is a soul intimately united with God; the human soul is more intimately united with God than with its own body. "I am not surprised that the common run of men, or that the Pagan Philosophers only consider soul in its relation and union to body, without acknowledging the relation and union it has with God; but I am surprised that Christian Philosophers, who should prefer the spirit of God to that of man, Moses to Aristotle, Saint Augustine to some wretched commentator of a pagan philosopher [read: Averroes], consider soul as the *form* of body, rather than as made in, and for, the image of God, which is to say, according to Saint Augustine, for Truth, to which alone it is immediately united. 'Tis true soul is united to the body, and it naturally is its *form*, but it is also true that soul is united to God in a much closer and more essential way." Soul can be without its body; it cannot exist without God. Original sin has so weakened the union of our soul with God, and so powerfully reinforced its union with our body, that we mistake the present state of man for its natural condition. Aristotelianism is the correct philoso-

phy of fallen nature. As a necessary consequence, it has perverted ethics. If soul is more united to its body than to God, then its body is for soul the cause of its beatitude; bodily pleasures are the supreme good; on the contrary, in a philosophy like that of St. Augustine where soul is intimately tied up with God, it expects from God, and only from Him, "its life, its light and its felicity." So anthropology, epistemology, metaphysics, and ethics are as many particular aspects of one and the same Augustinian and Christian truth.

38. *Traité de la morale*, I, c. 9.
39. *Ibid.*
40. *Méditations cartésiennes*, VI, 17.
41. *De la nature et de la grâce*, 3ème discours, Part I, v.
42. David Hume, *A Treatise of Human Nature*, Book I, Part III, sec. 14.
43. In this regard, see the extraordinary *Correspondence avec de Mairan*, edited with introduction by J. Moreau (Paris: J. Vrin, 1947); Mairan puts Malebranche on the spot to show in what sense he is *not* a Spinozist.

VIII. Blaise Pascal

1. BLAISE PASCAL, b. Clermont (now Clermont-Ferrand, France), 1623; d. Paris, 1662. Educated by his father, never saw the inside of a classroom; not yet sixteen, he wrote his *Traité sur les sections coniques* (Treatise on Conic Sections), 1639; in order to help his father working in a public taxation department, conceived and turned out a calculating machine "to perform all sorts of arithmetical operations" (1640); carried on experiments to verify the conclusions of Torricelli: *Abrégé du traité du vide* (Abridgment of a Treatise on Vacuum), 1651; death of his father, 1651; worldly life until 1654, accumulated observations on man; worked on two treatises, *De la pesanteur et la masse de l'air* (On the Weight and Mass of Air) and *De l'équilibre des liqueurs* (On the Equilibrium of Fluids), then his *Traité du triangle arithmétique et quelques autres petits traités sur la même matière*, 1654; a treatise then announced under the remarkable title of *Géométrie du hasard* (Geometry of Chance) has, unfortunately, never been written; at that time found himself on the threshold of infinitesimal calculus; Monday, November 23, 1654, mystical experience dated in the personal document called the *Mémorial*; being under the influence of Jansenism, he wrote, against the casuists, the pamphlets known as the *Provinciales* ("Letters of Louis de Montalte to a Provincial of his friends and to the RR.PP. Jesuits on the subject of the ethics and politics of the said Fathers," seventeen Letters published from 1656 to 1657; first collective edition, 1657; not a theological masterpiece but a literary one which created modern French prose); still interested in mathematical research: *A General Method to find the Centers of Gravity of all sorts of Magnitudes* . . . etc., 1658; more and more completely dedicated to works of charity and to personal religious life, accumulated material for a projected *Apologie de la religion chrétienne* (Apology for Christian Religion) whose collected fragments are known under the title of

Pensées; always weak, his health wholly deteriorated (*Prayer for making good use of sickness*); his last words were: "Let God never forsake me!"; died August 29, 1662, thirty-nine years old.

Collective editions: *Oeuvres complètes de Pascal*, ed. Léon Brunschvicg, E. Boutroux, and F. Gazier (14 vols.; Paris: Hachette, 1908-1921). More accessible and priceless: *Blaise Pascal. Pensées et Opuscules*, ed. Léon Brunschvicg (Paris: Hachette, 1897), many reprints. The collection *La Pléiade* contains another volume of selected works edited by Jacques Chevalier. Among countless editions of *Les Pensées*, two deserve special mention: *Reproduction en phototypie du manuscrit des Pensées de Blaise Pascal*, by Léon Brunschvicg (Paris: Hachette, 1905); B. Pascal, *Pensées*, edition paléographique . . . , ed. Zacharias Tourneur (Paris: Librairie Philosophique J. Vrin, 1942; copy of ms. Bib. Nat. 9202, fonds français, including all the corrections of Pascal's own hand). For a simple edition of good quality: Blaise Pascal, *Pensées précédées des principaux opuscules*, ed. Geneviève Lewis (Paris: La Bonne Compagnie, 1947).

Biographical: *Vie de Blaise Pascal*, par Madame Périer sa soeur (fundamental; written by Gilberte Périer, sister of Pascal); in L. Brunschvicg, *Pensées*, pp. 1-40; in G. Lewis' edition, pp. 1-57. On the whole, the best biography is the annotated edition of the *Pensées et Opuscules* by Léon Brunschvicg, himself a French philosopher of note who generously devoted years of his life to the works of a thinker whose thought and beliefs were widely different from his own.

Bibliographical: Nobody has ever been able to study Pascal in a spirit of complete objectivity; a detached attitude is not compatible with the nature of the subject, but studies on Pascal gain in philosophical interest what they lose in objectivity. Among many others: Emile Boutroux, *Pascal* (Paris: Hachette, 1900). A. Hatzfeld, *Pascal* (Paris: F. Alcan, 1901). Jacques Chevalier, *Pascal* (Paris: Plon, 1922). Léon Brunschvicg, "Le génie de Pascal," in *Blaise Pascal*, ed. G. Lewis (Paris: Librairie Philosophique J. Vrin, 1953, pp. 115-247). In English, see H. F. Stewart, *B. Pascal* (London: Milford, 1942). H. F. Stewart, *The Secret of Pascal* (Cambridge: Cambridge University Press, 1941). E. Caillies, *The Clue to Pascal* (Philadelphia: Westminster Press, 1943). Sister Marie Louise Hubert, *Pascal's Unfinished Apology, a Study of the Plan* (New Haven: Yale University Press, 1952). P. Mesnard, *Pascal* (London: Harvill Press, 1952). E. Mortimer, *Blaise Pascal* (New York: Harper, 1959).

2. Slightly hyperbolical interpretation of an anecdote; Gilberte Périer relates that, being quite young and his father refusing to teach him mathematics, he set about it himself and, by means of lines and circles, which he called *bars* and *rounds*, he found something that was the thirty-second proposition of Euclid, Book I., G. Périer, *Vie de Blaise Pascal*, ed. L. Brunschvicg, pp. 4-6, and p. 6, note 1. The proposition at stake is that the sum of the angles of a triangle equals two right angles. All references will be to the school edition of L. Brunschvicg (Paris, 1897) and any reprint.

3. Problem of the cycloid (seventeenth-century French: *la roulette*). See L. Brunschvicg, *Blaise Pascal*, pp. 135-136.

4. Brunschvicg, *op. cit.*, p. 127.

5. Principal text, *De l'esprit géo-*

métrique, pp. 164-196. According to Geneviève Lewis (*ed. cit.*, Introduction, p. xvi), the second part of this essay, published by herself under the title of *De l'art de persuader* (in her own edition, pp. 112-126), is an independent work, anterior to section 1, dated by Brunschvicg *c.* 1658, by herself *c.* 1654.

6. Pascal has made a halfhearted attempt to describe in a more precise way the method to be followed in demonstrating any sort of conclusion. The "art of persuading" (i.e., of giving perfect methodical proofs) is to give clear definitions of the terms to be used; to lay down evident axioms or principles by which the conclusions will be proved; in the demonstration, always to substitute the definitions for the defined objects. Here are rules concerning these three points:

Rules concerning definitions: (1) never to define anything that is either self-evident or clearer than the terms used to define it; (2) never to leave any obscure or equivocal terms undefined; (3) to use in the definition of terms only perfectly known or already explained words.

Rules concerning axioms: (1) never to use an axiom (or principle) without making sure it is granted, however clear and evident it may be; (2) to lay down, as axioms, only things that are self-evident.

Rules concerning demonstrations: (1) never undertake to demonstrate things so clear by themselves that you can resort to nothing clearer to prove them; (2) always prove slightly obscure propositions and in proving them only use either most evident axioms or already granted or demonstrated propositions; (3) always substitute mentally the definitions for the defined so as to avoid equivocations in their terms.

Of these eight rules, three are not absolutely necessary; to wit: to define no perfectly clear term in definitions; to make sure that all axioms are granted as evident; in demonstration not to demonstrate things well known by themselves. There is no harm in doing those things, on the contrary; but the five other rules are absolutely necessary; to wit: in defining, to define all, however slightly, obscure or equivocal terms, and never to use a term not perfectly known or already explained; with respect to axioms, only to beg perfectly evident ones; in demonstrating, to prove all propositions by evident axioms or already demonstrated propositions, and to avoid equivocation in terms by mentally substituting the defined for the definition.

These rules have nothing new, but to apply them outside geometry would be an entirely new thing. And it would not be an easy one! See Brunschvicg ed., pp. 189-190. In the Lewis edition, *De l'art de persuader*, pp. 118-121.

7. Pascal, *Pensées*, ed. Brunschvicg, sec. I, 1; pp. 317-319; join art. 2-4.

8. "The knowledge of the first principles, such as there is of space, time, movement, numbers, is as solid as any one of those which reasoning provides. And it is on these cognitions of *heart*, of *instinct* [italics ours], that reason must lean and found all its discourse. The heart feels that there are three dimensions in space, and that numbers are infinite; then reason demonstrates that there are not two square numbers of which one is double the other. Principles are felt, propositions are concluded; and the whole with certitude, though by different ways. Now it is as useless and as ridiculous for reason to require

from the heart proofs of its first principles, in order to assent to them, as it would be ridiculous for the heart to require from reason a feeling of all the propositions which it demonstrates, in order to subscribe to them." Pascal, *Pensées*, ed. L. Brunschvicg, *ed. cit.*, sec. IV, n. 282, pp. 459-460. Ed. Lewis, pp. 264-265. In the same passage Pascal infers two consequences of capital importance, to which we shall have to return: (1) this powerlessness to demonstrate principles should render reason modest without ruining our certitude (since reason is not our only source of certitude); (2) the truth of revelation is perceptible only to the heart, and since revelation is essentially divine, man cannot give religion to man by resorting to reasoning only.

9. "Those that are used to judge by feeling understand nothing in matters of reasoning, for they want presently to penetrate at a glance and are not used to seek for principles. And the others, on the contrary, who are used to reason from principles, understand nothing in matters of feeling, being always in quest of principles and unable to see at a glance." Pascal, *Pensées*, *ed. cit.*, sec. I, n. 3, p. 321; ed. Lewis, p. 131.

10. On Méré, his friendship with Pascal and its alleged consequences for the evolution of Pascal's mind, see the carefully weighed and substantial remarks of L. Brunschvicg in the introduction to the Second Part of his own edition of the *Pensées*, pp. 115-117. Those interested in knowing Méré will want to know about another friend, Miton (cf. Brunschvicg, *op. cit.*, pp. 117-119).

11. Pascal, *Pensées*, ed. L. Brunschvicg, fragment *De l'esprit géométrique*, pp. 173-184.

12. Exercises can help to realize some impossibilities. For instance, if space is made up of indivisibles, a square double of another one should contain twice the same number of points; which is impossible, since no square number is double of another one. The difficulty: How can one cross an infinite number of points in a finite time? results from an illusion. Since both time and space are divisible to infinity, we actually cross an infinite number of parts of space in an infinite number of parts of time, which is not absurd.

13. Pascal, *Pensées*, ed. L. Brunschvicg, p. 183. Pascal adds this concluding remark that, although infinitely different, the two infinites are so related that the knowledge of one of them leads to the knowledge of the other one. Indeed, in numbers, if it is possible to multiply one of them by 100,000, for instance, it must likewise be possible to take one hundred thousandth part of it; so the possibility of increasing numbers to infinity implies the possibility of diminishing them to infinity. Those who do not grasp these fundamental notions will never understand geometrical demonstrations. On the contrary, those who do understand them will find themselves in a position to understand their own nature (as will presently be seen), and the reflections of a man about himself, if they are right, are more important to him than geometry.

14. Pascal, *Pensées*, ed. L. Brunschvicg, fragment 282, p. 459; note particularly: "We know we are not dreaming . . ."

15. Ibid., fragment 78, p. 361, cf. fragments 77 and 79. See also p. 361, the remarks made by Marguerite Périer, note 1.

16. Ibid., fragment 298, p. 470. That

the majority rule is a form of the rule of force, fragment 299, p. 470, and fragment 301, p. 471. On the variations of justice: "Why do you kill me?—What? don't you live on the other side of the water? My friend, if you lived this side, I would be a murderer and it would be unjust to kill you that way; but since you are living on the other side, I am a brave man, and it is just," fragment 293, p. 464. Cf. fragment 294, pp. 465-468; note, p. 466, the Jansenist touch: "No doubt there are natural laws, but that beautiful corrupted reason has corrupted everything." Same remark concerning fragment 297: We have no rules of true justice left; had we such rules, "we would not consider it a rule of justice to follow the usages of one's own country." Observe that Pascal is here speaking of personal experience: "I spent a long time of my life in the belief that there was a justice; and in this I was right, for there is one, to the extent that it pleased God to reveal it to us. But I did not understand it that way, and that is where I was wrong, for I believed that our justice was essentially just and that I was qualified to know and to judge it. But I found myself so many times unable to judge right that I finally conceived some mistrust of myself, then of others. I saw all men and countries changing, and so, after many changes of judgment concerning true justice, I knew that our nature was but a perpetual change, and, since that time, I did not change any more," *ed. cit.*, fragment 375.

17. Pascal clearly alludes to Descartes in his criticism of the dogmatics, but their chief representative figure, in his mind and writings, is Epictetus. The antithesis be-

tween Montaigne, who teaches man wholly to mistrust himself, and Epictetus, who, in moral problems, teaches man to trust himself entirely, is one of the recurring themes of Pascal's reflections. The classical text on this point is the *Conversation of Pascal and Mr. de Sacy on Epictetus and Montaigne.* This is the stylized report of such a conversation written by a man who, having at his disposal the papers left by Pascal, made excellent use of them in reporting his part in the discussion. Mr. de Sacy, one of the "Solitaries" of Port Royal, has never read Epictetus or Montaigne; after listening to an exposition of their doctrines by Pascal, he answers that he himself had found in St. Augustine the essentials of what these two philosophers have said, plus what is required to bridge their opposition. For a thorough study of the composition of the work, see Pierre Courcelle, *L'entretien de Pascal et de Mr. de Sacy, ses sources, ses énigmes* (Paris: Librairie Philosophique J. Vrin, 1961).

18. Fundamental text: fragment 72, *Disproportion of man*, in *Pensées*, ed. cit., pp. 347-358.

19. This theme has been developed by Pascal in *Pensées* that count among his more beautiful from the literary point of view; among others, *ed. cit.*, fragments 347 and 348, p. 488; fragment 358, p. 493; fragment 397-400, p. 509; fragment 416, p. 514; fragment 418, p. 515.

20. The irony of Pascal often ridicules the *divertissements* to which man resorts in order to forget his misery; for instance, *Pensées, ed. cit.*, sec. II, fragments 166-171, pp. 405-407. For a complete exposition of the problem, from initial boredom to its various remedies, sec.

II, fragments 131-143, pp. 388-399.
21. Essential text in *ed. cit.*, sec. VII, fragment 425, pp. 518-520.
22. *Pensées, ed. cit.*, sec. IV, fragment 282, pp. 459-460. On faith: fragments 277-281, pp. 458-459.
23. It is difficult to know if Pascal would admit, in the present condition of man, demonstrations of the existence of God. In his primitive condition, such proofs would have been useless; are they now possible? On this point, Pascal observes that metaphysical proofs are so intricate that they can help few men; moreover, these men are impressed by the proofs only while they are seeing them; last, thus to know there is a God does not imply the knowledge of Jesus Christ. Only those who communicate with God through Christ know at once their misery and their mediator with God: *Pensées, ed. cit.*, sec. VII, fragment 543, p. 570.

This does not mean that Pascal takes no interest in the rational aspect of the problem, but his aim is less to prove the existence of God than to convince atheists that there are good reasons why they should assent to the proposition: there is a God. Such is the meaning of the famous *pari de Pascal*: Pascal's bet there is a God. It has been criticized as a proof of the existence of God.

It was not intended to be one. Addressing atheists, some of whom were heavy gamblers, Pascal puts the problem to them under the form of a gambling proposition. If you bet there is a God, and there is none, you lose nothing, except perhaps some finite goods in this life; but if there is a God, you win an infinite good after death; see *Pensées, ed. cit.*, sec. III, fragment 233, pp. 434-442.

In his Introduction to the *Pensées* (pp. 273-274) Léon Brunschvicg has excellently interpreted the argument. It supposes that reason is as unable to prove there is a God as to prove there is no God. Moreover, it takes stock of the fact that, anyway, we have to bet, and indeed, in the absence of proofs, we are betting in saying there is no God as much as in saying there is one. The question then is, practically speaking, how should one bet? By betting there is a God, I gamble finite goods for an infinite one. No hesitation is possible.
24. Pascal, *Pensées*, sec. VII, fragment 434, *ed. cit.*, pp. 528-534, and fragment 435, pp. 534-535.
25. *Ibid.*
26. For the *Mystery of Jesus, ed. cit.*, sec. VII, fragment 553, pp. 574-578. For the *Mémorial* of Nov. 23, 1654, *ed. cit.*, pp. 142-143.

PART 4   THE GOLDEN AGE OF METAPHYSICS

IX. Benedictus Spinoza

1. BENEDICTUS SPINOZA, b. Amsterdam, 1632; d. The Hague, 1677. Was raised an Orthodox Jew, thoroughly trained in Jewish theology, read medieval Jewish thinkers, Renaissance Stoics, and Neo-plato-

nists, learned Latin and began reading Descartes; was solemnly excommunicated from the Jewish community in 1656 for his belief that extension is present in God; lived quietly corresponding with learned men and making a living grinding lenses; published only one book in his lifetime, Parts I and II of *René Descartes' Principles of Philosophy* (published in 1663 with *Metaphysical Thoughts* added). From 1658 to 1660 wrote the *Short Treatise on God, Man, and His Well-Being*. Developed his thought further after 1660 in the *Treatise on the Healing of the Understanding*, which was not finished, perhaps because he decided upon using the geometrical order of exposition. Finally, the *Ethics Demonstrated According to the Geometrical Order* was completed in a draft form, containing three rather than the final five parts, in 1665. Then launched the explosive *Theologico-Political Treatise* in support of Jan DeWitt's effort to have the Reformed Church disestablished. In 1673, Spinoza's growing fame, spread abroad by those who had talked with him and written to him, resulted in his nomination to a chair at Heidelberg, which he refused because he wanted to keep his freedom. During that time he was busy revising and expanding the *Ethics*, but when he got ready to publish it in 1675, the uproar that was stirred up about it made him decide to withdraw it from the printers. The *Ethics* appeared just after his death in 1677, along with the *Treatise on the Healing of the Understanding* and an unfinished *Political Treatise*, started not long before his death.

Biographical works: A. Wolf, *Life of Spinoza*, published with his translation of *A Short Treatise on God, Man, and His Well-Being* (London: Black, 1910); S. von Dunin-Borkowski, S.J., *Der Junge De Spinoza* (Münster: Aschendorff, 1910); and S. von Dunin-Borkowski, S.J., *Aus den Tagen Spinozas* (4 vols.; Münster: Aschendorff, 1933-1936).

Collective edition: *Opera*, ed. C. Gebhardt (4 vols.; Heidelberg, 1925). The major works in English, translated by R. H. M. Elwes, *The Chief Works of Benedictus Spinoza* (New York: Dover, 1951).

Doctrinal: Richard McKeon, *The Philosophy of Spinoza* (New York: Longmans, Green, 1928). L. Roth, *Spinoza* (London: Benn, 1929). Stuart Hampshire, *Spinoza* (Baltimore: Penguin Books, 1954). H. Wolfson, *The Philosophy of Spinoza* (2 vols.; Cambridge: Harvard University Press, 1934) (also same in one volume, 1948), especially helpful for medieval Jewish background. On relations with Descartes, see P. Lachièze-Rey, *Les origines cartésiennes du Dieu de Spinoza* (Paris: Alcan, 1932). For an analysis of the *Ethics*, see H. H. Joachim, *A Study of the Ethics of Spinoza* (Oxford: Clarendon, 1901) and *Spinoza's Tractatus de intellectus emendatione: A Commentary* (Oxford: Oxford University Press, 1940). H. F. Hallett, *Benedictus Spinoza: The Elements of His Philosophy* (New York: Oxford University Press, 1957). David Bidney, *The Psychology and Ethics of Spinoza* (New Haven: Yale University Press, 1960).

2. This means, of course, that Leibniz had to reject Cartesian elements not only in Spinoza but also in Malebranche. We shall see later, however, that Leibniz' independence from Descartes was incomplete.

3. Spinoza states the principle explicitly: "The order and connection of ideas is the same as the order and connection of things" (*Ethics* II, Prop. VII).

4. *Ethics* I, Third Definition.

5. "By attribute I understand what the intellect perceives as constituting the essence of a substance" (*Ethics* I, Fourth Definition).

6. Spinoza's doctrine should not be confused with Leibniz' notion that every particle of reality, every "monad," is actually animated. The Spinozistic pantheistic substance once assumed, there immediately follows an airtight parallelism between the two orders of body and spirit. Every body, from the simplest atom to the most complex assemblage of individual bodies into a composite like the human body, has its ideational counterpart, its exact intelligible representative in the parallel order of idea-modes; the slightest modification in one is accompanied by an exactly corresponding modification in the other, without causal interaction between the two orders of modes. There is no need of such interaction precisely because both orders are modal emanations of one and the same infinite reality. To attain the same unity without falling into pantheism, Leibniz, in addition to animating each monad, is obliged to postulate that each mirrors within itself all the rest of the universe and all the possible changes thereof.

7. *Ethics* II, Prop. XX.
8. *Ibid.*, Prop. XXVIII.
9. *Ibid.*, Prop. XLI.
10. Effects, according to Spinoza's own definition, are "affections of the body, by which the power of acting of the body itself is increased, diminished, helped or hindered, together with the ideas of these affections" (*Ethics* III, Definition 3).
11. *Ethics* III, Prop. XI.
12. *Ibid.*, Prop. LVIII.
13. *Ethics* II, Prop. XLIX, *Scholium.*
14. *Ibid.*, Prop. VII.
15. *Ethics* V, Prop. VI.

16. *Ibid., Scholium.*
17. *Ibid.*, Prop. XIV.
18. *Ethics* I, Prop. XV; *Ethics* V, Prop. XIV.
19. *Ethics* V, Prop. XV.
20. *Ethics* I, Prop. XVII, *Scholium.*
21. *Ethics* V, Prop. XXXII, Corollary.
22. *Ibid.*, Prop. XXXVI. Descartes, we must notice here, suggested as much when proving that God alone could be the adequate cause of the idea I have in the *cogito* of the infinitely perfect divine nature.
23. *Ibid.*, Prop. XXIII.
24. *Ibid., Scholium.*
25. *Ibid.*
26. PIERRE BAYLE (1640-1707), a Frenchman from Foix whom nonconformist convictions constrained to flee to Rotterdam; author of the influential *Dictionnaire historique et critique,* published in 1697, an alphabetic catalogue of every error, stupidity, and superstition he could discover. A worshiper of reason, Bayle does not attack the Faith directly, but rather by raising, as occasion demands, every conceivable difficulty and problem. By the time one has run through the whole list, so many problems have been so skillfully assembled that a direct attack on the Faith would seem superfluous. The encyclopedists found in Bayle's *Dictionary* many ready-made weapons in their battle against "superstition." W. Bolin, *Pierre Bayle, Sein Leben und seine Schriften* (Stuttgart, 1905). A. Cazes, *Pierre Bayle, sa vie, ses idées, son influence, son oeuvre* (Paris, 1905). Jean Delvolvé, *Essai sur Pierre Bayle. Religion critique et philosophie positive* (Paris, 1906). Cf. Pierre Bayle, *Textes choisis,* edited by Marcel Reymond (Paris, 1948).
27. Pierre Bayle, *Dictionnaire,* art. "Spinoza."

x. Gottfried Wilhelm Leibniz

1. GOTTFRIED WILHELM LEIBNIZ, b. Leipzig, 1646; d. Hanover, 1716. Was the son of a philosophy professor at Leipzig. His father died when Leibniz was six, but he still had a wonderful family library at his disposal. He wrote *Metaphysical Disputation on the Principle of the Individual* for his degree at Leipzig (1663), showing familiarity with late scholastics. He was refused for doctorate in law because of his age, but was accepted at Altdorf and offered a professorship, which he refused because he preferred a more active life. In 1666, he published a project for a kind of philosophical symbolic logic (*Dissertation on the Art of Combination*) to end dispute in philosophical problems ("Gentlemen, let us calculate!" would henceforth be the approach to difficult problems). His writings in law won him the more active post he was looking for; he joined the staff of the Elector of Mainz. The year 1672 found him in Paris to persuade Louis XIV that Egypt would be a more suitable object for his military attentions than Holland; but apparently Louis le Grand found more suitable subjects to talk to than Leibniz, so the diplomat had plenty of time to reflect on the Cartesian mathematical method in chats with Malebranche and Arnauld, and above all with the eminent physicist Christian Huyghens, who inflamed Leibniz' already great interest in mathematics. Dissatisfied with the Cartesian mechanistic view of the material world, Leibniz began to think of other alternatives; the first fruit of these reflections was a new sort of mathematical conception, the calculus (which Newton worked out also about the same time, around 1676). Returning to Germany (Leibniz had a new job now with the Hanoverian prince), he stopped to talk with Spinoza and to copy some notes from the *Ethics* manuscript. At Hanover he was historian and librarian of the House of Brunswick. Active in scientific societies, he carried on a learned correspondence, worked for the reunification of Christendom, founded and was first president of the Prussian Academy of Sciences, founded the first journal of German studies, *Acta Eruditorum*. He left behind a mountain of writings; his whole life long he wrote philosophy and engaged in scientific reflections.

Principal philosophical works: Other than those already mentioned, the following are among the more significant treatises: *The Discourse on Metaphysics*, 1686; a treatise answering Locke, especially Locke's attack on innate ideas, *New Essays Concerning the Human Understanding*, completed 1704, but not published until 1765; *Essays on Theodicy*, written in 1710 to answer Bayle's objection that the fact of evil and the goodness of God are rationally irreconcilable; in *The Principles of Nature and Grace* (1714) his philosophy is succinctly presented, and again in the *Monadology*, first published in 1720. Many important thoughts are to be found in short opuscules and even fragments which are gradually being published only in our own century. As these works are being published, it is encouraging to note that they do not tend to change the essence of what is already known of Leibniz' mind from the earlier available material.

Biographical and doctrinal: G. E.

Guhaver, *Gottfried Wilhelm, Freiherr V. Leibnitz* (Breslau: F. Hurt, 1846). Bertrand Russell, *A Critical Exposition of the Philosophy of Leibniz* (London: Allen and Unwin, 1937). Kurt Huber, *Leibniz* (Munich: Oldenburg, 1951). H. W. B. Joseph, *Lectures on the Philosophy of Leibniz* (Oxford: Clarendon, 1949). Yvon Belaval, *Pour connaître la pensée de Leibniz* (Paris: Berdas, 1952). J. Moreau, *L'univers leibnizien* (Paris: F. Vitte, 1956). Herbert Carr, *Leibniz* (New York: Dover, n.d.). Ruth Saw, *Leibniz* (Baltimore: Penguin, n.d.).

Collective edition: The Prussian Academy of Sciences began a complete critical edition of Leibniz' work about 1923. It is to contain forty volumes in seven series; to wit: (1) general, political, and historical correspondence, 11 vols.; (2) philosophical correspondence, 6 vols.; (3) mathematical, scientific, and technical correspondence, 5 vols.; (4) political writings, 4 vols.; (5) historical writings, 4 vols.; (6) philosophical, theological, and juristic writings, 6 vols.; (7) mathematical, scientific, and technical writings, 4 vols. So far, only two volumes of philosophical interest have appeared, a volume of philosophical correspondence, *Philosophischer Briefwechsel* (Darmstadt: Reichl, 1926), and a volume of philosophical writings, *Philosophische Schriften* (Darmstadt: Reichl, 1930). There are two older collections, edited by Gerhardt, upon which one must in the meantime rely: *Die mathematischen Schriften von G. W. Leibniz* (7 vols.; Berlin: Asher, 1849-1863), and *Die philosophischen Schriften* (7 vols.; Berlin: Weidmann, 1875-1890). Important supplements: L. Couturat, *Opuscules et fragments inédits de Leibniz* (Paris: Alcan, 1903); G. Grua, *G. W. Leibniz, Textes inédits* (2 vols.; Paris: Presses Universitaires de France, 1948).

English translations: *Leibniz Selections*, ed. P. Wiener (New York: Scribner, 1951). *Leibniz' Discourse on Metaphysics, Correspondence with Arnauld and Monadology*, tranlsated by G. R. Montgomery (Chicago: Open Court, 1902). *The Monadology*, translated by H. W. Carr (Los Angeles: University of Southern California Press, 1930). *New Essays Concerning Human Understanding*, translated by A. G. Langley (3d ed.; LaSalle, Ill.: Open Court, 1949). *Theodicy*, translated by S. Huggard (New Haven: Yale University Press, 1952).

On Leibniz and his times: André Robinet, *Malebranche et Leibniz* (Paris: J. Vrin, 1955). Rudolf Meyer, *Leibniz and the Seventeenth Century Revolution*, translated by J. P. Stern (Cambridge: Bowes and Bowes, 1952). W. H. Barber, *Leibniz in France, from Arnauld to Voltaire* (New York: Oxford University Press, 1955).

2. In a letter to Remond, Leibniz related the steps in the movement that brought him to metaphysics: "After I had freed myself of the usual scholastic philosophy, I fell upon the writings of the moderns, and I can still remember going for a walk one day at the age of fifteen in a little wood near Leipzig called Rosenthal, and on this walk I reflected whether I should retain substantial forms. Mechanism finally triumphed and induced me to devote myself to mathematics, into whose depths, to be sure, I did not penetrate until later under Huyghens, whose acquaintance I made in Paris. But when I sought the ultimate grounds of mechanism and

of the laws of motion themselves, I saw to my surprise that it was not possible to find them in mathematics, and that I should have to return to metaphysics" (Leibniz to Remond, 10 Jan. 1714; cf. *Philosophische Schriften*, Vol. III, p. 606).

3. *First Truths*, translated and edited by T. V. Smith and Marjorie Greene, in *From Descartes to Kant* (Chicago: The University of Chicago Press, 1940), pp. 340-346.

4. *Ibid.*, p. 341.

5. In the Introduction to the *New Essays on the Human Understanding*, Leibniz asserts the inherent intelligibility of all things, and even goes so far in his reaction to Locke's insistence that there is much we do not and cannot know as to declare that anything conformed to the natural order can be known by some creature. Here is the passage: ". . . One must deny (at least in the natural order) that which is not intelligible nor explicable. I maintain then that substances, material and immaterial, would not be conceived in their bare essence without activity; that activity is of the essence of substance in general, and finally, that the conception of creatures is not the measure of God, but that their force of conception is the measure of the power of nature, everything conformed to the natural order being conceivable or understandable by some creature. . . . In the order of nature God does not arbitrarily give indifferently to different substances this or that quality; he will only give those which are natural to them, i.e., those which can be derived from their nature as explicable modifications." Although the excess rationalism of this passage can be attributed to Leibniz' reaction to Locke's occult-

ism, we can still reconcile it with Leibniz' insistence, even in this same Introduction, that much of our knowledge consists of contingent judgments and, worse, is determined by confused perceptions which work their effect on us without their presence even being apperceived. In the passage just quoted, Leibniz speaks *de jure;* in his psychological analyses of how we actually understand things, he speaks *de facto.*

6. *First Truths*, ed. cit., p. 341.

7. *The Principles of Nature and of Grace*, in T. V. Smith and Marjorie Greene, *From Descartes to Kant*, p. 364. (All italics are Leibniz'.)

8. *Ibid.*

9. *Ibid.*, p. 365.

10. *Ibid.*

11. *Ibid.*, p. 365.

12. *Ibid.* (Italics ours.)

13. *First Truths*, p. 341.

14. *Ibid.*, p. 343.

15. *Ibid.*, p. 345.

16. *Ibid.*, p. 342.

17. *Ibid.*

18. *Ibid.*

19. *Ibid.*, p. 343.

20. *Ibid.* Cf. *The Cartesians Move toward Occasionalism.*

21. *Ibid.*

22. *Ibid.*

23. *Ibid.*

24. "A Letter of Leibniz on His Philosophical Hypothesis, etc.," in *The Philosohpical Works of Leibniz*, translated by G. M. Duncan (New Haven: Tuttle, Morehouse and Taylor, 1890), No. 15, pp. 92-93.

25. "So what St. Thomas acknowledged concerning separated intelligences, which he declared never differed in number alone, must also be said of other things" (*First Truths*, p. 341).

26. In the intriguing notion of body

as *mens momentanea* mentioned in an early work, we see Leibniz at work reducing the universe to one essential force manifested in many infinitesimal points, each of a different intensity. The real trick here is to make matter a kind of less talented reality. "No force (*conatus*) without motion endures beyond the moment except in mind. Now what in the moment is force, is in time the motion of a body: here appears the door leading to the true distinction between mind and body that has heretofore been explained by no one. For every body is *mens momentanea*, or mind lacking in memory, because *mens momentanea* or body does not retain a force beyond the moment—either its own force or that of another body opposed to it" (*Die philosophischen Schriften von G. W. Leibnitz*, herausgegeben von C. J. Gerhardt [Berlin, 1880], Vol. IV, p. 230).

27. The Principles of Nature and Grace, ed. cit., p. 360.

28. Ibid., pp. 360-361.

29. Ibid., p. 361.

30. Ibid.

31. Ibid.

32. Ibid.

33. Ibid., p. 362.

34. Ibid.

35. Ibid.

36. "Soul" is the term for an entelechy monad capable of feeling or sentiment; "Spirit" is the term Leibniz actually uses for the human soul, alone capable of apperception.

37. Introduction to *New Essays on the Human Understanding*.

38. Nature and Grace, pp. 362-363.

39. Necessary and Contingent Truths, in Smith and Greene, *op. cit.*, p. 348.

40. Ibid.

41. Ibid., pp. 349-350.

42. Ibid., p. 350.

43. Leibniz' correspondence with Clarke, Leibniz' fifth paper, para. 1-9 (*Philosophical Works of Leibniz*, ed. Duncan [pp. 254-256]).

44. Ibid., para. 7.

45. "The motive inclines without necessitating; that is, without imposing an absolute necessity. For when God (for instance) chooses the best; what he does not choose, and is inferior in perfection, is nevertheless possible" (Correspondence with Clarke, Leibniz' fifth paper, para. 8).

46. Necessary and Contingent Truths, in Smith and Greene, *op. cit.*, pp. 350-351.

47. We are talking here about the freedom, the degree of self-direction, possessed by creatures capable of the highest degree of perception. It is only beyond the limits of the chains of "efficient causality" that there can be the kind of freedom that involves reflective self-possession and the grasp of ultimate goals. But even the lowest monads possess some freedom, in the sense that they develop from out of themselves and are to some extent self-directing. No action of any monad is either completely determined or completely undetermined. The difference between the lowest monad and the highest is one of degree of determinateness.

48. Necessary and Contingent Truths, p. 351.

49. Ibid., p. 347.

xi. Christian Wolff

1. CHRISTIAN WOLFF (often spelled "Wolf," from "Wolfius," the Latinized form of the name), b. Breslau, 1679; d. Halle, 1754. After some theological studies, turned to philosophy and completed his studies at Leipzig, 1703; became acquainted with Leibniz and was appointed professor of mathematics at the University of Halle, 1706; but he soon began to teach philosophy and he did so in a rationalist spirit which earned him the hostility of his "pietist" colleagues. Expelled from the country, he migrated to the University of Marburg, where he taught from 1723 till the "philosopher king," Friedrich II, acceded to the throne of Prussia in 1740. He then was recalled to Halle, where he taught till his death.

The works of Wolff divide into two classes, those which he wrote in Latin and those which he wrote in German (thus becoming, after Leibniz, the main creator of the German philosophical vocabulary).

Latin works: *Philosophia rationalis, sive logica methodo scientifica pertractata et ad usum scientiarum atque vitae aptata* (Frankfurt and Leipzig, 1728). *Philosophia prima, sive ontologia methodo scientifica pertractata qua omnis cognitionis humanae principia continentur* (Frankfurt and Leipzig, 1730). *Cosmologia generalis methodo scientifica pertractata, qua ad solidam imprimis Dei atque naturae cognitionem via sternitur* (ibid., 1731). *Psychologia empirica methodo scientifica pertractata, qua ea quae de anima humana indubia experientiae fide constant, continentur . . .* (ibid., 1732). *Psychologia rationalis methodo scientifica pertractata, qua ea, quae de anima humana indubia experientiae fide innotescunt, per essentiam et naturam animae explicantur et ad intimiorem naturae ejusque auctoris cognitionem profutura proponuntur* (ibid., 1734). *Theologia naturalis methodo scientifica pertractata* (2 vols.; *ibid.*, 1736-1737. *Philosophia practica universalis methodo scientifica pertractata* (2 vols.; *ibid.*, 1738-1739). *Jus naturae methodo scientifica pertractatum* (8 vols.; *ibid.*, 1740-1748). *Jus gentium methodo scientifica pertractatum* (Halle, 1750). *Philosophia moralis sive ethica methodo scientifica pertractata* (4 vols.; Halle, 1750). *Oeconomica* (*ibid.*, 1750).

German works: *Vernünftige Gedanken von den Kräften des menschlichen Verstandes und ihrem richtigen Gebrauch in der Erkenntniss der Wahrheit* (Halle, 1712). *Vernünftige Gedanken von Gott, der Welt und der Seele des Menschen, auch allen Dingen überhaupt* (Frankfurt and Leipzig, 1719). *Vernünftige Gedanken von der Menschen Thun und Lassen zur Beförderung ihrer Glückseligkeit* (Halle, 1720). *Vernünftige Gedanken von der Absichten der natürlichen Dinge* (Frankfurt, 1723).

Doctrinal: F. W. Kluge, *Christian von Wolff, der Philosoph* (Breslau, 1831). K. G. Ludovici, *Ausfürlicher Entwurf einer Vollständigen Historie der wolffischen Philosophie* (3 vols.; Leipzig, 1736-1738). Same author: *Sammlung und Auszüge der sämmtlichen Streitschriften wegen der wolfischen Philosophie* (Leipzig, 1738). W. Arnsberger, *Wolfs Verhältniss zu Leibniz* (Heidelberg, 1897). H. Pichler, *Ueber Wolfs Ontologie* (Leipzig, 1910). Mariano Campo, *Christiano Wolf e il razionalismo precritico* (2 vols.; Milano: Vita e Pensiero, 1939).

2. Two main causes have contributed to win Wolff the favor of the schoolmen. First, although a rationalist and a Protestant, Wolff was careful to stress the perfect agreement of his philosophy with

the teaching of Scripture. Next, he carefully retained the philosophical terminology of the scholastics, not, however, without adapting it to the needs of his own philosophy. At the same time, Wolff always insisted that, while agreeing with that of the scholastics, his own language could be made to agree also with that of Descartes. Many departures from the language and method of Thomas Aquinas in modern scholasticism are due to the influence of Wolff. Here are a few examples borrowed from his *Ontologia* (the word itself is a case in point). (The work is divided into paragraphs with a continuous numbering.) On retaining the language of the schools, *Ontologia*, para. 7-22; how to do so, para. 11-14.—*Principium contradictionis* and *principium rationis sufficientis:* the principle of contradiction applies to essences, that of sufficient reason applies to existences; definition of the latter: "Per rationem sufficientem intelligimus, id, unde intelligitur, an aliquid sit," para. 56; "Propositio quod nil sit sine ratione sufficiente cur potius sit, quam non sit, dicitur principium rationis sufficientis," para. 77; the principle is Leibnizian in origin and dominates the doctrine of Wolff; without it, Wolff says, the world becomes a *Schlaraffendland.* —*Causality:* "Ratio illa in causa contenta, cur causatum vel simpliciter existat, vel tale existat, et illud ipsum quod *causalitatem* appellarunt scholastici," para. 884.—As understood by Wolff, the notion of cause includes all the preceding determinations: "Causa est principium a quo existentia sive actualitas entis alterius ab ipso diversi dependet, tum quatenus existit, tum quatenus tale existit," para. 881.—The very way of dividing philosophy into

Ontology, Cosmology, Psychology, etc., has come to the modern scholastics from Wolff, as well as their general tendency to use an analytical method of exposition in their philosophy: P. Gény, S.J., *Questions d'enseignement de la philosophie scholastique* (Paris: Beauchesne, 1913).

3. Order of key notions as given in Wolff's *Ontologia* (the numbers indicate paragraphs): *Something:* "Aliquid est cui notio aliqua respondet," para. 59.—*Possible:* "Possibile est, quod nullam contradictionem involvit, seu, quod non est impossibile," para. 85.—*Being:* "Ens dicitur, quod existere potest, consequenter cui existentia non repugnat," para. 134; cf. "Quoniam illud existere potest, quod possibile est [para. 133], quod possibile est, ens est," para. 135.—*Essence:* "Essentia primum est quod de ente concipitur, nec sine ea ens esse potest," para. 144. "Per essentiam ens possibile est," para. 153. This way to conceive essence agrees with that of the schoolmen: "Sane Franciscus Suarez e Societatis Jesu, quem inter Scholasticos res metaphysicas profundius meditatum esse constat, in *Disputationibus Metaphysicis*; tom. I, disp. ii, sec. 4, para. 57; essentiam rei id esse dicit, quod est primum et radicale ac intimum principium omnium actionum ac proprietatum quae rei conveniunt," para 169. All this, Wolff thinks, agrees with the teaching of both Descartes and Thomas Aquinas, for the simple reason that Descartes had learned it from the Jesuits; *loc. cit.—Existence:* "Existentiam definio per complementum possibilitatis," para. 174 (a nominal definition). "Existentia entis contingentis nonnisi modus ejus est," para. 316 (as such it is not included in essence and requires a sufficient rea-

son).—*Substance:* "Substantia est subjectum, cui insunt essentialia et attributa eadem, dum modi successive variant," para. 770; Wolff considers himself on this point in agreement with the schoolmen as well as with Descartes, para. 771-772. On the part played by Wolff in the history of the notion of being, cf. E. Gilson, *Being and Some Philosophers* (Toronto: Pontifical Institute of Mediaeval Studies, 1949), pp. 112-121.

4. Definition of the *essentialia*, para. 142-143; of attributes and modes, para. 148; since, unlike attributes, modes do not necessarily belong to the essence, the sufficient reason of a mode always is some antecedent mode, or else some other being, para. 162; that existents are fully determined beings, para. 226; so they have their own principle of individuation: "Per principium individuationis intelligitur ratio sufficiens intrinseca individui"; schoolmen call it *haecceitas*, para. 228.

The creation of the world is accounted for by Wolff in truly Leibnizian spirit. The infinitely perfect being, which is by itself, causes the existence of all the rest. When its efficient cause exists, a "possible" becomes an "existible" (*Theologia naturalis . . . ,* I, para. 224); the power of God is such a cause, since it is the power of conducting possibles to actuality (I, para. 222); there always is a motive for the perfect being to will, or not to will, something (I, para. 312); mere possibility does not account for actual existence (I, para. 315); the motive of the divine will is the representation of the best (I, para. 389); from among all possible worlds, God has selected this one because it contains more perfection than they; had God made another choice, there would be no "objective reason" for

it and the principle of sufficient reason would not be respected (I, para. 325); so this world is the best possible one: "Mundus, qui existit, est omnium possibilium perfectissimus" (I, para. 386). This conclusion inevitably raises the problem of the existence of evil in that most perfect of all possible worlds; Wolff has discussed it at great length, especially I, para. 370-375, and I, para. 546-614. The principles laid down by Leibniz in his *Theodicy* dominate Wolff's discussion of the problem.

5. Cosmology applies the conclusions of ontology to the consideration of the totality of existing beings. It divides into "scientific general cosmogony" (directly derived from ontology) and "experimental cosmogony" (derived from observation: see Fr. Bacon). General cosmogony paves the way to *a posteriori* proofs of the existence of God to be given in Natural Theology: *Cosmologia generalis* (ed. 1721), para. 1-6.

6. "Mundus propemodum se habet ut horologium automaton," para. 117. Wolff says the world is very much like a clock, but not quite, because in it some of the parts enjoy freedom. On the other hand, the watchmaker is always able to modify the structure and functioning of the clock; so also God is able to act upon the world from without and to alter the course of events. This divine intervention in universal mechanism is called a miracle, and indeed "the all-powerfulness of God extends to all possibles."

7. Wolff agrees with the notion (common to Bacon, Descartes, and Leibniz) that all physical changes should be explained by the structure and composition of bodies; to do so is to resort to a "mechanica philosophia," para. 75; conse-

quently, all bodies are machines: "Quoniam corpora sunt entia composita, compositum omne machina est," para. 120. Every simple substance is endowed with a force of *inertia*, which accounts for its aptitude to resist ("resistibilitas"), para. 129-132, as well as with a moving force ("vis motrix"), para. 137. These two forces account for all changes taking place in bodies, para. 138. Matter is extension endowed with the force of inertia, para. 141 (a "nominal" definition). The moving force consists in a continuous effort to change: "Vis motrix consistit in continuo conatu mutandi locum," para. 149.

8. The active or moving force of a simple body must be conceived as a substance, para. 169. The effort (*conatus*) of the substance is the reality of motion, para. 173. The force of inertia is but a confused phenomenon, similar to sensible qualities; such things look like substances but are not (Wolff calls them "phenomena substantiata," para. 299-300). Bodies are aggregates of simple substances, para. 176. There is nothing substantial in bodies except simple substances, para. 177. Internal principles of bodies, when irreducible to others, are called elements, para. 185. Elements are called "atoms"; these divide into two classes (1) "material elements," further divisible in themselves, but which, in fact, no actually existing cause is able to divide; (2) "atoms of nature," which are indivisible in themselves as having no parts: "Atomus naturae dicitur, quod in se indivisibile est, ideoque partibus destituitur, in quas resolvi possit," para. 186.

9. The problem of the "communication of substances" (i.e., the possibility for two distinct substances to act and react toward each other)

has lost some of its acuity in the doctrine of Wolff. The "harmony" of all substances is not a supposition, it is a fact. As an intelligent cause, God can produce causes so conceived that they themselves will produce effects; that chain of causes and effects (which is a fact) requires no other explanation; on the connexity of causes and effects, para. 23-33, leading to this conclusion: "Si agens intelligens causam ideo producit, ut existere possit causatum, nexus rerum successivarum consistit in dependentia causati a causa et dependentia finis a medio, et actionis causae efficientis a fine simul," para. 34; cf. para. 53. Now all finite beings can be connected between themselves (para. 44) and their whole constitutes the world, para. 48.

The question of *how* that harmony was first achieved and still is being preserved is an entirely different one. This time the answer cannot be a fact, but a hypothesis. The more probable hypothesis will therefore be the true one. Wolff is chiefly interested in the problem with respect to the union of soul and body. See below, note 11.

10. Rational psychology is the science of that which is possible by the human soul ("scientia eorum quae per animam humanam possibilia sunt," *Psychologia rationalis* . . .[1735], para. 1). As all substances, souls are simple and endowed with a tendency to change, para. 56-58. Every soul represents to itself the universe according to the situation of its body and to the mutations taking place in its sense organs, para. 62. All changes in the soul originate from sensations, para. 62 (which does not mean that sensations are their causes; see below, note 11). Thus to be representative of the universe is for

the soul its very *essence:* "Essentia animae consistit in vi repraesentativa universi materialiter et constitutione organorum sensoriorum limitata," para. 66. The representative force of the soul is its very *nature*: "Natura animae in eadem vi repraesentativa consistit," para. 67. Affectivity follows from the soul's innate effort to change; more precisely from the perception of this effort, or tendency of the soul ("conatus mutandi perceptionem," para. 480). This awareness in the soul of being able to perceive plays an essential part in Wolff's doctrine of appetition and will; he calls it *percepturitio*, para. 481 (awareness of the possibility of a perception to be); that aptitude to foresee possible sensations enables us to pursue pleasant sensations and to avoid unpleasant ones, para. 488-489; hence the contrary movements of desire and aversion, para. 496; all pleasures and pains are therefore intuitive cognitions of perfection and imperfection, para. 500. Cf. *Psychologia empirica*, para. 511 and 518. On rational appetite (or desire) and rational aversion, *Psychologia rationalis*, para. 517-529. Note the opposition *voluntas* and *noluntas* (*de voluntate et noluntate*). The term *noluntas*, often considered an innovation made by Renouvier (in French, *nolonté*), was already familiar to Wolff.

11. The better part of the second volume of the *Psychologia rationalis* . . . (1734) is devoted to the problem of the *how* of the union of soul and body. Simply to say that there is interaction of soul and body is to say nothing, for indeed the problem now is to know how such an interaction could take place. The more generally received answer is that God actually imparts to substances their powers to cause effects in other substances as well as in themselves (*influxus physicus*); this is to turn nature into a permanent miracle, since it is the continuous seat of divine interventions (*Psychologia rationalis*, para. 588). Another answer to the question is Malebranche's system of "occasional causes," a not very probable one, para. 608. The third and better answer is the "pre-established harmony" such as Leibniz understood it. In that system, there has been one single miracle: creation. God having established perfect reciprocal agreement between bodies and minds, all the world history could develop in a purely natural way: "praestabilitio harmoniae inter animam et corpus est miraculum in creatione rerum facta, sed ejus deinceps vi naturaliter in singulis hominibus perpetuo consequitur perceptionum ac appetitionum animae et motuum corporis ubi est mutuo consentientium coexistentia," para. 629. Wolff insists on the fact that the harmony and relations of mind and body remain identically the same, however we may choose to account for it, para. 631; liberty is equally conceivable in the system of *influxus physicus* and in that of "pre-established harmony," para. 632-633. So the system of pre-established harmony is extremely probable ("Systema harmoniae praestabilitae admodum est probabile," para. 638); it is simpler and clearer than the others: "simplicius enim est aliis et liquidius," para. 639; the hypothesis is that of Leibniz (para. 639); should anybody be too dense to grasp the meaning of the doctrine, let him follow the system of *influxus physicus* and reject the better one, but at least he should put no malice in his rejection of it, para. 640.

12. The *Theologia naturalis* divides

into two volumes, each of which constitutes a complete whole in itself. Vol. I contains the *a posteriori* demonstration of the existence of God along with all that can be known of God that way. Vol. II contains the *a priori* demonstration of the existence of God along with all its consequences for our knowledge of his nature. The moments of the *a posteriori* proof are as follows: There is being by itself because according to the conclusions of *Ontologia* (para. 309) there is necessary being, and since such being has in itself the sufficient reason for its existence, being by itself necessarily exists. Since Scripture calls such a being God, there is a God (*Theologia* . . . , I, para. 69). The visible world is not being by itself, because it is not simple; hence it is by another (*ibid.*, para. 50-51). The cause of the visible world therefore is God: "Per Deum intelligimus ens a se, in quo continetur ratio sufficiens existentiae mundi hujus adspectabilis et animarum nostrarum" (*ibid.*, para. 67).

13. Theologia naturalis, I, para. 72.

14. Ibid., para. 31.

15. Ibid., para. 34.

16. The *a priori* proof is found in Vol. II. Wolff agrees with Leibniz, against Thomas Aquinas, that the argument of St. Anselm becomes valid if one begins by establishing the possibility (i.e., non-contradictory nature) of the idea of God. This can be done as follows: The supremely perfect being contains all compossible realities in their highest degree (*Theologia naturalis*, II, para. 6); such a being is infinite (II, para. 10); that absolutely supreme degree of reality excludes all possible defect (II, para. 11); reality in its absolutely supreme degree is possible (II, para. 12); the

absolutely perfect being is possible (II, para. 13); since existence is a perfection, the supremely perfect being necessarily exists (II, para. 20); the consequence necessarily follows from the fact that, in Wolff's doctrine, existence is a perfection belonging to essence; hence, since God is the supremely perfect being, he cannot lack existence, so *Deus necessario existit* (II, para. 21).

17. There is in Wolff a series of notions which it is useful to know in order to grasp the meaning of Kant's reaction against "dogmatism" in metaphysics. First that of "reality": "Realitatis hic nomen venit, quicquid enti alicui vere inesse intelligitur, non vero per perceptiones nostras confusas inesse videtur" (*Theologia naturalis*, II, para. 5); next, that reality is the absolutely highest degree of existence. Let us explain this: All existence is either contingent or necessary; now these are the only conceivable degrees in the order of existence (i.e., an existent cannot be anything else than either possible or necessary); so the absolutely supreme degree in existence is necessary existence, and since reality includes in itself actual existence, there is nothing higher, in the order of being, than actual reality (II, para. 20). Hence follows the famous ontological argument denounced by Kant: "Deus necessario existit. Deus enim continet omnes realitates compossibiles in gradu summo [para. 15]. Est vero idem possibile [para. 19]. Quamobrem cum possibile existere possit [para. 133 *Ontol.*], existentia eidem inesse potest; consequenter cum sit realitas [para. 20] et realitates compossibiles sint, quae enti una inesse possunt [para. 1], in realitatum compossibilium numero est. Jam porro existentia necessaria est gradus absolute summi [para. 20]. Deo igitur competit existentia necessaria, seu, quod perinde est, Deus necessario existit [para. 21]." The notion Kant will oppose is precisely that of actual existence conceived as one among the other possible realities. *18. The Philosophia moralis . . . ,* divides into five parts (five volumes published from 1750-1753): the main topics are as follows: I, Intellectual Virtues; II, Virtues of the Will; III, Duties toward God; IV, Duties toward Oneself; V, Duties toward Others. Ethics is the science of how man can freely make his actions to agree with natural law (I, para. 1); it teaches man how actually to acquire the supreme good; its end thus is the felicity of man; it presupposes all the other parts of philosophy (I, para. 7-8). It particularly presupposes the universal practical philosophy, or philosophy of action (*Philosophia practica universalis . . .* [1738-1739]) of which ethics is but a part; to wit: the part of universal practical philosophy that applies its own principles to moral problems. The central notion of Wolff's ethics is that of good and evil in the order of morality. Morally good are all the actions tending to the acquisition and conservation of the essential perfection of mankind in general and of every man in particular: "Actiones bonae seu committendae tendunt vel ad conservationem perfectionis essentialis, vel ad acquirendum accidentalem, vel ad conservationem generis humani et in specie familiae suae ejusque perfectionem, vel ad conservationem

perfectionis essentialis et acquisitionem accidentalis aliorum, vel denique ad perfectionem communem sociorum atque status eorumdem" (*Philosophia moralis*, II, para. 115). Wolff goes on to say that, from what precedes, it is easy to discover the root of all natural goodness in moral acts. It also shows how natural obligation is rooted in human nature itself. In fine, this teaches us that natural law, "whose sufficient reason is given in human nature itself, extends to all the actions to be performed by man." In accordance with the general inspiration of the philosophy of Leibniz (religious naturalism), Wolff concludes that such was the reason God could not have given man another law than natural law. This does not mean that to him the Christian law is worthless; but it does mean that the Christian law is good precisely because it is a perfect expression of natural law. Quite apart from its general trend, which is arguable, Wolff's ethics abounds in pertinent, useful, or noble moral advice. As an instance of what Wolff can do when at his best—and then he is very good indeed—one could read Part V, chap. 1, para. 1-53, on how to prepare oneself to practicing duties toward others, "De praeparatione ad praxim officiorum erga alios." From the point of view of the general conception of man typical of the eighteenth century Enlightenment, Part V brings to historians of ideas and literature priceless information. The whole enormous structure is dominated by its eighth proposition: *Finis ethicae est felicitas hominis.*

PART 5   A GOLDEN AGE IN ENGLAND

XII. The Cambridge Platonists

1. We have mentioned most often Whichcote, Smith, Cudworth, and More, but others are also grouped with these thinkers. Powicke, in the book listed below, includes chapters on Nathaniel Culverwell and Peter Sterry; de Pauley, in addition to quoting Lancelot Andrewes' sermon "On the Candle of the Lord," devotes chapters to Richard Cumberland, Culverwell, George Rust, and Edward Stillingfleet.

2. BENJAMIN WHICHCOTE, b. Shropshire, 1609; d. Cambridge, 1683. Graduated A.B., Emmanuel College, Cambridge, 1629; M.A. in 1633; B.D. in 1640; Fellow in the same Puritan-background college from 1633 and Sunday afternoon lecturer in Trinity Church from 1637 with great success. In 1644, named Provost of King's College, to his distaste, and Vice-chancellor for 1650-1651. With the Restoration, royal disfavor chased him to a series of respectable pastorates, finally terminating in thirteen years in London. His works consist of sermons and letters.

Collective edition: *The Works of the Learned Benjamin Whichcote, D.D.* (Aberdeen, 1751).

3. JOHN SMITH, b. Northamptonshire, 1616; d. Cambridge, 1652. Also Emmanuel College background, taking eight years to B.A., owing to bad health; M.A. 1644, and made Fellow of Queen's College, 1644, and in same year, dean. Considered at his early death an encyclopedia of holy learning, although a man of great humility and of unstinting generosity. Enthusiastic student of Plotinus, and deeply sincere Christian.

Works: Known for the ten *Select Discourses*, ed. Worthington (London, 1660). (Modern editions available; e.g., ed. H. G. Williams [Cambridge, 1859].)

4. RALPH CUDWORTH, b. Somerset, 1617; d. Cambridge, 1688. Another Emmanuel alumnus and Fellow in 1639. The most theoretical of the Cambridge group, wrote the immense (900 folio pages) *The True Intellectual System of the Universe*, published with a *Treatise Concerning Eternal and Immutable Ethics* (Edition by John Harrison [London, 1845]). Elected Master of Christ's College, 1654, where he lived until he died.

5. HENRY MORE, b. Lincolnshire, 1614; d. 1687. B.A. from Christ's College, the only one of our group not from Emmanuel; became Fellow at Christ's, 1639. Lived a quiet and contemplative life at Cambridge and the country home of Lady Conway, an intimate friend. More was the most ethereal of a rather ethereal group, so much so that he was even said to have smelled of violets! A lyrical and poetizing person, he too was steeped in Plotinus, but alas, also in pseudo-mystical and magical lore —the last of the Platonists.

Works: Main writings collected in *Divine Dialogues* (London, 1688); *A Collection of Several Philosophical Works of Dr. Henry More* (London, 1662); *Philosophical Poems*; also *An Explanation of the Grand Mystery of Godliness*, 1660. Works on the Cambridge Movement: John Tulloch, *Rational The-ology and Christian Philosophy in England in the Seventeenth Century*, in two volumes, of which Vol. II is entitled *The Cambridge Platonists* (Edinburgh and London, 1872). F. J. Powicke, *The Cambridge Platonists* (Cambridge, Mass.: Harvard University Press, 1926). W. C. de Pauley, *The Candle of the Lord* (London, 1937). E. Cassirer, *The Platonic Renaissance in England*, trans. Pettegrove (Austin: University of Texas Press, 1953).

6. Quoted by F. J. Powicke, *The Cambridge Platonists*, p. 127.

7. John Smith, "The Excellency and Nobleness of True Religion," chaps. iii and vi, in *Select Discourses*, pp. 361 ff and 392 ff.

8. Both quoted by Powicke, *op. cit.*, pp. 48-49.

9. Henry More, *Psychathanasia*, Book III, canto iv, st. 16.

10. Lancelot Andrewes, *Sermons* (1843 ed.), Vol. V, p. 319.

11. John Smith in the Discourse on

"The Excellence and Nobleness of True Religion."

12. Henry More, *op. cit.*, Book II, canto i, st. 7, p. 108.

13. Ralph Cudworth, *True Intellectual System*, Book I, chap. iii, sec. xxxvii, nos. 2, 5, and 11.

14. *Ibid.*, Book I, chap. iv.

15. John Smith in the "Discourse of the Immortality of the Soul."

16. ANTHONY ASHLEY COOPER, Lord Shaftesbury, b. 1671; d. 1713. Pioneer modern aesthetician, also moralist, great student of the Platonists, felt that all beauty and order in the world are the realization of a spiritual principle to which they lead back. His ethics is an aesthetic social eudaimonism. Principal work: *Characteristics of Men, Manners, Opinions, Times* (3 vols.; 1711).

17. The Cambridge influence on Shaftesbury is developed by E. Cassirer, *The Platonic Renaissance in England* (Austin: University of Texas Press, 1953), chap. vi.

XIII. John Locke

1. JOHN LOCKE, b. Wrington, near Bristol, 1632; d. Oates, 1704. Entered Christ Church, Oxford, 1652, where his views changed from the Puritanism of his youth to the broader outlook of the Church of England. Most active in scientific pursuits (he was Boyle's assistant), he found philosophy ("scholastic") uninspiring. Later he started reading Descartes, which at last convinced him that something could be done in philosophy. After receiving a medical degree, Locke was medical assistant to Lord Ashley (subsequently First Earl of Shaftesbury), ultimately becoming a patronage secretary to that peer

when he was made Lord Chancellor in 1672. From 1675 to 1682, poor health forced him into temporary retirement, which he spent in France developing his philosophical views. It was during that period that he expanded *An Essay Concerning Human Understanding*, two drafts of which he had already completed in 1671; the first edition was published in 1690. Locke was home in England only a short time when Shaftesbury's opposition to James II forced him to flee to Holland. The Glorious Revolution enabled him to return to England again in 1689. Not only did the *Essay* soon appear, but in the same year the *Two Treatises of Civil Government*. He published about this same time works on education, tolerance, and *The Reasonableness of Christianity*. Locke's views had become perfectly latitudinarian. Belief in Christ was the only necessary requirement for being a Christian. Although a member of the Board of Trade and Plantations, Locke spent most of his time at the country estate of friends, where he died peacefully in his seventy-third year.

Biographical: Lord King, *The Life of John Locke* (new ed., 2 vols.; London: Colburn and Bentley, 1830); and H. R. Fox-Bourne, *The Life of John Locke* (2 vols.; New York: Harper, 1876).

Collective edition: *The Works of John Locke* (10th ed., 10 vols.; London: Johnson, 1801).

Doctrinal: R. I. Aaron, *John Locke* (New York: Oxford University Press, 1937). D. J. O'Connor, *John Locke* (Baltimore: Penguin, 1952). For the political philosophy, see S. P. Lamprecht, *The Moral and Political Philosophy of John Locke* (New York: Columbia University Press, 1918); J. W. Gough, *Locke's Political Philosophy* (New York: Oxford University Press, 1950); J. W. Yolton, *John Locke and the Way of Ideas* (New York: Oxford University Press, 1956); E. L. Tuveson, *Imagination as a Means of Grace: Locke and the Aesthetics of Romanticism* (Berkeley: University of California Press, 1960); R. Polin, *La philosophie morale de John Locke* (Paris: Presses Universitaires de France, 1961).

2. *Essay Concerning Human Understanding*, Book I, chap. i, p. 2.
3. *Ibid.*
4. *Ibid.*, p. 4.
5. Letter to Edward Clarke, January

1, 1685, in *The Correspondence of John Locke and Edward Clarke*, Vol. I, ed. B. Rand (Cambridge: Harvard University Press, 1927), p. 117.
6. *An Essay Concerning Human Understanding*, Introduction, p. 5.
7. *Ibid.*, p. 7.
8. *Essay*, Book I, chap. ii, p. 22.
9. "By *determinate*, when applied to a simple idea, I mean that simple appearance which the mind has in its own view, or perceives in itself, when that idea is said to be in it" (*Essay*, "The Epistle to the Reader").
10. Locke underscores the element of *should* when he declares that a given word should stand for an idea that has been made sufficiently definite and articulated. "I say *should* be, because it is not everyone, nor perhaps anyone, who is so careful of his language as to use no word till he views in his mind the precise determined ideas which he resolves to make it a sign of. The want of this is the cause of no small obscurity and confusion in men's thoughts and discourses" (*ibid.*).
11. A word of caution, which holds not just for Locke but for all philosophers, is in order here. In elaborating a description of *experience*, a philosopher cannot proceed as though he had something lying out in front of him, an object which he has only to recount; "experience" is a reality englobing the "objective" and the "subjective" in the unity of a cognitive act; it is a complicated, bipolar phenomenon; indeed it is not a phenomenon at all, but the appearance of all phenomena in consciousness. Hence we should never be surprised to discover that a given "description" of experience is in fact a tissue of good intuitions and historically inherited, uncriticized presuppositions capable

of frustrating the philosopher's attempt to justify systematically his personal conviction.

Locke leaves little doubt about his basic personal human convictions in the matter at hand, and his fundamental intuition is sound indeed: Our "ideas" are surely not mere fantasies, but real knowledge about an objective world acquired in experiential contact with real things. But when the man assumes the technical role of *philosopher* and thus sets about the serious business of describing the "history" of how we build up our mature experience from some sort of original data, then uncriticized presuppositions are liable to obscure his sight.

12. *Essay*, Book II, chap. i, #2.

13. *Ibid.*, #4.

14. *Ibid.*, #3.

15. *Ibid.*, chap. ii, #1.

16. Which raises a good point: How distinct are the odor and the feel of a lily? The odor is the odor *of a lily*, and consequently tends to be the presence of the whole lily, so that we might say that it carries with it the whole *feel* of the flower. When I look at a blossom from five feet away, I can *see* the softness. One might reflect on this fact of experience if he wishes to understand the error of introducing the *abstraction* of distinctness into our fundamental perceptual experience.

17. *Essay*, Book II, chap. vii, #7-9.

18. *Ibid.*, #7.

19. *Ibid.*, #2.

20. *Ibid.*, #3.

21. *Ibid.*, chap. xii, #6 and 4.

22. *Ibid.*, #7. It was Locke's ambition to classify under these three categories all our complex ideas. In so doing, he introduced under each of the classifications a number of subdivisions. *Modes*, for example, are discovered to be of two kinds, simple and mixed, the simple modes combining ideas *of the same kind* to form complex modal ideas like space, duration, infinity; the mixed, combining *different sorts* of simple ideas to form complex conceptions like wrestling, hypocrisy, or beauty. In regard to the "how" of these combinations, Locke makes a remark that casts another light on his "realism." The mind, in putting together simple modes, usually patterns itself closely on combinations already existing in nature; but in putting together mixed modes, it often proceeds much more independently, concocting what Locke calls *notions* to signify that they are the mind's own fabrication. Moreover, even if once upon a time someone's mind may have been guided by observed complex unities in developing a conception like wrestling or hypocrisy, from then on men usually derive such ideas second hand, from custom, education, even from dictionary explanations. For most of us these concepts are nothing but "notions"; i.e., mere intellectual constructions. If Locke went no farther than just pointing out the possible transmission of such conceptions by other than experiential reference to the unities in nature upon which they are based, there would be no problem. But as he gets deeper into his descriptions of mixed modes, he tends to emphasize more and more the gratuitous and independent nature of the notions, even stressing that their interest lies purely in themselves, without any reference to natural external entities. Such an outcome is another development that is again not unexpected in view of Locke's having granted each atom of a simple idea a kind of independent content, making of it a building block ready to enter into an infinity of combinations within the spirit,

and without the need of any further reference back to the reality from which it originally came.

23. Essay, Book II, chap. xxiii, #1.

24. Ibid., #2.

25. Essay, Book III, chap. iii, #11.

26. Ibid., chap. vi, #2 and 3.

27. The empiricist tradition has steadily manifested a talent for seizing on an aspect of cognitive experience in which there are obvious limitations, and from that jumping to the conclusion that mankind can never expect its knowing faculties to do better than the worst performance they have been able to discover, despite the fact that we do manage to do so, all day, every day. A stick appears to bend in the water, a mirage appears on the desert, sugar tastes sour to a sick man; conclusion, we can never depend on the senses, for we can never be sure whether, in the present instance, they are not deceiving.

28. Essay, Book III, chap. vi, #7.

29. Ibid.

30. Ibid.

31. One could catalogue astonishing feats of the infantile mind generalizing, symbolizing, relating, naming. But the bachelor philosophers of old had little opportunity to observe babies, the more so as, in any case, young children were seldom educated under the care of their parents.

32. Essay, Book II, chap. xxi, #1 and 2.

33. Ibid., #4.

34. Ibid., chap. xxvii, #7. Locke common-sensibly points out that we can mean several different things when we speak of the identity of man. We can, as Descartes had said, think of the concept "man" as reflecting an identity of *substance*. We mean then by "one and the same man" one and the same "something" possessing a given series of attributes. But we can also mean by "man" a certain kind of *living organized body*; in this case "one and the same man" means "the same continued life communicated to different particles of matter, as they happen successively to be united to that organized living body" (*Essay*, Book II, chap. xxvii, #7). In such cases, the idea in our minds, of which the sound "man" is the sign, is nothing else but that of an animal of a certain form. "For I presume it is not the idea of a thinking or rational being alone that makes the idea of a man in most people's sense, but of a body, so and so shaped, joined to it; and if that be the idea of man, the same successive body, not shifted all at once must, as well as the same immaterial spirit, go to the making of the same man" (*ibid.*, 8).

Finally, we can mean by "one and the same man" one and the same *person*—one and the same "thinking intelligent being, that has reason and reflection, etc." (see the full quote in the text). In terms of Locke's philosophical position, it is this last that is important, and it is within the perspectives of this personal unity of consciousness that the whole *Essay* unfolds.

35. Ibid., 9.

36. Ibid.

37. Essay, Book IV, chap. i, 2.

38. Ibid., chap. ii, 1.

39. Ibid., chap. iv, 4.

40. Ibid., 5.

41. Ibid.

42. Ibid., 8.

43. Ibid., 6.

44. Ibid., 11.

45. Ibid., chap. iii, 10.

46. Ibid., 11.

47. Ibid.

48. Ibid., 12.

49. Ibid., 13.

50. Ibid., 14.

51. *Ibid.*
52. *Ibid.*, 29.
53. *Ibid.*, chap. ix, 1.
54. *Ibid.*, chap. x, 3.
55. *Ibid.*, chap. xi, 3.
56. *Ibid.*, 8.

57. *Ibid.*, 4-7.
58. See *The Second Treatise of Civil Government*, chap. ii.
59. *Ibid.*, chap. v.
60. *Ibid.*, chap. ix.
61. *Ibid.*, chap. viii.

xiv. The Influence of Newton

1. ISAAC NEWTON, b. Woolsthorpe, near Nottingham, 1642; d. London, 1727. Constructed complicated machines even as a child; went to Cambridge, entering Trinity in 1661; he was not twenty-five years old when he discovered the calculus, the law of the composition of light, and the law of gravitation. He became a professor at Cambridge, but moved very slowly in maturing to the full fruition of his great synthesis the ideas that had been with him from an early age. Finally, he published the *Mathematical Principles of Natural Philosophy* in 1687. In his fifties, Newton interested himself actively in public affairs and became Master of the Mint, a job he seemed to enjoy. From 1701 on, he lived in London all the time, having resigned from Cambridge. The *Optiks* was published in 1704. Newton was president of the Royal Society.

Biographical and doctrinal: L. T. More, *Isaac Newton, A Biography* (New York: Scribner, 1934). Herbert Butterfield, *The Origins of Modern Science* (London: Bell, 1950). G. N. Clarke, *Science and Social Welfare in the Age of Newton* (2d ed., Oxford: Clarendon, 1949). A. D. Morgan, *Essays on the Life and Work of Newton* (Lasalle, Ill.: Open Court, n.d.). E. N. da C. Andrade, *Sir Isaac Newton* (New York: Doubleday Anchor Books, 1958). E. A. Burtt, *Metaphysical Foundations of Modern*

Physical Science (New York: Doubleday Anchor Books, 1954).

Collective edition: *Opera quae extant omnia*, ed. Morsley (5 vols.; London: Nichols, 1779-1785).

2. Consider this tribute from no less a Frenchman than La Fontaine:

Les Anglais pensent profondément;
Leur esprit, en cela, suit leur tempérament;
Creusant dans les sujets, et forts d'expériences,
Ils étendent partout l'empire des sciences . . .

(La Fontaine, *Fables*, livre XII [1694], "Le Renard et les raisins.")

Translation:

The English think deeply,
Their spirit, in this, follows their temperament;
Digging into subjects, and strong in experiments,
They everywhere extend the empire of the sciences.

3. For a summary of the history leading up to Newton's synthesis, see the very readable study of Herbert Butterfield, *The Origins of Modern Science, 1300-1800* (London: Bell, 1950), pp. 106 ff.

4. According to Pemberton (*A View of Sir Isaac Newton's Philosophy* [London, 1728], p. 407), Newton claimed he had been misunderstood, that he had not intended "attraction" to explain anything but only to turn man's attention to a phenomenon which

has yet to be explained. In "Scholium generale" at the end of the third book of the *Principia*, he writes: "The ground of the quality of weight I have not yet been able to deduce from phenomena, and I do not allow myself to invent hypotheses." Actually, Newton was not a proponent of the notion that a force like attraction could really operate across an empty space. In both the *Principia* (2,11) and the *Optiks* (Queries 18-24) he suggests calling centripetal force "impact" (*impulsus*) rather than "attraction" (*attractio*) because the most likely hypothesis is the assumption of an ether everywhere, which is rarer close to the heavenly bodies than at a great distance from them; in this

way, light and warmth might also be explained.

5. Note in the hero-worshiping poem to Madame du Chatelet on the subject of Newton.

6. Newton's rational theology is contained in the "general Scholium" added to the second edition of the *Principia*, published in 1713; also in *Optiks*, Queries 28 and 29, and in the letters to Bentley.

7. Compare this remark in the Scholium, "Ordinary people conceive magnitudes only in relation to sensuous things," and his statement, at the close of Definition 8, that the "true, physical manner of conception is opposed to the mathematical"; *vere et physice* in opposition to *mathematice tantum!*"

PART 6 THE PHILOSOPHIES OF THE HUMAN MIND

xv. George Berkeley

1. BISHOP GEORGE BERKELEY (pronounced Barclay), b. Kilkenny, Ireland, 1685; d. Oxford, 1753. Went to Trinity College, Dublin; in 1707, became tutor; read Descartes, Locke, Malebranche, Newton, and Clarke. He was very exercised over the problem of Hobbes and proposed immaterialism as the only thorough answer; the *Philosophical Commentaries*, two notebooks written in 1707-1708 (but only discovered and published in 1871, re-edited more accurately in 1944), already contain this hypothesis; then in 1709, at the age of twenty-four, Berkeley published his findings as they clarified the problem of sight, in *An Essay towards a New Theory of Vision*; the following year came his masterpiece, the *Principles of Human Knowledge*; then in 1713, the *Three Dialogues*

between Hylas and Philonus. That year he left to spend eight years abroad. He was introduced to court circles in London by his countryman, Jonathan Swift; as the companion to the son of the Bishop of Ashe, he spent five years on the Continent, mostly in Italy. In 1720 he published a criticism of Newtonianism in terms of his own earlier works, *De Motu*. In 1721 he was called back to become Dean of Dromore in Ireland, and in 1724 of Derry. He returned to England to lobby for his idea of establishing a college in the Bermudas in order to raise the culture of the colonists and to advance the conversion of the Indians. In 1728, after four years of effort, having, he thought, obtained the backing he needed, he set sail for America and wound up in Newport, Rhode Island, where he spent three years waiting, while the Prime Minister made off with the needed funds for more urgent government projects. While here, he wrote *Alciphron, or the Minute Philosopher*, and built a house in Newport, Whitehall. When it was finally clear that Sir Robert Walpole was not coming through with the money, Berkeley left his books to Harvard and Yale and his house to Yale, and in 1731 returned to England. Another mark left by Berkeley, besides his books and the house, which still stands, was his name. In the nineteenth century, the university town in California where the main campus of the University of California is now located was given the name of Berkeley by a fervent admirer. In 1734 he published the *Analyst*, a criticism of basic notions in mathematics paralleling his earlier examination of physical concepts in *De Motu*. In the same year, he was appointed Bishop of Cloyne, and for twenty years zealously worked for the betterment of his flock. His last work of importance was *Siris: A Chain of Philosophical Reflections and Inquiries Concerning the Virtues of Tar-Water* (1744), which treats us to all of the bishop's wisdom, including his cure for dysentery. In 1752 he retired to Oxford, where his son was residing, and died there a few months later.

Biographical and Bibliographical: A. A. Luce, *The Life of George Berkeley, Bishop of Cloyne* (London: Nelson, 1949). B. Rand, *Berkeley's American Sojourn* (Cambridge, Mass.: Harvard University Press, 1932). T. E. Jessop, *A Bibliography of Berkeley* (New York: Oxford University Press, 1934). Claude Lehec, "Trente années

d'études berkeleyennes," in *Revue Philosophique*, April-June, 1953.

Collective editions: The older edition, *The Works of George Berkeley*, edited by A. C. Fraser (2d ed.; 4 vols. Oxford: Clarendon, 1901), is being replaced by a more critical edition, *The Works of George Berkeley, Bishop of Cloyne*, edited by A. A. Luce and T. E. Jessop (London: Nelson, 1948 ff). The most important philosophical works are grouped in one volume, edited by M. W. Calkins, *Berkeley: Essay, Principles, Dialogues, with Selections from Other Writings* (New York: Scribner, 1929).

Doctrinal: A. A. Luce, *Berkeley's Immaterialism: A Commentary on His "Treatise concerning the Principles of Human Knowledge"* (London: Nelson, 1945). G. D. Hicks, *Berkeley* (London: Benn, 1932). G. A. Johnston, *The Development of Berkeley's Philosophy* (New York: Macmillan, 1923). John Wild, *George Berkeley: A Study of His Life and Philosophy* (Cambridge: Harvard University Press, 1936). A. A. Luce, *Berkeley and Malebranche: A Study in the Origin of Berkeley's Thought* (New York: Oxford, 1934). H. M. Bracken, *The Early Reception of Berkeley's Immaterialism, 1710-1733* (The Hague: Nijhoff, 1959). J. J. Laky, *A Study of George Berkeley's Philosophy in the Light of the Philosophy of St. Thomas Aquinas* (Washington, D.C.: Catholic University of America, 1950). E. A. Sillem, *George Berkeley and the Proofs for the Existence of God* (New York: Longmans, Green, 1957). G. J. Warnock, *Berkeley* (Baltimore: Penguin, 1943).

2. The nominalist holds that only

the concrete thing is real and that all so-called universal ideas have absolutely no foundation in things but are merely arbitrary verbal constructions. The antithetical reaction is an idealism that would locate the source of all universal unity of our ideas in the mind. Many philosophers hold the middle position that "somehow" we have access to a potentially universal principle in things. Locke, for example, liked to leave the impression that we could form general ideas that have some real relevance to things. He discovered that he was unable to explain that relevance in terms of his fundamental epistemological decisions. Berkeley, in moving in to attack the Lockian general ideas, points out that real universal ideas would constitute a grasp of real "absolute natures" in things. He has little trouble showing that Locke's philosophy is unable to justify belief in such natures. No universal element can survive the shredding-machine of Locke's initial simple-idea analysis.

3. Berkeley quotes Locke in *Three Dialogues between Hylas and Philonus*, I.

4. *Principles of Human Knowledge*, I, 9.

5. *Ibid.*, 10.

6. *Ibid.*, 11.

7. *Ibid.*

8. *Ibid.*, 17.

9. *Three Dialogues*, I.

10. *Principles of Human Knowledge*, I, 19.

11. *Ibid.*

12. *Ibid.*, 28.

13. *Ibid.*, 29. The argument is Descartes'.

14. *Ibid.*, 30. Cf. Descartes' Sixth Meditation.

15. *Ibid.*, 31.

16. *Ibid.*, 32.

17. *Ibid.*, 49.

18. *Ibid.*, 48.

19. *Ibid.*, 148.

20. *Ibid.*, 149.

21. *Ibid.*, 147.

22. Cf. *Philosophical Correspondence between Berkeley and Samuel Johnson* in *The Works of George Berkeley*, ed. by Luce and Jessop (London: Nelson, 1948 ff), II, 285-286.

23. *Principles of Human Knowledge*, I, 118.

24. *Ibid.*, 13.

25. *Ibid.*, 120.

26. *Ibid.*, 130.

27. *Ibid.*, 131.

28. *Philosophical Correspondence between Berkeley and Samuel Johnson* in *The Works . . .*, II, 279.

29. *Principles of Human Knowledge*, I, 124.

30. *Ibid.*, 62.

31. *Ibid.*, 65.

32. *Ibid.*

33. *Ibid.*, 109.

34. *Ibid.*, 155.

35. *Ibid.*, 153.

36. Berkeley's "optimism" is more intemperate even than Leibniz'. In the "best of possible worlds" there was admittedly *evil*, resulting from the unavoidably finite nature of creation. But Leibniz would in all likelihood have been alarmed by what Berkeley is implying in the passage just quoted; to wit, that although the world is finite, it is nonetheless all good. Can there be limited perfection which nonetheless is all-perfect? Can the idea of metaphysical evil really be abandoned? These are the questions Berkeley's stand raises but into which he does not probe.

37. *Three Dialogues between Hylas and Philonus*, III.

38. Diderot, *Lettre sur les Aveugles*, *Oeuvres*, ed. Naigeon, II, 218.
39. *The New Theory of Vision*, sec. 11.

40. Voltaire, *Eléments de la Philosophie de Newton*, Part II, chap. vii; *Oeuvres*, XXX, 147.

xvi. David Hume

1. DAVID HUME, b. Edinburgh, 1711; d. same, 1776. Younger son of the laird of Ninewells, went to Edinburgh about 1721. The family was not rich, so David had to shift for himself; read for the bar for a while, worked for a merchant in Bristol, but his "passion for literature" led him finally, from 1734, to spend three years studying in France. It is not known exactly what he read, but surely he knew Locke, Berkeley, Hutcheson, Malebranche, and Bayle. He brought the completed *Treatise of Human Nature* back to London to publish it, which was accomplished in 1739 and 1740. Its failure to attract much attention persuaded Hume to write in a more popular style. Retiring again to Ninewells, he published in 1741-1742 two volumes of *Essays Moral and Political*, which were an instant success. In 1746 Hume ventured into affairs, becoming secretary to General St. Clair, whom he accompanied on a military expedition to France and, in 1748, on a diplomatic mission to Vienna and Turin. That year he published his *Philosophical Essays concerning Human Understanding*. This work included the *Enquiry concerning Human Understanding*, a more popular restatement, with many changes, of the first part of the *Treatise*. In 1751 appeared *An Inquiry concerning the Principles of Morals*, a rewrite of the third part of the *Treatise*, then, almost at once, a volume of *Political Discourses*. In 1751 he began living in Edinburgh, where he could enjoy such friends

as Adam Smith, the economist, and William Robertson, the historian. In 1752 he became Keeper of the Advocates' Library in Edinburgh and began writing, in several volumes, the *History of England*. In 1763 he went to Paris as acting secretary to the Embassy, where he remained, the center of admiring attention, for two years. His last years were happy ones in Edinburgh. He provided in his will for the posthumous publication of *The Dialogues concerning Natural Religion*, finally published in 1779.

Biographical: J. Y. T. Grieg, *David Hume* (New York: Oxford University Press, 1931). E. C. Mossner, *The Forgotten Hume: le bon David* (New York: Columbia University Press, 1943), and *The Life of David Hume* (Austin: University of Texas Press, 1954).

Collective editions: *The Philosophical Works of David Hume*, edited by T. M. Green and T. H. Grose (4 vols.; London: Longmans, Green, 1874-1875)—which is not a complete collected works. More commonly consulted are the following editions edited by L. A. Selby-Bigge: *A Treatise of Human Nature* (Oxford: Clarendon, 1888); *Enquiries concerning the Human Understanding and concerning the Principles of Morals* (2d ed.; Oxford: Clarendon, 1902).

Doctrinal: N. K. Smith, *The Philosophy of David Hume* (London: Macmillan, 1941). D. G. MacNabb, *David Hume: His Theory of Knowledge and Morality* (London: Hutchinson, 1951). J. Laird,

Hume's Philosophy of Human Nature (London: Methuen, 1932). B. M. Lang, *David Hume* (London: Benn, 1932). R. Metz, *David Hume, Leben und Philosophie* (Stuttgart: Frommann, 1929). R. W. Church, *Hume's Theory of Understanding* (Ithaca: Cornell University Press, 1935). H. H. Price, *Hume's Theory of the External World* (Oxford: Clarendon, 1940). R. M. Kydd, *Reason and Conduct in Hume's Treatise* (New York: Oxford University Press, 1946). A. B. Glathe, *Hume's Theory of the Passions and of Morals* (Berkeley: University of California Press, 1950). J. A. Passmore, *Hume's Intentions* (Cambridge: University Press, 1952). C. W. Hendel, *Studies in the Philosophy of David Hume* (Princeton: Princeton University Press, 1925). A. Leroy, *La Critique et la religion chez David Hume* (Paris: Alcan, 1930). A. Basson, *David Hume* (Baltimore: Penguin Books, 1958). G. Deleuze, *Empiricisme et subjectivité; essai sur la nature humaine selon Hume* (Paris: Presses Universitaires de France, 1953).

2. Hume acknowledges that "experimental" cannot have exactly the same meaning in natural philosophy, where we are dealing with an "object" other than the subject himself, and in moral philosophy, where the subject is precisely his own object; but he does not pursue this point at all, so that the assumptions implied by the reflective descriptive method are left quite in the dark.

3. *A Treatise of Human Nature,* Book I, Part III, sec. 1.

4. *Ibid.,* i, 2.

5. For an idea of the importance of the imagination as a theme in recent philosophy and for an indication of the variety of conceptions of its nature and role, consult, for instance, M. Heidegger, *Kant und das Probleme der Metaphysik* (2d ed.; Frankfurt: Klostermann, 1951), pp. 117-167; J. P. Sartre, *L'imaginaire* (2d ed.; Paris: Presses Universitaires de France, 1956); same, *Psychology of the Imagination* (New York, 1948); Mikel Dufrenne, *La phénoménologie de l'expérience esthétique* (Paris: Presses Universitaires de France, 1953); same, *La Notion de l'a priori* (Paris: Presses Universitaires de France, 1959).

6. *A Treatise of Human Nature,* Book I, Part III, sec. 14.

7. "Since these philosophers, therefore, have concluded that matter cannot be endowed with any efficacious principle, because it is impossible to discover in it such a principle, the same course of reasoning should determine them to exclude it from the Supreme Being" (*ibid.*).

8. *A Treatise of Human Nature,* Book I, Part I, sec. 4.

9. *Ibid.*

10. *Ibid.,* sec. 5.

11. *Ibid.,* sec. 2.

12. *Ibid.*

13. *Ibid.,* Part III, sec. 2.

14. *Ibid.* A rather bold mechanistic assumption. St. Thomas would object that the universal condition Hume has just laid down is true only of the narowest range of material causes, the sort that of course have to be experienced here and now to be known, the most contingent of causal experiences!

15. *Ibid.*

16. *Ibid.,* sec. 3. Hume's way of arguing should once again serve to teach us not to concede points of method too easily. For if we too lightly agreed when he argued that whatever is distinguishable can exist distinctly, what resistance can

we offer when he claims there is
therefore no bond of conceptual
necessity joining the ideas "beginning to exist" and "having a cause"?
17. Ibid.
18. Ibid. The italics are Hume's.
19. Ibid., sec. 7.
20. Loc. cit., note.
21. Ibid., sec. 7.
22. Ibid., sec. 8.
23. Ibid., Part IV, sec. 2.
24. Ibid.
25. Ibid.
26. Ibid., sec. 5.
27. Dialogues concerning Natural Religion, IX.

28. Ibid.
29. Ibid., XII.
30. Ibid.
31. A Treatise of Human Nature, Book II, Part III, sec. 9.
32. Ibid., Book III, Part I, sec. 1.
33. Ibid.
34. Ibid.
35. Ibid.
36. Ibid., sec. 2.
37. Ibid.
38. Ibid.
39. Hume, "Of the Standard of Taste," *Essays Moral, Political and Literary,* ed. Green and Grose (London, 1898), p. 268.

XVII. Condillac

1. ETIENNE BONNOT DE CONDILLAC, b. Grenoble, 1715; d. Castle of Flux (near Beaugency), 1780. Scanty information on his early education; of weak constitution and with poor sight, managed to carry his studies far enough to enter the great Seminary of St. Sulpice (Paris) and to learn theology at the Sorbonne; ordained a priest (1740), he never exercised active ministry but frequented literary and philosophical circles; read Locke (in French) and Newton (in Latin), then the metaphysicians of the seventeenth century; from 1746 to 1758, published his main philosophical works; from 1758 to 1767 was preceptor of the son of the Duke of Parma, an occasion for him to gather the material he was to use and publish in his *Course of Studies*; after some years in Paris he bought for a niece the castle and estate of Flux and retired there to spend in peace the rest of his life. A fellow of the Academy of Berlin (1749) and of the French Academy (1768), he continued to go to Paris from time to time, soon to return to the semi-seclusion of his library.

Main philosophical works: *Essai sur l'origine des connaissances humaines* (Essay on the Origin of Human Knowledge), 1746; *Traité des systèmes* (Treatise of Systems), 1749; *Traité des sensations* (Treatise of Sensations), 1754; *Extrait raisonné du traité des sensations* (Reasoned Abstract from the Treatise of Sensations), published along with the *Traité des animaux* (Treatise of Animals) in 1755.
Collective edition: *Oeuvres philosophiques de Condillac,* ed. Georges Le Roy (3 vols.; Paris: Presses Universitaires de France, 1947, 1948, 1951); Vol. I contains all the philosophically significant works.
Biographical: Baguenault de Puchesse, *Condillac, sa vie, sa philosophie, son influence* (Paris, 1910). G. Le Roy, "Introduction à l'oeuvre philosophique de Condillac," in *Oeuvres philosophiques de Condillac, ed. cit.,* Vol. I, pp. 1-35.
Doctrinal: G. Le Roy, *Oeuvres philosophiques de Condillac, ed. cit.,* Vol. III, pp. 569-574. J. Didier, *Condillac* (Paris, 1911). Raymond Lenour, *Condillac* (Paris, 1924).

Georges Le Roy, *La psychologie de Condillac* (Paris: Boivin, 1937). Dewaule, *Condillac et la psychologie anglaise contemporaine* (Paris: Alcan, 1891). R. Mondolfo, *Un psicologo associazioniste, E. B. de Condillac* (Palermo, 1902). Didier, *Condillac* (Paris: Bloud, 1911) (collection "Science et Religion"). Hans Havemann, *Der Erkenntnistheoretische Standpunkt Condillacs* (Jena: Vopelius, 1912). Victor Delbos, *La philosophie française* (Paris: Plon-Nourrit, 1919), chap. xi. Capone Braga, *La filosofia francese ed italiana del Settecento* (3d ed.; Padova: Cedam, 1947), I, pp. 99-159. Raymond Lenoir, *Condillac* (Paris: Alcan, 1924). Schaupp, *The Naturalism of Condillac* (Lincoln, 1926). Radovanovitch, *La théorie de la connaissance chez Condillac* (Geneva, 1927). C. von Brockedorf, *Wahrheit und Wahrscheinlichkeit bei Hobbes und Condillac* (Kiel: Lipsius und Tischer, 1937). R. Biazrri, *Condillac* (Brescia: La Scuola, 1945).

2. I. Newton, *Philosophiae naturalis principia mathematica*, Book III, Scholium generale.

3. Locke, *Essai sur l'entendement humain*, translated into French by Pierre Coste, 1700. This still is the only complete French translation of the *Essay*. In fact, the Coste translation enjoys the privilege of having been revised by Locke himself.

4. Voltaire, *Philosophical Letters*, letter XIII.

5. "One should distinguish two kinds of metaphysics. The one, ambitious, wants to pierce all mysteries: It promises to discover nature, the essence of things, the most hidden causes; in fact, it contents itself with very vague notions and it accumulates errors. The other proportions its ambitions to the weakness of the human mind; seeking only to see things such as they are, it acquires few cognitions, but those it acquires are solid and safe. Philosophers have particularly practiced the first kind of metaphysics, they considered the other one as secondary in importance and hardly deserving the name of metaphysics. Locke is the only one I believe I should except; having limited himself to the study of the human mind, he has successfully achieved his object" (Condillac, *Essai sur l'origine des connaissances humaines*, Introduction, ed. G. Le Roy, Vol. I, p. 3). All the following quotations will refer to this edition, Vol. I.

6. *Traité des systèmes*, chap. i, p. 123b.

7. *Ibid.*, pp. 123b-124a.

8. *Ibid.*, chap. ii, "On the uselessness of abstract systems," p. 125 a-b, cf. ch. p. 6, art. 2, pp. 144b-145b.

9. *Ibid.*, chap. ii, p. 127. As an instance of the ridiculous confidence of philosophers in the power of abstract deduction, Condillac related the speculations of Wolff concerning the size of the inhabitants of Jupiter (chap. iv, p. 133, note 1).

10. *Ibid.*, chap. vii, p. 150a.

11. *Ibid.*, chap. viii, sec. 2, art. 5, pp. 163-164.

12. *Ibid.*, chap. x, "Eighth and Last Example: Spinozism refuted," pp. 169-194. On the definitions by *that which*, art. 1, definition 3, pp. 170-171. An interesting development on the fact that Spinoza made non-Cartesian applications of the Cartesian principle that "one can affirm of a thing all that which is included in the clear and distinct notion one has of it," p. 194a. For instance, this penetrating remark: Spinoza rejects creation because he has no clear and distinct idea of it; then

he adds that, since existence is not included in the notion of finite beings, they must be caused; "now, how can it be that the finite beings, which do not exist by themselves, nevertheless exist without creation taking place?" The only way out for him is to say that finite beings are modes of the substance. An admirable curtain fall, indeed, at least in words. For the conclusion of these various critiques, chap. ii, pp. 194-195.

13. *Ibid.*, chap. xiv, p. 207. An aspect of the doctrine of Condillac usually neglected: his analysis of the object and methods of political sciences. He is entitled to a place in the history of social and political doctrines: *Traité des systèmes*, chap. xv, "Of the necessity of systems in politics and of the views and precautions with which they should be conceived," pp. 207-210. After his retirement to Flux, he became a Fellow of the Royal Society of Agriculture of Orléans; the same year (1776) he published a treatise on *Le commerce et le gouvernement considérés relativement l'un à l'autre;* in *Oeuvres complètes,* Vol. II, pp. 242-267. On the relation of this work to the school of the "physiocrats," see the bibliographical note of G. Le Roy, Vol. II, pp. 241-242, note 2. The writings listed are those of Quesnay, Mirabeau, Dupont de Nemours, Mercier de la Rivière, abbé Baudeau, le Trosne, abbé Roubaud, Saint-Péravy, Turgot (including the affair between Turgot and Dupont de Nemours, p. 242). The history of philosophy here blends with that of economics. On the school of the physiocrats, Le Roy refers to: G. Weulersse, *Le mouvement physiocratique en France de 1756 à 1770* (2 vols.; Paris, 1910);

same author, *Les Physiocrates* (Paris, 1931). On Condillac's own economics, Lebeau, *Condillac économiste* (Paris, 1903).

14. *Traité des systèmes,* chap. xiv, p. 207.

15. This key to the doctrine of Condillac is found in his own introduction to his *Essai sur l'origine des connaissances humaines,* ed. G. Le Roy, Vol. I, p. 5. What Condillac says there of Locke in general terms becomes quite clear as he develops his own position.

16. Condillac, *Essai . . . ,* Part II, sec. 2, chap. iii, 32-35, pp. 112-113.

17. *Ibid.,* I, 1, 2, line 11, pp. 8-9. Note the decisive lines: "There are three things to distinguish in our sensation: (1) The perception we experience; (2) that we relate it to something outside of ourselves; (3) The judgment that what we relate to things does actually belong to them." To which he adds: "There is neither error nor obscurity in that which takes place in us, nor in its being related by us to something outside"; line 11, lines 35-38.

18. For what follows, *ibid.,* I, 21, 16, p. 14; and I, 2, 2, lines 17-19, pp. 14-15. In the slow course of his analysis, Condillac from time to time provides useful recapitulations: 16, p. 14; 74, p. 28; 107, pp. 36-37.

19. There is no real distinction between sensations, perceptions, and ideas in the doctrine of Condillac. Ideas are all perceived objects of the mind. Things cannot be otherwise (since, in the last analysis, the only content of the mind is sensation, or transformed sensation). Nor should one worry about the use Condillac makes of the word "soul." He does not doubt one moment the existence of a subject to which sensations are related. This

subject (soul) is immaterial, as sensations themselves are. Wholly taken up with his personal project of a genealogy of man's knowing powers, Condillac takes all those certitudes in his stride, as natural evidence implied in sensation.

20. *Essay* . . . , I, 2, 4, 35, p. 19.
21. *Ibid.*, 2, 5, 46, p. 21.
22. *Ibid.*, 2, 6, 48, p. 22.
23. *Ibid.*, 2, 6, pp. 23-24.
24. This historical problem has been solved by the excellent editor of Condillac, Georges Le Roy, Introduction, pp. xvii-xviii and xx-xxi. In his *Elements of the Philosophy of Newton* (1738), Voltaire had borrowed from Berkeley's *Essay of a New Theory of Vision* (1709) fruitful remarks on the association of visual and tactile data in sensations, but he had left out what could suggest that, in Berkeley's own mind, these remarks were tied up with an idealistic metaphysics. Condillac, who, as was said above, could not read English, made good use of the part of the doctrine of Berkeley presented by Voltaire; it suited him perfectly and he quoted it without suspecting its idealistic implications.
25. The *Letter* of Diderot is included in *Oeuvres de Diderot*, ed. by André Billy (Paris: La Pléiade, 1946). The passage under consideration is to be found on pp. 865-866.
26. Condillac, *Reasoned Abstract from the Treatise of Sensations*, p. 325a.
27. *Ibid.*, p. 325.
28. G. Le Roy has stressed the paradoxical fact—paradoxical yet true —that Condillac has borrowed from Berkeley's psychology of tactile impressions several arguments used by him in the refutation of Berkeley's idealism: *Oeuvres philoso-*

phiques de Condillac, Vol. I, p. xxi and p. 250, note 24. The very title of the Second Part of the *Treatise* announces the nature of the problem and its solution: *Of Touch, or of the Only Sense that Judges by Itself of External Objects.*
29. *Treatise* . . . , II, iv, p. 253. For the preceding sentence, see *Abstract* . . . , Abridgment of the Second Part.
30. *Treatise* . . . , Part III, title, p. 275.
31. This exposition closely follows the *Reasoned Abstract* . . . , Abridgment of the Second Part, pp. 329-331. See the important variants, p. 329, note c. The complete demonstration is found in the *Treatise* . . . , II, iv, with note 25 on the corrections of Condillac (pp. 253-254); then in chap. v, also with variants, pp. 254-258: "How a man limited to touching discovers his own body and learns that there is something outside of himself." Note: when the hand touches its own body, if the hand says "I," the body answers "I"; the ego that feels modified in the hand is the same that feels modified in the body. On the contrary, when the hand touches a foreign body, the ego that feels modified in the hand does not feel modified in that body. On account of this experience, the statue judges "its modes of being to be entirely outside of itself."
32. Condillac, *Logic or the First Developments of the Art of Thinking*, *Oeuvres philosophiques*, Vol. II, p. 371.
33. In France, the influence of Condillac was largely tied up with the rise of the school of ideology, of which more will be said later. In Italy, the influence of Condillac was partly due to the fact that he spent about ten years at the court

of Parma. On the history of this influence, M. F. Sciacca, *La filosofia nell' età del Risorgimento* (Milano: Vallardi, 1948), pp. 6-114: "Seguaci e critici del Condillac."

XVIII. The Reaction against Locke

1. THOMAS REID, b. Strachan, near Aberdeen, 1710; d. Glasgow, 1796. Son of a minister, studied at Marischal College; first publication: an *Essay on Quantity*, in Philosophical Transactions, 1748, wherein he discussed the attempt made by Hutcheson to apply mathematical method to moral problems; rector of King's College (University of Aberdeen), 1752; published his celebrated *Inquiry* in 1764; not without hesitations, left Aberdeen for a much better position at the University of Glasgow, where he taught from 1763 to his retirement in 1781. He then collected and restyled the lectures he had been giving at Aberdeen and Glasgow and published them under the title of *Essays . . .* ; Reid died at Glasgow in 1796.

Main writings: *An Inquiry into the Human Mind on the Principles of Common Sense* (Dublin: Alex. Ewing, 1764); *Essays on the Intellectual Powers of Man*, 1786; *Essays on the Active Powers of the Human Mind*, 1788.

Collective editions: *Works*, with notes by G. N. Wright (2 vols.; London, 1843). Also with selections from letters by William Hamilton (2 vols.; Edinburgh, 1872). French translation (important for the history of French eclecticism) *Oeuvres complètes*, ed. by Theodore Jouffroy, with fragments from Royer-Collard (6 vols.; Paris, 1828 ff).

Biographical: Dugald Stewart has presented to the Royal Society an *Account of the Life and Writings of Thomas Reid*. The text is found in the edition of Reid's works by G. N. Wright, Vol. II, pp. 1-76; also in Dugald Stewart, *Biographical Memoirs of Adam Smith, LL.D., of William Robertson, D.D., and of Thomas Reid, D.D.*, read before the Royal Society of Edinburgh, 1811 (with portraits). Thurot (Jean-François), "Vie de Reid," in *Oeuvres posthumes* (Paris, 1837).

Doctrinal: Adolphe Garnier, *Critique de la philosophie de Thomas Reid* (Paris, 1840). J. F. Ferrier, "Reid and the Philosophy of Common Sense" (1847), published in the author's *Lectures . . .* , ed. Grant and Lushington (London, 1866), Vol. II, pp. 407-459.

2. Reid will be quoted from the G. N. Wright edition, in 2 vols. The opening remarks on his predecessors are taken from Reid's Dedication of his *Inquiry*, ed. cit., II, p. 395. He never thought of doubting the principles of human understanding until the publication of Hume's *Treatise of Human Nature*, 1739: "The ingenious author of that treatise, upon the principles of Locke who was no sceptic, has built a system of scepticism, which leaves no ground to believe any one thing rather than its contrary." The next sentence is typical of Reid: "His (Hume's) reasoning appeared to me to be just; there was therefore a necessity to call in question the principles upon which it was founded, or to admit the conclusion" (p. 396). If the principles of Locke were right, Berkeley and Hume themselves were right. Hence, for Reid, the necessity to challenge the principles themselves; this was the origin of his own philosophical inquiry.

3. This critical examination of the history of modern philosophy since the time of Descartes, along with the genealogy of Hume's skepticism, is found in *Inquiry* . . . , Introduction, Vol. II, pp. 404-410. While relating the origins of what he calls the low state of philosophy in his own time (a fact which very few were then noticing), Reid indicates at once what he will suggest by way of remedy: common sense. This also gives the reason for his personal opposition to skepticism: Reid could not admit the "sceptical system" of Hume without reluctance, nor could he believe that any sound mind would feel satisfied with it. The starting point of his opposition is not an abstract notion, but rather, it is the immediate feeling that no normal man is a skeptic. On the contrary, men live by belief; they all act in the conviction that they will achieve something by their effort: If the day laborer did not believe he would be paid, he would not work; even Hume wrote his book in the belief that it would be read; seizing upon this occasion to indulge in a piece of bad theology, our D.D. adds the remark that "the *unjust live by faith* as well as the *just*" (Vol. I, p. 396).

4. *An Inquiry into the Human Mind*, Introduction, vii, *ed. cit.*, II, pp. 409-410.

5. *Ibid.*, Introduction, I, vii; II, p. 410.

6. This invitation to respect the infinite complexity of human nature is one of the standing positions to be met in the history of philosophy. St. Augustine was one of its greatest exponents; in modern times, Reid has been one of the first

to voice it against the oversimplifications of associationisms: "Is the mechanism of the mind so easily comprehended, when that of the body is so difficult? Yet by this system, three laws of association, joined to a few original feelings, explain the whole mechanism of sense, imagination, memory, belief, and of all the actions and passions of the mind. Is this the man that nature made? I suspect it is not so easy to look behind the scenes in nature's work. This is a puppet surely, contrived by too bold an apprentice of nature to mimic her work. It shows tolerably by candlelight, but brought into clear day, and taken to pieces, it will appear to be a man made with mortar and a trowel" (*An Inquiry* . . . , chap. i, Introduction; Vol. II, p. 409). Such a passage could have been written by Bergson against Taine and Spencer. In other passages, the "ideal system" is called "the Cartesian system." In such cases, Reid always is careful to specify that neither Descartes nor Locke knew they were on the road to skepticism; "Bishop Berkeley was the first who discovered it." Here is one of the more perfect summaries given by Reid: "Thus we see that Descartes and Locke take the road that leads to skepticism without knowing the end of it; but they stop short for want of light to carry them farther. Berkeley, frightened at the appearance of the dreadful abyss, starts aside, and avoids it. But the author of the "Treatise of Human Nature," more daring and intrepid, without turning aside to the right hand or to the left, like Virgil's Alecto, shoots directly into the gulf:

"There Pluto pants for breath from out of his cell,

And opens wide the grinning jaws
  of hell."

(*An Inquiry* . . . , chap. vii, 3;
Vol. II, p. 585.
7. *Ibid.*, chap. v, ix; II, pp. 455-457.
8. *Ibid.*, chap. vi, v; II, p. 472. Note
the penetrating remarks on the inconsequence of Locke, who, after
initiating the notion of "secondary
qualities," did not realize it was a
meaningless one; how could there
be secondary qualities of bodies?
According to his own principles
and reasonings, these are "no qualities of bodies at all." Common
sense, that sovereign mistress of our
opinions, led him to use words in
opposition to his own hypothesis.
9. *Ibid.*, pp. 473-474. The "hypothesis" which all took for granted was
"that all the sensations we have
from things, were the forms or
images of these external things"
(pp. 471-472); this was the father
of the frightful progeny; the
mother was the Lockian principle
of the dissimilitude of our sensations from things.
10. *Ibid.*, chap. ii, ii; Vol. II, p. 413.
Sketched in the *Inquiry*, this part
of the doctrine is fully developed
in the *Essays*, which, in Dugald
Stewart's own words, were taught,
as to their substance, "annually,
for more than twenty years, to a
large body of the more advanced
students, in this University (Glasgow) and for several years before,
in another University (Aberdeen)."
Dedicated June 1, 1785. In the *Essays on the Intellectual Powers of
Man*, Reid carefully distinguishes
between (1) the possible meanings
of *ideas;* in the Cartesian and Lockian sense, it is a mere fiction to be
eliminated (*Essays*, I, xxvii, Vol. I,
p. 16); in a loose sense, it can be
used to mean any object of thought:
I, xix; I, p. 11; (2) *impression*, a

change caused in a *passive* subject
by the operation of an external
cause; (3) *sensation*, an *act* of the
mind that can be distinguished
from all others (note "all") by
this, "that it has no object distinct
from the act itself": I, 34; sec. 12,
I, p. 19; (4) *perception* "is most
properly applied to the evidence
which we have of external objects
by our senses." Reid adds: "The
perception of external objects by
our senses is an operation of the
mind of a peculiar nature, and
ought to have a name appropriate
to it. It has so in all languages. And,
in the English, I know no word
more appropriate to express this
act of the mind than perception"
(*Essays*, I, xii; Vol. I, p. 6). This
is a good example of how philosophies are wholly contained in their
initial definitions. The definition of
idea eliminates Descartes; that of
sensation (as distinct from impression) eliminates Hume; that of perception (a word much abused by
Hume: I, xiii, I, p. 7) eliminates
Berkeley. These distinctions exem-
plify what Reid calls "observation"
in "pneumatology" (or science of
the mind). It also shows its difficulty. On the other hand, Reid observes with satisfaction that, once
they are established by observation,
all the rest necessarily follows.
11. *Ibid.*, chap. ii, iii; Vol. II, p. 413.
12. "Why sensation should compel
our belief of the present existence
of the thing, memory a belief of
its past existence, and imagination
no belief at all, is what I believe
no philosopher can give a shadow
of reason for, but that such is the
nature of these operations; they are
all simple and *original*, and therefore inexplicable acts of the mind"
(*op. cit.*, chap. ii, iii; Vol. II, p. 414).
Reid takes it as a fact that man is
able to distinguish at once sensa-

tion from memory; hence the primitive distinction between the two classes of primitive judgments by which these two primitive facts are being attended.

13. Loc. cit., p. 415.

14. Op. cit., chap. ii, iv; Vol. II, p. 415. The expression used by Reid in this passage, "belief and knowledge," refers to the classical doctrine according to which knowledge properly begins with judgment; that is, at the moment when truth and error begin to be possible.

15. Condillac is not named, but Reid knows his doctrine. See in the *Inquiry* . . . , II, v, Vol. II, p. 417: "Two theories of the nature of belief refuted . . ." ". . . Of this kind surely is that modern discovery of the ideal philosophy, that sensation, memory, belief, and imagination where they have the same object, are only different degrees of strength and vivacity in the idea . . . etc." Reid objects to this, that the same argument "might as well be used to prove that love implies only a stronger idea of the object than indifference." In a deeper vein, he remarks that to maintain that sensation, memory, and imagination differ only in degree, and not in kind, is as shocking to common sense as to maintain that "a circle, a square, and a triangle, differ only in magnitude, not in figure." So Reid claims for inner experience the power immediately to apprehend specific differences between the various operations of the mind. To grasp the meaning of this point is to get at the bottom of the psychological empiricism of Reid, so different from the notional empiricism of Condillac.

16. Inquiry . . . , chap. ii, v; Vol. II, pp. 417-418.

17. Ibid., Conclusion, p. 587.

18. Reid has never submitted a complete list of the principles guaranteed by common sense; given their nature, it was not possible for him to do so. However, he gave important indications on the subject in his *Essays*. These embody the subject matters of the lecture courses he gave at Aberdeen, then at Glasgow; a first list is found in his *Essays on the Intellectual Powers of Man*, Essay VI, chap. vi, ed. G. N. Wright; Vol. I, pp. 439-458. The chapter concretizes for us his notion of "principles." Reid divides them into six classes according to the sciences to which they belong. Principles are (1) *grammatical*, for instance: every complete sentence must have a verb, etc.; (2) *logical:* no proposition can be true and false at the same time, etc.; (3) *mathematical:* any mathematical axiom; (4) in matters of *taste*, fine arts, etc., for indeed taste may be true or false and, if so, it must have principles of its own; (5) in *morals:* a generous action has more merit than a merely just one, etc.; (6) *metaphysical*, among which three deserve particular attention: (a) that the qualities perceived by the senses must have a subject called body, and that the thoughts we are conscious of must have a subject we call mind; (b) that whatever begins to exist must have a cause which produced it; (c) that design and intelligence in the cause may be inferred with certainty from marks and signs of it in the effect. From this last principle (purposiveness) the existence of the Deity can be proved more incontrovertibly than from any other proposition ever formed by human reason (*Essays*, VI, ix, p. 455); see demonstration in VI, x and xi, p. 456. A list of the principles proper to *morals* is found in *Essays on the*

Active Powers of the Human Mind, Essay V, chap. i, *ed. cit.,* Vol. II, pp. 312-319. All such propositions are principles because, being evident, they can be neither learned from experience nor demonstrated by reason.

19. *Inquiry* . . . , Conclusion, 3; Vol. II, p. 582.

20. JAMES BEATTIE, b. Laurencekirk, 1735; d. Aberdeen, 1803. Studied at Marischal College, and after modest beginnings was appointed professor of moral philosophy there. More religiously minded than Reid, he joined the common-sense school in its fight against the skepticism of Hume. Beattie visited London for the first time in 1771 and lived a peaceful life, not without its sorrows, but finding consolation in philosophy and poetry.

Main philosophical writings: *An Essay on the Nature and Immutability of Truth in Opposition to Sophistry and Scepticism* (Edinburgh, 1770; 3d ed.; London, 1772). Included in a volume of *Essays,* among which "On Poetry and Music, as They Affect the Mind" (Edinburgh: W. Creach, 1776; 2 vols., Dublin, 1778). *The Theory of Language* in two parts. Part I: "Of the Origin and General Nature of Speech." Part II: "Of Universal Grammar"; a new edition enlarged (London, 1788). *Evidence of the Christian Religion Briefly and Plainly Stated* (2 vols.; Edinburgh, 1786 [2d ed. 1789 and several times reprinted]). *Elements of Moral Science* (2 vols.; Edinburgh, 1790-1793; 3d ed. with index, Edinburgh, 1817). Beattie's best-known poem, *The Minstrel,* went through many editions, among them *The Minstrel,* a new edition to which are prefixed "Memoirs of the Life of the Author," by A. E. Chalmers (with portrait) (London, 1866). The first part of Beattie's poem was translated into French by Chateaubriand (in *Considérations sur les littératures étrangères*).

All successful authors have adversaries. Two deserve to be mentioned. Right after his first *Essay on the Nature . . . of Truth,* there appeared another one: *The Essay on the Nature and Immutability of Truth . . . , by Dr. Beattie, shown to be sophistical and promotive of scepticism and infidelity. With some remarks on priestcraft, etc.* . . . By a Professor of Moral Philosophy in the College of Common Sense (London, 1773). The author was Priestley. A more insidious attack was included in Buffier, *First Truths . . . ,* translated from the French. To which is prefixed "a detection of the plagiarism, concealment and ingratitude of the Doctors Reid, Beattie and Oswald," 1780. This Oswald is James Oswald, author of an *Appeal to Common Sense in Behalf of Religion* (Edinburgh, 1866-1872).

Biographical-doctrinal: C. Mallet, *Mémoire sur la vie et les écrits de James Beattie, philosophe écossais* (Paris, 1863). On the general history of the school: James McCosh, *The Scottish Philosophy* (London, 1875).

21. DUGALD STEWART, b. Edinburgh, 1753; d. Edinburgh, 1828. Studied Edinburgh, went to Glasgow in 1771. There Stewart heard Reid, but being a very precocious young man (he then was nineteen), he acted as a substitute for his father in the chair of mathematics at the university (1772). He succeeded his father in 1778; shifted to philosophy and became a professor of moral philosophy at the same university in 1785 and ceased to teach in 1809.

Main writings: *Elements of the*

Philosophy of the Human Mind . . . (3 vols. [with addenda to Vol. I]; London-Edinburgh, 1792-1827). *Outlines of Philosophy for the Use of Students in the University of Edinburgh* (Edinburgh and London, 1793; 7th ed., enlarged, Edinburgh, 1844). *The Philosophy of the Active and Moral Powers of Man* (2 vols.; Edinburgh and London, 1828).

Collective edition: *The Collected Works of Dugald Stewart*, ed. Sir Hamilton, Bart. (10 vols.; Edinburgh, 1854-1858).

22. For instance, *Essays on the Intellectual Powers of Man*, chap. viii; ed. Wright, Vol. I, pp. 458-471.

23. The exact sentence runs as follows: "To pass by Malebranche's notion of seeing all things in the Ideas of the Divine Mind, as a foreigner never naturalized in this land" (Reid, *Inquiry*, chap. vi, ed. Wright, Vol. II, p. 473). Whether there are such things as an "English philosophy," or as German, French, Italian, or American philosophies, is a debatable point. It is beyond doubt, however, that there were, and are, "philosophical schools" or schools of philosophy that can and must be thus qualified. Differences in languages, nationalities, geographical situations, systems of education, intellectual and religious traditions, not to mention the elusive, yet real mental idiosyncrasies (English empiricism, German idealism, French psychologism, etc.), are contributing to create geographically and historically localized streams of philosophical speculation that can bear labels of origin. This, however, is a very rough approximation of reality: a Scotsman, like Hume, felt at home in French philosophical circles; a man who, like Reid, spent his life in Scotland escaped influences

predominant in other countries. Reid had already used at least the formula when he spoke of "remarkable differences between the French and English schools of metaphysics" (*Essays on the Intellectual Powers of the Mind*, Essay II, chap. ix; ed. Wright, Vol. I, p. 106).

24. Roughly speaking, that country was part of Piedmont, cap. Torino; from 1721 to 1860, Piedmont formed, along with Savoia and Sardinia, what was called the Sardinian States. For geographical reasons, the language spoken in Savoia was French; this accounts for the fact that Gerdil, Joseph de Maistre, and others, although Savoyard born, wrote their works in French. Still, as will be seen, their thought escaped the influence of contemporary French philosophical circles; it even was in reaction against it.

25. The only constructive contribution to philosophy, on the French side, that can be considered Christian in its inspiration was that of Claude Buffier, S.J. (1661-1736): *Traité des vérités premières et des sources de nos jugements* (Paris, 1717). *Cours de sciences sur des principes nouveaux et simples: propre à former le langage, l'esprit et le coeur* (Paris, 1732) (included all his writings). It is significant that Buffier was to be hailed as a predecessor of Condillac and a precursor of the nineteenth-century school of ideology. More curious still is the fact that, over forty-five years before Reid, he attempted a justification of the prime and supreme truths by appealing to common sense. In fact, the scholastic doctrine of the natural light of reason and of intellect conceived as the faculty of principles offered possibilities in that direction. Unfortunately, Buffier failed to develop the

metaphysical presuppositions and implications of the doctrine. As was said above, the whole school of common sense was accused of having plagiarized Buffier, whose notion of common sense was, in fact, different from that of Reid.

26. SIGISMOND GERDIL, b. Samoëns (Savoia), 1718; d. Rome, 1802. Studied at the college of the Barnabites (Annecy) and entered their congregation; his versatility earned him the favor of Pope Benedict XIV; professor of philosophy at the University of Torino, 1749; professor of moral philosophy at the same university, 1754; preceptor of the young Prince of Piedmont, the future Charles Emmanuel IV, King of Sardinia; created a cardinal by Pius VI, he was elected pope by the Conclave of Venice in 1800, but the political veto of Austria prevented him from ascending the Holy See.

Main philosophical writings: *De l'immatérialité de l'âme démontrée contre Locke par les mêmes principes par lesquels ce philosophe démontre l'existence et l'immatérialité de Dieu* (Turin, 1747) (Of the immateriality of the soul demonstrated against Locke by the same arguments by which that philosopher demonstrates the existence and immateriality of God). *Défense du sentiment du P. Malebranche sur la nature et l'origine des idées, contre l'examen de M. Locke* (Turin, 1748) (Defense of the opinion of Fr. Malebranche on the nature and origin of ideas against its examination by Mr. Locke). *Réflexions sur la théorie et la pratique de l'éducation contre les principes de M. Rousseau* (Turin, 1763) (Reflections on the theory and practice of education against the principles of Mr. Rousseau). *Principes métaphysiques de la mo-*

rale chrétienne (Metaphysical principles of Christian morals), in four parts; posthumous work published in *Opere*, Vol. II, pp. 1-119; perhaps the most perfect of all the philosophical works of Gerdil.

Collective edition: *Opere* edited inedite del Cardinale Sigismond Gerdil, della Congregazione de' Chieri Regolari di S. Paolo (20 vols.; Roma: Vincenzo Poggioli, 1806-1821).

27. "Le premier et seul objet de nos connaissances est l'être." *Principes métaphysiques* . . . , Book I, principle 1, in Gerdil, *Opere*, Vol. II, p. 3. Since, on the other hand, "l'Idée de Dieu, ou l'objet immédiat de l'esprit qui connaît Dieu, ne peut être distingué de Dieu lui-même" (*op. cit.*, sec. 8, chap. i; Vol. IV, p. 190). Gerdil's position seems to be dangerously near the theological error called "ontologism." This, however, is a question for qualified theologians to answer. History only can define the data of the problem.

1) Gerdil intends to follow the tradition of Augustine, Malebranche, and Thomassinus. He accumulates passages taken in Augustine and Thomassinus in order to justify his own position. Even the words "to see God" (*videtur Deus*) are found there: Thomassinus, *Tractatus de Deo Deique proprietatibus*, VI, 10, 2 ff, as quoted by Gerdil, *Défense* . . . , Preliminary Dissertation, 5-9, in *Opere*, Vol. IV, pp. 16-20.

2) In Gerdil's doctrine, to see God is not to see the essence of God as in the beatific vision; it is to see the idea of Being of which the archetype is God, and which is immediately caused in us by the very essence of God.

3) Gerdil calls this sight of the notion of Being a sight of God because the notion is God himself

present to us as its efficient and formal cause.

4) A comparison can help us understand Gerdil's position: In St. Thomas Aquinas, God is immediately present to all his effects, and he is present to them by essence, because his essence is their cause; God is in his effects causally. In Gerdil, God is immediately present by essence to the human understanding, as efficient and formal cause of the notion of Being, which (since God is Being) is the notion of God.

5) The reason for the difference between the two doctrines thus becomes apparent. In Thomas Aquinas, the presence of God to human understanding enables it to be, to operate, and, by its own operations, to conceive in the natural light of reason the abstract notion of being and its properties. In the doctrine of Gerdil, God's presence provides not only the knowing power of man, but its very object, which is Being, which is God. All this comes, in Gerdil's doctrine, from having eliminated the active power of human understanding, its "agent intellect."

28. Op. cit., Vol. II, pp. 4-5.

29. Principes métaphysiques . . . , Book I, principles 2-4; Vol. II, pp. 5-7.

30. Ibid., Book I, principles 5-8; Vol. II, pp. 8-16. *Défense du sentiment du P. Malebranche . . . ,* sec. VII, pp. 161-168. Note that, being confused feelings, sensations are not in God, as ideas are, but they are modifications of soul caused by the action of God (*op. cit.*, sec. VIII, ch. ii; Vol. IV, pp. 167-177).

31. Dissertazione della esistenza di Dio e delle Immaterialità delle nature intelligenti, in *Opere,* Vol. II, pp. 352-353. On the God of St. Thomas Aquinas, *ibid.*, pp. 356-357.

Note that the philosopher often opposed by Gerdil, here and elsewhere, under the Italianized form "Obbesio" is Thomas Hobbes.

32. Principes métaphysiques . . . , Book II, principles 2-9; *Opere,* Vol. II, pp. 19-35. "If Mr. Locke wants to know what direct and immediate view of God we have, I shall answer that that view consists in this, that when we think of God, the immediate object of our mind is Being." Thus conceived as containing all possible reality, Being simply "is, because it is." Moreover, Being is at once conceived as infinite, immutable, simple, eternal and immense, self-knowing and self-loving. "That is what we see by a direct and immediate sight of the idea of God considered in Himself, and it is very different from anything that can be imagined about Cherubims, Seraphims, etc." (*Défense du sentiment du P. Malebranche . . . ,* sec. VIII, ch. i; in *Opere,* Vol. IV, pp. 196-197). This confirms one of his main objections to the thesis of Locke, that the idea of God is in us a complex idea formed by our mind by associating several simple ideas. On the contrary, the idea of God is simple, since all its attributes are included in the notion of unrestricted being (*ibid.*, pp. 187-198). Moreover, that idea is not an abstract notion empty of content; on the contrary, it is the notion of total and infinite reality (*loc. cit.*, § 17-18, Vol. IV, pp. 200-201).

33. Principes métaphysiques . . . , Book II, principle 9; *Opere,* Vol. II, p. 35.

34. Ibid., Book II, principle 10; Vol. II, pp. 36-38. Join principle 10 and p. 39, the extraordinary reference to Thomas Aquinas, *Contra Gentiles,* II, 43. As in Malebranche, the philosophical thesis that God is the

only cause of our cognitions, including the feelings of pleasure and pain, prepares the theological conclusion that God is the only conceivable cause of man's beatitude.
35. The refutation of Rousseau is included in the *Opere*, Vol. I, pp. 1-146. The title, as given in this edition, is *Anti-Emile ou Réflexions* . . . , etc. Only Vol. I of *Emile* is taken into account. The work refutes by discussing particular theses rather than going to the roots of the doctrine. On certain points his arguments rest upon a complete misunderstanding of Rousseau's true position. For instance, he seems to believe that Rousseau wants to bring men back to savagery. On other points, however, his criticism anticipates the future objections of J. de Maistre and of De Bonald. For instance: Rousseau intentionally considers in Emile his "human condition" (i.e., Emile as a man) and not his social condition; Emile is an abstract man, whereas real men are soldiers, lawyers, businessmen, etc. (*Opere* I, p. 7). The isolated man Rousseau has in mind does not exist; nature made man for society, so it is impossible to educate Emile for himself without at the same time educating him for others (Refl. 4, *op. cit.*, pp. 12-13). The so-called state of nature never existed; men never went on all fours; moreover, it is not true that society debases men; it improves them, unless, of course, we feel like maintaining that science and virtue are degrading influences. Are Socrates and Newton degenerates? (*Op. cit.*, pp. 22-23.) Rousseau objects to educational methods that appeal to reason, because reason is the goal to be reached by education, not its starting point; to which Gerdil answers: "Not at all. The condition of rea-

son when education begins is not at all the condition of reason when education reaches its end" (p. 55). It is interesting to compare his own views on education with those of Rousseau: *Plan des études pour un jeune seigneur*, in *Opere*, Vol. I, pp. 169-181. *Plan des études pour Son Altesse Royale Mgr le Prince de Piémont*, in *Opere*, I, pp. 185 ff. In philosophy, he recommends Bossuet, *Traité de la connaissance de Dieu et de soi-même*, as a textbook in metaphysics. Interesting to consult, his *Histoire des sectes des philosophes;* on Descartes, *Opere*, I, pp. 263-268; on Malebranche, pp. 268-270. "That is what Malebranche calls seeing in God; a metaphorical expression, little accurate, and which easily invites the ridicule under which one has tried to bury it" (p. 269). On Voltaire criticizing Pascal: he may be right on some details, but "it is the snake gnawing the file" (p. 277).
36. *Principes métaphysiques* . . . , Book III, chaps. ii-vii; pp. 48-70.
37. *Ibid.*, chap. viii, pp. 71-73.
38. *Ibid.*, Book IV, chaps. i-iii, pp. 81-88.
39. *Ibid.*, chaps. iv, vi, xi, and xiii; pp. 88, 98, 100, 101, 108-119.
40. Gerdil subscribes to the fundamental principle of Descartes that all that which the mind conceives clearly and distinctly must exist in reality such as it is conceived (*Immateriality of the soul* . . . , VIII, ii, 3; Vol. III, p. 181). On the notion of substance: "All that which we conceive, which has its own existence and is thereby distinguished from everything else, is a substance. The way a thing exists is a mode" (*op. cit.*, II, i; Vol. III, p. 84). There is no distinction between the notions of mode and of quality. In a round piece of iron, the substance is iron, roundness is

the mode or quality. Gerdil denounces the Peripatetics for turning abstract notions into things (*op. cit.*, III, i; Vol. III, p. 5).

41. A rather paradoxical reproach addressed by Gerdil to Voltaire is that of "going back to the substantial forms or to something like them" (*L'immatérialité de l'âme* . . . , Part IV, pp. 107-115). "Some new philosophers whose writings are otherwise praiseworthy for their polished tone and their good taste" (*ibid.*). Gerdil attacks d'Holbach's account of the intellectual acts of the human mind by means of physical sensibility. With the author of *The System of Nature*, no conversation was possible. *Osservazioni sul modo di spiegare gli atti intellettuali della mente humana per mezzo della sensibilità fisica proposto dall' Autore del Sistema della Natura*, in *Opere*, Vol. III, pp. 283-327.

42. Gerdil's literary eulogy pronounced after his death and printed in his complete works remarkably illustrates the situation of Christian philosophy in Gerdil's own time: "The number of the partisans of the English philosopher (Locke) grew much smaller; quite a few left him . . . and the sublime opinions cultivated by Plato, admired by Cicero, illustrated and purified by the great Augustine, ordered by Malebranche, put by Gerdil in the clearest light, were adopted by them and made theirs. It is therefore quite justly that his work *On the Nature and Origin of Ideas* earned him from M. de Mairan, the most famous Secretary of the Academy of Paris (to say nothing of other highly authorized testimonies) the title of the restorer of good philosophy, and, from the most wise Benedict XIV, that of its repurifyer" (*Elogio literario del card. G. S. Gerdil*, by Francesco Luigi Fontana, in *Opere*, Vol. I, pp. xviii-xix).

PART 7 THE AGE OF THE PHILOSOPHERS

XIX. D'Alembert and the Idea of an Encyclopedia

1. JEAN LE ROND D'ALEMBERT, a foundling picked up on the steps of the church of St. Jean-le-Rond, November 17, 1717. After brilliant studies, he refused to study law, and still more resolutely medicine, "the most ridiculous thing invented by men"; devoted himself to mathematics: *Memoir on Integral Calculus*, 1793; *Memoir on the Refraction of Solid Bodies*, 1741; *Treatise of Dynamics*, 1743; *Memoir on the General Cause of Winds*, 1746; a Fellow of the French Academy of Sciences, of the Academy of Berlin, and of the French Academy, he began to handle philosophical problems in 1751, with his *Preliminary Discourse* written as an introduction to the *Encyclopedia*. He was later to publish an *Essay on the Elements of Philosophy* . . . , 1759, and various polemical writings; offered high positions by Frederick II of Prussia, Christina of Sweden, and Catherine II of Russia, he accepted only modest pensions; died Paris, October 27, 1783.

2. *L'Encyclopédie ou Dictionnaire raisonné des sciences, des arts et des métiers, par une société de gens de lettres, mis en ordre et publié par M. Diderot, de l'Académie royale des Sciences et des Belles-Lettres de Prusse, et quant à la partie mathématique, par M. d'Alembert, de l'Académie royale des Sciences de Paris, de celle de Prusse, et de la Société royale de Londres.* The *Discours préliminaire des éditeurs* was the work of d'Alembert—chronology and vicissitudes of the publication *see* Diderot, *Oeuvres,* ed. André Billy (Paris: La Pléiade, 1946), Introduction, pp. 15-21.

The preface of d'Alembert is quoted from the school edition: *Discours préliminaire de l'Encyclopédie,* ed. with Introduction and notes by A. V. Pierre (coll. "Les Classiques pour tous"; Paris: A. Hatier, n.d.). Another separate school edition is: *Discours sur l'Encyclopédie,* by F. Picavet (Paris, 1919). Collective edition: *Oeuvres philosophiques,* ed. Bastien (Paris, 1805). On the doctrine: Maurice Muller, *Essai sur la philosophie de Jean d'Alembert* (Paris, 1926).

3. P. 67.

4. Pp. 62-63.

5. P. 70.

6. P. 11.

7. P. 20.

8. P. 21.

9. P. 19.

10. P. 22.

11. A matter of personal taste, but also a Cartesian feature. The judgment of Condorcet, which will be quoted at the conclusion of this sketch of d'Alembert, is confirmed by the following remarks of the *Discours:* "[the theologians] . . . feared, or seemed to fear the blows a blind reason could inflict on Christianity: how could they not see that Christianity had nothing to fear of so weak an attack? Sent from heaven to men, the so ancient and so just veneration of the people for the Christian religion had been guaranteed forever by the promises of God himself. Besides, however absurd a religion may be (a reproach that only impiety can direct against our own), it never is the philosophers who destroy it; even when they teach truth, they content themselves with showing it without constraining anybody to know it; such a power exclusively belongs to the all-powerful Being." The rest of the passage should be read as a remarkable sample of what d'Alembert himself called his "half-attacks." Theologians never hesitated to understand them as full ones and to react accordingly.

12. Pp. 40-41.

13. The place of "revealed theology" is expressly reserved, but it is included, as one of the knowledges of Reason, under the general category of Philosophy, in the subdivision: Science of God.

14. His own view of what happened is simple. Detesting the Middle Ages, d'Alembert thinks that the only way to get rid of their influence was to go back to antiquity. This was the task performed by erudition; its usefulness was to lead modern men to the study of *Belles-Lettres,* but the time of erudition is over. The anti-humanism of d'Alembert is as complete as that of Descartes, and more vocal. See pages 45-48, especially, as typical of the spirit of the Enlightenment, the passage on page 47; speaking of erudition, d'Alembert remarks: "It today is a kind of merit not to appreciate it; it even is a merit which many people deem sufficient. It would seem that the scorn in which those *learned* men are now held is intended to compensate for the exaggerated esteem in which they used to hold themselves or for the unenlightened approval of their contemporaries." Commenting on the time wasted on the study of dead languages, d'Alembert is led to an intelligent remark. Latin had at least the merit to be a common

language, used by all scientists (Newton could write in Latin) and by all philosophers (Bacon, Descartes, Spinoza, etc.). Since the French decided to write philosophy in French, the English philosophers did the same with English; "Germany, where Latin seemed to have sought for a refuge, is little by little losing its usage; I have no doubt they will soon be followed by the Swedes, the Danes and the Russians." Before the end of the eighteenth century a philosopher wishing to get informed of what his predecessors said, will have to burden his memory with seven or eight different languages and, after consuming in their study the more precious part of his life, he will die before beginning to learn. The use of Latin in matters of literary taste

is ridiculous; it would be very sensible to revive it in matters of philosophy and sciences where only precision and clarity are needed. One may wish to see that usage re-established, but one should not hope for it. The eighteenth century sees the slow beginnings of a sense for historicity. Hegel is only fifty years away. But the attitude of representative men like d'Alembert in the very heart of the century is a measure of the immense distance still to be traversed.

15. P. 32.
16. Pp. 29-30.
17. D'Alembert, "Eléments de philosophie" in *Mélanges de Littérature, d'Histoire, et de Philosophie*, nouvelle édition (6 vols.; Amsterdam, 1759), Vol. IV, pp. 5-6.

xx. Diderot, the Soul of the *Encyclopedia*

1. DENIS DIDEROT, b. Langres, 1713; d. Paris, 1784. Son of an artisan from whom he learned a respect for artisanry later to permeate the *Encyclopedia;* then at Paris (Collège Louis le Grand—Jesuit); became a student of Paris left-bank life rich in adventures of a less than philosophical sort, that throw light on the naturism of his ethics, itself but a speculative justification of his moral laxity. At first a deist, he soon ceased to be a Christian; then ceased even to be a deist; in 1742 became acquainted with Rousseau, who introduced Condillac to him; arrested in 1749 for the publication of his *Letter on Blindmen for the Use of Those Who See,* he spent three months in the Tour de Vincennes; from 1751 to 1772 his life coincided with the stormy history of the publication of the *Encyclopedia.* In 1765,

as a friendly gesture to help Diderot, Empress Catherine II of Russia bought from him his personal library, with the stipulation that he retain the use of it during his lifetime; in 1773, Diderot, who hated to travel, yielded to Catherine's insistence that he come to Russia; went to St. Petersburg, where he received a friendly welcome and had long philosophical conversations with the Empress; returned to Paris in 1774, where he spent the last ten years of his life in peace; in 1778 he had for the first time occasion to meet Voltaire, whom he deeply admired, in Paris; in 1784, Diderot fell sick; a flat was rented for him, at the expense of Catherine II (he was by no means a pauper); he died there, July 30, 1784. The *Encyclopedia* had been condemned by Rome, September 3, 1759; on the eve of his death, Diderot is said to have told friends: "The first step toward philosophy is unbelief."

Main philosophical writings: *Principes de la philosophie morale ou essai sur le mérite et la vertu* (Principles of Moral Philosophy Being an Essay on Merit and Virtue, trans. by Shaftesbury), 1745. *Pensées philosophiques* (Philosophical Thoughts), 1746. *La promenade du sceptique* (The Skeptic's Walk), 1747. *Lettre sur les aveugles à l'usage de ceux qui voient* (A Letter on Blindmen for the Use of Those That See), 1749. *Pensées sur l'interprétation de la nature* (Considerations on the Interpretation of Nature), 1754. *Entretien entre d'Alembert et Diderot* (A Conversation between d'Alembert and Diderot); followed by *Le rêve de d'Alembert* (The Dream of d'Alembert); and by *Suite de l'entretien* (A Sequel to the Conversation), *c.* 1769, posthumously published in 1830.

Collective editions: *Oeuvres complètes*, by J. Assezat and M. Tourneux (20 vols.; Paris: Garnier Frères, 1875-1879). Selected works, including the *Letter* and the d'Alembert trilogy in *Oeuvres de Diderot*, ed. André Billy (Paris: La Pléiade, 1946). A good choice of Diderot's philosophical works is found in Diderot, *Oeuvres philosophiques*, ed. Paul Vernière (Paris: Classiques Garnier, n.d.). Same collection, *Oeuvres esthétiques*, ed. Paul Vernière (Paris, n.d.).

Biographical: André Billy, *Vie de Diderot* (2 vols. with plates; Paris: Flammarion, n.d.). The main source is the abundant correspondence, particularly with Grimm (4 vols.; Paris, 1830); with Sophie Volland (3 vols.; Paris, 1930); inédite (2 vols.; Paris, 1931). L. G. Crocker, *The Embattled Philoso-*

pher (East Lansing, Mich.: State College Press, 1954).

Doctrinal and, most of the time, also biographical: K. Rosenkranz, *Diderots Leben und Werke* (2 vols.; Leipzig, 1886). Ducros, *Les Encyclopédistes* (Paris, 1900). R. L. Cru, *Diderot as a Disciple of English Thought* (New York, 1913). J. Mouveaux, *Diderot, l'encyclopédiste et le penseur* (Montbéliard, 1914). P. Hermand, *Les idées morales de Diderot* (Paris, 1923). R. Hubert, *Les sciences sociales dans l'encyclopédie* (Paris, 1923). J. Le Gras, *Diderot, et l'encyclopédie* (Amiens, 1928). J. E. Barker, *Diderot's Treatment of the Christian Religion in the Encyclopedia* (New York: King's Crown, 1941). Y. Belaval, *L'esthétique sans paradoxe de Diderot* (Paris: Gallimard, 1950). L. G. Crocker, *Two Diderot Studies: Ethics and Esthetics* (Baltimore: Johns Hopkins, 1952). O. E. Fellows and N. L. Torrey, *Diderot Studies* (2 vols.; Syracuse: Syracuse University Press, 1950-1953). A. G. Fredman, *Diderot and Starhe* (New York: Columbia University Press, 1955). A. Vartanian, *Diderot and Descartes* (Princeton: Princeton University Press, 1953).

2. WILLIAM MOLYNEUX, b. Dublin, 1656; d. Dublin, 1698. Asked Locke the problem now known as "the problem of Molyneux." Both agreed it should be answered in the negative. Berkeley also agreed, adding, however, that even to clear-sighted men, shapes, sizes, and distances are not directly perceived by sight only. Himself a translator of the *Meditationes* of Descartes (along with the objections of Thomas Hobbes), Molyneux was well aware of the philosophical significance of his question. The problem was complicated by

the observation published by the physician Cheselden in the *Philosophical Transactions of the Royal Society*, 1728. William Cheselden, b. Somerley, 1688; d. Bath, 1752. A physician famous for his successes in operating on cataracts described the first impressions of a young man born blind. These confirmed the conclusions of Locke, Molyneux, and Berkeley; they even seemed to confirm the point of view of Descartes (and, before him, of Aristotle) that sight is a kind of touch. As was said above, Voltaire included the conclusions of Berkeley in his own *Philosophy of Newton* (1741). Condillac had read Locke and Voltaire when he wrote his own *Essay on the Origin of Human Knowledge* (1746). Diderot published his *Letter* in 1749; his own discussion includes all the answers already given to the problem of Molyneux and the known interpretations of the observation of Cheselden. In 1754, Condillac takes up again the discussion of the problem in his *Treatise*, not, as it seems, without making good use of some of the remarks of Diderot. Each one of those who shared in the discussion contributed personal views; the contribution of Diderot was his insistence on a more realistic appraisal of the condition in which the patient finds himself right after the operation. Despite personal differences and variations, all agree that the recently operated patient could not tell at once the sphere from the cube.

3. Diderot quotes from *The Life and Character of Dr. Nicholas Saunderson, Late Lucasian Professor of the Mathematicks in the University of Cambridge: by His Disciple and Friend William Inchlif, Esq.* (Dublin, 1747). Diderot reproduces plates illustrating the tactile method used by Saunderson and (this is to Diderot the whole point) illustrating, for the benefit of clear-sighted men, the kind of tactile image of a colorless space a blind man can form.

4. This passage motivated the first prosecutions against Diderot, his arrest and his imprisonment at Vincennes. The point is that the formation of the world, including what it exhibits of order as well as of disorder, does not require the existence of a supreme Intelligence. As this was ruining the possibility of all knowledge of God *a creatura mundi*, it practically amounted to a denial of the existence of God. This was not even theism, it was straight atheism. On the credit side, note, in what precedes, Diderot's imaginative anticipation of the Darwinian "struggle for life" conceived as the survival of the fittest.

5. Both "theism" and "deism" were words currently used from the seventeenth century onward by authors who wished to clear themselves of the suspicion of "atheism" without having to confess to any particular form of religion. The best thing to do is therefore to follow each author's choice of word. Kant was, it seems, the first to attempt to draw a technical distinction between the two words, so it would be committing an anachronism to extend this distinction to authors such as Voltaire and Rousseau, who would not even have grasped its meaning, which is tied to the whole of the *Critique*. The element common to both terms is rejection of atheism, coupled with the affirmation of the real existence of an object of thought called "god," whatever meaning one may attach to the word.

6. We here avoid the *lapsus* of one

of d'Alembert's editors; in the passage of the *Preliminary Discourse* where d'Alembert writes *nous*, he means the French *we*, not the Greek *nous* (intellect).

7. The very title of the *Conversation* proves at least that, even though it is a wholly fictitious one, Diderot has in mind the positions of his friend d'Alembert. Moreover, the object of his attack exactly answers the development of the *Discourse* in which d'Alembert affirms the distinction of mind and body, the harmony of mind and body, and the existence of a supreme Intelligence accounting for their harmony. These three positions are expressly denied by Diderot. The theism of d'Alembert is here replaced by the plain atheism of Diderot.

8. Remember the position of Locke, according to whom it is neither evident nor demonstrated that matter cannot think.

9. Diderot sometimes gives an impression that he is materializing the doctrine of Leibniz, in which everything is made up of living and knowing units (the monads). At any rate, Leibniz had already been led to stress the law of continuity in nature. Taken in itself, this was one of the oldest themes familiar to the Western mind (Arthur O. Lovejoy, *The Great Chain of Being, A Study in the History of an Idea,* William James Lectures, Harvard, 1933 [Cambridge, Mass.: Harvard University Press, 1936]). Leibniz never tires of repeating that nature takes no jumps: *natura non facit saltus*. It should also be kept in mind that this notion of a continuous structure of the universe was then in the air. See Robinet, *De la Nature* (4 vols.; Amsterdam, 1761-1766), with a fifth volume published in Amsterdam in 1767 with

this subtitle: *A Philosophical View of the Natural Gradation of the Forms of Being, the Essays of Nature Learning to Make Man* (Lovejoy, *op. cit.*, p. 368, note 53; on the doctrine of Robinet, pp. 270-283).

A too neglected philosopher can be remembered in connection with either Diderot or Condillac: CHARLES BONNET of Geneva (1720-1793). On account of some analogies with Condillac in the method of exposition (the statue), it must be specified that Bonnet projected as early as 1748 the treatise he was to publish later: *Essai de psychologie ou Considérations sur les opérations de l'âme* (London, 1775), followed by an *Essai analytique sur les facultés de l'âme* (Copenhagen, 1780). This would be the Condillac side. On the science-fiction side recalling Diderot, though likewise independent of him, *Palingénésie philosophique* . . . , 1770 (*Philosophical Palingenesia,* or *Ideas on the Past Condition and the Future Condition of Living Beings*). See Lovejoy, *op. cit.*, pp. 283-286. For an introduction to Bonnet, G. Capone Braga, *La filosofia francese,* I, pp. 160-168. Collective edition: *Oeuvres d'histoire naturelle et de philosophie* (Neuchâtel, 1779-1783).

10. This notion of a fumbling Nature whose results are obtained by trial and error haunted Diderot's mind. Obviously, it entailed a wholly atheistic view of nature. It accounts for his interest in monsters and misfits of all sorts. The *Letter on Blindmen* was followed in 1751 by a *Letter on the Deaf and Mute for the Benefit of Those That Hear and Talk*. In another sense, it also tied up with the possibility that any being follows from another being and brings about the rise of another one. This favored the general notion of a nature con-

tinually turning out new types of beings. Such is the Nature of Diderot, a truly Heraclitean stream of transitory and never self-repeating situations and things: *Considerations on the Interpretation of Nature*, LVIII. On the other hand, since Nature tries everything once and rejects the misfits, it is not surprising that parts of one model can be found again in another model. Diderot sees Nature indefinitely varying the same mechanism and, so to speak, trying to produce many different animals by simply lengthening, shortening, multiplying, or modifying the same organs. From arms to wings, there are many possible stages. Hence the fact that ever-changing Nature is at the same time the seat of many correspondences between different beings. They are different, but they resemble each other because they all are produced by the same means: *Considerations . . .* , XII.

1. Very active as an art critic, Diderot wrote several treatises on problems of aesthetics; among others: *Traité du Beau* (*c.* 1750) written for the *Encyclopédie; Essai sur la peinture* (1760); *Pensées détachées sur la peinture, la sculpture, l'architecture, et la poésie* (1781).

2. Part of it might perhaps be explained by the brutal assurance with which Diderot asserts his views in all domains. Unsuspecting readers should also be warned that coarseness and vulgarity are parts of Diderot's making. His excuse is that he so often wrote for himself only, or for a very small number of friends, works that were to be published long after his death. Nevertheless, the way he reveals the illegitimate origin of d'Alembert in his *Conversation* cannot have been considered good taste by those who first read it; not to say

anything of d'Alembert himself. In fact, Mlle. de l'Espinasse resented the impudence with which he had atributed her a share in the famous conversation. Through d'Alembert, she asked Diderot to destroy the trilogy. Obviously, it was not done.

13. Around Diderot are found several materialists whose doctrines differ little from his own, the more so as he himself had a hand in some of their works. The exact extent of that collaboration is not known.

JULIEN OFFRAY DE LA METTRIE, b. Saint-Mâlo, 1719; d. Berlin, 1751. At first a Jansenist, he gave up theology for medicine. He was an army surgeon in active service when he published his *Histoire naturelle de l'âme* (Natural History of the Soul), 1745; he was dismissed from the army in 1746. Banished from France, he went to Holland, published *L'homme machine* (Man a Machine), 1748, and subsequently was banished from Holland. He then sought and found a refuge near King Frederick II of Prussia, who gave him the title of Royal Lecturer. The general inspiration of *Man a Machine* is well expressed by the title. He explicitly refers the reader to the Cartesian thesis (upheld by Malebranche himself) that animals are entirely accountable for by extension and motion only. Himself a competent practitioner, he was well informed in matters of anatomy and physiology. The body appeared to him as consisting of organs each of which has its own structure and whose association constitutes the whole. He insisted on the relative independence of the parts within the whole. Like all other animals, man can be explained by the organization of the organs proper to him; organized matter differs from non-organized matter in that it has motion. Realizing that, after all, machines as such have no motion, he amended his general thesis in later writings: *Man a Plant: Animals More than Machines*, 1750. *Philosophical Reflections on the Origin of Animals*, 1750. Two more writings published in 1751 and 1752 develop a pure sensualism in matters of morality.

PAUL DIETRICH D'HOLBACH, b. Hildesheim, Germany, 1725; d. Paris, 1789. Lived in Paris where, being very wealthy, he played constant host to the Encyclopedists. An atheist and a materialist, he would publish his works under assumed names. Such was particularly the case of *Le Système de la nature et du monde moral* (System of Nature and of the Moral World) par M. Mirabaud, secrétaire perpétuel et l'un des Quarante de l'Académie française, 1770. The alleged author had been dead ten years. Quotations from the book will be found under "Voltaire," note 21. He reduced all phenomena, physical and moral alike, to matter and motion, motion being held to be an essential property of matter. A strict determinism prevails everywhere. D'Holbach wrote a number of violently anti-religious works, directed against revealed religions in general but particularly against Christianity and priests. All religions are harmful; priests should everywhere be replaced by physicians. The doctrine aims at founding a new system of ethics which consists in identifying with pleasure the fundamental motive of human actions; societies should be organized in such a way that it be the interest of each and every individual to act for the greater benefit of the social body. It is the business of the state to see to it that personal interest and morality coincide. The moral problem must therefore be solved

by the political power; a non-religious education should train future citizens to act for the benefit of all; the legal system should also promote this harmony between personal well-being and common good; among other works favoring this view: *Ethocratie ou le gouvernement fondé sur la morale* (Ethocracy or Government Founded on Ethics), 1776; *La morale universelle* (Universal Ethics), 1776. When all is said, the *System* remains his major work. Catholic refutations are listed in R. Hubert, *D'Holbach et ses amis* (Paris, 1928), p. 220.

CLAUDE ADRIEN HELVETIUS, b. Paris, 1715; d. Paris, 1771. A receiver general, he became extremely wealthy. Read Locke with enthusiasm and followed the general trend of the Encyclopedists toward a materialistic interpretation of the *Essay*. Helvetius' main work, *De l'esprit* (On Spirit) (Paris, 1758), was condemned and burned. In 1772, one year after his death, his *De l'homme* (On Man) was published in Amsterdam; it is an amplification of the first work. Collective edition: *Oeuvres complètes* (London, 1776). *De l'esprit* expresses the same convictions and betrays the same interests as those of d'Holbach and La Mettrie. What is personal with him is, if not the notion itself, this being common to all the Encyclopedists, at least the all-importance he attaches to the notion of education. All men are made alike by nature, yet they all are different. What causes these differences? Education. On the part of the educated, the basis for education is attention; attention itself depends on interest and on passion, which are always bound with the quest of pleasure and the avoidance of pain. On the strength of these principles, it should be possible for education to mold men after a common pattern, abolishing the individual inequalities and training everyone to delight in actions beneficial to the common good of society. Virtuous actions are such as contribute to the welfare of the country; education will have achieved its end if it places children in surroundings that will determine in them the kind of passions from which virtues inevitably flow. Problems related to education were then coming to the fore in consequence of the common opposition of the Encyclopedists to religion and to Christian education. The state was for them the only possible successor of the Church as an educating authority; hence their common conclusion that ethics is ultimately one of the political powers of the state, as the state is responsible for the acquisition and preservation of common good.

On the speculative side, the main thesis is that *"physical sensibility* and *memory* are the productive causes of all our *ideas,* and that all our *false judgments* are effects of either our *passions* or of our *igno-*

rance" (italics Helvetius'). At the psychological level, the doctrine is a rehash of Condillac: "all *judgment* is but *sensation,*" "judging is feeling" (*De l'esprit,* Discourse I, chap. i). At the metaphysical level, Helvetius shows some practical prudence: "I shall perhaps be asked whether these two faculties are modifications of a spiritual or of a material substance. That question, once discussed by the philosophers, debated by the Fathers, and revived in our own days, does not necessarily enter the plan of my work. That which I have to say about spirit agrees equally well with both hypotheses. I only shall observe on this subject that, had not the Church fixed our belief on that point one could not but grant that no opinion of that sort is susceptible of demonstration." Like many other problems of the same kind, this one could be solved only by resorting to "the calculus of probabilities." A most extraordinary proposition indeed. The result of that possible calculation is not hard to guess. On the opinions upheld at the time of the Fathers, see Discourse I, chap. i, note 5.

XXI. Voltaire

1. FRANÇOIS-MARIE AROUET DE VOLTAIRE, b. Paris, 1694; d. Paris, 1778. Born of a petit-bourgeois family, rapidly made a fortune and immediately launched into the career of a typical successful writer whose literary talent, wit, and sense of publicity secured him a lasting hold on public opinion. Voltaire was the first, and he remains perhaps the greatest, of the modern publicists. He took the pen name of Voltaire in 1719 (in his tragedy, *Oedipe*); from 1726 to 1729, years of exile in England, which were to

be of decisive importance for his intellectual formation; his discovery of Locke and Newton dates from those years. In 1734, his *Philosophical Letters* reveal the depth and amplitude of that English influence; same year, *Treatise of Metaphysics,* written for Mme. du Chatelet, who kept it to herself. In 1736, an *Epistle on the Philosophy of Newton;* made a Fellow of the French Academy, 1746; accepted an invitation extended to him by the Prussian King, Frederick the Great, stayed at his court from

July 1750 to March 1753, after which they part company very ill pleased with one another. After trying various places, Voltaire migrated to Switzerland (Lausanne, then Geneva), until in 1760 he finally settled on the estate of Ferney (today Ferney-Voltaire), in France, so as not to be bothered by the Protestant ministers of Geneva, while being close enough to the Swiss border to be able to cross if the French police gave trouble. Voltaire spent there the rest of his life, always writing, especially philosophical novels and many signed or anonymous essays in which he carried on a very effective anti-Christian propaganda. Watched by the police, these writings were peddled and smuggled into Paris; with the years, this intensely present self-exiled writer became a legendary figure. In February 1778, he decided to return to Paris, where he was given a welcome that turned into a sort of apotheosis. Acclaimed by the French Academy, by the actors and public of the *Comédie Française* as well as by the crowds, he could not stand the strain and died there on May 30 of the same year. Voltaire then was eighty-four years old; this was eleven years before the French Revolution of 1789. He had left with a friend this short statement: "I die worshiping God, loving my friends, not hating my enemies, and detesting persecution."

Main works of philosophical interest: *Lettres philosophiques,* first published in English translation, 1733, then in French in 1734 (standard edition by G. Lanson, 2 vols.; Paris: Société des textes français modernes, 1909). The title *Lettres anglaises* often designates the *Lettres philosophiques. Traité de la tolérance,* 1763. *Dictionnaire philo-*

sophique portatif, 1764, revised with additions in later editions, all anonymous. *Questions sur l'encyclopédie,* 1770. The *Remarks on Pascal* (or *Remarks on the Thoughts of Pascal*) was first published in 1734, in the *Lettres Philosophiques,* as the "Twenty-fifth Letter, on the Thoughts of M. Pascal."

Collected works: *Oeuvres complètes,* ed. Louis Moland (52 vols.; Paris: Garnier, 1883). Easily obtainable editions of philosophical works: *Dictionnaire philosophique,* ed. Julien Benda and Raymond Naves (Paris: Classiques Garnier, 1954), contains the 118 articles published under that title by Voltaire with their complements published by him in his *Questions sur l'encyclopédie. Lettres philosophiques* or *Lettres anglaises,* suivies du texte complet des *Remarques sur les Pensées de Pascal,* with Preface and Notes by R. Naves (Paris: Classiques Garnier, 1956). The philosophic novels and tales have often been reprinted; illustrative of Voltaire's ideas are (among others): *Zadig ou la destinée, Micromégas, Histoire de Jenny*; complete reprinting of the 1775 edition by Henri Benac (Paris: Classiques Garnier, n.d), and also in one volume (Paris: Bibliothèque de la Pléiade, n.d.).

Biographical-bibliographical: Gustave Desnoireterres, *Voltaire et la société du dix-huitième siècle* (8 vols.; 1867-1876). Georges Bengesco, *Bibliographie des oeuvres de Voltaire* (Paris, 1882-1890). Gustave Lanson, *Voltaire* (Paris: Hachette, 1906).

Doctrinal: E. Saigey, *La physique de Voltaire* (1873). G. Pellissier, *Voltaire philosophe* (Paris, 1908). V. Delbos, *La philosophie française* (Paris, 1919), pp. 153-168. G. Lanson, *Voltaire* (Paris: Hachette, n.d.). Raymond Naves, *Voltaire et l'encyclopédie* (Paris: Les éditions des presses modernes, 1938). M. M. H. Barr, *Voltaire in America, 1744-1800* (Baltimore: Johns Hopkins, 1941).

2. ELIE FRÉRON, b. Quimper, 1718; d. Paris, 1776. Conducted his fight against Voltaire in his periodical *Lettres sur quelques écrits de ce temps* (1749-1754) continued till his death under the new title of *L'année littéraire*. Fréron was a very intelligent man and not a bad literary critic, but he is remembered only as the victim of Voltaire's sarcastic wit.

3. On Calvin, among many other passages, see *Dictionnaire philosophique*, art. *Dogmes*, ed. R. Naves, p. 173. Observe that Calvin is not being opposed on any Catholic, theological, or religious ground, but only as a representative of religious fanaticism. Voltaire has used the name of two sixteenth-century heresiarchs, Laelius and Faustus Socinus, who both denied the Trinity and the divinity of Christ, to embody his own religious ideal. See in *Lettres philosophiques*, Letter vii: "On the Socinians, or Arians, or anti-Trinitarians," ed. R. Naves, pp. 30-32. In it, Voltaire relates that "le grand Monsieur Newton" did that opinion the honor to favor it. Its most resolute supporter is "the illustrious Dr. Clarke." Voltaire also calls them "unitarians." In another passage he mentions Newton, Locke, and Clarke among the Socinians. See *Essai sur les moeurs*, chap. cxxxvi, and chap. clxxxxii where "theism" and "socinianism" are considered practically identical: "Most of the socinians have at last joined that party"; i.e., what Voltaire calls "theism." Voltaire seems to have played with the idea of calling him-

self a socinian because, in the last analysis, they are theists, and theists are "more attached to Plato than to Jesus Christ, *more philosophers than Christians*" (italics ours). On Voltaire's socinianism, see the notes of R. Naves to his edition of the Seventh *Lettre philosophique*, pp. 197-203.

4. This leaves open the possibility of a natural theology such as the brand of Deism to which Voltaire always makes profession to adhere; since the God of Deism was such as he himself made It to be, Voltaire had no reason to oppose it. What he objected to was faith: "What is faith? Is it to believe that which looks evident? No; it is evident to me that there is a necessary Being, eternal, supreme, intelligent; this is not faith, it is reason. I have no merit to think that that Being eternal, infinite, whom I know to be virtue and goodness itself, wants me to be good and virtuous. Faith consists in believing, not that which looks true, but that which looks false to our understanding. The Asiatics can believe by faith only the voyage of Mohammed to the seven planets, the incarnations of the god Fo, of Vishnou, of Xaca, of Brahma, of Sammonocodom, etc., etc., etc. They submit their understanding, they are afraid to examine, they do not want to be impaled, or burnt; they say: 'I do believe.'" These remarks are immediately followed by an interesting commentary: "We are very far from making here the slightest allusion to the Catholic faith. We not only venerate it, but we share it (*Non seulement nous la vénérons, mais nous l'avons*): we only are speaking of the mendacious faith of the other religions of the world, that is, of that faith which is not faith, but only consists in

words." (*Dictionnaire philoso-phique*, art. *Foi*, II: ed. R. Naves, pp. 203-204.)

5. *Dictionnaire philosophique*, art. *Fanatisme, ed. cit.*, p. 197. There would be no point in reporting the sarcasms of Voltaire in the *Dictionary;* they lack philosophical substance. In order to substantiate what precedes, one instance at least can be mentioned, that of Voltaire's tireless attacks against the Old Testament. His method is simple: it consists in interpreting what was a history of the Jewish people and a revelation of the divine law as a series of examples for men to imitate. For instance, after quoting a series of twenty murders or so committed by Jewish kings or princes, "to say nothing of many other minor murders," he complains that, for an inspired history, the subject is not very edifying (art. *Histoire des rois juifs, ed. cit.*, p. 234), as if these were not so many stories of "crime and punishments." Elsewhere, he completely misses the meaning of Hebrew poetry and mistakes the violent invectives of the prophets against crimes committed by the Jewish people for prescriptions to commit them (art. *Ezéchiel, ed. cit.*, pp. 190-194). He sometimes adds insult and hatred to sarcasm. Coupled with his detestation of the Old Testament, there is in Voltaire a recognizable vein of anti-Semitism. The two motives blend in his hatred of both when he speaks of "the Jews, our masters and our enemies, whom we believe and whom we detest" (art. *Abraham, ed. cit.*, p. 2). This mixture has led Voltaire to curious *non sequiturs* of the type: I hate the Jews, therefore . . . Here is one: "We abominate the Jews (*nous avons les Juifs en horreur*) and we want to find in all that which was writ-

ten by them and collected by us the mark of the Divinity. There never was more palpable contradiction" (art. *Salomon, ed. cit.*, p. 385).

6. *Dictionnaire philosophique*, art. *Tolérance, ed. cit.*, p. 401. *Traité de la tolérance*, 1763.

7. *Questions sur l'encyclopédie* (1770), art. *Ame*, sec. iv in *Dictionnaire philosophique*, ed. R. Naves, Notes, p. 432.

8. *Questions sur l'encyclopédie*, art. *Bornes de l'esprit humain* (reprinted in *Dictionnaire, ed. cit.*, p. 473); and under the same title, *Dictionnaire philosophique, ed. cit.*, p. 60; Montaigne is named both times.

9. *Dictionnaire philosophique*, art. *Matière, ed. cit.*, p. 297.

10. Locke, *Essay*, Book IV, chap. iii, 6.

11. *Dictionnaire philosophique*, art. *Ame, ed. cit.*, pp. 7-15. Cf. *Questions sur l'encyclopédie*, art. *Ame*, sec. ii: *Des doutes de Locke sur l'âme*, reprinted in *Dict. philos., ed. cit.*, pp. 426-428. See the note of Voltaire quoting the passage where d'Alembert says that Locke created metaphysics just about as Newton created physics: *ed. cit.*, p. 427, note 2. It is often said that Voltaire considers the soul to be material; in fact, we do not know enough about the soul to be sure that it is material. "We call soul (*anima*) that which animates. We know little more because of the limits of our intelligence. Three-fourths of the human kind do not go farther; they do not bother about the thinking being; the other fourth is seeking; no one has found, nor will find" (*Dictionnaire . . .* , art. *cit.*, p. 7). Cf. the *Thirteenth Lettre philosophique, On Mr. Locke, ed. cit.*, pp. 64-67.

12. "Chinese Catechism," Second Conversation, in *Dictionnaire phi-*

losophique, ed. cit., pp. 69-70. Of course the ideal situation would be to have a nation of philosophers; since no such nation exists, it is a problem how far superstition should be destroyed. "One wonders whether a people of atheists can subsist. Methinks one should distinguish between the people properly said and a society of philosophers above the people. It is very true that in all countries the populace needs to be firmly held in hands, and that if Bayle had had five or six hundred peasants to govern, he would not have failed to announce to them a rewarding and punishing God. But Bayle would not have spoken of him to the Epicureans, who were wealthy, peace-loving people, cultivating all social virtues, especially friendship," etc. Voltaire concludes: "And so the dispute seems to me to be settled insofar as society and politics are concerned." (*Questions sur l'encyclopédie*, art. *Athéisme*, sec. i, reprinted in *Dictionnaire philosophique, ed. cit.*, p. 459.

13. Art. *Théiste* in *Dictionnaire philosophique, ed. cit.*, pp. 399-400.

14. Art. *Enfer, Dictionnaire philosophique*, pp. 178-180.

15. "I maintain that no philosopher could ever rest assured that Providence does not prepare punishment for the wicked and rewards for the good; for if they ask me who told me that God punishes, I shall ask who told them that God does not" (*Dictionnaire philosophique*, art. *Fraude, ed. cit.*, p. 211). This article is reproduced in the *Questions on the Encyclopedia*, with this additional remark: "Above all let us remember that a philosopher must announce a God, if he wants to be useful to human society" (*ed. cit.*, p. 545, note 150).

16. The thesis that "all is well," upheld by Alexander Pope, is opposed by Voltaire in his own poem *On the Disaster of Lisbon*. His conclusion is: "All will be well some day, such is our hope; all is well today, that is our illusion." At the philosophical level, he opposes the *Theodicy* of Leibniz, who, he says, has sided with Plato. Personally, he observes in true Voltairian spirit, "after reading both more than once, I confess my ignorance, as I am wont to do" (*Questions sur l'encyclopédie*, art. *Bien* [*Tout est*]). Cf. *Dictionnaire philosophique*, under the same title, the article where Voltaire protests against the easy way in which philosophers dispose of the problem: "The origin of evil is an abyss of which no one has been able to see the bottom" (*ed. cit.*, p. 56). Pope has simply availed himself of the data on the problem collected by Bolingbroke and Shaftesbury despite their arguments.

17. Dictionnaire philosophique, art. *Fin, Causes finales, ed. cit.*, pp. 199-202; the present quotation is to be found p. 200.

18. P. 201.

19. Questions sur l'encyclopédie, art. *Causes finales*, sec. ii, *ed. cit.*, p. 542.

20. Ed. cit., p. 19.

21. Voltaire was resolutely opposed to the mechanistic conception of nature developed by d'Holbach in his *Système de la Nature*, 1770. In his own *Questions sur l'encyclopédie*, art. *Causes finales*, sec. i, *ed. cit.*, pp. 538-542, Voltaire objects to the "eloquent and dangerous passage" of the *System of Nature*, Part II, chap. v, which, however, he quotes in full. D'Holbach's position is that all the effects attributed to the power of God should be attributed to "the power of nature, which produces all the animals we see by means of the combinations of matter, itself in continuous action; the accord of the parts of those animals follows from the necessary laws of their nature and of their combination." Some say that we cannot have the idea of a work without having at the same time that of a worker distinct from his work, but "nature is not a work." It has always existed by itself; it is in it that everything is made. Nature is an immense workshop provided with all the materials and tools it needs in order to operate. It makes for itself its own tools. This materialism is still more radical, in a sense, than that of Diderot, which required extension, motion, and sensibility as first principles of things. D'Holbach only needs extended matter and motion. In short, the *Monde* of Descartes minus God. Remember Pascal's remark: "Descartes would like to do without God. . . ." To this atheistic mechanism, Voltaire opposes his own articles on "Atheism" and on "God," in the *Dictionnaire philosophique*, as well as his considerations in favor of final causes which, of course, entail the existence of a provident "worker."

22. One of the most violent diatribes against the Jews is the note 81 of *On the Thoughts of Pascal*, ed. R. Naves, pp. 297-298. Himself the prey of anti-Semitic fanaticism, Voltaire cannot forgive Pascal for trusting "fanatic usurers," robbers, bloodthirsty and superstitious men. Who would believe that God singled out that barbarous tribe to entrust it with his secrets?

23. After a lengthy denunciation of all the fanatics, Jansenists and Jesuits, Papists and Calvinists alike, Voltaire concludes, "Pascal was geometer and eloquent; the union of these two great merits then were very rare; but he did not add to

them true philosophy" (note 89, *On the Thoughts of Pascal, ed. cit.*, p. 301).

24. "Such as it is, the human kind cannot subsist unless there be an infinity of useful men who own nothing at all; for certainly a well-to-do man will not leave his field in order to plow your own; and if you need a pair of shoes, no Master of the Rolls will make you one. Equality then is the most natural and, at the same time, the most chimerical thing in the world" (*Dictionnaire philosophique*, art. *Egalité, ed. cit.*, p. 177).

25. The "gens de lettres" collectively designated by Diderot as the co-authors of the *Encyclopedia*, have been described and defined by Voltaire in the article "Gens de Lettres" written by him for the *Encyclopedia*. He considers those of the eighteenth century far superior to their predecessors. Using a sound philosophy, they have eliminated many dangerous superstitions, and "thereby, they have in effect served the State." See *Lettres philosophiques*, Lettre xxiii, notes, ed. R. Naves, pp. 260-263; and *Dictionnaire philosophique*, art. *Lettres, Gens de Lettres ou Lettres*, ed. R. Naves, pp. 272-274.

On this point, however, Voltaire occupies a position all his own. With "the wise Locke," he is against the doctrine of innate ideas, and of course against the "vision in God" of Malebranche. At the same time he does not subscribe to the absolute empiricism of Locke, especially when it is a question of principles of moral conduct. There are no innate principles of action, but, "instead of those chimerical innate ideas, God has given to us a reason that gathers strength with age, and that teaches us all, when we are attentive, without passion, without prejudice, that there is a God, and that one should be just; but I cannot grant Locke the consequences he draws from this. He seems to get too near the system of Hobbes, from which however he is very remote" (*Le philosophe ignorant*, chap. xxxv, "Against Locke"). The usual attitude of Voltaire on the question does not resemble that of Condillac. If one wants to label it (an always dangerous operation in history), it should be called a straight rationalism, rather than a sensualism. This, however, must be kept in mind, that although practically all his future positions are contained in his early *Treatise on Metaphysics*, Voltaire has slightly altered some of them. For various reasons, of which caution is one, his philosophical language sometimes lacks precision.

PART 8 THE PHILOSOPHIES OF SOCIETY

XXII. Vico and the New Science

1. GIAMBATTISTA VICO, b. Naples, 1668; d. Naples, 1744. Studied theology and law, then spent nine years as a preceptor in the family of the Marquess Domenico Rocca; during those years he read Gassendi and Descartes without feeling convinced of the superiority of their doctrines over the classical type of humanistic wisdom; he also studied theological problems, especially that of liberty; in 1698 he obtained the chair of rhetoric at the University of Naples, which permitted him to live, on an exceedingly modest salary, without doing anything but writing and teaching. The final redaction of his masterpiece, the *New Science*, was published a few months after his death.

Main works of philosophical interest: *De nostri temporis studiorum ratione* (On the Way to Study Used in Our Own Times), 1709. *De antiquissima italorum sapientia ex linguae latinae originibus eruenda* (On the Most Ancient Wisdom of the Italians Learned from the Origins of Their Language), 1710. *De universi juris uno principio et fine uno* (On the One Principle and One End of Law),

1720; followed by *De constantia jurisprudentiae* (On the Constancy of Jurisprudence), 1722. In 1725 at Naples, first published redaction of the *Scienza nuova*; in 1744, publication of the final redaction of the work: *Principi di una Scienza Nuova d'intorno alla comune natura delle nazioni* (Principles of a New Science Concerning the Common Nature of Nations). An *Autobiography* and a *Correspondence* have been posthumously published, ed. Benedetto Croce, in the series *Scrittori d'Italia* (Bari: Laterza, 1911). The *Autobiografia* was added to some editions of the *Principi*, for instance by P. Viazzi.

Modern editions: *La Scienza Nuova Prima*, ed. Nicolini, in the series *Scrittori d'Italia* (2 vols.; Bari: Laterza, 1931); selected pages with Introduction and Notes by G. Flores d'Arcais (3d ed., enlarged; Padova: Cedam, 1943). Same editor: *La Scienza Nuova Seconda* . . . (3d ed., rev.; 2 vols.; Bari, 1942). *The New Science of Giambattista Vico*, translated . . . by T. C. Bergin and M. H. Fisch (Ithaca, N.Y.: Cornell University Press, 1948). G. Vico, *De nostri temporis studiorum ratione*, Introduction, Italian translation and Notes by Vincenzo de Ruvo (Padova: Cedam, 1941-1949).

Doctrinal: Jules Michelet, *Oeuvres choisies* with a "Discours sur le système et la vie de Vico" (Paris, 1837), as revealing of Michelet as of Vico. Benedetto Croce, *La filosofia di G. B. Vico* (Bari: Laterza, 1911). G. Gentile, *Studi Vichiani* (Messina, 1914). M. Cochery, *Les grandes lignes de la philosophie historique et juridique de Vico* (Paris, 1923). E. Chiocchetti, *La filosofia di G. B. Vico* (Milano, 1935). A. H. Packwood, *The Life and Writings of Giambattista Vico* (London: Allen and Unwin, 1935). A. R. Caponigri, *Time and Idea. The Theory of History in G. Vico* (Chicago: Regnery, 1953).

2. On the notion of "common sense," such as Vico understood it, see p. 699.

3. Note *il certo*: Vico does not say *il vero*, because although it conforms to rules, the natural law of each nation is a fact to be ascertained as such.

4. See Book I, *Dei Principi*. Since all nations are ruled by eternal and universal principles, it is not surprising that, at all times and in all countries, certain customs are universally observed. Vico counts three of them: all nations have some religion; all nations contract solemn marriages; all nations bury their dead.

5. Only fragments of the immense history of the couple poetry-theology have been written. Let it suffice to remark that the problem of their relationship had never ceased to be discussed since the times of Petrarch, Coluccio Salutati, and Boccaccio. Here Vico is taking his place in a time-honored tradition.

XXIII. Montesquieu

1. CHARLES-LOUIS DE SECONDAT MONTESQUIEU, Baron de La Brède et de Montesquieu, b. Château de La Brède, near Bordeaux, 1689; d. Paris, 1755. Educated Juilly (Oratorians); studied law and began a life of reading historians of all countries and all times as well as all the recently published accounts of travelers to Asia. A magistrate of the Bordeaux Parliament, he published (anonymously) the *Lettres Persanes* (Persian Letters), 1721, a witty if often licentious satire of French life in his own times; elected a fellow of the French Academy (1725), his election was annulled; in 1727, having settled in Paris, he was elected again, and this time the election was confirmed by Cardinal de Fleury. A period of traveling abroad followed (1728-1731) which

was undertaken and carried out with the idea of studying constitutions, legislations, manners of conduct, and usages in various countries: Germany, Austria, Hungary, Italy, Switzerland, Holland, and finally England, which was then the obligatory pilgrimage of all French intellectuals; he stayed there from 1729 to 1731. Back in France, he retired to La Brède and published the *Considerations on the Rise and Fall of the Romans*, 1734, followed in 1748 by *L'Esprit des lois*, the success of which was very great. Having nearly lost his sight, he contented himself with writing minor works. Besides, no man can write twice what is the work of a lifetime, but he continued to answer objections and to write additions to his masterpiece. Then he had to stop: "I had conceived the design to give more extension and depth to some passages of this work. But I have become incapable of doing so. My readings have weakened my eyes and it seems to me that what I still have of light is but the dawn of the day when they shall shut themselves forever. . . . In the deplorable condition in which I find myself, it was not possible for me to put the last touch to this work; I would have burned it a thousand times had I not thought that it is a good thing to make oneself useful to men till the last breath."

Main works of philosophical interest: *Réflexions sur la monarchie universelle* (Reflections on Universal Monarchy), 1724. *Considérations sur les causes de la grandeur des Romains et de leur décadence* (Considerations on the Rise and Fall of the Romans), 1734. *L'Esprit des lois* (The Spirit of Laws), 1748.

Collective editions: Montesquieu, *Oeuvres complètes*, ed. with notes by Roger Caillois (2 vols.; Paris: Bibliothèque de la Pléiade), Nos. 81 and 86 of which Vol. I contains a Bibliography by Marion Lièvre. *L'Esprit des lois*, along with all the documentation related to it (including the *Considérations*), is contained in Vol. II of this edition. Many separate editions of *L'Esprit des lois* are available, among which one will be found in the collection *Classiques Garnier*, 2 vols., ed. with notes by Gonzague Truc. Selections: *Choix de textes avec introduction*, by Paul Archambault (Paris, 1910).

Doctrinal studies: Albert Sorel, *Montesquieu* (Paris: Hachette, 1887). Henri Barckhausen, *Montesquieu, ses idées, son oeuvre* (Paris, 1907). Abbé Joseph Dedieu, *Montesquieu* (Paris, 1913). Victor Del-

bos, *La philosophie française* (Paris, 1919), pp. 169-189. C. E. Vaughan, *Studies in the History of Political Philosophy* (Manchester, 1925), Vol. I, chap. v. Henri See, *L'évolution de la pensée politique en France au XVIIIe siècle* (Paris, 1925). E. Durkheim, *Montesquieu and Rousseau, Forerunners of Sociology* (Ann Arbor: University of Michigan Press, 1960).

2. *De l'Esprit des lois*, Book I, chap. i. Unless otherwise indicated, all references will be to the *Esprit des lois*, book and chapter.

3. *Défense de l'Esprit des lois*, Part I, #i.

4. *De l'Esprit des lois*, Book I, chap. i.

5. *Ibid.*, chap. ii.

6. *Ibid.*, chap. iii. Giovanni Vincenzo Gravina (b. Reggiano, near Cosenza, 1664; d. Rome, 1718). Professor of Civil Law at the Collegio della Sapienza in Rome (1699); then professor of Canon Law. His complete works were published at Naples, 1756; selected works, Milan, 1819.

7. *De l'Esprit des lois*, Book III, chap. i. Aristocracy is considered by Montesquieu as a particular form of democracy, in which power is in the hands of a certain number of persons. On the laws relative to its nature see *Esprit des lois*, Book II, chap. iii, and Book V, chap. viii.

8. *Ibid.*, Book II, chap. ii.

9. *Ibid.*, Book III, chap. ii. Concern for education, so widespread at that time in French circles for reasons given above, is conspicuous in Montesquieu. The problem is developed in *L'Esprit des lois*, Book IV. The laws of education are the first ones we receive; unless education be calculated to prepare future citizens fit to live in a definite type of state, it will have missed its end.

On the strength of this principle, Montesquieu describes, not what education in general should be, but what it should be in every one of the three fundamental kinds of government: education in monarchies, IV, ii; in a despotic government, IV, iii; in a democratic government, IV, v.

10. Ibid., Book V, chaps. iii-vii.

11. Literally, despotism is a perpetually self-corrupting political regime: "The principle of despotic government ceaselessly corrupts itself, because it is corrupt in virtue of its own nature" (*ibid.*, Book VIII, chap. x). Other governments perish because particular accidents corrupt their respective essences, "this one perishes because of its inner viciousness, when accidental causes do not prevent it from getting corrupt. Such regimes only maintain themselves when circumstances due to climate, to religion, to the situation or to the genius of the people, constrain it to follow a certain order and to suffer a certain rule. Those things force its nature without changing it: the ferocity of the regime remains; it is, for some time, tamed" (*ibid.*). Generally speaking, "once the principles of government are corrupt, the best laws become bad and work against the state; when the principles are sound, bad laws have the same effect as good ones; the force of the principle carries all" (*ibid.*, Book VIII, chap. xi).

12. Ibid., Book XI, chap. iii. Note the formula: "In a state, that is in a society where there are laws, liberty can only consist in having the power to do that which one ought to will, and in not being obliged to do that which one ought not to will." Whereupon Montesquieu adds: "One should keep in mind what independence is and what liberty is. Liberty is the right to do all that which the laws permit, and if a citizen could do all that which they forbid, he himself would have no liberty left, because the others would also have that same power." The following chapter (Book XI, chap. iv) shows the difference there is, in the mind of Montesquieu, between the essential purity of a regime and its political perfection. Pure political forms of government are not necessarily good in all respects. For instance, "democracy and aristocracy are not free states by their nature"; i.e., if they are free, they are so in virtue of another reason than their nature. "Political liberty is found in moderate governments only." Nay, it is not always found even in moderate states; it is found there only when there is no abuse of power. Unfortunately, it is an eternal experience that every man wielding power tends to abuse it; he goes on until he meets limits. This is true even of political majorities.

13. Aristotle, *Politics* VI, 10, i. Locke, *Treatise on Civil Government*, chap. xii as quoted by Victor Delbos, *La philosophie française*, p. 185.

14. L'Esprit des lois, Book XI, chap. vi, "Of the Constitution of England."

XXIV. Jean-Jacques Rousseau

1. JEAN-JACQUES ROUSSEAU, b. Geneva, 1712; d. Ermenonville, near Paris, 1778. Lost his mother in the year of his birth; in 1772, the father left Geneva and Jean-Jacques was entrusted to a minister till 1724; in 1726, apprentice to an engraver in Geneva; in 1728, returning from a walk, he found the doors of the city locked and decided on the spot not to go back to work; went to Annecy, met Mme. de Warens, a convert from Switzerland, who sent him to the hospice of the catechumens in Turin; abjured Protestantism; was a valet to Mme. de Vercellis, then to the Count de Gouvon; went back to Annecy and spent five months in the seminary; did some traveling in France and Switzerland, visited Paris and went back to Chambéry, 1729-1732; stayed at Mme. de Warens', 1732-1740; preceptor to the children of M. de Mably, 1740; went to Paris and presented to the Academy of Sciences his project of musical notation, 1742; a secretary to the French ambassador in Venice, 1743-1744; went back to Paris, lived with Thérèse Levasseur, and in 1747 sent his first child to the foundling hospital; published his first book in 1750 (*Discourse on the Sciences and on the Arts*); in 1752 wrote *Le devin du village* (The Village Soothsayer), a musical comedy; first performed at the Paris Opera, 1753; reintegrated as a member of the Church of Geneva, he recovered his status as a Genevan citizen, 1754; settled at the estate of Mme. d'Epinay (L'Ermitage), 1756; quarreled with Mme. d'Epinay and settled with the Marshal of Luxembourg (in Montmorency), 1757; in 1762 his *Emile* was condemned in Parliament and he himself was threatened with arrest; flight from Paris; *Emile* burned in Paris; *Contrat Social* and *Emile* confiscated in Geneva, then burned, and Rousseau threatened with arrest; sought refuge in the territory of Bern; was expelled from there and repaired to Motiers, then part of the Prussian State, where Frederick the Great permitted him to stay; began to dress as an Armenian; expelled from Motiers; went to Strasbourg, Paris, and London, where he broke relations with Hume, 1766; went back to France (1767), where he resided in various places, among others Paris (1770); always a sickly man, Rousseau became more and more mentally unbalanced and suffered from a pronounced persecution complex; accepted the hospitality of the Marquess René de Girardin at Ermenonville, 1778; died there July 2, 1778.

Main philosophical works: *Discours sur les sciences et les arts* (Whether the restoration of sciences and arts [i.e., the Renaissance] has contributed to purifying morality), 1749; published 1750. *Discours sur l'origine de l'inégalité parmi les hommes* (Discourse on the Origin of Inequality among men), 1755. "Génie," art. in *Encyclopédie*, Vol. VII, 1757. *Lettre à d'Alembert sur les spectacles* (Letter to d'Alembert on Theater Plays), 1758. *Du contrat social* (On Social Contract), 1762. *Emile ou de l'Education* (Emile or On Education), 1762. *Lettres écrites de la montagne* (Letters Written from the Mountain), 1764. Autobiographical: *Les confessions de J.-J. Rousseau* (J.-J. Rousseau's Confessions), posthumous, first complete edition, 1789. For other autobiographical writings, see *Oeuvres complètes*, Vol. I.

Collective editions: Jean-Jacques Rousseau, *Oeuvres complètes* (5 vols. projected, Vol. I; Paris: Bibliothèque de la Pléiade, 1959), includes the *Confessions, Rousseau juge de Jean-Jacques, Dialogues, Les rêveries du promeneur solitaire, Fragments autobiographiques et documents biographiques*; in short, all the autobiographical writings. Vol. II, *La nouvelle Héloïse*, 1961; Vols. III, IV, V will later complete what promises to become the standard edition. C. E. T. Vaughan, *The Political Writings of J.-J. Rousseau*, with Introductions and Notes (Cambridge, 1915). *Correspondance générale de J.-J. Rousseau*, ed. Théophile Dufour (20 vols.; Paris: Armand Colin, 1924-1934).

Separate editions of Rousseau's main philosophical works are numerous. Among the easily available ones, and carefully edited: *Collection des Classiques Garnier*; *Les Confessions* (3 vols.); *Emile ou de l'Education* (1 vol.); *Contrat social*; *Discours . . .* ; *Lettre à d'Alembert . . .* ; *Considérations sur le Gouvernement de Pologne . . .* ; *Lettre à Mgr de Beaumont . . .* (1 vol.).

Biographical: Chronology by L. J. Courtois in *Annales J.-J. Rousseau* (Vol. XXV, 1923), and by Anne-Marie Pfister in *Oeuvres complètes* (Vol. I, pp. ci-cxviii). Life: See the abundant notes to the text of *Confessions* in *Oeuvres complètes*, Vol. I.

Bibliographical: a publication entirely devoted to Rousseau: *Annales de la Société J.-J. Rousseau*, 1905 ff. A. Schinz, *Etat présent des travaux sur J.-J. Rousseau* (Paris, 1941).

Lives and portraits: Jules Lemaitre, *J.-J. Rousseau* (Paris: Calmann-Levy, 1907). Emile Faguet, *Vie de Rousseau* (Paris: Lecène et Oudin, 1911). Ernest Seillière, *J.-J. Rousseau* (Paris: Garnier, 1921). Henri Guillemin, *Un homme, deux ombres* (Genève, 1943).

Doctrinal: Harald Höffding, *J.-J. Rousseau et sa philosophie*, translated from the Danish (1896) into French by De Coussange

(Paris: Alcan, 1912). Emile Faguet, *Rousseau penseur* (Paris: Lecène et Oudin, 1912). J. Fabre, *J.-J. Rousseau* (Paris: Alcan, 1912). Bernard Bouvier, *J.-J. Rousseau* (Genève, 1912). Pierre-Maurice Masson, *La religion de J.-J. Rousseau* (3 vols.; Paris: Hachette, 1916). S. Moreau Rendu, *L'idée de bonté naturelle chez J.-J. Rousseau* (Paris, 1929). R. Hubert, *Rousseau et l'Encyclopédie. Essai sur la formation des idées politiques de Rousseau (1742-1756)* (Paris. 1928). Irving Babbitt, *Rousseau and Romanticism* (Boston and New York: Houghton Mifflin, 1919; re-edited, 1947). C. W. Hendel, *J.-J. Rousseau, Moralist* (London and New York: Oxford University Press, 1934). E. Cassirer, *Rousseau, Kant, Goethe*, translated by J. Gutmann, P. O. Kristeller, and J. H. Randall (Princeton: Princeton University Press, 1945). F. C. Green, *J.-J. Rousseau* (Cambridge: Cambridge University Press, 1955).

2. The detailed account of the event by Rousseau himself is in one of his *Lettres à Malesherbes* (Letter 2 in *Oeuvres complètes*, Vol. I, pp. 1135-1136). This is the first account of the incident and the more reliable. Another one is found in *Confessions*, beginning of Book VIII. On the later testimony of Diderot, see *Oeuvres complètes de Rousseau*, I, p. 1428, or Georges Roth, *Histoire de Madame de Montbrillant* (Les pseudo-mémoires de madame d'Epinay) (Paris: Gallimard, 1951), Vol. III, p. 591. Literary portraits of Rousseau usually are for or against; attempts to remain dispassionate in picturing such an eminently passionate model seem somehow to miss the point. Still, this "objective" attitude leads to interpretations from which it is perhaps wiser to start in studying

Rousseau. Because he is liable to see things simpler than they are, Emile Faguet provides one such starting point, for instance, in his *Dix-huitième siècle*, pp. 327-333. However one may feel about Rousseau, one should not forget to take into account the morbid side of his nature. From the very beginning there were oddities in his behavior. Himself no angel, Diderot has written of Rousseau: "In truth, that man is a monster," and again, that his most resolute supporters could absolve him "of cussedness only by accusing him of madness" (*Histoire de Mme. d'Epinay*, ed. G. Roth, Vol. III, p. 589). To put it bluntly: he was not mentally normal. His persecution complex made him indulge in wild accusations, but apart from the fact that men of sound mind should have taken them for what they were—i.e., insanities—they were not all, nor always, without some foundation in facts. The archenemy of fanaticism, Voltaire, wanted Rousseau to be burned at the stake; and he denounced him in anonymous libels to the government of Geneva. In point of fact, Rousseau had to fly from four different countries in rapid succession; even granting that his books were responsible for the situation, one cannot help contrasting this with the comfortable life then led by his ferocious enemy, Voltaire.

3. *Letters to Malesherbes*, II, *Oeuvres complètes*, I, p. 1136. Rousseau has interminably explained himself to himself and to others, but this second letter to Malesherbes might well contain his most penetrating self-analysis. "A soul lazy and frightened by any care, an ardent temper, bilious, easily affected and excessively sensitive to all that which affects it,

seem not to be able to blend in the same character, and yet these two opposites make up the bottom of mine own" (*loc. cit.*, p. 1134). On his distaste for imposed effort ("Laziness"), see *Confessions*, XII, p. 638. On his sensitiveness to all impressions, open any of his works at any page. Naturally, he will turn this trait of his own temper into a doctrine; the "materialism of the wise man" will follow from it; the educational program of *Emile* will be based on the essential plasticity of human nature; the *Social Contract* will likewise attempt to mold man from without.

4. That unfounded feeling of essential righteousness provides the only psychological explanation for the ocean of sophisms in which Rousseau wallowed every time he was looking for self-justification. The only answer to his problems, was, of course, original sin, but since he was fundamentally just, he could not accept that truth. His personal ideal was "to be free and virtuous, above fortune and opinion, and self-sufficing" (*Confessions*, VIII, ed. cit., p. 316). A typical specimen of Rousseau's sophistry is to be found in the very same passage (pp. 356-357), where he explains why he took his third child (as well as the four other ones) to the foundling hospital. After invoking the laws of nature, of justice, of reason, and even of religion (pure and not yet corrupt religion), Rousseau calmly remarks, "If I was wrong in my results, nothing is more astounding than the security with which I trusted them. Were I one of those ill-born men, deaf to the sweet voice of nature, my hardening would be easy to answer; but no: I feel it and I say so openly: this is not possible. Never, not one moment in my life, was J.-J. a soul-

less father." The proof of it is that, later in life, he sometimes regretted what he had done; on the whole, he knew he had acted in the best interest of the children: "As a citizen and a father, I considered myself a member of Plato's Republic." In noting that his heart felt regrets, while his reason was very far from blaming him, Rousseau seems to forget his own principle of principles, that reason is always wrong in such matters, and feeling always right.

5. *La nouvelle Héloïse*, first sentence of the Preface.

6. E. Faguet, *Le dix-huitième siècle*, pp. 332-334.

7. The Academy of Dijon had received twelve memoirs. The winner, Abbé Talbert, had already been honorably mentioned in the preceding competition of 1750, when Rousseau's memoir had been crowned. On the competitors of 1754 and their respective memoirs, see Roger Tisserand, *Les concurrents de J.-J. Rousseau à l'Académie de Dijon pour le prix de 1754* (Paris, 1936). From original sin to the inequalities of nature and to passions, all answers had been tried; that of Rousseau stood alone.

8. The *Contrat social* provoked immediate reactions. Among them that of Bauclair (a physiocrat), *Anti-Contrat social, dans lequel on réfute d'une manière claire, utile et agréable les principes posés dans le Contrat social de J.-J. Rousseau, citoyen du monde* (La Haye: Frédéric Staatman, 1764). *Lettre d'un Anonyme à Monsieur J.-J. Rousseau* (Londres: Becket and De Hondt, 1766); the author was Elie Luzac, a Protestant of French descent living in Holland. While reading the *Contrat social*, Voltaire annotated his copy; his marginal notes have been published in the

complete works of Voltaire, Moland ed., Vol. XXX, and more recently by George R. Havens, *Voltaire's Marginalia on the Pages of Rousseau* (Columbus, Ohio, 1933); also in footnotes to the edition of the *Contrat social* by Bertrand de Jouvenel, with occasional replies by the editor.

9. *Du Contrat social ou principes du Droit politique* has been edited many times and often well. All good modern editions derive from that by Dreyfus-Brisac, *Du contrat social . . .* , with Introduction and Notes (Paris, 1896). C. E. T. Vaughan in *The Political Writings of J.-J. Rousseau . . .* , also in separate edition, 1918. Georges Beaulavon, *Du contrat social . . .* , with Introduction and Notes (3d ed.; Paris, 1922). Maurice Halbwachs, *Du contrat social* (Paris, 1943), particularly interesting as giving the reactions of a very distinguished sociologist. Bertrand de Jouvenel, *Du contrat social . . .* (Genève: Constant Bourquin, 1947), with an Introduction and annotations including all of Voltaire's marginal notes.

10. *Contrat social*, Book I, Introduction. This remark is explained by Rousseau in *Emile*, Book V: "Even domination is servile when it depends on opinion, for then you depend on the prejudices of those whom you sway by means of their prejudices. In order to lead them as you please, you must lead them as they please," etc. Book V of *Emile* contains a handy abridgment by Rousseau himself of the doctrine of the *Social Contract*.

11. *Emile*, Book V.

12. *Contrat social*, I, chap. vi.

13. "This is pitiable," Voltaire remarks, "if Jean-Jacques is flogged, is the republic also being flogged?" The remarks of Voltaire on Rous-

seau are seldom deeper than his remarks on Pascal. This, however, must be added: in the case of his remarks on Rousseau, Voltaire is not responsible for their publication.

14. Emile, Book V.

15. Contrat social, Book I, chap. viii.

16. In Rousseau's republic, the institution of the civil society, as a body politic, is a contract; namely, the social pact. Once instituted, the body politic still is wholly undetermined. The state of nature being over and replaced by civilization, it is necessary to define justice. This is done by establishing legislation. Just as the social pact gives it existence, legislation gives the body politic motion and will. Since the sovereign is the whole body politic, its will can only be a general will; that is, the will of all with respect to all. A law then is a decision enacted by the general will in view of a general object, which is the whole body of the citizens. So "the object of the laws is always general"; laws "never consider a man *qua* individual nor an action as particular." This is only possible where laws are enacted by the general will of the whole body politic; hence the conclusion: "All legitimate Government is republican" (*Contrat social*, Book II, chap. vi). In this system, one thing at least is not general: the invention of good laws. It takes a *quasi* divine man to discover the laws. That exceedingly rare man, the Legislator, only propounds them and tries to coax the people into accepting them; the body politic alone (by its general will) has power to enact them, though it is unable to invent them (Book II, chap. vii). "It would take gods to give laws to men" (*ibid.*).

17. Contrat social, Book III, chap. i.

18. Ibid., chap. iii.

19. Ibid., chap. iv.

20. All this is taken from *Emile*, Book I. *Emile* has been reprinted many times; there is an enormous literature about it; for instance, F. Vial, *Rousseau éducateur* (Leçons faites à l'école des Hautes Études Sociales) (Paris: Alcan, 1912). Same author, *La doctrine d'éducation de J.-J. Rousseau* (Paris: Delagrave, 1920).

21. The doctrine according to which man is molded from without by objects whose influence he passively undergoes was the matter of a book he would have liked to write on "the materialism of the wise man." Traces of it can be found in the *Nouvelle Héloïse* ("La méthode de M. de Wolmar" in E. Gilson, *Les idées et les lettres* [Paris: J. Vrin, 1932], pp. 275-298). Cf. *Confessions*, Book IX, *ed. cit.*, p. 409 and note. The complete title of the book would have been: *Sensitive Ethics, or the Materialism of the Wise.*

22. These developments are taken from *Emile*, Book II.

23. These developments are outlined in *Emile*, Book III.

24. Ibid., Book IV. *The Confession of Faith* divides into two parts: an exposition of Rousseau's own brand of Theism and his reasons for rejecting not purely "natural" religions. The relationship of Rousseau to Christianity is very complex, even more so than he himself knew it to be. On this problem, see the work of Pierre-Marie Masson listed above (note 1), and by the same author, *Edition critique de la profession de foi* (Fribourg [Suisse] and Paris: Hachette, 1914). Some critics think P.-M. Masson makes Rousseau a little too much a Catholic. This may be true, but it is very difficult to avoid that mistake without falling into the contrary one.

25. "Profession of Faith . . . ," in *Emile*, Book IV.

26. There was nothing wrong in seeking for a natural theology. On the contrary, the trouble was that, in fact, after criticizing all positive religions and rejecting them, including Christianity, Rousseau pretended to justify, by purely rational arguments, a god that was, in fact, the God of the Christian revelation. Rousseau takes the Christian God for granted, or at least what of Him suits his "conscience," after which he feels free to do away with Christianity. Having been a Catholic once, and a Protestant twice, he had received more religious instruction than he cared to remember. In the *Profession of Faith*, he calls his religion a "*theism* or the natural religion, which Christians affect to confound with atheism or irreligion, a doctrine directly opposed to it." This was not the point. Rousseau certainly was no atheist, and he once wrote a sentence which witnesses to the sincerity of his religious feeling: "My son, keep your soul in a condition always to desire that there be a God, and you will never doubt of Him." The question is, would there be "theism" in the mind of Rousseau if he had never known Christianity?

27. The word is found in the last sentence of the Savoyard curate who, as we remember, is the mouthpiece of Rousseau: "Dare to confess God among the philosophers; dare to preach humanity among the intolerants. You will be alone in your own party, perhaps; but you will carry in yourself a testimony that will permit you to dispense with that of men. Whether they love you or hate you does not matter. It makes no difference whether they read your books or despise them. Just say what is true, do what is right; what matters for man is to fulfill his duties on earth; and it is by forgetting oneself that one works for oneself. My son, personal interest deceives us; only the hope of the just deceives not." This is how the printed text actually reads. At the end of it, on the manuscript, Rousseau added a single word: "Amen."

xxv. Condorcet

1. MARIE-JEAN-ANTOINE-NICOLAS CARITAT, Marquis de Condorcet, b. Ribemont, 1743; d. Bourg-la-Reine, 1794. Author of mathematical works (*Essai sur le calcul intégral*, 1763. *Problème des trois corps*, 1767); a Fellow of the Academy of Sciences (1769) and of the French Academy (1782); elected a deputy at the Legislative Assembly (1791), then its president (1792); got himself involved in the defeat of the "Girondin" party; threatened with arrest, he went into hiding but finally gave himself up for fear of jeopardizing the life of those who were concealing him. Arrested and jailed, Condorcet committed suicide with poison given to him by his brother-in-law, the philosopher Cabanis (see next volume: *Ideology*).

Collective editions: *Oeuvres*, ed. O'Connor and François Arago (12 vols.; Paris, 1847-1849). *Choix de textes*, ed. J.-B. Sévérac (Paris, 1912). Condorcet's main work in the philosophical field is his *Tableau historique des progrès de l'esprit humain*, 1795 (posthumously published by the National Convention); republished in the Bibliothèque Positiviste (Paris: G. Steinheil, 1900), under the title quoted above. In fact, the work comprises two distinct parts: I, *Prospectus d'un tableau historique des progrès de l'esprit humain*, which was conceived as a general program of a work of vast dimensions of which only fragments were written; those fragments constitute the second part of the work: II, *Fragments d'un tableau historique des progrès de l'esprit humain*.

Biographical and doctrinal: L. Cahen, *Condorcet et la révolution française* (Paris, 1904).

2. In the *Prospectus* of Condorcet the notion of economics as a positive science still remained largely a philosophical view of the mind. The same remark applies to the article "Economie politique" in the *Encyclopedia*, written by J.-J. Rousseau. Those who, in the second half of the eighteenth century, really founded a science of economic facts were Adam Smith in England and, in France, the school of the so-called "physiocrats." Their head was Father Quesnay (1694-1774), physician to King Louis XV and to Mme. de Pompadour, who late in life turned his attention to that order of problems and published *Tableau économique*, 1758; *Maximes générales du gouvernement économique d'un royaume agricole*, 1760. The doctrine was popularized by Du Pont de Nemours: *Physiocratie ou Constitution essentielle du gouvernement le plus avantageux au genre hu-*

main, 1761. The epigraph inscribed by Quesnay at the beginning of his famous *Tableau* eloquently described his general intention: *Poor peasants, poor kingdom! Poor kingdom, poor king!* With his infallible gift for mocking all that was new and important, Voltaire directed his sarcasm against the doctrine in his satire: *L'homme aux quarante écus*. On the other hand, the physiocrats vainly attempted to win Rousseau to their cause. They favored the notion that there was a "natural order" of social facts, swayed by its own laws; the idea that society could result from a contract was foreign to their minds.

On the physiocratic movement: H. Higgs, *Six Lectures on the Physiocrats*, 1897. G. Weulersse, *Le mouvement physiocratique en France de 1756 à 1770* (2 vols.; Paris, 1910). Ch. Gide and Ch. Rist, *Histoire des doctrines économiques depuis les physiocrates jusqu'à nos jours* (6th ed., rev.; Paris: Recueil Sirey, 1944), pp. 1-55.

3. The main weapon against prejudice is education. Condorcet shared the common interest of almost all the Encyclopedists for educational problems. His ideas on the question are found in his *Project of Law for the Organizing of Public Instruction*, submitted to the Legislative Assembly (1792). In the high schools, three sections out of four were reserved for the teaching of sciences, the last one being devoted to the study of languages, ancient and modern.

4. Unlike Diderot, Condorcet was of the opinion that mathematics will always remain capable of unlimited development. This view was expressed by him in the "Tenth Epoch" of the *Prospectus . . .*, ed. cit., p. 172.

PART 9   GERMANY, FROM *AUFKLÄRUNG* TO CRITICISM

xxvi. Gotthold Ephraim Lessing

1. GOTTHOLD EPHRAIM LESSING, b. Kamenz, Saxony, 1729; d. Braunschweig, 1781. Son of a Lutheran pastor; first taught by his father, then, from 1741, in the Fürstenschule (school under the Prince's patronage), St. Afra in Meissen, where he came to know the classics and to love especially Plautus and Terence. At Leipzig University (from 1746 to 1748) he soon gave up theology and began to appreciate the full artistic and intellectual life of that city "where one can see the whole world in miniature" (letter to his mother, Jan. 20, 1749). Turned to writing plays at a time when the German theater was trying to find a style and a place for itself; Lessing wanted to be its Molière. Financial troubles and local pressures persuaded him to move on; he found himself in Berlin, where he worked on a newspaper, wrote little plays, and issued his first *Aufklärung*-like religious statement, *Gedanken über die Herrnhuter* (1750); in it he attacked Orthodox Lutheranism, but also overly-rational religion. In 1751, became literary critic for a newspaper, interrupted by a short stay at Wittenberg, where he wrote his *Lemnius-Briefen;* became most famous German dramatist overnight with the performance of the tragedy, *Miss Sara Sampson,* 1755. In this same year, he set out on one of those *Wandlungen* which seem to remain unavoidable

for young Germans even today, but it was soon interrupted by the outbreak of war; returned to Leipzig, then back to Berlin, publishing with Friedrich Nicolai and Moses Mendelssohn the *Briefe, die neueste Literatur betreffend* (Letters Touching on the Newest Literature) (1759-1760). For five years in the government service in Breslau, he wrote two of his most famous works: his masterpiece on aesthetics, *Laokoön, or On the Limits of Painting and Poetry*, and the play *Minna von Barnhelm,* which appeared in 1766 and 1767, respectively. In 1766 associated himself with the city theater in Hamburg, hopeful that at last the German theater was going to be born; he was disappointed, the theater failed, but Lessing at least could speak his piece on the subject, which remarks were gathered in the famous *Hamburgische Dramaturgie*, high point of the German revolution against imitating the classical French theater. In dire financial straits, he accepted a miserable post as librarian in Wolfenbüttel, Braunschweig. Traveled to Vienna to seek Eva König, the widow of a friend; during this period appeared *Leibniz vor den ewigen Strafen* (Leibniz before the Eternal Punishments); *Des Andreas Wissowatius Einwürfe wider die Dreieinigkeit* (The Objections of Andrea Wissowatius against the Trinity), and in 1771, the tragedy,

Emilia Galotti. Exceedingly happily married to Eva König in 1776, he saw her taken from him the next year at the birth of a child who also died. In the *Beiträge zur Geschichte und Literatur, aus den Schätzen der herzoglichen Bibliothek zu Wolfenbüttel* (Contributions to History and Literature, taken from the Treasures of the Libraries of the Counts of Wolfenbüttel), Lessing published the work of Samuel Reimarus (1694-1768), which, in the spirit of the *Aufklärung,* maintained the purely historical nature of religion and asserted that the Bible was full of errors; Lessing was soon engaged in polemics with the orthodox churchmen. From this period dates the long poem, *Nathan the Wise,* an attack against intolerance, and a plea for intellectual freedom (1779). His health weakened since the death of his wife, he died in Braunschweig in 1781 at the age of fifty-two.

Collective editions: *Gesammelte Werke* (9 vols.; Berlin: Aufbau-Verlag, 1954-1957); *Gesammelte Werke* (10 vols.; Leipzig: Göschen, 1841 f). *Lessings Werke,* ed. G. Witkowski (7 vols.; Leipzig and Vienna: Bibliographisches Institut, 1911 ff). *Lessings Werke,* edited by Boxberger and Blumer (14 vols.; Berlin and Stuttgart: Speman, 1883-1890). Handy collection in one volume, *Werke in einem Band* (Hamburg: Hoffman und Campe, 1958); contains major plays, *Laokoön, Hamburg Dramaturgy, Nathan the Wise.*

Biographical and doctrinal: T. W. Danzel and G. E. Guhaver, *G. E. Lessing, sein Leben und seine Werke* (2 vols.; 2d ed.; Berlin: Hofmann, 1880-1881). Thomas de Quincey, *Lessing,* in De Quincey's *Works,* Vol. 9, pp. 369-438. J. H. J.

Düntzer, *Erläuterungen zu Lessings Werken* (6 vols.; Leipzig: Martig, 1874-1885). A. W. Ernst, *Lessings Leben und Werke* (Stuttgart: C. Krabbe, 1903). E. K. B. Fischer, *G. E. Lessing als Reformator der deutschen Literatur* (2 vols.; 2d ed.; Stuttgart and Berlin, 1904-1905). H. B. Garland, *Lessing, the Founder of Modern German Literature* (Cambridge: Bowers and Bowers, 1949). Émile Grucker, *Lessing* (Paris: Berger-Levrault, 1896).

2. *Laokoön,* Abschnitten I bis VI.

3. *Laokoön,* XVI, *Abschnitt.*

4. *Nachlass von Entwürfen und Materialen zum "Laokoon,"* Entwurf B, XLIII.

5. ALEXANDER GOTTLIEB BAUMGARTEN (b. Berlin, 1714; d. Frankfurt, 1762), whose *Metaphysics* (Halle, 1739) Kant considered a model of careful, rigorous definition, and whose *Aesthetics* appeared in Frankfurt between 1750 and 1758. On Leibniz as source of Baumgarten's aesthetics, see H. G. Meyer, *Leibniz und Baumgarten als Begründer der deutschen Aesthetik* (Halle, 1874); and J. Schmidt, *Leibniz und Baumgarten* (Halle, 1875).

6. *Aesthetices finis est perfectio cognitionis sensitivae, qua talis. Haec autem est pulcritudo. Aesthetica,* para. 14.

7. *Oratio sensitiva perfecta est poema,* in *Meditationes de nonnullis ad poema pertinentibus* (Halle, 1735), para. 9.

8. Herder, *Werke,* XXX, 32 f.

9. E. Cassirer, *The Philosophy of the Enlightenment,* trans. Koelln and Pettegrove (Boston: Beacon Press, 1955), p. 357. Cassirer's presentation of the development of aesthetic theory during the *Aufklärung* provides a good introduction to the subject.

XXVII. Johann Gottfried Herder

1. JOHANN GOTTFRIED HERDER, b. Mohrungen, East Prussia, 1744; d. Weimar, 1803. Educated by his schoolteacher father to read Latin, Greek, and Hebrew and raised in the pietistic tradition, he went in 1762 to Königsberg, became a student in theology, a teacher at the Collegium Fridericianum, a regular at Kant's lectures, and an intimate of that extraordinary independent spirit, Hamann, who communicated to Herder his sense of the depth and richness of life and of the need to seek out God's revelations through the multiplicity of natural and historical manifestations in which he has willed it should appear. Hamann's lightning blazes of insight found in Herder someone willing to develop them more extensively in literary and historical meditations. He read Hume, confirming the antipathy for empty metaphysical speculation Kant and Herder had already communicated to him; Shaftesbury strengthened his taste for an aesthetic approach to reality; but above all Rousseau. His fame as a teacher spread; he was called at age twenty to the Cathedral School in Riga, where he remained from the end of 1764 until May 1769. There he began his literary development, taking off from Winckelmann's and Lessing's discoveries, writing the 67 *Fragments about the New German Literature* and 69 *Kritischen Wälder*. He discovered the original Leibniz and was enthused. In 1769 he traveled to France, got to know Diderot, returned through Holland, and spent time in conversation with Lessing in Hamburg. Out of this came the famous *Tagebuch*, full of historical-psychological meditations. After a short stay in Lübeck, Herder went to Strasbourg, where he spent the winter ill-temperedly recovering from an operation. It was during that dark winter that a twenty-one-year-old Frankfurt law student came to seek the by now famous man, there to learn about literary genius from the twenty-six-year-old master, and to discuss Ossian, Shakespeare, and folk poetry— Herder's interests at that period. The young man from Frankfurt, for the rest of his life, was to refer to Herder with great respect, as one who had helped him to find himself. His name was Johann Wolfgang Goethe. *On the Origin of Languages* and essays on Ossian and Shakespeare were the principal literary fruits of the stay in Strasbourg. In April 1771, Herder became pastor and court counselor to the Count Wilhelm von Schaumburg-Lippe in the little town of Bückeburg, oriented himself toward theology, and began developing his characteristic view of a unity between nature and history as part of a divine plan for educating humanity. He became attracted to Spinoza, as Lessing had before him. At the urging of Goethe, Herder accepted the post of General Superintendent in Weimar, 1776; there he continued his theological writings—*On the Spirit of Hebrew Poetry* dates from this period—and his work in aesthetics— *Plastik* and *Volkslieder* are two fruits of that effort. But the great work, in which all the elements in his thought are finally fused into a personal, unified philosophy, is the *Ideas for a Philosophy of the History of Mankind*, which appeared in four parts from 1784 to 1791. Toward the turn of the century Herder addressed himself to what he called *Metakritik*, a criticism of the Kantian critique that was not very successful. He was only sixty when he died.

Collective editions: *Sämmtliche Werke*, ed. B. Suphan (33 vols.; Berlin: Weidmann, 1877-1913). *Sämmtliche Werke, Zur schönen Literatur und Kunst* (13 vols.; Stuttgart und Tübingen: J. G. Cotta, 1861-1862).

Biographical and doctrinal: L. Bate, *Johann Gottfried Herder; der Weg, das Werk, die Zeit* (Stuttgart: S. Hirzel, 1948). S. H. Begenau, *Grundzüge der Ästhetik Herders* (Weimar: Böhlaus, 1956). R. Bürkner, *Herder, sein Leben und Werken* (Berlin: Hofmann, 1904). R. T. Clark, *Herder: His Life and Thought* (Berkeley: University of California Press, 1955). W. Dobbek, *J. G. Herders Humanitätsidee als Ausdruck seines Weltbildes und seiner Persönlichkeit* (Braunschweig: G. Westermann, 1949). A. Gillies, *Herder* (Oxford: Blackwell, 1945). C. Joret, *Herder et la renaissance littéraire en Allemagne au XVIIIe siècle* (Paris: Hachette, 1875). T. Litt, *Kant und Herder als Deuter der geistigen Welt* (2d ed.; Heidelberg: Quelle and Meyer, 1949). F. McEachran, *The Life and Philosophy of J. G. Herder* (Oxford: Clarendon, 1939). M. Montgomery, *Studies in the Age of Goethe* (London: Oxford University Press, 1931).

2. Herder at one point was so taken with Rousseau that he wrote, "Rousseau, komm sei mein führer!" (*Werke*, Suphan ed., 29, 265).

3. Diderot, *Lettres sur les Sourds et Muets*, in *Oeuvres* (Paris, 1798), II, 279.

4. See above, the section on Diderot.

5. Lebensbild, IV, 293.

6. Ibid., III, 208.

7. Ibid., IV, 317.

8. Zur Lit. und Kunst, XIX, 42.

9. Ibid., 65.

10. We have here invoked of course only the bare outlines of Herder's theory. He goes into considerable detail, naturally. For instance, he points out that painting, employing figures and color, is naturally dependent on costumes for their effect, while for sculpture they are not important. So too, color, extremely important for the one, is disturbing in the other, etc.

11. Lebensbild, IV, 271.

12. Zur Lit. und Kunst, XIX, 68.

13. Ideen zur Philosophie der Geschichte der Menschheit, "Vorrede."

14. Ibid., Book IX, I.

15. Ibid.

16. ... *der Schade selbst aber macht die Menschen klüger*, "but the unfortunate itself makes men wiser" (*Ideen*, Book XV, II).

XXVIII. Immanuel Kant

1. IMMANUEL KANT, b. Königsberg, 1724; d. same, 1804. Passed his whole life in the remote province of East Prussia. After a pietistic education at home and in the Collegium Fridericianum, entered the University of Königsberg in 1740, where he was aided by Martin Knutzen, an enthusiastic and very young man, trained in the Wolffian tradition, but Newton-minded and therefore critical of the excessive rationalism of Wolff. Kant read in Newtonian physics, and his first scientific treatises, written in the 1750's, already show preoccupation with the problem of setting off the Newtonian and the Leibnizian methods against one another. The little essay, *Monadologia physica*, is an especially remarkable example of this. In the essay of 1755, *Primorum principiorum metaphysicae nova Dilucidatio*, which Kant submitted in connection with his becoming a *Privatdozent*, we find him examining especially the principle of sufficient reason; and, although the approach is cautious, young Kant is obviously still far from challenging all the presuppositions upon which Leibnizianism reposes; for example, he does not question that things in themselves are adequately knowable. But Herder tells us that, by the time he had become Kant's student in the early 60's, the latter was attacking Leibniz, Wolff, and Baumgarten, was a "follower" of Newton, and showed himself deeply impressed by the moral philosophy of Rousseau. In effect, Kant had by this time gone farther than even Christian Crusius in attacking Leibnizian presuppositions; he was firmly asserting that philosophy should follow "a Newtonian method"; i.e., should work analytically to clarify indistinct givens by breaking them down to irreducible elements, and that these elements are experiential and for that reason not analyzable. The principal work of this period is an essay of 1764, *An Inquiry into the Distinctness of the Fundamental Principles of Natural Theology and Morals.* Rousseau opened new horizons for Kant; above all, by revealing to him the tremendous importance in itself of the *moral* order, which reinforced from another angle the Newtonian feeling that a metaphysics without imme-

diate practical bearing is chimeric. In the famous "Dissertation" of 1770 (*De mundi sensibilis atque intelligibilis forma et principiis dissertatio*), the important elements of the "critique" are already in place —but Kant by no means holds yet the essential key. Through correspondence with Lambert, he has already picked up this thinker's suggestion of a "form-matter distinction"; in the "Dissertation," space and time are held to be "forms" of sensible intuition. Moreover, the sensibility and understanding are distinguished as receptivity and spontaneity, respectively. It is only when Kant goes back to reading Hume in the '70's that the objective character of the object becomes a question for him —and that, after all, is *the* critical question. By the middle of the decade, his letters show that the critical viewpoint is fully evolved, but there is no sign of the psychology of the *Critique*—that is, of the mediating role of the imagination— nor of the three syntheses that are so prominent in the First Edition. It was the two-volume psychology of N. Tetens, published in 1776-1777, under the title *Philosophische Versuche über die menschliche Natur und ihre Entwicklung*, that suggested these themes to Kant. The indifferent and uncomprehending reception of the *Critique of Pure Reason* in 1781 induced Kant to write what he hoped would be the more accessible and unmistakable *Prolegomena to Any Future Metaphysics*, which appeared in 1783; and then he interrupted his work on an ethics to revise the *Kritik* for a second edition in 1787. Kant had issued a sketch of his moral philosophy at the same time as the *Prolegomena*, under the title *Foundations of the*

Metaphysics of Morals. The *Critique of Practical Reason* appeared in 1788, and the *Critique of Judgment* two years later. *Religion within the Limits of Reason Alone* (1793), *Perpetual Peace* (arguing for republican government and international law) (1795), and notes growing out of his disputes with the burgeoning idealist movement occupied his last years.

Collective editions: The Prussian Academy of Sciences Edition, *Gesammelte Schriften* (22 vols.; Berlin: Reimer and de Gruyter, 1902-1942). Cassirer edition, *Immanuel Kants Werke*, ed. E. Cassirer (11 vols.; Berlin: B. Cassirer, 1912-1918).

Biographical: An accessible biography is to be found in the eleventh volume of Cassirer's collection of Kant's works (see above). The classical German biographies of Kant are those of Borowski, Jachmann, and Wasianski. These are combined in the best-known English biography, J. H. W. Stuckenberg's *The Life of Immanuel Kant* (London: Macmillan, 1882).

Doctrinal: F. Paulsen, *Immanuel Kant: His Life and Doctrine* (New York: Scribner, 1902). E. Caird, *The Critical Philosophy of Immanuel Kant* (2d ed.; 2 vols.; New York: Macmillan, 1909). A. D. Lindsay, *Kant* (London: Benn, 1934). H. J. De Vleeschauwer, *La déduction transcendentale dans l'oeuvre de Kant* (3 vols.; Paris: Leroux, 1934-1937), the main conclusions of which are condensed into this survey of Kant's development, *L'Evolution de la pensée kantienne* (Paris: Alcan, 1939). H. W. Cassirer, *A Commentary on Kant's Critique of Judgment* (London: Methuen, 1938). Some guides to the *Critique of Pure Reason*: T.

D. Weldon, *Introduction to Kant's Critique of Pure Reason* (Oxford: Clarendon, 1945); A. C. Ewing, *A Short Commentary on Kant's Critique of Pure Reason* (London: Methuen, 1938); N. K. Smith, *A Commentary to Kant's Critique of Pure Reason* (2d ed. rev.; London: Macmillan, 1930); H. J. Paton, *Kant's Metaphysic of Experience* (2 vols.; New York: Macmillan, 1936); J. Maréchal, S.J., *Le point de départ de la métaphysique*, cahier III: La critique de Kant (3d ed.; Paris: Desclée, 1944). On the moral doctrine and/or Third *Critique*, see: H. J. Paton, *The Categorical Imperative* (Chicago: University of Chicago Press, 1948); P. A. Schilpp, *Kant's Pre-Critical Ethics* (Evanston, Ill.: Northwestern University Press, 1938).

2. De Vleeschauwer is convinced that Hume played a less essential role in Kant's coming to be disillusioned with metaphysics than Kant seems to credit him with. Rousseau's influence, however, he feels was tremendous. Most decisive of all were Kant's reflections on the success of Newtonian physics. Cf. De Vleeschauwer, *L'Evolution de la pensée kantienne* (Paris: Alcan, 1939).

3. *Prolegomena to Any Future Metaphysics*, in Smith and Greene, *From Descartes to Kant* (Chicago: University of Chicago Press, 1940), p. 788.

4. *Ibid.*

5. The *Critique of Pure Reason*, Introduction to the Second Edition, VII. It is typical of the spirit of the Second Edition to add that the two sources "probably" spring from a common but to us unknown root.

6. "Transcendental Aesthetic," Introduction, same in both editions.

7. Translated "faculty of representation," which loses the sense of an

"activity of setting up an object before us," *vorstellen* as an activity.

8. *Prolegomena*, p. 814.

9. Introduction to "Transcendental Aesthetic."

10. "Transcendental Aesthetic," para. 9.

11. *Ibid.*, para. 4.

12. "When we say that the intuition of external objects, and also the self-intuition of the subject, represent both, objects and subject, in space and time, that is, as they appear—this is by no means equivalent to asserting that these objects are mere illusory appearances. For when we speak of things as phenomena, the objects, nay, even the properties we ascribe to them, are looked upon as really given; only that, insofar as this or that property depends upon the mode of intuition of the subject, in the relation of the given object to the subject, the object as phenomenon is to be distinguished from the object as a thing in itself" ("Transcendental Aesthetic," para. 9, sec. III).

13. *Ibid.*, para. 7.

14. "General Remarks on Transcendental Aesthetic," para. 9, sec. II.

15. *Ibid.*

16. *Ibid.*

17. "Transcendental Logic," I.

18. "Transcendental Analytic," para. 4.

19. "All general conceptions—as such—depend for their existence on the analytical unity of consciousness. For example, when I think of *red* in general, I thereby think to myself a property which (as a characteristic mark) can be discovered somewhere, or can be united with other representations; consequently, it is only by means of a forethought possible synthetical unity that I can think to myself the analytical . . ." ("Transcen-

dental Analytic," para. 12, note 1).

20. *Ibid.*

21. *Ibid.*, para. 6.

22. *Ibid.*, para. 14.

23. In the course of the discussion to follow we have not attempted to describe every one of these judgments and categories. Any of the standard Kantian commentaries will do so. See for example E. Caird, *The Critical Philosophy of Immanuel Kant*, Vol. I (New York: Macmillan, 1909).

24. Descartes, *Second Meditation*.

25. "Transcendental Analytic," para. 6.

26. "Transcendental Doctrine of Judgment," First Analogy.

27. *Ibid.*, Second Analogy.

28. *Ibid.*

29. "Transcendental Doctrine of Judgment," chap. i.

30. *Ibid.*

31. *Ibid.*

32. *Ibid.*, chap. iii.

33. *Ibid.*

34. Kant uses this term to describe the effort to draw a conclusion from a principle like the soul, world, or God which is in fact devoid of content, representing as they do only formal functions.

35. "Transcendental Dialectic," Book II, Part 1, A 342, B 400 ff.

36. *Ibid.*, II, 2, A 406, B 433 ff.

37. *Ibid.*, III, 4, A 592, B 620 ff.

38. *Ibid.*, 5, A 603, B 631 ff.

39. Kant seems to be preparing the way for the third *Kritik*'s (*Critique of Judgment*) assessment of the experience of finality in nature.

40. "Transcendental Dialectic," III, 6, A 620, B 648 ff.

41. *Critique of Practical Reason*, Preface.

42. *Ibid.*, Introduction.

43. *Ibid.*, Part I, Book I, chap. i, Prussian Academy Edition, Vol. V, p. 21. All further references are to this edition.

44. *Ibid.*, p. 22.

45. "Categorical" not only suggests fundamentality and the unavoidable but refers to the categories of the understanding as transcendentally formative, not only of all knowledge, but also of all duty.

46. *Critique of Practical Reason*, Part I, Book I, chap. i, p. 20.

47. *Ibid.*, p. 28.

48. *Ibid.*, p. 32.

49. *Ibid.*, p. 30.

50. "Kant wanted to prove, in a way which would dumfound the 'common man,' that the 'common man' was right" (Nietzsche, *Die Fröhliche Wissenschaft*, p. 193).

51. *Critique of Practical Reason*, I, ii, 4, p. 122.

52. *Ibid.*, 7, p. 136.

53. *Ibid.*

54. De Vleeschauwer, *L'Evolution de la pensée kantienne*, p. 139.

55. Cassirer calls it one of the great paradoxes in the history of philosophy that Kant, in the third *Kritik*, was able "to construct" the main idea of Goethe's poetry, which is what he did in rooting in the one principle of judgment, the teleological order in nature and the feelings of the sublime and the beautiful (E. Cassirer, *Kants Leben und Lehre*, Vol. XI of *Immanuel Kants Werke* [Berlin: B. Cassirer, 1923], p. 292).

56. "The relation of our faculties which is implied in the determination of an object as beautiful, is bound up with a feeling of pleasure, and this pleasure by the judgment of taste is declared to be valid for everyone; hence, neither the pleasure which accompanies the consciousness of the object, nor our satisfaction with the perfection of the object as falling under the conception of the Good, can be the ground of that judgment. It can therefore only be a subjective adaptation in the idea of an object without any purpose or end, either objective or subjective, i.e., it can only be the mere form of purpose in the idea by which the object is given, which constitutes that satisfaction which, in the judgment of taste and pleasure, we determine, without a conception, to be universally communicable" (*ibid.*, *Werke*, Rosenkranz ed., IV, 68).

57. *Ibid.*, p. 93.

58. *Critique of Judgment*, I, 1, #28.

59. *Ibid.*

60. *Ibid.*, I, #23.

61. *Ibid.*, I, #26.

62. *Ibid.*, I, #23.

63. *Ibid.*

64. *Ibid.*, II, #58.

65. "Just as the ideality of the objects of sense as phenomena is the only way of explaining the possibility of their forms being susceptible of *a priori* determination, so the idealism of purposiveness, in judging the beautiful in nature and art, is the only hypothesis under which *Kritik* can explain the possibility of a judgment of taste which demands *a priori* validity for every one (without grounding on concepts the purposiveness that is represented in the Object)" (*Critique of Judgment*, II, 58).

CONCLUSION

1. Strongly recommended is the early work of Lucien Lévy-Bruhl, *L'Allemagne depuis Leibniz. Essai sur le développement de la consci-* ence nationale en Allemagne, *1700-1848* (Paris: Hachette, 1890). On the part played by the "philosopher king," Frederick II, see Part I,

chap. ii, pp. 82-127; Kant and Fichte, Part II, chap. iii, pp. 255-286; Hegel and the theory of the State, Feuerbach, Part III, chap. iii, pp. 388-424. On the personal attitude of Goethe toward the modern notion of nationalism, see Part II, chap. 2, pp. 242-248; on Schiller, pp. 248-254.

Selected Paperbacks

The following is not a bibliography but a selected list of titles in modern philosophy available in paperback format. (Information about the publishers mentioned appears at the end of the list.) Anyone who wishes to see a complete listing of works in modern philosophy in paper reprints or originals may consult the latest issue of *Paperbound Books in Print*, published quarterly by R. R. Bowker Co., 62 W. 45th St., New York 36, N. Y.

F. BACON	—*New Organon.* Ed. F. H. Anderson (LIBERAL ARTS) —*Selected Essays.* Ed. M. Patrick (APPLETON)
G. BERKELEY	—*An Essay Toward a New Theory of Vision.* Ed. C. M. Turtayne (LIBERAL ARTS) —*Three Dialogues between Hylas and Philonous.* Ed. C. M. Turtayne (LIBERAL ARTS) —*Treatise Concerning the Principles of Human Knowledge.* Ed. C. M. Turtayne (LIBERAL ARTS) —*Selections.* Ed. M. W. Calkins (SCRIBNER'S)
R. DESCARTES	—*Philosophical Works of Descartes.* 2 vols. Tr. E. S. Haldane and G. R. T. Ross (DOVER) —in *The Rationalists* (DOLPHIN) —*Selections.* Ed. R. M. Eaton (SCRIBNER'S)

G. GALILEI

—*Discoveries and Opinions of Galileo*. Ed. S. Drake (ANCHOR)
—*Dialogues Concerning Two New Sciences*. Tr. H. Crew and A. de Salvio (DOVER)
—*Dialogue Concerning the Two Chief World Systems—Ptolemaic and Copernican*. Tr. S. Drake (CALIFORNIA)

J. G. HERDER

—*God, Some Conversations*. Tr. F. H. Burkhardt (LIBERAL ARTS)

T. HOBBES

—*De Cive, or the Citizen*. Ed. S. Lamprecht (APPLETON)
—*Leviathan*. Ed. R. Peters (COLLIER)
—*Selections*. Ed. F. J. E. Woodbridge (SCRIBNER'S)

D. HUME

—*An Inquiry Concerning Human Understanding* (OPEN COURT; GATE)
—*Hume's Moral and Political Philosophy*. Ed. H. D. Aiken (COLLIER)
—*Inquiry Concerning the Principles of Morals*. Ed. C. W. Hendel (LIBERAL ARTS)
—*David Hume's Political Essays*. Ed. C. W. Hendel (LIBERAL ARTS)
—*Dialogue Concerning Natural Religion*. Ed. H. D. Aiken (HAFNER)
—*A Treatise of Human Understanding*. (MERIDIAN; DOLPHIN)
—*Selections*. Ed. C. W. Hendel, Jr. (SCRIBNER'S)

I. KANT

—*Critique of Pure Reason.* Tr. F. M. Muller (DOLPHIN)
—*Critique of Practical Reason.* Tr. L. W. Beck (LIBERAL ARTS)
—*Critique of Judgment.* Tr. J. H. Bernard (HAFNER)
—*Foundations of the Metaphysics of Morals.* Tr. L. W. Beck (LIBERAL ARTS)
—*Prolegomena to Any Future Metaphysics.* Tr. P. Carus (OPEN COURT)
—*Religion within the Limits of Reason.* Tr. T. M. Greene and J. R. Silber (TORCHBOOKS)
—*Perpetual Peace.* Tr. L. W. Beck (LIBERAL ARTS)

G. W. LEIBNIZ

—*Discourse on Metaphysics, Correspondence with Arnauld, Monadology.* Tr. G. Montgomery (OPEN COURT).
—*Selections.* Ed. P. P. Wiener (SCRIBNER'S)

G. E. LESSING

—*Laocoön.* Tr. E. A. McCormick (LIBERAL ARTS)
—*Nathan the Wise.* Tr. B. Q. Morgan (UNGAR)

J. LOCKE

—*Essay Concerning Human Understanding.* 2 vols. Ed. A. C. Frazer (DOVER)
—*Treatise of Civil Government.* Ed. C. L. Sherman (APPLETON)
—*Two Treatises of Government.* Ed. T. L. Cook (HAFNER)
—*Selections.* Ed. S. Lamprecht (SCRIBNER'S)

M. de MONTAIGNE

—*The Complete Essays of Montaigne.* 3 vols. Tr. D. M. Frame (ANCHOR)
—*Selections from the Essays of Montaigne.* Tr. D. M. Frame (APPLETON)

C. de MONTESQUIEU

—*The Spirit of the Laws.* Tr. T. Nugent (HAFNER)

I. NEWTON

—*Opticks.* Ed. I. B. Cohen (DOVER)
—*Principia.* 2 vols. Tr. A. Motte and F. Cajari (CALIFORNIA)

B. PASCAL

—*Pascal's Pensées.* Tr. W. F. Trotter (EVERYMAN)

J. J. ROUSSEAU

—*The Confessions.* Tr. J. M. Cohen (PENGUIN)
—*The Emile of J. J. Rousseau.* Tr. W. Boyd (TEACHERS COLLEGE)
—*The Social Contract.* Ed. C. Frankel (HAFNER)

B. de SPINOZA

—*Chief Works.* 2 vols. Tr. R. H. M. Elwes (DOVER)
—*Writings on Political Philosophy.* Ed. G. A. Balz (APPLETON)
—*Ethics.* Tr. W. H. White (HAFNER)
—*Selections.* Ed. J. Wild (SCRIBNER'S)

G. VICO

—*The Autobiography of Giambattista Vico.* Tr. M. H. Fisch and T. G. Bergin (CORNELL)
—*The New Science of Giambattista Vico.* Ed. T. G. Bergin and M. H. Fisch (ANCHOR)

F. M. A. de VOLTAIRE

—*Candide, Zadig and Selected Stories.* Tr. D. M. Frame (SIGNET CLASSICS)
—*Philosophical Letters.* Tr. E. N. Dillworth (LIBERAL ARTS)
—*Philosophical Dictionary.* Tr. W. Baskin (WISDOM)
—*The Living Thoughts of Voltaire.* Ed. A. Maurois (PREMIER BOOKS)
—*The Portable Voltaire.* Ed. B. Redman (VIKING)

KEY TO PUBLISHERS

Anchor

Anchor Books. Doubleday & Company, Inc., 575 Madison Ave., New York 22, N. Y.

Appleton

Appleton-Century-Crofts, Inc., 34 W. 33rd St., New York 1, N. Y.

California

University of California Press, Berkeley 4, Calif.

Collier

Collier Books, 111 Fourth Ave., New York 3, N. Y.

Cornell

Cornell University Press, 124 Roberts Place, Ithaca, N. Y.

Dolphin

Dolphin Books. Doubleday & Company, Inc., 575 Madison Ave., New York 22, N. Y.

Dover

Dover Publications, Inc., 180 Varick St., New York 14, N. Y.

Everyman

Dutton Everyman Paperbacks. E. P. Dutton Co., Inc., 201 Park Ave. S., New York 3, N. Y.

Gate	Gateway Editions. Henry Regnery Co., 14 E. Jackson Blvd., Chicago 4, Ill.
Hafner	Hafner Library of World Classics. Hafner Publishing Co., 31 E. 10th St., New York 3, N. Y.
Liberal Arts	The Bobbs-Merrill Co., Inc., 4300 W. 62 St., Indianapolis 6, Ind.
Meridian	Meridian Books. The World Publishing Co., 2231 W. 110th St., Cleveland 2, Ohio
Open Court	The Open Court Publishing Co., 1307 Seventh St., LaSalle, Ill.
Penguin	Penguin Books, Inc., 3300 Clipper Mill Rd., Baltimore 11, Md.
Premier	Premier Books. Fawcett Publications, Inc., 67 W. 44th St., New York 36, N. Y.
Scribner's	Charles Scribner's Sons, 597 Fifth Ave., New York 17, N. Y.
Signet Classics	New American Library of World Literature, Inc., 501 Madison Ave., New York 22, N. Y.
Teachers College	Columbia University, New York 27, N. Y.
Torchbooks	Harper Torchbooks. Harper & Row, Publishers, 49 E. 33rd St., New York 16, N. Y.
Ungar	Frederick Ungar Publishing Co., 131 E. 23rd St., New York 10, N. Y.
Viking	The Viking Press, Inc., 625 Madison Ave., New York 22, N. Y.
Wisdom	Wisdom Library Paperbacks. Philosophical Library, Inc., 15 E. 40th St., New York 16, N. Y.

INDEX

Index